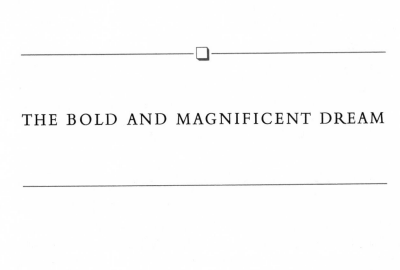

THE BOLD AND MAGNIFICENT DREAM

A special message to
the members of
THE FIRST EDITION SOCIETY

Every book has to speak for itself, of course, and there is not much point in saying "Here is what this book is about" when the book itself is there to tell you. It may be interesting, however, to show how the *The Bold and Magnificent Dream* took form.

It began with a set of assumptions and a conviction or two. First, we believed that people not necessarily enrolled in a college history course might conceivably enjoy reading about this country's history, and particularly about its origins and early development. This belief rested on two others: one, that the subject of history is, and of right ought to be, interesting and sometimes even exciting to read about (and that where it is not, the fault lies with the way it is written); and, far more importantly, that the history of the United States has a great deal to say to the modern world.

At bedrock lay a conviction we had had all along, and it was this that gave form and direction to our labors. We are unalterably convinced that one of the great, unique events in human history was the founding, survival, and growth of a nation conceived in liberty and dedicated to the idea that all human beings are created equal. Here was something new under the sun, and it had a compelling magic to it. The people are sovereign; whatever their fate may be, they are in sole charge of it; all of the safeguards put up to protect them from themselves are to be discarded, because they are their own saviors and their own source of strength. Win or lose.

This is familiar enough. What we found fascinating was the realization that this unique determination to build an entire nation and a whole way of life around the concepts of freedom and equality was not something brought forth by dignified and learned men from Massachusetts, Virginia, and other colonies, meeting amid snuff boxes and quill pens around the flicker of candle light on polished mahogany. These men—the Washingtons, Jeffersons, Adamses, Franklins, and the rest—simply put into words something that already existed.

For hundreds of years men in various parts of Europe had been working out different aspects of the idea of freedom. Freedom to worship (or indeed to abstain from worship), freedom to speak and write and move about, freedom to govern oneself in small matters and then in larger ones, freedom even to challenge and perhaps recast the venerable theory by which most Old World societies were run—the notion that there were fixed orders and grades of men, with some born to rule and own and control the sources of wealth and others born to serve and to labor, sons inheriting their fathers' rank and station without question—all of these freedoms, one at a time, separately, often at fearful cost in human suffering, were being hammered into shape in the hottest of fires. And in the strangest way each separate artifact was to be brought to America by one group or another, each in its turn to rub against the artifacts brought by others, until slowly over the years here and there the pieces began to fit together. Through the fires and revolts and bloody repressions in all parts of Europe, bits of America had been taking shape, generations and even centuries before white men knew that the American continent existed. It was a thousand-year process that stretched back to antiquity and picked up speed with the establishment and growth of white settlements in the New World; the process was slow enough and painful enough, by all odds, but it finally brought the American nation into being.

So America's story does not begin at Yorktown, or with anywhere else readily identifiable. It grows out of many separate stories, many of them lived by people who neither knew nor cared where America was. To understand America it is necessary to understand the world that produced it. And since what we are talking about, really, is one of the most priceless possessions of the human spirit—the concept of freedom for all men everywhere—we are equally convinced that to understand where the world is going and what its possibilities are it is necessary to understand America.

Bruce Catton

Will B. Catton

The First Edition Society

THE BOLD AND MAGNIFICENT DREAM

AMERICA'S FOUNDING YEARS, 1492–1815

by Bruce Catton
and William B. Catton

Illustrated by Dennis Lyall

THE FRANKLIN LIBRARY
Franklin Center, Pennsylvania
1978

For Kathryn Cherry Catton

CONTENTS

BOOK TWO: NEW NATION

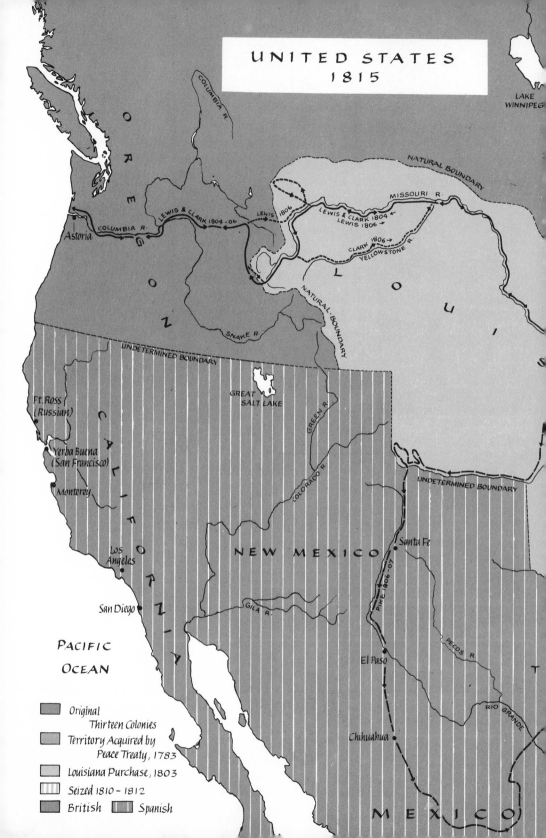

UNITED STATES
1815

LAKE
WINNIPEG

COLUMBIA R.

NATURAL BOUNDARY

MISSOURI R.

LEWIS & CLARK 1804-06

LEWIS 1806

LEWIS & CLARK 1804
LEWIS 1806

O R E G O N

COLUMBIA R.

Astoria

CLARK 1806

YELLOWSTONE R.

L O U I S

SNAKE R.

NATURAL BOUNDARY

UNDETERMINED BOUNDARY

GREAT
SALT LAKE

Ft. Ross
(Russian)

GREEN R.

Yerba Buena
(San Francisco)

Monterey

C A L I F O R N I A

COLORADO R.

UNDETERMINED BOUNDARY

Santa Fe

Los
Angeles

N E W   M E X I C O

PIKE 1806-07

San Diego

GILA R.

PECOS R.

PACIFIC

El Paso

OCEAN

RIO GRANDE

Chihuahua

Original
   Thirteen Colonies
Territory Acquired by
   Peace Treaty, 1783
Louisiana Purchase, 1803
Seized 1810 - 1812
British   Spanish

M E X I C O

THE BOLD AND MAGNIFICENT DREAM

PROLOGUE

LANDFALL

I T W A S a clear night, with the moon high over the port quarter and a bit past full. The three craft were running nicely before a brisk northeast wind and a strong following sea. The course was due west.

A few hours earlier, at sunset, after the flagship's party had gathered on deck for the routine of evening prayers and a chorus of the *Salve Regina,* the Admiral had made a little speech from the sterncastle. The good Lord, he pointed out, had blessed their voyage with fair winds and no mishaps, and had recently sent reassurances in the form of migratory birds and floating plants and sticks. By way of emphasizing his conviction that land could not be far off, the Admiral urged the night watch to keep an especially sharp lookout and offered a prize to the man who first sighted it. Expectations ran high as the little fleet surged westward through the October night. Even the doubters—meaning nearly everyone but the intrepid commander; only his promise to turn back soon, land or no, had quieted mutinous rumblings a day or two before—now felt that their venture into the unknown was about to be rewarded.

After a false alarm sounded by the Admiral himself four hours earlier, a lookout on *Pinta* made the landfall at 2 A.M. on October 12. Christopher Columbus and his excited mariners were peering through the moonlight at a coral island in the Bahamas, some thirteen miles long by six miles wide. Guanahaní, the natives called it; a reverently grateful Admiral would name the place for his Holy Savior. (San Salvador was a long way indeed, in place and circumstance, from the resplendent Oriental kingdoms which Columbus had sailed west to find. It lay some 275 miles north by west of the Windward Passage, just over 400 miles east by south of the Florida Keys. Quinsay, the "City of Heaven" celebrated by Marco Polo, was nearly half a world away, across an unknown continent and an unknown ocean.) During the daylight hours of October 12 the explorers coasted their new-found island, found a gap in the reefs and a good anchorage on the western side, and went ashore to exchange cautious greetings with naked copper-skinned folk who awaited them on the beach.

Columbus and his men went on to explore several other Bahamian atolls. Then—convinced that Japan, Marco Polo's Cipangu of the gold-roofed palaces, lay nearby; assured by helpful native guides that huge islands with gold-bedecked inhabitants lay to the southward—they found and coasted along parts of the northern shores of Cuba and Hispaniola. Cipangu remained elusive, but Hispaniola contained enough tangible evidence of gold to give the whole voyage (and the epoch it inaugurated) an enduring thrust. Early in the new year, with *Santa Maria* a stranded wreck on a reef near Cap Haitien, the party set sail for home in the two caravels; the Admiral transferred his flag to *Niña*. On March 4, 1493, a winter gale drove her into Lisbon bearing a commander and crew with some tales to tell, a few captured natives, some gold dust and other samplings from the transatlantic shores, and an unfathomable new dimension for the future of humankind.

BOOK ONE

NEW WORLD

PART ONE
THE HERITAGE

CHAPTER 1

Of Things Hoped For

E UROPE'S RESPONSE to this exploit only seems sluggish by the standards of an electronic age that could follow and savor every step of man's trip to the moon as it actually occurred. The epochal significance of what Columbus had done could better be grasped by later generations, beneficiaries of his legacy and the advantages of hindsight. His contemporaries, enjoying neither, had not been scanning the western horizon for his return, and news of it filtered casually eastward from Lisbon at the unhurried pace of routine mail couriers on horseback or coastwise packet. Only the thin upper layers of a European society still overwhelmingly rural, provincial, and illiterate were in a position to receive and assess the story at all.

And yet, given these circumstances, Europe reacted quickly and decisively enough. The expeditions that would find new continents and trade routes, found new empires, and rechart the earth's configurations and the course of human history were all fitted out within a generation of *Niña's* abrupt appearance in the Tagus in 1493. Indeed, what mattered most about this event was the reception it got. Christopher Columbus had had this enterprise in mind, to the point of obsession, for some twenty years.

That he could devise and ultimately win approval in high places for such a scheme is partly a tribute to his vision and powers of persuasion; it also says something about the intellectual and psychological climate of his era. And the era is worth a glance.

For this was the Europe of the Renaissance. If the term is deceptively simple and often misleading, the period must yet be adjudged one of the liveliest and most fruitful in the history of Western man. Let a few broad brush strokes try to suggest the contours. After making due allowance for continuity, the persistence of old forms and viewpoints, and the capacity of Renaissance enthusiasts to overdramatize and overestimate what was happening, the age remains one to conjure with—revolutionary in itself, harbinger of revolutions to come.

The unsurpassable quality of its art can be exemplified by St. Peter's in Rome, built because a Renaissance Pope sought to enshrine the spectacular creativity of his era and blend the Christian and classical traditions in an enduring monument; the artists he could engage to design and adorn the structure included Bramante, Michelangelo, and Raphael. Although the period made no comparable strides in science, many of its artists had a scientific eye for details of human anatomy and a scientific mastery of spatial perspective; such concerns pointed toward the scientific breakthroughs of the seventeenth century. Birthplace and vital center of the Renaissance lay in the cities of northern Italy, which were developing techniques and a world view that would draw Western Europe into the modern era as irresistibly as the Pied Piper lured the children of Hamlin town. Long before Columbus sailed, the tone and outlook in these Italian towns had become individualistic and secular to a degree unknown in the Middle Ages.

It was a time of heightened scholarly interest in the West's Greco-Roman and Judaeo-Christian heritage. This heritage, along with the documents, artifacts, languages, and traditions composing it, was assiduously re-examined, reinterpreted, and (in the view of men intoxicated by a sense of identity with the glory that was Greece and the grandeur that was Rome) rediscovered and reapplied. Renaissance scholars could hail the deeds of Columbus and other explorers in properly classical terms: it was Seneca who had prophesied the coming of an age "when the Ocean will loose the chains of things, and a huge land lie revealed. . . ."

This concept of a classical golden age, which had flourished and then died with the fall of western Rome, to be succeeded by a dark and stagnant middle period, and which was now being reborn as the stifling medieval constraints were thrown off, was what gave the era its name; these ardent classicists called their scholarly endeavors a Renaissance. They liked to call themselves Humanists, with the same persistent immodesty, and their enthusiasm for antiquity often had something of the cult and the fad about it.

They preened and they postured, but there was substance beneath the erudite affections. Modern critical scholarship, historical perspective, educational philosophy, diplomatic practice, and political thought can trace most of their origins here. The leading Humanists were not closet scholars but publicists and activists, men of affairs, self-made teachers or writers or poets who often served as advisers or secretaries to kings and princes, prelates and popes. They communicated their taste and outlook—later their desire to reform and save the Christian Church—to more than one generation of educated townsfolk and ruling families, and their prestige and influence were great, at times decisive.

Informing much of this artistic and intellectual effort was a compelling new vision of man: man here and now, on his own, endowed by his Creator with the power to make his own destiny. Preeminent among Renaissance scholars was the Florentine, Pico della Mirandola, who quoted God as telling man that he was "constrained by no limits, in accordance with thine own free will. . . . We have made thee neither of heaven nor of earth, neither mortal nor immortal, so that with freedom of choice and with honor . . . thou mayest fashion thyself in whatever shape thou shalt prefer."

This was heady stuff, beyond doubt—the kind of spirit that made things happen. It was eventually accompanied by a new sense of optimism and confidence, a feeling that Latin Christendom stood on the threshold of a great new era. Even the most coolheaded and judicious of the Humanist philosophers was touched by it: "I anticipate," Erasmus confided to a friend in 1517, "the approach of a golden age."

If this intellectual activity was largely confined to the university towns and urban centers, especially in northern Italy, there were other currents that ran more broadly and deeply. From about 1450 the population of Europe, after a century and a half of stagnation and decline, began a sustained rise that would continue until the early 1600s. This growth, manifest in all parts of the continent, had a corresponding effect upon the economy. Increased demand sent prices upward; trade and production flourished. Towns grew apace. Pressure on the existing food supply drove cultivators back onto marginal and less productive lands that had been abandoned during the prolonged contraction after 1300. A growing surplus of labor acted to force wages downward and rents upward, thus tending to transfer income to landlords and employers at the expense of peasants and artisans.

As the well-to-do classes prospered, the trade in luxury goods underwent a boom that stimulated international trade and capital accumulation. It also encouraged, where possible, the diversion of acreage away from cereal crops in favor of meat and dairy products, wines, and industrial raw materials like flax, wool, and dyestuffs. The great Italian trading cities, Venice and Genoa, continued (as they had for centuries) to reap fat middlemen's profits in the luxury trade with Constantinople, the Levant, and the Orient, importing spices, fine textiles and metalwork, precious stones, and the like, and distributing them throughout Europe. Thriving cloth and arms industries in northern Italy and the Netherlands enriched a network of producers: skilled artisans in the Flemish and Italian towns, English and Spanish wool growers, continental mineowners, and above all the merchant-capitalists who financed and organized every phase of production and distribution.

The expanded output of central European mines—silver, copper, iron, lead, zinc—had a multiple effect. It enhanced the wealth of the German towns and banking houses that underwrote the mining operations; it sustained Europe's supply of metallic currency for decades prior to the great influx from Mexico and Peru; and it sharply stimulated technological innovation and organizational technique. The mundane bulk traffic in timber, salt, fish, and grain also reflected the general economic upsurge. The shipbuilding industry, of course, throve on all of this. Antwerp in the Netherlands, where the most important lines of trade converged, became the financial and commercial capital of all Europe in the early sixteenth century.

What enabled this complex network of trade routes and production centers to function properly was an increasingly sophisticated apparatus for the gathering, distributing, and marketing of goods. The basic instruments of capitalism—commercial partnerships and agencies, credit trading, currency transfers, bills of exchange, banking facilities, marine insurance, double-entry bookkeeping—were being forged, tempered, refined, and utilized. (The Pied Piper Italian cities developed these instruments, and exported them.) The inexorable solvent of a market economy was at work upon medieval custom, law, manor, and guild. Money and contract were taking their place beside birth and status as determinants of human relationships and human worth. A capitalist economy, in short, was emerging. The process was a long way from completion at the end of the fifteenth century, but it had advanced far enough to alter the tempo, prospects, and conditions of European life.

Technological change did not proceed at breakneck speed during Columbus' time, but portentous advances were being made in a few key areas. The invention of movable type and the printing press around the middle of the fifteenth century was a revolution in itself, of course; it is impossible to imagine the patterns of Renaissance, Reformation, or world exploration unfolding as they did in the absence of the printed word. Cumulative advances in shipbuilding and navigation during the fifteenth century had even more relevance for the Columbus expedition. European shipwrights evolved strong, weatherly craft, sparred for both square and lateen rig, that could withstand Atlantic gales, tack against the wind, and maneuver handily along uncharted coasts. Proficiency in mapmaking, determining latitude by celestial navigation, and charting one's position by dead reckoning had all developed to the point where long voyages into the unknown were possible.

Meanwhile, steady improvements in firearms, cannon founding, metallurgy, and the draining and ventilation of mines were having continual effects, ultimately decisive, upon the art of war, the expansion of Europe, and the industrial process. (Men were already at work upon the line of development that led directly from deeper mine shafts to more effective pumping machinery, which in turn, someday, would summon forth the steam engine.) The day of the musketeer and arquebusier, siege gun, fieldpiece, and ship's broadside had fairly arrived—signaling, sooner or later, ruin or subjection for such diverse entities as mounted knight, feudal castle, Moslem war vessels in the Indian Ocean, and native warriors as far apart as Tenochtitlán and Malacca.

Political changes, too, were afoot. Certain rulers, enhancing their power with the new weapons and liquid assets that technological and economic gains had made available, were moving to suppress or absorb countervailing power centers and build effective national monarchies on the foundation of the territorial state. The ruling houses that had fairly succeeded in doing this by 1500 were those of England, France, Portugal, and the Spanish kingdoms. These centralizing tendencies, visible as far back as the eleventh century, had been arrested by the long period of stagnation, destructive wars, and other difficulties that beset much of Europe after 1300, but in recent decades the trend had reasserted itself. Neither supranational entities like Church and Empire nor smaller units like barony and city-state could match the vigorous national monarchies in commanding citizen loyalty, preserving order, mobilizing resources, and welding the combination into effective, expansive instruments of political power. Commercial enterprise and advantage, skillfully deployed, enabled the Venetians and later the Dutch to provide exceptions to this rule, but only for a time. The future belonged to the nation-state, and the future was already visible by 1500.

In short, Western society was more than ready to act on the news Columbus brought home. Well before his arrival Europe was astir—stretching and flexing its muscles like some great hungry carnivore about to go on the prowl.

The motives that drove Europeans in search of distant shores again and again during the fifteenth and sixteenth centuries were a fairly predictable sort, perhaps. Yet they made a fascinating mix— durable, contradictory, explosive, powerful. As a force in human affairs this mixture was by way of being the place whereon to stand that Archimedes had called for, whence the earth could be moved. And the combination proved capable of endowing the society that would later take shape on the North American mainland with a tone and an aura it would never lose.

At bottom lay a vision Western man had had since ancient times: the notion, compounded imprecisely of melancholy, longing, and hope, that a better land and a better life existed somewhere, far off on the mystic border between reality and dream. A vague mythology took shape over the centuries as poets and philosophers kept invoking the image, or variations on it. They bespoke wondrous places overflowing with milk and honey, where trees and flowers blossomed year round, birds sang in perpetual sunshine, and the season was always mid-May. People of primeval innocence dwelt there, and life was simple and good. The very names were evocative: Arcadia, the Fortunate Isles, the Elysian Fields, Hesperides, Avalon, the Islands of the Blest.

If these were little more than classical versions of Eden before the fall—the man looking backward to a golden age of lost innocence, longing for the possibility of making a fresh start in a rich and unencumbered land—they had a focus of sorts. In so far as they had a temporal location at all, these regions tended to lie across the Western Ocean beyond the known world, off toward the sunset. The Elysian Fields and Avalon lay vaguely in that direction; so, more explicitly, did Hesperides. Plutarch wrote of Spanish sailors who had been to the Islands of the Blest. Seneca, as we have seen, predicted that a huge western land would someday be revealed, and on Ptolemy's second-century map the farthest habitable regions to the westward were labeled the Fortunate Isles. Somewhere in that direction, too, lay fabled wealthy Atlantis, portions or offshoots of which were reputed to have survived after the mighty lost continent itself sank beneath the sea.

Later generations kept adding accretions to this body of Arcadian legend. An Irish saint named Brendan, in the sixth century, and an Irish prince named Maeldune, some two hundred years later, were each said to have discovered islands full of strange marvels in the far Atlantic. A group of Iberian bishops and their followers, fleeing the Moslem invasions of the eighth century, had supposedly sailed west and settled in an island or archipelago named Antilla, where their descendants were said to dwell in happy utopian communities. (The actual Caribbean islands would derive their collective name from this legendary land.)

The number and variety of imaginary islands increased steadily over the years. In human imagination, long before it was discovered, America had come to embody that faith which St. Paul had referred to as the substance of things hoped for and the evidence of things not seen.

The hopes grew more poignant. During that long time span—roughly, the fourteenth and fifteenth centuries—when the Middle Ages are depicted as in decline and giving way, via the Renaissance, to the modern era, the prevailing outlook across much of Western Europe was one of malaise and insecurity. Its components included world-weariness, sadness, fear, and a sense of imminent doom. Renaissance optimism was not widely observable much before 1500. "At the close of the Middle Ages," Johan Huizinga has observed, "a sombre melancholy weighs on people's souls. . . . A general feeling of impending calamity hangs over all." This was not merely an affliction of the intellectual element, where such attitudes are endemic and chronically stylish. In so far as telltale glimpses are afforded by contemporary legal records, chronicles, sermons, poems, and the like, the gloom and fear affected every stratum of society, and ran deep.

And there was reason enough for such a view. Everything seemed to have come loose; the aspects of life that had given the High Middle Ages their vitality, their confidence, and their sense of achievement had fallen into disarray. In this sense, certainly, the depiction of an age in decline, a civilization that had lost its bearings and outlived its capacity to meet human needs, was reasonably accurate. (The mood and situation bear no little resemblance to that of the late twentieth century.) Economic stagnation and depression beset the entire continent, even injecting proletarian revolts, bankruptcies, violence, and bitter class conflict into the bustling Italian cities. Europe's population declined steadily, at times catastrophically; recurrent epidemics like the dreaded Black Death ravaged town and countryside and depopulated whole regions.

The Roman Church, that all-encompassing source of spiritual authority, inspiration, guidance, comfort, and salvation, had fallen upon evil days. The papacy lost incalculably in prestige and influence after decades of "captivity" at Avignon followed by decades of schism in which rival popes laid claims to the office and hurled anathemas back and forth. Evidence of decay, corruption, and failure within the hierarchy were matched by ominous signs of heresy, skepticism, and worldliness among the faithful. The conditions and state of mind that ultimately produced the Reformation were visible long before.

As symbol and reflection of these weaknesses, the borders of Christendom were contracting before the sustained onslaught of a younger and apparently more vigorous faith. Islam had been a threatening, aggressive neighbor on Europe's flanks since Charlemagne's time; now, under the banners of the ascendant empire of the Ottoman Turks, it was posing the gravest threat of all. The Turks conquered most of the Balkan Peninsula during the fourteenth century, defeated Christian forces in battle after battle, and started moving up the Danube Valley into Hungary. Turkish sea power began pushing Genoa and Venice out of their bases and colonies in the Levant. Mighty Constantinople, capital of the seemingly imperishable Eastern Roman Empire for a millennium and now all that was left of it, fell to Turkish armies in 1453. At the other end of Europe, it took Portuguese and Spanish Christians more than four hundred years to reconquer the Iberian Peninsula from its Moslem overlords; the stubborn Moors were not driven from their last stronghold, in Granada, until the year Columbus sailed.

Yet Europeans, despite the Moslem threat, seemed more interested in fighting among themselves. Feudal and dynastic conflicts raged almost constantly, devastating much of France and the Low Countries and keeping England and the Iberian Peninsula in turmoil. The four horsemen of the Apocalypse—war, famine, pestilence, death—rode grimly across the land; violence, disorder, and suffering seemed to have become the norm. It is not surprising that Italian Humanists looked eagerly to antiquity as a golden age and strove to see it reborn, or that Europe stared more longingly than ever across the ocean sea.

———□———

Then, too, in their less lugubrious moments people were simply curious—avidly so, in the turbulent years of the late Middle Ages. A fascination with the bizarre, the freakish, and the wonderful helped give stories of distant regions their popularity. Much of the lore about strange regions overseas was heavily spiced with tales of monsters and fountains of youth, demons, lands of fire, humans with tails, and other marvels.

The zones of legend and fact gradually came together during the fifteenth century, as the twin frontiers of human knowledge and human longing were extended into the Western Ocean toward similar goals. The Canaries, claimed and eventually colonized by Castile, seemed to fit the location of the Fortunate Isles on Ptolemy's ancient map. The Azores, discovered and rediscovered piecemeal by the Portuguese over several generations, corresponded to cartographers' placement of St. Brendan's isles. As actual Atlantic islands kept appearing, belief in the mystical ones was reinforced. Pierre Cardinal d'Ailly, Bishop of Cambrai, the early fifteenth-century geographer whose version of the width and far boundaries of the Atlantic heavily influenced Columbus, believed that an Earthly Paradise (a high, fertile region containing a Tree of Life, whence issued a fountain that fed four of the world's great rivers) lay near the Fortunate Isles. The old idea of a perfect land in the west had lost none of its appeal; D'Ailly's Earthly Paradise, along with Antilla, were among the spots Columbus hoped to find on his way to Cathay.

The tough mariners, of all nations, who kept edging their little craft out beyond the borders of the known were a bold and hardy lot. But they had all the superstitions and credulity of their calling and their time; they kept exchanging, and crediting, sworn tales of islands glimpsed on the horizon at sunset or through the morning mist. Rumors and old yarns abounded. The Portuguese were said to have stumbled across Antilla during Prince Henry's time (returning home, so the story went, to find gold in the sand they had scraped for ballast off some distant beach).

And it was not all rumor and sea tale. People in the Atlantic ports and fishing villages probably still swapped vague stories of the actual Norse trips to Vinland and Markland of four centuries before. European mariners kept charting real islands below the horizon, including some that had been known about and then "lost" in earlier times: the Canaries, for example, and the Portuguese outposts of Madeira and the Azores. The westernmost of the Azores was not found until 1452, and the pattern encouraged the belief that there were more to come. Things kept drifting ashore—non-European bodies, carved bits of wood, exotic plants and seeds.

The very air became alive with expectation. By Columbus' time, a sense—feel, hope, conviction—of *something out there*, beyond land's end, had grown strong enough to be compelling. Some of the stories that drifted about the Atlantic docks and grogshops may have been true: by 1492 there were people in the maritime trade who either knew something or thought they did. Columbus had little trouble recruiting men for his expedition.

The medieval influence upon the age of discovery contained an impulse that went well beyond a credulous taste for the outlandish and a longing for Arcadia. The concept of chivalry still flourished. Urbane Italians with their Greco-Roman values might scoff at this outworn trapping of the past, but notions of chivalry had a tenacious hold upon the Western imagination. For decades after Columbus' return, accounts of New World discoveries, whether firsthand, secondhand, or fictitious, often submerged factual reporting beneath an odd double image of happy innocent natives (dwellers in Arcady, Nausicaa welcoming Odysseus) and tales of medieval derring-do: Elysium criss-crossed with accounts of knightly exploits, dragon slaying, evil spirits, fair damsels, and the like.

The urge to participate in the business of exploration and empire building owed a great deal, then, to the same quests for honor, adventure, and grail that had inspired generations of medieval knights. The Spaniards, in particular, were entranced to the point of obsession with chivalric deeds and ideals. This mentality included the kind of fixations and absurd posturing that later intrigued Cervantes, although the conquistadors were cut from tougher cloth than Don Quixote. And while Spain contained the greatest number, latter-day Rolands and Lancelots could be found all over Europe. One of the best known, Chevalier Bayard of France, was a contemporary of Columbus—a medieval throwback who won much of his renown battling, *sans peur et sans reproche,* as part of a French army that invaded and plundered Renaissance Italy. Political and economic changes had dislocated thousands of Europeans for whom the paths of glory exerted an irresistible attraction: footloose adventurers and underemployed mercenaries, down-at-heel knights, fighting-cock hidalgos who had spent a career battling the Moors, restless younger sons of impoverished noble families. They came to the port towns in droves to join the expeditions that fitted out in the quickening aftermath of *Niña's* return; many of the exploits that enabled Portuguese squadrons to dominate the oceans east of Suez and built a New World empire for Spain were performed by men in search of glory.

Glory, of course, was not all they sought. When recrudescent chivalry and love of adventure, curiosity, and Arcadian yearnings are given their due, it was another pair of driving wheels that provided Europe's global expansion with its principal thrust. The metaphor is used advisedly. The incentives in question were *paired,* as inseparably as wheels joined by an axle, and neither the driving force nor the people who were propelled by it can be understood save in the context of dual motives.

They were not hard to identify: a desire to advance the frontiers of Christendom and coincidentally to find wealth. God and gold. The former was as genuine an urge as the latter, and cynics of a later, more secular era would be wrong to underestimate the spiritual half of the combination. (Patriotism and self-interest would form a similar, comparably potent pair of drivers in modern times.)

The faithful had two goals in mind—to find and convert heathen souls (in India, Africa, the Orient, lands yet unknown), and to outflank Islam by making contact and common cause with Christian societies and outposts that were thought to exist in distant places, the result of migrations and missionary enterprises of long ago. Most talked about and sought after among these potential allies was Prester John, a legendary Christian prince who was reputed to rule a wealthy and powerful empire somewhere off to the south or east of Moslem territory—in Africa, it was thought, or perhaps in India. The old crusading spirit was still very much alive in parts of Europe; indeed, in a world that had gone so sour and so awry at home, the prospect of winning new souls for Christ and driving back the infidel Turk had a heightened appeal.

The appeal looked all the better when it promised to pay a secular dividend or two. As Columbus' venture suggested, the explorers usually set out in the twin hope of finding new lands and new ways of getting to old ones; both targets were expected to contain wealth. It had been two hundred years since Marco Polo's return from Cathay and the court of Kublai Khan, but his account of the unbelievable splendor and richness of the Orient—what he had seen and what he had heard about—had never been forgotten; it exercised a growing pull on European minds in the restless, questing atmosphere of the late fifteenth century. Contact and travel between Europe and the Orient, overland through the

Asian deserts and oases along the venerable route of the silk caravans, was more frequent during Marco Polo's time than during
Columbus'; the overland route was largely closed to Europeans
after the decline of the well-disposed Mongol Empire in the fourteenth century and the hostile presence of the Ottomans at the
near end of the journey. But the West's growing maritime com-
petence after 1400 encouraged the belief that an ocean route to the
Orient might now be within their grasp.

They wanted to grasp not only Marco Polo's Cathay and Cipangu but the nearer, no less storied wealth of Ormuz and of Ind;
not only precious metals, reportedly so abundant all across Asia,
but spices—an almost equally valued commodity. Indeed, in
medieval and Renaissance Europe spices were a high-priced necessity. Shortage of winter fodder forced Europeans to slaughter
most of their livestock every autumn, with the result that preser-
vatives were in great demand. The only one produced locally was
salt, and the other items that made aging meat palatable came
from semitropical regions: cinnamon from Ceylon, pepper from
India and Indonesia, nutmeg and mace from Celebes, ginger
from China, and—most valuable of all—cloves from the Moluccas near New Guinea, already world famous as the Spice Islands. Precious stones, Chinese silks, and Indian cottons were
also prized commodities in the West, but spices were what gave
the Oriental trade its special value and drawing power.

Here governmental objectives converged neatly with those of
individual fortune seekers and did much to explain the effective
partnership of public and private interests that undertook most of
the voyages of discovery. Europe had long had an unfavorable
balance of trade with the East—meaning, in this context, everything from Constantinople and Alexandria to China and the
Spice Islands. Since spices and Oriental luxury goods cost far
more than the raw materials and woolens that the West could
offer in return, European specie drained steadily eastward to
make up the deficit. Some of this currency stopped to enrich
those enterprising distributors of spices and Oriental goods, the

Venetians and the Genoese, but the Continent was a net loser. For a time the expanding output of central European and German silver mines helped keep this currency shortage from becoming critical, but it could not cure the imbalance or stem the outflow. Governments, always hungry for revenue, grew increasingly anxious to preserve and enhance national currency supplies— which helped explain the royal willingness to authorize exploratory voyages. The specie drain could be rectified both by discovering new sources of precious metals and by obtaining direct access to spices at their source, thereby avoiding the heavy cumulative charges levied by a chain of Chinese, Hindu, Moslem, and Italian middlemen.

Spices and the Orient were powerful lures, but what shimmered with growing intensity at the very core of European imagination were visions of gold. The Far East, in this vision, was virtually paved with it. Gold exercised a hypnotic fascination upon the minds of most explorers, equally so upon the imagination of Old World publicists who compiled accounts of the voyages. As the discoveries proceeded, every new island was expected to contain the yellow metal, and was scoured for it. Every native anklet or nosepiece and every ounce of metallic dust gave rise to new rumors—both before and after the Aztec and Inca conquests had yielded their treasure—of great stores and mountains and rivers of gold in the new lands.

By this time the Western image of the New World had become hopelessly blurred. Europeans had no sooner begun to double-expose a medieval landscape across the Arcadian original when explorers reported back that a few Indian tribes engaged in cannibalism and other barbaric practices. This discovery, which lost no fat in the telling, fed Europe's fascination with monsters and Gothic horrors; it also fostered an image of bestial demonic savagery which clung to the American Indian even more tenaciously than that of its polar opposite, the guileless happy innocent. Small wonder that the real Indian, who in all his variety bore scant resemblance to either stereotype, never emerged from behind them until he had been subjected or destroyed.

Meanwhile, corresponding polar images of the New World took shape together as well: the Garden of Eden alongside a savage untamed wilderness full of mystery and terror. The dialectic juxtaposition of happy fertile garden precariously balanced between corrupt Old World civilization and barbaric wilderness would later define an emergent self-image in British North America. And almost from the start, both the innocent Arcadian and the bloodthirsty savage would be depicted as bathing in gold dust and festooned with precious stones. Truly the hopes and fears of all the years were somehow met in that kaleidoscopic European vision of a land to the westward.

— □ —

And so, armed equally with cross, sword, and pocketbook, Europeans set forth into unknown waters. Their ablest leaders, when asked what they sought, summed it up eloquently enough. "Christians and spices," Vasco da Gama told Hindu questioners. (He found few Christians, but his first voyage to India stirringly dramatized the value of the spice trade. Returning to Europe in 1499 after a two-year absence, with only two vessels remaining of the four he had set out with, Da Gama brought back cargoes worth sixty times the cost of the entire expedition.) And on the other side of the world, the conqueror of Mexico and the treasure house of the Montezumas put it equally well. We came, Cortés said, to serve God and grow rich.

CHAPTER 2

Empires in Their Brains

T HE PORTUGUESE, who had been fitfully engaged in this dual quest for three quarters of a century when Columbus put into the Tagus in 1493, greeted his news with misgiving. He claimed, unequivocally, to have found what he had set out to find —the Orient. Unless he could be proved wrong Portugal's own ambitions there were in jeopardy. Five years earlier a Portuguese expedition led by Bartholomew Diaz had discovered and rounded the Cape of Good Hope, thereby demonstrating the existence of an eastern route to the Orient. But political problems at home had prevented Portugal from following up Diaz' Discovery, and now this confident Genoese in the pay of rival Spain was exhibiting trophies from lands he had found by sailing west, and insisting that they were outliers of Cipangu and Cathay!

The Portuguese were puzzled. They had been properly skeptical when Columbus, who was no stranger in the royal court at Lisbon, had twice sought their sanction for his Indies expedition before applying to Isabella and Ferdinand. The theory of a spherical earth dated back to antiquity and had won general acceptance in learned circles long before Columbus; all that impeded the project of sailing west to reach the Orient was continued uncertainty as to how much ocean had to be crossed. What had bothered Lisbon about Columbus' scheme was his calculation—derived from Ptolemy, Marco Polo, D'Ailly and other cartographers, and his own computations—that Japan lay some 2,400 nautical miles west of the Canaries.

This struck the Portuguese, correctly, as much too close. Ptolemy had greatly overestimated the width of the Asian land mass, Columbus had overestimated it even more, Marco Polo had placed Japan several hundred miles farther off the mainland than it actually was, and Columbus had badly underestimated the length of a degree of longitude. Japan is five times farther west of Europe than Columbus claimed, and Lisbon had suspected as much. With logic on their side, they had turned him down, preferring to look for Asia in their own way. It was left for the Spanish monarchs to approve Columbus' project.

And now he had obviously found *something*. Portuguese skepticism wavered, although they need not have worried. With Africa already rounded and Da Gama's decisive voyage only a few years in the offing, they were far ahead in the race to the East. They were also having the better of it, at least for a time, in the search for wealth. Indeed, for half a century or more on either side of the Columbian expedition this small kingdom on Europe's farthest fringe played an important role in world affairs. Pioneer and leader in the great age of discovery, Portugal would be briefly but brilliantly rewarded for its efforts: riches, commercial preeminence, overseas empire on three continents, the status of great world power.

There is something suggestive about the ingredients and circumstances of this phenomenon. A similar pattern can be traced in the earlier ascendancy of the Venetians and the Norsemen, and in the later achievements of Britons, Dutchmen, and New Englanders. To an extent, and on a larger scale, the pattern can also be detected in Western Europe's steady rise to world dominance after 1500—a process which Portugal can fairly be said to have launched.

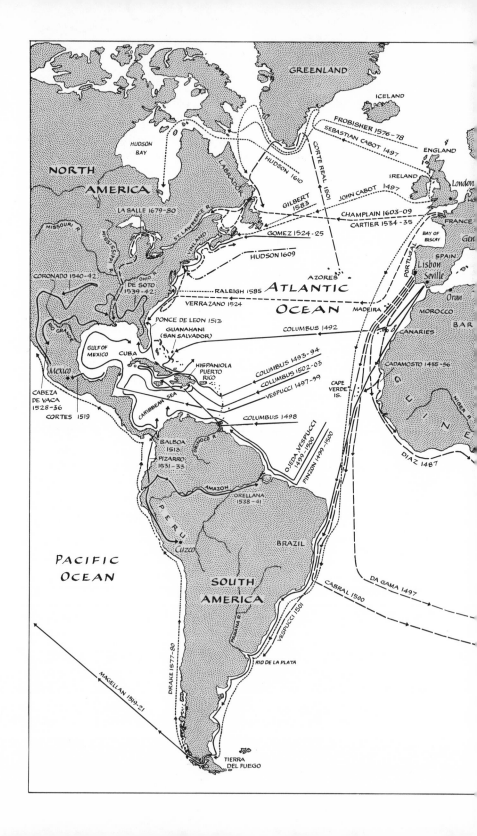

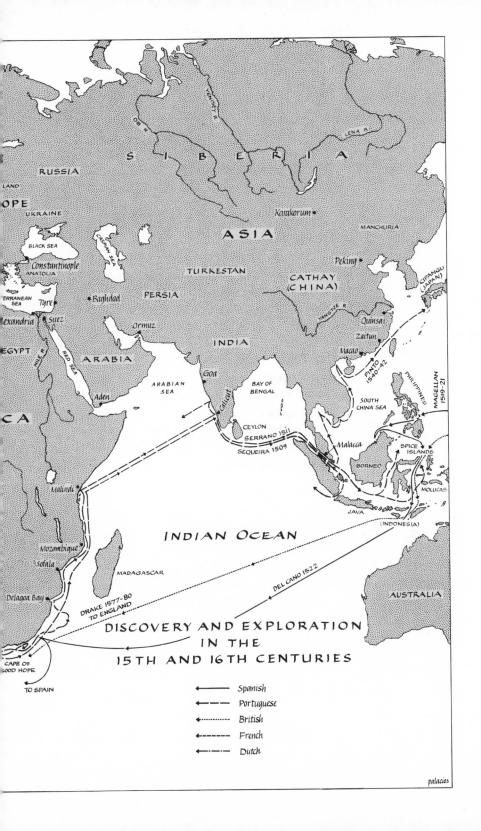

DISCOVERY AND EXPLORATION
IN THE
15TH AND 16TH CENTURIES

←	Spanish
←---	Portuguese
←······	British
←------	French
←-·-·-	Dutch

palacios

Consider the Portuguese example for a moment. In the larger European society the country was remote and peripheral, yet strategically located when horizons began to lift. Relatively poor in the basic economic resource—abundant arable land—her people had to look elsewhere for sustenance and surplus. Utilizing what lay near at hand—timber, fish, salt—they became a nation with an unusually large proportion of folk whose livelihood (far more than in agriculture) depended upon enterprise, boldness, innovation, movement: fishermen, shipbuilders, and merchants trading for the corn they could not grow; pointed seaward, townward, and outward rather than inward and downward to the land. (Thus it had been centuries earlier, when folk in northeastern Italy, seeking to escape the barbarian onslaughts that were engulfing western Rome, took refuge in the inhospitable marshy lagoons at the head of the Adriatic. They went on to make a town, build boats, and peddle marsh products like fish and salt for grain; from these hardscrabble origins did Venice begin its rise.)

Add to this Portuguese mix, finally, a proud aristocracy that dwelt on big estates, possessed more power than wealth, and looked pugnaciously about for ways to preserve the former and enhance the latter. Jealous of the energetic townsfolk, conditioned and impoverished by endless wars against Moors, Spaniards, and one another, these nobles volunteered with alacrity for any overseas venture—crusade, conquest, exploration—that offered promise of glory and gain.

During the fifteenth century Portugal had another key human resource in the person of Prince Henry, dubbed "the Navigator" by later English writers. It was he who laid the specific foundation for the little kingdom's startling achievements. Animated by a typical mixture of crusading zeal, scientific curiosity, and a desire to advance his country's fortunes, Prince Henry established an observatory and maritime workshop on Cape St. Vincent, at Portugal's southwestern tip, and recruited shipmasters, cartographers, pilots, and astronomers from all over. Drawing upon all that had been known and guessed and theorized by ancient, Arab, and contemporary geographers, Henry's corps of specialists pooled their talents and created a great laboratory for the advancement of maritime knowledge and the arts of navigation and seamanship.

Though Portuguese mariners remained busy to the westward, expanding the frontiers of their Atlantic fisheries and making important colonies out of Madeira and the Azores, the prime focus of Prince Henry's attention was Africa. The way around that little-known land mass, if one could be found, might open a path to India, Prester John, and the Spice Islands; such a route might also reveal the source of the gold dust and other interesting items that Moorish caravans brought north across the Sahara to Mediterranean ports. With Henry's encouragement the captains took their little caravels ever farther down the coast of Africa and learned to beat back home against the northeast trades.

Progress was slow and fitful, but by 1450 the overseas ventures began to pay off. Sugar, a tropical product Europeans had learned about long ago from the Arabs and craved ever since, was cultivated in Madeira and flourished there, greatly to Portugal's benefit. Africa, once the Guinea coast had been reached, exceeded all expectations; Portugal established warehouse fortresses at strategic points and began a lucrative trade in gold, ivory, slaves, and melegueta pepper, an inferior but acceptable substitute for the Eastern varieties.

The journals of a Venetian trader named Alvise da Cadamosto, who entered Prince Henry's service in the 1450s, suggest some of the appeal that these voyages of exploration had for Europeans while Columbus was growing up. Henry, Cadamosto wrote admiringly, "had caused seas to be navigated which had never before been sailed, and had discovered the lands of many strange races, where marvels abounded. . . ." The prince's men at Cape St. Vincent spoke so enthusiastically about their travels, Cadamosto went on, "that I with the others marveled greatly. They thus aroused in me a growing desire to go thither." The Portuguese government, not wanting to attract usurpers, tended to be secretive about the details of their discoveries, and Cadamosto's descriptions of the African shores he visited in Henry's service are among the few firsthand accounts of this important enterprise.

(One is repeatedly struck by the way in which those ubiquitous Italians left their mark upon the shape of things to come—capitalism, Renaissance, the non-European world. It was also a Venetian whose account of his sojourn in Kublai Khan's empire gave Europeans of a later era their incurable urge to explore strange waters in order to see what he had seen. It was a Genoese who discovered the New World and a Florentine who first called it such, voyaging far enough beyond Columbus along those uncharted coasts to realize that this was more than an appendage of Asia; mapmakers soon affixed his own name to the two new continents. It was another Italian, John Cabot, only three or four years after Columbus, who explored enough North American shoreline to give England its original claim to New World territory; yet another, Verrazano, performed a like service for France in the 1520s.)

After Prince Henry's death in 1460 the Lisbon government, in between wars, backed further ventures—east and then south along the interminable African shoreline, till Diaz returned with the news of Good Hope in 1488. Four years after listening to Columbus boast of his findings in the far Atlantic, the Portuguese dispatched Vasco da Gama on the voyage that would reach India and open the eastern sea route once and for all. In 1500 Cabral, following Da Gama's route, touched Brazil on his way south and gave his monarch a stake in the New World. Then in quick succession Da Gama, Almeida, and Albuquerque established Portuguese naval supremacy in the Arabian Sea and the Bay of Bengal, planted bases in the Gulf of Aden and at Ormuz, Goa, the Malabar coast of India, and Malacca, ventured into the South China

Sea, and reached the Moluccas. Eastern spices and luxury goods began going to Europe by way of Lisbon. The Arab and Italian middlemen had been outflanked at last.

— □ —

So Portugal easily won the race to the Orient's golden shores, although Christopher Columbus would die believing he had reached them. It would be several years after *Niña*'s return before other explorers began to establish that he had not, and several more before they learned that his New World contained golden shores of its own. But the Spanish sovereigns were sufficiently impressed by that first transatlantic voyage to authorize a second under Columbus' command, on a grander scale. In the fall of 1493 the Admiral of the Ocean Sea set out with seventeen vessels to explore new islands, resume contact with the garrison he had left on Hispaniola, and continue the search for gold and the Grand Khan.

The Spaniards never found this potentate, but by following in Columbus' wake they were able to find lands that formed the basis for the greatest of the European colonial empires. Castile, Aragon, and Andalusia had as large a quota of skilled mariners, sharp-eyed traders, and adventure-hungry hidalgos as Portugal did, and they were raring to go. Columbus himself went on to discover most of the Caribbean islands and parts of Central and South America, including the delta of the Orinoco, whose vast deposit of fresh water along that stretch of coast led him to regard this as one of the four great rivers flowing from that fountain in the Earthly Paradise.

And after Columbus, for the next five decades, came a parade of other explorers and conquistadors whose names still give off echoes: Amerigo Vespucci, concluding that this was indeed a New World and leaving his name on two continents; Balboa, sighting a great unknown ocean from his peak in Darien; Magellan on his way past the Río de la Plata and around South America and on across the Pacific; Cortés, moving inland to the Aztec capital; Pizarro and his cutthroat kinsmen discovering and looting the Inca empire in Peru; Ponce de Leon finding and naming Florida on his quest for gold and the youth-giving fountain; De Soto moving far into the interior of North America and dying on the banks of the mighty river he had found; Coronado traipsing across the Rocky Mountain plateaus and Kansas prairies looking for the golden cities of Cíbola; Cabeza de Vaca making his incredible trek from the Gulf Coast of Florida to the Gila Valley in Arizona and summing up the entire age of discovery (and more) in a sentence: "We ever held it certain that going toward the sunset we would find what we desired."

From these primary trails the lesser paths of exploration, conquest, and settlement ramified, until the Spanish Crown found itself heir to a vast region centered on the Caribbean and spanning large portions of both Americas. New Spain became a great cornucopia of things Europeans wanted or soon learned to want— sugar, tobacco, cocoa, cotton, dyestuffs, gold, endless quantities of silver from the mines of Mexico and Peru. Old World transplants, including rice, grapes, olives, mulberry trees, and especially livestock, throve there too. Most resident tribes, notwithstanding the best efforts of Church and Crown, were either put to work or exterminated, or both; it did not take the Spaniards long to disabuse the Caribbean natives of their original notion that these strange seaborne visitors had come from heaven. Within half a century of Columbus death in 1506 a rich domain based on tropic plantations, vast herds, silver mines, and white-walled mission houses had taken shape beneath the gold and crimson banner of Castile, while the sight of laden galleons bringing the treasure of New Spain to Seville each year had begun kindling covetous fires in the capitals and outports of England, France, and Holland.

Thus did the strange new world overseas come into Europe's

ken and begin revealing its wealth and its potential—nursed, in James Russell Lowell's apt phrase, by stern men with empires in their brains.

—□—

One other portion of the backdrop remains to be examined. The Portuguese and Spanish voyages marked the beginning of a great expansive thrust that would continue until Western Europe dominated the planet and superimposed its values and priorities across those of other peoples. The immediate dynamics—economic, political, technological, psychological—have already been touched upon. But there were deeper intellectual currents and collective character traits involved in this drive toward global hegemony, and they are worth a glance. They included a uniquely malleable and adaptive society, a powerful set of impulses derived from Europe's mercantile community and an equally powerful set derived from its religion—all interacting with a fortuitous combination of time, circumstance, and condition to prepare and account for the West's phenomenal rise. (The same forces, some centuries later, would interact with a similarly fortuitous combination of time and circumstance to explain the rise of the English-speaking society in North America.)

The proving ground and seedbed for all this interaction was that complex epoch between the fifth and fifteenth centuries A.D. which historians have called the Middle Ages. No attempt to provide partial answers—there are no other kind—to those abiding questions of who and what we are, and whence, and why, can avoid conjuring with these intangible qualities of character and intellect and cultural inheritance. They were bred into the very marrow of Latin Christendom, and of all its progeny.

At first glance, medieval Europe appears an unlikely choice for the mantle of future world primacy. It was (rather like Portugal within its own dominions) on the farthest fringe of the great belt of civilizations that girdled Eurasia from Japan to Gibraltar. The older centers—Mideast, India, China—distinctly overmatched Western Europe in terms of wealth, extent, population, relative stability of local institutions, level of cultural refinement and technology, and power.

Actually, Europe's comparative backwardness both concealed and conferred a host of benefits. All of the world's civilizations had experienced recurrent disruptions and setbacks born of internal strife, war, and barbarian incursions and invasions often amounting to engulfment and conquest. But nowhere else did political, social, and economic disintegration proceed as far or strike as deeply as in Europe during and after western Rome's collapse in the fifth century A.D. No other civilized area lapsed so far into barbarism or experienced greater institutional disruption. Law, order, and social cohesion all but vanished beyond the local level or the vicinity of kings and their tribal hosts. Trade and commerce languished where they did not disappear; the almost deserted Roman highways led past decaying towns and abandoned estates. Only the diocesan headquarters showed fitful signs of life. The lamps of learning flickered and burned low.

Rome fell, and Rome's western dominions were reduced, in the main, to as primitive a level as civilized man could occupy and still claim the title. But the bewildered ex-citizens of the vanished empire and the shaggy Germanic tribesmen who had overrun it mingled haphazardly and co-operated in the slow process of putting a civilization back together. They were building, almost literally, from the ground up, and it would be a few centuries before they got far enough to feel assured that they were going to make it.

Make it they did, however. Even in the darkest period—before the bright, brief heyday of the Carolingian empire offered tangible evidence of Europe's vitality and potential—the shifting cluster of counties and petty kingdoms were able to keep some lighted windows open. A few churchmen, tribal kings, and surviving patrician families retained a precarious but determined grasp upon the language, law, theology, and learning of imperial Rome. Enough of the priceless classical heritage stayed alive to build on and, equally important, to keep its scattered repositors keenly aware of how much they had lost and how far they had to go.

What emerged from this painstaking, up-by-the-bootstraps construction on an attenuated but vital Roman-Christian base was a remarkably flexible and innovative society. To be sure, medieval Europe had its share of folk who strove to suppress change by stern invocations of dogma and authority. Such efforts, together with the hostile comments of Renaissance critics who saw only the declining, anachronistic phase, have given the Middle Ages an undeserved reputation for sterility and restrictive narrowness. The charge, for example, is often made against such medieval hallmarks as feudalism, manor and guild, monasticism, chivalry, scholasticism with its elaborate logic, the Holy Roman Empire, and the extended controversy between kings and popes over who had the authority to invest bishops. But in origin, and for long periods, these institutions and concepts were highly workable, providing cohesion and direction to a society in sore need of both. Only in that time of affliction after 1300 did medieval institutions begin to yield diminishing returns. When all the defects are acknowledged, it remains true that in no other part of the world did tradition assume less hallowed and less rigid forms; no other people were so self-consciously aware of their limitations, so ready to borrow and incorporate and adapt what other societies had to offer. In law and government, science and technology, war and peace, religion and philosophy, agriculture and trade, whatever passed for conventional wisdom was subject to frequent questioning, re-examination, and revision.

As an eager cultural borrower, medieval Europe first looked east along the Mediterranean to the sources nearest at hand—to the Levant, where the oldest centers of human civilization came down to water's edge; and to Constantinople, proudly outlasting Rome as imperial and cultural capital by a thousand years. Italy provided the conduit, which remained at least partly open even during the West's darkest years in the sixth, seventh, and eighth centuries. The Byzantine Empire retained its foothold in southern Italy throughout this period, and hostile Arab sea power never won control in the eastern Mediterranean. Commercial revival in northern Italy in and after the ninth century enlarged Europe's Eastern contacts by freighting them along with silks and spices in the argosies of Venice and Genoa, thereby enabling the West to keep in touch with Byzantine and Arab intellectual activity when those two rival cultures enjoyed their most creative and dynamic eras.

Circumstances gave Western adaptive tendencies an important boost during the twelfth and thirteenth centuries, when medieval Europe was at its zenith. The conduit this time was that great belt of steppe and tundra that runs above and roughly parallel to the chain of Eurasian civilizations all the way from Manchuria to the Carpathians—the most important highway in human history until Western navigators mastered the ocean sea. From time immemorial this vast wild grassland had been thoroughfare, staging area, and breeding ground for hardy nomadic tribesmen who kept sweeping across its long gradients and down onto adjoining civilized areas as raiders, conquerors, or refugees cast loose by even stronger hordes farther back. The stuff of different cultures had been interchanged along this route, far from tranquilly, ever since warlike Indo-European charioteers thundered out of the steppes to infiltrate or overrun nearly every settled portion of Eurasia some fifteen centuries before Christ. Civilized societies were chronically subject to these violent incursions for the next three thousand years as a succession of assorted Hunnish, Avar, Magyar, and Tartar tribes surged restlessly out of central Asia.

The process climaxed between the eleventh and fifteenth centuries with a series of nomadic onslaughts of unprecedented

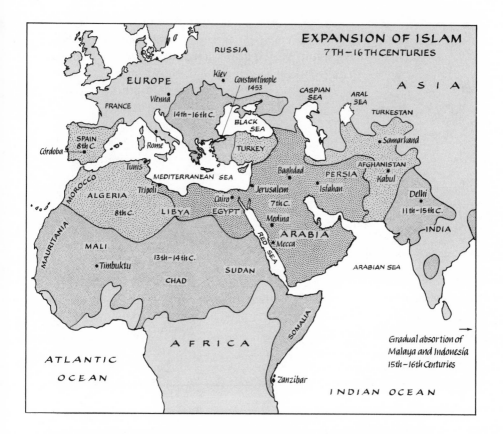

scope and impact. The cultural cross-pollination that accompanied these irruptions from the steppe was considerable; the spores were carried or set in motion by bands of semicivilized, incredibly tough Turkish and Mongol horse soldiers whose long proximity to the more settled, sedentary regions had given them a curiosity and an appetite without sapping any of the combative spirit and powers of endurance bred into them by generations of nomadic wars and wanderings.

Turkish warrior bands poured repeatedly across the Persian

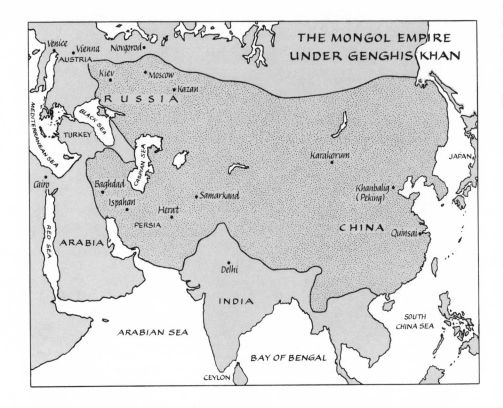

plateau and into the Middle East to become Islam's sharpest cutting edge. They expanded the Crescent at sword's point east and west, conquering more and more of India from the overmatched Hindu states while other bands pushed into Anatolia and over the Hellespont into southeastern Europe across the crumbling ramparts of Byzantium. The Moslem faith also expanded southward across the Sahara, down the east coast of Africa, and into Indonesia.

Established society was even more churned up by Genghis Khan and his tireless Mongol troopers, who took their wiry mounts and their helmets with the horsetail plumes across most of the Eurasian land mass in the thirteenth century. Incomparable fighters, brilliantly led, the Mongols conquered everything between the Ukraine and the South China Sea. They engulfed China, Siberia, Turkestan, and Russia, penetrated the Mideast, and were rolling toward the Japanese islands, southeast Asia, the Nile, and the Elbe before their flood crested. Once settled in as rulers rather than invaders, the Mongols proved keenly interested in other cultures and receptive to other ideas; it was during their continental dominion that the Polos and other European travelers moved in relative peace across half the world and saw the achievements and splendor of the East.

Having far more to take than to give, Europe was a cumulative gainer from these years of intermittent exposure to other cultures. Western society began responding most actively, moreover, just as the older civilizations underwent periods of intellectual stagnation. India tended to rigidify into conservative patterns after the tenth century; Byzantium became a declining force in the eleventh; dogma and mysticism stifled Moslem intellectual endeavor after the twelfth; China froze into complacency and isolation in the fifteenth, shortly after the Ming rulers overthrew the descendants of Genghis and Kublai Khan.

While medieval scholars pored over the elements of Greek, Arab, and Indian learning that filtered back to them—including important items in the fields of astronomy, medicine, mathematics, optics, and other sciences—the fitful currents from the East also bore such items as the stirrup and the lateen rig, the concept of chivalry, *The Arabian Nights* and other stories and poems, chess, cards, the compass and related instruments, the elements of printing and papermaking, and, in all likelihood, gunpowder.

If circumstance worked to the West's advantage in the matter of drawing upon other cultures, nature had conferred another set of benefits. None of the Eastern civilizations could match Europe's combination of temperate climate and good soils, rich timber and mineral resources, and long indented coastline full of good harbors and rivers reaching far into the interior. With each irregular advance in the varied technologies of agriculture, trade, industry, government, and navigation these physical assets grew in importance.

———□———

Meanwhile, harsh necessity had bred a class of men with an unparalleled aptitude for making good use out of whatever lay at hand. Europe's commercial element had evolved along somewhat different lines from their counterparts in older societies, and the resulting differences in comportment and outlook were crucial. The great Byzantine, Arab, Hindu, and Chinese merchants dwelt in larger cities and handled greater fortunes; they probably had an edge in matters of refinement and urbane sophistication; they certainly gave away nothing in terms of cupidity, shrewdness, or bargaining skill. But the merchant in Constantinople, Baghdad, Ormuz, or Peking was apt to be a dealer in luxury goods, submissively dependent upon the ruling class to whose tastes he catered and in whose capitals he dwelt. His enterprise was constricted by the parasitical nature of his trade or industry into currying princely favor or anticipating court tastes; he prospered best during quiet times and tended toward political timidity and fear of change.

The big Western merchants also owed their fortunes to the luxury trade, but in most instances they had had to go and create their markets rather than having one ready-made by the demands of an all-powerful imperial court. The Westerners, in short, had come up the hard way. Self-reliant and enterprising, they also tended to be aggressive—not merely in the commercial but in the physical sense, for they often had to do their own pacifying in the areas they served. The Italian pack trains and caravans that brought the splendors of the Orient to parochial manors and abbeys in Europe's interior came as aliens, armed and on guard against despoliation by resident robber barons, bands of wandering barbarians, or touchy local villagers who regarded strangers as enemies.

The other commercial rays that pierced the gloom of early medieval Europe were cast by the Scandinavians—another of those hardy fringe groups that went down to the sea in ships because their homeland could not support them all. Here the Swedes and Danes and Norwegians resembled the Venetians and Portuguese, save that they were more remote from commercial centers or trade routes or anything else except salt water—which they mastered totally. These Norsemen wrote history with a firm and heavy hand. They wrote a remarkable amount of it, too, casting wiry tentacles of plunder, commerce, exploration, and conquest as far distant from their native fjords as the Hellespont, the English Channel, the Mediterranean, and the St. Lawrence.

A few boatloads of them bucked the Atlantic gales westward past Iceland to Greenland and on to touch here and there along the North American mainland, leaving faint ambiguous traces but no permanent imprint; knowledge of this exploit, which eleventh-century Europe could neither digest nor follow up, disappeared somewhere in the Northern mists. Other Scandinavian bands went from the Baltic eastward to the great river highways that wind across European Russia; they traded and fought their way through scattered Slavic communities, some of which they welded together to form modern Russia's ancestral nucleus; and on across the Black Sea to Constantinople, where some of them, when the attempt to conquer it failed, hired out as Byzantium's imperial guard while others swapped furs, timber, and other Northern products for Eastern goods which they distributed back along the dark river routes all the way home.

The more ambitious of their forays amounted to full-scale invasions—as with the Danes who founded an ephemeral North Sea empire by conquering parts of Ireland and most of Britain; or the Normans who carved out a duchy near the mouth of the Seine, gave their name to it, and went on to reshape the destinies of France and England; or the Norman mercenaries who went all the way to the Mediterranean and created a kingdom in southern Italy by fusing an improbable mixture of resident Byzantine Greeks and Moslems under their leadership to form an effective government.

But mostly the Norsemen descended on Western Europe as raiders and plunderers, putting their dragon-prowed long ships up the inlets and rivers and looting with brutal thoroughness. As soon as terrified Europeans were able to equip enough armored knights to beat off these attacks, the Norsemen made the easy transition from piracy to trade and proceeded to stimulate commercial activity all along Europe's northern coasts.

Even merchants who had not begun as pirates in the Norse fashion had to learn how to fight them off or compete with them. This was true of the Germans and Dutch who traded along the Baltic and North Sea coasts, and of the Provençals, Catalans, and Portuguese who had to make their way in Mediterranean commerce between the powerful Italian cities and Moorish and Arab corsairs from North Africa. The entire European mercantile community thus became imbued with warlike traits, having learned their calling at a time when travelers away from home had to provide their own means of self-defense.

This pugnacious self-reliance had two major by-products. Merchant caravans threading warily through the interior tended to make camp and plant outposts in the administrative centers, lay and clerical, that had survived from Roman days, or beside an abbey or fortified manor that offered a measure of protection while customers were being lured. To the extent that these small mercantile outposts prospered, they began attracting artisans, shopkeepers, and other folk until they overshadowed the older settlement and formed the nucleus of new, predominantly commercial centers.

But these merchant townsmen were still essentially interlopers, outside the prevailing scheme of things—neither peasant
nor noble, neither Church nor Crown, forced to carve their own
niches, make their own law, build their own institutions, and define themselves as best they might. Their most pressing task was
to work out a satisfactory political relationship with the larger
jurisdictions—barony, bishopric, nation, empire—in which
their town lay. Varying in detail, these arrangements usually included a degree of autonomy for the town, sometimes amounting, as in the case of many Italian and German cities, to outright
independence. The merchant oligarchs who wielded this autono-
mous authority thus acquired a high degree of political awareness. Since the ways of towns and trade roused a chronic
suspicion and jealousy among peasants, landlords, churchmen,
and monarchs alike, the merchant class had to keep its political
faculties honed sharp. Such skills, placed alongside inbred aggressiveness, made for as dynamic a network of commercial opera-
tors as the world had yet seen.

Secondly, although the biggest profits were in the luxury
trade, there was never enough of this to go around, especially in
those shoreline areas (from the Mediterranean clear around to the
Baltic) where good harbors and marshy or mountainous coastal
terrain made the sea more hospitable than the land and drove disproportionate numbers into maritime pursuits. Since the Venetians and the Genoese had a virtual lock upon the Oriental traffic,
at least before Da Gama, lesser traders turned their hands to bul-
kier, cheaper items like fish, salt, grain, coarse cloth, timber—
and, of necessity, catered to a poorer but broader market. Dealers
in these bulk commodities were generally a harder lot than the
silk and spice merchants; they had to compete more fiercely and
range more widely to show a profit at all.

Efforts to peddle rough woolens or salt herring by extracting a
scarce copper or two from stolid peasants and village artisans
marked the beginning of a process whereby larger numbers of
common folk were drawn into the international market econ-

omy. This development was in its infancy during Columbus' time, but the bulk trades were expanding as population grew; they would form the mainstay of seventeenth-century Dutch and English commerce, and they pointed straight toward the Industrial Revolution.

And in one humble but far-flung branch of commerce—the fisheries—the mass market was already in existence and playing a crucial role. Religious fast days and recurrent meat shortages created a great demand for salted or dried fish, and the long rivers that placed most of Western Europe within reach of the seacoast enabled the demand to be met. It was undoubtedly the ongoing search for new supplies of food fish and new places to sell them, more than any other single factor, that pulled medieval Europe away from its landlocked rural isolation. The fisheries were primary school and training ground for mariners, shipwrights, and traders alike: Viking and Venetian, Portuguese and Spanish, French and Dutch, English and German seafarers first learned their skills there, and went on, eventually, to build larger craft and go in search of bigger game on farther shores.

This nascent mass market points to yet another distinctive feature of European life. There as elsewhere, to be sure, power and wealth rested largely in the hands of an aristocratic ruling class. But lesser mortals like clergymen, traders, townsfolk, and even peasants played a larger role than in other cultures. Men of commerce, as we have seen, were influential out of all proportion to their numbers or social rank, and even the humblest folk had begun a bit of halfpenny buying and selling on the world market. The Church offered many careers, including posts in high places, to aspirants of low birth. If much medieval literature devoted itself to romantic tales and chivalrous exploits, it was also true that the vernacular was everywhere displacing Latin as a written tongue, and at times the doings of such ordinary folk as millers and friars found their way into literature. Townsmen below the rank of merchant were developing a political consciousness. Progress in weapons like the longbow and the pike reached down to bestow new importance upon ordinary men.

Though both the theory and the tendency existed, divine right and absolute monarchy of *"L'état, c'est moi"* dimensions were still some distance in the future. European rulers, strong though the ablest of them became, never achieved the exalted supremacy of khan or sultan. Kingly claims to power and authority were hedged by a two-way concept of rights and obligations. Law, Church, and custom placed sanctions and imposed duties on prince and landlord as well as vassal and serf. Even the humblest of the latter had a few claims, and the rights of property constituted an important, expandable offset to royal prerogatives.

The power of taxation, for example, rarely became unilateral or absolute, though many a monarch strove to make it so. For the most part, the king had to bargain, cajole, manipulate, and play politics with his wealthier subjects in order to raise adequate revenues. His power was considerable, but he did not rule by fiat, and the constraints upon his authority contained the rudiments of representative assemblies and constitutional government. Peasant claims were often honored in the breach, to be sure, and ways around the sanctions against arbitrary seizure and confiscation were sometimes found. Yet such rights and sanctions did exist. The concept of private property offered one strong counterpoise to royal authority. There was nothing remotely democratic or egalitarian about the distribution of power, wealth, or status in the Middle Ages, but European life did contain a grass-roots dimension (and potential) that no other society could exhibit.

——□——

The insatiable dynamism that characterized Western Europe also owed an incalculable debt to Latin Christianity. Though they were comparably important, none of the other major religions

permeated its cultural matrix in a comparable way. The other
faiths offered compensations and stimuli of a different kind; the
precepts that could exalt, comfort, or inspire an Eastern Orthodox, Moslem, Hindu, Buddhist, or Confucianist believer might
invite comparison with Latin Christianity in terms of depth or
subtlety, but hardly in terms of the persistent, nagging, inescapable, here-and-now complexity of its doctrine. Christian theology fairly bristled with unresolved contradictions and tensions,
both within its body of doctrine and in the innumerable ways in
which it related to daily life: to politics, the pursuit of knowledge
and gain, the structure of society, and every aspect of personal
behavior.

The Christian conscience and awareness of sin added a compelling ingredient to the volatile European temperament. Where
they did not make for good conduct they almost guaranteed feelings of guilt, which neither the confessional nor the deathbed be-
quest could fully assuage. Only the most hardened businessmen
could avoid an awareness that their calling involved constant flir-
tation with the deadly sin of avarice. Backsliding and indifference
were doubtless as frequent in this as in any era, and yet medieval
Europe generally deserves its cognomen as an age of belief. And
for the thoughtful believer, whether ruler, trader, scholar, peasant, or priest, Christianity was housed within the spirit like a
tightly coiled spring. Such a person might pursue any of several
courses, but the one avenue denied him was that leading toward
complacency, inactivity, or enduring peace of mind.

Efforts to compartmentalize or synthesize these contradictions
eventually broke down, even during the period when the spiritual unity of Latin Christendom and the hierarchy of its value
system enjoyed the widest acceptance. The opposing dictates of
faith and reason kept colliding. Questioning never ceased; enduring consensus proved impossible.

Christianity also accounted for that mixture of eager curiosity
and supreme confidence with which Westerners set about studying other times and places to see what they could learn and ac-

quire. Contrast this attitude with that of the Chinese, who before 1500 were far better equipped than Europe for world exploration and expansion. China's one major oversea venture convincingly demonstrated this; between 1405 and 1433 the Chinese government dispatched an admiral named Cheng-ho with a series of huge expeditions into distant waters. Cheng-ho's fleets visited the East Indies and Malacca, probed westward to Siam, Ceylon, India, the Persian Gulf, the Red Sea, and the east coast of Africa, and established Chinese hegemony over the entire Indian Ocean. Dwarfing the biggest European ventures of a century later, each of these expeditions deployed dozens of large vessels and thousands of men. They were prosecuted at a time when tiny Portuguese craft were still creeping in ones and twos down the Atlantic coast of Morocco. And they brought back marvels and trophies enough to have stood any European court on its ear.

Yet the Chinese rulers, having mounted an expansive thrust that might have turned modern history upside down if they had followed through, abruptly called off the whole undertaking and went on to prohibit further maritime ventures. China turned inward. Their curiosity was apparently canceled out by a conviction, which the Mongols had lacked, that anything they might discover elsewhere was bound to be inferior to what they already had. The Ming emperors built upon an age-old Chinese view of foreigners as inferior barbarians. So Cheng-ho's great fleets went home, never to return, and the way was cleared for the Portuguese.

It is impossible to imagine the West turning back in this fashion. Utterly convinced of the superiority of their faith, yet prompted both by its teachings and by the evidence around them that they were far behind the achievements other and earlier peoples had recorded, Latin Christians diligently searched distant lands, antiquity, and their own souls in the belief that they could thus better their condition and fulfill their potential, and that God would reward such quests. A desire to learn and improve braced by a confidence in ultimate triumph made a potent combination indeed. The influence of Christianity upon the West's formative years was pervasive, profound, and indelible.

———□———

All of this, and more, was part of Europe's medieval heritage. The period often depicted as backward, narrow, and superstitious also developed and bequeathed the university, the English common law, the mechanical clock, and an abiding curiosity that never permitted orthodoxy to stifle dissent. The Renaissance did not rise abruptly out of the Middle Ages like a tall mountain towering over a flat plain; there was no sudden flash of light in a hitherto dark world, though many Humanists and later scholars liked to picture it that way. The Renaissance simply built upon intellectual and cultural forces that had been at work for hundreds of years.

This process was interrupted, to be sure, by the stagnation and turmoil of the fourteenth and fifteenth centuries, when the vitality of the High Middle Ages seemed to have lost its force. But the momentum had been checked rather than lost, and penning it up for a few decades had only contained it as a closed chamber confines steam under mounting pressure, or thunderclouds hold an electric charge.

In sum, what had evolved in the millennium since Rome's fall was by all odds the most dynamic, aggressive, adaptive people on the face of the earth. Their culture, to an extent unequaled anywhere else, was shot through with tensions, contradictions, and opposing thrusts—between church and state, city and country, faith and reason, law and violence, might and right, God and mammon. These unresolved contradictions made for an incurable, explosive restlessness. When this perpetually dissatisfied, questioning yet confident folk perfected the tools (of war, seamanship, commerce) wherewith to go into distant places and take what they could find, the results were foregone.

These impulses undoubtedly intensified during the Renaissance. If the term can be applied to a civilization, it is not inapt to observe that Latin Christendom was on the make—consciously, pugnaciously, defiantly. The continent was led by people who wanted something and had already started after it: in art, letters, politics, trade, and over the horizon. They were lively times; even at this distance the sense of excitement and achievement communicates itself. Spirits and minds had been released, new worlds had come into view, and forces fairly set in motion would continue until every aspect of human existence was altered. Beyond the decades of dynastic and religious wars and shifting power balances that were among the immediate results of Western Europe's efforts to slough off segments of its medieval past, vaulting toward ascendancy in the centuries after Columbus, was the age of modern science, modern capitalism, and the modern nation state.

The Renaissance was still some distance from all of this, however, and there is danger of exaggerating the scope and speed of the changes it witnessed. For the great majority of Europeans—tillers of the soil, with attendant clusters of local artisans and other rural specialists—life in the bright age of discovery and self-styled rebirth went on about the way it had for generations, still bound by the unvarying rhythm of the seasons and the narrow horizon of manor and village, church and mill. The heady winds of the Renaissance blew here hardly at all, unless it was to send troops of armed men clanking across the landscape in the service of some far off prince. (And these, after all, had clanked through Europe since the dawn of history; only the garb and the gear had changed.) The merest crumbs and trailing fringes of the rich trade in spices, silks, and silver that quickened the tempo in seaports and market towns from Novgorod to Lisbon ever dropped within the purview of these rural toilers; their annals remained short and simple as of yore.

For all its excitement, its sense of hope and a new day dawning, its deathless achievements in arts and letters and on the high seas, the Renaissance did little to alter the ageless imbalance, as old as human civilization itself, between the privileged few and everyone else. This was an age that glorified the exceptional man, the superior talent, the creative genius—and produced more than its share of such. It helped carve avenues to the top that enabled these gifted achievers to claim eminence alongside men of noble birth (even as economic growth was making room in high places for the merchant prince). But the Renaissance looked upward and outward, rarely downward, and viewed ordinary mortals with lofty unconcern. Ordinary folk had always counted, to be sure, in the eyes of the Church, where their souls stood equally with others at the gates of heaven's grace; and a few of them mattered more immediately and temporally in the Swiss cantons, some of which had evolved a species of democratic government. (Whether invigorated or merely spun restlessly off by their unique political system, thousands of these hardy Swiss hired out as mercenaries to Renaissance princes; for a few decades they were the best infantry in Europe.)

Yet the Renaissance worked no changes in the European power structure, which remained firmly within the grasp of royal families, landed aristocracies, and urban oligarchies. Both the peasantry and the ragged urban proletariat in the manufacturing cities of Flanders and northern Italy were occasionally stirred into rebellious outbursts when the system bore too heavily upon them, but their revolts always ended in bloody suppression and defeat. Economic expansion after 1450 served, at least in the short run, to reinforce this power imbalance, as income tended to redistribute itself in favor of the well to do.

So too, for a time, with the epochal voyages of discovery. If they lifted Latin Christendom's horizons and led Europeans to the fabled golden Indies, east and west, they also led to that ill-starred African coastline where cloth and copperware and hawks' bells would buy not only gold dust and melegueta pepper but human beings. The mighty New World empire that extended Spanish dominion from the Rio Grande to Tierra del Fuego within two generations of Columbus' last voyage was built partly upon silver, sugar, dyestuffs, and livestock and more basically upon the plundering and virtual destruction of one people and the forced labor of another. The immediate sum of Renaissance activity overseas—behind the claims that Indian souls were being saved for Christ and the glib rationalization that the black human cargoes for whom Portuguese traders chaffered on the Guinea coast were slaves already—was to enlarge rather than diminish the already formidable area of human subjection and exploitation.

What remained in short supply in Europe and most of the rest of the civilized world and was in no way remedied by the first exploits of Europeans in Africa, the Orient, or New Spain, was *room*—arable soil in temperate climate, on acres not already burdened with an entrenched legal pyramid of feudal titles or established claims based on conquest. For a time during the twelfth and thirteenth centuries many Germans and other Europeans had moved eastward to colonize the relatively empty plains beyond the Elbe, while reclamation of swamps and forests had made substantial new acreage available to peasant cultivators in parts of France and England. But that had been a long time ago, and the topheavy process of infeudation had loomed over nearly all of it. The tangled and increasingly complex human equation that constituted European civilization had never really included the factor, even at considerable remove, of large amounts of cultivable, sparsely occupied real estate to which no very formidable prior claims existed. And this, too, in the vague shadowy regions above the Spanish Main, was what Christopher Columbus had found.

CHAPTER 3

This Other Eden

THE HARBOR of San Juan de Ulua was no more than an anchorage in the lee of some low-lying shingle reefs a quarter-mile offshore. The biggest of these had deep water close along its inshore side, enabling ships to tie up against it and enjoy protection from the north winds that scoured this section of the Mexican coast.

On this September day in 1568 the Spanish and English ships were moored to the reef side by side in a tightly packed row, like so many suckling pigs. The English squadron numbered seven in all, mostly small vessels, with two large fighting ships that had been lent to the expedition by Her Majesty Elizabeth I. Although the presence of the queen's ships attested to the English government's interest in the enterprise, it had been a private trading venture, fitted out for the purpose of acquiring blacks along the African coast and selling them to the labor-scarce settlements and plantations along the Spanish Main. The Spanish vessels included a few small craft and a fleet of about a dozen cargo ships just arrived from Spain, convoyed by two galleons. A mastless hulk, living out its days as a floating storehouse and separated from the nearest English ship by a narrow strip of open water, marked the dividing line between the two squadrons.

Tension hovered over the crowded anchorage. A few miles up the coast was the town of Vera Cruz, where Cortés had landed to begin his great conquest in 1519, and where the road to Mexico City began its ascent into the high interior plateau. An unhealthy spot with no sheltered harbor of its own, Vera Cruz contained a handful of dwellings and enough warehouses to store the silver, hides, and other products that came down from the interior by mule train for transshipment to Spain. Each year a large convoy sailed from Seville to supply the colonists and pick up the wealth of the New World; part of this fleet would go to San Juan, wintering in that desolate anchorage to refit and take on cargo brought by coasters from the warehouses at Vera Cruz. Virtually empty except when these annual visitors were present, San Juan consisted of some huts for the slave stevedores, a warehouse or two, a chapel, and, on the reef commanding the entrance to the anchorage, a few batteries manned by a small garrison.

The tension was readily explainable. Although England and Spain were at peace, the English ships in San Juan were interlopers. Only traders licensed by the Spanish Crown and enrolled in the monopolistic merchant guild of Seville were legally entitled to operate in Spanish America. Spanish colonial officials were under stern admonition to enforce these regulations, and because the chronic violations invariably provoked the wrath of the government at Madrid, no one in San Juan or any other colonial port could pretend ignorance.

But the monopoly at Seville seldom provided enough to satisfy the needs of the Spanish colonists, most of whom were more than willing to transact illicit business whenever an unlicensed foreign trader dropped by. This put local officials on the spot, and the result was usually a kind of tacit compromise, beginning with a set of maneuvers that were half charade and half in earnest. The visiting merchant, his formal request to land and do business having been officially refused, would proceed to act like a pirate (which often required little or no acting). He would bombard the town in more or less desultory fashion and perhaps put armed men ashore. After a few minutes or hours of this, depending upon the earnestness of either party, they would arrange a cease-fire and get down to business, and the local governor would later try to persuade higher authorities that his community had been forced to trade at gunpoint.

The English vessels in San Juan de Ulua had been trading and shooting their way along the Spanish Main in just this fashion for the past six months. Their commander, John Hawkins of Plymouth, was a notorious and not unwelcome figure in Spanish America. This was the third time he had crossed the ocean with a cargo of slaves and manufactured goods to poach upon Seville's New World monopoly, and he had done so well on the earlier ventures that Queen Elizabeth herself had been induced to buy a share of this third expedition.

Actually, San Juan had not been on Hawkins' itinerary. Bad weather had driven him there, and all he really wanted was a quick refit for the homeward voyage—although he still had a few dozen unsold blacks below decks whom he would dispose of for Mexican silver if he could. After the local garrison had fired a salute at his incoming ships in the mistaken belief that they were the expected *flota* from Seville, Hawkins moored his ships to the reef, took possession of the batteries, and assured the authorities that his intentions were peaceable and that he would promptly be on his way. A day or two later, while his provisioning and repairs were in process, the sails of the incoming *flota* appeared on the horizon.

Dispatching a local dignitary in a small boat with a message for the Spanish admiral, Hawkins proposed that the two squadrons agree to coexist peacefully in San Juan until his own vessels were ready to leave, and that they exchange hostages as an insurance against violations. His forces commanded the entry to the anchorage, and it did not take the Spanish leaders long to accept. Hostages were exchanged and the two squadrons traded salutes while the newcomers moved cautiously behind the reef to moor alongside the Englishmen.

Now John Hawkins had been operating in the pugnacious, semipiratical world of sixteenth-century maritime commerce for a long time, and he had no illusions about the spot he was in. The Spaniards greatly outnumbered him, and Spanish officialdom regarded his presence in the Indies as an intolerable affront. Antagonism between England and Spain had been heating up in recent years, fueled by a variety of conflicting interests back home. Moreover, as soon as the Spanish fleet anchored he learned that it carried no less a personage than the viceroy-designate of Mexico, Don Martín Enriquez, a Castilian grandee who had come to take up his new post. To Don Martín the Englishman was a lawbreaker and a pirate, and a Protestant heretic to boot, beyond the pale of concepts like honor and fair dealing. Even as he pledged his acceptance of Hawkins' terms, the viceroy had begun making plans to violate the truce and capture or destroy the English ships as soon as opportunity offered. And Hawkins suspected as much.

When it came, the Spanish attack took the form of a concerted rush upon the island batteries and an attempt to warp the hulk, now full of armed men, close enough alongside the nearest English ship to permit boarding. The onslaught was launched clumsily and prematurely, enabling Hawkins to cut his two largest ships free and begin bombarding the packed row of enemy vessels moored to the reef. This cannonade soon wrecked the two galleons, but the Spaniards meanwhile succeeded in overrunning the batteries. They could then direct an effective fire upon Hawkins' ships, which were trapped inshore and had trouble clawing out to sea. English losses in prisoners and casualties were heavy. In the end Hawkins lost all but two of his squadron, including his flagship. He escaped with the other royal vessel and a small craft commanded by a young mariner from Devonshire named Francis Drake.

— □ —

It had begun. Spain and England were swinging around to confront each other through the shifting patterns of European politics. The battle at San Juan was neither the first nor the last episode in the chain of events that brought this about, and it would be another twenty years before the Armada. But the Hawkins expedition fairly bristled with omens. It was token and symbol of great changes then afoot in England. Spain had not seen the last of Francis Drake, and the New World would soon learn more about his countrymen.

By the time the battered remnants of Hawkins' expedition reached home, England had been enjoying the relative stability and order of Tudor rule for the better part of eighty years. Trends with origins far back in English history had been allowed to gather force under optimum conditions for three or four generations, and in Elizabeth's time the curves by which one might chart these tendencies began to zigzag decisively upward. Powerful currents were being generated. Without them the Englishmen who planted overseas colonies in later years would not have gone where they went or done what they did, or been what they were. The Tudors and their era are worth a look.

England in the late fifteenth century stood in sore need of such rulers. Generations of wars with France, punctuated by the Black Death and sporadic peasant revolts and followed by decades of domestic strife growing out of the Wars of the Roses, had created conditions of turmoil and disorder from one end of the land to the other. "There is no country in the world," the Venetian envoy noted, "where there are so many thieves and robbers as in England; insomuch that few venture to go alone in the country excepting in the middle of the day, and fewer still in the towns at night, and least of all in London." Unruly noblemen, whose bands of armed retainers rode about despoiling or expropriating the property of weaker neighbors, set the king's justice at naught in many districts by bribing or intimidating local juries.

The first Tudor, Henry VII, had the right combination of firmness, sagacity, and understanding to pull the kingdom together and give his distraught countrymen the kind of leadership they needed. Law and order were restored, and not even the turbulence and stress accompanying the religious shifts that marked the reigns of his successors could more than temporarily disrupt the king's peace.

——□——

The English economy, long sluggish, began to expand. This was partly a reflection of changes taking place all over Europe after 1450: a sustained rise in population and in prices, with corresponding effects upon trade, the growth of towns, and the distribution of wealth. This process was accelerated in England by Henry VIII's confiscation of the monasteries in the 1530s, which transferred much prime real estate into the grasp of the country's most ambitious and enterprising men. The new landlords, erecting their manor houses on the ruins of empty abbeys and priories, pursued aggressive policies that further stimulated rents, prices, and productivity.

Much of England's growing prosperity was made of woolen cloth. Famous since early medieval times for their good pasture, fat sheep, and prime raw wool, Britons later learned how to process what they had once been content to stuff in woolsacks for export to Flanders or sale to Venetian merchant galleys; by about 1400 the wheel, shuttle, and loom had replaced the sheepwalk as mark and measure of economic growth.

The fulling process, in which the newly woven cloth was pounded in an unlovely mixture of alum and special soil ("fuller's earth") in order to cleanse it of grease and dirt, underwent an improvement during the Middle Ages that gave the English industry a great advantage over continental rivals. The fulling mill, wherein water-powered hammers pounded the cloth clean, proved vastly superior to the older method of stomping it with human feet. Conditions of terrain and rainfall limited the employment of fulling mills in the Netherlands and northern Italy, the first great centers of cloth manufacture, whereas English streams had a more consistent and reliable rate of flow. Spinning and weaving had long been rural pursuits in England, followed part time by thousands of families to supplement meager farm income. Since fulling mills could be located at hundreds of scattered rural sites, the merchant clothiers who ran the woolen industry were able to keep it dispersed—and hence conduct and expand it free from the cramping restrictions of town guild regulations and the violent class antagonisms that had eventually undermined the urbanized medieval cloth industries of Flanders and Florence.

The English Crown had furthered the domestic woolen industry by importing skilled weavers, willing emigrants from social convulsions and destructive wars in France and the Low Countries. Englishmen thus learned how to make the long-fibered "new drapery," which weighed a fraction as much per yard as the older short-fibered yarns, enjoyed a wider market because of its lighter and more attractive texture, and required fewer skilled workers to produce, so that it could be made and sold far more cheaply than the older cloth. By the Tudor period English woolens were in demand all over Europe.

English captains had not only goods to sell but orders to fill, and they ranged into distant seas to satisfy the wants of clothiers, tradesmen, producers, and landed gentlemen with money to spend. These people wanted Oriental silks, spices, and precious stones; Mediterranean oils and wines and fruit; rich brocades and hand-crafted metalwork from the shops in Istanbul, Italy, and the Netherlands; and exotic products from the American tropics like sugar and coffee, cocoa and tobacco. The booming cloth industry needed dyestuffs, available in half a hundred places the world over including spots as old as Tyre and as new as Brazil. Shipyards wanted Baltic hemp and mast timber and naval stores.

Englishmen built more and bigger vessels in order to carry all these items. They penetrated the Baltic and the Mediterranean, began poking along the Guinea coast, and eyed the Spanish Main. Groups of them chartered companies on a joint-stock basis to trade with Muscovy and the Levant, Africa and India. No longer did Italian and Hansard merchants dominate English trade. The economies of central and southern Europe, which had quickened during the Renaissance, languished during the latter sixteenth century, and primacy began passing northward and westward—to Amsterdam, London, Paris, and the lands that flanked the Narrow Seas.

Along with commercial expansion, England experienced a burst of industrial development after about 1550 that foreshadowed the more famous revolution of two centuries later. A thriving woolen industry was only part of the story. Religious, political, social, and technological changes were combining to give the island kingdom a big head start in the area of producing large quantities of standard low-cost items for what amounted to a mass market.

The English Reformation, the confiscation of the monasteries, and the (by continental standards) relatively spare dimensions of the monarchy and aristocracy meant, among other things, that for the nation as a whole there was less demand for luxuries and costly high-quality items to adorn cathedral, court, and castle. The expanding tastes of wealthy merchants and landlords took up some of this slack, to be sure. But the market for finely crafted luxury goods was smaller in England than on the Continent, and many English producers were stimulated to look in other directions.

Technology and natural resources abetted them in two key areas. The development of the blast furnace, for example, enabled iron manufacturers to melt and then cast the ore—a great improvement over the old process of repeated heating and hammering by which wrought-iron products were made. The blast furnaces, unlike the forges, could use the cheap lower-grade ores with which England was abundantly supplied, and the casting process wasted less of the ore in the form of slag. These economies enabled ironmongers to make quantities of durable everyday items—pots, pans, nails, horseshoes, rods, and the like—at prices ordinary folk could afford. (The casting process also led to an increased output of cannon, to the benefit of the new royal navy that Henry VIII had built.)

A growing timber shortage had even greater consequences. As the forests dwindled, the demand for fuel induced manufacturers to experiment more and more with coal—another prime English resource now moving toward the center of things. It took awhile for artificers to develop the types of closed crucible and kiln that made coal firing an effective process. They did this, essentially, during the century that began with the accession of Elizabeth I. Newcastle entered upon its grimy heyday, and the smoke clouds from coal fires in a thousand industrial shops made London dirtier and darker every year.

The advent of blast furnaces and a coal-burning economy was epochal—the first great step on the road to industrialization. The two chief components of the Industrial Revolution were now being utilized in earnest. They were still separate components; it would be another two centuries before Englishmen learned to use coal as a fuel in iron metallurgy or harness the steam that a coal fire could generate. But the quest had begun before the end of the Tudor era. Men already realized that pumps powerful enough to drain the deepening coal shafts in the Tyne and Severn hillsides needed a better source of power, and some of the first fumbling experiments with a jet of steam dated from this period. Another incidental feature of the Tudor-Stuart coal industry involved the placing of parallel wooden rails on long gently inclined roadways out from the mineheads, so that wagons full of coal could be trundled down to dockside by gravity. Here, too, a vital component of industrialism awaited only a solution to the riddle of steam.

More immediately, the advent of coal and iron changed not merely the look and the smell but the very texture of English life. Capital investment in industry began a small but significant growth along with the smoke and soot. The cheapness and abundance of coal enabled Englishmen to make quantities of homely, unpretentious items that could affect ordinary houses, ordinary kitchens, and ordinary living habits—things like beer, alum for the woolen industry, soap, starch, earthenware, refined sugar, salt, lime, brick, wrapping paper, cheap window glass. A productive system based so largely upon the output of low-cost consumer goods had social as well as economic implications, and England was becoming a nation apart in more ways than one.

English society had all of the conventional Western gradations, although a few details differed suggestively from the continental norm. A small hereditary aristocracy, possessing disproportionate amounts of land, power, and status, ranked above a much larger landed group known as the gentry or squirearchy— baronets, knights, and men with enough real estate and enough quarterings to put "Esquire" after their names and classify as gentlemen. Below the gentry was an even bigger layer of independent farmers: the famed English yeomen. Some yeomen were freeholders who owned enough land (the legal minimum in Tudor England was a tract with an annual value of forty shillings) to qualify for the franchise. The term also applied to leaseholders who farmed comparable amounts of acreage. The great majority of rural Englishmen were in a bottom category that included tenant farmers with small or marginal holdings, hired hands, servants, day laborers, and the chronically unemployed or unemployable poor.

One or two points about these country folk are worth noting. Serfdom had all but disappeared. This was true in most of Western Europe, but the English yeoman had no real counterpart across the Channel—where the peasantry, though legally free and often in possession of their own land, were socially degraded, politically powerless, and economically oppressed. For the English yeoman it had been different. He had a proud tradition dating back to the Hundred Years' War and shared by no comparable group anywhere in the Western world. What helped give the yeomanry their special quality was the longbow. Their mastery of this formidable weapon, which had originated in the wild Welsh marches and which no other Europeans learned how to use, enabled English armies to win their spectacular victories over the French chivalry at Crécy, Poitiers, and Agincourt. As an antidote to the psychological stigma of inferiority attached to serfdom and the peasantry, nothing could match the sense of one's own worth that came with the ability to drive a shaft through chain mail into the vitals of a mounted knight. The legacy endured; the English bowman had acquired a skill and an outlook that enabled his descendants to walk into the modern era with their heads held high. Social degradation and political apathy were never part of the yeoman's experience.

Non-rural elements—amounting, by the early seventeenth century, to some 25 per cent of the population—formed a comparable social pyramid. The urban elite shaded downward from great merchants to lesser merchants, together with a few proprietors of major industrial and mining establishments, then on down to various master craftsmen and a middling group of tradesmen, shopkeepers, sea captains, and skilled artisans. Below these stood a larger lower-middle grouping of journeymen, clerks, house servants, fishermen, draymen, and mill hands; at bottom was an even larger assortment of dock workers, seamen, day laborers, apprentices, marginally employed folk, and all of the vagabonds and oppressed flotsam of an urbanizing society. A professional hierarchy of judges, barristers, dons, government functionaries, clergymen, and students cut irregularly across class and town-country lines.

What chiefly distinguished the English social structure was its relative fluidity. To be sure, class lines were drawn and class distinctions mattered greatly. But the deep, virtually impassable gulf between lords and commoners that existed in most European countries was bridged, in England, by the intermediate categories of squirearchy and yeomanry. Social movement within and across these boundaries was not infrequent. Mobility was further enhanced by a two-way flow between town and country; many wealthy merchants joined the gentry by buying country estates, and primogeniture drove the younger sons of earl and squire to seek careers in trade or the professions. In England, to a greater extent than on the Continent, fuzzy gray areas rather than sharp bands separated the social ranks.

—□—

By the end of the Tudor period England had evolved a remarkable political system based upon an elaborate set of interlocking human agencies—Crown, Parliament, and Privy Council; a national system of law and justice; and a maze of local governmental units and functionaries. The structure was confusing, complex, surprisingly workable, and uniquely English.

With Magna Carta in 1215 the English barons had won the right to consent to taxation, and the notion proved expandable. During the thirteenth century the periodic conferences between king and barons were enlarged, piecemeal, to include the knights and their urban equivalent, the burgesses. These folk had already acquired a substantial measure of self-government, electing men of their own class to administer the affairs of borough or shire in conjunction with royal judges and officials. The knights, squires, and burgesses were respected community leaders, and it made sense to seek their co-operation and assent in matters of taxation and other national policies—especially since the English monarchy chose to function without a large bureaucracy.

Hence it became the practice to have each shire and borough send two elected representatives to Westminster to sit with the king and his barons in council and talk things over; these talk fests or discussions became known as parliaments. At first the elected knights and burgesses mostly listened and acquiesced, but as the years passed their role broadened. They presented petitions from their communities, gave advice (usually when asked), enacted and sometimes initiated legislation, and increasingly gave their consent—what began as a political expedient was later regarded as a necessity and ultimately claimed as a right—to revenue measures.

As their experience and self-confidence grew, these elected representatives began meeting separately now and then, rather than with the barons, in order to discuss their collective response to some kingly demand. From this informal and occasional practice the bicameral body of Lords and Commons emerged during the fifteenth century. Though still very much a subordinate branch of government in Tudor times, Parliament already had great prestige, a proud tradition, and a tendency to look upon many of its functions as rightful powers. Its very existence persuaded many Englishmen of middling and low degree, whether they were actually enfranchised or not, that they had some sort of stake in their government. (Comparable representative institutions had evolved in most European countries during the Middle Ages, but nearly all had been discredited or weakened by the wars and political turmoil of the fourteenth and early fifteenth centuries. As a result, continental monarchs moving to consolidate their realms could either dominate these bodies or ignore them— whereas in England the element that emerged from that dismal period in the worst condition was the nobility, which had both discredited and decimated itself during the Wars of the Roses.)

The Tudors shrewdly turned all of this to their purpose, strengthening the monarchy by working with and through Parliament rather than over its head. Henry VII transformed another important instrument of royal government—the Privy Council —from a faction-ridden and unruly body of great barons into a powerful, well-knit corps of trusted ministers, mostly clergymen and lawyers with experience in public affairs. These devoted civil servants were able to curb and subdue the fractious nobility. They also sat in the House of Commons as the king's ministers and instructed and guided that body in the ways of legislative government.

The Crown's search for revenue and authority had also helped create an effective legal system. From the eleventh century, royal officials were dispatched with growing regularity to ride circuit through the shires and try important cases in the king's name, execute the king's orders, and implement his policies. These circuit judges soon resorted to the practice of swearing in local inquest juries in order to amass information for tax purposes and also, secondarily, to help settle local disputes. The functions and jurisdictions of the king's courts, judges, and juries were steadily extended and regularized. If equal justice under law was still, in Tudor England, badly flawed by the advantages that accrued to wealth, power, and social status, two vital elements in an equitable legal system—jury trial and due process—had become fairly well established. Englishmen of humble station had some chance of obtaining a just verdict in the king's courts.

The bedrock for this intricate legal structure was the English common law, which had emerged out of innumerable judicial decisions over the centuries and was applied by a professional corps of judges and lawyers, educated in their own schools—the Inns of Court, in and about London—and free from clerical or royal domination. The common law was a great unifying force; Englishmen tended to be proud of it, and popular allegiance to monarchy and commonwealth flourished accordingly. Those gritty Norman rulers who originated the system had built better than they knew. In their ceaseless drive to contain the barons and strengthen the Crown they had put together a legal system—in contrast to the Continent, where Roman law prevailed—resting in part upon the principle that the king neither made the law nor stood above it.

The English political system also flourished at the community level, where the royal practice of working through local notables rather than a central bureaucracy had paid large dividends. The Crown commissioned these people to serve without salary as coroners and, after the middle of the fourteenth century, as justices of the peace. It steadily added to the administrative, executive, and judicial functions of these offices, thereby saving large sums and forging a strong supportive link between throne and populace.

Below and beside the JPs were a cluster of local institutions like the parish and the manor court, and a whole array of local officials: constables, churchwardens, aleconners, sextons, commissioners of the poor, and so on. These offices, together with occasional jury duty, gave not merely the gentry but many lesser folk a taste of participating in local government. The Englishman's sense of having a stake in his community, of being in some small way a part of the system, was widespread, and it extended well below the privileged orders. The process was by no means democratic. Town and shire were ruled by tight little oligarchies; the poor had no real voice. But at the local level the sense of participation went deep and was not wholly illusory.

The English also underwent their own version of the Protestant Reformation during the Tudor years. The most prominent early landmarks were Henry VIII's break with Rome and his subsequent confiscation of the monasteries; the former put the English Church on an independent course (before any very pronounced sense of direction in matters of doctrine had become manifest), and the latter enriched a significant cluster of peers, gentleman capitalists, merchant investors, speculators, and ambitious yeomen, all of whom thenceforth had a vested interest in the new order. But neither the king's dynastic and marital concerns nor the departure of the monks and friars was at the heart of the matter. None of Henry's moves would have succeeded if a decisive majority of English men and women had not given their tacit approval. This they did—not because any great number of them had yet formed a very precise notion of what the Church ought to become, but out of a quiet, pervasive dissatisfaction with the way it was.

This discontent was over 150 years old when Henry VIII and

his Privy Council secured the acts of Parliament that replaced the Pope with the reigning monarch as head of the English Church. It had boiled over in the late fourteenth century with John Wyclif and the Lollards, who wanted a simpler, more pious faith, a vernacular Bible (which Wyclif had prepared), and emphasis upon preaching rather than ritual.

The fourteenth-century Church was unresponsive. It defined the Lollards as heretics and persecuted them relentlessly, clung to its ancient privileges, and continued all of the practices—simony, pluralism, the sale of pardons—that had inspired growing resentment over the years. The abbeys and priories, with some exceptions, came to seem less and less relevant to daily English life, more and more a privileged and useless world apart. Popes continued to appoint non-English favorites to sinecures in the English Church. The neglected lay clergy went about their tasks with little aid or guidance from above.

Anti-clerical sentiment consequently throve, especially in the towns; there was one bit of late medieval irreverence to the effect that if Abel had been a priest, no jury in London would have convicted Cain. Lollardry went underground but did not perish. Dissatisfaction grew even stronger in the early sixteenth century when Renaissance Humanism led a few of England's keenest intellects to inveigh against Church abuses and monkish obscurantism. The majority of Henry's subjects were undisturbed, and many were pleased, when the break with Rome took place.

Anti-clerical nationalism rather than Protestantism marked this early phase of the English Reformation. For a few years the English Church occupied an ill-defined way station only a short remove from Catholic orthodoxy. Henry VIII was no Protestant; he had moved vigorously to suppress Lutheranism in England before his quarrel with Rome and opposed Protestant heresies afterward. Yet way stations are always temporary stopping places, and the English Church soon slid beyond the one Henry had created for it. This headstrong monarch had not called for them, but spirits from the vasty deep were coming nonetheless. Protestantism was on the move all across Europe, and Englishmen soon became stirred by issues that went far beyond vernacular Bibles, monastic sequestration, and image breaking. The Church moved fitfully in a Protestant direction during the reign of Henry's son Edward VI (1547–53), swung back toward allegiance to Rome under the guidance of his devout Catholic daughter Mary (1553–58), then went about on the Protestant tack once and for all with the accession of Mary's half sister Elizabeth.

The new queen wanted to restore peace and harmony in her troubled realm, which had witnessed sporadic harassment and persecution of Catholics under Edward and a harsher, more sustained attack on Protestants under Mary. The result was a broad compromise based on royal headship and the English Bible, the recently issued Book of Common Prayer, and a form of worship that left much to the discretion of individual clergymen and their flocks. As administered by the skeptical and politic Elizabeth, the Anglican settlement contained enough leeway and vagueness in matters of doctrine and ritual to keep a majority of worshipers in the fold, including many who inclined in a more Protestant direction and others with lingering Romish sentiments.

Yet the Elizabethan compromise, too, was a way station. Religious ferment on both sides of the Channel continued. The Church of England was flanked on one side by a few Lutherans and assorted sectaries, including a handful of despised Anabaptists, the outspoken social radicals of their day; and on the other by an irreducible residue of staunch Catholics. But the most characteristic and vital element on the English religious scene during Elizabethan and Stuart times was Puritanism, which grew up *within* the Anglican establishment and greatly influenced it.

The Puritans favored a simpler form of worship, earnest evangelical sermons based on biblical texts, and an end to virtually all that Anglicanism had retained of Romish ritual. On the matter of church organization they split into three groups, two of which remained within the Anglican fold as long as they could. One wanted to replace the episcopal hierarchy with a federation of synods and presbyteries composed of ministers and lay elders; the second wanted more or less complete congregational autonomy. A third group, similarly in favor of independent congregations, soon despaired of achieving this within the Church of England and became out-and-out Separatists. Elizabeth did not approve of many Puritan tendencies and occasionally undertook to stifle or bring to heel its more outspoken votaries, but Puritans did not stifle easily and were not given to falling into line; their influence within the Church continued to grow.

Puritanism's appeal, though it cut across class lines, had the least impact at the top and bottom layers of society. It did particularly well among the more aggressive, capitalistically inclined gentry, the more aspiring yeomen, and the more energetic merchants, traders, artisans, and mariners. It tended to be stronger in the south and east and in the clothing districts, stronger still in the towns and seaports, strongest of all in London.

—□—

No treatment of the American past can avoid trying to come to terms with the Puritan faith and character, which stamped themselves indelibly upon the English colonial experiment and its heirs and assigns. Puritanism drew upon a variety of European sources but most heavily upon the one that emanated from Geneva, and the effort to fathom this complex faith must begin with a brief glance at John Calvin and his implacable message, cold as dry ice and as quick to burn.

The importance of the individual human soul is at the core of Christianity. Notwithstanding scriptural injunctions to render unto Caesar and obey one's master and reminders of the unimportance of life on earth compared to life hereafter, the thrust of Christ's teaching contained temporal implications of another sort. There was the Sermon on the Mount, for example, not to mention that barbed warning about the ways in which the least of these my brethren were treated.

Individual worth and human equality in the eyes of God were Christian principles, but the effort to make life on earth conform to them faced awesome difficulties. For long periods the Church made little apparent headway on this difficult course, which it could only follow in slow zigzags like a ship tacking against a stiff head wind. The dead weight of the past, the status quo, and the interests of the great and powerful were all arrayed against it. These were strong head winds indeed, and for centuries the Church could do little more than invoke Christ's message and hope that some of it would take. Some of it did, but Caesar continued to reign. The social order seemed to require it, and man, after all—the Bible said this, too—was depraved, born to sin since Adam's fall.

The Calvinists and other early Protestants were little disposed to question any of this. Indeed, one of their main concerns was that the Church had become lax on the subject of human depravity, and was encouraging the belief that good works and repentant contributions could free the soul from eternal torment, as though God's grace were something that could be bargained for, and bought. By their own lights they were not revolutionaries at all, but conservatives—bent on reforming and purifying the Church, not breaking with it. The Reformation's chief concern was with the relation between man and God, and the life hereafter; not between man and man, here and now.

Yet John Calvin and his spiritual progeny were revolutionaries in spite of themselves. What they insisted upon doing, these grim torchbearers of Reformation, was to look at the Christian message head on, staring wide-eyed at the deep unfathomable core of it, at God in His awful omniscience and man in his utter depravity, at the things the early Church fathers had really said about salvation and damnation.

Now this was gazing directly into the sunlight, at noonday. It was peeling away all the layers of protective insulation that the Christian Church had donned over the years, since the sun at noonday—an eternity of damnation—was more than most men

could face. Here was part of the great tension, the powerful contradictory pull of Christianity—the pull between God's justice
and His mercy, between man as a little lower than the angels and
man as a fallen brute.

Enter, here, the inadvertently revolutionary aspects of the Calvinist reformation. For the Calvinists did more than reinvoke the
image of an omnipotent God who in His infinite wisdom had
predestined the fate of every human soul. They also called upon
man to ponder the meaning of this awesome proposition as it affected his own fate. Predestination, taken straight, would seem to
eliminate any role whatsoever for the human will. But the imperative summons from Geneva calling upon man to contemplate the state of his soul carried an unavoidable implication.
Humans did, it would appear, have the power to think—to respond, and perhaps even to choose. Having slammed the door
against the idea of free will, the Calvinists almost immediately
slipped the window open for it.

Calvinism was not merely a call to contemplation but a call to
action. History offers few examples of a creed that engendered a
more thoroughgoing activism among its adherents. For Calvin
himself, it was enough that people should devote themselves to
their calling as a matter of love and duty to their Maker—for the
greater glory of God. To serve God well was its own reward.
What happened after death had already been determined, and
Calvin, like Martin Luther and other Reformation leaders, was
firm in his insistence that good works were not enough. Justification was by faith, and by faith alone. And only God could know
for sure whether a person's faith was of the right caliber.

But the Calvinists had set something in motion here that refused to stand still. They demanded a return to the study of the
Bible, the unadorned Word of God; they continued to believe that
Christianity was built upon the three-legged stool of God's omnipotence, man's depravity, and justification by faith. Yet the
spiritual hunger that led thousands of people to respond to this
message began to enlarge the sphere in which the human will was

active. Good works were somehow important; no one was working any harder than the Calvinists. And the human will almost *had* to count for something; at least it was difficult to imagine that souls were as powerless and inert as so many pebbles along the shore, among which God strolled, stooping occasionally to pick the good ones.

The Puritan response to the Calvinist dilemma was the covenant theology. God, without sacrificing His omnipotence, had consented to bind Himself in a contract with man, laying down the conditions whereby salvation might be achieved. Man had to *believe*—justification by faith. In return, as His part of the bargain, God would show man *how* to believe, how to prepare his soul for the entry of divine grace by which one achieved salvation and became a saint—one of God's elect.

This regenerative experience, wherein God touched man with the covenant of grace, became the keystone in the arch of Puritan theology. A Puritan's entire life was to be spent in preparing himself for the receipt of God's grace, then in demonstrating to the satisfaction of those already chosen that he had in fact undergone such an experience, and finally in showing by his conduct that the experience had been real and not false. The Puritans who came to New England in the great migration of the 1630s were believers in this covenant theology. It offered a measure of reassurance, an explicit guide to human conduct (thanks to the Bible), and a fairly well defined contractual obligation by which the awful uncertainty about the future of one's soul could be avoided.

Puritans well appreciated the danger they were in. Their chief quarrel with the Church of England in the early seventeenth century was that it had come under the leadership of men who ascribed too large a role to human will in the process of salvation. The Puritans regarded this as heresy and labored mightily to root it out, but it kept returning, for their own doctrine kept encouraging it. If the path toward an emancipation of the human spirit be likened, once more, to a matter of beating incessantly to windward, then the Puritans were perhaps sailing a point or two closer to the wind on this hazardous course than they would have liked to admit. Refine it though they might, their covenant of grace was essentially a contract that it took two parties to fulfill, and in fulfilling his part man was in some way engaged in an act of will: he was more than a pebble on the beach. Moreover, the Puritans were carrying further a process that their Reformation forebears had set in motion—that of stripping away the intermediaries between man and God. The only one they retained was the Bible.

Here they had come to grips with another of the great tugs of war to which Christianity subjects its followers—the attempt to balance faith and reason. (Christianity abounds with such antagonisms, and the Puritans wrestled with nearly all of them. They kept losing, but each battle brought them imperceptibly closer to the wind.) For in the matter of the Bible they demanded not only a ministry educated enough to interpret it but a congregation educated enough to understand and study it. They were by no means the first Christians to believe that they *had* reconciled faith and reason, to maintain that man's rational faculties, properly employed, would lead to a reinforcement of his faith.

The Puritans were people of few illusions, but they had permitted themselves one here, and it was a big one. The notion that reason would end by supporting faith was itself an act of faith. It was also a thundering endorsement of human potential.

This endorsement was being countersigned, so to speak, by revolutionary progress in the area of scientific inquiry. During the century that began in or about 1570 man not only found answers to some of the riddles of the universe; he devised a method whereby many of the rest would be unlocked in their turn. Modern science had its origins in this period, and the outlines of the modern world came into sharper focus (almost literally) as man's eye began scanning the hitherto ill-charted realms opened up by the microscope and the telescope.

Flowing essentially from the same wellsprings of mind and spirit that had set the Reformation currents in motion—a craving for better answers, better approaches, something more satisfying than ancient dogmas cloaked in the chain-mail garb of Absolute Authority—the new scientific impulses beat with growing force against the ramparts of prevailing wisdom. Three great changes in procedure underlay the scientific revolution of the late sixteenth and seventeenth centuries. As never before, scientists learned to appreciate the importance of precise quantitative measurement. Secondly, they came to rely upon observation and experiment. What was new here (the Greeks and the Arabs, after all, had observed and experimented) was the realization that these practices offered the only valid proof of a hypothesis. The third and most revolutionary change took place in the realm of mathematics. It was accelerated and made easier by such innovations as logarithms (invented by a Scot in the early seventeenth century), the replacement of Roman by Arabic numerals, and the adoption of the modern practice of adding and subtracting from right to left in place of the ancient, cumbersome method of going from left to right. Modern math fairly burst into existence. Men formulated and employed concepts like probability, continuous function, and periodic recurrence, all of which rendered intuitive insights susceptible of abstract proof.

All of these developments were part of a general European phenomenon in which England merely shared; the great names of the period—Kepler, Tycho Brahe, Galileo, Pascal, Descartes, William Harvey—attest to the cosmopolitan nature of the endeavor. But England characteristically achieved its portion of the general breakthrough in a different way: not so much from learned circles downward as from the ground up. The real challenge to prevailing orthodoxy came from an assortment of curious, energetic craftsmen—surveyors, gunners, navigators, metallurgists, glassmakers, mechanics, mariners—who were quietly remaking English life. Their thirst for knowledge outpaced that of university or court and provided the matrix for England's contributions to the scientific revolution.

What amounted to an adult education movement appeared in Elizabethan times in response to demand from these folk, many of whom had attended grammar schools recently founded by merchants who disliked clerical control. London institutions like the Surgeons' Hall, the College of Physicians, and the Society of Apothecaries began sponsoring public lectures in navigation, mathematics, surgery, geography, artillery, and related subjects. Responding to the same demand, English presses and authors far outstripped their continental neighbors in the output of cheap, up-to-date scientific texts, almanacs, and handbooks in the vernacular. Some of the purchasers of such works were able to attend the college founded in the late sixteenth century by Sir Thomas Gresham, a wealthy London merchant. Gresham College established professorships in law, divinity, medicine, geometry, and astronomy, among others. The lectures were in English, and the teaching relied not upon ancient texts but upon demonstration and experiment, with emphasis on applied as well as theoretical aspects.

The whole movement was utilitarian, confident, experimental, anti-authoritarian. Its adherents were of a piece, intellectually, with one of Elizabeth's most learned and gifted courtiers, who summarized the new outlook in a wry epigram. "I shall never be persuaded." Sir Walter Raleigh remarked, "that God hath shut up all the light of learning within the lanthorn of Aristotle's brains."

Nothing quite like this was happening on the Continent, where scientific advance owed much less to the stirrings and promptings of ordinary folk. Only in England had this element, thanks to Tudor rule and the Channel moat, enjoyed so long a period of relative peace wherein to pursue and speculate about their tasks. Stimulated, perhaps, by the Reformation's ongoing challenge to orthodoxy, these English tradesmen and craftsmen grew similarly skeptical of scientific dogma. What, in short, *was* true? And how did one find out? The lanthorn of Aristotle's brains had been called into question, and recent findings had placed other ancient texts in like disrepute. Curious operatives turned instead to measurement, quantitative precision, observation and experiment, applied mathematics. There could be no turning back. The needs of state, and of cannon foundries, shipyards, surveyors, navigators, customs officials, mining engineers, and others, kept placing higher premiums on accurate data and improved techniques.

Intellectuals and universities were following, not leading. According to historian Christopher Hill, William Gilbert's study of magnetism had its origins in his observation of foundry workers and his talks with navigators; William Harvey's theory about the circulation of the blood took shape as he watched pumps at work in mine shafts and on shipboard. "The nearest that 16th- and early 17th-century scientists could get to a lab . . . ," Hill concluded, "was in the workshops of metal-workers, glass-makers, paper-makers, dyers, brewers, sugar-refiners—new industries, or industries in which new processes had been introduced."

It was neither accidental nor unimportant that so much of this grew out of the same social strata and intellectual environment wherein Puritanism flourished. The Puritans tended to be highly congenial to the new science. Both movements were questioning old dogmas and often marched hand in hand in these years, faith and reason supporting each other in a confident assault upon conventional wisdom. Relatively backward scientifically until this startling surge of activity manifested itself, the island kingdom soon became a world leader in such key areas as optics, astronomy, mathematics, surveying, instrument making, and navigation. The skills that helped scatter the Armada, sent expeditions to the New World, and ushered in the modern era were forged in the England of Elizabeth.

—□—

What tied all of these economic, social, political, religious, and intellectual developments together during the latter half of the sixteenth century was conflict with Spain. France, England's traditional enemy, was weakened by protracted civil wars, while the power of Hapsburg Spain waxed steadily. From its Iberian base the Spanish Crown bade fair to dominate Europe and most of the known world, especially after Portugal and its valuable footholds in Africa, Brazil, India, and the East Indies were conjoined to the Spanish throne in 1580.

The nervous antagonism with which Englishmen came to regard this formidable aggregation was honed sharp by the religious question, which glinted off every facet of European politics for over a century after Martin Luther's quarrel with Rome. In ensuing decades the Reformation triumphed in parts of Germany and nearly all of Scandinavia, made inroads in Bohemia, Hungary, and Poland, moved toward success in Scotland and England, and kept peppering the religious cauldron with new theories and controversies from assorted headquarters in the Rhine Valley and Geneva. Protestantism also, greatly to the interest of Englishmen from their close vantage point across the Narrow Seas, provided much of the impetus for bitter civil wars in France and the Spanish Netherlands.

Long in disarray and retreat, the Roman Church eventually mobilized for a counterthrust. It undertook an intensive review and reform of its discipline and dogma, with an eye to improving conditions in areas still loyal to Rome and regaining the allegiance of Protestant areas by any combination of persuasive tactics— word and sword, reason and rack, conversion and conquest— that the situation might require. Its chief instruments, along with a reinvigorated papacy, were the indefatigable members of the Society of Jesus (founded by a Spanish Basque in the 1530s) and the temporal power of His Catholic Majesty Philip II of Spain.

The English began to see what this might mean for them during Mary Tudor's brief reign. Determined to bring her country back to the Roman fold, that zealous ruler not only conducted a drive against heresy in which some three hundred English Protestants were executed and hundreds more driven into exile. She also married Philip, which threatened to reduce England to the status of client state in the great Spanish Empire. Mary's death in 1558 removed this specter temporarily, but the memory and the danger remained. With Elizabeth's accession the Marian exiles returned, bearing sterner brands of Protestantism and overjoyed to be back home. "God is English!" one of them exulted as he stepped ashore, summarizing the fusion of national and religious zeal in three words.

The widowed Philip, anxious to offset French influence in Scotland, sought for a while to win the hand of Elizabeth. By the time it became apparent that the new queen would not accede to such a match the enmity between the two countries had increased sharply, prodded by episodes like that at San Juan de Ulua. Spanish influence soon came to be involved in the intrigues that hovered about the person of Elizabeth's cousin Mary, Queen of Scots, whose very existence imperiled Elizabeth's throne, England's domestic tranquillity, and the unstable Anglican compromise.

Luckless, romantic Mary held all of the tangled threads, at least for a time. Forced by scandal and religious strife to flee her own country and seek refuge in England in 1568, where she remained a prisoner of her cousin's for the next nineteen years, Mary was a devout Catholic. She was also, as a great-granddaughter of Henry VII, the rightful heir to the English throne whenever the childless Elizabeth might die.

Meanwhile the English had expressed their patriotic-religious sentiments in a variety of ways. They cheered and often aided and abetted the Huguenot rebels in France and the Dutch Protestant rebels in the Low Countries. Their sympathy for the embattled Dutch stopped short of war, but it went to the point of capturing Spanish treasure ships bound up the Channel with pay for the army that labored for years to crush the Dutch revolt. Catholic Spain, long before the Armada sailed, had become the enemy.

God was English, and many of England's budding commercial, maritime, and scientific skills were employed against the Spanish menace. National attention was thus increasingly drawn to the Atlantic. From the Bay of Biscay to the Caribbean, wherever the life lines of Spain's far-flung empire offered targets or its outposts offered markets, Englishmen became active. John Hawkins neatly symbolized all of this—devout Protestant, enterprising merchant who had mastered the arts of navigation by sending his ships to three continents, ardent patriot who sailed partly in the service of his queen and later helped command the naval forces that defeated Philip's Armada. Religious, commercial, and nationalist zeal were intermingled and mutually supportive; pocketbook, Bible, and flag were parts of a single design emblazoned on England's coat of arms. (To give the symbol its grimly apt final touch, Hawkins' own crest was a Negro bound with a cord.)

Thus did England emerge from continental appendage to Atlantic power, her ambitions lifting with the western horizons that drew her mariners onward. Literate Englishmen in Elizabeth's day began reading the works of a lawyer named Richard Hakluyt and a clergyman cousin of the same name, whose pamphlets and publications described the sundry voyages of New World exploration and discovery since 1492. The Hakluyts offered an explicit, well-reasoned summons to their countrymen to strike at Spain and enhance the nation's fortunes by planting colonies and creating an empire overseas.

This idea was first translated into action by two enterprising courtiers, Sir Humphrey Gilbert and Sir Walter Raleigh. Gilbert got as far as Newfoundland, but was lost in a storm near the Azores in 1583 before a colony could be established. Picking up the project, Raleigh financed an exploratory voyage to North America a year later, and sent an expedition under another prominent gentleman adventurer, Sir Richard Grenville, to plant a small colony on Roanoke Island off the Carolina coast in 1585. Though they had made careful plans, neither Gilbert nor Raleigh ever quite mustered resources or colonists in sufficient amount to make these initial ventures successful. War with Spain diverted attention from the Roanoke colony, and when reinforcements reached the place in 1591 they found that the tiny band of settlers had disappeared without trace.

But the vitality and zeal that animated this generation of Englishmen had continued to strike blows at the power of Spain. Francis Drake paid his old score from San Juan de Ulua many times over, plundering towns along the Spanish Main, returning from a trip around the world in 1580 in a ship bulging with captured Spanish treasure, "singeing Philip's beard" with a destructive raid on Cádiz in 1587. Elizabeth's reluctant, long-deferred decision to execute her cousin Mary in that same year helped convince Philip, long resentful of English depredations, that it would advance both Spanish and Catholic fortunes if he conquered that troublesome kingdom. "If Your Majesty should place a dependent on the throne of England, which is at present stirring up the Netherlands, troubling the Indies, and infesting the ocean," an adviser urged him, "there will be no one in Christendom left to provoke you." So the Armada sailed to its unhappy rendezvous with storms—God seemed indisputably English in 1588—and sea dogs like Drake and Hawkins and Grenville.

These were stirring times for that loose network of politically involved, scientifically curious, acquisitive, staunchly Protestant folk, in London and the outports and the clothing districts, who along with their sovereign made this reign one of the great ones. Elizabeth was not merely Good Queen Bess but Gloriana, and the voices that would render the era unforgettable were already speaking. This was the England of Edmund Spenser and Ben Jonson, Christopher Marlowe, Sir Philip Sidney, Francis Bacon. The impulses, transmitted in part by means of those grammer schools that Puritan merchants kept founding, reached into places like the Avon River town of Stratford, and by the end of Gloriana's reign theatergoers of every social rank could feel their pulses quicken when the playwright had John of Gaunt speak in praise of "This royal throne of kings, this sceptered isle, This earth of majesty, . . . This other Eden, demi-paradise, . . . This happy breed of men, . . . This blessed plot, this earth, this realm, this England." It was with such spirit that the nation moved to the threshold of her imperial years.

———□———

A word of caution. There were big exceptions to all of this. England contained areas that change had barely touched, placid communities where village life and open-field agriculture had altered little since Plantagenet times, remote backwaters where crudity and provincial isolation reigned as they had in the days of Ethelred the Unready. The invigorating forces were not always blended or in harness: some devout Puritans were suspicious of the new science and the new economy, while many moneygrubbing tradesmen and artificers were indifferent to science, education, and religion alike. On the other hand, there were educated, curious, commercially minded, patriotic English Catholics. And there were untold thousands in the middling and lower ranks of society who had been brutalized or broken—or simply untouched—rather than exhilarated by what was happening.

All of these were part of England too. But they were on the margin, and this was not their time. For the nation was caught up in one of those great tidal movements by which a past age is left behind. And it was the people on the crest of this wave—that confident array of Protestant landowners, merchants, lawyers, artisans, divines, scientists, and farsighted ministers and courtiers —who would later stand atiptoe when this day was named. If the period can be defined, in part, as England's battle between medieval past and industrial-imperial future, these were the folk who fought on St. Crispin's Day.

———□———

This was vastly exhilarating, but it was not quite enough; the impetus that would draw large numbers of people into colonizing ventures had yet to appear. Elizabethan times were, if anything, too good, too busy, or too full of promise for most English men and women to entertain many thoughts about emigration.

Then the mood began to alter. The great wave of the future, it turned out, carried a wicked undertow. The half century that began in the 1590s was different—a time, in Carl Bridenbaugh's apt phrase, of vexed and troubled Englishmen. The tempo of confident scientific advance continued, but the social, political, and economic atmosphere became heavy with uncertainty.

Friction between Crown and Parliament increased, as did antagonism among Puritans, Anglicans, and Catholics. Even Good Queen Bess, tired and infirm, lost a measure of her political skill and sensitivity in her last years, and her successor turned out to be lacking in these qualities from the start. (Mary Queen of Scots had her revenge, finally, when her son James came to the throne of England upon Elizabeth's death. But Mary Stuart's line proved, on balance, as consistently unlucky and inept as she had been.)

It would be wrong to blame too much on James I, but he contributed his share. He was less effective than his predecessor as head of state, both in responding to public sentiment and in conducting foreign affairs. England suffered a humiliating defeat in the East Indies at the hands of the Dutch, as the two Protestant nations began competing for the spice trade. James's well-intentioned policy of preserving the peace with Spain, after Elizabeth's long and costly war with that country, was pursued to the point of frequent accession to Spanish demands; patriotic Englishmen saw this as truckling and kowtowing, and were galled by it. Blunders and setbacks also marked English diplomacy during the Thirty Years' War.

James's reign featured a variety of court scandals, together with the sale of offices and grants of lucrative monopolies and patents to influential favorites. Monopoly grants in the trade or manufacture of a commodity were nothing new, but people had long resented the practice, and Elizabeth, knowing this, had moved to eliminate many Crown-sponsored monopolies. But James needed revenue and found it convenient to resume the practice of selling exclusive rights to favored groups of businessmen and courtiers, and his subjects grumbled.

They were further troubled by the possibility of conspiracies against the state, most of which had an ominously Romish cast. Jesuits, Spanish agents, and native Catholics had schemed more than once to put Mary Stuart on the throne in place of Elizabeth, and these elements continued active in later years. Early in the new century the nation was shocked to learn of the greatest conspiracy yet—an ambitious Catholic attempt to blow up not merely the king but Parliament. The Gunpowder Plot was foiled at the eleventh hour, but rumors and fears of other conspiracies remained alive.

Social turmoil appeared to be increasing—due in part to sheer growth. London had contained perhaps 50,000 inhabitants when Henry VII came to the throne in 1485; when Elizabeth died in 1603 it numbered over 200,000, and it added another 100,000 or so during the first quarter of the seventeenth century. Tension, crime, and disorder inevitably accompanied such a pace and such a multitude, and observers were also worried by conditions in the towns and rural areas. The stability that had characterized much of the Tudor era seemed to be breaking down.

The gravest and most perplexing troubles were economic. The English economy had always been subject to ups and downs, but depressions in the early Stuart years tended to be more severe and prolonged, affecting a larger segment of the population. Tudor expansion had drawn more and more people into commercial production and made them more dependent upon items like the price level, the wage rate, the profit margin—all of which had a way of fluctuating sharply and mysteriously. The large number of families whose incomes derived partly or wholly from the woolen industry were hard hit by severe, protracted depressions in the cloth trade.

In sum, life in England for many ordinary folk had taken on a grim and nettlesome quality, containing more threat than promise. This feeling was enhanced by the venerable Christian belief, held to the point of deep conviction by most Puritans, that when things go wrong it is a sign of God's displeasure, possibly even of His wrath. Evidence could certainly be adduced (court scandals, depressions, diplomatic and military setbacks) to support the notion that God had grown angry with England. From here it was a short step to the bolder idea that perhaps it was God's will that His people should go elsewhere to worship Him.

Only a handful of would-be colonists had volunteered for the pioneer appeals of Gilbert and Raleigh. In the early seventeenth century they began coming forward by the hundreds, then by the thousands. Beneath the infinitude of reasons that prompted such a momentous decision lay a widely shared feeling that something had gone wrong in England and that a brand-new start in distant lands might be the best answer.

Not untypical of these troubled folk was a conscientious, well-to-do squire who dwelt in Groton Manor, Suffolk. His yeoman grandfather had risen to the ranks of the gentry by purchasing a tract of confiscated monastery land from the Crown in the 1540s. The grandson, born in the year the Armada sailed, had become a standard member of the squirearchy—educated at Cambridge and in the law at one of the Inns of Court, a justice of the peace and respected leader in his community. He was also a devout Puritan who did not like the way things were going. "This country," he wrote, "grows weary of her Inhabitants."

He had exchanged views of this sort with like-minded friends in recent months, but now he had something quite specific to think about. A group of Puritan merchants and landowners, most of whom he knew well, had recently incorporated with a view to establishing a colony in America, wherein folk of their persuasion could erect the kind of community and church they believed in. They wanted the squire of Groton Manor to participate and lend his known talents for leadership to the enterprise.

So after much hard thought, earnest conversations with his wife, and the kind of deep soul searching that marked every Puritan decision, John Winthrop left for Cambridge in the summer of 1629 to meet with the directors of the company that had taken the name of that stretch of New England coast where they proposed to plant the new colony, along Massachusetts Bay.

PART TWO
THE SETTLEMENTS

CHAPTER 4

Where None Before
Hath Stood

ENGLAND IN the early seventeenth century contained a
large and growing number of people who were sufficiently dissatisfied or worried by what they saw around them to
be ready to emigrate. The same mixture of forces that had underwritten the nation's rise during the Tudor era was now on the
verge of summoning forth a colonial impulse, which in turn,
during the Stuart years, would lead to the creation of the first
British Empire. The process was far from systematic, but it was
conscious and, on the whole, purposeful. The Empire was not
put together, as has sometimes been observed, in a fit of absent-
mindedness. Rather, it emerged haphazardly, out of a series of
unco-ordinated enterprises. These enterprises, and the impulse
that underlay them, were key determinants of the future New
World society—England's way of transmitting its own strongest and most distinctive features to a new environment.

Colonization was partly a matter of bringing various impulses
together, mobilizing and harnessing them. The components
were all there, including the examples set and the lessons learned

by the unsuccessful ventures of Sir Humphrey Gilbert and Sir Walter Raleigh. On the individual level, there were all those vexed and troubled Englishmen, more numerous now, and more vexed than in the days when Gilbert and Raleigh had been able to enroll a few dozen of them. And on the national level, people in high places were still aware of the cluster of imperial ideas so ably put forth by publicists like the Hakluyts. They had devised a formula which no later arguments in favor of colonies would improve upon: discovering gold and a Northwest Passage to the Orient; converting the North American Indian to Protestant Christianity; planting overseas settlements that would assist the navy and provide raw materials, new markets, and home and opportunity in safely distant spots for England's restless poor. There was something here for everybody. Religious, social, and commercial motives had been neatly blended in a plan designed to benefit individuals while enhancing England's strength and strategic position in her struggle with Catholic Spain.

These arguments, dating back to the 1580s, retained much of their plausibility and relevance twenty years later, but recent experience suggested that a restructuring of priorities was in order. Gold and the Northwest Passage remained elusive. At the same time, the Crown seemed as little disposed under James as it had been under Elizabeth to do more than grant permission and bestow its general blessing upon colonial enterprises. No English monarch during the Tudor-Stuart era was prepared to consider actual investment in colonization. That must come, as it had in the building of the Spanish Empire, from private sources. As for converting the Indians, English Protestantism was now even more preoccupied with the nagging, disruptive problem of how to define its own creed. Protestants would begin migrating soon enough, but for reasons that had little to do with converting Indians in competition with Rome.

The formula that finally began to produce results combined the essential elements—land, profits, religion, and the national interest—in ways that said a good deal about the kind of empire the English were going to build and the kind of society that would gradually take shape in their new overseas dominions. The key element, by which the needs and aspirations of prospective colonists were yoked to those of the nation, was land.

Probably no single word, at least in the secular realm, had more important or revealing connotations for the English people. Land was talisman, pole star, magnet, key—the ultimate social security, in every sense of that phrase. Only gold had a comparable drawing power. Yet gold worked a different and narrower sort of magic, turning everyone who touched it into Midas. Land could do this to people, too, but it could do far more. It was a many-sided concept, as varied in its hold upon the folk who went after it as in its actual physical qualities. The New World contained vast unknown quantities of it, beckoning mysteriously, compellingly, from beyond that long irregular wooded shoreline of North America which the explorers of several nations had already coasted and begun to probe.

England was in flux. So was much of continental Europe, but history and geography had combined to develop the island kingdom along somewhat different lines, and England was better situated to adjust to the forces of change, and finally to take advantage of them. The course of Western civilization had entered the first rapids, with faster and more turbulent stretches yet to come. England, responding most readily, would end by leading the way through them. In so doing, she would become for a time the greatest power in Europe and in the world, and in their vanguard, she would plunge first over the awesome cataracts of industrialization.

This was all in its early stages at the beginning of the seventeenth century, but it was perceptible; the speed of the current had quickened enough to be felt. English men and women exhibited every variety and combination of human response to the challenge of change—bewilderment, frustration, confusion, anger, excitement, fear, enthusiasm. Some floundered, hopelessly out of their depth; some clung to the past and sought desperately to pre-

serve it; others looked eagerly ahead and leaped to take advantage
of the new opportunities. Still others, including some of the most
prudent and practical, sought to arrange things so they could
have it both ways.

To a greater extent than in any other society, the Englishman's
many-faceted concept of land spoke in one way or another to all
of these responses; wherever one stood with regard to change,
land offered him something. And just as Englishmen began feeling all of this most acutely, the New World real estate to which
their government laid claim moved into their ken and gave their
concept of land an exciting new dimension.

For ordinary country folk, a freehold offered status and independence. If they were commercially minded, it offered opportunities for profit in the raising of produce for sale in distant
markets. For members of the gentry and the nobility, possession
of enough acreage conferred the highest status and most attractive way of life that Englishmen recognized—that of the great
landholder, with his manor, his retainers and his tenants, and the
power and influence these conferred. For such a landlord who
wished to move with the times, large holdings under proper
management could be made to yield large returns indeed. For
townsfolk—merchants, traders, master craftsmen, dealers in
this and producers of that—rural acreage had the same double
value: it offered a way into the ranks of the gentry, and if it could
be made to produce the right things in sufficient quantity it
would be a source of profit.

Land as the source of independence, status, profit, wealth,
power, influence—there was nothing particularly English or in
any way new about this. But the English had extended landownership or the possibility of landownership further down the
social ladder than in most European societies. The process of
moving away from the feudal, or lord-and-vassal, concept of
land tenure had thrust many former English serfs into the ranks
of freeholders; it had thrust an even larger number into the ranks
of leaseholders, who owned their own labor and exclusive right

to what they produced in return for payment of a money rental. This leaseholding population stood poised in an uneasy halfway house between the full citizenship of freeholding and the subordination of hired hand or servant. When the economy behaved erratically, both the upper and the lower doors to this halfway house stood open. With good luck, an aspiring tenant might buy some acres of his own; a little bad luck could lead to an abrupt descent into the ranks of the laboring landless poor. Economic fluctuation touched the higher spots on this ladder as well. Freeholders and even members of the gentry and nobility could find themselves wiped out or hopelessly in debt if prices took an unexpected turn. The difficulty of finding a place for second and other extra sons in a society committed to primogeniture added greatly to the pressure upon existing acres and the appeal of new ones.

Understandably, then, land became the keystone in the elaborate arch of colonization arguments, the one appeal that was legal tender in all quarters. For the fearful and the hopeful, the backward-looking and the expectant, leaseholders, freeholders, country squires, courtiers—land offered a way up or a way out or a way back. Sir Humphrey Gilbert and Sir Walter Raleigh had understood all of this perfectly, and land had figured prominently in their colonizing schemes. They had hoped to carve out great domains for themselves and get support by granting lesser estates to other gentlemen who would join the expedition, while attracting recruits at the lower level by promises of freeholds and leaseholds on good terms.

Incentive and experience had been acquired from slightly earlier ventures as proprietary colonizers in Ireland, which Elizabethan England had set out to conquer in the interests of the throne, the state, the Protestant faith, and land-hungry courtiers and second sons. (The prominent part played by men like Gilbert, Raleigh, Sir Richard Grenville, Edmund Spenser, and other noted Englishmen in the subjection of Ireland prompted a telling observation from Sir George M. Trevelyan: "It has been said," he wrote, "that the Elizabethan eagles flew to the Spanish Main while the vultures swooped down on Ireland; but they were in many cases one and the same bird.").

The Gilbert-Raleigh New World enterprises had been well planned and well reasoned; they fell victim, essentially, to bad timing. War with Spain during the last fifteen years of Elizabeth's reign diverted the nation's attention and its resources. The pool of prospective colonists was not yet large enough. Most important, the merchants, whose resources and skills would prove indispensable for the first colonial successes, were not yet ready to participate on a sufficiently large scale. Raleigh and Gilbert could never quite sustain those first American ventures, and the merchant community still saw greater promise and more return in areas like the wool industry, the Mediterranean, the Baltic, Muscovy, or Africa.

But it all began to come together at the turn of the century. The war with Spain ended in 1604, liberating a substantial portion of the national energy. While fear and envy of Spanish power remained, the various religious and political antagonisms that would push England into civil war a few decades later were already beginning to be felt. The disruptive effects of economic change and growth were touching more and more lives. And the London mercantile community now had capital and interest to spare for colonial enterprise. The schemes, investments, and migratory impulses that would lead to the creation of a new overseas empire had reached the point of coalescence.

In the beginning, for English colonizers, was Virginia. Land, throughout this founding century, remained the primary inducement for both the sponsors and the settlers, but it took a strong injection of mercantile methods and skills to make the first colony a workable proposition. And it was Virginia's success that made the later ventures possible.

London was England's hub, and it was London that put together the winning combination. Sir Walter Raleigh, nearly bankrupted by his Roanoke ventures, had transferred his charter rights to a group of London merchants, and early in the new century their interest had matured to the point of taking action. The London mercantile community contained able men. Their experience in the Muscovy Company, the Levant Company, the newly formed East India Company, and many lesser enterprises had taught them how to mobilize and deploy capital. A group of them organized the Virginia Company of London, obtained a charter from the Crown in 1606, and recruited colonists with an eye to establishing a beachhead that would form the basis for a permanent settlement. Drawing upon their experience, their connections, and their resources, these men proceeded to experiment until they devised a formula that made their little colony work. The sum of their efforts pointed the ways in which Englishmen would finally succeed in building an empire, and contained a visible outline of the kind of empire it was going to be.

Finding a satisfactory formula proved difficult, and the price of success in Virgina was high—in lives, in human suffering, and in money. Nearly two decades of struggle and trial elapsed before the small Virginia settlements could maintain themselves as going concerns, and by this time the company that had created them had gone bankrupt and lost its charter. But a great deal had been learned. The varied ingredients that would enable England's colonial ventures to thrive and prosper had been selected and tried.

The two basic ingredients were money and organization. These the Londoners provided by employing the device of the joint-stock company, an ancestor of the modern corporation which was able, by pooling resources, selling shares, and spreading the risk of loss, to mobilize capital in amounts far exceeding the resources of courtier-colonizers like Gilbert and Raleigh. Although the joint-stock company as a purely commercial venture was not to be employed in the founding of many future colonies

—English merchants learned from the Virginia experience that investment for profit in the actual planting of a colony was not likely to pay off—the company organization proved adaptable, in Virginia and later in New England, to the governing of a colony. This would have important consequences.

These merchant adventurers appreciated the value of publicity, and no little portion of their capital and energy was spent on promotional literature. Their enterprise, obviously, could not succeed without a labor force. Some of it could simply be hired; other recruits became shareholders by investing their labor as part of the joint stock and agreeing to work for a given number of years before claiming their share of the corporate profits. But Virginia was designed as more than a factory, staffed by wage earners; it was to be a settlement, or plantation, in the terminology of the day, staffed by full-time colonists who would live as well as work in the distant outpost. And whether the people came as hirelings and servants, as investors, or simply as settlers, they had to be induced.

The Virginia Company began with the devices and arguments they knew about—tracts, broadsides, and printed sermons setting forth the appeals that publicists like the Hakluyts had formulated years earlier, with due emphasis upon the prospects of finding gold and a new passage to the Indies, the chance to strike a blow for England against Spain and for Protestantism against Rome, the temporal and spiritual gains to be derived from converting the heathen red man and trading with him. The promotional literature also made specific appeals to prospective husbandmen and artisans, speaking of the opportunities that awaited every occupation in the New World.

A few years of this sort of thing enabled the Virginia Company to recruit enough people to staff the Jamestown settlement and keep it going, despite the appalling mortality rate of the early years. Gradually, however, the promotional literature took on a new emphasis. The patriotic, religious, and even the profit motives began to be subordinated to a deeper and more basic appeal

—that of persuading men and women to come forward and emigrate as permanent settlers in a New World, builders of a new society. In the short eighteen years of its existence, the Virginia Company developed promotional techniques that would be a vital part of the colonization process from that time forward.

While the company raised money and recruited settlers, its leaders wrestled with the problem of how best to manage affairs, both in the home office and in the overseas outpost. The first important lesson was that some form of centralized authority, both at headquarters and in the field, was necessary. Management was originally in the hands of councils—one appointed by the Crown to oversee company affairs in London, and a subsidiary body chosen by the Royal Council, entrusted with leadership in the colony itself. The effect of this diffusion of authority was a near-fatal lack of leadership.

A companion venture under that 1606 charter, the Plymouth Company, backed by Bristol and other West Country merchants jealous of London influence, was authorized to plant colonies in a vast tract overlapping the Virginia Company's grant and to the north of it. The Plymouth group planted a settlement at the mouth of the Kennebec in 1607 while the Londoners were busy at Jamestown, but the northern venture failed and was abandoned in little over a year, chiefly because the overseas council with its hopelessly dispersed authority could do no more than divide into factions and wrangle while the settlement withered for lack of leadership.

The same fate almost overtook Jamestown in its early years and would probably have done so but for the strong hand of Captain John Smith. After a year of floundering and quarreling, the survivors of the first Jamestown landings turned in desperation to this tough, contentious, able man, "all brasse without and golde within," whom they had expelled from the council when the expedition first landed. Under Smith's iron authority the straggling little settlement acquired enough strength and order to be able to survive.

Learning from these examples, the company in 1609 procured a revision of its charter that made greater centralization of authority possible. At home, the governing council—roughly equivalent to a modern board of directors—became a stronger body, with virtual one-man rule vested in the post of company treasurer. The individual who held this position and provided a crucial amount of strong leadership during these early years was another Smith—Sir Thomas Smith, one of London's wealthiest and ablest merchants, a shrewd, devout, and learned man. At his urging the cumbersome device of a subsidiary overseas council was replaced by the office of governor, appointed by the company and having "full power and authority" to run the colony. The example of one Smith was thereby institutionalized by another, and for a time the colony was run along the lines of a military outpost—which in many respects it was.

A new joint stock was created in 1609, with both money and labor represented by shares that would go into a common pool for seven years. During this time all overseas property and profits remained in company hands and enterprise was communal, with each man working for the company and drawing what he needed from a company storehouse, land and profits to be divided pro rata when the seven years were up. Meanwhile a succession of governors ruled Virginia with a firm hand under a code that combined martial and civil law at the expense of individual liberty.

The second major lesson the company learned was by way of being the reverse side of the first one, and it was even heavier with future significance: however necessary centralized authority might be during a settlement's early years, Englishmen did not in the long run take kindly to it.

The first indication of this came from the stockholders, or adventurers, as Englishmen who joined the company by venturing their capital in it were called (as opposed to "planters," who actually went overseas and invested their labor). Dissatisfaction among the adventurers led to a revision of the charter in 1612 whereby control over company affairs was transferred from the treasurer and Crown-appointed council to a "Court and Assembly" of all shareholders, meeting periodically. The new charter retained the governor's absolute authority overseas, but the settlers and planters were growing restive under the tight regimen of a military outpost, and the system began to fray at the edges. The communal labor system went against the English grain and was a constant irritant, and the governors soon began modifying it by allowing individuals to farm a few acres privately, in return for specified amounts of labor in the company fields and a small contribution in kind. Even worse, the colony was not making money. When the seven-year plan ended in 1616, far from having profits to divide among contributing planters and adventurers, the company only had larger debts. Enthusiasm about Virginia, among both settlers on the scene and prospective immigrants back home, had waned. The flow of newcomers all but ceased.

It had now become clear that if settlers were going to be attracted to Virginia and kept happy after they got there, they would have to be given a chance to acquire some land of their own and some kind of voice in managing their own affairs. Land and self-government: the colonial impulse derived from these, and the entire colonial edifice would be built upon them—not because rulers, founders, or organizers especially wanted it that way, but because ordinary Englishmen were not prepared to come forward in sufficient numbers if these items were not included in the package.

The Virginia Company figured this out after a decade of experiment and adjusted its policy accordingly. All it had to divide, at the end of that seven-year joint stock, was land. The settlers and planters were clamoring for it. They were clamoring even harder, now, because after years of search and unsuccessful trial it appeared that the Chesapeake colony had finally found a cash crop in the form of tobacco. The company changed front and obtained a new charter in 1618 with clauses that marked the great turning point for Virginia and pointed the way ahead for all of British North America.

Under the new plan, the company would keep certain substantial estates for itself, paying dividends (it was hoped) from the revenues and cultivating it by means of seven-year leases to those emigrants who came over at company expense. Existing planters and adventurers would receive land grants in accordance with the size of their investments. And henceforth every new settler who paid his own passage would receive a fifty-acre tract of land, with an additional grant for every person, child or adult, whom the newcomer brought with him or whose later passage he might finance.

This was the famous headright system, a recognition by the company that the chance to acquire a few acres of one's own was the greatest single inducement to prospective colonists. The headright was used in nearly all of the English colonies, sooner or later. In keeping with the new emphasis, company promotional literature thenceforth stressed the theme of permanent settlement as a desirable end in itself. Englishmen were being invited to come and help build new societies, not merely to labor for a commercial organization. And they were being invited to settle as landowners rather than as tenants or hirelings.

The second momentous feature of the Virginia Company's new charter was the clause creating a general assembly. Consisting of two representatives from each private settlement and two from each of the company's four estates or tracts, the assembly was to meet at least once a year, and its enactments would have the force of law in the colony. Moreover, company instructions from London would not go into effect until the assembly had ratified them. The governor, aided by a council of his own choosing, would continue to be the executive officer, but his absolute authority was gone. The strict martial and civil code was replaced by the English common law.

The company hoped by this farsighted measure to harness its own interests with those of the private plantations that had begun to spring up and grow after the ending of the seven-year joint stock. The first duly elected assembly met at Jamestown with the governor and his council in midsummer of 1619. The little session lasted less than a week, driven to quick adjournment by malaria and the stifling July heat. But as a precedent for England's nascent empire, it had no peer.

The company had found the formula that insured success for its infant colony, but its own fortunes went from bad to worse. It had sunk great sums of money in Virginia, but it never returned a farthing in dividends, and its debts mounted steadily. Under new management at home after 1619, the company redoubled its promotional activities and granted a number of land patents to various subsidiary corporations formed by groups desirous of planting new private settlements in Virginia. (One such patent was issued to a group of English Separatists who had first emigrated to Holland and now wished to try their luck in America; history would know them as the Pilgrims.) A national lottery was pushed with enough zeal to provide proceeds whereby several hundred newcomers were transported at company expense. An even larger number, attracted by the new dispensation, came on their own.

But if individuals prospered, the company continued to lose. Grumblings against it, both in England and in Virginia, became louder. The colony could not accommodate so rapid an influx, and the mortality rate was appalling. A surprise Indian attack in 1622 took more than three hundred lives and nearly pushed the little settlements back into Chesapeake Bay. Desperate for revenue, the company obtained a monopoly from the Crown on the shipment and sale of all Virginia's tobacco. This inspired such fierce resentment among private growers that a royal commission was named to investigate the company's affairs. These, it was revealed, were a sorry mess. Hopelessly bankrupt, the company lost its charter under judicial proceedings in 1624 and went out of existence.

Virginia now became a royal colony, with a governor appointed by and responsible to the Crown. It looked for a time as though Virginia's political status under the Stuarts, who were no great admirers of representative government, would revert to the centralized authority of the early charters. But Charles I, who acceded to the throne shortly after the Virginia Company's dissolution, had weightier things on his mind than the details of colonial policy, and in the absence of specific orders, his governors learned an instructive lesson in the ways of English colonists with absolute rule when it was three thousand miles away. The first royal governor was Francis Wyatt, who was a stranger to Virginia and intelligent enough to perceive that he could not govern intelligently without advice and assistance from knowledgeable folk on the scene. He quickly adopted the practice, which had been followed informally during the company period, of choosing a body of local notables to act as his council. The council, though appointed from above, displayed an independent spirit from the start; it proved indispensable, and became an important and permanent part of Virginia's governmental structure.

Wyatt had no authority to convene the representative assembly, whose future under royal administration was very much in doubt. But he convened it extralegally in order to determine colonial sentiment on a particular question, and in the absence of orders to the contrary from home, the little House of Burgesses continued an ad hoc existence. The delegates met every year on their own to discuss colony affairs and petition the king to confer the authority they had had under the company charter. These petitions were ignored for a time as governors came and went, but full authorization for annual assemblies was granted with the return of Governor Wyatt in 1639. The Crown retained the company's original power of appointing the governor and disallowing colonial laws, but the assembly had persisted and would endure. The first settlers to quit their native land in favor of colonial existence had not forgot to pack and bring along that well-developed sense of what it meant to be an Englishman.

—□—

By this time the first great wave of English migration had crested, and several new colonies had sprung into existence. Maryland was conceived and developed along the proprietary rather than the corporate line. The Stuarts much preferred landed magnates to London merchants, and the latter had learned a lesson from their Virginia experience; henceforth the commercial element would invest in the transportation and supply of colonists but not in colonization. But the older, half-feudal dream of a great landed estate, with earnest tenants and sturdy yeomen tugging at their forelocks while the lord of the manor rode by, continued to play a prominent part in seventeenth-century colonization schemes. Stuart England, first and last, abounded with aristocrats, courtiers, and the extra sons of gentlemen whom religious, political, or economic change had adversely affected, and who longed to regain status and fortune in some princely domain overseas. The Stuart kings were surrounded by such men, especially after the accession of Charles I.

The Maryland grant was made to George Calvert, a former high government official with considerable interest and experience in the home-country side of colonial activity. Well connected at court, Calvert became a Catholic in the mid-1620s, resigned his government post, and was elevated to the peerage as Lord Baltimore, in which capacity he forwarded his proprietary plans. These had begun with a generous grant in Newfoundland, where he tried to establish his barony in 1628, emigrating with his family and a few dozen settlers. But trouble with French privateers, followed by a taste of Newfoundland winter, persuaded him to leave, "determined," as he put it, "to commit this place to fishermen" and seek his domain in warmer climes. He first tried Virginia, but the governor's council disapproved his Catholicism and did not make him welcome. He then besought a grant in the territory just south of Virginia, but King Charles had just awarded this to another would-be proprietor, and Baltimore ended with the Maryland grant instead.

Although it had not been his first choice, the terms of the charter were all that an aspiring feudal magnate could have wished for. And they revealed something of the sort of allies the House of Stuart wished to have. Lord Baltimore's authority in Maryland was well-nigh absolute, more sweeping than that of the king in England. He held all the land and had all the power of legislative, executive, and judicial appointment. He could found towns and boroughs, bestow titles, create courts, make the laws, and pass all of this power to his heirs. The only restraints were the Crown's right to regulate trade, control foreign affairs, receive one fifth of all precious metals, and disallow Maryland statutes that clearly contravened the laws of England. The only other restriction was that the proprietor's laws required the people's advice and consent; he alone, however, could initiate legislation.

Now this was a long look back toward the great feudal baronies of a much earlier time. Maryland prospered, almost from the start, and so, in a way, did the Calvert family. (The first Lord Baltimore died and was succeeded by his eldest son before the two ships with Maryland's first settlers left England in 1634.) But the Maryland proprietorship never took more than a step or two down the road to the past. The "advice and consent" clause was all the colonists needed. They had the Virginia example of a representative assembly before them, right down Chesapeake Bay; and the Calverts were tolerant realists who preferred the substance of things actually obtainable to the shadow of what lay out of reach. They foresaw Maryland as a refuge for English Catholics, a few of whom came and received large estates from the proprietor. But the majority of immigrants were Protestants, who wanted a few freehold acres rather than a great estate. Seeing this, the Calverts followed the Virginia example and began giving out hundred-acre headrights to attract settlers. It worked. The newcomers borrowed further from Virginia and devoted most of their attention to growing tobacco, now well established as a cash crop that could thrive in the Chesapeake region.

The first general assembly was summoned by the proprietor in 1635, met in the presence of the governor (the second Lord Baltimore's brother) and his council, and immediately adopted parliamentary procedure and started testing and extending the boundaries of its rights and privileges. In 1638 the assembly defiantly rejected laws sent over from England and demanded the right to initiate legislation. This was granted in a limited way before the end of the year, and although the proprietor did not relinquish the principle, he steadily gave ground in fact. Maryland, like its near neighbor, developed fairly early along the basic English lines of an elected assembly and freehold farms.

Colonizers were also at work in other portions of the Western Hemisphere, including one attractive region far to the south of Chesapeake Bay. The lure of a more hospitable climate and the chance to strike at their favorite enemy drew a few prospective founders and settlers toward the islands where Europe's first acquaintance with the New World had begun. One tiny outpost, the Bermudas, was discovered by chance in 1609 when one of a fleet of ships bound for Virginia was driven ashore on the major island by a hurricane. The Londoners promptly decided to plant a colony there as well as in Virginia. A subsidiary company, run by the same adventurers, was chartered in 1615 to govern the island colony, which flourished right from the start. Bermuda had several attractions—excellent climate, long growing season, no hostile Indians, coral reefs offering protection against pirates and enemy privateers—and it was the only corporate colony that paid much of a return on its investment. By 1629 the little islands had almost as large a population (some 2,000) as the entire Virginia colony.

The warm sunshine, mild winters, and good tobacco crops enjoyed by the early Bermuda colonists added greatly to the possibilities some Englishmen already saw in similar islands in the West Indies, where, since the time of Hawkins and Drake, English, French, and Dutch privateers had been prowling for Spanish treasure ships and doing what damage they could to Spain's New World empire. Spain was still, despite internal weaknesses and a visible onset of her long decline, the foremost European state in the first half of the seventeenth century. Most of her rivals' overseas enterprises during those years were launched partly or primarily for the purpose of forestalling, outflanking, harrying, or reducing Spanish power.

Spain's enemies had known since Hawkins' time that this power in the New World was vulnerable. Their attention became particularly drawn to the Lesser Antilles, a handsome, fertile chain of islands extending in a long arc east and south from Puerto Rico to the Venezuelan coast. Transatlantic voyagers were familiar with these islands. Many of the ships bound for British North America went there by way of the West Indies, taking advantage of the northeast trades on Columbus' old route and touching at one or another of the Antilles for fresh water and provisions before sailing north on the last leg of the voyage. Spain had always been too absorbed with the major centers of her empire, farther west, to occupy these islands effectively, and her rivals were willing to recognize Spanish claims to a monopoly in the New World only in those areas where Spaniards were present in force. After 1600 the rivals grew bolder and began moving in on the Lesser Antilles. While the French established footholds on Guadeloupe and Martinique, the English planted outposts on St. Kitt's, Barbados, and Nevis in the 1620s and occupied a half dozen smaller islands in the Leeward chain during the following decade.

These English ventures were of the proprietary type, prosecuted by land-hungry adventurers who lacked the resources or influence to work on the scale of the Calverts. The little West Indian proprietaries were able to make a go of it, despite Spanish objections to their presence. Tenants and small landowners were readily attracted to these fertile islands, where tobacco, cotton, dyewoods, and a variety of tropical products could be grown. More than 20,000 Englishmen had settled in the Antilles by 1640.

The West Indian proprietors learned what founders of mainland colonies were also learning, and permitted a substantial measure of self-government to the inhabitants.

Until about 1650, European thoughts about the New World were still largely conditioned by the position of Spain, which continued to have the only empire of consequence in the Western Hemisphere. Most of the scattered English ventures—Virginia, New England, Bermuda, the Leeward Islands—had been conceived and forwarded with at least one eye upon the Spaniards, and the tiny French settlements in Canada and the Antilles had a similar strategic background. But the most active Europeans on the scene during this period, both along and beyond the Spanish Main, were the Dutch, who engrossed much of the Spanish colonial trade when the two nations were at peace and captured or destroyed what they could of it when the two nations were at war. Dutch interest in transatlantic colonization was limited to commercial and strategic objectives, and the search for trading advantage was subordinate to the search for bases and opportunities whence to launch attacks upon Spain.

It was with such ends in view that they organized the Dutch West India Company in 1621. The directors, unlike most of their enterprising fellow countrymen, were more interested in striking at Spain, out of religious and nationalist zeal, than in simply amassing profits. The company did indeed show handsome returns now and then, but most of them were poured into privateering activities in the Caribbean or sunk into a prolonged, expensive, and ultimately futile campaign designed to wrest Brazil from the Portuguese.

Yet the Dutch made their mark by means of that energetic company. Its greatest coup came with Admiral Piet Heyn's capture of an entire Spanish silver fleet off the north coast of Cuba in 1628. A few years later the company planted a base in the island of Curaçao, off Venezuela, and made it an entrepôt that virtually monopolized the lucrative trade with Spain's needy colonies, prosecuting from a point close at hand, on a large scale, what John

Hawkins and his ships had begun doing three quarters of a century before.

Though it was by way of being a side show to the Caribbean operations, the Dutch West India Company also established a chain of small outposts on the North American mainland along the lower Delaware, Hudson, and Connecticut rivers. The company engaged extensively in the fur trade, rubbed elbows with and finally absorbed a tiny Swedish colony on Delaware Bay, began using its well-placed little port at the mouth of the Hudson as an entrepôt for trade with the neighboring English colonies, and handed out some princely estates in the Hudson Valley. But New Netherland attracted relatively few settlers; it was always conceived and administered more as a company trading post than as a genuine colony. And after 1650 it stood in danger of absorption by the more populous, faster-growing English colonies on its flank.

CHAPTER 5

Cities on a Hill

T HE DUTCH venture in New Amsterdam was in its infancy
when another manifestation of the English colonial impulse
began the settlement of New England. Here the impulse was primarily religious, although it would be wrong to draw too sharp a
distinction between God-fearing New Englanders and commercially minded Chesapeake and West Indian planters. The Southern colonies contained a full share of devout folk who subscribed
to essentially the same moral code and strove as sternly to enforce
it as did the founders of Massachusetts Bay; and New England
drew many settlers with their eyes peeled for new opportunities
and chance of gain. Nevertheless, any examination of the origins
of New England must begin with the religious motivation.

It came, essentially, in two varieties: a simple desire to go
where one could worship in peace and be left alone, as with the
Pilgrims who landed at Plymouth Rock; and a great sense of
being on a mission for God, to build, in the wilderness, the kind
of spiritual community He intended that people should inhabit,
as with the Puritans who came to Massachusetts Bay ten years
later. The latter impulse was the stronger and more significant,
by far. Yet the Pilgrims, too, made their mark. Numberless thou-

sands who came after them were the same sort of unsung folk, coming for the same quiet reasons. The tiny band that immortalized Brewster and Bradford and *Mayflower* and the other down-to-earth names should still be rendered passing honors, for in that early transit of civilization from England to America they carried something crucial.

In their humble way the Pilgrims cut across nearly all of the great lines that were carrying England toward a New World empire and Western Europe toward the modern era. They were Separatists, who unlike the majority of English Puritans had carried their convictions to the point of separating from the Church of England rather than seeking to reform it. They came mainly from the ranks of the yeoman farmers and country artisans, yet the Puritan appeal transcended class lines: the leader of the Scrooby congregation was a well-to-do gentleman named William Brewster, at whose fine moated manor house the little group gathered to worship in the early years of the seventeenth century. Brewster was a man of affluence and distinction; he had been a diplomat in the service of Queen Elizabeth, and he had picked up his Puritanism as a student at Cambridge. Cambridge-educated, too, was the pastor of this little flock, the Reverend John Robinson, described by a man of different religious persuasion as "the most learned, polished, and modest spirit that ever separated from the Church of England." One of the worshipers was a farmer's son named William Bradford, still in his teens at Scrooby, whose latent skill as leader and writer would soon offer quiet proof that neither gentility nor higher education had a lock upon greatness.

The England of these years was not a congenial place for Separatists, and in 1608, about the time John Smith was giving the ragged Jamestown settlement its first taste of leadership far to the westward, the bulk of the Scrooby congregation moved to Holland. They stopped first in Amsterdam, but this mighty seaport, already entering upon its great period as the commercial and financial hub of the Western world, was too much for these impecunious rural Englishmen. In 1609 they moved to Leyden, where most of them stayed for the better part of a decade, unmolested in their faith. Though far smaller than Amsterdam, Leyden was also part of the wave of the future, with its great university and busy shops and textile factories. Holland was tolerant enough, but it was too worldly and too commercial for the staid Pilgrims, who remained rural English in outlook and preference.

So they moved again. Brewster was acquainted with Sir Edwin Sandys, an urbane member of Parliament who had recently become treasurer of the Virginia Company. Puritanism and Separatism did not offend Sandys, and he obtained a town-plantation patent for the Pilgrims in 1619 entitling them to found a settlement in Virginia. Though a few dozen of the Leyden congregation were prepared to go, they lacked sufficient means; Brewster had sold his property to help finance the earlier move to Holland. A hardfisted group of London merchants agreed to advance the money, but their terms bound the Pilgrims into a seven-year joint-stock arrangement like the one Virginia had already tried and found wanting. The Pilgrims had no taste for the plan but accepted it in the absence of an alternative. It worked no better than the Virginia system had, and when the disgusted settlers in the Plymouth colony elected to buy their way out of the unsatisfactory contract in 1627 it took them seventeen years to pay off the debt.

The Pilgrims had ties with one more of the threads that had begun binding the Old World to the New. Sometime during their preparation they encountered the ubiquitous John Smith, late of Virginia and more recently returned from a prolonged fishing expedition along the Atlantic coast of North America. Smith was a gifted and thoughtful observer, and his voyage had culminated in a widely circulated pamphlet published in 1616, entitled "A Description of New England" and replete with maps. Other names (Northern Virginia, Norumbega) had been applied to this stretch of coast, but Smith's was the one that stuck. He had been sufficiently impressed by what he saw of New England to call it "the Paradise of these parts."

The Pilgrims took due note. Smith apparently offered his services to their venture in the capacity of military officer and guide, but they turned him down "to save charges," as Smith wryly noted, "saying my books and maps were much better cheap to teach them, than myself." They chose a peppery little captain named Miles Standish instead, but they went equipped with John Smith's useful observations about the transatlantic shores.

They went on the *Mayflower* in the fall of 1620—about one hundred of them, of whom one third were Pilgrim Saints from the Leyden congregation and the rest employees and servants recruited by the London underwriters. By the time they made their first landfall off Cape Cod in early November, after a rough two-month crossing, they decided that it was too late in the season to beat down the coast toward Virginia territory; a quick reconnaissance revealed sheltered waters and good anchorages inside Cape Cod. Besides, they were equipped with Smith's pamphlet and maps and might have been disposed to settle in "the Paradise of these parts" rather than in Virginia anyway.

———□———

Before landing, they made one of those on-the-spot decisions that has become a historic landmark for Americans, a small early milestone along the road to independence and self-government. Aware that they were about to settle in unexplored land to which they had no title under their patent, the little group agreed to form their own government, elect officers to pass and administer laws, and be bound by the laws and ordinances thus enacted. They carefully prefaced this document with a pledge of loyalty to King James.

This was the Mayflower Compact, enduring symbol of the self-governing instincts of the English colonists. It deserves the attention and credit it has received, and for more than the reasons customarily given. The Pilgrims were probably aware of the dramatic possibilities. Like all good Puritans, they had a keen sense of history and of human actions as fulfilling part of God's grand design; and what they were doing seemed natural enough in any event, for the compact was no more than a secular version of the covenant which—again like all good Puritans—they believed to form the basis of church organization and man's relation to God. The theological underpinning of this little procedural guide for those about to enter a state of nature was clearly set forth: "We, whose names are underwritten . . . do . . . covenant and combine ourselves together into a civil body politic. . . ." What they were doing also had its practical side, and indeed seemed no more than common sense. They saw the compact as a stopgap, a way of giving their wilderness community a framework that would enable it to function until the venture was properly legalized by higher authority.

But the Saints also had a more immediate end in view. In proposing this covenant they were not simply acting out an Englishman's innate craving for law and order. The people they explicitly wanted to bind by the compact were the non-Pilgrim members of their little party, those artisans and servants recruited in London. Some of these latter, when the decision to land at Plymouth rather than go to Virginia was being made aboard *Mayflower,* had been heard to remark that this freed them from all authority, that they could now proceed to do exactly as they chose in the new land. Anxious to prevent this kind of self-serving independent action and subject these wayward tendencies to their own strict sense of what a community ought to be, the Saints drew up the compact and secured the adherence of enough non-Saints as to give themselves (the Saints were, after all, a minority of the *Mayflower's* party) a chance to control the settlement.

This they succeeded in doing. Forty-one adults signed the compact, and thus became freemen entitled to vote. Nineteen of the signers were Saints; there were also two sailors, four servants, and sixteen Londoners among the self-created freemen. Two among the latter element voted with the Saints in the first election, enabling them to choose one of their own members, John Carver, as governor by a majority of one vote. They retained this control. When Carver died during that first grim winter ashore, he was succeeded by thirty-year-old William Bradford, who led the Plymouth Colony for nearly all of the next thirty-six years, until his death in 1657.

In short, the compact was not only an innovation but an expedient, designed not only to provide a basis for law and order but to give the framers a chance to run things. It worked, serving both the higher and the more immediate purpose. The groups of Englishmen who began making the decision to migrate in the early seventeenth century always seemed to include a few who knew exactly what they were about.

Although the Plymouth group soon got a patent, validating their title, from the successors of that company of West Country merchants who had planted an abortive settlement at the mouth of the Kennebec—this organization was now known as the Council for New England—the Pilgrims never got the royal charter they hoped to obtain. Their Mayflower Compact served as the sole basis for their government for as long as the little colony had an existence of its own. It remained modest in numbers and small in size, being completely overshadowed after 1630 by the larger settlements with their nucleus at Boston, and before the end of the century it was absorbed into the Massachusetts Bay colony.

But they had done their work well, this small band of Saints and strangers. They had survived, prospered in a modest way, and shown what Englishmen could do on their own. No one ever put it better than Governor Bradford did, reminiscing later in life about these founding years: "Thus out of small beginnings greater things have been produced by His hand that made all things of nothing, and gives being to all things that are; and as one small candle may light a thousand, so the light here kindled hath shown unto many, yea, in some sort, to our whole nation."

What the Pilgrims of Plymouth did in modest roman type, so to speak, in the interest of their own future security, the Puritans of Massachusetts Bay did in flaming italics, on behalf of themselves and (as they viewed it) all Protestant Christendom. The same innovative and expedient qualities were on exhibit, too, including a few that manifested themselves before the main body of believers left England.

The great Puritan experiment had its origins in 1623, when a Dorchester clergyman named John White persuaded a group of West Country merchants to form a company and found a settlement of farmers and fishermen, attended by Puritan ministers, on Cape Ann, a few miles north of the infant Plymouth colony. A handful of other tiny, semipermanent fishing and fur trading posts had already sprung up here and there along the New England coast, and interest in the region John Smith had charted and described in his pamphlet was growing.

English Puritans, many of whom were affluent merchants and landowners, were becoming particularly interested. Their willingness to back schemes like the Reverend John White's at Cape Ann and the larger enterprises that soon followed it suggests that they were thinking in terms of possible religious havens rather than of profits. They were shrewd men, and the experiences in Virginia and on the Kennebec had indicated that colonization was a bad investment financially, whether the colony itself survived or not. The Dorchester investors proved the truth of this by disbanding in 1626, although the nucleus of their Cape Ann settlement persisted; most of the inhabitants were centered around the village of Salem.

The Reverend White, meanwhile, was determined to enlarge and build upon this outpost. Like most Puritan divines, he was well educated and well acquainted among the gentry and in legal, medical, and business circles where men with Puritan inclinations or convictions abounded. There was a kind of informal network of such folk in England, centered in the seaports of the south and west, the eastern clothing districts, and above all in London. It was to London that White went for a follow-up to his Cape Ann settlement, and London contained several Puritan merchants who were willing to back him. They obtained a patent from the Council for New England (successor to the old Plymouth Company of 1606 that had planted the defunct settlement on the Kennebec), organized themselves as the New England Company, and sent a shipload of colonists to Salem in 1628.

The situation in England, as far as Puritans were concerned, was becoming ominous. And things seemed to be moving toward a climax. Quarrels between Crown and legislature over revenues and the king's prerogative had erupted in angry confrontations. Charles I, denied the funds he wanted by a watchful Parliament, had resorted to forced loans and other forms of unparliamentary taxation. A later Parliament had denounced this as illegal and forced the king to repudiate recent arbitrary actions in return for the money he wanted. The king saw to it that Parliament was lectured about royal supremacy over legislative bodies. When Parliament defiantly resolved that the king's principal source of revenue was illegal, Charles responded in the spring of 1629 by dissolving Parliament and making it known that he would henceforth govern without it. He did so for the next eleven years, and England lurched down the highroad toward civil war.

A darkening political scene was accompanied by thunderclouds on the religious horizon. In politics, the Stuart kings were would-be absolutists, believers in divine right; in religion, they veered toward a brand of high-church Anglicanism which Englishmen of other persuasions—and particularly the Puritans— found harder and harder to distinguish from outright Catholicism. This trend first became visible with the rise to prominence of William Laud, whom Charles made Bishop of London in 1628 and Archbishop of Canterbury a short time later.

Laud's religion was totally unacceptable to the Puritans (and vice versa), and the man who headed the Church of England under Charles I was every bit as zealous and determined as they were. Laud worked diligently to strengthen the episcopal and ritual side of the Church. While his bishops issued commands, visited parishes, and sat on newly reactivated spiritual courts in a sustained drive to root out unorthodoxy among suspect clerics and laymen, Laud strove to improve the quality as well as the doctrine of the Anglican clergy. Striking directly at Puritanism, he prohibited the kind of exhortatory preaching and lay-supported lecturing that good Puritans had long employed; he removed Puritan ministers from the pulpit in wholesale fashion.

Worst of all, in Puritan eyes, Laud was an Arminian—a believer in the doctrine that man could achieve salvation by good works and free will. This was the antithesis of predestination, hence anathema to good Calvinists; it appeared all the more heretical and dangerous to Puritans because in their own covenant-and-regeneration theology they had made a compromise with predestination and were watchfully, almost guiltily, on guard against any further attempts to expand human power at the expense of God's.

Laud's doctrines, and his determination to root out dissent, would soon leave the Puritans with no alternatives save conformity, silence, emigration, or revolt. And it was not in their nature to look kindly upon those first two choices.

This state of things was incipient when John White and his London backers formed the New England Company in 1628. But Puritans had been sniffing danger for too long to mistake the direction of the wind, and it was blowing harder. The next Parliament revealed its sense of how things fit together by denouncing popery, Arminianism, and illegal taxation in virtually the same breath. It was this body that Charles promptly dissolved with the clear intention of not summoning another. During these climactic months the New England group moved with speed and dexterity. Sensing that time was short and a haven overseas imperative, they sought to enlarge their base by communicating with influential fellow Puritans like John Winthrop, and began making plans for their departure.

If they were to try their luck overseas, they were determined to have as much security as they could get for their venture, and their first concern was to obtain adequate title to the land they wanted to occupy. All they held so far was a patent from the Council for New England, and there were doubts as to just how valid this claim might be. A royal charter, issued directly from the Crown to themselves, would be safer. It would also be hard to get. Charles had recently announced that he would grant no more rights of government to trading companies, and he could hardly be expected to go back on this policy when approached by a trading company full of Puritans. But Parliament had not yet been dissolved, and both houses were full of men with Puritan inclinations, including a few with influence. By means that remain unclear and must have involved finesse, they procured a royal charter from the king only a week before he dissolved Parliament for the last time in 1629.

The New England Company thereby became the Massachusetts Bay Company, a corporation empowered, through governor and assistants elected by the members, to control all properties and make all laws in the territory to which it received title, between the Merrimack and Charles rivers on the New England coast. The terms of this charter followed closely after those granted to the Virginia Company in 1612.

That this particular group of Puritans could have obtained such a charter from this particular king represented a coup in itself, but the incorporators of the Massachusetts Bay Company, already busily engaged in bringing kindred spirits like John Winthrop into their ranks, had devised yet another maneuver to bolster the security of their enterprise. The king's blessing, in the form of the charter, had been a necessary first step. But what the Crown had given the Crown could take away, as the recent annulment of the Virginia Company's charter attested. King Charles might possibly have been persuaded to sign this charter without being quite aware of the exact nature of the incorporators, but Bishop Laud, already moving toward a dominant position in the Church of England, would know who the Massachusetts Bay people were and what to do about them. New settlements in far-off Massachusetts would not be a safe refuge for Puritans if the government ever renewed its acquaintance with that charter.

The Bay Company leaders, whether they had engineered the creation of this loophole or merely spotted it later, took advantage of the fact that the charter stipulations did not include a prescribed place for the company to hold its quarterly meetings and maintain its headquarters. Most charters did include such a stipulation, usually specifying the city where the bulk of the incorporators resided. No one had ever questioned the principle, which was obviously assumed to be operative here as well, that companies undertaking overseas enterprises would keep their headquarters in England.

Yet this charter was silent on the subject, and the company leaders seized the opportunity thus offered. Meeting at Cambridge in the summer of 1629, they decided to move charter, place of meeting, and company headquarters overseas along with the actual colonists. Transferring the document and the whole government of the colony to Massachusetts removed the possibility that control might later fall into the hands of investors with different ends in view; it also placed a broad ocean between the charter and the investigative authority of an unfriendly government.

For what these men had in mind was no mere trading company outpost but a community of Saints, governed according to the terms of the charter and good Puritan doctrine. John Winthrop, present at this meeting, thereupon agreed to join the company and emigrate with the others. A few days later a General Court of the freemen of the company—in modern parlance, a meeting of the stockholders—assembled and ratified this proposal; those who did not choose to emigrate agreed to relinquish control and transfer or dispose of their interest to those who did. A kind of caretaker government was retained in London to settle financial matters growing out of this decision and perhaps also to serve as a blind. (William Laud, true to Puritan anticipation, moved against the Massachusetts Bay Company as soon as he found a pretext.

But he did not learn until 1635 that the charter had crossed the ocean. It took him two years after that to obtain a court decision revoking the document, and by this time Charles and his ministers had their hands too full with more pressing matters to take further action against Massachusetts.)

In October 1629 the freemen met again and elected John Winthrop as governor. An advance guard of some four hundred colonists had been dispatched to Salem that spring, as soon as the charter was approved. During the spring and summer of 1630 a total of seventeen ships left England for Massachusetts Bay. On board, in addition to an abundance of provisions and livestock, were Governor Winthrop and a handful of other freemen, the company charter, and about one thousand prospective settlers, recruited by a well-planned and well-financed campaign.

In June 1630 the flagship *Arbella* and three of her consorts dropped anchor off Salem, to be greeted rather wanly by the arrivals of the preceding year and a few earlier settlers. After a few weeks of reconnoitering, Winthrop and the other leaders decided to locate the principal settlement around the spacious, island-studded harbor formed by the confluence of the Charles and Mystic rivers. The great Puritan migration had begun. Some 20,000 English men and women would follow this vanguard to Massachusetts Bay before the decade had passed.

There were in the Winthrop party and in the shiploads that came later a number of folk whose main concern was with economic opportunity and a fresh start. Much of the English social structure was represented—landed gentlemen of substantial means, like Winthrop and several others; a sprinkling of merchants, lawyers, and tradesmen; a wide range of urban and rural craftsmen, especially from the clothing districts; a solid core of yeoman farmers who had left freeholds or leaseholds in the old country to try their luck on acreage in the New World; and a considerable scattering of small tenant farmers, agricultural laborers, unskilled workers, servants, and other humble folk.

But the heart of this migration was unmistakably, incontrovertibly religious. It had far more than its share of ordained ministers, and of Bible-reading laymen who could follow a learned sermon, discourse ably upon points of doctrine, and even lecture from a biblical text. No representative cross section of English society, the group was disproportionately low in aristocrats, courtiers, the very poor, the lazy, and the dissolute; disproportionately high in men and women with some education and substance, no little piety, and a tough inner fiber. The Reverend William Stoughton, reminiscing in a Boston sermon thirty-odd years later about those who, like his father, had left England to build Massachusetts in the 1630s, epitomized them with no more than mild exaggeration: "God sifted a whole nation that He might bring choice grain over into this Wilderness."

The essence of the Bay Colony's appeal to prospective colonists had been drawn from God's Holy Word, which was rod and staff to so many in this generation of Englishmen. Apt quotations abounded. St. Matthew, in the Geneva version of Scripture that remained popular in many Puritan homes and pulpits even after the work authorized by James I appeared in 1611, had quoted the Lord as promising His people that "from the wilderness unto the great sea toward the going downe of the sunne, shall be your coast." And in a sermon to a portion of that first wave of migrants in 1630 the learned and eloquent Reverend John Cotton, whose influence upon the new colony would be equal to Winthrop's own, took his text from the Geneva version of the second book of Samuel: "And I will appoint a place for my People Israel, And wil plante it, that they may dwell in a place of their owne, and moove no more, neither shal wicked people trouble them any more as before time."

All varieties of English Puritanism were represented, albeit not equally. There were ordinary Anglicans who wore their Puritanism lightly (Puritanism shaded imperceptibly off into standard or low-church Anglicanism in many matters of doctrine and belief; the distinction becomes sharp only when outspoken Puritans are contrasted with the equally outspoken followers of Archbishop Laud). An untold and probably somewhat larger number of these Puritan emigrants were of the Presbyterian persuasion, while still others were out-and-out Separatists.

But the greatest number, including the dominant element, consisted of Non-separating Congregationalists, still bent on remaking rather than quitting the Church of England. It was this group that set the tone in Massachusetts Bay and created the religious and political institutions by which the new colony was shaped and led. The leaders of this dominant faction, though they occasionally differed among themselves, were a strong-willed and purposeful group who knew what they were about and placed the stamp of orthodoxy upon it. For the next generation or so, they were able to persuade dissenters and doubters of the error of their ways, the wisdom of silence, or the advisability of going elsewhere.

Their creation on the shores of Massachusetts Bay is worth looking at, because much of the Puritan character and eventual legacy to America was built into it. As Winthrop and the other guiding spirits conceived it, they were embarked upon a special errand, or mission, for their Maker. The basis of every society, in their view, was a covenant with God, whereby the people contracted to obey His commands and do His will in return for His blessing. England was failing, visibly failing, to live up to the terms of its covenant with God, and these emigrant Puritans were now upon a special commission, designed to provide the English people with the means of restoring their covenant and regaining their favor in God's eyes.

This was an awesome responsibility, as the Puritans well knew. They were entering into a new covenant with God, of an exceptional kind. And, as Winthrop warned his fellows, "when God gives a special Commission, He lookes to have it stricktly observed in every Article." The nature of this special commission was simply stated. They were to try to construct a model community, a Bible Commonwealth, based upon what the Scriptures revealed of God's intent, a society centered on, and conceived in the interest of, a community of Saints—God's elect, His chosen people. These would proceed to demonstrate, in a land untrammeled by the sinful ways and evil conditions then besetting England, that it was possible to walk uprightly and obey the command of God.

It was not to be an isolated exercise, a refuge only for escapees and dissenters, as at Plymouth. The Winthrop group was running a demonstration program, creating a prototype, and they were very conscious of being on the center of the stage. As Winthrop put it to his fellow passengers on board the *Arbella,* as she surged against the cold westerly winds of the North Atlantic spring, "Wee shall be as a Citty upon a Hill, the eies of all people are uppon us." The notion of being engaged upon a noble experiment for the benefit of the rest of mankind would long outlast this original Puritan application of it. They were indeed building a prototype, to a far greater extent than they realized.

At the heart of this holy experiment in the wilderness would be a few features common to all English Puritans and a few that identified this particular strand. It would derive its authority from the Bible, it would define its authority in terms of the kind of covenant God had reportedly agreed to make with man, and the government deriving from this covenant would be, through the magistrates, the close working partner of the ministry.

This much would have been acceptable to nearly all Puritans. But the leaders of the Massachusetts Bay group were determined to base their enterprise upon two or three additional items that other Puritans found it hard to accept. To begin with, they were still avowedly within the Church of England; this placed them at odds with the Separatists (and there was more latent separatism within the Massachusetts Bay Colony's ranks than anyone realized at the outset). Secondly, they insisted upon congregational autonomy, having repudiated not only the episcopal hierarchy,

with all its trappings, but also the pyramid of lay elders and ministers that presbyterians believed in. Here the immigrants were opposed by a great many of their English brethren. And thirdly, the
Bay Colony Puritans insisted upon limiting church membership
to the regenerate—the Saints. Others would have to attend
church, contribute to its support, and be subject to the laws of the
community. But they could not qualify for membership or participate in the communion sacrament until they had demonstrated, to the satisfaction of the minister and all the Saints in the
congregation, that they had undergone a genuine conversion experience and were now filled with God's grace. This was the most
radical departure from English practice, both Anglican and Puritan, where church membership had always been defined in accordance with Roman Catholic tradition as coequal with the entire community.

In demanding this combination of principles as a basis for their
new society, the Massachusetts Puritans were embarked upon a
collision course with all manner of trouble. They were constructing an edifice upon incompatible architectural principles, and
sooner or later something—eventually, quite a bit—was going
to give. Yet what eventually emerged, as the New World and the
passage of time altered old contexts, was a remarkably supple and
workable structure. For they seasoned their high principles with
strong dashes of common sense, and it was more than accident or
good luck that enabled their experiment to survive and adapt to
changing circumstances. The builders of the Bay Colony were
essentially practical and innovative folk, with a keen eye for what
worked.

These qualities are best illustrated by a look at what they did with
that charter. Obtaining it in the first place, and then deciding to
take it to Massachusetts with them, had demonstrated a shrewd
political sense that would not desert them when they reached the

New World. In creating a government, Winthrop and his small band of fellow architects began with the charter stipulation that the freemen (i.e., shareholders) of the company should make all laws for the governance of the colony and elect a governor, deputy governor, and eighteen assistants (in effect, a chairman and board of directors) to execute the laws and preside between the quarterly meetings of the shareholders. This was fairly standard procedure for business corporations, then and since. But this company was attempting to adapt the structure of an economic institution to purposes for which it was not intended—that is, the actual government of the colony.

Now the Winthrop group was in a peculiar situation. Only about a dozen freemen, or shareholders, had come over with the *Arbella* fleet, and nearly all of these had been chosen assistants (that is, directors) in the election back home before they sailed; Winthrop himself had been elected governor. So when this little band met in Massachusetts they could wear two hats. As the only shareholders on the scene, they could have met and voted to elect themselves again as governor and directors, and thus retain all of the executive, legislative, and judicial power in their own hands. Instead, they performed a rather neat maneuver, in which the provisions of the charter were both expanded and contracted, although nobody else quite realized this until later; Winthrop and his associates were careful to talk about the charter without actually showing it to anyone outside their own ranks.

In any case, at their first shareholders' meeting—referred to in seventeenth-century terminology as a General Court—they threw open the gathering to non-members, presumably most of the adult males in Salem and vicinity, and won their assent to the proposition that hereafter the freemen would confine themselves at their annual meeting to electing assistants. These assistants, in turn, would choose the governor and deputy governor and assume the lawmaking power.

By this device, and with the general and perhaps somewhat confused consent of their fellow colonists, the leaders made the company charter into a kind of political constitution, in which the shareholders were redefined as voting citizens and the governor and assistants, or board of directors, were transformed into a combined executive and legislative body. But the Winthrop group had only begun to adapt the charter to the kind of reality they envisioned for Massachusetts Bay. At the next meeting of the General Court, also thrown open to non-members, those adult males who could qualify as Saints were admitted to company membership as freemen and hence (by action of the preceding meeting) to the ranks of voting citizens of the commonwealth. Winthrop and the assistants had thus expanded the charter by admitting Saints to membership, but they had contracted it by transferring the lawmaking power from the freemen to the assistants—who, together with the governor, now in fact held all of the legislative, executive, and judicial authority in the new government.

And they had won the assent of the new citizenry to all of this, although it was still not known that the terms of the charter were being so stretched and distorted. In securing community assent to the new system and admitting the Saints to voting membership, Winthrop was being politic but not democratic. He and his little oligarchy had the seventeenth-century notion of authority as flowing downward from God, not upward from the people. And in making the legislature subject to popular election they had no intention of making it subject to popular control. Winthrop knew that, as Englishmen, the settlers would be more inclined to accept the authority of the magistrates if they had had a hand in selecting them. If the Puritans were not democrats, neither were they believers in the kind of arbitrary authority then being exercised back home by the House of Stuart. Deriving their authority from God, rulers were accountable to God, and this, it was felt, placed sufficient hedges upon their power.

For Winthrop was at pains to point out that this was not merely a political but a religious operation. The charter could be seen as a kind of covenant, and here the governor was standing on firm Puritan ground. The covenant theology contained a two-stage process: men first covenanted with God, agreeing to live by His commandments, and then covenanted among themselves, forming governments and pledging to live together by the terms of the contract with God. Admitting the Saints to membership in the corporation simply made them parties to the covenant whereby the colony would be governed. Winthrop could have employed no surer means of gaining the support and adherence of the general body of Saints.

But these Saints were Englishmen, and it did not take them long to work modifications of their own upon the charter. In 1632 the citizens of one town sounded an enduring English note when they objected to a tax as having been levied without their consent. Winthrop persuaded them that the magistrates, having been elected by an annual General Court, were in fact like a small Parliament; hence the voters were represented. But he agreed to a compromise whereby the representation became more direct; the next General Court voted that each town would hereafter send two deputies to confer with the magistrates on matters of taxation. Winthrop also persuaded the magistrates, rather against their will, to bow to community sentiment and agree to make the governor and deputy governor elected by the freemen rather than by the assistants. When a vital principle was not at stake, Winthrop was more disposed to compromise with public sentiment than were many of his more imperious associates. The flexibility that the Massachusetts government came to have owed much to their first governor's responsiveness and political sense.

However, in bending to public sentiment on one hand he made enemies on another. Other leaders were jealous of his power and prestige, and opposition grew. In 1634 it culminated in a demand to see the charter. Upon examining the document people learned that lawmaking power had originally been vested in the freemen, not in the assistants. The citizens, meeting in General Court, immediately demanded that this right be returned to them. They also realized that there were now (thanks to population growth and Winthrop's liberality in extending the franchise) more citizens than could conveniently gather four times a year to make laws. From this emerged the system of electing two representatives from each town to serve, along with the governor and assistants, as the legislative body. The generality of voters would elect these deputies and other officers once a year, as before.

The General Court, as the legislature was thereafter called, drew up a code of laws for the colony in 1641. Three years later it divided into a bicameral body, with an upper house composed of the assistants and a lower house composed of the two elected deputies from each town. By these stages, in less than a decade and a half, the original company charter had evolved by a process of give and take into a full-fledged and effective government.

The process had demonstrated, once again, the innovative qualities that Englishmen tended to take with them when they went overseas. It also provided an excellent example of how thoroughly English Puritanism had blended the economic, political, and religious areas of human existence, each reinforcing and contributing to the others. Thus charter had become constitution by way of covenant; a company had become a government in which the citizens were Saints.

— □ —

The government set up by the community of Saints proved enduringly workable. But it is hardly surprising that a society based upon so complex and powerful a doctrine, inhabited by such strong-willed believers, and subject to the pressures of population growth as hundreds of new migrants arrived each year, proved unable to contain so many people and so much doctrine within a single body politic. Massachusetts became subject to disaffected out-migrations, or hivings off, less than five years after the first settlers arrived, and the process continued until by the 1640s a whole cluster of small New England colonies had come into existence.

The string of little fishing villages stretching north and east from Salem along the coast were all drawn into the Bay Colony's orbit. The old Council for New England, whose existence consisted mainly of a series of futile gestures, protested during the 1630s that Massachusetts was infringing upon its territory. It granted the land north of the Merrimack to a pair of would-be lords proprietor, who in turn divided the region into the separate grants of New Hampshire and Maine. But their efforts to exploit these territories made no headway against the expanding Bay Colony, which dominated the former area until the 1670s and the latter until the early nineteenth century.

Expansion southward was another matter. The Plymouth settlements discreetly minded their own business and maintained a separate existence until 1691, when the Bay Colony absorbed them. But Massachusetts found itself boxed in along the rest of its southern border, chiefly because this region was settled by folk who were there because Massachusetts could not hold them, and who were as strong-minded and resolute as the people they had left. Two clusters of settlements became the centers of new colonies in the 1630s—one around Hartford, in the lower Connecticut Valley, and the other around New Haven, on Long Island Sound. These departures from Massachusetts arose from differences that were political rather than doctrinal; both the Connecticut and New Haven settlements (they were not merged until the 1660s) were communities of Puritan Saints with religious and political institutions patterned closely after those of the Bay Colony. The Reverend Thomas Hooker and his flock took off to found Hartford in 1636 because they found the Winthrop government too arbitrary, and the Reverend John Davenport took off to found New Haven in 1637 because he considered the Winthrop government too lax.

It is also possible that both of these eminent divines found the religious atmosphere in Massachusetts a shade too stifling because it was so completely subject to the influence of the Reverend John Cotton. Cotton had a powerful personality and a good mind and a large following (many of whom, Roger Williams caustically observed, "could hardly believe that God would suffer Mr Cotton to err"). The process here at work demonstrated one of Puritanism's inherently divisive tendencies, on the purely personal level, in that the strong wills required to master and stay on top of such a body of beliefs often found it difficult to stay on top of them together.

In any case, both the Connecticut and the New Haven outmigrations proceeded on the basis of no authority save their own, into regions to which neither they nor Massachusetts held title. And like the *Mayflower* pilgrims and other groups of Englishmen in like situations, they drew up their own covenant-charters to serve as a basis for government and authority until higher validation could be obtained. Since England was itself entering that stormy period when final authority had no agreed-upon location, this validation proved impossible to get until the dust settled with the Stuart Restoration in 1660.

The move to Connecticut revealed some of Puritanism's divisive tendencies; the move to what eventually became Rhode Island revealed just about all of them: doctrinal, attitudinal, personal, and on across the board. Rhode Island became an enduring symbol of more than one kind—a lonely beacon of toleration in a dark sea, a refuge for what were called the otherwise-minded, a haven for dissenters who dissented from one another as soon as they got there, a hissing and a byword in the eyes of more orthodox neighbors, a strange and ill-assorted collection of the high-minded zealotry, grasping ambition, and inveterate quarrelsomeness that Puritanism was capable of spinning off.

Although no examination of Rhode Island can avoid making a centerpiece out of the inimitable, irrepressible Roger Williams, the origins of the little colony are best understood in terms of the schismatic tendency built into the spirit of Protestantism. The

Bay Colony Puritans had a particularly difficult time with this problem because of their commitment to the idea of congregational autonomy, which meant that there was no formal higher command—bishops or presbyteries—to enforce orthodoxy. Congregational Puritans further compounded their difficulty by urging all worshipers to read and meditate on the Bible for themselves rather than passively receiving dogma from the clergy. No single item in the Puritan creed was as naïve as their confident belief that right-thinking people would read and interpret the Bible in the same way. No Puritan denied for a moment that God's Holy Word was the ultimate and binding authority; the trouble came in determining exactly what the Scriptures meant. The Puritan impulse, carried to its logical extreme, was separatist.

Now Roger Williams was an avowed Separatist, and no one of his time was more inclined to carry something to its logical extreme—and on beyond. He was one of many restless talents that the religious upheavals of this era had produced. Bright, Cambridge-educated, well known and well connected in Puritan circles, persuasive, outspoken, opinionated, and altogether charming, young Williams came to Massachusetts only a few months after the Winthrop group did, and for much the same reason: "Bishop Laud," he said, "pursued me out of the land." Winthrop and the other members of the Bay Colony establishment knew and liked him, and made him welcome.

But the gifted young minister became a source of controversy almost immediately. He refused an offer to preach in a Boston church, saying that he had separated from the Church of England because it was contaminated by admitting unregenerate persons to communion. Now the Massachusetts churches did not do this; only Saints—the regenerate—could take communion. But Williams pointed out that the Massachusetts churches were avowed Non-separatists. Hence, though they might keep the unregenerate from communion, they were contaminated nonetheless because they had refused to separate from the contaminated Anglican Church.

Winthrop and the other leaders could only shrug and shake their heads at this kind of purity, but Williams had barely begun. He went down to Plymouth, where the folk were Separatists like himself, but he soon left the Pilgrim colony because, in his judgment, they were not separatist enough. When members of the Plymouth congregation returned for visits to England they sometimes attended Anglican services; this association with contaminated worship was enough to contaminate the whole Plymouth enterprise. Williams finally went the limit on this line of reasoning, holding that it was wrong for a regenerate man to pray in the company of unregenerate men. After studying those around him, he concluded that all existing churches were somehow contaminated, and that he could only in good conscience take communion with his wife. (Apparently he never entertained doubts about her.)

Meanwhile, the young maverick had galloped through the Puritan vineyard trampling on orthodoxy right and left. Not even his own charm nor Winthrop's patience, both of which were considerable, could finally contain him within the bounds of Massachusetts. He terrified both the Bay and Plymouth colonies by announcing that neither of them held valid titles to the land they occupied, because the English king had had no right to give it away in the first place. The land belonged to the Indians. (In this and other views about fair treatment for the red man, Roger Williams was centuries ahead of his time.) He challenged the oath Massachusetts required of non-freemen (that is, non-church members) to support the colony, on grounds that regenerate magistrates contaminated themselves by tendering this oath to the unregenerate non-freemen.

He went from there to insist, again generations ahead of his time, upon complete separation of church and state. This called into question the very essence of the Massachusetts system, based as it was upon the most intimate partnership between church and state. His unending drive to keep the Church as unspotted as possible led him to challenge yet another cardinal Puritan principle, that of requiring attendance at church by non-members, though only Saints were permitted to take communion. This distinction, for Williams, was not enough. Only the regenerate should be there at all: "Forced worship," he said bluntly, "stinks in God's nostrils." And once he realized that the absolute purity he sought was impossible, he turned completely about and stood four-square for liberty of conscience.

All of this was far more than Massachusetts could tolerate, though it took some five years of intermittent controversy before he left for good. After his early sojourn at Plymouth, he had returned to accept the pulpit of a church in Salem, and from then on the establishment was hamstrung in its efforts to silence him by its commitment to the congregational principle. His charm and eloquence kept much of his own congregation behind him, despite the dangerously unorthodox nature of many of his views. Reasoned discourse could not persuade him; pressure could not intimidate him. He finally went too far when he asked his congregation to denounce all the other Massachusetts churches as being impure. This a majority of them refused to do, and he thereupon left, taking a few hardened followers with him, in the winter of 1635.

He went to the Narragansett region, bought a tract of land from the Indians, named his little plantation for divine Providence, and permitted full liberty of conscience among those who settled with him. Williams was no democrat. He regarded himself as a medieval lord of the manor and did not take kindly to sharing his authority; he embraced religious toleration not out of respect for dissenting views but because he believed that the peace of the community required it. No cursory account can do justice to this complex and contradictory figure; at Providence plantation, a very special offshoot of the English colonial impulse had taken root.

—□—

Rhode Island would have been distinctive enough on this basis alone. But there were other seedlings to be planted around Narragansett Bay. Though she herself did not remain long, Mrs. Anne Hutchinson was another refugee from Massachusetts who left her mark upon the origins of this strange new colony. And Mrs. Hutchinson, if more elusive, is every bit as striking a figure as Roger Williams. Like him, she had restless intelligence, an abundance of charm, the courage of her convictions, and a mind of her own. And she was altogether too much for the ruling elders of Massachusetts Bay.

Anne and her husband, whom Winthrop described as "a man of very mild temper and weak parts, and wholly guided by his wife," arrived in Boston in 1634. The stronger half of this combination began to make her mark almost at once. She was one of those devout and energetic Puritans, with which the faith abounded, who liked to hold weekly discussions in order to analyze and explore the previous Sunday's sermon and other points of theology. In England she had been a devoted admirer of the Reverend Cotton, when he preached in Lincolnshire, and with Cotton's departure for the New World it was only a question of time before the Hutchinsons came after him. Anne was soon an active member of the Boston congregation that had chosen Cotton as one of its two ministers. It was her bold analysis of Cotton's theology, in those weekly seminars, that led Mrs. Hutchinson and her rapt followers—for she was every bit as persuasive as the great Reverend Cotton himself—into serious trouble.

One of the Puritans' major difficulties was that they were fated to walk an eternal tightrope precariously poised over various forms of heresy. The least bit of overcompensation to avoid one form could plunge the believer headlong into another. Their chief concern during these years was to avoid the Arminian heresy toward which Archbishop Laud was guiding the Church of England—the notion that good works and free will were active agents in the achievement of salvation. Now the Puritans, like good Calvinists, insisted that man was passive in his vital process; the Covenant of Grace was bestowed by God, and regeneration was an experience which a person simply underwent, as an empty vessel is filled with water.

But like most points of doctrine, this one had a gray twilight zone rather than a clear-cut boundary. The conversion experience was all-important to the Puritan. He was constantly being abjured to prepare himself for it and to search his soul for signs of it. This process of preparation—attending to sermons, prayer, Bible reading, private and public soul-searching—was the gray twilight zone. For it became deceptively easy to expand the preparative process until man had in fact played an active rather than a passive role in the receipt of God's grace—in short, Arminianism. Laud and his followers had embraced this heresy openly, but good Puritans were constantly sliding into it, or were in danger of doing so.

John Cotton was among those conscientious divines who strove mightily to be on guard against this tendency and to keep his flock from straying accidentally into the forbidden Arminian pasture. This meant continued reassertion of the sound Calvinist doctrine of divine omnipotence and human helplessness, and Cotton was very good indeed at keeping his parishioners on the straight path when they seemed about to stray.

Unfortunately, the path was less safe than it looked, because the Puritans had insisted upon making man's spiritual odyssey a perpetual tightrope. Mrs. Hutchinson, in her approving expositions upon the Reverend Cotton's texts, fell off on the other side. She did this by carrying the doctrine of human helplessness to its ultimate extreme. In effect, nothing man did beforehand could affect the entry of the Holy Spirit into his soul, and none of the things he did afterward—upright conduct, faithful church attendance, and the like—afforded any clue as to whether the conversion experience had been real or false. "The Holy Spirit," Mrs. Hutchinson maintained, "illumines the heart of every true believer." Such a person, having been saved—that is, completely possessed and taken over by the Holy Spirit—could thereafter commune directly with God. Moreover, a truly regenerate individual, being now in effect a creature of the Holy Spirit and in direct touch with God, could tell as if by instinct whether or not others—laymen or ministers—were truly regenerate.

Now Anne Hutchinson was a brilliant woman, and she had employed some first-rate theological reasoning in expounding and extending the Reverend Cotton's views. But she had also destroyed the entire basis of the Bible Commonwealth and plunged headlong into a heresy even more frightening than Arminianism. She was denying the whole elaborate process by which people demonstrated, to their ministers and peers, that they had had a genuine conversion experience. She was equally repudiating the notion that upright conduct and good behavior were signs that such an experience had taken place. Worst of all, she was taking leave of that absolute irreducible bedrock of Puritan theology— the Scripture as the supreme and only reliable authority about God's intent and His instructions to men. She had overleaped the community of Saints, the educated ministry, and—with her assertion that a person filled with the Holy Spirit could commune directly with God—the Bible itself.

This notion of direct personal revelation struck at the roots of the Puritan faith and seemed to point toward anarchy—total chaos. Horrified, the Bay Colony leaders moved to counter this dangerous doctrine. Anne had many supporters, and for a time in the mid-1630s the government, ministry, and community were badly divided. Cotton himself remained one of Mrs. Hutchinson's admirers but stayed on the fence in much of the theological dispute. The gifted woman would neither recant nor admit the error of her ways. Nor would she cease expounding her views to fascinated listeners, and it looked for a time as though the Bay Colony might split into two irreconcilable parts.

In the end, orthodoxy triumphed. Anne's wit and intellect were more than a match for those of her opponents. But Winthrop and other leaders possessed enough power, influence, and political skill to mobilize most of the colony's ministers and, finally, the weight of community opinion against her. She acquitted herself brilliantly at her trial, although her frank assertion, at the end, that she was herself receiving immediate personal revelation from God was too much for all but a handful of her followers. She, and they, were excommunicated and banished. One of her supporters, the Reverend John Wheelwright, took a few kindred spirits across the Merrimack and founded the town of Exeter in what later became New Hampshire, but the expanding Bay Colony soon absorbed this settlement.

The Hutchinsons themselves and a few followers went south to the Narragansett region in 1638 and established the village of Portsmouth not far from Providence. (The luckless Anne stayed there only a few years, still a party to quarrels. Soon widowed, she moved with her children to New Netherland and was killed in an Indian raid in 1643.) By this time Roger Williams' trail had been traveled by several other folk whose spirits, ideas, or temperament could not be contained within the Bay Colony's brand of orthodoxy, and other settlements had begun to sprout here and there along that irregular stretch of coastline west of Cape Cod. With folk like Williams and Hutchinson for openers, one begins to understand why the little colony that struggled into existence on the basis of these settlements never hid its light under a bushel or let anyone forget it was there.

Another of the early founders was an eccentric and controversial prophet named Samuel Gorton. Like Mrs. Hutchinson, albeit less charmingly and more cantankerously, Gorton believed in direct personal revelation. His preachings, which he based upon the unblinking claim that God was speaking to him directly, had a disruptive effect wherever he went. (The verdict of one contemporary, who termed Gorton "a proud and pestilent seducer, and deeply leavened with blasphemous and familistical opinions," should be taken as less than a whole description; Puritan communities had a way of thus stigmatizing those who took issue with prevailing doctrines.) Gorton avoided expulsion from Mas-

sachusetts by departing voluntarily, later got expelled from
Plymouth, and went to settle with the Hutchinsons in Portsmouth, where he again got expelled. Once established in a little
plantation of his own south of Providence, he settled down to
preach his brand of truth unmolested and ceased causing trouble.
Other inspired prophets, meanwhile, were also gravitating to the
area. Little wonder, certainly, that Williams chose liberty of conscience as the only possible basis for a colony formed out of such
elements.

Rhode Island became even more than a haven for independent
spirits, oddballs, and far-outers. A strong dash of unabashedly
secular ambition was added to this bizarre recipe for a colony in
the person of William Coddington, a thoughtful merchant who
followed Mrs. Hutchinson from Boston to Portsmouth, later
quarreled with her, and moved south to establish the town of
Newport, which he hoped to make the base for a great baronial
estate. He prospered, and Newport went on to become a thriving
seaport in later years.

Noting that the unfriendly Bay Colony seemed on the verge of
absorbing these contentious settlements and reimposing orthodoxy, Roger Williams hastened to England and succeeded in obtaining a charter in 1644 for the little cluster of communities. The
document validated their claims to a separate existence and entitled them to form their own government as best they might. Distracted by civil war, Parliament asked only that such government
"be conformable to the laws of England, so far as the nature and
constitution of the place will admit."

The heterogeneous group of villages thereafter coexisted, not
always smoothly, and defended themselves against the encroach-
ing tendencies of hostile neighbors. They survived as a colony on
the basis of individualism, representative institutions, and religious toleration, all of which permitted prophets to preach their
various doctrines and ambitious men to put large estates together
and explore commercial possibilities. Indeed, Rhode Island's
early and ongoing attraction for aspiring landed magnates, more

than a touch of whose aspirations he shared, led Williams to reflect ruefully later in life on the direction his little experiment in liberty of conscience was taking. "I fear," he wrote John Winthrop's son in 1664, "that the common trinity of the world— Profit, Preferment, Pleasure—will be here the *tria omnia,* as in all the world besides: . . . and that God Land will be as great a God with us English as God Gold was with the Spaniard."

It was a prediction that could be applied equally well to the entire set of English colonies.

CHAPTER 6

Lord Protector, Lords Proprietor, Lords of Trade

THE RELATIONSHIP between England and her scattered overseas possessions entered a new phase after 1640. On the one hand, the civil war and its attendant political changes gave the new colonies a decade and more when they were left largely to their own devices. The Crown's interest in them had never been more than spasmodic; under the stress of civil war this interest disappeared altogether—as indeed, for a time, did the Crown itself. The intermittent neglect that was so important a feature of American colonial development was much in evidence in the 1640s and 1650s.

Yet the beginnings of a countertendency were also visible. Parliament was led to give serious thought to the general place of the colonies in the English system for the first time—partly out of the need to re-examine all constitutional relationships after the execution of the king, partly in response to certain refractory and assertive tendencies on the part of colonial governments, chiefly because of the commercial threat posed by the Dutch. Oliver Cromwell, who tended to take a large view and lead with a firm hand, had a pronounced imperialist outlook. Further re-examination inevitably came with the restoration of the monarchy in 1660, by which time a move to define and tighten the bonds of empire was under way. The haphazard and unsystematic era of English colonial development had ended. For over a century thereafter, Englishmen on both sides of the ocean would be intermittently, increasingly engaged in the task of working out an imperial relationship that somehow met everyone's need, native Britons and their provincial cousins alike.

By and large, the colonists tended to regard the Puritan and parliamentary triumphs in the English civil war with a jaundiced eye. The Chesapeake and West Indian colonies reaffirmed their allegiance to the House of Stuart and refused to recognize parliamentary supremacy. This was not unexpected, but the triumphant English Puritans were taken aback by the tone of the response from the Massachusetts Bay colonists, who rather pointedly insisted upon going their own way. They maintained strict neutrality in the civil war, trading with Roundheads and Cavaliers alike, and indeed throwing open their ports to all shipping. They formed a confederation with the other New England colonies of Plymouth, New Haven, and Connecticut (pointedly excluding Rhode Island) for the purpose of promoting mutual concerns in foreign affairs, religion, and Indian policy. When Parliament went so far as to offer to pass legislation favorable to Massachusetts interests, Governor Winthrop cautiously refused this and other offers of aid, on the farsighted grounds that in "after times," as he put it, "hostile forces might be in control, and meantime a precedent would have been established."

The 1640s abounded with such acts and expressions of colonial independent-mindedness. During the war years Parliament, often hard pressed, had been in the position of supplicant. But with the execution of Charles I in 1649 the English government looked overseas again and took a harder line. Colonial ties to England had hitherto been entirely through the Crown, either directly, as with Virginia, or through the proprietary grants or company charters issued by the king. Now the king was gone, and a new constitutional relationship would have to be established.

Parliament moved to do this in 1650 with a statute declaring its supremacy over the colonies and demanding their submission to its authority. The act required all vessels engaged in English colonial trade to obtain a license and placed an embargo upon all commerce with those colonies that had espoused the Stuart cause. The act also created a commission which went overseas to investigate conditions in each colony and receive official acknowledgments of parliamentary supremacy.

Ironically, the only colony that maintained consistently unsatisfactory relations with the parliamentary and interregnum governments in England was Massachusetts. Constant bickering and mutual disillusionment marked the relations between the Puritans who governed Massachusetts and the Puritans who came to power in England. The latter development had once been eagerly awaited by the builders of the Bible Commonwealth, but their spiritual brethren back home showed no interest in the working model on exhibit in Massachusetts other than to carp at it. The Bay Colony was proud of its ability to maintain orthodoxy by stamping out dissent; Oliver Cromwell had concluded that toleration was the only way to keep English Protestants from tearing one another apart, and the Commonwealth sharply rebuked the Boston government for its harsh policy against non-conformists.

Smarting from this repudiation in matters of religious policy, the Bay Colony retaliated by paying almost no attention to the mother country's policies and instructions. Acting very much like an independent nation, Massachusetts conducted its own foreign affairs through the Confederation of New England, minted its own coins, expanded its jurisdiction by absorbing settlements outside its original boundaries, and generally went its own way. The Cromwell government was too busy with weightier matters to take strong action against this wayward offspring, but her posture would be remembered in later years.

Meanwhile Parliament had taken another long step toward the establishment of an imperial system with the passage of a Navigation Act in 1651. The act decreed that all colonial trade—between one colony and another, between the colonies and England, and in commodities from Asia, Africa, and elsewhere in America—had to be conducted in English (including colonial) ships. Goods going to the colonies from Europe also had to be sent in such ships, or in vessels belonging to the country whence the goods originated.

The act of 1651 was a turning point, big with consequences. The principle of commercial regulation was an old one, widely accepted in England and elsewhere, and Parliament had enacted many statutes concerning colonial trade before this—preferential tariffs, import duties, and so forth. But this was the first comprehensive attempt to view the empire as part of an integrated whole. For over a century the English government would proceed to extend and systematize the principles set forth in the Navigation Act of 1651. And the workings-out of this system of imperial trade regulation would henceforth do much to determine the shape and structure of the Empire. The act of 1651 also indicated that the major emphasis in imperial thought, to a greater extent than ever before, would be commercial.

What brought the Empire into sharper focus for the English during the Commonwealth period was the threat posed by a new rival. The early colonial ventures had been prosecuted, in part, as a counterthrust against the power of Spain. The idea of tightening the bonds of empire came in response to the Dutch. This skilled and active people, while fiercely involved for the better part of eighty years in fighting first to win and then to maintain their independence from Hapsburg rule, had carried commercial enterprise to the same pinnacles of wealth, power, splendor, and cultural achievement as the Venetians had done two and three centuries before.

As traders the Dutch were dominant everywhere, absolutely without peer. They swarmed all over the world's sea lanes—in the Baltic and the Mediterranean, the North Atlantic fisheries and the wine and salt trades. They wrested the Spice Islands from the Portuguese and took over that rich traffic, sent their ships to China and Japan, lodged themselves on Ceylon and Java, competed with the English for the India trade. They invaded the slave and ivory traffic of the Guinea coast and established a base at the Cape of Good Hope. Dutchmen infiltrated the Caribbean and supplied the Spanish Main from their base at Curaçao, enlarged their foothold on the coast of Brazil, handled furs and other colonial goods from their outpost at the mouth of the Hudson. Their engineering, mining, agricultural, land reclamation, and banking skills were in demand all across Europe. Amsterdam, as the wide-eyed little band of worshipers from Scrooby could briefly attest, had become the busiest and richest city on earth.

The handful of tiny provinces jammed into the marshy flatlands between the Zuider Zee and the mouths of the Rhine had achieved a spectacular economic pre-eminence, best summarized in Daniel Defoe's brief description early in the eighteenth century. "The Dutch," he wrote, "must be understood as they really are, the Middle Persons in Trade, the Factors and Brokers of Europe . . . they *buy* to *sell* again, *take* in to *send* out, and the greatest Part of their vast Commerce consists in being supply'd from All Parts of the World, that they may supply All the World again."

The Navigation Act of 1651 reflected England's sudden awareness that the Dutch, along with dominating every other branch of commerce, had almost completely usurped the trade to and from England's colonies, both on the mainland and in the West Indies. Active before in these areas, they had quickly achieved a commanding position there when England's own commerce was disrupted by the naval phase of their civil war, in which Cavalier and Roundhead privateers struck hard at each other's shipping.

The weapon that made Dutch supremacy possible, along with unmatched enterprise and trading shrewdness, was a new type of trading vessel they had perfected in the 1590s known as the *fluit,* or flyboat. The *fluit* combined cargo capacity, sailing qualities, and cheap construction costs in a way that enabled the Dutch to outstrip all competitors. The skippers of these well-handled, well-sheathed little vessels could offer better prices, greater variety of merchandise, cheaper freight rates, and more reliable delivery than Londoners or anyone else. Unable to compete with the Dutch, the English resorted to navigation acts as a means of excluding them.

Parliament had seen the problem; but Cromwell's England had its hands full, and these early attempts to regulate imperial trade amounted to little more than earnest finger waggling. To be sure, the Navigation Act contributed to the outbreak of an inconclusive war with the Dutch—the first of three that these bitter commercial rivals would fight—but the colonists themselves paid little attention to the act except to voice objections. Signs that settlers in America might look at the situation in their own way came from as far apart as the West Indies and Massachusetts Bay. "Shall we be bound to the government and lordship of a Parliament in which we have no representatives?" asked the legislature of Barbados in 1651. "This would be a slavery far exceeding all that the English nation hath yet suffered." Massachusetts chimed in with a similar assertion: "Our allegiance binds us not to the laws of England any longer than while we live in England, for the laws of the Parliament of England reach no further."

The colonies were here claiming the status of self-governing dominions, in effect, which suggested that the task of defining an imperial relationship satisfactory on both sides of the Atlantic would be a ticklish one. During the first Dutch war, Connecticut, Massachusetts, and Rhode Island all managed to go on record protesting, as illegal, the seizure of Dutch vessels by English warships in colonial waters, unless a colonial legislative body had authorized such seizures. As for the provisions of the Navigation Act, in the absence of enforcement machinery the colonists tended to ignore them and continued trading with the Dutch while it was to their advantage to do so.

——□——

The period of the civil war and interregnum in England witnessed two other developments of future importance to the mainland colonies: a pronounced increase in the strategic and economic value of the British West Indies, and a surfacing of political and religious radicalism in the mother country.

Oliver Cromwell himself played a part in advancing the course of empire in the Caribbean. Cromwell had some thoughts about the value of a properly run empire, and given time and energy to spare for this subject, which he never had, he might well have moved with his customary firmness to bring the straggling colonies into a more disciplined relationship with England. But Cromwell's only real effort in imperial matters was directed at the Caribbean, and at expansion of the Empire, not internal restructuring.

Cromwell was an imperialist of the old, or Elizabethan, school, in that he still regarded Spain as England's primary opponent and operations against Spain as a worthy national goal. He regretted the outbreak of war with the Dutch, fellow Protestants and long-time allies in the struggle against the Hapsburgs, and he did what he could to bring the first Dutch war to a speedy end. He then sent an expedition under the command of Admiral William Penn to conquer some of the larger Spanish holdings in the Caribbean area. Although the attempt to invade Hispaniola proved a disastrous failure, Penn's forces went on and succeeded in conquering the lightly held Spanish island of Jamaica in 1655.

Though Cromwell was disillusioned by the West Indian foray

and died thinking it a failure, the conquest of Jamaica proved highly important. The fertile island became the capital and focal point of England's Caribbean possessions—their most productive single unit, an entrepôt for commerce between England and New Spain, and a distributing center and staging area for a growing slave trade that supplied the Spanish Empire, England's other island possessions, and her mainland colonies.

At about this time, too, the English planters in Barbados, St. Kitts, and the other West Indian islands were completing an economic transition to the exclusive cultivation of sugar cane, for which the Caribbean lands were remarkably well suited. The acquisition of Jamaica and the switch to sugar production marked the beginning of a century and more of sustained prosperity for the British West Indies. The demand for sugar and molasses products proved insatiable.

Concentration upon large-scale sugar production was heavy with consequences. It inaugurated a boom in the slave trade, as planters imported quantities of blacks to labor in the cane fields. The influx of blacks touched off an exodus of most of the middle-class and lower-class white population, many of whom migrated from the West Indies to the mainland colonies. Meanwhile, the sugar islands quickly became the most valuable and prized portion of the British Empire. West Indian politics and strategy thereafter played a major role in English diplomacy. Wealthy absentee sugar planters from Barbados, Jamaica, and the Leewards became a power in English politics, acquiring landed estates in the mother country, seats in Parliament, and an influential voice in imperial policy while their overseers and factors ran the huge plantations in the Caribbean islands and drove slave gangs up to and beyond the limit of their endurance in the backbreaking tasks of sugar cultivation. Neighboring Guadeloupe and Martinique, on the basis of the same product grown in the same fashion, became comparably rich and important in the French Empire.

Furthermore, as we shall see, the West Indian concentration

upon sugar at the expense of everything else gave the mainland colonies, especially those north of Maryland, an opportunity to create prosperity for themselves within the workings of the imperial system.

———□———

Back home, Oliver Cromwell and the forces he had helped set in motion made another sort of indirect contribution to the future of colonial America. For a time the New Model Army that Cromwell led to victory over the Royalist cause was the most effective fighting force in all Christendom, possibly in all the world. Cromwell's veterans had the élan that comes with success and the discipline deriving from deep religious commitment and a belief in the righteousness of their cause. But the Ironsides were a bit more than Bible-reading, psalm-singing sectarians doing battle for the Lord. The English civil war, like all such conflicts, had its revolutionary side, and pointed in all manner of directions, like a wildly swinging compass needle, before the nation settled uncertainly upon its new course. Most of the soldiers in Cromwell's army were drawn from the middling and lower ranks of society, and they had discussed more than theology around their campfires.

Taking up arms against their king, whose authority had long been defined and accepted as God-given, had been a big step, and it had set folks to thinking. If the power of God's anointed could be set aside, then perhaps, just possibly, all social relationships were up for grabs. As horrified conservatives had been saying all along, the process of challenging authority and the existing order had no logical stopping place. While English Puritans had fought mainly from religious convictions, their challenge had clearly gone beyond religious matters; the House of Stuart's resolute defense of the Anglican episcopate was based on the intimate connection they had seen all along between spiritual and temporal authority. "No Bishops, no King!" James I had snapped early in his reign, in answer to the Puritans. His son Charles saw that bet called.

Some of the campfire conversations in the New Model Army explored the implications of this matter of challenging authority, and a few earnest groups came up with some radical answers indeed. The most important of these groups formed behind the leadership of impassioned John Lilburne, who had been risking his neck in defiance of authority for years. They were known, significantly, as the Levellers.

In the welter of proposals churned up during the tense debate in the 1640s over the future of the monarchy and what might replace it, the Levellers quite frankly enunciated the idea of a republic based on democratic and egalitarian principles, among which they specified liberty of conscience, equality before the law, and protection of individual rights against the coercive powers of the state. This was downright revolutionary, and Englishmen of property and standing momentarily overlooked their other differences to draw back in alarm. Radicalism of such dimensions was two centuries or more ahead of its time in England. But its very appearance in an aristocratic, class-conscious, tradition-bound society was suggestive, not only in terms of the road ahead for Great Britain, but as to what might happen when the same ideas occurred to people in less trammeled surroundings.

——□——

The religious counterpart of John Lilburne and the Levellers, in Cromwellian England, was George Fox and the Society of Friends. The Quakers were among several sects that stood on the far left wing of seventeenth century Protestantism. They were an offshoot of the same brand of Reformation radicalism that had produced the Anabaptists—and, like them, subject to harassment and persecution on both sides of the Atlantic during their early years.

The Quakers based their doctrine on the notion of the Inner

Light, an extension or manifestation of the Spirit of God, which resided in every human soul. They were mystics; the Inner Light could be felt and perceived rather than rationally demonstrated or logically analyzed. They were egalitarians who questioned all forms of deference to rank or submission to authority. And they were activists, at least in their early years, exhorting others wherever they went to find the Inner Light within them and be faithful to it.

Their insistence upon proselytizing was partly what made them so unwanted among the devout of other persuasions. The Quakers might emphasize silent meditation in their own meetings, but in the outside world they regarded it as a duty to propagate their faith, not least in communities where this was forbidden. A few of them were willing, and some were apparently determined, to be martyrs. And some succeeded, for the seventeenth century had its share of leaders with a strong predilection for making martyrs out of nonconformists. Small numbers of Quakers began coming to America in the 1650s, where a few were executed and several others banished by the watchful Massachusetts Puritans. With the exception of wide-open Rhode Island, the so-called Children of Light were not much more welcome in the other colonies.

What made Quaker doctrine such anathema to the Puritans was the principle of the Inner Light. The original Protestants had, as it were, got rid of the Pope; and the Puritans, as they left the Church of England, had got rid of the bishop, interposing only the Scripture, as interpreted by an educated ministry, between man and God. No Puritan (as Anne Hutchinson had learned) would go further than this. Man could only approach God through the Scriptures, and the minister was needed in order to see that the Scriptures were correctly read.

The Quakers were a good example of an ongoing tendency in Protestantism: once begin peeling away the intermediate units in the chain of command between an individual and his Maker, and the process (rather like that of challenging authority by executing kings) is apt to continue indefinitely. The Puritans had learned to live without Pope or bishop, but they were horrified when the Quakers went them two better, so to speak, and eliminated minister and Scriptures. Every Quaker was in effect his own minister, and they called the Bible "a declaration of the fountain, and not the fountain itself." The Spirit of God dwelt in every person, not merely in a few Saints whom God had chosen. And one did not need to demonstrate that he had achieved sanctification, in the Puritan manner, by a rigorous combination of soul searching and Scripture-based oral exam before a flinty-eyed board of experts composed of the minister and Saints who had already passed. For the Quaker, it was simply a matter of communion and meditation, alone or with others, until he realized, not that the Inner Light had suddenly come to him, but that he had in effect learned how to turn it on.

Small wonder, certainly, that the Puritans were scandalized; they would do anything but renew their affiliation with Rome before they tolerated such heresies. The notion of direct and immediate personal revelation was anathema, one which they had recently had to extirpate from their ranks in the person of Mrs. Hutchinson. Now the Quakers had made this pernicious doctrine the very center of their faith.

Moreover, the Quakers, in sharp contrast to the Puritans, were perfectionists, and their message contained that which made the human spirit soar. George Fox had put it this way: "Now was I come up in Spirit thro the flaming sword into the paradise of God. All things were new; and all the creation gave another smell unto me than before, beyond what words can utter. I knew nothing but pureness, and innocency, and righteousness, being renewed into the image of God by Christ Jesus to the state of Adam; which he was in before he fell."

This was going the distance, and there was nothing exclusive about the Quaker claim. What Fox had found within himself was "the true light, which lighteth every man that cometh into the world." If the Puritans (to invoke that nautical metaphor once

more) were sailing a point or two closer to the wind than most of
their predecessors, as regards human potential, then the Quakers
were sailing right into the teeth of it—and virtually without sails
or masts, as though they had discovered the principle of the steam
engine. Preposterous or no, they were taking this idea to America
with them and bruiting it about.

The Restoration period marked the beginning of a new phase in
the development of the British Empire. During the interregnum,
Parliament had begun to pass legislation defining the imperial relationship, and the government under Charles II and his successors extended and took steps to implement this legislation. By
1700 a recognizable imperial structure and consciousness had
taken shape. The process was far from complete, but England's
overseas possessions were no longer the random assortment of
virtually self-governing colonies that had sprung into existence
before 1650.

English leaders were learning to think in imperial terms. Diplomacy, economic policy, military and naval strategy, and other
aspects of statecraft would henceforth be formulated and conducted within the imperial context, and no little amount of such
activity would be shaped, at times dictated, by considerations of
empire. The days when prospective colonizers would simply be
permitted to embark, armed with royal patent and royal blessing,
to go their own way in the distant wilderness, were almost gone.

Almost, but not quite. As Charles II began his reign a new
burst of colonizing activity induced a temporary reversion to the
old method of bestowing huge chunks of power, authority, and
land upon private individuals. The king agreed with his advisers
in the matter of strengthening the bonds of empire; there were
royal revenues as well as benefits to English mercantile and manufacturing interests to be derived from a successful regulation of
colonial trade. But Charles II was under conflicting pressures, and

he was (alone of the four Stuart monarchs) a flexible and politic ruler, shrewd enough to listen to more than one set of voices even if this sometimes meant contradicting one policy with another.

Not least among the voices beating at the royal ear were those raised by various courtiers, nobles, and squires who had supported the Stuart cause during its darkest days, often at the cost of their estates and fortunes. Charles could not repay these folk by bestowing largesse from his exchequer, which was nearly empty, but there were still millions of empty acres in the American wilderness at his disposal. The enduring English dream of regaining or acquiring status and wealth as the lord proprietor of some vast estate had lost none of its magic, and it had an especial appeal among the Tory landed interests that had staked so much upon the House of Stuart. Turning to the map, Charles could see that the mainland colonies in North America were clustered in two widely separated areas, one along the New England coast and the other about Chesapeake Bay. Between these two clusters were the small, cosmopolitan trading centers and scattered farms along the lower Delaware and Hudson rivers that comprised New Netherland. Along the great stretch of coastline from the capes of the Chesapeake to the Spanish forts in Florida there were no white settlements at all.

The result, over the next few years—with the help of a second war with the Dutch, in which New Netherland was captured and became a possession of the English Crown—was a series of huge proprietary land grants to highly placed favorites and creditors, with terms and provisions modeled after those awarded to the Calverts in Maryland in the 1630s. From these grants, sooner or later, emerged the colonies of New York, New Jersey, Pennsylvania, Delaware, and the Carolinas. By the end of the century British North America comprised an uninterrupted chain of possessions extending along the Atlantic coast from the Kennebec to the Savannah.

Charles made all but one of these big proprietary grants in the early years of his reign. The Carolina patent, embracing all the territory between Virginia and Spanish Florida, was issued in 1663 to eight English gentlemen of the highest political standing and influence. Like the original Maryland patent, the Carolina grant conferred sweeping rights and powers upon the proprietors. Basing their project on the hope of attracting settlers from elsewhere in the New World rather than from the mother country, the Carolina founders included freedom of worship, a legislative assembly, and headrights in the package designed to lure colonists.

Some elaborate planning went into the Carolina venture, most notably the famous Fundamental Constitutions drawn up in 1669 by one of the eight proprietors, the reflective Earl of Shaftesbury, and his energetic secretary, John Locke. The document envisioned orderly settlement on an intricate check-and-balance system, with blocks of land reserved for proprietary estates, other large blocks set aside for a home-grown hereditary nobility, and the rest to be held by small freeholders. Shaftesbury was a keen student of ideal governments and systems, but his plan was too cumbersome and elaborate for conditions in the wilderness. What finally made it unworkable was not its aristocratic bias but its attempt to impose order and system upon the process of settlement. When colonists finally came, they simply refused to be bound by the grid-square pattern of counties and subdivisions in the Shaftesbury blueprint.

Settlement in Carolina proceeded slowly and on a small scale until after the turn of the century. The two regions in which the early colonists clustered were so far apart that the proprietors eventually split the territory and provided a government of sorts for each half. North Carolina consisted of a few tiny rural settlements around Albemarle Sound in the northeastern corner of the colony, inhabited mainly by surplus Virginians spilling south from the Old Dominion to try their luck in a new area. In the early years it was little more than a straggling outpost of Virginia, evolving a representative assembly, a system of local government, and a small farm-planter economy after the Virginia pattern.

South Carolina before 1700 consisted almost entirely of the thriving little community of Charles Town, founded in 1680 and inhabited by a heterogeneous mixture of French Huguenots, Scots, and Barbadian Englishmen whose cultural and religious differences were far outweighed by a common fund of energy and ambition. These early South Carolinians explored far into the back country, rubbed elbows with nearby Indians and Spaniards, launched a brisk trade in furs and deerskins, and raised food to sell to the hungry West Indian colonies until rice and indigo provided a larger economic base in the 1720s and after.

South Carolina's development then offered a double irony. Long after the pretentious Shaftesbury-Locke Fundamental Constitutions had been abandoned as unworkable, the colony evolved a class of great landed aristocrats with a role and influence along the lines Shaftsbury had envisioned for such a class. And some of its leading members turned out to be immigrants from Barbados and other British West Indian islands, who had fled those colonies because the shift to sugar production and big plantation units worked by slave labor had crowded them out. Some of them were attracted to the Carolina country (as the proprietors had hoped), and as soon as opportunity offered, they organized large plantations and imported black slaves in a pattern identical to the one that had crowded them out of the West Indies a few years before.

The recipient of Charles's next big proprietary grant was his brother James, Duke of York, Lord High Admiral of the Royal Navy, and commander of the expeditionary force that captured New Amsterdam from the Dutch without firing a shot in 1664. It fitted both the rank and the temperament of this future English king that he should receive one of the most princely domains (from Delaware Bay to the mouth of the Connecticut, plus lands in what would later become Vermont and Maine) and one of the most sweeping grants of authority (it was well-nigh absolute)

ever bestowed by the English Crown. New Netherland became New York and passed into the hands of its new proprietor as soon as the Dutch struck their colors.

The Duke of York relinquished parts of his domain: a royal commission awarded Connecticut the eastern portion of the former Dutch colony, the Maine grant was absorbed by Massachusetts, and the region between the Delaware and the Hudson was ceded to a pair of the Carolina proprietors. But he kept the valuable middle portion centered along the fine river valley, with its fur-trading post at Fort Orange, renamed Albany, at its upper end, and the seaport on Manhattan Island at its lower. He in no way molested the religion, customs, or property of the erstwhile Dutch colonists, who had grown accustomed to authoritarian rule under the West India Company and accepted James's not dissimilar authority with scarcely a murmur. The proprietor continued the Dutch practice of giving away much of the land in huge manorial tracts to a few favored magnates.

Population grew slowly, though faster than it had under the Dutch. The fur trade and the commerce of the busy little port on Manhattan remained the colony's mainstays. The proprietor's first governors were an energetic lot who created, under the terms of the patent, a fairly complete set of institutions of local government while keeping the real power firmly in the proprietor's hands. They governed paternalistically, without an assembly, and it remained for some Puritan freeholders, who had left New England to settle on Long Island during the Dutch era, to raise the fine old English point that they were being taxed without their consent. The proprietary government staved off demands for a representative assembly for nearly twenty years, finally permitting one in 1683. The Dutch legacy, along with picturesque architecture and delightful customs (ice skating, sleighing, Santa Claus), included a working alliance with the powerful Iroquois tribes in the region west of Albany.

King Charles was also responsible for the New Jersey grant, ratifying his brother's cession of that region to Lord Berkeley and

Sir George Carteret in 1665. These two gentlemen proceeded to divide their new grant between them, and for the next twenty years the Jerseys passed through a bewildering variety of proprietary hands and conflicting claims. This process left a maze of contested and clouded titles, enough to give New Jersey residents something to quarrel about for generations. The eastern half was settled mainly by Puritans migrating out of New England; the western half, building upon a small nucleus of Dutch, Swedish, Finnish, and Puritan farming communities along the lower Delaware, soon passed into the hands of some Quaker proprietors and received an influx of Quaker settlers in the 1670s. Both halves of the colony enjoyed freedom of worship and respresentative assemblies, but conflicting land claims and the overshadowing influence of New York on one flank and Philadelphia on the other would long distract the history of New Jersey.

While this wave of colonizing activity went forward, England moved to tighten the reins of empire. The newly conquered island of Jamaica and all of the West Indian proprietaries were made royal colonies in the 1660s, with governors appointed directly by the Crown. In the matter of commerce, the government implemented and extended the principles contained in the Navigation Act of 1651, designed to keep colonial trade out of foreign hands. This first act had been so poorly enforced and full of loopholes as to be almost a dead letter. It took two more wars with the Dutch and a series of enactments extending over the period 1660–73, known collectively as the Navigation Acts, to establish English control over the colonial trade.

These acts laid down several specific rules. All trade between England and her colonies, or between one colony and another, was to be in English (including colonial) ships. The definition of such ships was tightened by requiring that the master and at least three fourths of the crew be English (again including colonists);

ships not built in England or her colonies would have to be formally registered in England in order to qualify. Colonial imports from Europe, with a few important exceptions like wine and salt, could be shipped only by way of England, where they had to pay a duty and be reloaded; this gave English merchants a monopoly of the colonial import trade. Finally, certain enumerated products—most West Indian goods, together with tobacco—could be shipped only to England or to another English colony. This enabled English merchants, refiners, distillers, and other processors to monopolize the most sought-after colonial products, like sugar, molasses, ginger, cotton, dyewoods, and tobacco, hitherto dominated by the Dutch. Evasions of this act by colonial shippers were blocked by an amendment in 1673 requiring the payment of duty on enumerated items at the point of departure. Colonial governors were now required by oath to enforce these acts and keep records of the vessels trading with their ports, so as to permit checking up on possible violators.

Though some smuggling and illicit trading persisted in every colony, the Navigation Acts largely accomplished their objective. The Dutch were driven out of their profitable position in the intercolonial trade, and England's monopoly on this increasingly valuable portion of her entire overseas commerce was not seriously threatened after the 1670s. The colonies themselves were able to make their way satisfactorily under the rules laid down by the Navigation Acts, though not without some chafing and some cheating, chiefly because each colonial region developed an economy that permitted it to prosper within the confines of the system.

The act of 1673 also provided for the introduction of English customs officials, paid servants of the Crown, into colonial ports for the collection of the export duty and the general enforcement of the navigation system. Two years later a standing committee of the Privy Council known as the Lords of Trade and Plantations was created, explicitly charged with making and supervising policy regarding colonial affairs. This body developed its own administrative staff, which grew in size as the Empire did and became a kind of permanent secretariat, responsible for collecting information, making reports, and otherwise assisting the Lords of Trade on colonial affairs.

This represented an important new element. A large and growing body of men had come into existence—royal ministers, bureaucrats, customs officials, and the like—whose careers and fortunes would be bound up with the administration of empire. As it grew, the imperial mechanism offered opportunities high and low—for the devoted civil servant, the placeman, the corruptionist, the fortune hunter. At their best, these officials strove with some success to bring order out of the jumble that marked the early colonial system. At their worst, they would contribute enormously, perhaps in the end decisively, to the rift that would someday drive colonies and mother country apart.

CHAPTER 7

Friends and Kings

T HE CAROLINA, New York, and Jersey patents had been
awarded in a cluster, early in Charles II's reign; some sixteen
years elapsed before he was induced, under changed and interesting circumstances, to confer one final grant of New World land
and authority upon a lord proprietor. The powers conferred,
though broad enough, indicated the growing trend toward consolidation of royal authority over the Empire. Unlike its predecessors, this grant extended a specified number of miles
westward rather than "from sea to sea"; provincial laws were explicitly made subject to approval or disallowance by the Privy
Council; colonists were allowed the right of appeal from proprietary to English courts. Strict obedience to the Navigation Acts
and co-operation with royal customs officials were enjoined
upon the new colony, and the proprietor was required to maintain an agent in England to be answerable before courts or royal
commissions regarding violations or evasions of regulatory laws.

The old grants had contained no such clauses; imperial consciousness had grown considerably since the Restoration. And
shortly after the issuance of this charter the Lords of Trade and
Plantations enunciated the policy that there would be no further

proprietary grants in America or delegations of "further powers that may render the plantations less dependent on the Crown." The mother country had made its last territorial giveaway.

The recipient was William Penn, a recent convert to the Quaker faith that other Protestants, including the Anglican establishment that had returned to power with the House of Stuart, found so objectionable. All of the intellectual and political ferment, flexibility, paradox, and innovative power that Tudor-Stuart England had generated—in sufficient amount to supply both the island kingdom and its nascent empire with some of their most distinctive and enduring qualities—were on exhibit in the making of that charter. Its background afforded a small representative panorama of the whole colonial impulse.

Trace the lines backward for a moment. William Penn's father was an admiral who had fought with distinction for Oliver Cromwell in the 1650s. The grateful Protector had rewarded Penn with several Irish estates, which enabled him to accumulate a modest fortune and live like a gentleman. Toward the end of the Protectorate he spent a few weeks in the Tower for some real or imagined crime against the state but was soon released for lack of evidence. He thereupon left London to live the good life on his Irish acreage, send his son William to Oxford, and support the Restoration in 1660. The admiral preferred amity to quarrels; he was a friend of Oliver Cromwell, and a short time later he was a friend of both the returning king and his brother James, Duke of York—close enough, apparently, to lend these impecunious brothers the handsome sum of £16,000 at some point during their return to power.

Meanwhile his son, who had inherited charm and political sense, was managing to get himself thrown out of Oxford for outspokenly non-conformist religious beliefs. A few years later, after a fashionable continental tour that was supposed to confirm him in the attractions of a gentleman's life, young William became exposed to Quaker preaching in Ireland and soon became a convert. His embrace of a creed that good Anglicans and good

Puritans vied with one another in detesting infuriated the admiral, who had envisioned a distinguished career for his talented son.

But the son's conversion was obviously genuine and permanent, and the admiral had learned long ago, at sea, to keep his station in any sort of gale. The two were fully reconciled before the elder Penn's death in 1670, by which time young William had spent a few months in the Tower of London and a few more in Newgate Prison for refusing to deny or conceal his religious beliefs. He emerged from these experiences with firmer convictions than ever about his faith, and about the rights of individuals in matters of law, taxation, the ballot, and liberty of conscience.

He began to think seriously in terms of a haven somewhere for religious dissenters. His father had left him a comfortable inheritance that included a good name, a good head, a good income from those Irish estates, good connections, and an old promissory note, never presented but not forgotten, of the House of Stuart. Penn was one of a group of Quakers who bought into the Jersey proprietary in the 1670s with a refuge for the Society of Friends in mind. Now in 1680, convinced that a larger and less encumbered grant was necessary, he was applying to his father's old friend for his own grant of land in the American wilderness, so that members of his faith could do in peace what it was against the law for them to do in Charles's England.

The king, too, could look back down an interesting trail as he considered William Penn's application. Penn had maintained amicable relations at court in the years following the admiral's death. It was a measure of this particular monarch and this particular Quaker that they could remain friends and discuss a matter like this across the wide gulf that separated them in religion and politics.

Follow the trails again for a moment. Charles's father had headed the regime and pursued the policies that drove John Winthrop and his Puritan followers to Massachusetts Bay half a

century before. There they had upheld their own brand of orthodoxy with the same fierce intolerance that Archbishop Laud and
his monarch had employed in upholding theirs. In the name of
this Puritan orthodoxy, Winthrop had harried and finally banished the intractable Separatist Roger Williams, whom he liked
and respected, and the founders of Massachusetts and Rhode Island had thereafter pursued their differing faiths in antagonistic
proximity.

Then civil war and Puritan triumph had come to England.
Laud and the first Charles had paid with their heads for their beliefs, and iron-willed Oliver Cromwell had come to power. Puritanism incarnate, he had dispatched Admiral Penn to take from
Spain in the Caribbean; at home, he sought a policy of toleration
for his sect-torn country, disavowing the harsh conformitarian
model erected by John Winthrop overseas and doing what he
could to protect George Fox and his new faith from persecution,
while vainly seeking to legitimize the interregnum government.

Then the Restoration. One of the first tasks of the new king,
whose father had been executed by men of the Puritan persuasion, was to hear the petitions of spokesmen for two Puritan colonies overseas seeking royal approval of their charters. One of
these colonies was Rhode Island, still functioning under the document Roger Williams had prepared years before and got approved by Parliament during the civil war. The other was
Connecticut, whose founders had also drawn up their own constitution and lived by it for over twenty years without the faintest
shadow of authority from the mother country. Both colonies,
very much on their good behavior now, had come hat in hand to
King Charles, aware that with a stroke of the royal pen he could
validate or destroy the legal basis of their existence.

Charles must have been struck by the irony of it all. The petitioner from Connecticut was its governor and one of its early
founders, none other than John Winthrop, Jr., whose father had
left England thirty-odd years earlier because Charles's father had

made things too warm for him. The younger Winthrop, like the younger Penn and the younger Charles, combined personal charm with a good deal of skill and astuteness as politician and negotiator. He was a man of parts, this junior Winthrop—popular governor, competent doctor, distinguished scientist, the first colonial, and one of the few, to be made a Fellow of the recently formed Royal Society of London. Winthrop won approval of his charter, thereby validating Connecticut's legal existence as a self-governing colony under its Fundamental Orders. New Haven was absorbed within Connecticut, which also obtained a "sea to sea" clause extending its western boundary. All in all it was a liberal gesture, which in the presence of a less tolerant monarch or a less skillful petitioner might not have been forthcoming.

Moreover, once he had achieved his goals the genial Winthrop turned about and helped the Rhode Island petitioner get royal approval for that charter as well. Though Winthrop echoed a widely held sentiment in terming Rhode Island a "road, refuge, asylum to evil livers," he had enough respect for old Roger Williams and the principle at stake to help plead his neighbor's case and be instrumental in winning it. The Crown granted Rhode Island's charter in 1663 largely, as one official put it, because of "the good opinion and confidence we had in the said Mr. Winthrop."

So the other self-governing colony was affirmed in a charter that would be its constitution, as colony and state, for 180 years. The provisions guaranteeing Rhode Islanders their right to self-government resembled those of Connecticut, with the addition of a clause that Roger Williams had made a governing principle from the time he first went to Narragansett Bay: whatever the laws of England might be, no one in Rhode Island would ever be "molested, punished, disquieted, or called in question, for any differences in opinion in matters of religion." Thus did the younger Winthrop secure for Williams, from a Stuart king, what the elder Winthrop—and nearly everyone else of his day—had regarded as an unworkable and subversive principle. In approving these charters for Connecticut and Rhose Island, the king asked only that the governors and other officials of the two colonies affirm their loyalty to the English Crown and acknowledge its supremacy.

The paths had gone on crossing and recrossing. While Charles was regaining his throne, young Penn was developing the detestation of conformity that would get him expelled from Oxford, and the Massachusetts Bay Colony was trying and executing four Quakers who had migrated there and disregarded colonial laws forbidding them to preach their faith. A few years later had come Penn's conversion and the beginnings of his search for a haven where people could worship as they chose.

In search of such a spot during the early 1670s, his friend George Fox left for a long tour of America. He stopped at Jamaica, which Admiral Penn had helped capture; he visited Barbados, where colonists of the middling sort were beginning to leave because the sugar planters were enlarging their holdings and importing slaves. He went on to the mainland, inspected Virginia and then Maryland, the Delaware Valley, New Jersey, Long Island. He concluded his journey by visiting Roger Williams in Providence, where the two doughty old believers hashed out their respective faiths. Williams had left his doors open for Quakers as for everyone else, though he regarded the Children of Light as utterly wrongheaded and misguided, and railed against their blasphemous doctrines with all the zeal of a Massachusetts Puritan. One would like to have been present at that conversation between George Fox and Roger Williams.

After returning to England, Fox accompanied Penn on a visit to the Continent in 1677. They met Germans from a variety of Pietist sects, many of whom, like the Quakers in England, were eager to escape persecution. Then the trails led back to the English court. Fox and Penn had agreed by this time that the land between the Delaware and Susquehanna valleys offered the best site for their project, and Penn went to Charles for royal approval.

So the worldly king gave his perfectionist Quaker friend the charter he sought, with a sardonic backward glance, one suspects, at the tangled bit of history that had brought them together. These two men understood and liked each other. Everything went smoothly. The £16,000 credit that Penn had inherited from the old admiral afforded Charles no more than a pretext he might use in explaining why he had approved the grant; he had owed, and avoided paying, larger sums than this. Penn knew that the government would not be displeased at this relatively inexpensive way of getting rid of a troublesome group. The king, more tolerant than many of his Tory-Anglican supporters, may have been moving to spare Penn and his coreligionists from further acts of official harassment.

In any case, the charter was carefully and diplomatically drawn, designed to avoid giving offense or raising hackles. It circumscribed the proprietor's power in keeping with the new trend toward imperial consolidation, as we have seen. It carefully avoided mentioning holy experiments or havens for non-conformists. It spoke instead of such unexceptionable purposes as converting Indians, enhancing English trade, and enlarging the Empire. Laws could be initiated and promulgated by the proprietor, subject to the advice and consent of the freemen. His power to appoint judges, pardon criminals, and otherwise create and administer a system of justice was subject only to the familiar prohibition that nothing be contrary to the laws of England. The charter was fully approved in the form Penn requested in 1681.

Penn thus received title to the great tract lying west of the Delaware between Maryland and New York. To protect his colony's access to the sea, he persuaded the Duke of York to cede him that part of erstwhile New Netherland lying along the western shore of Delaware Bay, just below Pennsylvania. The Duke agreed, and these three so-called Lower Counties, seldom known as Delaware until near the end of the colonial period, became part of Penn's holdings and a close affiliate of Pennsylvania. The same governor and charter of privileges held sway over both areas, although the three Lower Counties were permitted to have their own assembly.

Penn's blueprint accurately reflected his philosophy, which contained several ingredients that offset the soaring idealism of his faith. He had read Algernon Sydney, James Harrington, and John Locke as well as George Fox; he had studied law and acquired a sense of history, and in politics he was an enlightened liberal rather than a radical. Liberty of conscience of course was fully guaranteed. He was equally determined to protect civil liberties, having learned from his sojourns in the Tower and Newgate to appreciate them. No more liberal land terms had yet been offered American colonists: 50-acre headrights, 200-acre tenant farms at low rentals, 5,000-acre estates plus a town lot for £100. The pamphlets he circulated in England and on the Continent to advertise these terms and attract settlers were scrupulously accurate and precise in setting forth the conditions the emigrants could expect to encounter. Shiploads of Quakers and a sprinkling of other non-conformists from Wales, England, Ireland, Holland, and Germany began to arrive in 1682. Pennsylvania, with its neatly laid out capital between the Delaware and Schuylkill rivers, sprang quickly into a busy and prosperous existence.

Pennsylvania was an immediate and continuing success, but it was no utopian democracy. Devout believer in Quaker doctrine though he was, Penn was also a man with the tastes and outlook of an aristocrat, and his first government reflected some of this. He made himself governor and reserved the right to reject all legislation. Lawmaking, justice, appointment, and administration were placed in the hands of an elected council drawn from among the substantial landowners "of best repute for wisdom, virtue, and ability"—in short, a propertied elite. The franchise was limited to taxpayers. Below this council was a large representative assembly, which could accept or reject but not initiate legislation. He did not even want to accord this group the power to debate or amend.

While Penn was actually present in the colony—he built himself a great country estate on the banks of the Delaware, imported thoroughbred race horses, and was rowed from his country seat to Philadelphia in a resplendent six-oared barge—his magnetism and charm made this aristocratic form of government work reasonably well. But during his periodic absences in England the colonists resented it furiously and demanded a larger share of political power. Penn agreed to a revision of the system by issuing a Charter of Privileges in 1701 providing for a governor and council appointed by the proprietor, with royal confirmation, and a full-fledged representative assembly elected by property owners with the power of debate and initiation as well as advice and consent.

Penn's thriving experiment did not let notions of brotherly love interfere with a propensity to quarrel. Bitter, prolonged battles broke out over landholdings, quitrents, the border with Maryland, the rights and powers of the assembly and the proprietor. The Quaker immigrants who dominated Pennsylvania politics for the first few decades include several men of substance, like Penn himself, and this Quaker elite proved neither the most benevolent nor co-operative of leaders. Yet when all of these qualifications have been noted, the fact remains that Penn's creation was the most successful, the most tolerant, and the most liberal of England's colonies. Its heterogeneous and growing population learned to live prosperously together, if not without friction, then without falling apart, and without banishing or persecuting the otherwise-minded.

—□—

Meanwhile, the Restoration government had continued its campaign to bring the colonies more directly under royal control, notwithstanding the king's occasional susceptibility to appeals for granting proprietorships and validating charters. Penn had obviously been a special case. As for the earlier examples of

Rhode Island and Connecticut, it is possible that in approving their charters and thereby passing up the chance to establish royal control the king had bigger game in view. The two small New England colonies had been eager to co-operate; confirming their charters had earned their gratitude and might create loyal counterweights against their overweening neighbor to the northward. Charles had no taste for stirring up unnecessary trouble. But if there was to be a showdown collision with the colonies over questions of royal authority, English governing officials could perhaps unite in wanting that collision to be with Massachusetts.

This colony's persistent attitude did much, over the years, to sharpen the government's desire to bring its empire under more effective control. Massachusetts leaders had been stiff-backed in their dealings with the Long Parliament, the Commonwealth, and the Protectorate; they continued to be stiff-backed in their dealings with the restored monarchy. Bay Colony leadership was beginning to stir complaint and resentment on the part of its own citizens, too. There were not a few Boston merchants and other independent-minded folk who had about had it with the rule of the Saints. Some of these complaints came to the attention of the English government; and Charles decided, as the second Dutch war ended in 1664 with New Netherland suddenly falling into English hands, to send a royal commission overseas, with the dual assignment of tidying up the Dutch conquest and taking a long look at conditions in New England.

Once the commission had overseen the transfer of authority in New Amsterdam from the Dutch to the English, it visited Connecticut. The commissioners agreed to move that colony's border with the erstwhile Dutch possession westward to the point where Governor Winthrop wanted it, and gave Connecticut their blessing. They were similarly pleased by the co-operative attitude and expressions of good will that they found in Rhode Island and Plymouth.

Then they went to Massachusetts, where the colonial government did everything in its power to forestall, circumvent, and obstruct their investigations. This reception confirmed many of the internal complaints and much that outsiders had long believed about the posture of Bay Colony leadership. The commission's report to King Charles included the frank recommendation that the Crown revoke the Massachusetts charter and administer the colony directly.

For the next few years the English government was too involved with more pressing matters closer to home, including the plague, the London fire, domestic political changes, and a third war with the Dutch (in which New York was briefly recaptured), to pay much attention to its unco-operative province. By the mid-1670s, however, England was ready to resume the process of tightening up the Empire. The Lords of Trade commissioned an agent named Edward Randolph to inspect and do the tightening up in Massachusetts.

Heedless of its internal critics, the Bay Colony's government continued on its unswervingly defiant course and gave the hard-nosed and controversial Randolph a very difficult time indeed. Randolph reciprocated, and Massachusetts ultimately lost a series of legal battles. The New Hampshire settlements were wrested from its control and organized as a separate royal colony in 1679. To keep its jurisdiction over Maine, many of whose inhabitants had grown restive and resentful, Massachusetts was forced to buy up all the rights of other claimants to that territory. Finally, legal action initiated by the Lords of Trade in an English court resulted in a decision in 1684 invalidating the Bay Colony's charter and thus removing the rights that it had used to shield itself from royal control.

James II acceded to the throne in the following year, and the process of bringing the colonies under royal authority changed from a canter to a gallop. The erstwhile Duke of York was an able administrator and distinguished naval officer who believed in getting things done fast. In governmental matters he was an authoritarian; in religion, a papist. His real abilities were fatally hampered by the fact that his policies ignored or sought to short-circuit nearly everything that had happened in his country's politics and religion since the accession of Elizabeth I. He had three years in which to act before the forces that culminated in the Glorious Revolution combined to overthrow him.

In colonial affairs he moved with vigor and determination. He embarked upon a sweepingly ambitious program to organize the American empire into two great viceroyalties administered by the Crown, along the Spanish model. One of these, which he called the Dominion of New England, was to include all of the New England colonies together with New York, New Jersey, and, eventually, Pennsylvania. The Dominion would be administered by a royally appointed governor and council. There was no provision for a representative assembly in this new structure, and the existing colonial legislative bodies were to be abolished. James and the Lords of Trade apparently envisioned a like structure to embrace the region from Maryland south to the West Indies.

The first governor of the Dominion of New England was Sir Edmund Andros, onetime professional soldier and governor of proprietary New York, who arrived in Boston in late 1686 to take up his new duties. He lacked the bureaucracy adequate for so huge a task. Though able and conscientious, Andros was also short on tact and patience, and as blind to the historical realities of colonial America as his royal master was to those in the mother country. Local rebellious movements overthrew his colonial regime at about the time that James was ousted from the throne of England.

James's successors, William III and Mary II, undid the extreme centralization represented by the Dominion of New England but took steps to continue the process in more acceptable ways. With the Dominion at an end, New York was made a royal colony along Virginia lines. Massachusetts also became a royal colony in 1691, with a governor appointed by the Crown and a council nominated by the lower house and confirmed by the governor. All enactments of the legislature became subject to the governor's veto and royal disallowance. The old Plymouth Colony was merged into Massachusetts, whose rights to Maine were also confirmed under the new royal patent. Freedom of worship was established, and the franchise, restricted under the old charter to church members, was redefined to conform to the standard English property qualification of a forty-shilling freehold.

The trend toward a more uniform system of direct royal administration continued into the new century. New Jersey became a royal colony in 1702. With the buying out of the Carolina and Bahama proprietors by the Crown a few years later, all but four of the North American colonies had come under royal control. (Bermuda had lost its company charter and become a royal colony in 1684.) Rhode Island and Connecticut remained undisturbed under their self-governing charters after the collapse of the Dominion of New England in 1689. William III brought Pennsylvania and Maryland under royal authority in the 1690s, but Penn regained his proprietary rights in 1694 and the Calverts were restored in Maryland in 1715.

The king moved to reinforce the imperial structure even more decisively with two key measures in 1696. One was a comprehensive new Navigation Act that tightened shipping registration procedures, bound the governors more closely into the enforcement mechanism, and enlarged the colonial customs service. It also empowered customs officials in the colonies to issue the kind of general search warrants, known as writs of assistance, then being employed in England, whereby vessels and warehouses could be entered and searched for illicit goods. Most important, the new Navigation Act created a set of vice-admiralty courts for the colonies, to try cases of alleged violation of trade regulations and thus remove such cases from the colonial common-law courts, where local juries seldom found against violators.

William's other measure was the replacement of the Lords of Trade and Plantations with a new agency designed to improve and centralize colonial administration—the so-called Board of Trade. An advisory body in which Privy Council and Parliament

were represented, but consisting mainly of full-time colonial experts, the Board of Trade was entrusted with general oversight of
colonial affairs. Aided by firm royal backing, at least in its early
years, the Board became an influential body whose recommendations tended to form the basis for parliamentary legislation and
royal decrees. Through these recommendations, the Board often
had the decisive voice in selecting and instructing royal governors and in disallowing colonial laws.

The reign of William and Mary signaled yet another crucial
shift in emphasis for the Empire. William was a member of the
House of Orange, which had been instrumental in guiding the
destinies of the Dutch Republic from its very inception. He had
been Stadholder of the United Provinces (the office that was as
close to the position of ruler as the unwieldy Dutch federal system possessed) since 1672, and he ruled both countries jointly
after 1689. William was doubly related to the House of Stuart,
from one of those exercises in dynastic cross-pollination that European statesmen loved: his mother, named Mary, had been
James II's sister, and his wife, also named Mary, was James II's
daughter. It was this marriage to his first cousin that enabled the
architects of the Glorious Revolution to invite them to the throne
of England as joint sovereigns replacing the ousted James, with
no great sacrifice of the principle of legitimacy.

The point was that in coming to England, William had not
abandoned Holland, whose interests were very much on the new
king's mind. For nearly a generation the Dutch had been subject
to the growing pressures and aggrandizing tactics of Louis XIV,
who had built on the work of talented ministers to make France
the strongest power on the Continent. Expanding in all directions, France pursued aggressive designs in the Austrian Netherlands and the Rhine Valley which brought it into repeated collision with the Dutch.

William had formed a continental alliance against Louis, and his accession to the throne of England enabled him to draw that nation into it; the ensuing war lasted from 1689 to 1697. This conflict marked the beginning of a century-long series of wars between France and Great Britain, in which great commercial interests, European hegemony, and imperial rivalry on three continents were all at issue. A fateful new backdrop for English colonial development had been slid into place.

From the 1660s, operating under mercantilist principles and autocratic authority, the French Crown had poured resources and energy into the development and expansion of its overseas empire. As a result, sparked by the boldness of explorers like La Salle and the ruthless guidance of governors like Frontenac, the straggling, underpopulated, long-ignored French colony on the St. Lawrence had grown into an aggressive extension of the mother country back home. It was a strange sort of colony, but under vigorous leadership it worked. From its chief centers at Montreal and Quebec, linked by a scattering of feudal seigneuries and peasant farms along the great river, Canada reached outward until it assumed continental dimensions, yet beyond that small nucleus on the St. Lawrence it was no more than a vastly distended trading post and military base strung together by frontier forts and men in canoes.

Count Frontenac deployed a motley but effective assortment of hard-bitten *coureurs de bois,* Jesuit missionaries, soldiers, royal officials, and Indian allies. Together they extended French sway across the Great Lakes, down the Ohio and Mississippi valleys, and over the Great Plains. They pressed harder and harder upon the English colonial frontiers along the Appalachian foothills. Trappers from South Carolina encountered Frenchmen in the Alabama country, while others led Indian attacks on settlements in Maine and New York.

A century earlier, Englishmen had begun launching colonial ventures with an eye to outflanking the Spaniards; fifty years later they were integrating and regulating their scattered possessions in order to beat off the Dutch. Now England and her colonies were locked in a great struggle with the French, for stakes that included nothing less than the destiny of the North American continent.

—□—

And in the course of this pioneer century of colonizing activity, an empire with a recognizable if rather loose-jointed federal structure had emerged. A network of officials responsible to Crown and Parliament exercised control over trade and foreign policy and constituted a kind of court of last resort over colonial laws and actions; the day-to-day domestic affairs of each colony were firmly in the hands of the colonists themselves, functioning through a welter of institutions ranging downward from provincial assemblies to innumerable local units—county, borough, corporate town, vestry, congregation, court—that Englishmen overseas had put together pretty much on their own, adapting English models to American conditions as they saw fit.

Face to face on the uneasy friction points in the middle, where the imperial and the provincial gears were supposed to mesh, stood the governor with his powers of veto and appointment (backed ultimately by all of the prestige and resources at the disposal of the British Crown) and the assembly with its powers of legislation and taxation (resting ultimately upon the will of the community expressed through the mechanism of a reasonably liberal franchise). In each colony these two key units of government were probing and testing the limits of each other's authority; these struggles afforded miniature overseas versions of the long contest between Crown and Parliament in England, so recently resolved in the latter's favor by the Glorious Revolution of 1688.

If there was an omen here for what would someday happen to the contest between royal governor and colonial assembly, few detected it at the time. The Empire worked; a balance, of sorts, between central and local authority had been struck. But it would require statesmanship and understanding and a give-and-take disposition—of the kind displayed at crucial points, for example, by the younger Winthrop, the younger Penn, the younger Charles—to keep this rather ramshackle mechanism in proper working order.

And the order was constantly subject to new stresses; the context was fluid. The accelerating imperial rivalry between Great Britain and France would dominate European politics for over a century and impinge constantly upon the welfare, security, outlook, habits, and opportunities of the English colonists. So, in a different way, would the assorted ambitions, scruples, and intelligence held by those royal ministers, officials, and placemen whom England would assign the task of making its empire work.

Moreover, the colonists themselves had been at it long enough, now, to be something more and something less than transplanted Englishmen. Generations were coming of age in the Chesapeake colonies and New England that knew only America. It was a different land, and it was molding a different people.

PART THREE

THE LAND AND
THE PEOPLE

CHAPTER 8

Before We Were the Land's

"THE LAND was ours before we were the land's," Robert
Frost wrote. "She was our land more than a hundred years
before we were her people." Yet in a sense we were "her people"
almost from the start. The settlers from the Old World migrated
with their heritage and sought to transplant it but, from the moment of their arrival, what they found here began to work upon
them. "The cleft dust was never English dust," Stephen Vincent
Benét observed; "the catbird pecked away the nightingale." If the
society that emerged owed a great deal to its European and particularly its English origins, it would owe an equal amount to the
realities imposed by the land and the people who were already
here. The result, eventually, would be a civilization unlike any
other existing on earth, with an identity and characteristics peculiarly its own.

First there was the red man. A quick comparison of the Indians
encountered by the Spaniards in the sixteenth century with those
encountered by the English in the seventeenth suggests the importance of this influence. The eastern portion of North America
was inhabited by several dozen tribes of the Algonquin, Iro-

quoian, Muskogean, and Siouan language groups. Although the details varied, their mode of life was a pastoral blend of farming, fishing, and hunting. They dwelt in villages, with a rather rudimentary political organization based on a complex of family, clan, and tribal loyalties. These Indians were thinly spread across the American landscape. Most of the villages were small; seldom did entire tribes contain more than a few thousand members. They were still essentially a Stone Age people, and although the North American Indian had much to teach the European newcomers, neither his political, economic, and social development nor his numbers posed a formidable problem for the English settlers in the long run.

By contrast, the Spaniards had encountered the most advanced and populous of all the Indian groups in the Western Hemisphere. At their highest, the Aztec, Maya, and Inca cultures invited comparison with the best in Western Europe, and they gave Spain's New World empire much of its form, not to mention much of its wealth. Politically, the dominant Indian societies in Mexico and Central and South America were authoritarian, tightly ruled by a narrow elite. The masses were relatively tractable. Skill, boldness, and good fortune enabled the conquistadors to subdue the native oligarchies fairly quickly. Taking over at the top, the Spaniards simply continued for their own ends the kind of exploitation that Aztec and Inca leaders had practiced for centuries.

Spain thus fell heir both to an incredible amount of mineral wealth and other treasure and to a large subject population. Most Spanish colonists therefore settled and dwelt among these folk, and because there were fewer empty acres and relatively fewer opportunities at the middling and lower ends of the scale, people from Spain did not emigrate to the New World in anything like the volume that emigrated from the British Isles a century later. The culture that finally emerged in Spanish America was unmistakably Spanish, and yet it was also an unmistakable mixture, in every sense of the word, of the Spanish and Indian stocks. What the Spaniards might have done with a nearly empty continent will never be known, but the course of their empire was shaped right from the start, and fundamentally, by the nature and number of the people who had got there first.

In English North America the Indians were less advanced, and there were far fewer of them. These differences immediately began to shape the nature of the English experiment in a variety of ways. To begin with, the venture was not based upon outright conquest. The English simply landed and undertook the process of settlement; their initial contacts with resident tribes featured a cautious interchange in which tenuous friendship or uneasy coexistence was more in evidence than hostility at first. The English had learned something about colonization from the earlier Spanish and Portuguese efforts, and more directly from their own experiences in Ireland. But only a few of these lessons could be applied to conditions in North America, and the process of adapting to new surroundings owed a great deal to the readiness with which the Indian taught the newcomers the relevant parts of his knowledge and his skills. Although the English colonies tended to take shape and grow on a trial-and-error basis, much of the trial and many of the errors were spared them by the co-operation and example of these red-skinned guides, who showed them the lay of the land and how to get about in it and how to dress for it, and what to find there that would sustain life.

The wide-eyed newcomer learned about wigwams and birch-bark canoes, snowshoes and toboggans. He learned to use the river trails and the deer trails that wound into the interior; he learned where the fish and game were, and what they were; he copied the Indians' method of slash-and-burn agriculture, planting his crops among the stumps in the burned-out tracts. He soon discovered that the Indian moccasin, leggings, and other garb were better adapted than English clothing for travel through the dense forests that carpeted the eastern seaboard right down to water's edge. The Englishman's diet and his dress underwent substantial alteration, to which the enrichment of his language with Indian words bore witness: succotash, moccasin, squash, pumpkin, raccoon, muskrat, tobacco, tomahawk, mackinaw, moose, hominy.

The North American tribes exercised certain deeper influences as well. These tribes were small and the country was immense: this part of the continent looked virtually empty. It was there for the taking, and before long the English set out enthusiastically to take. The red man had been guide and instructor; he now became, as the nearly empty acres beckoned, an enemy. Most Englishmen already had a highly developed sense of their own racial and ethnic superiority, and the Indian was simply in the way. He must move, stand aside, or be eliminated. The dismal record of clashes between the white and the red cultures began fairly early, and in spite of the examples of friendship made famous by Squanto and Pocahontas, enmity became and remained the rule.

This enmity was sharpened by a basic difference between the English and Indian concepts of landownership. The notion of individual private property in land had never taken hold among the American Indians. They recognized such things as territorial rights for fishing, farming, and hunting, and indeed the tribes could wage frequent war with one another over such rights. But the land, and the fruits thereof, were something to be used and enjoyed in common by the entire family or tribe. Until the moment the white man threw them out they never really understood the white man's concept of individual landownership. In few, if any, of the innumerable treaties calling for the sale or cession of tribal lands did the Indians realize they were giving up as much as the English believed they were getting. The furious antagonism born of this misunderstanding has lasted for the better part of four centuries.

———◻———

There were one or two subtler influences of a related sort. Some of the things the Indian had to teach were going to be learned the hard way, and the slow way. Closely tied to the red man's ideas about land use was his reverence for nature and his enduring attempt to live in harmony with it. Communal use and harmony stood in stark contrast to the prevailing European idea of private ownership and conquest, of land as something to be exploited, mined, used up, taken over. Most of it had in fact been used up and taken over before the white man began to realize that the red man might have had the right idea all along. This realization, to be sure, came too late to do the Indian much good. (For that matter, it may have come too late to do the white man much good, either.)

Not all North American Indians were political primitives. Some of their institutions, notably the confederacy that had been put together by the Iroquois tribes, eventually attracted the attention and won the respect of more than one astute colonist. Benjamin Franklin concluded that the colonies might well profit from the Iroquois example. In 1754, proposing that the mainland colonies form a union within the British Empire, Franklin observed that "it would be a strange thing if Six Nations of ignorant savages should be capable of forming such a union, and be able to execute it in such a manner as that it has subsisted ages and appears indissoluble; and yet that a like union should be impracticable for ten or a dozen English colonies, to whom it is more necessary and must be more advantageous, and who cannot be supposed to want an equal understanding of their interest." The Iroquois league indirectly left its mark, later, upon the structure of the United States Government and upon some of the procedures by which congressional committees learned to function.

It cut closer to home than that. Several Indian tribes had developed a strong belief in the essential freedom and dignity of the individual. Much of their culture and much of their political organization were based upon this concept, and represented a workable attempt to reconcile the age-old antagonism between the needs of the group and the needs of the individual. There were observant colonists who learned from this and used the Indian example to sharpen their own concepts of individual worth and dignity.

One final influence remains to be noted. Europeans, of course, were interested in the Indian from the moment they found him. White observers, struck by the contrast between European civilization and the societies of the less advanced tribes, soon detected and emphasized a utopian quality in Indian life. They exaggerated this almost beyond recognition, to be sure. But beneath all of the distortions and rhapsodical invocations of Noble Innocent Red Men lay a substratum of truth. Life, at least among the more fortunately situated tribes, *did* offer greater simplicity, a larger measure of freedom and, as outsiders viewed it, more happiness, than were the lot of most Europeans.

This idealized and oversimplified view of the American Indian eventually had a significant influence upon one of the most important strands in European political thought. Philosophies erected upon the premise of man originating in a state of nature were mightily reinforced by what appeared to be actual examples in the New World. From Montaigne through John Locke to Jean-Jacques Rousseau, this vein of political thought contained revolutionary ore; Rousseau was contrasting the American Indian with the European when he sounded his famous tocsin to the effect that man had been born free and was everywhere in chains.

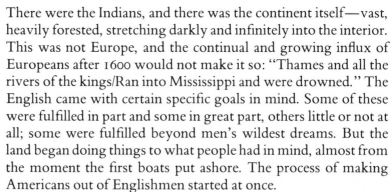

There were the Indians, and there was the continent itself—vast, heavily forested, stretching darkly and infinitely into the interior. This was not Europe, and the continual and growing influx of Europeans after 1600 would not make it so: "Thames and all the rivers of the kings/Ran into Mississippi and were drowned." The English came with certain specific goals in mind. Some of these were fulfilled in part and some in great part, others little or not at all; some were fulfilled beyond men's wildest dreams. But the land began doing things to what people had in mind, almost from the moment the first boats put ashore. The process of making Americans out of Englishmen started at once.

First, and by all odds most important, was the sheer abundance of the land in America. This aspect of the English colonial experiment was downright revolutionary, and it transposed everything the colonists did or sought to do into a new key.

Title to this land and the methods of acquiring it varied, as we have seen. In some cases a company, as in Virginia and Massachusetts, received large grants of vaguely bounded North American real estate in their charters from the king, while in others the land was granted in princely amounts to various lords proprietor; company or proprietor would then rent or retail parts of their acreage to actual settlers. After 1700, in all but a few instances, the land was administered directly by the Crown operating through the provincial government. On the local level, some plots were staked out and settled by entire communities, later parceled out to individuals by the town fathers; this was the custom in most of New England, although by the eighteenth century the lure of empty acres was breaking down this orderly pattern even there. Elsewhere the size, location, and mode of individual acquisitions were unsystematic almost from the start.

Europeans emigrated with elaborate concepts of land tenure in which early capitalist and traditional feudal elements were confusingly mixed. They applied these concepts as best they could, but the continent was too much for them. The eastern half was thickly wooded and the quality varied, but for the family that was willing to apply the backbreaking effort of felling trees and clearing undergrowth, there was good land right along the coast. For the more venturesome families, willing to do these things amid howling wilderness and Indians and incredible isolation, there was an inexhaustible supply in the back country. Once you got to it, acreage was there virtually for the taking.

And the repeated efforts of chartered companies, lords proprietor, colonial governments, and king and Parliament to maintain undue control over the disposal of all that acreage broke to pieces upon this irreducible fact. There was more arable land here than Europeans had ever dreamed of, and only a few Indians stood in the way. The ratio of land to people was the exact opposite of that obtaining in most of Europe, and attempts to create recognizable versions of Old World society on this side of the Atlantic would have to adjust accordingly.

Consider a few of the basic effects for a moment. To begin with, possession of land worth a certain amount conferred the franchise in England. As local governments took shape in North America it was the customary practice to grant full citizenship, including the right to vote, to freeholders with a given amount of acreage. But whereas this group, from the yeoman farmers and burgesses on up through the gentry, had constituted a distinct minority of the male population in England, land was so easy to get in most of British North America that societies containing a majority of small independent landowners emerged fairly quickly.

There were great disparities in the size of the holdings, to be sure; some men acquired large farms, a smaller number acquired vast estates. But even for the poorer individual there was real estate to be had—good or indifferent, legally or by squatter's pre-emption, at greater or less distance from existing settlements. Colonial governments, perennially eager for settlers, learned that the most attractive single inducement was the offer of a parcel of land. Colonies south of New England soon resorted to one or another version of the headright system, which made at least a small farm available to anyone who could pay his passage. Similarly, the town fathers who apportioned holdings in the New England communities usually saw to it that all male residents above the rank of servant received some sort of freehold allotment. And for whites, at least, poverty and servitude were not necessarily permanent handicaps.

Possession of a few stump-filled, rock-strewn acres in some New England river valley or of a densely wooded tract along the Delaware or the James conferred citizenship. This meant the franchise; what mattered even more was that it conferred independence and status—freedom. Landownership emancipated one from the obligations and subordination of tenantry and hired labor, and this was a powerful lure. It helped explain the steady expansion of British North America, once the hardships of the founding years were over, and it guaranteed that the societies here could never develop more than superficially along European lines.

Several related effects derived from this one. Labor, skilled and unskilled alike, found itself in a new and exhilarating position in most of the English colonies. The needs of new and struggling communities combined with the abundance of land to make labor scarce as it had never or rarely been scarce in Europe. This in turn raised wages to heights undreamt of in the Old World, and it also raised the status of artisans and laborers. Skills in such demand had to be treated with respect, and at the first indication of a sneer or a snub, a sensitive worker might decide to chuck it and try his hand at farming or move to some other community where he would be accorded more respect. Nowhere in Europe did the artisan and laboring classes enjoy such advantages, or such options. (The process was much slower, but a similar development, deriving from a similar excess of demand over supply, began to take place in the status of women in colonial America. Despite powerful traditions to the contrary, the age-old role of woman as subordinate and inferior creature, in the family and before the law, began a slow but visible erosion in the English colonial settlements.)

Another corollary to cheap abundant land was a society that by prevailing European standards was unbelievably fluid and mobile. There were limits to this, of course. Old World notions were too strong and deep-rooted to give way easily, and belief in rank and deference and social hierarchy was widely held on this as on the European side of the Atlantic. But the reality of a widely diffused landownership kept chipping away at the notions.

The abundance of land also slowed the pace of economic development even as that pace was quickening in Western Europe and particularly in England. The labor shortage in British North America was chronic and persistent; wages remained high, and industry faced a corresponding handicap. There was an especial shortage of skilled labor. The tendency was to encourage domestic handicraft and led many colonists to become jacks-of-all-trades, with negative effects upon productivity and the quality of craftsmanship. The most obtainable land—that is, the cheapest —tended to be in the uncharted back country, which of course kept retreating westward as the edge of settlement advanced. The independence that went with owning one's own land was paid for not only in the process of grubbing trees and clearing stumps; for society at large, the price was a widely dispersed group of small and virtually self-sufficient landowners, producing little or no surplus, poorly connected with the more settled areas, contributing little to the economy either as consumers or as producers.

Notwithstanding the commercial nature of many of the colonial ventures, and indeed of much of English society in the seventeenth and eighteenth centuries, notwithstanding the obvious ambition and get-ahead, go-ahead traits evinced by many of the settlers themselves, a powerful offsetting factor during the colonial period was this tendency to scatter, to go beyond the established settlements, to carve out a few acres on one's own. For many of these wandering, restless spirits the profit motive was less important, at least for a time, than a quite unphilosophical desire for independence—the hitherto undreamt-of opportunity simply to be left alone. For America, the long road leading to industrialization would eventually become a superhighway whose travelers hurried forward faster and faster; but in its early years it was little more than a circuitous footpath meandering slowly and haltingly through the wilderness.

In short, America was not only land but frontier land. If the effects of this upon character have been exaggerated, they are impossible to ignore. The coastline itself was frontier at first—

Plymouth, Boston, Chesapeake Bay, and the other scattered headlands and harbors where tiny new communities were being planted. A generation or two later the frontier began its slow inexorable move inland, ever deeper into the dark forests. The process would gather momentum and continue for the better part of three centuries and find its great interpreter (at about the time the process ended) in Frederick Jackson Turner.

One need not go the distance with Turner and his disciples in order to recognize that the frontier did indeed leave its mark upon the colonists and their descendants. Frontier conditions reinforced or encouraged, if they did not actually create, certain qualities of character and temperament, and it ought to be possible to refer to these qualities without getting starry-eyed. They included individualism and self-reliance, a kind of tough egalitarianism, and a growing dislike of privilege, all of which would lie at the very core of American political, social, and economic activity during the nineteenth century and afterward.

Frontier conditions undoubtedly bred less attractive qualities as well. The pioneers did co-operate—in barn-raisings, quilting bees, and so on—but the enforced isolation and concurrent feeling of being on one's own undeniably eroded the sense of community that had been a hallmark of English society. Frontiersmen were apt to be boisterous and quarrelsome, narrowly provincial, distrustful of strangers, quick to protest, impatient of authority or legal restraint. Whether or not the colonist actually donned leggings and moccasins and walked the trackless forest, he was subject to influences and pressures that bore little resemblance to those he had experienced in the Old World.

The facts of geography, then, were decisive in explaining the differences that set off England's colonial experiment from the parent society. These facts were also going to determine a great many other things.

The ocean itself was an elemental fact of geography. It placed an insuperable burden of distance between what England planned or directed with regard to her empire and what actually happened there several storm-tossed weeks and three thousand miles later. Its teeming fisheries on the banks off America's long northeastern coast gave Boston an emblem and New England a prime resource to offset its thin and rocky soils.

The irregular Atlantic coastline, with its many good harbors and bays and rivers leading into the interior, permitted settlement to take place at a great number of points and diffuse itself along the entire seaboard. One need only glance at the Pacific coast of North America, with its scarcity of good harbors and avenues to the interior between Puget Sound and San Diego, to realize what a different course American history would have followed had the country been settled from that direction.

The dense woodlands carpeting most of the eastern seaboard added another dimension. Timber resources and water power in the innumerable streams made lumbering a common secondary or alternative occupation to farming, gave the royal navy a new and needed supply of masts, and placed the material for colonial houses, towns, ships, tools, and furniture close at hand in the same sort of unbelievable plenty that characterized the land itself.

As the colonies grew and matured, geography affixed them with certain fateful attributes that would help determine the entire course of American history. In the southern mainland colonies, once various initial attempts to find gold or plant silkworm culture or recreate feudalism or make yeoman farmers out of English convicts had failed to pan out, it was discovered that conditions of soil and climate and growing season permitted the cultivation of crops for which a large European demand existed: tobacco in the Chesapeake colonies, later rice and indigo in South Carolina. The economy of the colonial South was built upon these staple crops, and the society and outlook of the South—during and long after the colonial period—were built in turn upon the economy.

In Virginia and Maryland, for example, the predominant crop was tobacco. Because tobacco cultivation wore out the soil within three or four years, planters concluded that success depended upon large landholdings—the larger, the better. Because English commercial policy sought to regulate the important tobacco trade and the way it was conducted, the margin of profit on a single hogshead of tobacco tended to be small; this conferred another advantage upon the big producer. Because Chesapeake Bay and its network of tributaries drained nearly all of eastern Virginia and Maryland, most planters could locate right on navigable water and ship their crops directly overseas. One important consequence was an absence of towns or an urban middle class, since most of the import-export business in the Chesapeake region could be done directly by the colonial planter with English or Scottish merchants, who sailed right to his wharf and picked up his crop, took it to England and sold it for him, filled his orders there for manufactured goods and luxury items, and sailed back next year to begin the cycle over again.

The premium upon large estates at the expense of smaller proprietors and urban centers resulted, eventually, in the rise of a powerful landed aristocracy in the Chesapeake colonies. A comparable pattern emerged farther south, although the port of Charleston in South Carolina, serving as entrepôt and social center for the surrounding area of rice and indigo plantations, offered an exception to the prevailing condition of rural predominance.

The Southern colonies took on one additional and related characteristic. The planter's other great need, along with enough acreage, was an adequate labor supply. The early planters, and many later ones, did what they could with indentured servants from the Old World, buying the contracts that bound those folk to a given term of labor, perhaps five or seven years. From the planter's point of view this system had two drawbacks. He stood to lose the servant's labor just as the man's skills had been fully developed, and the proximity of frontier wilderness made it difficult to prevent or recapture runaways.

The solution, tried tentatively on a small scale until late in the seventeenth century, was to import blacks from Africa or from the West Indies, where Negro slavery was firmly established in the Spanish Empire and also in the English, French, and Dutch Caribbean islands. After 1700 the institution became the dominant labor system in the planting colonies. It took root slowly and rather haphazardly, but deeply. And something recognizable as The South had emerged, long before the end of the colonial period.

——□——

The inescapable logic of geography led the Middle and New England colonies in a different direction. The growing season was shorter, and staple, semitropical products that throve in the Chesapeake and Carolina country were ill suited to the colder Northern climate. Ship timbers and masts alone excepted, the output of the Northern colonies did not have the kind of booming English market that made tobacco so important in Virginia and Maryland. Markets for the products of Pennsylvania, New York, and New England could be found, but the people there had to go in search of them.

This they did, with growing success—selling horses, livestock, meat, barrels, lumber, flour, and grain to the West Indian sugar planters in return for Spanish silver, English sterling exchange, or tropical goods that did have a ready European market; using these to buy what they needed in Europe; bringing back West Indian molasses to convert into rum, which could then be used to acquire slaves along the Guinea coast for sale to those same West Indian planters. Mediterranean Europe ate the best of New England's fish and the teeming slave populations of the West Indian sugar islands ate the worst of it; New Englanders carried it to both places, in their own ships.

And so complex patterns of trade gradually evolved, reaching from Boston and New York and Philadelphia to the Caribbean, the Mediterranean, the English Channel, the coast of Africa, the Grand Banks. The Northerners handled most of this trade themselves, and because commerce thus became important in the Northern colonies, towns became important—and shipbuilding, and all of the skills and enterprises that commercial towns require. This was especially true in New England, where unfailing harvests of rocks on the rugged hillsides encouraged more and more settlers to try their hands at something else instead of or along with farming: logging and lumbering and fur trading in the interior, fishing along the coast, or off-season labor in the boatyards, ropewalks, distilleries, and other maritime industries in the little seaports that came to dot the New England coast from Passamaquoddy to Long Island Sound. Agriculture continued to command the full- or part-time attention of the great majority of colonists in the North, but the tone and orientation were unmistakably more urban and commercial than anywhere in the South.

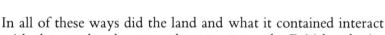

In all of these ways did the land and what it contained interact with the people who came there to stamp the British colonies with their own special features—varying from province to province and region to region in ways that would prove significant, yet sharing certain common traits that set them off more and more as time went on from the society that had fostered them.

CHAPTER 9

Choice Grain to the Wilderness

B Y THE early years of the eighteenth century an identifiable
American society had emerged, still recognizably English
yet unmistakably different. Many of the leading strands in the
complex fabric that was British North America already pointed
clearly toward Lexington and Concord and Yorktown; some
pointed, only a little less clearly, toward the longer-range future
—toward the Age of Jackson and continental expansion, Manifest Destiny and sectional controversy, civil war and the rise of
industry.

Of prime importance was the sheer fact of population growth.
In 1650 there were perhaps 50,000 English-speaking settlers in
North America, centered almost entirely in the coastal regions of
Chesapeake Bay and southern New England. By 1700 this popu-
lation had grown to about a quarter of a million, still heavily con-
centrated in those two regions but with smaller bridgeheads
established and pushing inland from such newer centers as New
York, Philadelphia, and Charles Town. The eighteenth century

was the spectacular growing time for Great Britain's mainland colonies. The figures are little more than educated guesses, the best of which suggest that there were over 600,000 colonists by 1730, well over 1,000,000 by 1750, and something close to 2,000,000 by 1770.

By the latter date, although there were still sizable blocks of sparsely settled land here and there, even near the coast, the edge of settlement had pushed well inland and begun penetrating the foothills of the Appalachians. One advance guard was already moving into the upper Ohio Valley, another through the Cumberland Gap along Daniel Boone's trail to Kentucky. The major seaports—Boston, Newport, New York, Philadelphia, Charleston—had achieved the status of small cities; Philadelphia, then the leader with a population of perhaps 35,000, had become one of the largest urban centers in the British empire.

After 1700, in short, the beginning-time, the period of struggle merely to survive and maintain a precarious foothold in the New World, was well past. The seaboard colonies were going concerns, and rapid population growth, with all of its benefits and problems, had become a leading fact in American colonial life.

—□—

This fast-growing society displayed a well-defined class structure, varying somewhat from place to place but having enough common characteristics to make possible a general description. Three classes, loosely defined in the terminology of the day as "better sorts," "middling sorts," and "meaner sorts," had emerged in every colony.

At the top stood a fairly distinct colonial aristocracy. It lacked the titles, most of the pretensions, and nearly all of the privileges of its counterparts in England and Europe; it was self-made rather than hereditary; it had arisen, often quite recently, from modest middle-class circumstances; and it was not rich by European standards. Nevertheless, each colony's politics, society, and economy were led and dominated by a small group of landed or mercantile families, who had come to occupy most of the key positions and won recognition and deference from the classes below them.

The middling sort, the most important element in colonial society, was composed primarily of independent landowning farmers, together with the equally independent, equally property-conscious artisans, shopkeepers, and tradesmen in the villages and towns. Shading imperceptibly off below the middling sort was a large and fluctuating group of tenant farmers and journeymen who in prosperous times might climb upward into the middle class and in depressed times might slide as easily downward into the ranks of the meaner sort.

These, in town and country, were much like the poor in Europe—farm hands, dependent artisans, free servants, apprentices, day laborers, sailors. In the very lowest ranks, at least temporarily, were the indentured servants, and, more permanently, those drifters and improvident marginal types who existed to a greater or lesser extent in every town and on the fringes of every rural community—folk whose lack of skill, incentive, health, or luck had mired them at the bottom of the heap.

By the eighteenth century the American heap had acquired a large and formidable layer even beneath the lowest classes, and here all resemblance to the European class structure ceased. For under the poorest, humblest, and most debased of white settlers, of which every colony had its share, lay the institution of slavery—African slavery, composed entirely of blacks and based frankly and explicitly upon the fact of color difference.

Blacks were brought to mainland North America within a dozen years of the establishment of the first permanent settlement at Jamestown, but they were negligible, in numbers or importance, until around 1700. By then, however, and increasingly thereafter, slavery was firmly established, especially in the Southern colonies, and the black population grew every bit as spectacularly as the white. Toward the end of the seventeenth century, when the institution began its real period of growth, perhaps 8 per cent of the colonial population were slaves. By the 1760s this proportion had climbed beyond 20 per cent. Nine out of ten of them were in the Southern colonies, with perhaps a third concentrated in Virginia alone. Only in South Carolina had blacks become a majority, but they comprised 40 per cent of the inhabitants of Virginia and about one third in Maryland, North Carolina, and Georgia.

Despite this concentration in the staple-producing South, slavery was established by law in all of the colonies, questioned in none, and more than marginally present in parts of the North. In New York, where a pre-emptive overlay of great landed estates had acted to discourage white settlement, blacks in the 1760s made up no less than 13 per cent of the population. They exceeded 7 per cent in Rhode Island, approached 7 per cent in New Jersey, and stood at around 5 per cent in Delaware. Only in New England and Pennsylvania, where as occasional seamen, artisans, and house servants they composed about 2 per cent of the total inhabitants, were blacks a negligible quantity.

An infinitesimal minority of blacks, mostly in the North, had achieved freedom, although the term had a special and qualified meaning. It was an uneasy, precarious, ill-defined halfway house between slavery and the full citizenship to which only people with white skins could aspire. But fenced in as it was by the enduring suspicion and hostility of the white community, those slaves who knew about freedom wanted it desperately. It was at least a step upward.

In any case, a caste system based on color lay underneath the European class system, and nearly every generalization that can be made about the transatlantic society is in one way or another dependent on that fact. The forced immigrant from Africa and the voluntary immigrant from Europe were becoming Americans together; not least among the many factors making for "Americanness" was the presence of the two races and the challenge posed by their co-existence.

—□—

A brief regional review of the colonial class structure displays variations in detail but no important difference in the prevailing pattern. In the New England colonies the aristocracy was primarily urban, based upon commercial wealth and allied or auxiliary professions and skills; a few fortunes in Rhode Island also derived from large estates devoted to the raising of horses and livestock for export to the West Indies. Below the prosperous first families of Boston, Newport, and a few smaller towns was the largest and most stable middle-class element in all of British North America. Each of the townships that constituted the basic political unit in New England contained its own substantial families and local elites, yet wealth and land were distributed more equitably in most New England communities and shared in by a higher percentage of the total male population than anywhere else on the planet. This stable, orderly region also had its quota, in village, town, and city alike, of landless and dependent poor.

The situation in Pennsylvania and New Jersey resembled that in New England. Philadelphia occupied the role of Boston as chief distributing and marketing center, with wealthy Quaker and Anglican merchants exhibiting much the same diligence and self-assurance as their Puritan counterparts to the northeast. The ethnic composition of the Middle Colonies was more heterogeneous, and farms tended to be larger; but they were like New England in the size and preponderance of their middle-class farming element, in the general prosperity of that element, and in the relatively equitable distribution of wealth.

The same could not be said for New York, which contained one of the most powerful groups of great landed families to be found anywhere in America, and correspondingly fewer opportunities for enterprising yeoman farmers. The colony had some of these, to be sure; it also had a mercantile element based on the Manhattan seaport and an influential fur-trading element based on Albany. But New York had a more uneven distribution of wealth, a smaller middle class, a larger tenant population, more slaves, and a higher incidence of poor and disaffected sorts than any other Northern province.

Below Pennsylvania lay the South, already distinguishable from the Northern settlements in tone, social composition, and outlook. Slavery and a high proportion of blacks, staple-crop agriculture with large landholding units, and a more decidedly rural society gave the South its regional identity. Yet even here the variations were considerable.

The Chesapeake colonies, where tobacco dominated the economy and bulked large in men's thoughts, contained a well-entrenched, energetic, tightly knit aristocracy of great planters, no towns worthy of the name, and a substantial number of degraded poor whites. Yet both Virginia and Maryland also possessed a middle class of yeoman farmers and small planters, prosperous and enterprising in the best colonial tradition. If this middling element was smaller than in Pennsylvania or New England, it was of greater consequence than the traditional Southern stereotype would indicate.

North Carolina, though slavery was firmly rooted and one third of the inhabitants were black, was the least Southern of the Southern colonies. There were big tobacco plantations with their first families in the northeast, adjoining Virginia, and big rice plantations with their first families in the Cape Fear region adjoining South Carolina, but for the province as a whole the American norm of small and middle-sized farms was more in evidence than elsewhere in the South. The towns were few and small, barely more than villages; the general level of prosperity was lower, the incidence of poverty and bare self-sufficiency somewhat higher, than in the North. But North Carolina represented a distinct modification of the standard Southern image.

South Carolina had the newest and wealthiest of the colonial aristocracies. The second quarter of the eighteenth century was a boom period there: sustained high prices for rice and indigo, and plenty of good land on which both crops could be grown. The result was rapid expansion, rapid accumulation of wealth, a rapid importation of slaves until they outnumbered the white population by a ratio of three to two, and a pattern of life (at the top) more frankly given over to the pursuit of pleasure than anywhere else in British North America. The big South Carolina planters owned more land and more slaves than the first families of Virginia and Maryland. Unlike the Chesapeake planters, the South Carolinians divided their vast holdings into manageable units, placed each in the hands of a resident overseer, and avoided the rural plantation life with its English gentry overtones in favor of stately town houses, cooling Atlantic breezes, and the urban pleasures of Charleston—the one town of any consequence south of Philadelphia. In no mainland colony was wealth more unevenly distributed or plantation slavery more predominant. Though not without its quota of small farmers, small planters, and townsfolk catering to Charleston's elite or serving the rice and indigo trade, South Carolina had strayed conspicuously farthest from the colonial middle-class norm.

As for Georgia, the southernmost colony and much the youngest, less than a generation old at the middle of the eighteenth century, important changes were afoot. These changes offered an instructive lesson, by which the entire colonial experience might be read. It added up to this: what the majority of settlers wanted, especially if they wanted it badly enough, was sooner or later going to prevail over anything to the contrary that planners or founders might have had in mind.

Philanthropic and imperial interests had conjoined to prepare a well-planned blueprint for Georgia. It was to be a haven for England's debtors and other sturdy unfortunates, who would receive small but workable tracts of free land in the unsettled country below the Savannah River and who would be available, in their sturdy and rugged independence, as a ready-made citizen soldiery protecting the more settled British colonies from the incursions of hostile Spaniards and Indians operating out of Florida. The blueprint was duly tried out. Assorted felons, debtors, and other prisoners were recruited, brought over, and given their fifty acres, with the careful stipulation, written into law, that all such grants without a male heir would revert to the trustees. The other stipulations, equally in the interest of maintaining a stable force of border guards, forbade rum and slavery.

This was eighteenth-century philanthropy at its best, and no set of rules could have gone more completely against the colonial grain. Fifty acres permitted no more than bare self-sufficiency. Rum, here as in most of the New World, was regarded as little less than a necessity of life. And the ban on slavery, well intentioned and healthy though it was, ran into unfortunate timing: Georgia was founded and the settlers arrived just when neighboring South Carolina entered upon its boom years, with fortunes being made in the cultivation of rice and indigo on large plantations by slave labor. Georgians could see all of this happening, not only across the Savannah but right under their noses; a few South Carolinians took up large tracts in Georgia and brought their slaves with them in order to take advantage of the boom, in casual defiance of the new colony's rules.

Public pressure against these rules mounted steadily, and not long after the middle of the century the whole blueprint collapsed. Large holdings, entailable with or without a male heir, were permitted; so rum; so was slavery. And in the generation just preceding the Revolution, Georgia began its first period of growth and development as a thoroughly Southern colony, importing blacks and creating a plantation system as fast as it could.

—□—

West of the towns and settled farming regions along the coast lay an irregular and ill-defined area known simply as the back country; by the mid-eighteenth century this region had begun to exhibit certain social patterns of its own. For the Northern colonies, the westward movement had gone about as far as it could then go. The best and most accessible land in western Massachusetts and Connecticut was pretty well taken up. New Englanders had also begun moving northward into New Hampshire, Vermont, and southern Maine, but this expansive thrust paused uncertainly at mid-century in the face of the continuous threat posed by imperial France and her Indian allies. The influence of landed proprietors and Albany fur traders combined to curb the flow of migration into frontier New York; in Pennsylvania, where the tide of settlement had reached the Susquehanna and in a few places crossed it, the same cloudy danger zone that New Englanders faced farther north, beyond which hostile French and Indians lurked, acted to stem or divert the westward movement until after the Seven Years' War. The most active area of back-country migration during the second quarter of the eighteenth century was in the Southern colonies—into the Piedmont regions of Maryland, Virginia, and the Carolinas. The farm country was good here, in places excellent; the Indian menace, if it still existed, was much reduced by the comparative inaccessibility of the area to the prodding efforts of imperial France.

Much of the bustle, energy, confusion, and hectic pace that later generations of Americans would experience accompanied this process of settling the back country. With regional variations, the same sort of thing was observable all along the frontier, from New England on down. Order was at a discount. Land titles tended to be cloudy, and disputes, at law and sometimes at gunpoint, correspondingly more frequent and more bitter. Rude cabins were thrown up and trees were girdled in a hurry. Many individuals and families eked out a squalid, precarious existence in conditions that travelers from the more settled regions could only regard as barbarous; nearby, in contrast, newcomers might establish prosperous farmsteads that struck outside observers as positively idyllic.

The former condition was observed, for example, among recent Scotch-Irish arrivals in interior North Carolina. "The clothes of the people consist of deerskins, their food of johnny-cakes, deer and bear meat. A kind of white people are found here who live like savages. Hunting is their chief occupation." The idyllic contrast was noted at about the same time by an observer of some new German settlers in the Shenandoah Valley in the 1760s: "They know no wants and are acquainted with but few vices. Their inexperience of the elegancies of life precludes any regret that they have not the means of enjoying them; but they possess what many princes would give half their dominions for—health, contentment, and tranquility of mind."

As Richard Hofstadter has pointed out, both of these pictures are true enough, yet neither accurately describes what was really going on when settlers streamed into the back country. Crude savagery and idyllic self-sufficiency were phases that most colonists sought to escape as soon as they could clear enough acres to grow a marketable surplus. In much of the back country there were rivers providing avenues of sorts to the seaboard markets, and in most new communities the crude egalitarianism usually associated with the frontier soon gave way to the kind of haphazard inequality that variable combinations of luck, incentive, and enterprise acted to bring about.

A prime mover in this process of back-country settlement was the land speculator—a far more representative and important character in the building of America, for better and for worse, than is sometimes recognized. Mark them well, these speculators. They are ubiquitous if sometimes shadowy figures, present whenever a boom or the promise of a boom or the chance of persuading someone else of the promise of a boom exists. Their predecessors helped organize the first companies and the first movements by which the first Englishmen crossed the Atlantic. We shall meet them again during the early national years, and again during the railroad heyday, and in the mining towns of the Far West, on the Great Plains, and always on the urban frontiers, from seventeenth-century Manhattan to twentieth-century Levittown—drawing up maps and prospectuses, organizing companies, staking out claims, buttonholing legislators, hiring agents to circulate among prospective customers. The speculator was composed of varying quantities of dreamer, salesman, patriot, and con artist, on a scale that ranged from pennyante pitchman to continental empire builder. He tended to know his way around in politics, and he had a quick tongue, a quick imagination, and a keen eye for the main chance. In all of this he was thoroughly American, whether of the seventeenth, eighteenth, nineteenth, or twentieth century. More often than not, he provided the agencies, printed material, organization, and machinery whereby individuals, families, and groups were induced to pull up stakes and brought to this or that portion of America.

These speculator-adventurers were hard at work during the settling of the back country before the Revolutionary War. Their efforts undoubtedly added to the confusion and the conflicting land titles, the inequities in distribution and price of land; they also contributed greatly to the speed with which this hitherto uncharted region was peopled and built up.

With equal speed, the crude, isolated, hastily thrown together settlements were transformed into back-country replicas of the older societies whence these folk had come. Hard on the heels of the pioneer farmers came a scattering of artisans, ministers, lawyers, merchants, rootless vagabonds and ne'er-do-wells, desperate men a step ahead of the law, and sundry other types that went into the making of a colonial community. In the Southern colonies, too, came planters or would-be planters, sometimes with a slave or a handful of slaves. Buzzing energetically to and fro with all these newcomers were some of the speculator-adventurers whose schemes and political connections and prospectuses had helped set the tide in motion in the first place. And from this motley assortment not merely farms but villages and small towns and a class structure emerged in a few short years, as roughhewn and recent as the new buildings and the trails that led there, yet consisting of the same identifiable hierarchy of better sort, middling sort, and meaner sort that characterized the social structure of British North America as a whole.

— □ —

Two items distinguished American colonial society most sharply from those of Western Europe. It was more fluid, and the middle class was proportionally larger and more important.

Class lines were drawn, of course, and the established social hierarchy was never seriously questioned. But these lines were undeniably easier to cross than in Europe, even than in England, and this difference was widely recognized. The degree of mobility in any society is a relative matter, depending upon the object of comparison. Europeans, especially of the upper class, tended to view the fluidity in colonial America as bordering on anarchy; they were impressed chiefly by the greater ease with which the social ladder was mounted—or descended—than in the Old World. Yet by the standards of nineteenth-century America the situation in the colonies seems far more stable, the mobility more circumscribed.

There is scattered evidence to indicate that class lines in America were hardening somewhat and that mobility, especially into the upper ranks, was becoming more difficult at about the middle of the eighteenth century. This change was to prove relevant to the tangle of thoughts and reactions that Americans began having as the controversy with the mother country assumed revolutionary proportions. But until this counter trend set in, and for most of the first half of the eighteenth century, when due allowance is made for the exaggerations of shocked conservatives and Old World aristocrats, the mainland colonies offered a degree of social mobility unknown anywhere else on earth.

This mobility operated into and out of a middling element that was both larger and more influential than in other Western societies. (The Dutch and the Swiss afforded possible exceptions to this statement, but the circumstances in both cases were so different that meaningful comparisons are difficult to make.) The American colonies struck many observers, foreign and domestic, as consisting almost entirely of a huge, spread-eagle middle class. This was noted despairingly or admiringly, depending on the observer's politics. It was noted most frequently, of course, in those colonies where middle-class dominance was most evident. As a writer in the *Pennsylvania Journal* in 1756 put it: "The people of this province are generally of the middling sort, and at present pretty much upon a level. They are chiefly industrious farmers, artificers, or men in trade; they enjoy and are fond of freedom, and *the meanest among them* thinks he has a right to civility from the greatest."

This was an exaggeration, even in the eighteenth-century Pennsylvania of Benjamin Franklin, but it was inspired by a fundamental truth. Notwithstanding the power, wealth, and influence of the upper classes and the deference generally accorded them, notwithstanding the widespread existence of poverty, colonial America was first and last a middle-class society. The norms, standards, and values were set here, and even before the democratizing influences of the revolutionary, Jeffersonian, and Jacksonian eras had been felt, ultimate power resided here, and nearly everyone knew it.

In every colony the better sort led, but most of them knew or sensed that the freeholding farmers and property-owning townsfolk who were generally content to follow their lead would withhold this support when the leadership tried to move in directions the middling sort found unacceptable—as had been the case, for example, in Georgia. The middling sort had the franchise, which gave them a potential majority in provincial legislatures and New England town meetings. They also exercised the more subtle, less tangible, but ultimately more compelling influence of public opinion—the weight of community sentiment. When this opinion was largely of one mind about something, that was the way things were going to move, as James Oglethorpe and many other lords proprietor had already learned, and as the British king and Parliament and their cadre of officials would find out in their turn.

For most colonial elites, the matter of arranging to lead where the middling sort wanted to go was seldom very difficult. Partly this derived from political sensitivity, an awareness of where the votes and the decisive political power resided. But mainly it stemmed from the simple fact that, almost without exception, these colonial elites were of middle-class origin themselves—if not self-made, then only a generation or two back. Only a negligible handful of the English upper classes came to America; Crown officials and their retinues to one side, colonial leadership was home-grown and self-made. Some Southern planters, New York patroons, and Yankee merchants, as their holdings expanded, might come to feel enormously superior to the ordinary farming folk; they might surround themselves as completely as possible with the trappings of Old World aristocracy—in their clothing, equipages, homes and furnishings, the education of their children, in their manners and what a later generation would call their life style. But the great majority of these colonial aristocrats never really transcended the pervasive middle-class values that have lain so consistently at the center of the American experiment.

—□—

These values have been noticed before, innumerable times. They have been invoked so frequently, and usually in such reverent and admiring tones, that the invocation has become a kind of litany, a stylized cliché. But certain concepts become clichés, after all, because they contain a truth, and few things were truer in colonial America than the fact that bourgeois values reigned supreme.

Put as briefly as possible, these values revolved around the work ethic, which made cardinal virtues out of industry, frugality, honesty, and self-reliance. The colonist's religion also made virtues of these qualities, as did his experience on the frontier. And of course his European origins had bequeathed them, well developed and in working order. The bourgeois mentality had been emergent in Western Europe, and above all in Holland and England, for some time before the first English ships and colonists set sail.

What made the crucial difference in America was that there were almost no competing values to offset this bourgeois emphasis. The wilderness did not contain, nor was it possible to transplant, a titled hereditary nobility, a crown and court, a living legacy of armored knights and turreted castles, a truly established church that was everywhere accepted, with a tradition centuries old and all the pomp and panoply of cathedral orders and episcopal hierarchy.

The result was that the work ethic flourished in the mainland colonies like the green bay tree. Few vices were subject to as much condemnation as those connected with indolence. The class distinctions accepted by the colonists rested not upon pedigree, coat of arms, or title but upon personal achievement, measured chiefly in material terms. Acceptance of class differences, and of corresponding differences in wealth and property, was accompanied and tempered by a growing conviction that people should rise or fall according to their talents and virtues. Attempts to duplicate the manners and customs of the English gentry or nobility could only be made within this context.

Hence the colonial elites, whatever their pretensions or pipe dreams, were a *working* aristocracy, imbued with a bourgeois sense of responsibility that betrayed their bourgeois origins. Except for the pleasure-hunting rice planters who had got rich so quickly in eighteenth-century South Carolina—men who let overseers run their plantations and provincial government atro-

phy almost to the vanishing point—the folk at the top of the colonial hierarchy minded both their own affairs and those of their
provinces with an energy and dedication that did much to explain
the general success of colonial governments and the essential harmony that prevailed between the middle and upper classes.

This harmony was further enhanced by the fact that what the
upper classes had, the more ambitious members of the middle
class might get, either in their own lifetime or in that of their children. By the same token, there was a general disposition on the
part of the "meaner sorts" to accept the system and work within
it. For the poor man with ambition and energy—and the colonial
era contained thousands of such—it was clear that he could "better himself" more easily here than anywhere else on earth. And
for that sizable portion of the lower classes who were permanently mired in their low estate, there was no real disposition to
question the system or do more with one's frustrations than
brood or toil or drink or idle the waking hours away.

All of this helped to explain the unremitting energy with
which colonial society went about its tasks. It also had an enormously stabilizing effect. There were strong counter tendencies
at work, but the emphasis upon diligence and self-reliance made
for a sensible, steady, disciplined people. Unless deeply challenged, they would prefer the moderate approach. The middle-
class consensus had a built-in stability that even revolutionary
times, when they came, could not seriously impair.

The bourgeois motif struck yet another chord. Stable and
steady though they might be, colonial Americans were nonetheless a society of climbers—acquisitive, materialistic, assertive
folk who looked hungrily upward and contemptuously downward. They had a way of measuring merit and value in monetary
terms, and they operated with a powerful conviction, which little
in their own experience did anything but strengthen, that those
who failed to make it—that is, poor folk—had failed because of
some grave moral defect or congenital inferiority, and hence

were deserving of neither sympathy nor assistance. The middle-class temperament contained a hard and calculating quality, and it, too, was operating in an environment with few offsetting forces.

———□———

Obviously the colonists were considerably more and considerably less than one large happy family working industriously together toward a single goal. Each colony offered a wide range of political disputes and antagonisms. The settlers did not learn the ways of representative government merely by solemn play acting. They learned their politics well, and thoroughly, in the only way that it can be learned—by hashing out their differences in the political arena.

These differences were inevitable, arising from the welter of conflicting needs and demands of people living in a growing and increasingly sophisticated society. Continual political battles occurred in each colony over the basic questions of land, currency, religion, representation, taxation, the role of government, Indian policy, and the like. Class antagonism frequently entered these disputes, and it would be fatuous to assume that colonists of middling or low estate were uniformly content with the leadership of the better sort, or that the better sort consistently governed in the best interests of all. Many of the disputes were sectional—protracted and sometimes bitter conflicts between the eastern and western areas of a colony, in which frontiersmen demanded fairer representation and a higher allocation of tax moneys for roads, defense, and so forth than the older, well-entrenched eastern sections were willing to grant. These disputes were often further complicated by the role of the English government, which tended to have firm ideas of its own about Indian, land, and currency policies, the treatment of dissenting religions, and other matters. Except for a few brief instances, however, clashes between colony and mother country were of secondary importance until after 1760; the colonists gained most of their political experience battling one another.

Some of these disputes were fairly rugged. Middle-class stability and moderation did not prevent colonial Americans from losing their tempers and occasionally resorting to more robust methods than those of debate, petition, and majority vote. There were several serious rent riots in New York, sparked by the bitter resentment of struggling tenants on the large estates of the patroons. Proprietary New Jersey experienced a similar clash. Examples of armed struggles between the eastern and western sections of a colony ranged from Nathaniel Bacon's rebellious movement in Virginia in the 1670s to those of the Paxton Boys in Pennsylvania and the Carolina Regulators ninety years later.

Sectional and class antagonisms existed, but they were less important over the long run than harsh factional disputes between rival groups of upper-class leaders. Indeed, it was in these quarrels between competing factions of the colonial elite that people of middling and low degree often became more active and more aware. Ignored by his leaders in quiet times, the ordinary colonist found politics coming in search of him during the long factional contests. (The normal process whereby a ruling group courted the favor and sought the support of lesser folk, in the interest of beating out a rival faction, was a vital early step toward greater mass participation in politics. Other steps would follow.)

A complex range of political disputes was not the only disruptive force at work. One of the outstanding features of colonial development was the high proportion of those who came here in some form of bondage. This had numerous consequences and implications—beginning, of course, with the brute fact of slavery; a distressingly large portion of the colonial structure was being built on the forced labor of human chattels.

And while the wealth piled up by the black bondsman's unrequited toil began to accumulate, with an unseen rate of interest compounding itself silently and inexorably on the debit side of the ledger, the white bondsman, too, came and helped build

America. It has been estimated that as many as half—and outside of New England, where the process never really took hold, considerably more than half—of all the white immigrants during the colonial period came as indentured servants.

This is neither as simple nor as attractive a story as it is often made out to be, although the picture had its brighter side. Some of these bonded immigrants were redemptioners—Europeans of some little substance who often came with their families and a modest store of tools and personal possessions. Usually they were able to pay a portion of their passage money and bonded themselves to redeem the unpaid portion by laboring for someone else for a specified term of years: one or two, or perhaps as many as four, depending upon the amount of passage money they had had to borrow. A far larger number were indentures, people with no money at all and no possessions beyond the clothes on their backs, coming under a contract that could be bought and sold (as could the bearer, while working out its terms) and called for a specified number of years of labor in return for passage and board and keep. A great many, too, were convicts, at least in the sense that they came from English prisons—debtors, perhaps, or those found guilty of one of the innumerable petty crimes which carried heavy prison sentences under the harsh penal code of the times. A few in this final category had committed or been convicted of more serious offenses, and not a few, whatever the extent or reality of their guilt, had become more or less hardened criminals simply by too long association in the brutalizing confines of an unenlightened prison system.

The brighter side of this picture, and the one that receives most attention, is the happy ending that a beneficent system had in store for many of these newcomers once they had worked out their terms. It was the first version of the great American success story—or perhaps the second, if the survival and achievements of those initial settlements in Virginia and Massachusetts be accounted the first. America was here being the fabled land of opportunity from the very start, permitting thousands of penniless folk to come over, labor awhile in servitude, and then achieve independence and success by their own efforts once they could begin working for themselves.

And many thousands did just this; the large colonial middle class included a substantial number of people who came out of poverty in this fashion, and even more who were descended from that element. Certainly the redemptioners, most of whom were from continental Europe rather than from England, and whose origins were a shade less humble than those of the indentures, often moved rapidly from their period of servitude into the ranks of the independent landowning farmer. Many indentures and ex-convicts were also able to do this.

But the success story is only part of the story. One of the most careful studies of indentured servitude in America has estimated that some 10 per cent of the bondservants went on to become freeholding farmers; another 10 per cent achieved comparable status as artisans, overseers, and the like. The rest—eight out of ten—flouted the traditional success story by failing to make it. Some died during their servitude; others drifted back to the Old World; the majority simply took up permanent residence, as it were, in the ranks of the American lower class—sufficiently beaten down by their experiences in either the Old World or the New, or both, to be unable to take advantage of the opportunities America offered. Many indentures, including some of the very poorest and not a few of the convicts, were sold for the term of their contract to Southern plantations, where most were assigned the arduous, endless chores of manual labor required by tobacco or rice culture. Paupers from the London slums were ill prepared for field work in the hot Southern climate. It is hardly surprising that most of them failed to survive this experience or make a go of it afterward.

This is worth a comment or two. The law governing indentures, and the mere possession of a white skin, gave the white bondsman several large advantages over his black counterpart toiling beside him or on the next plantation; only a willful misreading or ignoring of the total evidence can lead one away from the bedrock conclusion that nobody's lot in colonial America was as bad as that endured by the black man. The psychic adjustments demanded of the black slave and the white bondsman in, say, the Virginia tobacco country were basically different in that the slave had no hope whatever for the future. For him things would never get any better; except as age or illness altered the nature of his tasks, things were not even going to change much. The white bondsman could at least see the end of his servitude somewhere ahead.

Yet this probably did most of the white laborers little good. Many blacks would willingly have traded with them, no doubt, but for most derelicts or convicts out of Hogarth's London there was no such word as "hope," no notion of a future that might be better. The built-in advantages of being white in the land of opportunity were of little use to such folk. Opportunity was something they could hardly imagine, let alone actually pursue. The average planter was neither a sadist nor a fool; it was natural for him to work white bondsmen harder than he worked blacks, on the cruel but economically sensible theory that the white laborer would only be there a few years and might as well be worked to the limit before he departed, while the black man represented a permanent investment whose resources should be husbanded more carefully. For this and other reasons, all too many white indentures emerged from their labor experience with neither the incentive, the spirit, the skills, nor the energy to swim well in the middle-class mainstream.

If not all white indentured servants represented the lowest dregs of English society, nor labored till they broke at the thankless tasks of plantation agriculture, the fact remained that the flow of white migrants to the New World, once the great Puritan exodus of the 1630s had ended, included a pump at the Old World end of the line that needed priming more frequently than is generally realized, and in ways that need more attention than they usually get. Voluntary newcomers never arrived in sufficient numbers during the colonial period to fill a fraction of the demand. Small settlements might endure and survive in the far-off wilderness, but the architects of the colonial enterprises wanted to make a profit. For this, empty land was only half of it. Profit would not come until settlers, buyers, tenants, producers, and consumers—in short, people—were established there in sufficient quantity to make the whole thing go.

This was elementary, of course. But it was far easier to see the need for warm bodies than it was to get enough of them over here. On both sides of the English Channel there were enterprising men who proved capable of doing this—a motley and not overly attractive assortment of merchants, ship captains, recruiting agents, propagandists, thugs, and various related dealers who collectively acted as middlemen in the complicated business of getting folk to the New World. There were men of similar ilk, similarly engaged, in the older and bigger business of bringing blacks from Africa to the New World. The trade in white bodies required a bit more finesse and subtlety but was not strikingly different.

The point is that not very many of the poor folk wanted to go —not nearly enough of them, at any rate, to satisfy even the minimum demand. America would someday become a great magnet, attracting poor Europeans by the million and exerting its attraction in every corner of the Old World. This process, which was central to one of the greatest migrations in all human history, also required its complex machinery of ships, agents, recruiters, and brokers. But the latter group had one big advantage over their seventeenth- and eighteenth-century forebears in the immigrant trade—the real reputation that America as a great land of opportunity came to have after 1800. The country became its own best selling point; even the most exaggerated hopes of Mediterranean or Eastern European emigrants in the late nineteenth century, even the embellishments and exaggerations contained in the brochures of the transatlantic steamship companies, were built upon a solid substratum of truth: the land *was* good; opportunity *did* exist; this was known.

No such reputation surrounded colonial America, at least not for the poorest of migrants. By the eighteenth century the opportunities available to farmers and artisans—those already in the middle class or close enough to it to peek in the window—were acquiring a deserved reputation in England and parts of Western Europe. But for the very poor it was different. Many of them lacked the incentives and the skills necessary for middle-class status, and many were so submerged in the ignorance and squalor that went with their condition that America was not even a name to them, certainly nothing more than that.

This the assortment of middlemen set out to rectify. At their worst, they were outright crimps cruising the slums and grogshops in search of defenseless folk and employing a combination of muscle, gin, and fast talk to get their senseless or befuddled victims off the streets and aboard ship. Children were sometimes lured by offers of sweets. If this beginning of a voyage across the ocean was the fate of a small minority, a much larger number were conned into signing indentures by fabulous and altogether deceitful promises and descriptions of what awaited them in the New World. Many others, including those with a few possessions and a little money to apply toward the expense of the trip, found themselves ultimately stripped of all this by a series of unknown extra charges and fees that kept being levied, so that they arrived on the farther shore as penniless as their poorer brethren.

Thus migration for many began under unfortunate auspices. Some came under duress and larger numbers were grossly deceived; still more were fleeced. Add to this, for all save that minority who could afford to go as fare-paying passengers, and not for all of these, a long ocean voyage under conditions of discomfort, peril, sickness, and high mortality only a notch or two better than those endured by Africans on the middle passage. Cap it off with a reception in the New World in which indentured servants were herded together, hastily spruced up, and sold off like so many cattle; while the redemptioner and fare-paying arrivals, if they lacked full command of the language or their senses, were apt to find themselves separated from what remained of their cash by official-looking "helpers" at dockside. The totality of this experience left a whole range of physical and psychic scars. It is hardly surprising that some never healed.

—□—

Homogeneity was altered in a different way by the increasing infusion of non-English elements into the colonial bloodstream. This did not become noticeable until late in the seventeenth century and assumed its largest proportions in the eighteenth, when the seaboard colonies entered upon their great period of sustained growth. Of greatest signficance was the large-scale influx of men and women of African descent. Next in importance were those from the Rhine Valley and the north of Ireland. By the Revolution, the German element in colonial America may have numbered up to 8 per cent of the total population, and the Scotch-Irish—descendants of Scots who had migrated to northern Ireland during the early seventeenth century—may have numbered 10 per cent.

The Germans were mainly redemptioners, though some also came as indentures and others as full-fare freemen. They filled up and expanded the back country in eastern Pennsylvania and the Susquehanna Valley, then pushed on southwestward to form many new settlements in western Maryland, the Valley of Virginia, and interior Carolina. They added strong dashes of Lutheranism and various brands of Pietism to the colonial religious mixture; they tended to be politically passive, socially self-sufficient in their well-knit communities, and economically invaluable as skilled and devoted husbandmen who made their farming regions the most productive and well kept of any in America.

The Scotch-Irish added something special to the colonial brew. They tended to be hard cases politically—unyielding Presbyterians, schooled and scarred by generations of turmoil in Ireland, caught in the middle between oppressed Irish Catholics and the Anglican establishment, hated from both sides, returning the hatred at compound interest. (Where Ireland was concerned, the English, whose overall record as colonists does not compare unfavorably with that of other Western nations, were mired from first to last in a deeper bog than any that dotted the landscape of the Emerald Isle. Even their better-intentioned efforts never turned out right, and such efforts were usually overshadowed or canceled out by all of the heavy-handedness, myopia, prejudice, arrogance, and fumbling ineptitude of which the British at their worst were capable. Ireland represented perhaps the only truly unsuccessful Tudor policy; their successors for the next four centuries built upon these initial mistakes in the same vein, and not a generation passed but what more chickens came home to roost.)

What the Scotch-Irish brought to America, along with their devout Presbyterian animosity toward Papists and Anglicans alike, was a political activism of the querulous and boat-rocking variety. These folk were tough, stubborn, touchy, combative, and full of energy. Like the Germans, many of them went to the back country, where they farmed less skillfully and lived less quietly than their Rhenish neighbors. Their political impact was considerable, and it reverberated in both directions: as the most truculent and activist of frontier settlers, they battled the Indians with the same fierce joy and no-quarter antagonism that marked all their other struggles, and thus provided colonial America with a tough frontier cordon for which settlers in the more established areas had reason to be grateful; yet at the same time the Scotch-Irish became the angriest and most belligerent critics of the seaboard areas, demanding that more sums be spent for defense against Indians and loudly protesting the underrepresentation of frontier counties in provincial assemblies. Not even the original Puritans had added as much ginger to the flavor of American politics.

In addition to the Germans and Scotch-Irish, there were smaller but still sizable migrations from Scotland and Ireland proper, and from the Netherlands, the latter folk adding to the persistent Dutch stock in the Hudson Valley. Even smaller dashes of Swedes, Finns, Welsh, Swiss, and French added something to the ethnic variety. Though few in number, a sprinkling of French Huguenots rose to wealth and prominence in more than one colony. At a conservative estimate, more than nine in ten colonists were English or of English descent as late as 1690; by the end of the Seven Years' War, the English preponderance was no more than three in five.

Collectively and cumulatively, the waves of migrants had an intangible but perhaps decisive effect upon the developing character of this colonial people. It was a biased rather than a representative sample of British and European populations, as the high incidence of indentures and redemptioners suggests. "The rich stay in Europe," De Crèvecoeur observed, "it is only the middling and the poor that emigrate." Every possible human ingredient was being thrown into this transatlantic stew, but a few elements were outstanding. A great winnowing process was under way. In the most obvious sense, the grinding hardships of ocean crossing and wilderness clearing and frontier existence proved a cruelly effective way of eliminating many of the weak; toughness of body and of spirit was being bred into most of the survivors.

The great Puritan migration of the early seventeenth century left indelible marks, and many of the sober freeholding newcomers of later years—for these men of modest property kept coming, along with the indentures and the very poor—were of like quality. The Reverend Stoughton had said it: "God sifted a whole nation that He might bring choice grain over into this wilderness." If not all of this grain was choice in Stoughton's highminded sense, nearly all of it was choice in the sense of growing qualities and staying power; the harvests would someday be unforgettable. The best brief description of the leading human qualities was supplied by the eighteenth-century British agriculturist Arthur Young, who had done some thinking about this. "Men who migrate," he wrote, "are from the nature of the circumstances the most active, hardy, daring, bold and resolute spirits, and probably the most mischievous also."

Different though they were, these newcomers had a few broad things in common. In one way or another their lives had been disrupted or threatened by a tangle of economic dislocation and hardship, religious strife, political persecution, war and attendant social turmoil—all of which, in England and in much of the Continent, were taking place as part of the tremendously complicated process whereby the Western world careened into the early stages of the capitalist and nationalist era. Nearly everyone, especially in the middle and lower echelons of European society, was affected by this, felt the pressures, received the buffets that accompany change.

Nearly all were affected, yet only a few came, and in the absence of ways of measuring the difference, one is led to conclude that certain traits set the emigrants apart. Arthur Young had gone to the heart of it; this much more, perhaps, can be ventured. The push, from Europe, was probably more important than the pull. These people were not so much going *to* something as *from* something, and what they were leaving had a grim pattern to it—conflict, upheaval, uncertainty, turmoil, loss or the threat of loss. Things looked bad; these folk wanted out. Even the perils of a transatlantic voyage to an unknown land—about which most of these prospective colonists had few illusions—were preferable to what they had experienced or seemed about to experience in the Old World. Others, equally oppressed, chose to stay at home. Apparently, then, the boldest spirits, the most impatient and restless, the most alienated, the most desperate and quarrelsome, were among those who decided to pull up stakes.

What had got to them, essentially, was the status quo: things as

they were. (The fact that the status quo itself was changing in unfathomable ways only made matters worse.) These people were
disposed to question and resent authority rather than accept it, to
take action rather than remain passive, to fight or run—or both
—rather than surrender.

At its peak, this translated itself into a soaring, almost boundless vision of what might be done in a new land, where authority
would be an ocean away and things would not be as they were,
where a model society with fewer blemishes than the one they
were leaving could be built. From such bold and at times utopian
visions, the aspirations ranged downward through various hopes
for new opportunities all the way to a mere blind, urgent desire to
escape. But from one end of this broad spectrum to the other,
forceful qualities of mind and spirit were at work: venturesome,
aggressive, abrasive qualities. These people did not all want the
same things, beyond the elemental notions of escape and a fresh
start. If, for a determined handful, this meant social engineering
and creating communities, for untold larger numbers it meant
simply a vague but compelling desire to go where they could be
left alone. "Get off my back" is a piece of twentieth-century
slang, distinctively American, which well summarized the prime
motivation and prevailing mood among immigrants to Britain's
mainland colonies. A people so motivated and of such temperament would leave their mark.

CHAPTER 10

The Dissidence of Dissent

T HE AMERICAN character is as elusive as a forest creature — something that can be glimpsed and detected but not captured or seen whole. One of the best ways of tracking it down is by following the religious trails.

The outstanding feature of religion in colonial America is that it was heavily, overwhelmingly Protestant. Even though Maryland was founded, in part, as a refuge for persecuted English Catholics, and even though the principle of toleration gained ground after 1650, Catholic immigration was insignificant; at the time of the Revolution, fewer than two in a hundred American churches were of the Roman faith. The number of Jews was smaller still; a few Jewish families, chiefly of Spanish and Portuguese origin, engaged in commerce in the colonial seaports, and in the 1760s made up less than one tenth of one per cent of the mainland population.

The first thing to note is that these Protestants lived up to their name. The protesting spirit was unquenchable. Protesting and challenging religious authority encouraged strong wills and independent minds that could subject prevailing economic or political doctrine to the same harshly critical scrutiny. Edmund Burke, from the distant vantage point of the English Parliament, saw what this meant. "The people are Protestants; and of that kind which is the most adverse to all implicit submission of mind and opinion," he observed in the 1770s. "This is a persuasion not only favorable to Liberty, but built upon it. . . . All Protestantism, even the most cold and passive, is a sort of dissent. But the religion most prevalent in our northern colonies is a refinement on the principle of resistance; it is the dissidence of dissent, and the protestantism of the Protestant religion."

Colonial Americans were not only Protestant; they were every variety of Protestant. Nowhere else in the Western world was there so great a multiplicity of sects. Protestantism contained a perverse and rather frightening logic which believers tended to back away from whenever they saw it, but there was no real escaping it. The process of questioning Truth is easier to start than to stop, and in a questioning atmosphere no truths are safe. Protestants did not plan it that way and did not care for it very much, but they had started something that led straight toward individual freedom of conscience. If this principle was still some distance short of universal acceptance at the end of the colonial period, the great number of denominations and sects indicates that the process had come a long way. (At the outbreak of the Revolution some 20 per cent of the colonial churches were Congregational and another 20 per cent were Presbyterian. Anglicans and Baptists each claimed about 15 per cent of the total; the Society of Friends, about 10 per cent. Perhaps 5 per cent were German Reformed and another 5 per cent were Lutheran. Smaller groups included the Dutch Reformed, the Methodists, and German Pietist sects like the Moravians, Dunkers, and Mennonites. Not all of the larger bodies were firmly united; Congregationalists and Presbyterians had split into New Light and Old Light factions, and there were already several varieties of Baptist.)

There were also a great many people who belonged to no church at all. This was probably truer even in the beginning, and even in such colonies as Massachusetts, than is generally supposed, and as the colonies expanded lustily in the eighteenth century the proportion of the unchurched increased. The secular current in America was always strong. Even pious New England in its most pious early years contained folk like the hardy immigrant who announced that the reason he and his fellows had come over was to catch fish, and every colony contained a substantial number of people who had little or no religion. The shaping influence of religion in American life was itself shaped by the presence of these folk.

In all of this there was a strong pressure toward religious toleration, even though nobody especially wanted it. Later Americans were proud that their country was a haven for liberty of conscience and separation of church and state; they can be just as proud, surely, even after they realize that their ancestors backed into these great principles.

To begin with, in none of the colonies outside of New England, and not in all of those, was any one religion strong enough to impose its will in the matter of conformity or establishment. The Anglican Church was eventually established in parts of New York and in most of the Southern colonies, but only in Virginia was it able to act like an establishment and even here it met stout resistance. Rhode Island never had an establishment, nor did Pennsylvania, Delaware, or New Jersey. Nearly every religious group found itself in a minority somewhere, and so had to argue for religious toleration in self-defense. With more and more sects endeavoring to co-exist cheek by jowl the idea of live and let live in matters of worship was no more than common sense. To be sure, devout believers got to this position slowly and with reluctance, and where they were strong enough they harried dissenters vigorously—even to the extent of hanging a few unrepentant Quakers in late seventeenth-century Massachusetts. But toleration and the right of dissenters to worship in public and aspire to full citizenship gained ground steadily after 1700.

Not least among the forces working toward liberty of conscience in America came from the Old World. Here the supposedly corrupt, tradition-bound mother country gave the colonies a lesson. In matters of toleration, England applied common sense and practical realism well before the colonies did—and this in the harshly intolerant world of the seventeenth century rather than the genially skeptical one of the eighteenth. Such dissimilar leaders as Oliver Cromwell and Charles II came to see that toleration of diverse beliefs made more political sense than persecution. It was the de facto toleration (uneasy and bitter though it was) during the Commonwealth period that robbed New England Puritans of their zealous conviction that history was flowing their way, and it was the worldly Charles who granted both Roger Williams and William Penn their libertarian charters. From the Restoration onward the British government acted more than once to curb or disallow the harsher examples of religious intolerance in the colonies.

—□—

Of all the elements in the colonial religious legacy, the one that deserves the most attention is the one that receives the most—the Puritans.

It is easy to distort or misunderstand the nature of their influence. They have been credited with too much and blamed for too much; they were children of controversy who have remained the subjects of controversy to this day, and all in all they are not easy to like. But their identity and purpose three and a half centuries ago remain indissolubly bound up with America's, and the nation must understand and acknowledge them before it can ever understand itself.

To begin with, the Puritans brought their faith to this country and put it to work. No more apposite word could possibly be found. Work was as important to the Puritans as it had been to John Calvin at Geneva, and what they built here, however else one might judge it, undeniably *worked*. Keeping eternally at it, they managed to do just what they had set out to do—create a

Bible Commonwealth in the wilderness, a viable community of Saints, run according to precepts they believed in and designed to serve as a model for all Christendom to follow. When the success of this model proved irrelevant a generation later, the New England Puritans (with characteristic soul-searching) adapted their system to an altered context. *Work,* in the sense of labor, continued apace; so, in ways that left the Puritans themselves a bit dazed and bothered, did *work* in the sense of success.

Puritanism in America, its trust in God and the efficacy of dry powder not one whit diminished, proceeded to have at the new continent in wondrous fashion. Dismayed though many of the original Puritans would have been by what happened to their ideas and institutions at the hands of later generations, they knew their Bible well enough to have derived a certain grim satisfaction from the passage about God moving in mysterious ways.

Indeed, the working out (how often that Calvinist word recurs) of the Puritan impulse in colonial America affords a good example of the way in which historical forces converge or mingle to bring about results that no single force or lesser combination could have produced. Political experience and heritage, environment, and economic development interacted to propel the colonists in a certain direction. These forces in themselves made for a strong-flowing stream which neither the American Indian nor the British government proved able to channel or contain. When conjoined with the Puritan current, the stream became a mighty flood, a great majestic artery on which people and ideas would move forward irresistibly, truly like the Mississippi, able to drown the Thames and all the rivers of the kings.

The Puritan affluent enriched the mainstream in crucial ways. The covenant theology—that complex and often murky line of reasoning by which the early Puritans had sought to make predestination palatable without losing it—led straight to the theory of the social contract, whereon the Revolutionary generation took its philosophical stand. Generations of New Englanders grew up believing that regeneration had been made possible by a covenant between God and man, and that later covenants between man and man, deriving from this one, were the true basis for godly human communities. The author of *The Social Contract* might later renounce the notion that God should go in search of Moses in order to speak to Jean-Jacques Rousseau; but Bible-reading New Englanders could accept John Locke the more readily because of what God had said to Abraham.

The Puritan belief in the autonomy of the congregation pointed with equal directness toward the notion of government by consent. Similarly tenacious and adaptable was their idea of a higher law, an ultimate guide to human conduct above and superior to man-made statutes. For Puritans this higher law was the Bible, the Word of God—which, properly studied, thoughtfully read, and carefully interpreted, was believed to contain all that man needed to know about what God expected of him.

Like so much in the Puritan arsenal, this was explosive stuff, and much would depend upon how it was used. In more secular terms, the higher law could become natural law, which human reason could discover, and by which human conduct and indeed the entire universe functioned—another theory which eighteenth-century revolutionaries would put to good use. Since the higher law in the form of the Bible was written law, it encouraged a belief in the importance of a written constitution, a supreme law of the land. Yet there were no limits to the heights of this higher law. For many of the Puritans' descendants, this remained the Bible, or what they read in it, and no man-made law, not even the Constitution that called itself supreme, could stand as high. Disobedience to the latter in the service of the former was not only justified but a duty. (The argument that would help break the nation in half in 1861 drew in part upon this line of reasoning, and upon the morality behind it.)

Beneath these notions of the convenant, the independent congregation, and the higher law that was God's Holy Word lay a principle that the Puritans themselves found distasteful and not a little frightening, but they could not prevent the thing from rising to the surface and glowing like a lighted buoy marking a difficult channel.

This concept was individualism, which drew more from the Christian tradition than from anything in the realm of politics or economics or secular theories of man and society. Now the Puritans were not democrats, and they are twisted all out of shape by latter-day attempts to make them appear so. They were far too persuaded of man's innate sinfulness and depravity to advocate individual freedom, and they believed firmly in authority and obedience to authority as the only safeguards against anarchy. Yet the individualist germ grew and thrived in the Puritan culture.

For the Puritan ideal of a literate flock, reading the Bible and holding reasoned discourse with their pastors, was an open invitation to the individual to step forward and realize his potential to the utmost. The belief in human frailty and sinfulness never wavered, but the Puritans issued this invitation anyway, and kept issuing it. People were to be educated, and they were to ponder the Word of God themselves, to the best of their ability. Behind the invocations of God's wrath and God's omnipotence, this was proclaiming that the human brain had the capacity to grasp truth and that this process was somehow indispensable to the achievement of salvation. For a group who steadfastly believed that "in Adam's fall/we sinned all," this represented an enormous vote of confidence in Adam's descendants.

Their faith being what it was, the Puritans could hardly avoid the notion that they were a chosen people. The idea took hold and remained strong long after the theology back of it had evaporated. The most prevalent secular version was the idea of Manifest Destiny and the American mission—the belief that we had been selected, because of superior attributes, to expand across the continent and, at least in influence, across the ocean beyond, and spread the blessings of our superior system to a benighted world.

Although they drew upon other sources as well, Americans owed to the Puritans more than to any other group the unquenchable zeal and energy with which each generation has gone about its tasks; also, the abiding concern for education, together with the belief that education is fundamentally a community responsibility. Puritans gave the country its first printing press and its first college, and they insisted upon both almost from the moment of their arrival. Notwithstanding a strong and recurrent streak of rowdyism, colonial Americans as a group were a responsible, sober, law-abiding, self-disciplined, and essentially moral people; the Puritan imperatives go far toward explaining this. Backsliding of course was constant (which never would have surprised the Puritans), but the norm remained and it stayed visible. Much that happened in American politics would not have been possible had this not been so.

Mention must also be made of those aspects that prompted H. L. Mencken's immortal description of Puritanism as the haunting fear that someone, somewhere, might be happy. Like all strong-willed folk, the Puritans had the vices of their virtues. They were often stiff-backed and contentious, heavily inclined to self-righteousness. They believed that sin could be identified and that sinners should be brought to judgment. They felt that government existed to enforce morality and that they were their brother's keepers, so they pried into his affairs incessantly. Convinced that they were about God's business, they had a tendency to justify their own conduct even when it was atrocious. And these traits, too, they would transmit to the American character.

The Quakers left a less pervasive mark upon America than the Puritans did, but it can be argued that they left a higher one. They helped begin an important dialogue which traces an irregular point counterpoint through American history: between the idealist and the realist, the starry-eyed visionary and hardheaded man of affairs.

The visionary often has trouble making himself heard. He

wants to talk about other things—like consequences, or long-range effects, or untried alternatives. Because much of what he has to say strikes the practical man as at best irrelevant and at worst dangerous or downright unthinkable, the visionary is apt to encounter a cold welcome. To make himself heard at all he has to shout, and interrupt, and pound on the table, which only adds to the hostility he arouses. The cold welcome and the hostility are apt to strengthen inclinations, already present in his temperament, toward zealotry and fanaticism (although the community often affixes the fanatic label upon anyone who merely persists in views that run contrary to its own).

The visionary is resented because he is the voice of conscience, derided because he dares to dream the impossible dream, hated because he insists upon thinking the unthinkable and voicing the unspeakable. To some he is a nuisance; to others, a mortal threat. But he keeps reappearing, and his role is vital. The course of American history would have been quite different without him.

The Quakers were the first of this breed to make themselves heard in America. They were perfectionists. The notion of human perfectibility, attainable through each person's discovery and nurture of the Spirit of God that glowed within him, struck practical men as preposterous, but it had a magic to it. George Fox had defined the Inner Light in terms of newness, and pureness, and innocency: the state of Adam. The message was particularly potent when its advocates stood in a new land, where the concept of an unsoiled Eden did not seem farfetched. The idea, like so many of those brought here by seventeenth-century religionists, would later shed some of its theological garb and emerge as part of the American dream: lost Adamic innocence regained in a new and pure land. And what gave this notion, finally, a power comparable to that of the Christian message from which it derived was the breathtakingly revolutionary proposition that over here man could in fact achieve the impossible, that his reach was infinite, that he could be whatever he wanted.

The Puritans were not without their strain of bold idealism;

they could not have built the Bible Commonwealth without it. But they always kept both feet firmly on the ground. Their idealism never lost touch with reality. They were visionaries, as Perry Miller pointed out, who never forgot that two plus two equals four. A dialogue among realists will be sane and shrewd, sensible and sober, but it will also have a low ceiling. Confining one's projects to the art of the possible can end by having a narrowing effect. The Quakers were the first Americans, really, to defy such boundaries—the first, in the words of a more recent American martyr, to look at what never was and say, Why not?

The Quakers were also universalists, convinced that the divine presence was in every human soul. They wanted to bring others to their faith, but only by exhortation and example. Unlike the great majority of early Protestants, they were genuine in their desire for liberty of conscience, in that they not only wanted it for themselves but were willing to extend it to others. Their belief in individual worth and dignity was protected from sliding toward anarchy by a strong communitarian sense; here they were very much children of their age.

Like the Puritans and others, the Quakers included stewardship among their virtues. It was one's duty to labor in this world for the glory of God and the good of mankind. Their corporate sense of responsibility, in the main, was stronger than that of their contemporaries. They worked a bit harder with the notion that poverty represented a moral claim on the wealth of others. And even more than the Puritans, they sought through the agency of their religious gatherings to regulate and promote community activity in the interest of the general welfare. Poor relief, loan offices, courts of arbitration to settle wage and contract disputes, an employment agency, and an office to advise and assist new immigrants were among the ongoing functions of the Quaker meetings in Philadelphia.

Like the Puritans, the Dutch, and other groups who made a living creed out of hard work, they prospered, and their rise to prosperity on the open market sharpened the same traits in them as it did everywhere else. The Quakers, one contemporary observed, were "a people that mistake their interest as seldom as any, being Men of Industry, and Experience, such as are intent upon their business, cunning in their bargains, and crafty upon all occasions for their own ends. And some we find of these Children of Light have been so much Wiser than the Children of This World, that 'tis now good advice to look to your pockets when you have any dealing with Quakers." Their devotion to simplicity in dress and manner did not prevent the wealthy Quaker merchants of Philadelphia from making their sober black garb out of the best broadcloth and surrounding themselves quietly with unostentatious elegance.

So the Quakers were human too, of course—as vulnerable as any high-minded folk to charges of hypocrisy. They were undoubtedly difficult to live with at times, a disturbing influence in other communities and even more of a trial in their own. Their obsessive purity in the matter of refusing to take any kind of oath before a magistrate or in court could lead them into absurd and at times paralyzing situations. Their moral disapproval of war combined all too readily, in the eyes of their critics, with a dislike of higher taxes to make them refuse to vote higher sums for defense against Indian depredations on the frontier. If this made moral and financial sense in Philadelphia, it could only kindle undying animosity among the embattled Scotch-Irish frontiersmen whose homes were being burned and whose families were being butchered.

Admit all of this, and then return once more to those bedrock Quaker principles. What matters most about such principles is not man's inevitable failure to live up to them but his insistence upon trying—his belief in them, as guides to conduct and action. The Quakers flew these principles from their masthead during their years of struggle and martyrdom, and would not haul them down during the years of prosperity and acceptance. They continued to proclaim the equality of all souls in the eyes of God and the essential brotherhood of man. They believed that equality and brotherhood demanded complete liberty of conscience. They were even further ahead of their time in believing that Christ's highest precepts led toward peace, not a sword; toward fair and honorable dealings with the Indian; and toward freedom for the African slave.

These were impractical notions indeed, in colonial America. But one shudders at the kind of society that might have developed if no one had arisen to proclaim them at all.

Colonial America underwent a religious experience during the second quarter of the eighteenth century that became known as the Great Awakening—the first great evangelical movement in American history. It had its Old World counterparts in the upsurge of Pietistic movements on the Continent and the wildfire spread of Methodism in England. They were all related, in one way or another, to the stresses produced by economic change and population growth. The pace of change was quickening, and few of the Protestant churches could cope with this until they had undergone some upheavals of their own.

The major denominations had lost their cutting edge by the eighteenth century. The price of toleration was a lessening of zeal and a growth of skepticism and indifference. Formalism and sterility and dry prepared sermons were creeping into religious discourse. The pulpit no longer resounded but was content to drone. Even Puritanism was riddled with the effects of time and success and establishment. Puritans had long tried to strike a balance between reason and faith, insisting that both were important: "Knowledge," as Winthrop had put it, "is no knowledge without zeal, but zeal is but a wildfire without knowledge." Like most of the Puritans' intellectual balancing acts, this one proved impossible to sustain when those early gifted acrobats passed from the scene. Later generations of ministers took what they had learned at Harvard or Yale into settled congregations and leaned harder and harder on the rational and intellectual side of their heritage. Eighteenth-century rationalism and even undertones of Deism began to infiltrate their sermons.

Churches found themselves increasingly given over to secular concerns—disputes over wills and boundaries and land titles, which could divide a congregation within itself; and disputes over the size of ministers' salaries, which was part of the community tax structure and could divide a congregation from its minister. Doctrinal disputes persisted, often in rather arid form— arguments over the relationship between faith and works in achieving salvation, even sharper ones over the riddle that had plagued Protestantism all along: the extent to which human free will played an active part in the saving of one's soul.

What went unappeased in all of this was spiritual hunger, which grew apace in the older areas and on the frontier alike as immigration and population growth disrupted normal patterns. Here and there a few ministers began experimenting with a more emotional and hortatory style, with a new emphasis on man's sinfulness and need for regeneration. Worshipers proved responsive, and preachers who followed this style found themselves in demand. The revivalist technique emerged quickly and soon became standard: emotional preaching and emotional responses, with variations and refinements of the hellfire-and-sinners-repent theme. Eloquent speakers like William and Gilbert Tennent of New Jersey, a Westphalian emigrant named Theodore Frelinghuysen, Jonathan Edwards of Massachusetts, and—most famous of all—the Englishman George Whitefield, began drawing huge audiences and swaying them mightily. Revivalism invaded nearly every sect and denomination and swept at one time or another through all of the British colonies except South Carolina. The overworked simile of a fire remains the most apt: revivalism tended to go through communities and across regions like a flame through dry leaves, blazing brightly for a while and then burning itself out. The phenomenon had largely run its course before 1750, although the technique did not disappear and outbreaks of revivalism would thenceforth be a recurrent feature of the American religious scene.

The Great Awakening had a large and varied impact—religious, intellectual, social, political, psychological. It can be (and has been) studied from any or all of these vantage points, and it left an identifiable if somewhat blurred and confusing imprint upon colonial life. Even a cursory glance at what happened and some of the reverberations can be suggestive.

To begin with, the Great Awakening picked up colonial religious institutions and practices and gave them a vast shake. Great numbers of colonists, obviously, had a deep craving for new and more satisfying spiritual experiences. The new evangelical approach spoke to these needs and tapped a big vein of pent-up emotional longing. Revivalism brought religion for the first time to thousands of the unchurched, in communities along the frontier or off the beaten track. It spoke with equal force to thousands of communicants in settled and established congregations that had grown bored or dissatisfied with the cold formalism of literate eighteenth-century sermons. The Awakening was undoubtedly responsible for both spreading and revitalizing the religious impulse in colonial America. Its positive influence, simply in bringing some form of God's Word into many people's lives for the first time, should not be underestimated.

On the other hand, the Great Awakening was divisive, bitterly and enduringly, as any phenomenon that rouses intense emotions and challenges the established way of doing things is bound to be. It split communities, congregations, and whole churches, notably the Congregationalists and Presbyterians, right down the middle. Some of the cleavages lasted for generations, and a few were permanent. It was difficult, from pew and pulpit alike, to be indifferent about revivalism.

The controversy was less a matter of theology—with the exception of Jonathan Edwards, the revivalist ministers were not particularly strong in this area—than it was of style and approach. If eighteenth-century rationalism had inclined the old

Puritan balance between reason and emotion in favor of the former, the revivalists tilted it sharply and violently the other way. Perhaps the Puritan equilibrium had been inherently unstable and inevitably temporary; in any case, the seesaw snapped in two during the revivalist agitation. The rifts were more complicated than that, to be sure, since they often superimposed themselves across existing controversies. But the heart of the religious quarrel touched off by the Great Awakening had to do with people's reactions to the revivalists' frankly and at times overwhelmingly emotional appeal.

Thousands were repelled, even horrified, by the revivalist surge. Among the more educated, and among the more staid and self-contained communicants, the outbursts seemed excessive and dangerous. For these people, enthusiasm was bad form, at the very least, and giving free rein to the emotions pointed in all manner of dangerous directions. Zeal, as John Winthrop had said, was but a wildfire without knowledge—and many of the revivalists seemed bent on proving his point. The gist of the revivalist message seemed to be that an intensely emotional religious feeling was not only a necessary but the sole condition of salvation. This was unsound doctrine, and it was also productive of social dangers. Community cohesion and deference to one's superiors were threatened. The authority of the ministry, a necessary safeguard to public morality, was being challenged. Some of the responses to the revivalists' appeal were frightening. Not a few gave way to uncontrollable frenzy or downright hysteria in the depths of their emotion. Control and order appeared to be in danger, and to sober observers the revivalist minister was no more than a rabble-rousing demagogue.

From a distance, some of the doctrinal disputes are rather confusing, and one suspects that they appeared so to many of the participants. On the issues of salvation and free will, Protestantism had wandered into an intellectual labyrinth in which all but the strongest and sharpest of minds could readily lose their way. But confusion and losing one's way are only stimulants to controversy, and the controversies raged. In some communities, things did seem for a while to be getting out of hand, lurching toward the extremes of anarchy which the anti-enthusiasts had detected all along in revivalism. A few of the cruder revivalist ministers had little or no education and denied that any was necessary. Some of the exhorters, moreover, were laymen—self-appointed bearers of the Word, who insisted that their zeal and private insights more than made up for their lack of theological training.

The issue of the conversion experience began cavorting through town like an overexcited dog that had slipped its leash. Many folk who had been swayed by revivalist oratory now claimed, with heartfelt sincerity, to have had the true experience of conversion; the Holy Spirit had entered their souls. From this quarter, now and then, came accusations that certain ministers of the non-revivalist persuasion were themselves *not* converted, hence not entitled to preach or worthy to be followed. Disputes of this sort could be heated and deeply divisive, and it is hardly to be wondered at that orthodox ministers and worshipers saw a mortal threat in the revivalist impulse.

Orthodoxy, it should be pointed out, was overreacting in its turn. Not all of the unsound theology was on one side of this controversy, and not all revivalist ministers were unlettered tub thumpers. The condition of many colonial churches was moribund when the Awakening swept through them; they had clearly stopped meeting people's needs. A balanced verdict would seem to be that the sum of the religious experiences during the Great Awakening was more salutary than harmful.

Sooner or later the fervor subsided and the revivalist flames flickered and died. But the religious landscape had been greatly altered, and colonial society had been led several steps further from its English origins and closer to its American future.

For one thing, the rift that the revivalist controversy had opened up between reason and emotion proved enduring. The old Puritan balance was never regained. None of the extreme fears of rationalist and conservative was realized, but the dispute had undoubtedly sharpened a deep-seated distrust flowing both to and from the intellectual portion of the community. Anti-intellectualism, in and out of religion, would henceforth be a stronger and more persistent impulse in American life. It had flexed its muscles and got up and prowled around during the Great Awakening—not least, be it noted, because the keepers of knowledge and citadels of wisdom were vulnerable and offered tempting targets.

There was a related social effect of more immediate consequence. In hundreds of towns and villages the stirrings were social and political as well as religious. When disputes over enthusiasm, conversion, and related matters entered a congregation, laymen found it almost impossible to avoid taking sides. The great prestige, influence, and authority of the New England ministry were severely shaken; in most places they survived and remained strong for generations, but the clergy never regained their old dominance. Worshipers, including many of the humblest sort, were being shaken out of years of lethargy and generations of deference; they were questioning their ministers, sometimes sharply criticizing them. They were being forced to make decisions for themselves upon important questions. With the decision came soul-searching and thought; these people were being activated. In some, at least, the experience took.

The line that led from the Great Awakening to the American Revolution was neither clear nor direct—few historical lines are —but such a line can be traced. Thousands of people, up and down the eastern seaboard, were being roused to new levels of action, thought, and awareness by religious questions, only a few short years before the colonists began taking a new, long look at their relationship with the mother country. Since the divisions growing out of the revivalist movement tended to cut sharply across class lines, an indirect political result could be glimpsed a little later: upper- and middle-class communicants who had mingled readily with humbler folk out of shared religious convictions in the 1740s found it less difficult and less strange to be making common cause with them over political questions in the 1760s. For some of these humble folk, moreover, the experience of self-assertion and participation would prove lasting.

Finally, the Great Awakening accentuated or reaffirmed certain other tendencies that were helping to make American society what it was. These included a many-sided and constantly shifting religious pluralism, with new schisms and sects continually adding to the diversity and strengthening the trend toward toleration and liberty of conscience. America would remain Protestant, but its Protestantism would remain splintered. Old habits of soul-searching were reinvigorated by the evangelical thrust. Whenever American society displays a tendency to grow comfortable and complacent, as parts of it were doing in the eighteenth century, the active Christian conscience, with all its awareness of guilt and sin, its jeremiads about decline and its calls to repent, is bound to reassert itself. It had done so before, many times (here and there in New England, the authentic voice or the ringing echo of the jeremiads could always be heard), but never during the colonial era did the voice reverberate into so many corners of society as during the 1730s and '40s.

Certain middle-class tendencies, including asceticism and the work ethic, were also reinforced. So was individualism, in that the challenge of revivalism (for both adherents and opponents) was to impel man to turn inward and search his soul for signs of God's grace. The terror and tension of being balanced between eternal damnation and salvation became, for many, *felt* terrors and tensions. And life, for such folk, became a matter of sharp, haunting contrasts and polar opposites, and these in turn became moral ones: hell and heaven, wrong conduct and right, evil and good, black and white. Old World and New, corruption and innocence, the worldly and the righteous. The person whose experience told him he had received God's grace had been saved; he had been saved because he was good. All decisions and events could now be viewed in moral terms, as a working out of God's will: what one did, or, by extension, what one's church, or community, or nation, or race might do, was good because it was part of the divine plan. And if God be for us, who can be against us? Religion and nationalism would strengthen and reinforce each other in many societies. In America the fusion would be well-nigh perfect.

CHAPTER 11

The Burden of Race

T HE BRITISH colonies were settled mainly by Protestants; they were also settled mainly by English-speaking whites, most of whom had had no previous contact whatsoever with darker-skinned peoples. The contacts in America, first with Indians and then with Africans, were of such a nature, and came at such a time in England's social, economic, and religious development, as to engender a steadfast and implacable brand of racism. It was not so much a matter of engendering, actually, as of uncovering—the real basis for this racism lay not in what the English saw or experienced but in what they were.

This was no mere surface blemish; its roots were embedded in the remote Western past and went into some of the deepest recesses of the human psyche—an angry, evil goblin from the caves of our ancestors, when all life was a mixture of brute survival and stark fear. That portion of the cave men who ultimately became Englishmen had traveled a particular route to get there, and they had come quite a distance. But some of the fears that had loomed beyond the firelight of those remote ancestors still lurked in the darker caverns of the human spirit. The overlays were fragile; at times of stress or uncertainty the fears would yet come out and prowl, or glare balefully from the shadows while men did unspeakable things to keep them at bay.

Racism was another English transplant that grew well here, like a vine that wove its tendrils tightly about the stalk of worthier plants, to grow and thrive as they did. Little that Americans would try to do or become was not marked by it. Only the presence and inspiration of those dreamers of the impossible dream would serve to counterbalance it and subject it to some kind of control. It was America's irony, and its tragedy, that the tree of liberty grew toward such majestic heights with this unlovely vine clinging about the trunk and growing among the branches. Irony, tragedy, and ultimate challenge as well—whether a people so encumbered, who have repeatedly staked their destiny upon reaffirmations of that impossible dream, can long endure.

With little in his own experience to prepare him for it, the Englishman accommodated to his rather sudden exposure and growing proximity to darker-skinned folk, normally enough, by forming stereotypes. These in turn served as both guidebook and justification for the way in which these new and different people were to be judged and treated. Stereotypes are a form of that categorizing which is a necessary component in the human perceptive process, a shorthand way of avoiding confusion and imposing order on the things one encounters. It is essential to think in categories, and it becomes convenient—a substitute for rigorous mental effort—to think in stereotypes; the simpler, the better. Stereotypes reveal more about their creator than about their object, and the Englishman revealed much of himself in the different images of red man and black man that guided his conduct toward these folk in the New World. The images derived less from what the Englishman saw than from what he wanted to see, which in turn was powerfully shaped by what he wanted to do.

This was particularly true in the case of the Indian. Vague notions of the noble savage quickly shifted when the English colonists began to look at the Indian from the territorial rather than the commercial or exploratory point of view; then the red man became a treacherous barbarian. The colonists methodically took his land, anticipated his response, endowed him with a whole range of negative qualities, and used these as a justification for taking the land, in a neat circular concept. The mold soon hardened. For the colonist and his descendants, as long as the Indian stood in the path of settlement, concepts of noble savage were relegated to effete Old World philosophers.

The shift in image was accomplished without much effort. A series of clashes in Virginia touched off a sudden Indian attack upon the white settlements in 1622, which led the Virginians to an instant and sweeping conclusion. "Our hands, which before were tied with gentleness and fair usage," one colonist wrote, "are now set at liberty by the treacherous violence of the savages, so that we may now, by right of war and law of nations, invade the country and destroy them who sought to destroy us. . . . Now their cleared grounds and all their villages (which are situate in the fruitfulest places of the land) shall be inhabited by us; whereas theretofore the grubbing of woods caused us the greatest labour." The ensuing war was followed, typically, by a peace treaty, which the Virginia Council deliberately threw aside in 1629, proclaiming in its stead a policy of "perpetual enmity" toward the Indians as being in the best interests of the colony.

And henceforth, with few exceptions, the settlers could see only negative qualities in the red man. One analysis, shortly after the massacre of 1622, blocked out the entire picture, calling the Indian "by nature sloathfull and idle, vitious, melancholy, slovenly, of bad conditions, lyers, of small memory, . . . by nature of all people the most lying and most inconstant in the world, sottish and sodaine, . . . lesse capable than children of six or seven years old, and less apt and ingenious. . . . " Samual Purchas, a leading English publicist and propagandist for colonization, described the Virginia tribes in the same vein. They were, he contended, "bad people, having little of Humanitie but shape, ignorant of Civilitie, of Arts, of Religion; more brutish than the beasts they hunt, more wild and unmanly than that unmanned wild Country which they range rather than inhabite; captivated also to Satan's tyranny in foolish pieties, mad impieties, wicked idleness, busie and bloudy wickedness. . . . "

English attempts to convert the Indians to Christianity, which had never been prosecuted with much vigor or success disappeared almost entirely. The negative image took hold, and the colonists conducted themselves accordingly. There were always some exceptions—a handful of forest-loving frontiersmen in the Natty Bumppo tradition, a handful of zealous missionaries and religious radicals like the Quakers, a few scholarly and dispassionate observers like Cadwallader Colden—but these were, quite literally, voices crying in the wilderness. The Anglo-American attitude was best summed up in the enduring aphorism about the only good Indian being a dead one, and this attitude would not begin to change until the red man had ceased to occupy land that the white man wanted.

The prevailing stereotype endowed the unfortunate Indian with many of the negative qualities that were also attached to the African, but for obvious reasons of different circumstance the red image never became quite as totally degraded as the black—or at least not until conquest and whiskey and subjection had stripped the Indian of his capacity to make serious trouble. Until that happened, the colonists hated the Indian but kept a measure of respect for him; he was a courageous, resourceful, and at times deadly opponent, with manly virtues the English admired.

With the black man it was altogether different. He was subjected elsewhere, and then brought here, in small random captive packages rather than as a people, with no chance to prove his prowess, no sympathetic Leatherstockings or Daniel Boones to observe his manly independence in the wilderness, no benign philosophers meditating about the virtues of the Noble Black Man. The African in the New World, and especially in British North America, had to carry the stifling dead weight of bondage about with him wherever he went, and some kind of negative stereotype was inevitable.

But it will not do to lay the trouble at the feet of slavery. The institution later perpetuated and strengthened the white man's view of the black man but did not create it; the origins of that view go further back than slavery and are imbedded more deeply in the Englishman's subconscious. Once again, as with the Indian, the English saw what they wanted to see in the African. But why they wanted to see these particular things by no means reduces itself to the proposition that what they wanted to see grew out of what they wanted to do. The thing went from there into deep imponderable questions that are somehow entangled with the roots of human existence.

By the time the first black men reached America the English stereotype had already been formed, and had assumed the shape and most of the details that it would retain thereafter. Most Englishmen did not have to fight, despoil, own, or even see a black man in order to form an opinion of him. That opinion sprang into existence fullblown, like Athena from the head of Zeus, almost from the moment that England learned there were such things as Africans at all.

This began before the colonial period. In contrast to Mediterranean Europeans, whose contact with people from Asia and Africa dated back to ancient times, only the barest handful of itinerant Englishmen had ever seen a black person, or had occasion to reflect about the existence of black persons, until the trading voyages of men like the Hawkinses to the Guinea coast in the middle of the sixteenth century. The slave traffic was of ancient origin, and the Portuguese had been at it for over a century, but Africa offered far more contrast and variety than most Europeans suspected. There were some powerful kingdoms and advanced cultures among the black societies along the Atlantic shore, and the few Englishmen who took time to look about them were duly impressed by much of what they saw. But the reports that went back home and fastened upon the public mind were of a different sort, and the English proceeded to build a rather elaborate image upon the basis of almost no substantive knowledge whatever. Imagination leaped in avidly and took over from the start.

It began with color—the ineffaceable and, for the English observer, startling fact of blackness. As Winthrop Jordan has pointed out, the English—well before the sixteenth century, and before the concept was in any way involved with human beings—had affixed *black* with a whole dismal catalogue of negative meanings. Black had come to mean "deeply stained with dirt; soiled, dirty, foul . . . having dark or deadly purposes; malignant; pertaining to or involving death, deadly; baneful, disastrous, sinister . . . iniquitous, atrocious, horrible, wicked . . . indicating disgrace, censure, liable to punishment." It was yoked in opposition to *white,* in the English mind, as filth was to purity, sin to virginity, baseness to virtue, ugliness to beauty, Satan to God. Thus *black* was a powerful and evocative symbol which surfaced whenever Englishmen came into contact with black-skinned folk or even heard about their existence.

Color consciousness of a peculiar sort, then, formed the foundation. It had been excavated, and was ready for the black man to occupy, well before he came along. With equal rapidity and a kind of consistent ingenuity, the English proceeded to erect a super-structure. The next outstanding fact about the African, in English eyes, was that he was a heathen, "without a God, lawe, religion, or common wealth." Quick to put two and two together, the Englishman readily linked the African's heathenism with his blackness and saw the hand of the Devil at work. Satan, one description had it, "has infused prodigious idolatry into their hearts, enough to rellish his pallat and aggrandize their tortures when he gets power to fry their souls, as the raging Sun has already scorcht their cole-black carcasses."

Sixteenth-century Europeans, English and other, were endlessly fascinated with tales of the bizarre, the grotesque, and the monstrous. Of all the varied details of black culture, high and low, that were there to be observed along the Guinea coast, the ones that received most attention in English travel accounts or translations were connected with savagery. The English were fascinated, as they had been by Spanish reports from the New World, by stories of cannibalism, mutilation, polygamy, and comparable customs. The tribes that engaged in such practices became the typical tribes; this was what Africans were like. The dominant metaphor in these descriptions revolved around words like "brutish," "bestial," "beastly." English traders on the Guinea coast could reinforce this image by their observation of captured slaves being herded about like beasts awaiting sale.

Having proceeded upward from blackness through heathenism and savagery to bestiality, the image makers proceeded to cap this formidable edifice with a kind of penthouse that contained the most fascinating element of all. Some of the early accounts of the Dark Continent associated the African with various apes that were known or supposed to reside there. The idea took hold. Speculation that the African might be related to the ape encouraged the conclusion that he might be subhuman, which in turn provided a convenient justification for enslaving him.

But the matter went deeper than this. The pervasive and compelling theme in the association of blacks with apes was that of sexuality, which clearly had an almost obsessive fascination for many observers. The English were ripe to be persuaded that Africans were a lascivious, oversexed, and wanton folk, as awesomely potent and lustful as so many apes or goats. Here the image really preceded the contact altogether, and it long preceded any English experience as slaveowners. In Francis Bacon's *New Atlantis,* the "spirit of Fornication" appears as a "little foul ugly Aethiop." Iago's consuming hatred for Othello abounds with such references: "I do suspect that the lusty Moor has leaped into my seat," he muttered, and later informed Brabantio that "an old black ram/Is tupping your white ewe." The English were not the only Europeans to become rabidly preoccupied with the black man's alleged sexuality, but they were among the first, and the most affected by it.

This stereotype was formed long before the English began coming to America, hence it will not do to ascribe prejudice against blacks to the institution of slavery. The order is all wrong. First came the image, so to speak, then the blacks, and finally the institution. The small number of blacks who were brought to the Chesapeake colonies during the second quarter of the seventeenth century came as indentured servants rather than slaves, and for a time no legal distinction was drawn between white and black indentures. Slavery was unknown in English law, and the nearest thing to it—villeinage, or serfdom—was obsolete and not very applicable anyway. The English colonists proceeded, tentatively at first but more systematically after about 1660, to devise their own law about slavery, and they devised it to fit the practice that had evolved first.

The Spaniards and Portuguese had faced no such problem when the institution became important in their overseas empires. Their legal systems were based upon Roman law, which had always recognized slavery—as a condition of circumstance, not of race—and which included certain immunities and protections for the person of the slave. Long accustomed to the institution and to people with dark skins, the Spaniards and Portuguese practiced slavery as a matter of course and staffed their slave-labor forces from Africa primarily because it was the best source of supply. They exploited their chattels with conscienceless greed and no little brutality, despite the earnest efforts of the Church to secure more humane treatment. But their notions of color difference were rather casual. They neither prohibited intermarriage, placed insuperable bars against emancipation, nor attached indelible stigma (and consequent social degradation) upon former slaves of black or mixed blood. Social barriers existed but they were relatively mild and easily crossed, and a thriving set of mestizo cultures emerged in Latin America. The Roman Church saw to it that the protections afforded in the Roman legal code and the benefits of Christianity were made available to the black. Hard though his lot was, the slave was believed to have a soul and the right to have it saved. His essential humanity was not denied.

By contrast, English slaveowners long resisted the occasional half-hearted attempts of the colonial Protestant churches to bring Christianity to the blacks. To expose them to Christianity would be to admit that they had souls and introduce them to troublesome notions about equality. Most blacks in the English colonies were denied much contact with the Christian religion before the second half of the eighteenth century.

From no tradition of slavery at all, the English devised an institution with none of the softening influences derived from Mediterranean culture. Hugely conscious of color differences from the start, they began to draw distinctions between white and black servants before the word "slavery" appeared in legislative debate or statute. The distinctions could be detected in the absence of written protective contracts for black indentures, in specific prohibitions of their right to bear arms, in sharper penalties for black than for white runaways. Though a few blacks seem to have attained freedom in seventeenth-century Virginia, the evidence suggests that most of the early black bondsmen, in contrast to white indentures, served not for a given term of years but for life. A standard penalty meted out to runaway indentures in colonial America was to add given amounts of time upon the term of their contracts; reference is made, in the Chesapeake colonies, to the inapplicability of this penalty to black runaways. Several estates with inventories including servants of both races placed a significantly higher evaluation upon the black servants than upon the white. Penalties against interracial marriage and cohabitation appeared fairly early—as did children of mixed blood.

By 1660, or thereabouts, the colonists were passing explicit slave legislation, codifying the practice that had built up over the preceding forty years. Within a short time all of the mainland colonies had enacted slavery into law, based frankly upon race. The institution thereafter contributed much to the perpetuation of the black stereotype, but the stereotype clearly had earlier and deeper origins.

Attempts to explain so tangled and murky a phenomenon as color prejudice will range from the obvious to the highly speculative and end by being neither complete nor satisfactory. Yet the English-speaking colonists, their descendants, and their unfortunate red and black fellow travelers were going to carry this thing with them into the far distant future. It would mark many of the steps they took and many of the turns in the road ahead, and neither America's heritage nor its destiny can be seen whole without coming to grips with the question.

A few generalizations would appear to be in order. Partly, of course, it was a manner of the times, and here it is not the English but the whole Western world, and the non-Western as well, that stand arraigned. The sixteenth century, when Englishmen first began learning things about Africa, and the seventeenth, when English colonists began to put Africans to work as slaves in North America, were harsh and essentially inhumane times—aggressive, violent, crude, destructive, brutal. It was a frankly exploitative world, and the offsets were few and fragile. Humanitarianism was virtually unknown, and Christianity was too preoccupied with its internal convulsions to exercise much of a meliorating influence. People were just beginning to soften cruelty with compassion in the treatment of their own kind; they viewed most strangers with suspicion and hostility, as threats to be beaten off or victims to be exploited.

The English brought to this general and inclusive proposition all of the specific bluster, belligerence, and chip-on-the-shoulder hostility of *nouveaux,* for that is what they were—still clawing their way up in European politics from the ranks of third-rate power on the fringes. As yet the English had acquired none of the complacent confidence of the older cultures along the Mediterranean. Sensitive and insecure, they could be expected to act with uncompromising harshness and lack of charity toward those less fortunate than they. Since the contacts with Africans and Indians had been sudden and rather startling, the English reacted with edgy aggressiveness, as befitted a people on the make.

Moreover, the Englishmen in the forefront of these contacts were from the edgiest and most ambitious stratum of English society. The victims or products of social turmoil at home, out to acquire what they could in a world they knew to be savage and unjust and full of uncertainty, they could not afford to view vulnerable strangers with the kind of detached tolerance available to a comfortable, stay-at-home aristocrat. England was thrusting its way up the political and economic ladder, and those in the vanguard of this process were the ones who shaped and spiced the racial stereotypes. Self-consciously on the rise, they were self-consciously English as well, with a pugnacious and well-developed sense of national identity sharpened by their insularity and the growing dislike of foreigners that had helped motivate their break with Rome.

Their religious and national senses were thus thoroughly intertwined, and the religious outlook contributed as much as the national. For this all happened while the English were becoming Protestants and defining, in heated debate and at times by violence, just what sort of Protestants they were going to be. Their Christian zeal drew its major inspiration from Christ's warning that He brought not peace but a sword. They were Christians at war—with heresy, and the forces of evil. They knew exactly what sin was and where the Devil resided. It was no more than God's will that sin be punished and His enemies destroyed, that creatures of the Devil had no souls or had lost them already—and could be used as righteous men saw fit.

Neither the Indian nor the African could expect much from this kind of attitude. A smallpox epidemic in an Indian village in

Massachusetts prompted the remark from John Winthrop that this was God's way of "thinning out" the natives in order to make room for the Puritans, one of whom referred to this same epidemic as a "wonderful plague." The Indians, Winthrop wrote, "are neere all dead of the small Poxe, so that the Lord hathe cleared our title to what we possess." And after the war with the Pequots in 1637, during the climax of which the Puritans surrounded several hundred Indian men, women, and children in a fort and burned them to death, the Bay Colony leaders recorded that God "had laughed at his enemies . . . making them as a fiery oven. . . . Thus did the Lord judge among the Heathen, filling the Place with dead bodies." The zeal that could see God's will in this sort of thing had no trouble shackling slavery upon those black limbs of Satan brought over from Africa.

The fusion of nationalism and religion was exuberantly summarized in three words by that returning Marian exile who had proclaimed that God was English. Most of the colonists believed this, too, which gave rise to the later notion that God, if not specifically American, had blessed this land and selected its inhabitants as His chosen people. And as far as race was concerned, it would be far into the second half of the twentieth century before it could even begin to occur to the offspring of those ethnocentric colonists, in the form of an apt, nervous joke, that God could be anything but a white male.

A white *male*—for this gets down to the nub. The racism that the English brought here, to flourish so luxuriantly in the New World environment, was finally a matter of sex and sexuality, a psychological fixation we can recognize more readily than we can explain. Here their time and nationality and religious inclination had implanted in most Englishmen a complex of attitudes about sex, sin, and morality that made the African stereotype a kind of hollow statue into which they poured all of their own fears and longings. If they had not found the African they would have had to invent him. These Englishmen knew what sin was, not merely from reading their Bible and attending church, but from having wrestled with it in themselves and seen it in action in Elizabethan England. One contemporary description of the Africans rang every change upon this theme: "They have no knowledge of God; . . . they are very lecherous, greedie eaters, and no lesse drinkers, and thievish, and much addicted to uncleanenesse; one man hath as many wives as hee is able to keepe and maintaine."

This fixation about black sexuality was magnified and compounded, later on, by the guilt that white colonists could seldom avoid feeling after cohabiting with black women. But the fixation, and the guilt as well, preceded such cohabitation or indeed any close contact with blacks. For here the Englishman, in attributing a whole catalogue of negative qualities to the African, with a kind of crescendo on the theme of sexuality, was externalizing evil—speaking of qualities he envied but knew to be wrong and dared not admit in himself, as if the sins in one's own soul could somehow be cleansed if someone else could be made the embodiment of them. The Englishman could engage in this delusion and cling to it tenaciously thereafter, at least partly because his intense Protestantism subjected him to unmerciful strains between his appetites and his sense of sin. Projecting the latter upon the black was at least a way of making the tension tolerable.

Whatever the exact causes, the Englishman's contact with people of other races came at a time when he was peculiarly vulnerable. And his racism was thereafter a part of him. For the folk on the receiving end, the results were predictable—for the red man, a long, violent retreat to the westward, which his rear-guard actions and counterattacks could slow but never halt, until he had been wiped out, broken, partially domesticated, or, for the most part, penned up on lands that the whites no longer wanted; for the black man, life sentence for himself and all his progeny in a labor system that he was able to withstand physically (at least in the sense that he proved as fruitful and multiplied as fast as free white colonists), and entrapment in a social system that placed him at the absolute bottom of the pyramid, surrounded him with barriers of caste that would have made a Hindu blink, and reminded him in every way that it could, from birth to grave, that he was where he was by virtue of his color, which in turn was a badge of congenital and immutable inferiority.

And what of the white man, firmly in the driver's seat, reaping all the benefits of this dual system of aggrandizement, secure in the conviction that God had willed the despoliation of red people and the enslavement of black ones? This conviction would eventually prove less secure than it looked. The Christian mental process, being human, has historically been capable of finding rationalization, if not justification, for almost everything believers wanted to do. But the Christian conscience, where people take their religion seriously—and the most important elements in colonial America did—tends to be a light sleeper. It is susceptible to the cold truth outside, and blanket-layer after blanket-layer of rationalization covered over it will not keep it slumbering for long . . . if the truth outside is cold enough.

The truth that the colonists erected and extended—a slave system based upon color prejudice—was cold enough, by all odds. For some generations, the collective conscience did little more than stir restlessly in the night. But the wind was rising, to beat with scriptural results against houses built on sand. They would deny, as long as they could, that it was conscience. Yet few among those who lived off of slavery, or in close proximity to it, could keep uneasiness at bay.

They tried to keep it at bay in the classic manner of a society that has got hold of a troublesome thing from which it derives both economic and psychological benefits. They closed ranks, erected rampart after rampart of legal, physical, and philosophical defenses of the troublesome thing, and enjoyed the benefits. (These defensive ramparts, backed by the weight of community opinion, were of firm and durable material; it was the ground on which the foundations rested that was sand.) During the colonial period, as the institution grew along with the rest of society and acquired a tradition and a momentum of its own, the whole thing seemed to be working quite well. It was not until the middle of the eighteenth century that the first stray voices began to be raised in protest. They were few in number, and they could be shouted down or ignored. The uneasiness and the conscience might make for troubled sleep and a bad dream or two, but during the daytime the sun shone; the comforts and benefits of the system were visible, and God still seemed in His heaven making all right with the world.

The creation of a rigid caste system based on color beneath a fairly fluid class system within the white community undoubtedly made the latter a more cohesive operation. The presence of an alien and despised race promoted white solidarity and did much to explain the general acceptance of planter dominance on the part of the great majority of Southern whites. The ambitious among these defined success in terms of acquiring enough acres and enough slaves to join the planter class; for such aspirants, there was no disposition to question the system by which they hoped to achieve success. For the rest of the community, the tendency to resent planter dominance had no real chance of assuming serious proportions because this posed a threat to white solidarity which nearly everyone agreed was all-important. The losers and failures in the white community were assuaged by the great supportive crutch of white supremacy, and this psychological balm to bruised and bitter egos—low as one might be, there was always a large group permanently mired beneath him—was probably as big a factor in accounting for slavery's powers of endurance as were the profits and luxurious way of life that it made possible for the great planters.

In any case, the system throve. Wherever it went, it became part of the American way of life; and what really held it together, beneath the elaborate legal mechanism, armed patrols, and overseers' whips, in back of all the wharfsides piled high with hogsheads of tobacco and barrels of rice, buried in the sand beneath the cellar, so to speak, was a great ugly grab bag containing all of the white man's deepest fears, guilts, lusts, and erotic fantasies. Because he had insisted upon making the black man, even before enslaving him, a bearer of his own sins, a living repository of what Winthrop Jordan called "the blackness within"; because, in effect, the white man was staring through a glass darkly, not at the black man at all but at a mirror image of himself, he had truly fastened onto something he could not let go.

Blackness was evil and had to be contained, sealed off, kept down. Therefore any thought of emancipating the Negro or admitting him to membership in society on anything like equal terms became absolutely unthinkable—as Hofstadter put it, "a monstrous, demonic, haunting, apocalyptic image." Civilization itself depended upon the maintenance of white supremacy.

Whites who lived where blacks were most numerous felt the thrust of these propositions most acutely. At about the same time, the tiny Quaker vanguard that had glimpsed the impossible dream and emerged with a totally different concept of human nature began to say, out loud, that slavery was a great unconscionable wrong.

Thus did the wind rise, hurling the first faint sounds of voices and distant drumbeats along the wharfsides piled high with hogsheads of tobacco and barrels of rice . . . and against the windowpanes of plantation homes and back-country farms, and down among the slave cabins as well. Americans had devised a peculiar yoke for the highest ideals and basest appetites, ensuring for themselves that the way ahead would lead not merely to great heights but through the valley of the shadow as well.

BOOK TWO

NEW NATION

PART ONE

REVOLUTION IN
THE MAKING

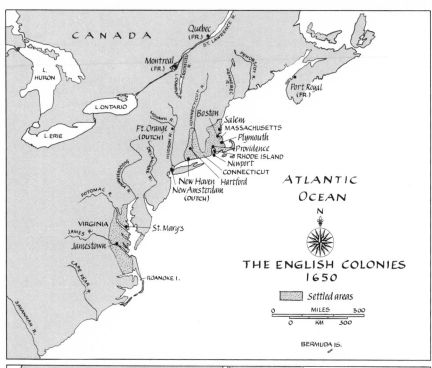

CANADA

Quebec
(FR.)

ST. LAWRENCE R.

Montreal
(FR.)

L.
HURON

L. ONTARIO

L. ERIE

PENOBSCOT R.

Port Royal
(FR.)

Ft. Orange
(DUTCH)

MOHAWK R.

HUDSON R.

DELAWARE R.

KENNEBEC R.

CONNECTICUT R.

Boston
Salem
MASSACHUSETTS
Plymouth
Providence
RHODE ISLAND
Newport
CONNECTICUT

New Haven Hartford
New Amsterdam
(DUTCH)

SUSQUEHANNA R.

POTOMAC R.

VIRGINIA

JAMES R.

St. Mary's

Jamestown

CAPE FEAR R.

ROANOKE I.

SAVANNAH R.

ATLANTIC
OCEAN

N

THE ENGLISH COLONIES
1650

Settled areas

0   MILES   300
0   KM   300

BERMUDA IS.

CANADA

Quebec
(FR.)

ST. LAWRENCE R.

Montreal
(FR.)

L.
HURON

Ft. Frontenac
(FR.)

L. ONTARIO

L. ERIE

PENOBSCOT R.

Port Royal
(FR.)

MOHAWK R.

Albany
NEW YORK

PENNSYLVANIA

HUDSON R.

DELAWARE R.

KENNEBEC R.

CONNECTICUT R.

NEW HAMPSHIRE
Exeter
Salem
Boston
MASSACHUSETTS
Northfield
Providence
RHODE ISLAND
Deerfield
CONNECTICUT
Hartford
New Haven

New York
Philadelphia

NEW JERSEY

SUSQUEHANNA R.

POTOMAC R.

MARYLAND

DELAWARE

VIRGINIA

JAMES R.

St. Mary's
Williamsburg
Norfolk

Jamestown

CAPE FEAR R.

NORTH
CAROLINA

SOUTH CAROLINA

New Bern

Brunswick

SAVANNAH R.

GEORGIA

ALTAMAHA R.

Charleston

Ft. King George

ATLANTIC
OCEAN

N

THE ENGLISH COLONIES
1700

0   MILES   300
0   KM   300

BERMUDA IS.

Settled areas

CHAPTER 12

From Colonies to Provinces

T HE DECISIVE period in colonial history began in the late seventeenth century and lasted until about 1760. At its outset the settlers along the Atlantic seaboard were hesitant colonials, unsure of themselves, their future, the location of authority, and the nature of their society. By the 1720s they were confident provincials who had redefined their social system and acquired a sense of direction. Within the next forty years they freed themselves from the constricting pressure of a hostile foe along their borders and began looking hungrily toward the great Western treasure house that lay open to them at last. By this time their way of life, outlook, and assorted ethnic and social conditions had made them distinctively more and less than Englishmen overseas, and by and large they sensed it. They had undergone a period—albeit this they would not fully recognize until afterward—when both revolution and new nation were in the making.

———□———

America in the late seventeenth century underwent what Clarence Ver Steeg has seen as a kind of collective identity crisis. It was a time of political stress, economic difficulty, and social instability, and the colonials betrayed enough unrest and anxiety to suggest that they had lost their bearings. Tumult of more than routine proportions beset Virginia, Maryland, New York, and Massachusetts now and again between 1675 and 1700. Although each episode had its own causes and features, a similar pattern ran through them all.

The uprising in Virginia that took its identity from a well-connected young planter named Nathaniel Bacon grew out of a dispute over Indian policy. Governor William Berkeley and his supporters advocated cautious defensive measures, while planters and farmers nearer the edge of settlement gathered behind Bacon's leadership and urged strong aggressive action. Repeated clashes with local Indians, who were being elbowed in turn by other tribes in a chain of interior migrations originating as far off as Canada, finally induced Bacon to defy the governor's orders and lead his followers on a big punitive raid into the wilderness in the spring of 1676.

Both Berkeley and Bacon were strong of will and quick of temper. The governor proclaimed Bacon a rebel, upon which he proceeded to act like one. Twice he led his forces into the colonial capital at Jamestown, forcing Berkeley to take refuge across Chesapeake Bay. On the second occasion Bacon burned the town and took virtual possession of the colony, but the whole movement collapsed when he suddenly died of dysentery in October 1676. Berkeley was able to restore his authority without difficulty and without needing the British troops sent over to aid him. He and a legislature of his persuasion dealt harshly with the rebels, confiscating property and hanging a few of Bacon's lieutenants.

Behind the Indian problem and the clash of two strong personalities lurked bigger issues. Virginia was suffering from depressed tobacco prices. The Navigation Acts forced all tobacco to be marketed in England before it could be re-exported to the Continent. This economic squeeze made new acreage more important than ever to the hard-pressed planters, but good land was no longer easy to get. Stuart favorites had received the enormous tract between the Potomac and Rappahannock rivers as a tax-free proprietary grant. Good acreage beyond the edge of settlement still belonged to the Indians, whom Berkeley wished to handle gently for the sake of peace and a lucrative fur trade (in which, his detractors pointed out, the governor and several of his associates had a big investment). Meanwhile taxes had risen. Berkeley and his clique had become the nucleus of an oligarchy which dominated the assembly, narrowed the franchise, and usurped many of the functions of local government.

Reason enough, then, for resentment to boil over when Nathaniel Bacon defied the governor in 1676. Yet the Bacon affair was essentially a clash between rival factions of leading planters, none of whom had yet acquired the secure social and political position that Virginia's first families would occupy in the eighteenth century. What really bothered Virginians in the 1670s was the gnawing uncertainty that had come to surround colonial life. Everything—economic future, social structure, the location and nature of political authority, the ability to acquire land—seemed in doubt. A dispute over Indian policy could thus become a rebellion, which in turn could sputter harmlessly out with the fall of a single leader.

Berkeley himself died the next year (on his way to London to explain his own highhanded conduct in the affair), but royal authority in Virginia clamped down harder than ever, and most of the reforms Bacon's group had tried to push through in their brief moment of power were undone. Yet Bacon would be remembered. His example would help prompt a later, securer generation of Virginia planters to occupy their privileged position with some sense of the responsibility which he had sought, however clumsily, to instill in the governing process.

Bacon's discontent had echoes among Virginia's near neighbors, where comparable problems of Indian policy, depressed tobacco prices, taxes, and land hunger were bound up with the question of proprietary rule. The leading landholders in both

Carolina and Maryland had divided into factions, one clustered about the proprietary government and the other in resentful opposition.

The Bacon movement spilled directly over into northern Carolina, which at this time was little more than a fringe along the Old Dominion's southern border, inhabited by migrant Virginians. Some of Bacon's followers fled there to escape Berkeley's vindictive return to power, and one of these refugees, John Culpeper, helped lead a rebellious uprising against proprietary authority in Carolina. It succeeded, set up a government of its own, and then co-operated so readily with the proprietors that Culpeper, who went to England to explain what had happened, was acquitted of charges of treason. His regime won official recognition and was allowed to stay in power.

The struggle was harder and more complicated in Maryland, where the Calverts sought to rule with a near-absolute hand. Their earlier concessions to the assembly had never been more than grudging, and in recent years they had paralleled Berkeley's policy of curtailing the franchise and dominating government at all levels. As in Virginia and Carolina, the quarrel was chiefly between rival groups of planters, although in Maryland it had the added ingredient of religious antagonism. The Calverts and most of their appointees were Catholic; the opposition therefore took on an aggressively Protestant cast, and all other grievances got yoked to the religious question.

In the fall of 1676, at about the time Nathaniel Bacon was seizing control in Jamestown, the Maryland quarrel also erupted when an anti-proprietary mob menaced the government. It was not much of an outbreak, but the proprietary group was so alarmed by events in Virginia that it cracked down hard on the dissidents, hanging two of their leaders. A sometime Anglican minister named John Coode helped lead a similar movement against the government in 1681, again to no avail. This time the leaders were charged with sedition and banished, but the anti-proprietary, anti-Catholic sentiment smoldered on.

It blazed up again, more effectively, as news of the Glorious

Revolution filtered to America in early 1689. Amid wild rumors in Maryland that Lord Baltimore was still pledged to the deposed Catholic king and would not recognize the new sovereigns, John Coode returned to help lead another uprising. This one called itself the Protestant Association, proclaimed its adherence to William and Mary, occupied the capital at St. Mary's, and formed a government. A newly elected assembly enacted long-awaited reforms in the electoral process and the machinery of local government; it also passed some stern anti-Catholic legislation and saw to a wholesale elimination of Catholics from office.

Since the Protestant Association's quarrel with proprietary rule coincided with the Crown's desire to bring all colonies under direct royal control, England upheld what had happened in Maryland and deprived the Calverts of their political authority, though not of their charter, rents, or land titles. Maryland was governed as a royal colony for the next twenty-five years. By the time the Calverts (now tactfully converted to Protestantism) regained their political rights in 1715, the dominant element in Maryland politics was firmly in control.

New York also staged an uprising during the hesitant colonial phase of the Glorious Revolution. Although the issues were similar, the complexity and sheer number of New York's political differences had no parallel. Even at this early date New York politics had acquired the inimitably Byzantine quality it has displayed ever since—perhaps because, alone among the mainland colonies, New York lacked anything like economic, ethnic, or religious homogeneity to soften its internal disputes. In any event, behind the seizure of power in 1689 by a German-born ex-soldier named Jacob Leisler, who had parlayed a favorable marriage and an aggressive intelligence into one of the colony's largest mercantile fortunes, lay some tortuous recent history and a tangle of conflicting interests.

Recall the outlines of that history for a moment. A Dutch outpost till its conquest by the English in 1664, then a proprietary fief of the Duke of York's, reconquered by the Dutch in 1673 and returned at the peace table a year later, New York resumed its proprietary status for about a decade. It became a royal colony with the accession of James II in 1685 and almost immediately afterward was submerged, along with its near neighbors, in the centralized administrative structure known as the Dominion of New England.

The one consistent strand in this series of abrupt governmental changes had been authoritarian rule, by James and his governors no less than by the executives of the Dutch West India Company. Meanwhile New York had increased its population fourfold since 1664. Mutual resentments overlapped and flourished: between the original Dutch communities and the newer Puritan settlements, between Presbyterians and Anglicans, between landed and commercial interests, artisans and merchants, Hudson Valley wheat growers and city exporters who obtained a legal monopoly of the flour market. Frequent governmental changes bred quarrelsome uncertainty about the security of land titles and the legality of quitrents and taxes.

Then there were external pressures. The French and their Indian allies competed fiercely against the Albany fur traders and menaced the frontier settlements, and enterprising New Englanders threatened to capture New York's foreign trade. Protestant settlers, at odds with one another about everything else, reacted with their usual edgy, rumor-prone hostility to the Catholicism of King James and some of his governors—an antagonism sharpened by the proximity of hostile papist Frenchmen to the northward.

Swatches of these fears and discontents coalesced long enough in 1689 to enable Leisler, a militia captain, to grab the reins of power. He summoned a convention of freemen, appointed a committee of public safety, proclaimed the sovereignty of William and Mary, called elections, and convened an assembly. In power for nearly two years, he worked closely with the legislature, set up new courts, abolished the city flour monopoly, and wrestled with other grievances. He had a large following that included many farmers, Long Island residents, city workers, and first families, although his enemies from all ranks were also numerous. The Albany area refused to recognize his authority until a murderous French and Indian raid on Schenectady in 1690 persuaded them to co-operate. His administration botched an attempted counterthrust into Canada but did manage to levy taxes, dispatch privateers, and improve fortifications in prosecuting New York's share of the recently declared war between England and France.

The denouement was sudden. In 1691, William and Mary sent a new governor and a few soldiers to New York to re-establish royal authority. When they demanded that Leisler surrender the Manhattan fort his militia occupied and turn over the government, he vacillated, made a belligerent gesture or two, and gave up. The only real muscle was employed afterward: Leisler and his chief lieutenant were tried for treason, found guilty, and hanged. It was a controversially harsh verdict that delighted his enemies, antagonized his supporters, and insured that the political cleavage in the wake of his movement would be enduring and bitter.

But the authoritarian days of James and the Dominion of New England were over. New York kept its representative assembly. The local elites, without once composing their factional rivalries, began moving toward a more secure position at the top of the colonial power structure.

A like pattern, partially distorted by one bizarre episode that had no counterpart anywhere else, unfolded in Massachusetts. Anxiety in and about the Bay Colony was given a sharp boost by the colonial period's worst Indian war, which broke out just as the same issue was kindling Nathaniel Bacon in Virginia. The tribes in lower New England had not bothered their white neighbors much for a generation. Some had been Christianized and half domesticated, others were contained on local reservations (their conduct and existence subject to a set of humiliating and repressive laws), and most of the remainder had been pacified by their growing dependence upon English weapons, blankets, and rum.

But the Puritans despised the Indian, maltreated him, and coveted his land too much to leave well enough alone. Goaded until his resentment passed the limits of endurance, the red man launched an all-out war in 1675. A proud but not overly effective Wampanoag sachem named Metacomet, known to the white community as King Philip, provided a name and focus for the conflict, although the coalition of Narragansetts, Nipmucks, Mohegans, and other Eastern tribes that joined the Wampanoags achieved its successes more in spite than because of his leadership.

Its successes were notable. The Indians devastated the lower New England frontier from Narragansett Bay to the upper Connecticut and Nashua valleys. They destroyed some twenty-five settlements, struck at villages in New Hampshire and Maine, killed or captured one tenth or more of the Bay Colony's adult males, did untold property damage, disrupted commerce, attacked or menaced communities as close to Boston as Sudbury, Concord, and Medfield, and very nearly drove the Puritan colonies into the Atlantic. (With a little more luck and a leader of, say, Pontiac's caliber they might have succeeded. This would have rewritten a large page of history, since the French were just embarking upon the belligerent course that would keep North America's future in doubt for another ninety years. Count Frontenac would assuredly have taken advantage of such an opportunity, and New England might well have become a fortified outpost of New France.)

As it was, their own heavy casualties and dwindling food supply coupled with determined white counterblows finally broke the back of the Indian offensive. Philip was captured and shot. Peace was restored in mid-1676, and most surviving members of the warring tribes were enslaved or driven out. But no tribe had been exterminated, and the remnants would be heard from again. If southern New England now appeared secure, peace did not come to Maine till 1678, and other displaced tribesmen would participate joyfully in the raids soon to be launched from Canada.

From this tribulation Massachusetts went on to a series of others, less destructive but almost as unsettling. Bay Colonists had no sooner dispatched King Philip when they encountered Edward Randolph, whom we have met. Clashes with this flinty English investigator ranged across the entire spectrum of Massachusetts law, trade, and custom, upon nearly all of which Randolph reported unfavorably. This in turn (as we have seen) led to legal proceedings against the charter, the loss of New Hampshire, Randolph's return as customs officer, stringent enforcement of the Navigation Acts, revocation of the charter, creation of the Dominion of New England, and the arrival in Boston of Sir Edmund Andros to administer it.

All of this happened within ten years of King Philip's war, and it is easy to see why the Commonwealth reverberated with fears and alarums. If the Puritans overreacted, as folk with so highly developed a sense of omen and apocalypse are wont to do, they had been sorely tried—and from their uneasy vantage point things seemed to be coming apart. The colonial assembly had been eliminated. Judicial procedure, trade regulations, the tax structure, the authority of the magistrate, the relation of church and state, the validity of land titles—in short, everything that gave cohesion and pattern to their existence—had been altered or placed in doubt. No one quite knew where he was; the rock on which Massachusetts thought it had built its house had apparently turned to sand.

Actually, the autocratic Andros was a fair-minded and not unperceptive man, and some of the changes he wrought or attempted were improvements. But his regime was alien in style and procedure, and fear of what it might do was as potent as resentment of what it actually did. Fears and resentments fed upon one another, and throve.

Not surprisingly, rumors of papist plots found ready listeners in Massachusetts in the 1680s. (One version had it that Governor Andros, who pressed the militia into service and led them to defend the Maine frontier against French attacks in the fall of 1688, planned to turn all New England over to France if James were deposed.) When news of William and Mary's accession reached Boston a group of dissidents swung into action. They jailed Andros, Randolph, and a few others, set up a committee of public safety, and called a convention which voted to re-establish the pre-Dominion form of government.

But the provisional regime floundered, unsure of its own authority and lacking recognition from England or more than tentative public support. They were out of their depth: the French were threatening by land and sea, expenses were mounting, taxes could not be collected. Sentiment in favor of a return to royal government mounted, and relief rather than resistance greeted its restoration in 1690.

Yet all the uncertainties persisted. The Dominion of New England was gone, but William and Mary would not restore the old charter, and the new one they issued in 1691 retained the royal governor and added to his powers, changed the basis of the franchise, and left important questions of land, taxes, courts, trade, and church governance open to future interpretation, and hence much in doubt. The creation of the Board of Trade, a new Navigation Act, and vice-admiralty courts in 1696 did nothing to allay these doubts.

The Puritan oligarchy that had dominated Massachusetts since Winthrop's day also faced another challenge. As a creed, Puritanism had lost its fine edge; the old zeal and sense of community were being eroded by baser concerns. The magistrate, the minister, and the pillars of the congregation were still influential figures and would long remain so, but they no longer had the field to themselves. The growing mercantile community in Boston and the smaller ports increasingly reflected the values of city, quarterdeck, and countinghouse rather than pulpit, and the merchants were now vying for dominance with the old oligarchy. The distinction between the two groups was not clear-cut, and it would be an exaggeration to equate the rise of a commercial element with the eclipse of the old order. The point is that in the 1690s neither group's position was sure, and their conduct reflected this. It is not surprising that ordinary folk shared in the uneasiness so evident at the top.

The most famous manifestation of this pervasive anxiety was the witchcraft mania that seized Salem village and afflicted several other communities in the early 1690s. It started when a pair of teen-age Salem girls attributed their recent odd behavior to having been bewitched. Before it ended, the Bay Colony was rocked by a series of sensational trials and outlandish testimony that took twenty lives, threw dozens of others in jail, and touched off a near epidemic of hysterical accusations. (Belief in witches was still common on both sides of the Atlantic, and not merely among the ignorant. Yet it seldom went to such lengths.) Sanity reasserted itself in 1693 and the craze subsided. But its extent, and the number of reputable leaders who presided over or delayed in speaking out against the proceedings, indicate that psychic anxieties ran from top to bottom.

—□—

The Salem tragedy, of course, was in something of a class by itself. The other episodes were political, and they shared some interesting features. They all grew out of factional power struggles, usually between ins and outs, with neither group securely established. Although the grievances and resentments were real enough, there was surprisingly little violence; the so-called rebellions resorted more to postures and gestures than to destructive action, and either success or collapse, or both, usually came with ridiculous ease.

Another significant point about these episodes is that resistance to authority never once questioned the ultimate source of power and authority in colonial America—the government of

Great Britain. It was not merely that the mainland colonies in the late seventeenth century lacked the means or cohesiveness for a revolutionary struggle; revolution never really occurred to them. Resistance was entirely local, aimed at local officials and conditions. The vision and confidence that can transpose local discontent into a higher key were missing, and obedience to the mother country was not even remotely at issue.

Yet many of the grievances that animated followers of Bacon, Coode, or Leisler have a familiar ring. A tightening of imperial control, the appointment by the Crown of heavy-handed officials to enforce new regulations, resentments growing out of real or potential changes in land, trade, tax, and Indian policies, old religious antagonisms that throve on rumor and were quick to detect conspiracies, a belief that local institutions, economic opportunity, and basic rights were being infringed upon or threatened—these bear no little resemblance to the issues in that fateful period after 1760, when the colonial path broadened steadily into a revolutionary highroad.

What really changed in the ninety-odd years between Bacon's Rebellion and the Stamp Act Congress was not the issues but the people reacting to them, and the context in which the reactions took place. These changes, many-sided and interlocking, formed a necessary precondition of the War for Independence.

Whatever the causes and nature of their collective despond, the colonies began emerging from it shortly after the turn of the century. Even the first round of Anglo-French colonial wars, which blazed intermittently for some twenty-five years and kept scorching New England's frontier with Indian attacks, had its positive side. The invasion routes ran both ways. The colonials occasionally carried the battle into enemy territory and tasted enough victory to emerge from the inconclusive struggle with their self-confidence rather more boosted than buffeted.

Further boosts were in store. The return of peace in 1713 launched a half century of almost unbroken expansion and prosperity for British North America. A long economic upswing in England and the West Indies and parts of Europe meant good markets for American raw materials. This drew more people to the land and more acres into cultivation; the rivulets of immigration from the British Isles and the Rhine Valley became swollen streams. Population growth in the mainland colonies was dramatic, sharp, and sustained. Opportunities rippled outward in all directions to touch local millers and lumbermen, artisans and itinerant peddlers, land speculators, New England rum distillers and fishermen, West Indian sugar planters, English manufacturers, merchants on both sides of the Atlantic, and nearly everyone with a marketable crop or skill.

While the towns and villages grew and the tracts of empty land along the coastal plain filled up and the edge of settlement inched westward across the Piedmont and into the first Appalachian ridges, colonial America took on more and more of the dimensions of a mature society. The economy began developing a relatively sophisticated network of financial institutions, credit instruments, trade routes, specialized agricultural regions, and enterprising merchant capitalists. Political institutions functioned with growing effectiveness. Notwithstanding the best efforts of royal governors and their retinue of appointees and allies, the balance of power in each colony came to rest more and more firmly in the hands of the provincial assemblies, with their core of experienced first-family representatives and their secure ties to the assorted town fathers, sheriffs, JPs, vestrymen, militia officers, and other worthies who administered local affairs.

Years of expansion and prosperity enabled the landed or commercial elites who dominated the political affairs of every colony to enhance and entrench their power, and eventually to function with all the easy self-assurance of people to the manner born. Their ranks remained more open to ambitious newcomers of modest origin than had ever been the case in Europe, but the colonial upper class showed signs of becoming more of a closed corporation as the century advanced. It was getting harder to enter, even harder to obtain full membership; and the options for the successful climber had narrowed. The establishment might be joined, if one had good cards and played them correctly. But it was too well established to be threatened, rivaled, or overturned, and even its factional struggles were more like family quarrels (bitter enough, but restricted to insiders) than all-out political wars. The lower and middling sorts now and then found things to gripe about under this oligarchic leadership, but in the main they followed it. By about the second quarter of the eighteenth century the anxieties that had lurked so near men's hearths and campfires during the generation of Nathaniel Bacon and the Salem trials were all but gone.

Indeed, something very like an opposite trait was forming, eventually to become a prominent feature of the emerging American character. Several decades of expansion fostered a mentality that looked upon growth—more people, more farms, more goods, more everything—as normal: part of the underlying and expected order of things. It was the mentality of the speculator and the developer. Its tendencies were to think big, plan on a boom, and discount tomorrow.

Such an outlook was not uniquely American, but there was something about the interaction between rapid growth and empty acres that gave it a kind of epidemic quality in this country. The whole community could get to thinking that way, and the speculator who laid his plans and placed his bet in anticipation of tomorrow's rise was less apt to be some fast-talking outsider— though such men were around—than the neighbor one had known for years, yesterday's sober merchant, staid town father, stolid farmer, or dignified first-pew holder. The growth mentality was a powerful enough trait, when enough people were under its influence at the same time, to carve a deep channel and make a good deal of history flow down it. This began to happen in America for the first time during the middle years of the eighteenth century.

Well, why not? For the colonists as a whole—always excepting slaves, wartime victims, the very poor, and the congenitally
unlucky—these were very good times indeed. Life in America
was no soft touch, but it offered rewards of a special kind, and the
sounds it gave off were evocative—church bells, lowing herds,
the chink-chock of ax blade against wood and mug against
counter top, soft hoofbeats on a dusty road, the rhythmic splashing of a mill wheel, wind in the rigging or among rows of corn.
These bespoke a set of intangibles that contained magic, of the
sort expressed in homely phrases like "breathing space," "elbow
room," "out from under," "on one's own," "a better tomorrow"—all of which were coming within reach of considerable
numbers of plain folk for the first time. The land was already
bright with hope and promise, and otherwise stolid and unimaginative men would stir when anything appeared to threaten it.

During most of these palmy decades, significantly, none of the
threats emanated from Great Britain. The British government
would eventually go about and steer toward its fast-growing colonies on a collision course, but for two or three generations after
1700 imperial policy had a haphazard, distracted quality to it, and
in all but a few areas the colonists were able to do about as they
pleased. This reinforced an already prevalent colonial belief to the
effect that doing as they pleased—specifically, controlling their
own local and internal affairs—was not only the way things were
but the way they ought to be; less a privilege than a basic right.

Yet in theory the collision course had been charted almost
from the first. For whenever the British took time to think
seriously about the colonial relationship, their thoughts were
clear and consistent—altered in no important fashion since
Tudor times and fundamentally at odds with the colonial viewpoint.

British imperial theory rested upon that loose conglomeration
of ideas and principles known as mercantilism, in which nation-

states were seen as competing for larger shares of the world's precious metals and other goods. A nation should strive toward the interrelated goals of economic self-sufficiency and a favorable balance of trade. Economic regulation and promotion, in the form of tariffs, tonnage duties, subsidies, bounties, and drawbacks, were the weapons of national policy by which these goals could be achieved.

Colonies had an important role in such a system. As producers of raw materials which the mother country lacked and would otherwise have to import from foreign sources, colonial possessions would lessen a nation's dependence upon rivals and strengthen its balance of trade. Furthermore, the colonials were expected to buy their finished goods from the mother country and thus provide an additional (and protected) market for its manufactures. The imperial trade mechanism called for a system of navigation acts designed to keep all important products and nearly all profits out of the hands of foreigners. (The initial round of British navigation acts, be it remembered, came in response to Dutch inroads upon American trade in the 1640s.)

This theoretical apparatus was less systematic than it looked, and it was not without internal inconsistencies, difficulties of application, or critics. But mercantilist assumptions in one form or another influenced European economic thought and more than one national policy in the seventeenth and eighteenth centuries, and the idea at least affords clues to what bureaucrats and royal ministers *thought* they were doing during the American colonial era.

The colonists were seldom disposed to question the economic side of their imperial status, at least until the whole relationship came up for review in the years just before Lexington and Concord. Throughout the preceding century they chafed under some of the commercial regulations and evaded or flouted others, but they generally admitted, right to the last, the mother country's right to control trade.

The rub came with the political implications. To the British these were no more than a logical extension of the economic relationship, whereas the colonials viewed political questions in a different light almost from the start.

As far as the English government was concerned, colonies existed solely for the benefit of the mother country—as strategic outposts, sources of wealth, areas of opportunity, and so on. They belonged to the Crown, and this fact was in no way altered by the Crown's policy of farming out the actual development of its overseas possessions to private enterprise. Whatever grants of land, political authority, and other chartered rights the monarch might bestow, he remained in the capacity of the Empire's feudal overlord, so to speak, with his corporate or proprietary grantees so many tenants-in-chief. What the king could bestow, he could revise or take away.

In British eyes, the rise of Parliament to ascendancy during the seventeenth and eighteenth centuries only reinforced the colonies' dependent status. Parliamentary authority over them was supreme. As Governor Sir Francis Bernard of Massachusetts explained it during the intense imperial debate of the 1760s, the English saw colonial governments as a species of corporation, empowered to make bylaws but existing entirely at Parliament's pleasure.

Since colonies were subordinate by definition and in perpetuity, there was a tendency in England to regard the colonists themselves as little better than menials or hired hands in the service of the mother country—subject to the protection of her laws and possessed of certain rights, to be sure, but inherently second-class citizens. In practice, English officials were usually prepared to concede somewhat more than that, and several ministers and royal governors came to respect the self-governing institutions and habits of the American colonist.

Still, the colonist's theory of his political status was diametrically opposed to the English view of it, first and last. The American governments, Francis Bernard told his countrymen, "claim to be perfect states, not otherwise dependent upon Great Britain than by having the same king"—in short, what a later and wiser Empire would affirm as dominion status. The colonial assemblies came to regard themselves as little parliaments having the same rights and powers as the parent body. The Glorious Revolution, which to the English had little or no overseas application, was seen in America as establishing or ratifying legislative supremacy over the executive—on their side of the Atlantic no less than in Westminster.

The same divergent views appeared at almost every step. The formal instructions that each new royal governor received from the Crown at the outset of his appointment were looked upon by the colonists as mere guidelines, to be altered or ignored as realities might dictate; the British regarded them as having the force of law, no less binding upon a colony than an act of Parliament would be. This ambiguity was never clarified.

As individuals, the colonists maintained all along that in coming to America they remained full-fledged English citizens, with all of an Englishman's rights and liberties—notably the right to vote their own taxes and in general to manage their own affairs. They conceded control over trade and foreign policy to the mother country and claimed the rest for themselves: self-governing dominions, in fact if not in name.

One problem was that the colonists failed to grasp the full import of the Revolution of 1688. Its major result was to weld the executive and legislative branches of the English government together, with Parliament now the senior member in what soon became a close working partnership. Colonial policy, whether issuing from the Crown as instructions to a royal governor or from Parliament as a regulatory statute, was in either case England administering an area over which the governmental partnership—the king in Parliament—had absolute control. Or so the British believed.

The colonists never fully understood the new relationship of Crown and Parliament. To them, 1688 only meant the establishment of legislative supremacy. From then on, in consequence, their attitude toward the English executive was ambivalent and confused. On the one hand, their loyalty to England was felt and expressed as loyalty to the king; their ties with England were seen as going through the Crown. (They saw little direct need for Parliament, since each colony had one of its own.) Yet the executive, represented in America by the royal governor and other appointed officials, was also viewed as an outside force which opposed, and sought to encroach upon, the power of the assembly. In beating back these encroachments, the assemblies believed they were upholding the verdict of 1688 over royal tyranny, never quite realizing—or refusing to admit—that the real power in opposition to them was the new senior partner in the English government.

The point is that Americans were making a series of claims and assumptions which England never conceded for a moment. Two incompatible concepts of empire had taken root and flourished on opposite sides of the Atlantic.

Yet for several generations, more or less by accident, they avoided a showdown. It very nearly arrived one hundred years ahead of schedule; the English government steered closer and closer to that collision course, albeit somewhat fitfully, during the half century that spanned the Protectorate, the Lords of Trade, James II, and William and Mary, when the bonds of empire were tightened and royal authority was asserted with increasing firmness.

But colonial agitation, as noted, was so bound up with local concerns that it never really came to grips with the imperial question. Their worries were always a bit off target—the Catholicism of a James or a Baltimore, the highhandedness of a Berkeley or an Andros, the legitimacy and personality of a Leisler. They were not prepared, psychologically or in any other way, to take a stand on the theory of empire they had already begun to evolve, even though the threat to it would never be graver than during the 1680s and '90s.

Then Great Britain altered course, early in the new century, and there would be no showdown for another sixty years. The colonists, as we have seen, used the time well; when the subject came up again they would be ready. Why did the English back away when they stood on the verge of establishing imperial dominance and making it stick? And why did they wait so long to try it again—by which time, as is clear at least in hindsight, it was much too late?

It is fairly easy for Americans to write this off as an example of British stupidity, arrogance, and shortsightedness. A case can be made; at times the eighteenth-century British government lived up to the worst that has been said about it. But the case is incomplete, and distorts by omitting too much. It is nearer the mark to observe that British policy makers did the best they could under the circumstances—and that circumstances were too much for them.

These circumstances came in all sizes, and one difficulty was that the colonies seldom ranked near the top on England's list of priorities. In colonial matters the English government usually looked the other way after 1700—sometimes because it had to, with more pressing things on its mind; and sometimes because it chose to, guided by shrewd leaders like Robert Walpole and the Duke of Newcastle who often felt that avoiding trouble was better than standing too hard on principle.

They can be permitted the belief that there were troubles enough already. England had become a great power contending bitterly, almost interminably, with her chief rival. The struggle with France extended past both ends of the eighteenth century: it began when William and Mary led a European coalition against Louis XIV in 1689, and it would not end until Bonaparte was in permanent exile on St. Helena. The two countries were officially or unofficially at war for more than half of this 125-year span, and in between times they were almost as earnestly recuperating, rearming, and jockeying for position. Their diplomats and statesmen were deeply involved in every slight shift in the intricate European balance of power.

The scope of the contest was global. France and Great Britain, newest pace setters in Western Europe's great outward thrust, were expanding powers whose interests and ambitions had become worldwide. They ranged from India to Gibraltar and from Newfoundland to Florida, and across the Seven Seas from Hudson Bay to the Indian Ocean, the Mediterranean to the Caribbean, the Gulf of Guinea to the Gulf of Mexico. The stakes included something like world hegemony.

Englishmen were equally busy at home. The country was getting rich, or at least a number of well-situated people were, and the process of amassing wealth was no less absorbing in eighteenth-century England than it has ever been. There was money to be made in land and trade, in textiles, in finance and public securities. Great Britain was steadily developing the institutions, the technology, and the surplus (of capital, labor, appetite) for its imminent, all-out plunge into industrialization.

The political arena was no less active. It took the English a good part of the eighteenth century to work out the details and implications of the intricate new relationship between Crown and Parliament made possible by their Glorious Revolution. This involved redefining and limiting the royal prerogative, transferring the ultimate responsibility of the emerging cabinet system from king to Commons, and testing the exact nature of parliamentary government. Since it was, at bottom, a contest for political power, the process was both absorbing and fascinating. But it became so much an end in itself that a sense of direction with regard to policy was easy to lose.

For one thing, there were few strong hands at the helm. The English monarchs between William III and George III tended to be passive rulers, and English ministers (until the appearance of William Pitt in the 1750s) were inclined more toward caution than boldness. In this period Great Britain owed her ascendancy more to strategic location, commercial enterprise, and the efforts of her hard-pressed armies and navies than to outstanding political leadership.

—□—

In the absence of such leadership, the machinery of empire had a kind of Rube Goldberg quality to it: much intricacy and motion to achieve small results. There were too many bases to be touched. The Board of Trade, an advisory body whose capacity depended largely upon the vigor of its president and that of the monarch, languished for decades after the passing of William III in 1702. Before it could even advance a recommendation it had to get the approval or acquiescence of every branch of government with a hand in colonial affairs—the Admiralty, the War Office, the Treasury, the commissioners of customs, the Bishop of London, the Secretary of State for the Southern Department (which meant southern Europe; the American colonies were thrown under his jurisdiction as a way of finding a pigeonhole for them). Even though most of these agencies were represented on the Board, this was a cumbersome procedure, and in practice it approximated Edmund S. Morgan's neat summary of the imperial mechanism: "The Board of Trade told the Secretary what to do; he told the royal governors; the governors told the colonists; and the colonists did what they pleased."

The negative judgment of British policy begins to find ammunition right about here. During most of these years the nation was more impressive than the people who ran it. The currents of intellectual and political change that had traced so lively a course in the sixteenth and seventeenth centuries flowed sluggishly now. Great Britain had grown complacent and wealthy, dominated by a powerful oligarchy of landed and mercantile interests whose inability to look beyond short-run advantage or take the large view was almost total.

While a few statesmen brooded over matters of European

power politics, the routine affairs of state and empire were left in the hands of lesser men, of whom the political order contained a great many. The English two-party system was emerging, and at this stage both Whigs and Tories were loose coalitions of factions and interest groups, to whom matters of patronage, influence, favoritism, personal loyalties and antagonisms, and putting together ministries on the basis of maneuver and expedient alliance were often more important than devising sound policy. Placemen and hacks abounded, and the use of one's office as a means of self-enrichment was taken for granted.

Despite all of this, Parliament kept an eye on the colonies and occasionally sought to exercise its authority. Its concern usually came in response to one or more of the powerful British interests —landed, military, commercial, industrial—whose influence counted. It passed laws aimed at placing limits upon the sale or manufacture of colonial woolens in 1699, hats in 1732, iron products in 1750. The needs of the royal navy produced a series of acts setting aside most of the vast colonial pine forests for the Crown, including much that the navy could never use. More and more colonial products were put in the enumerated category, which meant that they could be exported only to England. To meet the demands of West Indian planters, hurting from the competition of French rivals on Guadeloupe and Martinique, Parliament placed a prohibitive duty in 1733 upon the colonial importation of non-English molasses and sugar. It outlawed private land banks in 1741 and forbade colonial governments to issue legal-tender paper currency in 1750.

Most of these regulations were less impressive than they looked. It is doubtful that much colonial capital would have gone into woolens or hats in any case, when the English product was so abundant. Colonists continued to cut pine trees pretty much as they wished. Their iron industry throve in spite of all restrictions; it proved so valuable to the British during the French wars that they tended to let it thrive, and colonial furnaces and forges were producing an estimated one seventh of the world's iron by 1770.

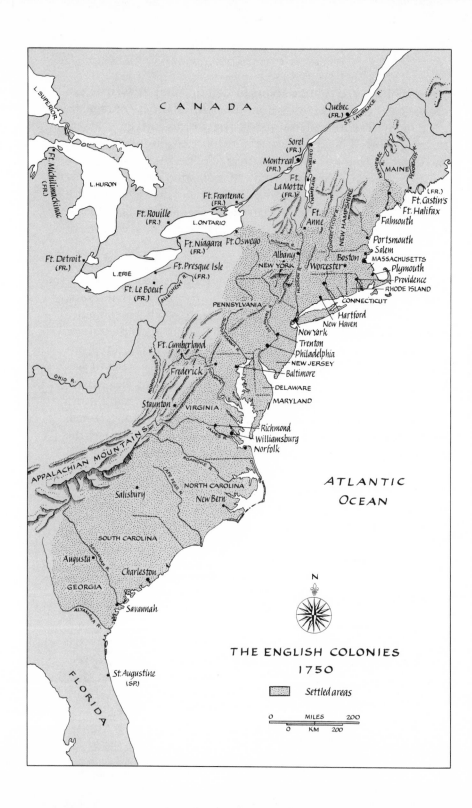

THE ENGLISH COLONIES
1750

Settled areas

0   MILES   200

0   KM   200

The Molasses Act of 1733 was rarely enforced; a fairly standard bribe persuaded customs collectors to look the other way when cargoes of French molasses entered colonial ports.

Most of Parliament's attempts to tighten the colonial reins were thwarted, either by the calculated laxity of ministers like Walpole and Newcastle or by the irremediable obstacles of time and distance. There was no regular mail service to America before the 1750s, and letters were months or years in transit when they did not go permanently astray. Reports from governors and other colonial officials often lay unread in Home Office files. By the time information could be gathered, bills passed, instructions written, and responses obtained, conditions might have so changed as to make the entire effort irrelevant. The Empire, in short, was not very efficient, which was precisely what the colonists liked best about it.

This benign inefficiency permeated the imperial mechanism for the greater part of fifty years. Its chief effect was to induce certain habits of mind in America that no one would recognize until something happened to alter the way things worked. Meanwhile being left alone became an indispensable component of the colonists' sense of well-being, and by the middle of the eighteenth century they had grown too accustomed, too strong, and too self-confident to submit to any other kind of handling.

CHAPTER 13

From Pawns to
Prime Movers

GREAT BRITAIN would have provided a tougher kind of handling had national policy not swung so decisively upon foreign affairs. France held the pivot, and few facts in our early history are more significant than this one. From about 1660 onward, as soon as the shadow of Louis XIV began to lengthen across Europe, the destinies of colonial America and Bourbon France were closely intertwined.

It was a connection well laced with irony: the Western world's prime examples of royal absolutism and local self-government drifting into conjunction, thence to jar each other forward, leapfrog fashion, toward goals neither side could have imagined when the association began.

French expansion toward the Rhine in the 1670s and '80s insured that when William of Holland came to the English throne Great Britain would actively join France's European foes. Meanwhile French imperial policy was being prosecuted with ambitious boldness. It transformed Canada from weak fur-company outpost to strong crown colony and sent Joliet and Marquette and La Salle on the great interior journeys that extended French sway from the Great Lakes to the Gulf. It also dictated the orders that sent Frontenac's soldiers and Indian allies through the northern forests to press savagely against the English colonial settlements. For the next eighty years France was the enemy in British North America—implacably hostile, unremittingly feared and hated.

Yet America's debt to France began right here, a century before a normal policy of calculated self-interest led the French monarchy into armed alliance with America's revolution in 1778 (and thereby led it perceptibly closer to the coming rendezvous with its own). Louis XIV's drive to impose conformity upon his Huguenot subjects forced thousands of them to emigrate, which badly weakened the French economy (another early step toward Bastille Day and the tumbrils) and enriched the societies of every country that received them. The industrious, talented refugees took up residence in Holland, England, Brandenburg, and not least in America, where their influence is attested by a sample roll call of Huguenot names: Revere, Bowdoin, Faneuil, De Lancey, Huger, Jay, Delano, Manigault, Vassar, Gallaudet, Bayard.

Elsewhere, too, the debt mounted. French power in Canada kept the British colonies penned in behind the Appalachians for decades, which insured that their growing strength would be all the harder to reckon with when the reckoning finally came. French pressure also induced Walpole and Newcastle, in the interest of not borrowing trouble, to pursue their policy of deliberate neglect; the French threat was what forced Great Britain to leave her colonies pretty much alone for over fifty years. This enabled them to develop to a point where resistance to any change in British policy would be not only possible but inevitable—and unbending.

And lastly, it was French response to colonial infiltration into the Ohio Valley after 1750 that drew Great Britain into the climactic phase of the struggle for North America, which culminated in the expulsion of France from the continent. This altered every condition by which England and her colonies calculated their relationship, freeing both from the reciprocal dependence that had muted the imperial dialogue since 1700. Britain's colonial policy abruptly hardened. It took the resulting confrontation little more than a decade to reach an impasse which only violence could resolve. All of this compels the conclusion that, without the France of Louis XIV and Frontenac and Montcalm, there would probably have been no American Revolution for the France of Louis XVI and De Grasse and Lafayette to assist.

The long imperial contest between France and Great Britain affords several revealing glimpses of the shape of things to come. In North America it began with the fur trade, which had been a paying venture ever since the first European explorers and settlers, eyes peeled for things of value, learned about the new continent's abundant wild life. What the animals were and how to get them they learned from the Indian, whose skills as trapper and hunter were matched only by the appetite he developed for the white man's weapons, blankets, tools, and drink.

The tribes that became most deeply involved in the fur traffic already had working rivalries of their own, and long before France and England came into open conflict the bitter enmity between Iroquois and Algonquin had got bound up with the white man's future in North America. The Algonquins were more numerous and scattered over a wider area, from East Coast Abenakis, Montagnais, and Micmacs to the distant Ottawas, Ojibways, Potawatomis, Miamis, and other Great Lakes tribes. But the Iroquois, operating out of their fertile Mohawk Valley-Finger Lake domain south of Lake Ontario, were more compactly settled and better organized.

French claims in North America centered on the St. Lawrence, and when they started penetrating this valley in earnest under Champlain in the early 1600s, geography decreed that their Indian contacts would be with Algonquin tribes. Befriending these folk, in the interest of peaceable expansion and a good fur traffic, the French casually aided them in a skirmish against the Iroquois, thereby making mortal enemies out of the most warlike, politically advanced tribes east of New Mexico. Algonquins thereafter tended to be well disposed, which aided French progress in exploring and laying claim to the interior. But the vengeful Iroquois befriended first the Dutch and then the English as those nations moved inland by way of the Hudson Valley. Competition for furs between French traders operating out of Montreal and Dutch or English companies based on Albany added its pressures to the long-standing Iroquois-Algonquin feud. The French got about better in the wilderness and got along better with the Indians (always excepting the Iroquois), but the English offered cheaper trade goods and could afford to pay higher prices for furs.

As the nearby animal population dwindled, Indian trappers ranged farther westward to supply the white man's markets, and fur-seeking Iroquois were soon clashing with western Algonquins all over the Great Lakes country. By the final quarter of the seventeenth century this rivalry for interior fur sources had acquired momentum and a hard core of violence, and was ready to converge upon the distant course of European politics.

Imperial designs were also clashing. Boundaries between English and French possessions in America—below the St. Lawrence, around Hudson Bay, and out West—had never been exactly determined or agreed upon, and French claims to the interior were in conflict with the grandiose sea-to-sea charter clauses of more than one English colony.

Out West. Included among the areas in dispute was a prize of such breathtakingly incalculable value that no one looking back at the contest can avoid a sense of awe. The Indians and the French voyageurs and the occasional English visitors to the area only knew their way about in parts of it—chiefly along the river highways, great and small, that coiled their way through an endless expanse of thick forests, rolling hills, flat grasslands, and cold blue lakes. These people could see the wealth in furs and fish and timber with which this territory abounded. But none in his wildest dreams could conjure up the whole of it.

The closely connected basins of the Great Lakes and Mississippi Valley together formed the heartland of North America: a huge triangle pointing southward, its apex at the mouth of the great river, its sides slanting northeast and northwest along the Appalachian and Rocky Mountain ridges, its northern base running irregularly east and west between Lake Ontario and the headwaters of the Missouri. It had already occurred to some of those who came and went and fought there in the eighteenth century that whoever controlled the Great Lakes–Mississippi country would control the continent. It was as yet only dimly apparent that such control would also confer possession of one of the richest and most important domains ever known to man.

While shadow images of red man, trapper, voyageur, priest, and soldier stalked one another across this nearly empty stage and the white Bourbon lilies still fluttered above the log forts at Michilimackinac, Niagara, Detroit, and along the great river, other images hovered in the wings awaiting their cue, and large portions of human history waited with them: pioneer farm families moving west in Conestoga wagons or Ohio River flatboats, on their way to build cabins and plant corn in the new states of the Old Northwest; Indiana hog drovers prodding their charges toward the Cincinnati packing houses; black slave gangs picking cotton or chopping sugar cane in the rich Mississippi bottomlands; twin-stacked paddlewheel steamboats crowding against the levees in St. Louis and New Orleans or whistling for landings at towns and villages along five thousand miles of river highway; oilmen drilling along the narrow Allegheny creeks; dusty longhorn herds pounding into the railhead cow towns at Fort Dodge, Abilene, Cheyenne; track gangs pushing Pacific railroads across the flat grassland and into the Rockies; prairie tribesmen fighting cavalry to a standstill but doomed as soon as the great buffalo herds had been reduced to acres of bones bleaching in the dust beside the tracks.

Still the images pressed forward: placer miners sifting for pay dirt along Colorado stream beds; loggers toppling cathedral stands of virgin timber in Michigan and Wisconsin while lumber schooners took on cargo in half a hundred little Great Lakes harbors; copper miners leaving rusty bootprints across the Keweenaw Peninsula or erecting giant smelters in Butte and Anaconda; coal shafts burrowing into the hillsides of West Virginia and Kentucky and southern Illinois; immigrants from the harsh dominions of the Romanovs and the Hapsburgs and the Ottomans and the Gulf States converging on Chicago to labor in the stockyards and mills and sweatshops; farm boys and combines harvesting their treasure from the soils of Iowa and Nebraska and the Dakotas; grain elevators towering over a thousand railroad sidings across the Middle West; electric power lines radiating their long spiderweb catenaries outward from Niagara and dam sites along the Tennessee.

And behind these loomed the greatest image of them all: the long, laden, flat-sided bulk carriers edging into the Soo Locks, an endless procession downward bound with prairie wheat for half the world or Lake Superior iron ore for the mills in Gary, Detroit, Toledo, Cleveland, Hamilton, Buffalo, and the smaller ports along Lake Erie's southern shore, each with its rows of hopper cars beside the coal and ore docks and its rail lines slanting southward to steel cities on the Mahoning or the smoking hill country in western Pennsylvania where two rivers meet to form a third.

The four Anglo-French wars that would clear the way for this many-sided drama occupied two distinct periods, separated by a generation of uneasy peace. The first conflict, known in America as King William's War, opened formally in 1689 following a dec-

ade of bloody encounters between Iroquois and French-Algon-
quin war parties in New York, along the St. Lawrence, and as far
west as Michigan and Illinois. This conflict went on till 1697. A
brief truce ended four or five years later in what the colonists
knew as Queen Anne's War, which lasted from 1702 to 1713.

A quarter century of peace, punctuated by sporadic Indian
raids and border clashes, gave way to the second round of wars in
1739. It began with conflict between England and Spain (growing
out of the same half-illegal, half-violent Caribbean traffic in
slaves and trade goods that had brought John Hawkins to grief
there nearly two centuries earlier) and soon widened into a third
Anglo-French contest, which the colonists called King George's
War. Another flimsy truce interrupted hostilities in 1748, but
within six years the American agents of the great rivals were at it
again; two years later the principals and their assorted European
allies were also fully engaged. This, the biggest and farthest-
ranging of the four conflicts, was known here simply as the
French War, later as the French and Indian War. It ended with
complete victory for Great Britain and the surrender by France in
1763 of all its vast holdings on the North American mainland.

Save for the fourth war, when the scope and scale of military
operations increased markedly, a consistent pattern underlay the
American side of this eighty-year struggle; the shifting details
were little more than variations on a theme. It was, at least for the
folk who had to pay most of the price, a dreary enough theme:
frequent raids by Indian and French-Canadian forces on the exposed frontier settlements in New England and New York;
counterincursions by Iroquois and English colonial parties upon
French Indian villages east of the Penobscot and French settlements along the St. Lawrence; privateering activity by both sides;
a few large amphibious assaults upon major French bases like
Port Royal, Louisbourg, or Quebec.

The New World theater was a gigantic affair. Most of the contests had a Southern phase, in which French, Spanish, and English
forces and their Indian allies attacked one another's villages and

forts or scouted the back country between Carolina and the lower Mississippi in search of strategic advantage, furs, and detachable tribal loyalties. (This kind of maneuvering went on in much the same fashion during the so-called peacetime interludes: the creation of Georgia in the 1730s as a frontier garrison between Carolina and Spanish Florida was a typical example.) Out West the activity consisted mainly of Indian skirmishes, the erecting of forts, and rough wilderness diplomacy aimed at preserving or breaking France's network of alliances with interior tribes. French and English units collided now and then in distant Hudson Bay, and there were several land and sea actions in the West Indies.

The forces were small by contemporary European standards. They usually fought in raw forested wilderness, over long distances and on roads little better than paths through the woods, all of which posed huge problems for supply and medical services and virtually precluded refinements like cavalry, artillery, or elaborate tactical maneuvers. Indians and colonial militia, both English-American and French-Canadian, did most of the fighting; the French could never spare more than a few hundred regulars from the homeland for duty in North America, and before 1750 the British limited their direct participation to a few naval and marine units, transports, and an occasional army regiment for some of the seaborne operations.

In short, there was little Old World professionalism and little enough place in which to employ it, and neither regular army discipline nor formal eighteenth-century rules and conventions counted for much. Although the wars featured plenty of bravery and occasional touches of gallantry, in the main they were fought with a no-quarter savagery in which red man, French Canadian, and English colonist would seem to have come off about evenly.

If they were small by European standards, the colonial wars were substantial enough to the people involved. For hundreds of settlers it began with days of tense silence emanating out of the dark forest and ended in an abrupt stark horror of scalping yells

and children's screams and butchery in isolated villages or frontier cabins. It often included long forced marches, as prisoners or
pursuers of French and Indian raiding parties, along the forest
trails connecting New England and Canada. These pursuers and
their sometime Iroquois allies visited the same sort of terror upon
French and Algonquin villages, when they could.

It was a rugged kind of warfare, and the folk who survived it
were a hardy lot. There was Hannah Dustin of Haverhill, Massachusetts, for example, whom the Abenakis captured, along with
another woman and a boy, in a raid in early 1697. After a six-
week trek through the late winter landscape of northern New England, Mrs. Dustin roused her two companions one night while
their twelve captors slept around a campfire. She proceeded to
kill ten of them, allowing a squaw and a boy to escape into the
woods. Then she methodically scalped all ten of her victims and
returned to Haverhill to rejoin her family and claim the £ 50
bounty—£ 5 per scalp—that the Massachusetts government
paid for such trophies.

The Canadians could point with pride to fourteen-year-old
Madeleine Jarret, daughter of a French officer who owned a sei-
gnory on the St. Lawrence a few miles below Montreal. At work
in the fields, surprised by an Iroquois war party while her parents
were absent, Madeleine ran to a nearby stockade and rallied a pair
of skulking soldiers and a handful of women and children into
manning the walls and standing off the dread Iroquois for a week
until a French relief force lifted the siege. Each conflict had its
quota of such heroics.

Although the fourth war had all of the remote edge-of-civiliza-
tion quality that distinguished its predecessors, it also had a dimension they lacked: the presence, alongside the red-skinned and
provincial forces, of a substantial number of British and French
regulars. They gave the French and Indian War a touch of the
color and pageantry of Old World conflict, including the two or
three episodes that constitute the sum of most people's knowledge of the colonial wars: Braddock's redcoats marching through

the Pennsylvania forest to deploy in formation and be slaughtered by French and Indian woods fighters near the Forks of the Ohio in 1755; gallant Montcalm and gallant Wolfe receiving mortal wounds as their troops collided in the best European parade-ground style on the Plains of Abraham outside Quebec in 1759, while the British fleet that had made Wolfe's assault possible tacked and maneuvered on the wide river below.

This fourth war was different in other ways, too. The first three were essentially standoffs, and whenever one side lost a bit of territory the other side usually gave it back at the peace table. Not so with the French and Indian contest. Far bigger than the others, it alone ended decisively. After generations of stalemate, Great Britain put together a winning combination in the 1750s. France began strongly, scoring a succession of triumphs. Then crusty egotistical William Pitt became Prime Minister in 1757 with the blunt announcement that he alone could save the nation, and calmly proceeded to make the boast good. While British money helped keep Frederick's Prussians in the field against France on the Continent, British commanders turned the war around. Clive destroyed French power in India; squadrons under Hawke, Boscawen, and Rodney drove the French fleet from the Western Ocean.

With Britain controlling the sea, New France was a cut flower in a vase. Pitt sent Amherst and Forbes and Wolfe to America to recoup the losses their predecessors had suffered and carry the war to the enemy. One by one the strategic French bastions fell before British and colonial arms—Fort Duquesne, Fort Niagara, Louisbourg, Fort Frontenac, finally Quebec and Montreal and the whole far-flung New World empire France had built.

—□—

In the course of this protracted series of conflicts the American colonists learned a few things about one another, their mother country, the outside world, and the bizarre incongruities of war.

As always, the sum of their wartime experiences was a mixed bag. Colonial governments, chronically short of hard cash, financed their campaigns against the French by issuing various forms of paper currency, and thus had their first exposure to the unpredictable ways of inflation, fiat money, and government indebtedness. Many individual colonists also discovered that there are handsome profits to be made by trading with the enemy—an early lesson in war's unfailing ability to make a mockery of moral standards and impose its own cruel logic.

The instances were numerous, and they increased along with the scope of the wars. At times the independent-minded Iroquois, disillusioned by English ineffectiveness and French attacks on their villages, chose to stay neutral. On such occasions Albany traders were not above trafficking with their rivals in Montreal—not only in furs, but to the extent that booty captured by Indians in raids on New England settlements had a way of turning up weeks later in Albany shops.

The practice was not limited to a few unscrupulous fur traders. British naval superiority sometimes prevented France from keeping all of its overseas forces adequately provisioned, and the normally good market for American meat and breadstuffs in the French West Indies was even better during wartime: what the French sugar planters did not take could be sold and transshipped to supply French soldiers—including those engaged in North America. In general, the wars acted as stimulants to the colonial economy, or at least to those segments of it that were in a position to supply the armed forces, regardless of flag. (The extent of this trade with the enemy during the French and Indian War appalled and angered the Pitt ministry when they learned about it, and contributed directly to the hardening of British colonial policy after 1760.)

Britain's impression of greedy colonial profiteering was balanced, in a way, by some impressions Americans picked up about the mother country and its inhabitants, especially its leaders. The sum of these impressions, along with pockets of resentment, was a vague but growing sense that Englishmen were somehow different from Americans—in manner, style, custom, outlook. This in turn contributed to an equally vague sense of American nationality, signs of which began to emerge during the middle years of the eighteenth century.

Each war afforded grounds for American resentment. A colonial attempt to launch a co-ordinated land and sea invasion of Canada in 1709 failed because the troops and ships London had promised to contribute never showed up (nor, for some months, did the misdirected letter blandly informing America of the change in plans). An even more ambitious effort actually got under way against Quebec two years later, but the British admiral in command of the expedition turned back after losing a few ships and several hundred men on reefs in the St. Lawrence, in what the colonists rightly viewed as a craven and inept performance. Hundreds of American volunteers perished of gunfire and disease in a monumentally mismanaged British assault in 1741 upon Spanish Cartagena in the Caribbean. And another major expedition against Quebec in 1746, toward which eight colonies contributed a total of nearly eight thousand men, failed to get started because the British regulars earmarked for the campaign were never sent. (Once again, it took London almost a year to offer an explanation: the redcoats had been diverted at the last minute for an abortive attack on the French coast.)

Two of the most successful colonial campaigns include a Massachusetts expedition in 1690 against Port Royal and a big intercolonial attack in 1745 upon heavily fortified Louisbourg, which with British naval assistance the colonists captured after a bold siege. Both triumphs were nullified when Great Britain gave the prizes back to France after hostilities ended. (In succeeding wars both Port Royal, in 1710, and Louisbourg, in 1758, were captured again, this time permanently. But the earlier impressions of hard-won victories wiped out at the conference table were the stronger ones. How long might it be, some Americans wondered, before Great Britain used the colonies themselves as bargain counters in the calculated give and take of European power politics?)

British heavy-handedness also left its mark. In the Louisbourg campaign of 1745 the government refused to cut the New Englanders in on a share of the booty and prize money that fell into the victors' hands after the fortress surrendered, thus casting a cloud of irritation over the genuine co-operation between royal navy and colonial militia by which the victory had been achieved. Closer to home, there was the matter of a well-meaning British commodore whose squadron visited Boston during the closing months of King George's War in the 1740s. He had so admired a colonial militia's recent defense of their Connecticut River fort that he presented its commander with a sword. But before leaving port the commodore resorted to a time-honored navy practice and sent a press gang into Boston to procure some extra crewmen for his ships. They duly picked up a few local citizens— whereupon an irate mob gathered, seized some of his officers, and made threatening noises. Although the provincial government and the Boston town meeting joined in condemning the mob and secured the release of the officers, the surprised commodore had to return the captured civilians and sail off. It was an episode which London would have done well to ponder.

The wars taught other lessons. Considerable numbers of young colonials experienced their first sojourns beyond the narrow confines of home and farm and village—on long wilderness marches, in camp, on British transports, in siege operations hundreds of miles from their native province. In other words, they tasted a few slices of army life, and the broader horizons, worldly wisdom, bad habits, and vague restlessness that are sometimes bequeathed by such an experience came home with them.

Among the new notions growing out of the colonial military experience was one that soon hardened into conviction and got incorporated as a central feature of the American creed: the belief that non-professional American frontiersmen and farmers were better fighters than regular soldiers. Proponents could cite chapter and verse, like the militia victories at Louisbourg in 1745 and Crown Point ten years later, and especially the defeat of Braddock's regulars. This was a highly selective reading of the evidence, and the confidence in the frontier farmer's superior virtues as a fighting man would prove a costly one. But it said something about an image of themselves and their environment that Americans were beginning to form.

Many of the campaigns, including some that succeeded and some that failed, featured a measure of intercolonial co-operation in the contributing of troops, supplies, money, and leadership. These co-operative lessons were learned slowly, and not by everyone; the line leading upward from isolated colonies toward confederation and national unity traced a zigzag course replete with instances of foot dragging and flat refusals to participate. Yet the idea was taking hold here and there that in certain matters of common concern the colonies could best solve their problems by working together.

This notion reached a peak of sorts at the outset of the French and Indian War, when no fewer than nine of the mainland colonies sent delegates to a conference at Albany in 1754 to consider questions of defense and Indian policy. The agenda included a detailed proposal for an intercolonial council and Crown-appointed "president general" which together would have the power to pass laws and levy taxes in the areas of defense and Indian affairs. Though the plan was conceived and presented by that persuasive, distinguished Philadelphian, Benjamin Franklin, nothing came of it at the time; the colonial governments neither considered Franklin's plan nor co-operated more than spasmodically in the war that followed. But the federal idea had been planted, and it had acquired at least one influential advocate. It would not appear as a totally novel or unthinkable concept when events resummoned it twenty years later.

—□—

Consider one last point about the Anglo-French conflict. If its cumulative effect altered the course of colonial history, the colonists managed near the end to exert a decisive influence upon the course of the conflict. It was a remarkable turn of events, prophetic of coming shifts in the location of power and in the capacity to make things happen.

For the first sixty years or so of the imperial contest, from the 1680s until the 1740s; the American colonies were mere pawns. Prime movers in the great struggle were monarchs, royal ministers, generals, admirals, courtiers. As always, the captains and the kings called the tune, and ordinary folk marched. Yet at mid-century, in one memorable instance, it was the other way round.

A vanguard of colonists—speculators, Indian traders, pioneers: people of the move—began spilling across the Appalachians and leaving their mark and staking their claims here and there in the rich uncharted Ohio Valley domain that France regarded as her own. This infiltration summoned powerful retaliatory moves by the French, which soon boiled over into open conflict; this in turn drew Great Britain into the war. But the great powers were responding, not leading. Initiative had passed from royal courts to buckskin-clad provincials in the remote American forest.

These new makers of history were an improbable but effective crew. They included skilled trader-diplomats like the Pennsylvania immigrants, Irish-born George Croghan and German-born Conrad Weiser, who succeeded in diverting the allegiance of several Western tribes from France to Great Britain in the 1740s and engineered Indian treaties that opened the Ohio country as a market for English trade goods. They included land-hungry climbers from the middling ranks of Virginia's planter aristocracy like young George Washington, militia officer and member of a land company that hoped to sell wilderness farm lots to pioneer families. (Washington's land company was one of several being formed during this period by combinations of colonial speculators and bargain-hunting British investors who pooled their influence to obtain big land grants from provincial governments and the Board of Trade.) Also present among the new movers and shapers were a few restless, wilderness-loving pathfinders like Christopher Gist and John Finley and Daniel Boone, variously exploring the Western country on behalf of trading companies, land companies, or small groups of prospective settlers.

Here were America's advance skirmishers, her point men— enthusiastic carriers of the rapid-growth and discount-tomorrow mentality created by a generation of prosperity and expansion back East, looking now beyond the mountains for new avenues to wealth. And the main body would follow, sooner or later: the vast vague tracts of forest acreage being marked out by the land companies up and down the Ohio Valley from the Kanawha to the Wabash, and the new trading fort that Croghan built in the Miami Indian town of Pickawillany (modern Piqua, in central Ohio) as a distributing center for the Western Indian trade, were unmistakable straws in the wind.

The French did not mistake them. First they sent an expedition through the Ohio country to harangue the Indians and bury lead plates here and there that proclaimed His Most Christian Majesty's title to the region. Then under the forceful Marquis Duquesne they countered in earnest. One unit wiped out the fort and village at Pickawillany in 1752, which jarred most Western tribes back into the French orbit. Other military detachments started building a new chain of forts designed to seal off the Ohio Valley against the colonial expansion.

For fifty years the French had slowly been tightening the huge arc of their Great Lakes-Mississippi Valley fortress chain. First they had connected lake and river by way of Green Bay and the Wisconsin, then by way of the Kankakee and Illinois, most recently by way of the Maumee and Wabash, placing forts here and there along each route. Now Duquesne planned to draw France's heartland defense perimeter along its easternmost edge. His troops began in 1753 by building Fort Presque'Île near the eastern end of Lake Erie and cutting a road south from there to the upper reaches of French Creek, where they erected Fort Le Boeuf. Then they seized an English trading post at Venango, where French Creek joins the Allegheny, and started building a fort there. Another party of soldier-workmen went down that river to the Forks of the Ohio, where the French proposed to anchor their chain with a big new fort to be named for Duquesne himself.

These first colonial ventures into the Ohio country had started something for fair. The French response touched off more activity east of the mountains. Virginia, whose energetic Governor Dinwiddie was also a member of one of those new land companies with big claims and big plans in the West, sent a small party under young Major Washington into the Allegheny Valley to remind the French that this was Virginia territory. Washington found them at newly completed Venango and Le Boeuf, where they politely wined and dined him, rejected his claims, and sent him home. But the Virginians persisted. When Duquesne's men returned to the Forks in early 1754 to commence that fort (bad weather and disease had forced the original party to return to Niagara the previous autumn), they found a small band of Virginians on the site, at work upon a similar project under orders from Governor Dinwiddie. The Frenchmen drove them off and began building Fort Duquesne.

Not knowing this had happened, Dinwiddie sent Washington with a force of Virginia militia into western Pennsylvania in April to protect the workmen. Washington found them at Wills Creek, on the upper Potomac near modern Cumberland, and learned of the French presence at the Forks. Continuing toward that point, he encountered a small French detachment about forty miles south of it on May 28 and impetuously attacked. The Americans killed or captured most of them, and Washington, reinforced by three more companies of Virginia militia, prepared to follow up his little victory. He erected a stockade, pressed northward, and then retreated to his defensive position upon learning that a superior force of Frenchmen and Indians from Fort Duquesne was moving toward him. The French besieged and attacked the Virginians, and after several hours of brisk action Washington agreed to a parley. Having no real choice but to surrender, he signed articles of capitulation at midnight. It was the morning of the fourth of July, 1754.

From here on the contest for Ohio moved beyond parleying and fort-building. Washington's defeat drew General Braddock and his redcoats overseas and across Pennsylvania to their bloody rendezvous along the Monongahela in 1755. France became supreme beyond the mountains. The Western Indians, emboldened by their ally's new show of vigor, launched murderous raids into the Susquehanna Valley and on down across western Maryland deep into the Virginia Blue Ridge. But Great Britain was now fully committed—drawn into war not for reasons of European power balance or commercial-imperial aggrandizement but to protect the interests and welfare of her North American colonies. The colonies, be it noted, had taken it upon themselves to define those interests as lying beyond as well as along the seaboard. From these origins the conflict broadened into full-scale war on three continents. Soon afterward the British found William Pitt, and it became a fight to the finish.

The French obstacle to America's having its way with the great interior heartland had at last been removed. The treaty ratifying this momentous development was signed in Paris in 1763, and the ink had not yet dried before the victors were fully embroiled in the controversy that would eventuate twenty years later in another treaty signed in Paris, ratifying the removal of the British obstacle as well.

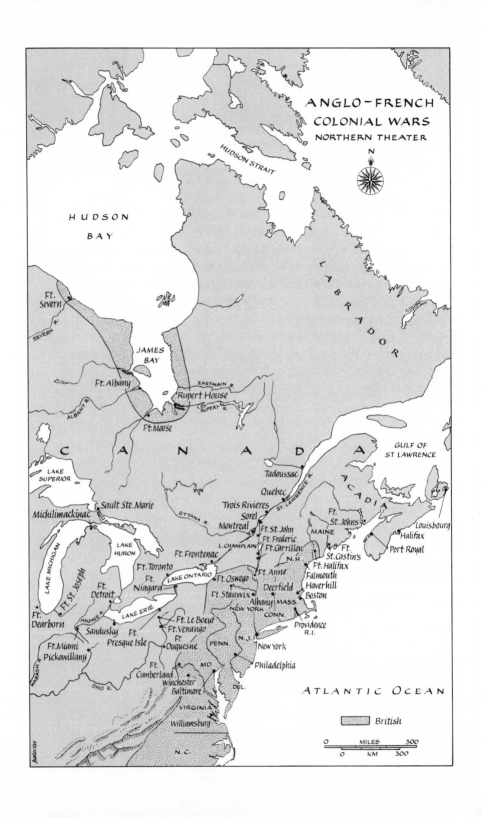

ANGLO-FRENCH
COLONIAL WARS
NORTHERN THEATER

N

HUDSON STRAIT

HUDSON
BAY

LABRADOR

Ft.
Severn

SEVERN R.

JAMES
BAY

Ft. Albany

EASTMAIN R.

Rupert House

ALBANY R.

RUPERT R.

Ft. Moose

C A N A D A

GULF OF
ST. LAWRENCE

LAKE
SUPERIOR

Tadoussac

Quebec

A C A D I A

Sault Ste. Marie

Trois Rivieres

OTTAWA R.

ST. LAWRENCE R.

Ft.
St. Johns

Michilimackinac

Sorel

Montreal

Ft. St. John

MAINE

Louisbourg

LAKE
HURON

Ft. Frederic

Halifax

LAKE MICHIGAN

Ft. Frontenac

L. CHAMPLAIN

Ft. Carrillon

Ft.
St. Castin's

Ft.
Halifax

Port Royal

Ft. Toronto

N.H.

Ft.
St. Joseph

Ft.
Detroit

Ft.
Niagara

LAKE ONTARIO

Ft. Oswego

Ft. Anne

Falmouth

MAUMEE R.

LAKE ERIE

Ft. Stanwix

Deerfield

Haverhill

Boston

Ft.
Dearborn

Sandusky

Ft. Le Boeuf

Albany

MASS.

Ft. Venango

NEW YORK

CONN.

Ft.Miami
Pickawillany

Ft.
Presque Isle

Ft.
Duquesne

PENN.

Providence
R.I.

N.J.

WABASH R.

OHIO R.

Ft.
Cumberland

MD.

New York

Winchester

DEL.

Philadelphia

Baltimore

VIRGINIA

ATLANTIC OCEAN

Williamsburg

British

N.C.

0   MILES   300

0   KM   300

padirias

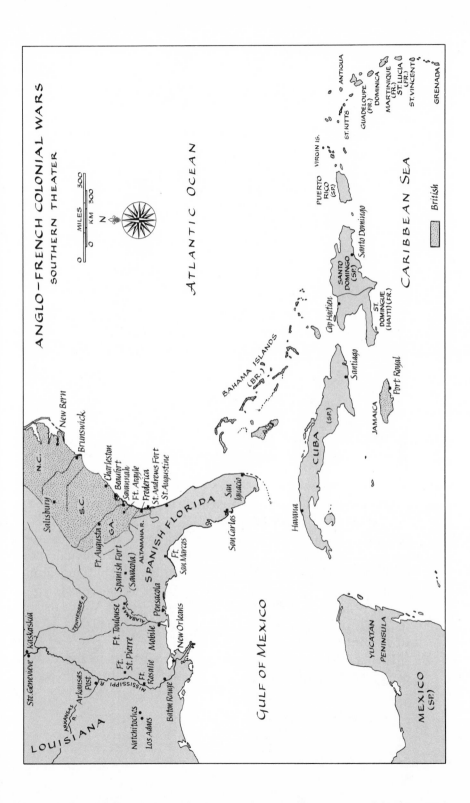

ANGLO-FRENCH COLONIAL WARS

SOUTHERN THEATER

MILES 300
KM 500

ATLANTIC OCEAN

LOUISIANA

Ste. Genevieve • Kaskaskia

ARKANSAS R.
Arkansas Post

Natchitoches
Los Adaes

Ft. St. Pierre
Ft. Rosalie

MISSISSIPPI

Baton Rouge

New Orleans

Ft. Toulouse

Mobile

Pensacola

Spanish Fort
(Sawacola)

ALABAMA R.

TENNESSEE R.

Salisbury

N.C.

New Bern

Brunswick

S.C.

Ft. Augusta

Charleston

Beaufort

Savannah

Ft. Argyle

Frederica

St. Andrews Fort

St. Augustine

GA.

ALTAMAHA R.

SPANISH FLORIDA

Ft. San Marcos

San Carlos

San Ignacio

GULF OF MEXICO

MEXICO
(SP.)

YUCATAN
PENINSULA

Havana

CUBA
(SP.)

Santiago

JAMAICA

Port Royal

BAHAMA ISLANDS
(BR.)

Cap Haitien

SANTO
DOMINGO
(SP.)

ST.
DOMINGUE
(HAITI)(FR.)

Santo Domingo

PUERTO
RICO
(SP.)

VIRGIN IS.

ST. KITTS

ANTIGUA

GUADELOUPE
(FR.)

DOMINICA

MARTINIQUE
(FR.)

ST. LUCIA
(FR.)

ST. VINCENT

GRENADA

CARIBBEAN SEA

British

CHAPTER 14

Inherit the Wind

IN THE spring of 1760 Benjamin Franklin wrote a pamphlet to reassure people who feared that the British Empire would soon break up. The American colonists were notoriously a prickly, stiff-necked breed, given to strong emotions that seemed to come up out of the Western Ocean storms, given also to strong delusions born no doubt of the wilderness midnight that lay beyond the mountains that hemmed them in. They were much closer to each other than they were to their proper overlords and kinfolk in Britain, and it began to seem likely—to some, at least —that sooner or later they would unite in wild revolt against the mother country. Franklin felt that this was not merely improbable but impossible. The colonies, he said, were basically non-cohesive. They could not even unite in self-defense, although the French and Indians along the western border were burning farm cabins and settlements and butchering farmers and settlers. Apparently the colonists preferred this to united action. Would they, then, ever unite against their own countrymen beyond the seas? It was inconceivable.

Franklin had reason to know what he was talking about. As deputy postmaster general for the colonies he had arranged a postal service that ran the length of the seaboard, and so had done more than anyone else to bring the colonies together, but if there was a lesson in all of this apparently no one had learned it. Franklin remembered the mixture of dead silence and horrified opposition that had greeted his Albany plan for an intercolonial governor and council in 1754, even though the need for some sort of common effort had never been greater. His proposal had circulated among the colonial governments just as ghastly frontier incidents west of the Alleghenies were signaling the onset of the largest and most threatening of the Anglo-French wars for empire: table stakes, and the loser does not even get carfare home; the destiny of all the colonies and the lives of a great many colonists balanced on the line.

Franklin, who had seen this coming a year or two before the actual outbreak of hostilities, concluded that in sheer self-interest the colonies ought to join hands to protect themselves. His plan for a federation had seemed no more than common sense. Begin, he suggested, by picking "half a dozen men of good understanding and address," lay out for them the right kind of plan, and send them through the colonies to discuss it with the leading men. He had faith that "reasonable, sensible men can always make a reasonable scheme appear such to other reasonable men, if they take pains and have time and opportunity for it." The central idea in Franklin's plan was that the program for defense would originate with the colonies themselves and would finally carry out plans they themselves had made; plans, it was emphasized, which they themselves would finance. This was a wholly new concept for the organization and direction of life in America, and it went straight to the heart of the underlying problem—which was that American life simply could not be directed from London because static England could not really understand dynamic America. Franklin planted this seed and waited for it to germinate.

No more than common sense, yet not enough people could see it that way. Proper germination time should have been in 1754, with new French forts being built and garrisoned in western

Pennsylvania and serious trouble obviously coming. Governor De Lancey of New York had seen this, and invited delegates from other colonies to meet at Albany and take thought about the matter. Having thought, the delegates had concluded that some sort of united action was needed and named a committee, including Franklin, to make suggestions. The committee recommended a plan embodying the essence of Franklin's idea for an intercolonial union, it was sent around to all the colonies in 1755—and one and all they turned it down, aghast at the thought of giving so much power to one central body. The idea died. This seed was going to need more time for germination.

Years later Franklin remarked that people on both sides of the Atlantic would have been happier if the plan had been adopted in 1755. The colonies would have been able to defend themselves, England would not have had to send troops overseas, and the long wrangle about finding some way to make the colonists pay for these troops, a brush fire that at last got wholly out of control, would have been averted. When he wrote his pamphlet he had good reason to say that England had nothing to fear. American feelings toward the homeland in 1760 were cordial. The colonists could see their immediate neighbors at close range and knew them for desirous, grasping, and often willful human beings who needed watching, but the English beyond the Atlantic were far off and appeared benign from a distance. The British hand at that time was fairly light. The colonists had developed a great, instinctive, unvoiced desire to stay out of anybody's leading strings, and although the government in London had imposed a number of rules to govern them these rules were so loosely enforced that most of the time they could be evaded. The colonies, Franklin remarked, were governed only at the expense of a little pen, ink, and paper: "They were led by a thread."

Yet Franklin felt obliged to hedge, and he added that when he called a union against England impossible, "I mean without the most grievous tyranny and oppression." The American people, he said, had property to protect and privileges to defend, and so by nature were conservative; "while the government is mild and just, while important civil and religious rights are secure, such subjects will be dutiful and obedient." There was just one thing to remember: "The waves do not rise but when the winds blow."

Like most great storms, the wind Franklin dreaded began quietly. In 1760 William Pitt, then dominant in the British government, ordered tighter administration of the Sugar Act. This law, by imposing prohibitive duties on foreign molasses, sought to compel the colonists to buy all their molasses from the British West Indies. Molasses was highly important in the colonial economy, especially in New England, where it was turned into rum which became the base for a growing export and coastal trade, and the British islands did not produce enough to satisfy the demand. This restrictive act had been on the books for a long time without bothering anybody very much because it never got more than token enforcement. The colonists had evolved an effective smuggling system, enhanced by the fact that customs officials could usually be induced to look the other way. All Pitt wanted now was a more efficient administration, but that was precisely what the colonists did not want because it was the inefficiency of His Majesty's imperial apparatus that made the act acceptable in the first place.

Now there was to be an end to laxity and to the soft cushion of judicious bribery; and to make matters worse, the customs officers were now empowered to go to court to get writs of assistance, a species of general search warrant that allowed officers to enter any premises at any time to search for smuggled goods. This aroused good men who had nothing to do with molasses, rum, or smuggling, because it smacked of unwonted and possibly illegal severity. Among those aroused was a brilliant, unstable Boston lawyer named James Otis, who argued against the writs so forcefully that John Adams considered him "a flame of fire" and wrote later that the seeds of American independence were planted then and there.

Still, this was a small swirling gust and not Franklin's great storm, and it blew itself out quickly enough. In this same year of 1760 George III came to the throne, quietly determined to rule rather than to reign, and he wanted a less forceful man than Pitt running things. Pitt retired, strict enforcement of the Sugar Act was more or less shelved, the writs were forgotten, and all seemed to be well. The new king appeared to be a decent likable man, and most colonists, watching at long range, concluded that he was a great improvement on the first two Georges.

Another small gust arose from the fact that the death of George II automatically voided all royal commissions so that new ones had to be issued—to all kinds of officials, including judges. The king could require such appointees to serve "at the king's pleasure," which meant that only he could remove them, but this had fallen into non-observance. Most royal governors, appointing judges in the king's name, sought to ease their own relations with the colonial assemblies by specifying that the judges were to serve "during good behavior." This system was now overhauled. When Governor Cadwallader Colden of New York named a chief justice he was ordered by London to make a "king's pleasure" appointment. The assembly responded with a bill authorizing salaries only for "good behavior" judges. Colden vetoed this, and the assembly then refused to vote the new justice any salary.

Here, in short, was a head-on dispute, although hardly of the kind that shakes empires. In the end the assembly backed down and accepted royal control over the judges, and another little gust had blown itself out. There was more to come, not especially damaging but indicating a vague thickening of the atmosphere.

It thickened noticeably in 1763, when the king issued a proclamation informing the colonists that they could not settle or take up Western lands beyond the sources of the rivers flowing into the Atlantic: in brief, the trans-Appalachian country with its rich Ohio Valley was declared off limits.

Now this proclamation was essentially a stopgap measure, designed to give Great Britain time to work out a permanent policy for the vast Western territories it had just acquired. Yet a permanent policy that would satisfy all the interested parties and points at issue was going to be a tall order; as Ray Billington has observed, British ministers had to devise a system that would meet the needs of "jealous provincials, greedy traders, land-hungry speculators, English merchants, rabid imperialists, sentimental humanitarians, and individualistic frontiersmen"—to say nothing of several Western Indian tribes already stirring resentfully at the postwar influx of white traders and settlers. Had these British ministers possessed the wisdom of a Solomon—and the line-up that followed William Pitt after 1760 was a long distance shy of that—they could not have found a formula for such an assortment.

The two groups whose Western interests were completely incompatible were the land speculators and the fur-trading companies. The former wanted to retail wilderness farmsteads and fill the West with settlers; the latter wanted to keep the settlers out and let the Indian and the beaver and the other denizens of the great Western forests have it all to themselves. The proclamation of 1763 was naturally pleasing to the fur companies, and to those few English humanitarians who advocated fair treatment for the Indians. But London was mainly playing for time, hoping to clear up the turmoil that was pouring into the Western country behind the traders' pack-horses and pioneer wagons. Meanwhile, land companies and prospective settlers could go to the new territories of Canada or Florida (which the British had obtained from Spain as another prize in the recent war.)

This was a reasonable beginning, but time was the one thing Britain's fumbling imperial mechanism did not have; forces set in motion out West by the surrender of New France had gone too far to be turned back. The traders and speculators and pioneers who thirsted after trans-Appalachian opportunities were already present in force and more were going west each year. Outside the recently captured and rebuilt French forts and their small red-coated garrisons there was no government and no administration to speak of between Lake Ontario and the Gulf of Mexico—not enough, at any rate, to keep unlicensed traders from cheating and debauching the Indians, or land company agents from trying to con them out of their hunting grounds, or new farm families from simply staking out homesteads on Indian land.

Proclamations from London were not going to restrain these folk, and the handful of royal officials on the scene were not much help. The British military commander in America was Lord Jeffrey Amherst, one of the stars on the winning varsity team Pitt had assembled against France. Indian affairs were then under Amherst's jurisdiction, and he might just possibly have been able to restore a measure of order. But Amherst's view of Indians was about as far down the road toward twentieth-century final solutions as eighteenth-century minds had yet traveled: his idea of dealing with the red man was to canvass the possibility of distributing germ-infested blankets among the tribes in hopes that they would all catch the smallpox and die of it. Lacking such blankets, he slashed the appropriations for the Indian Department in 1762 and terminated the established custom of giving presents as a way of sweetening relations with the tribes. Between Amherst on the one hand and the swarms of predatory newcomers on the other, the few Anglo-American officials with some experience and understanding of the Indian point of view could make no headway whatever.

In short, and as usual, the red man was fair game. He passed the limit of endurance in 1763, just as the British government four thousand miles away was trying to formulate a Western policy. An Ottawa chieftain named Pontiac, who lived near the British fort and trading post at Detroit, was stirred to action that spring. Angered by the treatment his people were receiving, assured by leftover Frenchmen that soldiers of the Bourbon king would soon be back to help the Indians drive the redcoats out forever, Pontiac led his warriors in an attack on Detroit in May. He also managed to put together a loose coalition of Western tribes—his own Ottawas, some Ojibways, Shawnees, Delawares, and a few others—for a concerted attack on English forts and settlements

in the West. By the fall of 1763, British relief expeditions had broken Pontiac's coalition and driven off his forces, but not before he
had captured Mackinac and Venango and almost every other fort
in the Ohio country, done a lot of killing and very nearly swept
the Anglo-American pieces off the Western board; at its peak his
offensive was besieging the last three British holdings beyond the
mountains: Detroit, Niagara, and the big fort at the Fórks of the
Ohio that England had renamed for William Pitt.

The Pontiac affair convinced London of two things: that some
version of the Proclamation Line had better be kept until the
Western Indians were pacified, and that it would be wise to enlarge the permanent garrison of British regulars stationed in
America. They therefore followed the boundary proclamation
with the announcement that the government was going to raise
the number of troops on duty in the colonies to 10,000—which
by past standards was a large number indeed.

This made sense in the wake of Pontiac, but it was noticed that
relatively few of the new regiments were to be stationed along the
frontier, where there were Indians to be overawed. They were ordered mostly to the seacoast—to overawe colonists, perhaps?
People were beginning to mutter. London might well have kept
in mind that some of the most substantial and influential men in
the colonies including both George Washington and Benjamin
Franklin, were interested in projects involving big land grants
in the now forbidden Ohio country . . . but it did not.

There was no great weight in any of these grievances, but they tell
something about basic attitudes. Clearly, the colonists at this moment were not looking ahead to independence, not even to
greater freedom; they were looking back to an era which, although they did not yet realize it, had ended when a new king
came to the throne in 1760: an era when the American colonies
were hardly governed at all and enjoyed a personal, down-to-

earth liberty so great that it went undefined. In the new attitude that began to be visible at London they felt that the freedom they already had might be under threat. Without quite realizing it, they had put a chip on the shoulder; things done in London would be examined with suspicious eyes. The colonists had never adjusted to the fact that as European ideas then ran, colonies existed for the sake of the homeland. They were there to be exploited, and the British were trying to exploit them, as if they were running a business rather than an empire; running it, unfortunately, with a bumbling incompetence that would have brought any business on earth to bankruptcy.

The next step came naturally, and suddenly the rising gusts began to blow with disturbing force. Facing a huge debt left by the Seven Years' War, Parliament was desperate for increased revenues, and America—where a good deal of the war debt had been incurred—seemed a logical source. So in 1764 there came a new Revenue Act, known here as the Sugar Act, which tried to raise money and plug up the customs leaks. It cut the duty on foreign molasses in half, or down to a level where the colonists could live with it, but it provided the kind of irritant they detested by tightening the collection machinery so that the new duty would actually be paid. The act of 1764 also extended duties on many other things and greatly lengthened the list of colonial products that could be exported nowhere except to England. All of this was natural enough, perfectly in line with the homeland's self-interest; it was time the national exchequer made something out of those rich American colonies. Yet the people who lived there were beginning to feel oppressed by such policies.

Then, on top of these grievances, came the Stamp Act; and all at once the inchoate colonial suspicions and resentments came together and for the first time the rising wind began to look dangerous.

The Stamp Act was avowedly a measure to raise money to defray "the expenses of defending, protecting and securing His Majesty's dominions in America." It required that every legal document, along with some that would not ordinarily be so classified, must bear a stamp to show that a tax had been paid. Transactions requiring stamps included almost everything that was put in writing and made a matter of record—commercial contracts, legal documents, newspapers, college degrees, even a license to run a tavern—and all of these were declared invalid if unstamped. It looked like a routine matter in London, which did badly need more revenue. But there were two points bound to create trouble.

In the first place, as Franklin pointed out, the tax was going to bear with especial weight on lawyers and publishers: "Every step in the law, every newspaper advertisement, is severely taxed." Going on from there, it irritated all clergymen, whose written sermons had to bear a stamp on each apostolic page; and it infuriated merchants and traders, who lived by deals that had to be written down and who now met the tax collector at every step in every transaction. Regardless of logic or justice, any tax measure which aroused the sustained and emotional opposition of the four groups that led in the formation of colonial opinion—lawyers, editors, ministers, and merchants—has to be ranked as a political blunder of colossal dimensions. A ministry that could devise and adopt a program of this kind was simply begging for trouble.

In the second place this represented a new method of raising money. So far the implicit understanding had been that Parliament would not impose direct taxes on the American colonies. Customs duties and trade restrictions were another matter; one might object to them if they were too heavy, but they embodied the exercise of what everybody considered a legitimate right of government. The Stamp Act was different. By its own preamble it was a money-raising devise pure and simple, voted by Parliament on its own hook, and one could argue that a right was being violated. No measure that raises taxes is ever popular with any people, in any country or at any time, and this one had the added handicap of introducing a disagreeable new tax by means which the people who were going to have to pay it considered illegal.

One of the things that made colonists feel like men was that only their own elected assemblies could impose direct taxes. This stamp tax was not only onerous; it was wrong. To resist it might well be a duty.

Here the colonists were following John Locke, who had written a scholarly justification for the Glorious Revolution of 1688 and laid down the principle that people should not be taxed without their consent. By this, of course, he meant the consent of Parliament as against the king, and he argued that the king had only certain specific powers; all the rest were reserved to the people through their representatives in Parliament. The colonists took this to mean that the people—themselves, in short—had certain natural rights which even Parliament, in which no colonist was represented, could not violate.

So now, to the intense surprise of government leaders who had supposed they were simply taking a routine step to raise money, the Stamp Act immediately kicked up a swirling storm. The colonists showed that they considered it an unendurable outrage, and they found a new slogan: "No taxation without representation!" Under this slogan they began to take direct action of unmistakable purport. In city after city—Boston, Newport, New York, Charleston—mobs went out and rioted, calling themselves Sons of Liberty and acting in notable harmony. They seemed to be composed of dock wallopers, sailors, and apprentices, but they clearly had been infiltrated by men of higher station often enough insultingly disguised in blackface. These mobs had heavy hands. They sacked the houses of customs officers, stamp distributors, and judges, hanged the king's officials in effigy, and forced the lieutenant governor of one province to take refuge on a warship. The Sons of Liberty in different towns kept in regular touch with each other, seeing to it that every flame of discontent was carefully nursed.

It was not just a matter of mobs. Oratory was also involved, and incendiary resolutions were voted by elected persons. In the Virginia House of Burgesses arose a fiery sprig named Patrick

Henry, who flung out a challenge that was to become famous. . . . Caesar, he pointed out, had Brutus, Charles I had Cromwell, and George III—and when certain shocked listeners interrupted him to declare this sort of talk treasonous, he blandly continued: ". . . . and George III may profit by their example." Then, bowing to one and all, he added that if this was treason they might make the most of it. Having spoken, he introduced certain resolutions, the chief one being an assertion that Virginians could be taxed only by their own assembly—to which was coupled a rider saying that anyone who denied this "shall be deemed an enemy of His Majesty's colony." Since His Majesty himself would unquestionably have denied it, this was perhaps a trifle strong, and the Burgesses passed the resolution but discarded the rider. (That made little difference: what went up and down the seaboard, via an effective communications system maintained by committees of correspondence and Sons of Liberty in each colony, was the unexpurgated version. Patriotic pulses beat faster.)

It had effects. The Massachusetts assembly called on all the colonies to meet in New York to consider united action, and in October 1765 the famous Stamp Act Congress convened on Manhattan Island, with ardent Christopher Gadsden of South Carolina calling on everyone to unite in defense of inalienable rights and crying: "There ought to be no more New England men, no New Yorkers, but all of us Americans!"

Just ten years had passed since the colonists had shown that not even fire and steel along the frontier or the threat of French armies and Indian allies sweeping in to destroy everything could make them take united action. Ten years, ending in a blissful peace . . . and now this, the thing Franklin had said could not happen. A powerful wind was blowing now, making waves big enough to be seen even from the banks of the Thames. The colonists were taking steps to unite. They were beginning hesitantly, reluctantly, but definitely to speak of themselves as Americans rather than as Englishmen, and they were willing to act. They demanded repeal of the Stamp Act. They passed a general declaration of rights insisting that only Americans could tax Americans, and they instituted a boycott of English-made goods. Talk of demanding representation in Parliament died down rather quickly; it was obvious that this was no remedy. Colonial representatives would be lost and outvoted at Westminster, taxes would be passed over their objections, and the great Lockean slogan would no longer serve. Stamp Act Congress, declaration of rights, boycott—what really mattered was that an act of Parliament had done what fire and murder on the frontier had not done; it had forced the colonists to realize, however imperfectly, that they had a common cause and ought to join hands. As omens go, this one was striking.

It was the violence of the colonial response that puzzled London—as indeed it puzzled Franklin himself, who felt that it would have been better to submit to the tax and work for its repeal. He and his associates, he wrote, had opposed passage of the act but they might as well have tried to keep the sun from setting: "But since 'tis down, my friend, and it may be long before it rises again, let us make as good a night of it as we can. We may still light candles."

Any doubts he may have had he expressed privately. When Parliament summoned him, as American agent in London, before the Bar of the House, he bluntly told the members that the colonists would never pay the tax "unless compelled by force of arms." Even that, he continued, probably would not work, and he posed a question to which the government was quite unable to find an answer: "Suppose a military force sent into America, they will find nobody in arms; and what are they then to do? They cannot force a man to take stamps who chooses to do without them. They will not find a rebellion; they may indeed make one."

The Stamp Act did not have a long life. King George was not at all moved by the colonial uproar, but he had come to feel that he could get along without his Prime Minister, George Grenville, whose desire to balance the budget had led him to cut down the king's civil list as well as impose a new direct tax on the colonies, and Grenville gave way to the Marquis of Rockingham. Rockingham learned that the merchants of London disliked the Stamp Act because the boycott voted by the Stamp Act Congress was reducing their profits; and in March 1766 Parliament formally repealed the law—passing a companion act that firmly asserted their right to tax the colonies even though (for the moment) the right was not being exercised.

When news of the repeal reached America it set off a great rejoicing. Parliament's assertion of its right to tax was ignored; what mattered was that the hated tax was withdrawn, and all up and down the coast people went out in the streets to celebrate— doing it all the more enthusiastically, perhaps, because the measures taken against the act had come a good deal closer to outright rebellion than most colonists were then prepared to go. All of this jubilation, it was noted, centered about renewed expressions of affection for King George III. Parliament had done an oppressive thing, but the wise monarch had brought about a reversal; in New York a grateful public paid for and erected a statue to this beloved king. (Ten years later the same public would pull the statue down and melt its metal to make bullets with which to shoot the king's soldiers.)

This outpouring of affection for the Crown was the surface indication of a misunderstanding that was fundamental to the entire American Revolution.

To an increasing extent the colonists were coming to look on themselves as bound to the Empire by their loyalty to the king. They were not represented in Parliament—could not practically be represented in it, did not really want to be, and in any case were not—and they felt that they owed Parliament little or nothing. They were the king's subjects and they wanted to remain so, but they were not subject to Parliament. What they were actually looking for, although the term had not yet been invented, was dominion status. Franklin had already outlined the idea, and both Thomas Jefferson and John Adams would do so before 1776 brought in a hardier concept, and it was clearly what more and more Americans were thinking about. They rioted, orated, and passed inflammatory acts against Parliament; it was the king who would make things right and hold everything together.

Now this feeling was becoming dominant just when the king was contriving to make Parliament his own instrument. He had perceived that Parliament was controlled by the Whigs and he understood how this was done, and he had worked patiently to set up controls of his own, forming a bloc of members known as the King's Friends who, through judicious use of royal patronage and outright bribery, would eventually have a balance of power in the House of Commons. The restrictive acts which, as the colonists saw them, were infringing on the liberties of the king's subjects were to a large extent the king's; in the years ahead they would be increasingly so, until finally delusions vanished. King George, not as a tyrant but simply as a monarch who had found out how the government was run, was ultimately the man against whom the colonists would rebel.

The results of this were far-reaching. The colonies had already affirmed that they owed Parliament neither loyalty nor accountability; once they discovered that the bonds which they considered so oppressive ran direct to the throne, they had no place to go—except the amazing road that ran from Bunker Hill past Independence Hall to Yorktown and The World Turned Upside Down. Hardly anyone had planned any of this, but there it was. The king had stepped into the line of fire and got hit by missiles that had really been aimed at a different target. The heartfelt rejoicings of 1766 had strange echoes.

For about a year there was comparative quiet. The Rockingham ministry was of short life and soon gave way to one headed by the great Pitt, a known friend of America. But Pitt's health failed and he left, the government falling into the control of the Chancellor of the Exchequer, an incomprehensible lightweight named Charles Townshend. He inherited two problems

—the perennial need for more revenues and the silently mutinous conduct of the New York assembly, which refused to vote money for the upkeep of the British garrison maintained there. Townshend dealt with the second one offhand, by putting through a measure suspending the New York assembly until it returned to obedience. (Americans saw this as a threat to liberty, although actually Townshend had had to resist an indignant faction in Commons that wanted him to send in the army and navy to knock the New Yorkers' heads together.) Then he remarked airily that it was easy enough to get money out of the colonies if you just went at it right: they objected bitterly to direct taxes but did not in the least mind paying indirect ones, and so he would raise the needed revenue by a new set of customs laws. Apparently he either had learned nothing at all from the Stamp Act furor or had learned the wrong lesson.

The Townshend Acts were fairly ferocious. They raised the import duties on a long list of items, from glass to paint to paper and tea, set up an American board of customs commissioners responsible directly to London, and reconstituted the writs of assistance which had caused James Otis to flame so brightly. The preamble stated flatly that the purpose was to meet the cost of administering justice and supporting civil government in America; in addition it announced that appointed officials and judges would draw salaries from London, which of course meant that these officials would feel compelled to heed what London said and need pay no attention to colonial assemblies. So here was taxation without representation all over again, in a sharper form than ever. By this time colonial leaders had developed fairly sensitive antennae for such points, and they took due note. Among those who took note was a singular genius named Samuel Adams.

Sam Adams had had much to do with the birth, growth, and activity of the Sons of Liberty, and had helped create the committee network that kept intercolonial correspondence circulating; all in all he was as dangerous an enemy to British rule as the North American continent then contained. An odd figure altogether, he had not enough voice to be an orator and not enough muscle to be a fighter. He was unable to keep his own affairs in order or even to support himself unaided—but he was a consummate revolutionist, one who knew how to bring on trouble and how to evoke the desired response to it, understanding propaganda and the uses of the "spontaneous demonstration" as well as any man who ever lived. The Townshend Acts played right into his hands, and when the customs men seized a ship owned by rich John Hancock a spontaneous demonstration immediately broke out on the Boston wharf where this ship was moored. A mob unloaded the ship's untaxed cargo in spirited defiance of authority, and the city's top customs official fled to Castle William, a fort on an island in the harbor. Then Adams went persuasively to work on members of the Massachusetts assembly, who did not need much persuasion anyway, and that body promptly denounced the Townshend Acts as taxation without representation, asserted that Crown officials must not be independent of colonial control, and invited the other colonial assemblies to endorse these sentiments.

Reaction in London was prompt and ill advised. The Massachusetts assembly was declared dissolved, and assemblies in other colonies were told to ignore the Massachusetts circular or be dissolved likewise—an order to which they paid very little attention—and eight warships and two regiments of regulars were sent to Boston to let Massachusetts know that there was a law in the land. This step was self-defeating. Before long even the British government could see that the cost of maintaining this force in Boston was far greater than the total revenue the Townshend Acts could possibly produce, and at last—in March 1770—Parliament repealed the acts en bloc, retaining only, at the king's request, the tax on tea just to show that the basic right to tax was not being abandoned.

Too little and too late. The British regulars were not popular among Bostonians, who looked on them as brutal instruments of tyranny and jeered at them as lobster-backs; and on the evening of March 5 a soldier doing sentry go in front of the Customs House was pelted with snowballs, rocks, and insulting epithets until at last he called out the guard. A couple of squads came to the rescue with loaded muskets and fixed bayonets, and with hundreds of angry men all around yelling and taunting and throwing things it was inevitable that some soldier would eventually fire his musket in reply. The shot rang out, other soldiers also fired, the crowd screamed and cursed and drew away . . . and four civilians lay dead on the pavement, two others had wounds of which they would die, and Sam Adams had another ball to field. Up and down the coast went the news: there had been a massacre in Boston, with ruthless mercenaries firing on peaceful citizens, pavements running with blood, and could any patriot consider this without feeling profoundly outraged?

Some patriots could, as a matter of fact. The soldiers were brought to trial and no less a patriot then John Adams, Sam's more balanced cousin (and in the end equally dangerous to the king's rule in America), appeared as counsel for the defense. The soldiers were acquitted; but Cousin Sam did not even stop for breath. He played the incident for all it was worth, and on each March 5 for years to come there would be parades, oration, and breast beating by Sons of Liberty all along the coast. The Boston Massacre lives on to this day as a grim reminder of the way innocent men can be persecuted by the minions of oppression.

The Boston Massacre was important as a fulcrum for the lever of propaganda, and as one more sign that opinion and emotion on both sides were hardening. Franklin, who missed nothing, looked past the riot to the intent back of the Townshend Acts, and from London wrote soberly to James Otis and Samuel Adams: "I think one may clearly see, in the system of customs to be exacted in America, by act of Parliament, the seeds sown of a total disunion of the two countries, though as yet that event may be at a considerable distance." All in all, the distance was not so great;

immeasurably shortened, in the spring of 1772, by direct action-
ists in Rhode Island, who saw in the customs acts precisely what
Franklin had seen. There was in Narragansett Bay a British revenue cutter, H.M.S. *Gaspee,* which under command of a lieutenant
in the royal navy had been diligently enforcing the customs laws
in an area which had not previously seen enough enforcement to
amount to anything; and one June evening while chasing a smug-
gler *Gaspee* ran hard aground on a sand bar a few miles south of
Providence. Out from nowhere came small boats full of smug-
gler-patriots, who swarmed aboard the revenue cutter, overpowered her officers and crew, sent them all ashore, and then
burned the hated instrument of tyranny to the water's edge.

The authorities of course responded by sending in ships and
men to search the waves and beat the bushes for the guilty parties,
who if taken would be sent to England for trial and would unquestionably be hanged. The authorities could catch no one, but
the manhunt aroused all of the patriot agitators. They rightly
supposed that if smugglers could be taken to London and hanged
they themselves might one day be served the same way, and here
was more ammunition for Sam Adams, who saw that all the colonies were told about this new menace. He got an especially
strong response from Virginia, where the assembly quickly
named a committee of correspondence (composed of Patrick
Henry, Thomas Jefferson, and Richard Henry Lee) to keep in
touch with the other colonies and raise the alarm whenever tyranny showed itself. This was probably the best support Adams
ever got, and soon there were committees at work in twelve colonies. Before long they had a great deal to do.

For now the king's ministry (led by a well-intentioned mediocrity named Lord North, Townshend having died) moved on
to take one of those steps which seem perfectly logical but which
ignore political realities so completely that they can only be described as acts of immense folly. Repealing Townshend's customs laws, Parliament had retained a tax on tea as symbol of its
right to tax the colonies; upon learning that the British East India

Company was in financial trouble, the ministry permitted tea to enter England duty free and gave the company a monopoly on the export of tea to the colonies. Since it would pay no duty the company product figured to sell more cheaply in America than any other brand . . . but Americans took a different view of the matter. As a monopoly, company tea could eventually sell for as high a price as the company might wish to charge. And besides, it was one more proof that what the colonists wanted in the way of imports, duties, and taxes generally had no relation at all to what they were likely to get.

So the corresponding committees got busy, good patriots proclaimed this tea business a hateful imposition, and when the monopoly's ships came in they got a bad reception. In Charleston the tea was unloaded but kept under bond in a warehouse. In Philadelphia and New York the ships were not allowed to unload, and they presently turned about and sailed for England. In Boston the atmosphere was equally frigid, but when the captains of the three ships prepared to weigh anchor the governor refused to grant clearance papers and the ships had to stay where they were, unable to do anything but wait helplessly for catastrophe.

Here was an open invitation to Sam Adams and his Sons of Liberty, who did not need to be invited twice. What promptly happened—on the night of December 6, 1773—was a gaudy uprising half humorous and half grim, that passed at once into living legend and also touched off the sequence of events that would turn Franklin's gathering storm into a hurricane: the Boston Tea Party, which saw patriots imperfectly and derisively disguised as redskins boarding the company's ships, lugging chests of tea up from the hold, and flinging them into the harbor, all to the tune of gay shouts, cheers, and a general chesty tarry-hooting around. The irrevocable act had at last been committed.

The tea party was the kind of destructive, defiant challenge that no government could ignore, and London responded with vigor. In the spring of 1774 Parliament passed the so-called Coercive Acts (promptly renamed Intolerable Acts by indignant patriots) and summoned the full might of the Empire to stamp out this teapot rebellion. The Coercive Acts began with the Boston Port Act, which closed the port until the tea was paid for and the king was satisfied that peace and obedience to law had been restored. A second act tightened government and administrative controls in Massachusetts, making colonial council, judges, sheriffs, and justices of the peace royal appointees to serve during the king's pleasure. A third was the Quartering Act, under which a royal governor could take over private houses anywhere he chose for lodging troops. King George was putting his sovereignty on the line; he told Lord North that the colonists now must either submit or triumph.

The colonists had no intention of submitting. The significance of the Intolerable Acts lies in the speed and intensity of the response to them: an all but automatic response, owing nothing to the plans and organizations of any revolutionists but coming straight from the hearts of people who had been aroused beyond the point of restraint. Massachusetts promptly set up a provincial assembly which in no time found itself governing just about the whole Bay Colony outside of Boston—an utterly illegal but highly effective instrument devised by men who in time of crisis turned instinctively to the processes of self-government. Other colonies made the cause of Massachusetts their own; most notably Virginia, whose House of Burgesses passed a resolution drafted by Jefferson, Patrick Henry, Richard Henry Lee, and George Mason denouncing the British occupation of Boston as a hostile invasion. When Governor Dunmore dissolved this seditious assembly the members immediately reconvened—unofficially, as completely illegal as the Massachusetts body—and set up committees to bring on united action. These Virginians had the support of their constituents. In Fairfax County a meeting presided over by George Washington pledged its support and declared that closing the port of Boston was "an attack on all British America." Earlier, Washington had written to George Mason saying that Britain was trying to subvert American freedom and that the colonists must act "to maintain the liberty which we have derived from our ancestors."

All the roads now began to converge. Illegal colonial assemblies met, denounced, and resolved, and their illegal instruments kept in touch and made one instrument out of many: there was a great meeting in Philadelphia, early in September 1774, delegates from far and near coming now to that unity of action which Franklin had considered impossible without vast stupidity at London, a brimming cup of which had recently been supplied . . . calling themselves, these delegates, the First Continental Congress.

CHAPTER 15

Truth Made Self-evident

THE WORDS men choose can say more than they seem to say. This was the *Continental* Congress, which suggests that the men convening and the men who sent them were beginning to see something portentous. They were not just discontented colonists, meeting as a colonial convention to demand settlement of grievances. They were men of a continent, with a new world at their disposal, and the very size of the great land mass and the fact that they saw themselves as its people was indication that they wanted something which the Empire could never give them. A little later on, Thomas Paine summed it up in words that expressed what more and more Americans were coming to feel: "'Tis not the affair of a city, a country, a province or a kingdom, but of a continent—of at least one-eighth part of the habitable globe." Some Englishmen saw it too, among them one William Eden, who came to Philadelphia three years later as member of an abortive peace mission. "It is impossible," Eden wrote a friend, "to give you any adequate idea of the vast scale of this country. I know little more of it than I saw in coming 150 miles up the Delaware; but I know enough to regret most heartily that our rulers instead of making the tour of Europe did not finish their education by a voyage round the coasts and rivers of the western side of the Atlantic."

The Continental Congress met and did what the occasion made possible. It had before it a bill drafted by Joseph Warren and passed by the Massachusetts assembly, which formally declared the Coercive Acts void and without substance, advised Massachusetts to establish itself as a free state, and urged the people to arm themselves. This bill the Continental Congress adopted and made its own, along with another designed to halt all trade with England. Then, on October 24, 1774, it adjourned, declaring that a Second Continental Congress would convene on May 10, 1775, to consider whether London was doing anything substantial about adjusting colonial grievances.

Things were moving faster now, and they had passed the point of no return. In the early winter of 1775 the Earl of Chatham (Pitt, friend of America, fighting against a dominant majority and against the decay of his own mind and body) introduced in Parliament a bill that would have given the colonists just about everything they asked. If the bill had passed, the Revolution probably would not have taken place . . . but it was quickly, irretrievably defeated. Parliament followed Lord North, who talked broadly of reconciliation but let the Intolerable Acts stand and reaffirmed the right to tax and after firing Franklin as postmaster general had his emissaries do their clumsy best to bribe him—so that Franklin, angry and disgusted, declared there was no chance for reconciliation, returned to America, and became one of the most radical of patriots, deadly because he had twice the capacity of any Englishman who opposed him. (It is possible to feel sorry for George III. At the high crisis in his country's affairs he was served by men like Townshend, North, Germain, and the incomparable Earl of Sandwich; who had to match wits with Adams, Franklin, Jefferson, Lee, Mason, and Washington. If ever men were woefully, shockingly overmatched, the king's ministers were, for a crucial decade.)

And General Thomas Gage, commander of the king's troops

in North America, who had been named captain general and governor-in-chief over contumacious Massachusetts and had put the Boston Port Act into effect, felt that if London yielded now it would lose its sovereignty altogether. England, Gage went on, would be better without colonies than to accept the terms the colonists were demanding, and he bluntly told his superiors in London: "It appears to me that you are now making your final efforts respecting America; if you yield, I conceive that you have not a spark of authority remaining over this country." There could be no peace, he added, until the Boston patriot leaders had been sent to England as prisoners.

Gage does not come down to this generation in very clear focus. We never quite *see* the man, and at times he seems nothing more than the total embodiment of the traditional military man who knew of only one solution, the vigorous use of unmeasured force, to solve the problems of empire at a time when empire and its possibilities were undergoing profound change. He plays his unhappy part just as the great story begins to take on its grade school textbook quality and becomes a succession of scenes from old battle paintings set off by names and phrases that have worn their way to the depths of the American subconscious. He somehow remains offstage, blocked out by shapes from a pageant everyone saw in childhood and kept, unforgettable, underneath every other national memory.

Gage had the quite sensible idea that if the government used force it must be sure to use enough force, and he saw that although occupied Boston was under control the rest of the colony was answerable only to that provincial assembly which in his view had no right to exist at all. He believed that "the troops must march into the country" if British power were to be maintained, and he began to prepare for such a move.

Massachusetts militia then was answerable to the provincial assembly's committee of safety, whose chairman was John Hancock, and this committee had been setting up in various militia units special groups known as Minute Men—expected, as the name suggests, to turn out, armed, on a minute's notice. Noting that Gage's army was beginning to move about, the committee concluded that when as many as 500 British soldiers appeared on any road outside of Boston it would mean that Gage was making a real effort to enforce the Intolerable Acts. In that case, it decreed, a colonial army of observation should be set up, and in a surge of pious hope it held that this army would act wholly on the defensive as long as it seemed reasonable for it to do so.

Gage had been busy trying to identify the men responsible for the Boston Tea Party and other seditious disturbances, and he had learned enough to convince himself that he chiefly wanted to arrest Sam Adams and John Hancock, who were thought to be hiding in or near the town of Lexington. He had also learned that the colonists had a store of powder and other military supplies concealed at Concord, which was not far from Lexington; and on April 15, 1775, he set up a marching column of some 700 light infantry drawn from several different battalions, with competent Major John Pitcairn of the marines in command. A plan for the guidance of these men was drawn up, good patriots learned of it, and on the night of April 18–19 two lanterns were hoisted in the steeple of Old North Church in Boston and Paul Revere began a ride—to sound the alarm, to set the Minute Men in motion, to summon spirits from the vasty deep, and to warn the provincial authorities that the king's troops were at last moving to that use of force which would change everything.

And now history becomes legend, taking shape first on the village green at Lexington, where there was a great confrontation which we know about before we even start reading. *Disperse ye Rebels . . . If they mean to have a war let it begin here . . .* and the volley that sent sparks straight to the magazine, six patriots lying dead on the grass, redcoats marching off for Concord and hard news going out to meet the Minute Men shivering their way along the country roads in the early light of dawn. Then a greater confrontation at Concord, where a rude bridge arched a placid New England stream and patriots for the first time fired on the king's soldiers and saw them fall dead, untaught mercenaries who had come three thousand miles to keep the past upon its throne; and the start of the long retreat, with the whole countryside alive with Minute Men behind stone walls, hiding back of trees and barns, fading back when the regulars broke out to charge them, coming together again farther on, making Major Pitcairn's march a nightmare that moved through a tantalizing, irregular fire storm that went beyond the teachings of formalized European warfare. In the end Gage sent out reinforcements, so that the column numbered perhaps 2,000 men, but they could not halt and make a regular battle out of it because the colonists refused to fight that way and the retreat continued, exhausting and ignominious, until the soldiers were back in Boston where the colonials dared not follow them. And off to the south went men from those committees of correspondence, carrying the word to New York and Philadelphia, to Virginia and South Carolina, that the main event had begun.

Looking back, we see the Revolution moving at top speed once patriots had fired on the king's troops. Actually it still moved very slowly, guided by events rather than by conscious thought. For a time it was formless, adrift on a current that could be neither resisted nor clearly understood. Minute Men and other colonial militia swarmed out to lay siege to Boston, or at least to surround it and confine the redcoats to its peninsula, yet this encircling army—really, a haphazard collection of untrained troops—which was defying royal authority was itself an orphan, responsible only to the Massachusetts provincial assembly, whose authority was tenuous but for the moment the only authority in sight. Nobody knew what these volunteer soldiers were supposed to do, a clear program being non-existent. Obviously, much would depend on the British response; on that, and on the doings of the faraway Second Continental Congress, which was to meet at Philadelphia on May 10 . . . on these, and on what the men of the suddenly embattled colonies really had at the bottom of their minds.

The British acted predictably. The response had begun to take shape before the news of Lexington and Concord reached London. Gage was powerfully reinforced, receiving troops that brought his strength up to 10,000 men; reinforced less powerfully by a top dressing of generals—Generals Sir William Howe, John Burgoyne, and Henry Clinton, with whom the colonists were about to get much better acquainted. Gage and these officers came to the obvious conclusion: the armed rabble that encircled them must be driven off, the troops to do it were at hand, and it was time for a showdown. This resolution came to a head when the armed rabble crossed Charleston neck on the night of June 16–17 and fortified Breed's Hill, a moderate height overlooking Boston Harbor. If cannon were planted there British ships would have to leave, and Gage could do nothing less than strike before this was done.

Meanwhile the Continental Congress learned about Lexington and Concord; learned also that a mixed New England force led by Ethan Allen and Benedict Arnold—two uncontrollable characters, if American military history contains any such—had seized the decaying British stronghold at Ticonderoga overlooking Lake Champlain, seizing thereby a gateway to Canada and also a great many cannon which would be most useful in the lines around Boston. A war of some indefinable sort had clearly begun, and Congress moved to adopt the army before Boston (the expression is John Adams') and on Adams' motion named George Washington to command it. Adams had the sound idea that to give the struggle a continental cast it would be well to put a Virginian in charge of the troops in New England, a move which disjointed the nose of the eminent John Hancock, who had supposed himself slated for this command. Congress also approved a plan to send an army north to seize Quebec and conquer Canada.

Having taken these warlike acts, Congress then formally announced that it was not raising armies "with ambitious designs of separation from Great Britain and establishing independent states," asserted that it had been forced to choose between submission to ministerial tyranny or resistance by force, and insisted that it was fighting the ministerial army and not the army of King George. Washington's appointment was in line with this declaration, serving notice that when it came to fighting the matter would be in the hands of a conservative of impeccable social standing rather than a hotheaded troublemaker like Sam Adams or Patrick Henry. Washington set off for Boston on June 23, 1775, and had gone only a short distance when he met galloping couriers bearing news that there had been a great fight at Bunker Hill.

Bunker Hill was a battle about which no one had thought clearly. The patriots fought it in the wrong place and the British fought it in the wrong way—and suddenly a confused uprising had turned into a major war that could not end without ending many other things as well. Seeking to deny Boston Harbor to British shipping, the patriots had moved on past Bunker Hill, a considerable height that would have served perfectly, to occupy lower, more exposed Breed's Hill. The British might have dislodged them easily enough by moving around to seize Charleston neck, but some sullen instinct for an outright collision—coupled probably with an angry desire to prove that no armed rabble could stand up to the king's troops in a fair fight —led them to make a reckless frontal assault on good marksmen protected by entrenchments. The mistake was terribly expensive. The New England farmers were as good as any soldiers alive under such conditions, and the British attack was thrown back with shocking casualties. In the end, colonial ammunition running low, the hill was taken, but the British had lost more than 1,000 men out of 2,000 in action: close to 50 per cent, an almost unheard-of figure for eighteenth-century warfare. (Among the dead was Major Pitcairn, who had led the Lexington-Concord thrust.) American losses were much smaller, some 440 out of 3,200 engaged, and although such revered patriots as Joseph Warren were killed American morale was high. Technically the British had won a victory, but in sober fact they had had a disaster. The Americans had shown that they could fight regular troops (under proper conditions) and they had the British tightly cooped up in Boston—the only place in all New England where royal authority could still be exerted.

Washington arrived in due time, and at Cambridge on July 2 he assumed command of the assembled militia. There were at that moment some 15,000 of them, although there was a great deal of coming and going and it was hard to keep an exact account; and now the army was the creature of the Continental Congress, not just of the provincial legislature. Significantly, it took on a new name, which it was to make great: from now on this was the Continental Army, and Washington's first task was to turn it from an informal convocation of militia units into an organized fighting force.

Washington's would-be army consisted chiefly but by no means entirely of Massachusetts men. New Hampshire had sent a strong contingent with a good leader, Colonel John Stark; 3,000 men from Connecticut were present, accompanied by tense, impatient Benedict Arnold, Rhode Island sent troops under a gifted amateur soldier, Nathanael Greene, who at war's end would stand second only to Washington in military stature. In an army that was strictly impromptu a bright amateur could rise fast: another one was a fat Boston bookseller, Henry Knox, whose innocent hobby had been the study of writings on military engineering. He made himself a military engineer now, laying out the entrenched lines by which the new army kept the British locked up in Boston, doing it so well that Washington marked him for a more active command.

Washington's first job was to get things organized along military lines. Many patriots objected to tight control on principle, and objected most bitterly unless they themselves got proper recognition; Washington confessed privately that he had never seen or imagined such scheming, chicanery, and selfishness, adding that if he had foreseen it nothing on earth would have led him to accept the top command. Still, the job got done, and in public

Washington was as serene and unperturbed as a commanding general need be. He was also aggressive, seeing the war as something much bigger than the lines around Boston. By order of Congress a force led by General Richard Montgomery was advancing on Montreal from Ticonderoga, with an eye to the conquest of Canada. (A good patriot would have said that this would enable Canada to join her sister colonies in striking down British oppression, a thing which as it turned out the Canadians had no desire to do. All but a handful of them were French-speaking Catholics, and King George had won their loyalty by a toleration act which guaranteed them full freedom to retain their language, folkways, and religion without molestation. New England was full of militant Protestants who considered this an outrage and were vocal about it; they were equally vexed because the king had extended Quebec's boundaries to include the whole trans-Appalachian West. The Canadians saw no reason whatever to join hands with them.) Washington wanted to strengthen this blow, and in the late summer of 1775 he sent 1,000 men up through the Maine wilderness under Arnold, who was to meet Montgomery on the St. Lawrence and join him in an assault on Quebec.

One contingent in Arnold's force was significant merely by its presence: two or three companies of riflemen from the Pennsylvania and Virginia back country. They were led by a huge, powerful, hot-tempered man named Daniel Morgan, a former wagoner from the Virginia frontier, who nursed a personal grievance against the British because during the French war he had had an argument with a British officer, had knocked the man down, and had been brutally flogged for it. The scars were still on his back, and now here he was leading Virginians and Pennsylvanians brigaded with New Englanders on a march to Canada: verily the great wind Franklin had talked about was blowing now, and the joint colonial action impossible fifteen years earlier had become a reality.

—□—

During all of this the warring colonists believed—or at least told themselves and others, in all sincerity—that they were firmly loyal to King George and were fighting simply to regain the liberties which his ministers had so basely taken away from them. Washington himself, when he reached Cambridge, expected to be back home in Virginia by the end of the year. Jefferson wrote (just before the invasion of Canada began) that he looked forward to a full reconciliation with Great Britain, and John Adams said that as late as October 1775 he could find no one in the Continental Congress who really wanted independence. Yet independence was proclaimed, fought for, and won by the very men who believed they were doing something else. Why?

In part, because George III saw what was going on better than the patriots did. On August 23, 1775, he issued a proclamation saying that the Americans were in "open and avowed rebellion" against his authority. Subjects who shot more than 1,000 of his soldiers in order to possess a hill from which they could drive his ships out of one of his own harbors did not strike him as loyal, especially when they followed this by sending an army far beyond their own borders to conquer a colony whose people had shown no signs of discontent. When the proclamation reached America men began to realize that they were in fact rebels, their protestations of loyalty blown to shreds by volleys fired down the slopes of that little hill overlooking Boston Harbor. If they were not talking about independence, people in London were talking about it, assuming with logic that men who behaved as the colonists were behaving had cut their old ties. Whatever they may have thought they were doing, they had in fact committed themselves.

Events carried people along. Shortly after the first of the year —1776, one of history's greatest years—the Continental Congress got several bits of news. It learned that Parliament, taking its cue from the king, had forbidden all trade with the rebellious colonies and declared all colonial ships lawful prizes with the crews subject to impressment in the royal navy. Congress also learned that the invasion of Canada had failed. Montgomery had taken Montreal, and after an incredible march through the wilderness Arnold had joined him near Quebec. On the stormy night and cold dawn of December 30–31, 1775, they had advanced through blinding snow flurries to make their assault. Montgomery had been killed, Arnold wounded, Morgan captured (to be exchanged later), and what was left of the exhausted little force was in full retreat to Ticonderoga.

Then from General Washington came news that the reorganization of the army had gone better than anyone really had a right to expect. His problem had been prodigious; he had had to disband one force and raise another in the immediate presence, as he pointed out, "of the flower of the British army," and he had done remarkably well. His new army, by mid-January 1776, contained more than 8,000 men, sworn to serve the Continental Congress instead of separate colonies. Their powers and their orders would come from that Congress; so would their food, clothing, ammunition and (if they ever got any) their pay. Of these men, some 5,582 were present for duty, and although this number was inadequate the deficiencies could be met for the time being by calling up various militia units. Meanwhile, determined to drive the British out of Boston, Washington had sent bookseller Henry Knox to Ticonderoga to fetch the artillery captured the summer before. Knox did this neatly despite heavy snows and a total absence of good roads, and from now on he was a gunner: the best artillerist in the Continental Army had begun his new career.

On the heels of this, King George laid his own ax to the ties that bound his unhappy subjects to him by announcing (so that the colonists could hear) that he had contracted with certain petty rulers east of the Rhine to hire regiments of German mercenaries for use in America. And while the members of Congress were digesting this, a displaced English scribbler named Thomas Paine brought out a pamphlet entitled "Common Sense."

Paine was in his thirties, a malcontent who had been employed in the British excise service, had been fired, and had agitated without success for higher pay for excise men. In 1774 Franklin detected a useful flame in the man and sent him to America bearing letters of introduction. He had been writing for different publishers in Pennsylvania since then, and now he had written a pamphlet which said what a great many people were beginning to think and said it with a passionate intensity that helped turn a drift in men's thoughts into a firm resolve. Paine derided the notion that a mere island should control a continent. Addressing himself to "ye that dare oppose not only tyranny but the tyrant," he argued that freedom beyond the Atlantic had been dispossessed and called on Americans to "prepare an asylum for mankind." Closing, he had flung out a line which he called on his fellows to adopt and make their own — "the free and independent states of America."

With that line soaring as a descant over the plainsong of things done as planned, events moved even faster. Knox got his guns to Washington's army and Washington planted them on Dorchester Heights, a commanding elevation which the British had incomprehensibly left unoccupied all these months, and this did what the occupation of Breed's Hill had been supposed to do: it made Boston Harbor an impossible anchorage for the king's ships. British commander in Boston now was Sir William Howe, Gage having been recalled after Bunker Hill, and Howe realized that the jig was up. On March 17, 1776, the British army and navy sailed for Halifax, to get reinforcements and devise a new strategy. (Going north with them were several hundred Massachusetts loyalists, who preferred King George to the Continental Congress.) Americans rejoiced over a great victory, Congress voted Washington its thanks and a gold medal, and Harvard made him a doctor of laws.

And elsewhere, some 1,000 hastily assembled patriots in North Carolina fell upon and savagely defeated a larger Tory force — already those loyal to the Crown were dubbed Tories — which had tried to march to the coast in the belief that an army of redcoats was about to arrive by sea. The Carolina back country was full of Scottish Highlanders who had fought under Bonnie Prince Charlie against George II, had fled to the New World after Culloden, and had settled in the rich interior valleys east of the Blue Ridge. There their resentment of discriminatory treatment at the hands of the seaboard patricians who ran North Carolina quickly displaced the lingering Jacobite resentments against the House of Hanover, and within a generation these ex-Highlanders and some of their fellow frontiersmen had become staunch supporters of George III. The back country was getting, as they viewed it, unfair taxes, corrupt justice, inadequate representation, and generally a bad deal, and in the 1760s they had challenged Eastern authority in an uprising known as the Regulator Movement. The Regulators had been dispersed after a brief skirmish but the resentments had smoldered on, and now that the hated Carolina establishment was lining up behind the patriot cause a great many of these unforgiving Westerners became ardent loyalists. But there were patriots in frontier Carolina too, and enough of these had stolen a march on their loyalist neighbors to give them a drubbing at the obscure battle of Moore's Creek—and the chance that western Carolina would become an impregnable Tory stronghold was gone. It produced Tories but no stronghold, and five years later Cornwallis broke the back of the king's cause trying to regain what the Highlanders and Regulators had lost at the very outset of the war.

By now the decisive step had to be taken. Early in May the Virginia assembly instructed Virginia's delegates in Congress to work for a declaration that the United Colonies were free. On June 7, accordingly, Richard Henry Lee rose to move "that these United Colonies are and of right ought to be free and independent states." Four days later Congress named a committee to prepare a declaration of independence: Roger Sherman of Connecticut, Robert R. Livingston of New York, Benjamin Franklin, John Adams, Thomas Jefferson. By common consent the drafting of the document fell to Jefferson, with interlineations and excisions by the others, and by July they were ready. On July 2 Congress took its stand, adopting Lee's resolution and asserting flatly that the colonies were absolved of their allegiance to the British Crown and that "all political connection between them and the State of Great Britain is, and ought to be, totally dissolved."

There remained the formal Declaration, and for several hours the Congress went over Jefferson's text word by word and line by line, making alterations here and there. Knocked out of this assertion of man's unlimited right to freedom was Jefferson's denunciation of Negro slavery as an "assemblage of horrors" for which King George was to be blamed. The king, clearly, was not at fault here, and anyway a great many of the delegates, including Jefferson himself, were slaveholders, and all in all the question of extending the principle of equality to the chattels who toiled so usefully in the fields was a bit more than the men of that era were ready to face. Face it men had to, but for the moment it was evaded. Aside from this the original document was approved with its powerful cadences unimpaired. And on July 4 a great bell was rung, with far-reaching echoes; and riding over these echoes were the words that moved further and grew ever more resonant, tossing the empires of the world into a mighty solvent and opening an endless road. . . .

"We hold these truths to be self-evident, that all men are created equal, . . . endowed by their Creator with certain unalienable Rights, that among these are Life, Liberty and the pursuit of Happiness." So governments got their authority from "the consent of the governed" and from nowhere else, and when a government destroyed those enumerated rights "it is the Right of the People to alter or to abolish it." Men are still acting on those words, and they always will. The idea has lost none of its power.

In a strange but logical way these powerful words came out of a ferment that had long been working. For about a generation the colonies had been experiencing their own version of a contest that had been taking place all over Western Europe: a conflict between aristocratic and democratic theories of society. The elite groups in every country—hereditary nobles, landed gentry, wealthy burghers, men in high office—had been trying to increase their power and privileges and close their ranks. At the same time outsiders—intellectuals, a few disaffected aristocrats, and a number of aspiring middle-class types who saw themselves being frozen out of the establishment—were demanding a more open society and a redistribution of power along more democratic lines. (The very poorest classes were not being heard from, but the debate had implications for them.)

What brought the debate to a head was the reassertion of a third force—that of central authority, which nearly everywhere in Europe meant the monarch. The Seven Years' War had been costly, kings needed more money, and there were innumerable disputes (as the colonists could testify) about who would pay how much and at whose command; most countries witnessed a contest over taxes and related questions between the central governments and the privileged orders. Not infrequently it was the Crown that came to stand for liberal reforms—notably of the tax structure, in a drive to remove upper-class exemptions—and in such cases the aspiring democratic elements might align themselves with the rulers. But in the colonies the aristocracy, in the name of resisting centralized tyranny, invoked "liberties" in the name of "the people" and thereby courted the outsiders. (They were egged on here, ironically, by the British Parliament, many of whose members were outspokenly critical of the way King George was acquiring power and influence in the House of Commons.)

With provincial elites invoking broad popular rights and liberties in their resistance to British tax laws, it is hardly surprising that "the people," thus encouraged, began to come outside and look around. And presently the colonial upper classes found themselves in the not overly comfortable position of leading a popular uprising which eventually became an outright revolution against legally constituted authority. When it got down to cases, in 1775, many of the elite were so scared by what they saw or sensed on the other side of the chasm that they turned back and reaffirmed their loyalty to England and the king, even if that meant selling or losing their homes and moving to Canada, or taking up arms against their fellow countrymen.

But most of the American upper class became patriots, even though when they finally got around to it the framers of the Declaration went the whole distance. They boldly proclaimed human equality—there was a revolutionary concept for staid aristocrats to espouse!—and inalienable rights that belonged at least in principle to all mankind. Thus far had the "better sorts" been led by the pressure of events and their view of the best course of action.

For this was not going to be a mere War for Independence now —not with that Declaration at the masthead. In seeking to re-establish the pre-1760 world where the colonists had been left alone and untaxed, the colonial leaders had taken their stand on one of the most sweepingly radical ideas men have ever entertained.

Why had they gone this long extra mile, these conservatives whose own interests would have been served by a more sober assertion? What had happened was that some of the best of them—the Jeffersons, Adamses, Washingtons, Franklins, and the like—had got hold of a new vision of society. The details were not in perfect focus, because as self-conscious members of the American upper class these men were not exactly unvarnished democrats . . . yet they had been taking a hard look at Old World aristocracy and they did not like what they saw. Britain offered the most disturbing example, being closest to home, and there were dismaying signs that the purse-proud corruption and debauchery visible there were taking hold in America as well. A great many Virginia gentlemen (and it is hard to imagine the American Revolution without *that* group) had become more fearful of going the way of British aristocracy than they were of casting their lot with a distinctly democratic theory of government and society in America . . . and they behaved accordingly.

The basis for that bold move was a growing faith, or a pious hope, that America was a new land and that in a new environment a new race of people might be emerging, purified of the vices and evils that pervaded European countries. Things here could be different—*must* be different; and so these men went the whole way, defining America in universal terms, as something that had a rich meaning for all people everywhere.

The man who could define the deep forces moving the American spirit better than any other who ever lived was Abraham Lincoln, and in February 1861, on his way to Washington, he made a stab at defining those forces in a brief address to the New Jersey legislature at Trenton. The men of the Revolution, he said, had fought for something greater than national independence— "something that held out a great promise to all the people of the world for all time to come." He had to grope for it, using the indefinite word "something" for a matter hard to define, and he returned to it the next day at Independence Hall in Philadelphia. What really held the Union together, he said, was the great idea that there was "something in the Declaration giving liberty, not alone to the people of this country, but hope to the world for all future time." He continued: "It was that which gave promise that in due time the weights should be lifted from the shoulders of all men, and that *all* should have an equal chance. This is the sentiment embodied in that Declaration of Independence."

The men who adopted the Declaration knew perfectly well that if things went wrong their signatures would lead them to an ugly death on the scaffold and in the reeking pit below the scaffold, where the hangman with his bloody knife would wait beside a little bonfire. They accepted this, and jested about it, Hancock by writing his signature extra large so that King George could read it without his glasses, Charles Carroll by adding "of Carrollton" to his name so that the executioner would not seize an innocent Charles Carroll by mistake. Franklin, when all had signed, quietly remarked that they must hang together now because if they did not they would assuredly hang separately, and well they all knew it.

So the thing was done, independence proclaimed, and that prodigious "something" began to reverberate down through world history. Clearly, this was not simply an act brought on by clever agitators, a stupid ministry, oppressive taxes, or the divergent views of men living on an island and men living on a continent. Profoundly and everlastingly, this was a thing done in accordance with the deepest spirit of the times; or perhaps the spirit of the times came to move in accordance with these words brought down from the mountaintop where great men had seen with eternal clarity what all men could hope to become.

PART TWO

WORLD TURNED
UPSIDE DOWN

CHAPTER 16

First in War

THE PEOPLE who had just proclaimed their freedom were
joyously and innocently overconfident. Their leaders were
sober enough, agreeing with John Adams that the war that had to
be won would be "long, obstinate and bloody." But optimism is
a prime American trait and it displayed itself early, refusing to let
a mean realism limit soaring hopes. When the British evacuated
Boston in March 1776, Washington promptly moved his army
down to New York, correctly assuming that Sir William Howe
would try to split the new nation by seizing its central land mass
and its most capacious seaport; but the soldiers who were paraded
in their camps on July 9 to hear the Declaration read seemed to
take it for granted that they would soon be discharged. Sentiment
back home ran the same way, and the make-up of the army reflected this. Washington simply had not been given the kind of
army he desperately needed and repeatedly called for, because the
people back home did not believe that it was really necessary.

Washington wanted a long-term army, which through discipline and hard experience would take on the skills and battlefield
cohesiveness that would enable it to meet the king's regulars on
equal terms; an instrument of central government, with state mi-

litia and Minute Men to be used only in local emergencies. This the people refused to give him. There was indeed a law permitting the Continental Army to enlist men for three years or the duration of the war, but there was also a provision for one-year enlistments, and most of the Continentals signed up for one-year terms. Congress could establish quotas for enlistments from the several states but had no power to make any state comply; it could say how large the army ought to be but could do nothing at all to make it that large. Inasmuch as it was never possible to build the Continental Army even close to the level Washington needed, the militia had to remain a principal reliance. It could be called up for brief periods, and the hope was that it would be suitably "stiffened" by intermixture with the Continentals.

Several factors were in play here. People making rebellion against a tyrannical government were not going to build up the power of their own central government if they could help it. They were not going to let any outside authority make a state, county, or other local agency raise more troops than the local people saw fit to raise. One of the things they were rebelling against was that tool of oppression, the standing army, and so they had no enthusiasm for raising a large standing army of their own. They would assuredly refuse to give anyone the power to make a man enter the army against his will.

Furthermore, experience seemed to show that the state militia (altogether a much more comfortable thing to live with than the Continental Army) could handle British regulars as well as any patriot could wish. Concord had been a militia victory, pure and simple, and it was militia who gave the British such a crushing repulse at Bunker Hill; militia, too, which at last forced Howe to get out of Boston. Men who believed that militia could carry the whole load were not being altogether unreasonable, even though they might be disastrously mistaken.

They were mistaken because from now on the war was going to be different. In the main it was going to be fought European style, and only the British knew how to fight that way. European warfare involved the marching, maneuvering, and climactic savage attack of steady, compact, closed-up masses of disciplined soldiers who fought by the numbers—*hut* two three four, fire one volley and raise a cheer and go on in with the bayonet—and nothing in the patriots' experience, training, or wildest imagination had prepared them for this. They were not prepared because there was nobody to teach them. Washington's army contained many former British army officers, but these men knew nothing about drilling troops. That was a job for the sergeants, and very well the sergeants did it. Unhappily the Continental Army contained few former British non-coms.

The bayonet seemed to be the decisive weapon. It not only killed men; it frightened the daylights out of them first, if they were raw Americans who had no bayonets themselves and did not understand what the things were all about in any case. To see a British battle line come in close, fire one volley, raise a full-throated cheer, and then advance on the run, steel points leveled —that, according to men who faced it, was the most terrifying experience war could offer. The worst thing about it was its inhuman unity of action. The advancing regulars halted all at the same moment, raised their muskets as one man, fired a concise thunderclap of a volley (raggedly aimed, but they all pulled trigger together), then cheered once, all together, and ran forward in an ordered mass four ranks deep, bayonets tilted as precisely as if someone had pulled a lever—all the more menacing because it was done by the numbers. This was a machine and if you got in the way it would kill you.

Few Americans had been given bayonets, those who did get them generally used them as spits for broiling steaks (when they had any steaks) and then threw them away; instruction in their proper use was not to be had. General Burgoyne quite properly told his officers to make their men rely on the bayonet: "Men of half their bodily strength, and even cowards, may be their match in firing; but the onset of bayonets in the hands of the valiant is irresistible."

Even this was not the worst of it. The Americans could not form those compact masses that could move deftly from road to field to hillside to riverbank and swing quickly into battle line at the end of it, because nobody had taught them . . . another price paid for the woeful lack of drill sergeants. The average American regiment marched in single file, Indian fashion, which meant that it straggled badly and took forever to form a battle line once it reached the field—where its continuing lack of elementary infantry tactics was an even worse handicap. A Continental officer at Valley Forge summed it up: "It was impossible to advance or retire in the presence of an enemy without disordering the line and falling into confusion." That was why American soldiers were so much more capable at defending Bunker Hill trenches, or at the informal hit-and-run business on the roads back from Concord, than they were on a regular battlefield. Fighting in their own way, they were as good as the best; fighting European style against professionals, they were lost.

There was some chance to improve this unhappy state of things in the Continental Army, where even the one-year man was in for a longer unbroken term than the militiaman and where the discipline was more impersonal and demanding; in the militia, substantial improvement was almost impossible. Where circumstances, luck, or folly compelled the British to fight battles like Concord or Bunker Hill the militia could do well, but that hardly ever happened any more. It was not going to happen in the summer of 1776, when Howe undertook to occupy New York, the lower Hudson Valley, New Jersey, and the heartland of the hopeful new nation. Howe appeared to be in no great hurry— European warfare in the eighteenth century tended to be quite leisurely—but he did apply a cool professional touch.

Howe's force began to arrive at the end of June, when 100 warships and transports came down from Halifax and the leading ships began drifting in past Sandy Hook, to drop anchor in the lower bay and send troops ashore on Staten Island. The expedition made an imposing display, and the patriotic belief that King

George and his ministry would stop fighting and concede independence began to die then and there. This was the first team,
powerfully reinforced, infantry under General Howe, navy
under his brother, Admiral Lord Howe—"Black Dick" to his
sailors, a competent sea dog who was liked and respected both by
his own lower-deck ratings and by the rebellious Americans
whose dream he was out to destroy. It was rumored that the
Howe brothers brought a proposition for peace, with a full pardon for all rebels except a few ringleaders like Sam Adams, John
Hancock, and Ben Franklin. They were in fact empowered to negotiate, but first they proposed to give Washington's upstart
army a beating

The strength was at hand for it. On August 1 Sir Henry Clinton brought in a strong force that had just made a dismal failure
out of an attempt to capture Charleston, South Carolina. A
doughty colonel named William Moultrie in a palmetto log fort
on Sullivan's Island had rebuffed a naval force inexpertly led by
Admiral Sir Peter Parker, while Clinton's infantry on its way to
attack Moultrie from the rear floundered helplessly in a tidal inlet,
unable to fire a shot or indeed to do anything at all except wait for
the navy to carry it away. (Army intelligence had reported that
the inlet was eighteen inches deep and could easily be waded; it
turned out to be seven feet deep, with a swift current.) So
Charleston was safe, and Clinton took his men up to New York.
Among them was a titled officer who would become well known
in America, Major General Lord Cornwallis.

The affair at Charleston was important. The British could have
saved themselves a good deal, including possibly the army Cornwallis finally lost at Yorktown, if they had been able to take and
hold Charleston in mid-1776. Failing, they had taken one unob-
trusive step toward ultimate defeat; and yet this summer was not
a time for patriotic rejoicing. A strong British army was being
built up in Canada, and when it was ready General Sir Guy Carleton would lead it along the Champlain-Hudson waterway to
New York; if his force and Howe's ever joined hands the new na-

tion would be split in two, perhaps fatally. It was hard to see how this could be prevented. At the moment there was nothing much to check the northern invasion except a scratch force Benedict Arnold was putting together on Lake Champlain in homemade war craft. Washington could do little to help. He had 19,000 men, mixed Continentals and militia, the largest American army he commanded during the entire war, but he needed every man because Howe had 25,000 with reinforcements in prospect.

Howe's 25,000 were massed on Staten Island. Howe could go wherever he chose, because his brother's fleet had complete control of all the waterways; this meant that the British could march with their flanks protected and no more trouble with Minute Men skulking from walled fields to farm woodlots to shoot perspiring lobster-backs who could not get at them with their bayonets. The American cause was very much on the defensive, and the famous Declaration was not two months old.

Washington's task was to defend New York, which then occupied only the southern tip of Manhattan. He kept more than half his army there, getting it well dug in to cover all possible landing places, and he put some 9,000 men over on the western end of Long Island, planting batteries on Brooklyn Heights to cover New York's wharves and docks; an enemy proposing to take New York would have to take Brooklyn Heights first. Washington had his men entrenched on good ground, with Nathanael Greene in command in Brooklyn.

There were two unfortunate developments. First, Greene took sick and command passed to General Israel Putnam of Connecticut—"Old Put," a legendary hero and a good fighting man but not quite up to command on a field where something more than straight-ahead slugging was required. Second, realizing that the British would probably move on the Heights from the south,

Putnam spread troops out in the open country to hold the approaches, tried to hold too much ground and so spread his men too thin. This relieved the British of the necessity for making a Bunker Hill attack on the Heights, permitting them instead to fight out in the open, European style, where they would have all the advantage. On August 22 Howe was ready, and he began ferrying his men across the lower bay from Staten Island to Long Island in small boats fully protected by British battleships, moving 15,000 soldiers across before sunset. Washington sent over reinforcements and the Continentals nerved themselves for a massive attack.

The massive attack was coming, but it did not come when and as the Americans expected. On the night of August 26 Henry Clinton formed a column of 10,000 men and led them far around to the east, passing the lines Putnam had drawn up so carefully, smashing an outpost on the extreme American left, and driving north past the flank and into the American rear, while other British units began tapping at the American front. The front held, for the most part; and on the far American right, crack British regiments were thrown back by William Smallwood's Maryland Continentals and John Haslet's Continental regiment from Delaware—units soon to be known as among the very best in the American army. But nothing could redeem the collapse on the left. Washington, hurrying over from New York, patched his broken forces together and grimly held on to the Heights, but if Howe had driven ahead with his offensive that afternoon he might have destroyed half of Washington's army.

Instead of doing that, Howe called a halt and had his men entrench in a broad arc enclosing the American position. With recollections of Bunker Hill too vivid for comfort, he did not care to make a frontal assault on Americans dug in on high ground; New York was going to fall sooner or later in any case, and it would be much less expensive to pin his foe down and let siege warfare take its course. Possession of the place seemed to be the important thing. The whole lower Hudson–North Jersey area was a stamping ground for Tory loyalists who would warmly support a British army in residence, the farming country round about would supply an abundance of food, the wide pastures of Long Island would provide the needed horses and beef cattle, and the rebellion could hardly hope to survive if this region were properly held for the king . . . especially since the conciliation program which the Howe brothers were about to propose would (it was supposed) greatly soften the rebels' determination. So Howe slowed his pace to a walk—and gave Washington just the time he had to have.

Washington used it without delay. Among the remarkable regiments in his army was Colonel John Glover's 14th Massachusetts Continentals, seafarers recruited in and around Marblehead, men who had learned how to handle small boats almost as soon as they had learned to walk, and their special skills now saved the Revolutionary cause. On August 29, 1776, contrary winds prevented Admiral Howe's warships from coming up to the East River to seal off the American line of retreat. Washington's officers collected an assortment of small boats and barges, Glover's men took charge of them, and after dark the army quietly abandoned its Brooklyn lines and made for the waterside, where the Marblehead soldiers ferried them over to the Manhattan shore. In a little more than twelve hours all were safely across, 9,000 men with their horses, guns, wagons, and supplies. An army faced with destruction had survived to fight another day on other fields.

But wars are not won by skillful retreats, and this army had gained no more than a reprieve. It had had more than 1,000 casualties, and many of its individualistic soldiers (finding hard marching and hard fighting less romantic than they had anticipated) simply faded away. When he reassembled his troops Washington had no more than 15,000, and this total would shrink even more as short-term enlistments expired, militia units reached the end of their terms, and the faint of heart continued to comb themselves out of the service. He was outnumbered two to one, and Howe had reinforcements coming.

Washington had to withdraw from Manhattan. The royal navy could take troops up both sides of the island and plant an overpowering force in his rear whenever the British chose, compelling an ignominious surrender. Howe tried a frontal advance first, however, driving Washington off to the north after stubborn actions at Harlem Heights and White Plains which indicated that when they fought on the defensive on good ground these soldiers were just as dangerous as they had been at Bunker Hill. In substance, Howe tried to drive the American army away instead of surrounding and capturing it. He was not the most energetic of generals, and besides he had a cloudy hope of making peace. He and his brother had been given broad authority, and to find out what terms would be offered Congress sent a top-level delegation—Benjamin Franklin, John Adams, and Edward Rutledge of South Carolina—to confer with them. This got no one anywhere. The British seemed to be offering, at best, total amnesty for all rebels who returned to their allegiance, and the least the Americans would consider was recognition of independence. After a meeting on September 11, negotiations were broken off and the armies could get on with the war.

The British got on with it fastest and best. When he was driven north from Manhattan, Washington left behind two Hudson River forts, Fort Washington and Fort Lee; these were now deep within enemy lines and the British promptly snapped them up, capturing some 2,000 men and munitions and supplies the Americans could not afford to lose. Washington got the bulk of his force over into New Jersey—a badly shattered army, steadily losing strength as enlistments continued to expire and imperfectly disciplined men concluded that they had had enough and set out for home. Howe sent a strong force under Lord Cornwallis to harry Washington out of New Jersey, detached another with naval escort to occupy Newport, Rhode Island, and the Hudson River was open for any use the British cared to make of it. If Carleton now brought his men down from Canada the game was about over.

———□———

Carleton did not quite make it. The royal navy had a strong squadron on Lake Champlain, and on October 11, 1776, this force came on Benedict Arnold's impromptu little flotilla back of Valcour Island and destroyed it after a sharp fight. Now Carleton could go ahead and use the lake as he pleased . . . and yet something about the way Arnold and his men had fought, probably also something about the extreme remoteness of the Champlain country and the mysterious loneliness of the surrounding forests with winter coming on made Carleton feel that this was no time to be hasty. Instead of driving on to reach the Hudson before snow fell, he held the invasion force in Canada. The move would take place next spring. Once again the Americans had gained a reprieve.

Which meant that the American cause would for a few crucial months be borne entirely on Washington's shoulder. (Not for the last time, either.) His army was visibly fading away, and Cornwallis, joined now by Howe in person, was pressing it hard; almost captured it, did compel it to get out of New Jersey and take refuge beyond the unbridged Delaware River, which was too deep for fording. Washington ensured the temporary safety of his army by sending out detachments to seize every rowboat, barge, or other craft on the Delaware, for miles upstream and downstream. The British could not get at him . . . but winter was coming on, he could do nothing where he was, and the hopes of Congress and the country centered very largely on this one man, on his firmness of purpose, his refusal to panic, and his indefinable ability to keep and hold the unswerving confidence of the ragged Continentals who would have to do the fighting. Patriot morale outside of the army went lower and lower; the obverse side of heedless optimism is pessimism looking down into the Pit, and that is just where people were looking now.

Howe had his troops scattered about New Jersey in snug winter quarters, buttoned up for cold weather in little towns where there were good taverns for headquarters and weatherproof stone houses for other ranks. For the Continentals there were bleak acres off to the west, beyond the turbulent impassable Delaware, with cold winds whipping around the campfires of despair. Nothing could happen until spring, and although by assembling all available troops Washington now could muster a total of 6,000 men he would have no more than half of them when terms of enlistment expired shortly after the first of the year. Howe could well afford to wait until spring and then round up the fragments and enforce the king's peace.

Except that George Washington had an idea; an idea that made nothing at all of the flood-stage Delaware brimming with grinding ice floes and made everything of the tattered soldiers who could do the impossible if this man demanded it. After dark on Christmas Day of 1776 he got 2,400 men on the frozen road and led them to the river at a place nine miles upstream from Trenton, New Jersey. (Two other columns were heading for other riverside assignments, but they never quite made it. This was the one that counted, George Washington moving at the head, national independence riding on its banners.) At the river John Glover's priceless seagoing regiment was waiting, with a fleet of broad scows used in season to ferry goods. Into these boats went the chilled files of soldiers, along with some of Henry Knox's artillery, Knox and Nathanael Greene and a doughty general named John Sullivan, and Washington himself in full regimentals, unconsciously posing for a famous painting that was a full century away from being painted. The boats moved out on the river in midnight darkness, the Marblehead men in control, depositing troops and guns on the Jersey shore, returning for another load, shuttling back and forth steadily until the whole army was across.

Then, at four in the morning, Washington led them south for Trenton, a town of perhaps a hundred houses held by three regiments of Hessians under Colonel Johann Rall.

These men were tough professionals who had helped chase Greene out of Fort Washington on the Hudson, capturing most of the garrison, almost capturing Greene himself; as he took his column on into the cold-crackling dawn Greene understandably acted like a man with a score to settle. Rall and his Hessians had celebrated Christmas in hearty German style, plenty of rum for the enlisted men and wine by the tavern fire for the officers. Pot-valiant in their ignorance, they held the colonials in hearty contempt and knew perfectly well they had nothing to worry about. When daylight came hardly anyone was awake, and the sleep-drugged heavy-feet who were brought clumping forth by the sudden crash of Henry Knox's guns wove unsteadily about under the weight of massive hangovers. Out into the streets they came stumbling, to meet the fire of angry Continentals who had lived for just this moment.

Meeting fire, they also met bayonets. Some of Washington's regiments had this weapon, and found that against men dazed by sleep, drink, and panic surprise it was marvelously effective. Colonel Rall came out to rally his men and went down with a mortal wound, an attempted counterattack failed completely, and in three quarters of an hour it was all over. Washington's army had taken 900 prisoners and had shot down or bayoneted another hundred or more. All of Rall's supplies and munitions had been taken, and the town itself was in full American possession. This had been done at minor cost: two men dead (frozen to death, actually; this was truly a wintry morning) and four wounded. The victorious army hustled its captives and booty back upstream, crossed to Pennsylvania with the help of Glover's men, and bedded down in its old camp—while Washington set out to see whether this army would remain in effective existence once the first of the year had passed.

It would. By some prodigy of persuasiveness, Washington

talked men whose enlistments were expiring into staying on for six more weeks. This done, he led his army back to Trenton to see whether another blow might be struck. He got there just in time to discover the approach of Cornwallis, who was coming in with 8,000 men to avenge the outrageous defeat inflicted on the Hessians. Sideslipping neatly, Washington moved forward past him, fell upon a British contingent at Princeton and routed it, and then evaded Cornwallis once more and marched—not back to Pennsylvania but northward to Morristown, New Jersey. Cornwallis gave up the pursuit and went into winter quarters; after all, gentlemen could hardly campaign in January and February in this unkempt colony of heavy snowfalls and bad roads. Washington's men went into winter quarters themselves and found that it was possible to face the coming year with a good deal of confidence.

The victories at Trenton and Princeton had been of great importance. On paper, they did not add up to much; in fact they were a turning point. Patriot hopes that had been on the point of vanishing were suddenly reborn. It was possible for the homespun army of mixed antecedents, inadequate training, and the briefest of traditions to take the offensive against British and German regulars and win stand-up victories. New Jersey, which had been lost, had been regained, and an area that was supposed to be full of Tories was suddenly hot for independence, proof of it being the readiness with which New Jersey militia regiments came in to serve in Washington's army. Part of this, to be sure, was due to the gross misconduct of the Hessian regiments occupying the colony; they had foraged and looted with German thoroughness and total disregard of the effect this might have on the feelings of the rebellious subjects whose affection King George was trying to reclaim, and these tactics destroyed loyalist sentiment right and left. In the main, however, the change came because the Americans began to look like winners. If Washington was getting new militiamen from New Jersey he was also getting them from Pennsylvania, which had seen no Hessians, and recruiting officers farther afield found that it had become a little easier to sign up new Continentals. Trenton had been a small victory and Princeton had been even smaller, but they had immense significance.

—□—

While all of this was going on, one more essential building block in the substructure of the new nation was quietly fitting into place. In December 1776 Benjamin Franklin settled in Paris as an agent of the Continental Congress.

There were two other agents: Silas Deane of Connecticut, who had been there since spring, and Arthur Lee of Virginia, who went over with Franklin. They were dedicated men and they worked hard, but it was Franklin who made the difference. As the scientist who had learned the secret of lightning he already had a substantial reputation in Europe; now he came on the scene as a quaint natural philosopher from the unlettered frontier, beaming with a backwoods innocence which a society addicted to Rousseau's gospel found irresistible. That his cherubic harmlessness hid an ability to play an intricate political game with Europe's most sophisticated diplomats would become clear only later, after he had picked up all of the chips and taken his winnings back home.

On the face of it America had little to expect from any appeal to the French court. Louis XVI had his limitations but he was after all the great-grandson of the Sun King, not in the least likely to look with favor on men who made war on the whole idea of kingship. His ministers had no reason to welcome the representatives of an aggressive democracy; they were noblemen, owing everything they had to their society's built-in system of inequality, not disposed to accept a declaration that all men are equal.

But the one thing they all understood about the situation in America was that it meant trouble for England. They would add to that trouble if they could do so without undue risk, because memory of defeat in the last war still rankled and there might soon be a chance to regain some of the territories lost on the Plains of Abraham. Before Franklin's arrival, Deane had been able to arrange for the export to America of a few modest shipments of gunpowder and other supplies, and with proper encouragement these shipments might be increased. The Comte de Vergennes, King Louis's foreign minister, was cautious but given to moments of effervescence when enthusiasm got the better of good sense. If England's difficulties became more serious he might respond favorably. Much would depend upon what happened in America during the year 1777.

As a matter of fact, what happened in America could easily have brought final victory to the British. They had devised a plan that would win the war if properly executed: move up the Hudson with one powerful army, move down from the St. Lawrence with another, leave a third force to keep everything under control around New York City, and the thing would be done—colonies hopelessly fragmented, their unity gone, their armies blown to bits. Washington would have to fight all out to prevent this, and his partly trained Continentals and mercurial militia would be racked up by British numbers and discipline. It was a good plan and the British had the needed resources. It remained to be seen whether they had the generals.

The beginning looked promising enough. To Canada the ministry sent a dashing officer who at least looked the part of a fine general, the resemblance being more striking in London than it proved to be in upstate New York: Sir John Burgoyne, sometimes referred to as Gentleman Johnny, who was to do what Sir Guy Carleton had tried to do a year earlier. Burgoyne was given an army of 7,000 men: British regulars, Hessian mercenaries, and a sprinkling of Canadian militia, not to mention an auxiliary force of several hundred Iroquois warriors whose explosive qualities made them allies of uncertain value. Burgoyne reached Quebec early in May 1777, took command, and started moving south on the historic Lake Champlain route. The idea was that Howe would meet him at Albany.

That at least was the way the War Office and General Burgoyne understood it. In a vague way General Howe probably understood it that way also, but he interpreted the understanding in a most eccentric manner. He decided that he could not move up the Hudson without first knocking out Washington, who was never there when Howe went looking for him. Then after wasting the entire spring and early summer moving fruitlessly about New Jersey, he concluded that he ought to capture Philadelphia.

That this would take him much farther away from Burgoyne just when the two ought to be meeting apparently meant nothing; Burgoyne would be all right once he reached Albany, Howe would leave 7,000 men at New York under Sir Henry Clinton to go upriver if Burgoyne needed help, and anyway Philadelphia was the American capital and in Europe to capture the capital was to win the game. And so, late in July 1777, Howe and 12,000 men boarded transports and sailed for Philadelphia. They took the long way around, going down to the Virginia capes and up the Chesapeake, and it was August 25 when they finally disembarked at Elkton, Maryland, some sixty miles southwest of Philadelphia. Washington had brought 11,000 men overland and was waiting on Brandywine Creek, in northern Delaware, ready to provide the stand-up fight Howe had so long been wanting.

By this time, instead of being well along with one co-ordinated campaign that would crush the whole rebellion, the British had managed to set up two separate, ill-co-ordinated campaigns; having delayed victory by sloth and confused purposes in the Southern theater, they were well on their way toward losing it altogether by bad luck and clumsiness up North. (An important factor in both cases, not yet fully recognized, was that American soldiers were becoming increasingly hard for British troops to handle.) As a result, instead of being a time when they closed out the war, the summer of 1777 turned final British defeat from a faint possibility to a distinct probability.

Coming down from Canada, slowed by a huge wagon train which the luxurious habits of the high command made necessary,

Burgoyne took Fort Ticonderoga without trouble and moved ponderously on toward the Hudson. At this point he was tripped up by the oldest and most fatal of all British failings in this war: a total inability to understand what made Americans tick. . . . The Green Mountain Boys, being known to hate restraint, most of their neighbors, and nearly the whole Continental Congress, would doubtless help the British, and so muskets and ammunition were given them with the king's compliments. John Stark's restless levies accepted these happily and used them with deadly effect to shoot British soldiers, and when Burgoyne sent 900 Hessians off to seize a depot of supplies at Bennington the Vermonters ambushed them and killed or captured the lot. . . . To frighten the countryside, British propaganda spread the word that Burgoyne's army included a big Iroquois war party, and although Burgoyne did his best to restrain them the Iroquois lived up to advance billing and made the only kind of war they understood—total war, complete with scalping knife and dreadful fire. This so infuriated the settlers that Burgoyne thenceforth had to campaign in a region that was anti-royalist beyond recall; swarms of militia turned out to destroy this army that had loosed such horrors on farm and town. . . . The British had also banked on the animosity between York State men and New Englanders, and the American army hereabouts was commanded by General Philip Schuyler, a good soldier but a New York patrician whom the New Englanders making up the bulk of the army viewed with suspicious dislike. Congress bowed to pressure and replaced Schuyler by General Horatio Gates, whose military capacity was lamentably modest but who somehow managed to please both Yorkers and New Englanders; and Washington sent up some Continentals, including Daniel Morgan (exchanged since his capture at Quebec) and his Virginia riflemen; and by now anti-British sentiment was so strong that it overrode local antagonisms anyway.

In other words, nothing worked out as planned. To make it worse Barry St. Leger ran into unmitigated defeat in the Mohawk

Valley and a big prop was knocked out from under Burgoyne's campaign.

Lieutenant Colonel St. Leger had brought a 2,000-man force of regulars, Hessians, Canadian militia, and Mohawk Indians up Lake Ontario to Oswego, planning to attack Albany from the west just as Burgoyne approached from the north. He was delayed by stubborn resistance at Fort Stanwix, and although he routed a relieving militia column led by Colonel Nicholas Herkimer and killed its commander, his own losses were heavy and he paused to pull his troops together. Then he learned that he lay in the path of an avenging tornado composed of 3,500 Americans led by hard-driving Benedict Arnold, who was worth more to the patriot cause this summer than the price he demanded for its betrayal two years later. (Actually Arnold had no more than 1,000 men, but he had carefully planted rumors which the luckless Britisher swallowed whole.) The Mohawks decided they had had enough and faded off into the forest, and St. Leger soon followed their example and took his shattered column back to Canada. Arnold led his triumphant band east to join Gates, furious because he had not been given command of the Northern army in Gates's place, as indeed he should have been. And Burgoyne was left to make the best of his way on to Albany, isolated and beyond help in a land where every man was his enemy. When Howe moved his forces up to do battle for Philadelphia, hundreds of miles to the southward, the Northern game was just about lost.

— □ —

Washington's Continentals were well posted on Brandywine Creek and when Howe made his assault, on September 11, 1777, they put up a sharp fight, losing at last when a column led by Cornwallis swung out and crushed John Sullivan's division on the far right—the same sort of flanking attack that had beaten the Americans at the battle of Long Island. Sullivan might have rallied his men and regained the lost ground, but the Continentals were still incapable of the swift battlefield maneuvering that was called for, and despite Sullivan's best efforts and sturdy fighting by the divisions of Anthony Wayne and Nathanael Greene the day was lost. Washington moved off in full retreat, having lost upward of 1,000 men, and Howe's road to Philadelphia was wide open.

Among the American wounded was the prince of all American storybook heroes then and thereafter, a young Frenchman abundantly named Marie Joseph Paul Yves Roch Gilbert du Motier, Marquis de Lafayette. A youthful idealist from a cynical court, Lafayette had crossed the Atlantic to serve George Washington, winning a commission when he convinced Congress that he wanted neither pay nor authority over troops; just a place on Washington's staff would be enough, because something about the great Virginian had touched him all the way across the sea. He and Washington seem to have worked out a father-son relationship of enduring firmness, in time Americans took him to their hearts as they took no other European, and his mere existence greatly helped the American cause in France. Now he was wounded. He would recover.

Howe was established in Philadelphia by the final week in September. For whatever it was worth, he possessed the rebel capital, although the rebel Congress had escaped and was coolly conducting the Republic's affairs from a temporary capital at York. Washington's army had also escaped, its morale undamaged by its costly defeat along the Brandywine, and Washington was disposed to use it. He moved forward, saw an opening, and on October 4 made a savage attack on Howe's advance at Germantown.

Here the Americans almost won a fabulous war-ending victory. They attacked in the mists of early dawn and wholly smashed the British front line, driving the fragments away in headlong rout, with Howe himself riding into the fire shouting and thwacking mightily with his sword to get the runaways back into line. His entire army was off balance, crack regiments of British and German professionals crumpled up by the rebel attack, and a dazzling possibility could be glimpsed . . . briefly. Then the solid brick mansion owned by the Chew family offered a rallying point, scrambling redcoats made an effective fort out of it; and the triumphant Continentals, instead of by-passing it and pressing their drive on the temporarily disorganized foe, wasted time and manpower in a futile attempt to take this place by storm. Elsewhere Washington's army displayed its old failing—lack of the tactical training needed for quick changes of position on the field—and in the end he had to lead them off in retreat once more, with another 1,000 casualties to lament. Defeat: and yet, this time, it had not *felt* like defeat, and the British took little pride in their victory. Howe's army, or a good part of it, had had to take flight and had come fairly close to total disaster, and with all its short-comings the rebel army had fought this fight on even terms. This vastly impressed such Europeans as were scanning the horizon for omens, and one may be sure that Franklin called it to people's attention in Paris.

Shortly after this, Congress gave heed to a motion brought in by the same Richard Henry Lee who sixteen months earlier had posed a momentous "and of right ought to be" resolution: demanding now that Congress say whether it was leading a loose alliance of sovereign states or a single independent nation organized for an enduring life. In November, digesting weighty battlefield news, Congress adopted and forwarded for ratification a document headed "Articles of Confederation and Perpetual Union Between the States." The states dawdled, ratification was delayed, and the Articles of Confederation were not overly effective, but the key idea of perpetual union had been planted.

Meanwhile a victory to make up for the one glimpsed and lost at Germantown had been won near Saratoga, by the Hudson River, far to the northward. Burgoyne had been roundly defeated and driven into a camp from which escape was impossible, and on October 17, 1777, he and his entire command—nearly 6,000, rank and file—surrendered to the army of General Gates.

Burgoyne had been doomed before he even knew that he was

in trouble. Loss of the flanking columns at Bennington and the Mohawk Valley did not disturb him much because he believed that the Americans could not raise an effective army in his front and that he could walk through any militia force that might appear. But an effective army was raised, greatly stiffened by tough Continentals from the South, stiffened even more by men like Morgan and Arnold, and Burgoyne was badly outnumbered before he realized what was happening. He floundered on toward the Hudson, with twenty miles of forest to penetrate; American axmen felled trees across the inadequate roadway and his progress fell to half a mile a day. Getting supplies down from Canada took forever, and getting them in the immediate neighborhood (which, once beyond the forest, contained rich farmland) was impossible because the whole area was alive with vindictive militiamen.

Burgoyne inched along, reached the Hudson at last, crossed it believing his troubles were over, and learned that he could expect no help at all from General Clinton. (This was not Clinton's fault; he simply did not have enough men to hold New York City and Newport and at the same time force his way up the Hudson and knock the obstacles out of Burgoyne's path.) Burgoyne's one chance now was to get to Albany, where there was food, equipment, and a rest from all striving. He began to move, and found that Gates with an army larger than his own stood squarely in his path. Across the open fields of Freeman's Farm the British and Hessian columns moved in to make their attack.

Waiting for them in the woods were Morgan's riflemen, who could kill soldiers half a mile away. They lurked unseen, shooting men who had no place to hide, and they had an uncanny way of signaling their presence to one another—a repeated incomprehensible turkey gobble, which British soldiers found as unnerving as anything they had ever run into: gobble-gobble-gobble, an unearthly bubbling war cry coming out of dim light where nobody could be seen, while backwoods riflemen shot down good infantry who could have cleaned them out at bayonet point except that they could not find them. Then Benedict Arnold swung into action with New England regiments and drove wavering regulars away, Burgoyne's assault columns hurried back to their camps, and the day was an American victory.

Now Burgoyne had no chance to avert disaster. His supplies were diminishing, his chance to replenish them gone altogether. The riflemen had his camps under fire, his German mercenaries were beginning to desert, and on October 7—just after Washington's near miss at Germantown—he made one final attempt to break out. There was furious fighting on the slopes beyond the Freeman's Farm clearings but British luck was no better than before, the riflemen were as deadly as ever, and Arnold led another hard charge that slammed the door shut for good and all. Ten days later, after formal negotiations, Burgoyne made formal surrender, Gates playing the part of the courtly victor with easy charm, luxuriating in the triumph better soldiers had won for him. The British army of the North ceased to exist, and the great dream of independence began to look very much like coming true.

Oddly enough, it looked less like it in Washington's camp than anywhere else. With Howe's army snugly settled in Philadelphia, Washington's battle-worn Continentals went into the bleakest of winter quarters at Valley Forge two dozen miles away and found themselves facing the worst winter and the severest trial of the war. Things came to a strange focus on the snowy, wind-whipped fields of this camp where no one was ever really warm or clean or decently fed; unless the men who camped there remained firm in the faith, all that had been won at Saratoga would be lost forever here in Pennsylvania. The American Revolution was a rhythmic progression from crisis to crisis, and this crisis was the worst of the lot.

Part of the trouble arose in the dim sheltered corridors of the high command. It is clear enough now that George Washington was the great irreplaceable, the one man without whom the war could not have been won, but it was not so clear at the time. That winter saw a queer, semi-secret plot to get Washington out of there and replace him with someone else. The plot seemed to center around a malcontent Irishman named Thomas Conway, who had served in the French army and had been commissioned a major general by Congress over Washington's objection. A subtle argument began to buzz and whine back of what men said openly: Washington always led his men to defeat, he was not really a skilled soldier, Gates had won battles and had forced a British army to surrender, Gates had a winning record and Washington did not and therefore Gates ought to have Washington's job. (This was two centuries before television began adjusting presidential campaigns to the mentality of the professional football fan, examining track records rather than basic principles. The sportscaster's scale of values dates back a long way.)

How much Gates knew about all of this is not clear, even now. There were men in Congress who supported him vigorously, fearing (or professing to fear) that Washington would eventually make himself dictator, and Conway certainly did his best to make Gates an active participant, but there are hazy edges to the affair. In the end a measure of sanity returned to the public servants who had nourished this insane notion, the so-called "Conway cabal" collapsed of its own weight, and no one heard any more of the argument that Gates should replace Washington. But the danger was real while it lasted.

Underneath everything, of course, was the army itself—the ragged Continentals of legend, never more ragged or more legendary than now. Washington had taken 15,000 men to Valley Forge, and by midwinter of 1778 nearly half of them were out of action from illness or lack of clothing. Some were just plain naked and could not even go out to build the cabins they were to live in unless they could borrow a pair of pants. It was common to see men doing guard duty without shoes, or going out in the snow naked to the waist to gather firewood. In the matter of rations they were no better off, and at times the army seemed about to go out of existence for sheer lack of basic supplies. Naturally enough there were many desertions, and an old handicap was vastly intensified: units whose terms expired were reluctant to re-enlist.

This was not because America did not have what the army needed. The trouble lay in the incompetence of the army's supply system, which was totally bogged down in a job beyond its understanding and performance. Late in the winter Washington turned the job over to Nathanael Greene, who did not in the least want it—an ambitious soldier, he protested that no quartermaster ever became famous—but as a good patriot he took the assignment and did exactly what needed to be done. By spring he had found stocks of food and clothing his predecessor had never heard of, men were properly fed and decently clothed once more, and the crisis was over. Later Greene returned to combat duty and won much distinction, but he never served the cause better than he did at Valley Forge.

Washington's army did more than survive this winter. When active campaigning was resumed in the spring of 1778 it was a far more effective battle instrument than it had ever been before, thanks largely to that improbable but priceless soldier, Baron Friedrich von Steuben, late of the Prussian army: an honest man who got here by dint of one of the neatest fakes in American history.

A captain in the service of Frederick the Great, Von Steuben had been on half pay for over ten years and in 1777 was looking for a job in any army that needed a good professional soldier. He drifted into Paris just when the French officials who quietly controlled the famous dummy trading corporation of Hortalez et Compagnie needed such a person. This corporation was sending large amounts of arms and other supplies to aid the American cause, and they were worried because Washington lacked the solid professional advice that would enable him to put them to the best use; when Von Steuben appeared, a man trained in Prussian staff lore and procedures, he was like the shadow of a mighty rock in a weary land. Let him go to America to give Washington's army the technical direction it needed.

There were certain angles. Congress was sick to death of European fortune hunters and it had laid down the law: neither generals' commissions nor generals' pay would be given to any more men from Europe. Meanwhile, the Conway cabal had saddled Washington with the ineffable Conway himself as inspector general, the post a proper military technician would be given, and Conway was openly declaring that only an officer from the army of the great Frederick could provide the shambling Continentals with Prussian drill and efficiency and redeem the desperate situation Washington had allowed to develop. Washington needed a man like Von Steuben even more than Hortalez et Compagnie did, but as the law stood he had no way to get him.

At which point Franklin and his French confidants staged their fake. They turned Von Steuben from a staff captain into a Prussian lieutenant general simply by buying him the proper uniform and equipping him with certain letters. The French then provided a temporary cash subsidy, so that Von Steuben was able to affirm that he wanted no pay from the Americans and no position in command: he simply wanted to serve General Washington, no strings attached. Franklin wrote to Congress recommending that this generous offer be accepted, Congress was properly dazzled —one of the great Frederick's lieutenant generals, offering to serve without pay on the staff rather than in the line—and over came Von Steuben, to be accepted and sent along to Valley Forge to meet Washington.

The two men hit it off from the start, despite the language barrier. Washington detailed two of his aides, Colonel John Laurens and Lieutenant Colonel Alexander Hamilton, to serve as aides to Von Steuben; both of these men could speak French (as could Von Steuben, to an extent), and Von Steuben's own military secretary, Pierre Duponceau, could speak French and German, and the communications problem was solved. Washington then defused Conway by appointing Von Steuben his *acting* inspector general. Conway could not protest; Washington had come up with exactly what Conway had been derisively demanding, one of Frederick the Great's top officers ready to train the army along Prussian lines . . . and before long Conway faded out of view and ceased to be a problem.

Von Steuben went right to work. He spent a few days getting acquainted with Washington's generals and inspecting the enlisted men in their quarters, greatly impressed by the quality of the soldiers. He had to write his own drill regulations first, and then—after these had been translated from German through French into English—he had to train a select company in their use, after which he had to split this company into separate teams of drill instructors. Each team, as soon as it had mastered the fundamentals, had to proliferate into new teams, until the whole army was toiling mightily on the drill field, day after day and week after week. An odd thing happened: Von Steuben was a Prussian martinet, he had a whole army full of touchy individualists for his awkward squad, and drill instructors are never popular —but suddenly it developed that General von Steuben was the best-liked man in camp. When one of his teams gummed up its assignment, which was forever happening, he would fly into a colossal rage, swearing in German, French, and what he supposed to be English, calling on his aides to swear for him, and winding up by making himself and everybody within range shout with laughter. He could laugh at himself and he could make the laugh contagious, and the army learned what it had to learn in an amazingly short time.

It learned how to swing from marching column into fighting line, and a battlefield maneuver that formerly would keep a brigade shuffling back and forth for two hours would get done in thirty minutes. Bayonets were provided, and men were drilled in their proper use. Even the smallest squad moving on the least assignment was required to march in proper military formation, and the day of sauntering casually from here to there came to an end. In the spring of 1778 the Continental Army got the professional touch it had so sorely lacked. Now it could meet British and Hessian regulars on equal terms.

———☐———

And one day that spring the army was paraded at Valley Forge to listen to the reading of a great announcement: formal news that an alliance had been signed with France and that the army and navy of Louis XVI would actively help Americans win their independence.

Back of this lay an intricate diplomatic game played unsentimentally for the highest stakes.

Franklin had been courting the French most carefully, so skillfully that the French thought they were courting him. Vergennes feared that a Britain reunited with her revolted colonies would be forever dominant in America, and he hoped that these colonies, once independent, would become a useful French satellite; he was wondering if he could persuade Franklin to accept a French alliance at the very moment when Franklin was prepared to do almost anything to get one. Burgoyne's surrender had brought this supersaturated solution to the point of crystallization. Early in 1778 Lord North's ministry offered everything the patriots ever wanted except outright independence. Congress flatly rejected this offer but Franklin went ahead and talked to the British anyway, being careful to let Vergennes know he was doing it. Vergennes worried, and infected the court with his worries, so that at Versailles it began to seem vital to get this American alliance. The finance minister, Turgot, realizing that the alliance would mean war and knowing full well that France was in desperate financial trouble already, warned King Louis that the country could not possibly afford it; King Louis ended by ignoring this advice and agreeing to the alliance. (Out of the bankruptcy that Turgot correctly predicted came the French Revolution, the execution of amiable King Louis, a new map of Europe, and a great deal more.)

Both Franklin and Vergennes, in short, went fishing in troubled waters and it was Franklin who made the catch. For his country he won all-important military and naval aid, cash loans of almost equal importance, an enlarged flow of munitions, and a pledge that France would not stop fighting until American independence had been established. What France won was less tangible: an intensification of England's troubles plus an American pledge to go on fighting until France could get a satisfactory peace. Having risked so much and won so little, the French needed reinsurance and accordingly sought the aid of Spain, making gamblers' promises in order to get it. Affairs got so tangled that the Americans, without realizing it, were now committed to go on fighting until Spain had regained Gibraltar. They did know that they had guaranteed France continued possession of her Caribbean sugar islands, although how that guarantee was to be made good is not entirely clear; they were probably not aware that both France and Spain calculated victory in this war as an extension of their New World empires at American expense.

So the American Revolution became part of a general European war, and for the time being America would be a secondary theater. General Howe returned to England, as he was bound to do once Burgoyne's surrender emphasized the complete failure of Howe's strategy. General Sir Henry Clinton was named to succeed him and ordered to get the army back to New York as quickly as possible and prepare to retrench; 5,000 men must be sent to the Caribbean, 3,000 more must go to Florida, and for the present England would do little more than hold onto what she already had. Early in June 1778 Clinton gave up Philadelphia and led his army of 10,000 men across New Jersey to New York. Washington set out in pursuit with 13,000—sharply trained men, now, who could be trusted not to trip over their own feet when they attempted the intricate ballet-dance steps of the battlefield—and on June 28 the Continental advance overtook Clinton's rear at Monmouth and began to fight.

Unfortunately the Continental advance was commanded by cantankerous Charles Lee, who had served long in the British army and who in the beginning was supposed to be the ablest professional soldier America had—an opinion to which Lee himself clung tenaciously long after everyone else had abandoned it. Along with belief in his own worth, General Lee was convinced that the American soldier was grossly inferior to the British regular and was capable of acting only on the defense. Now he was in command on a field where the British were outnumbered and at a disadvantage so that one hard, properly co-ordinated drive would rout them—and he went over to a confused defensive, refusing to support a dramatic attack by Wayne's men, withdrawing troops who should have stayed where they were, and altogether making a fine hash out of what ought to have been a sweeping triumph.

Washington learned what was up and galloped to the field in an enormous fury, swearing mightily, visible and audible over the smoke and uproar of battle, wholly demolishing the legend that has him all graven-image dignity, demolishing also General Charles Lee so that the man went entirely out of the war for good. In the end the fighting stopped, and that night Clinton's army withdrew and went on to New York, still alive but with its tail feathers badly singed; and the Continental Army had lost its last great chance to destroy its foe in one echoing clash on the field of battle. There would be bloodshed, pain, and sometimes bleak discouragement for several years to come, but north of the Chesapeake the time of high drama and great possibilities was over. The British could hold New York and a few outposts, and conduct raids along the coast and stir up the horrors of Indian warfare on the frontier, but they could not win anything important here. The Americans could still lose—they came uncomfortably close to it, once or twice—but the final decision would have to be made elsewhere.

—□—

It would be made in the South, where the attention of both France and Britain was becoming focused. The islands spotting the Caribbean were valuable because of their sugar; in London and Paris their acquisition and protection seemed more important than anything that might happen on the North American mainland. This began to be evident in the summer of 1778, when Admiral the Count d'Estaing brought a French fleet across the Atlantic just when the British were off balance because of the retreat from Philadelphia to New York. He might have made serious trouble in Delaware Bay, might have forced his way past the narrows and into New York Harbor, might have gone in with Washington's army to seize the great anchorage at Newport—Washington set aside troops for this purpose, and elaborate plans were made—but D'Estaing was hampered by restrictive orders which in effect told him not to get so entangled that he could not quickly go down to the West Indies, and these possibilities came to naught. Similarly, the British prepared to shift the center of gravity to the South so that troops could be quickly available for use among the sugar islands, and in the fall of 1778 a British expedition went to Savannah, routed a small American force, and regained possession of Georgia. Later, D'Estaing and a fleet with 6,000 French soldiers came down to drive the British out, but the weather was bad, D'Estaing hated to risk his ships on what must have seemed a side issue, a premature land attack failed, and at last the French re-embarked and sailed away with nothing accomplished.

By 1780 many Americans began to feel that the French alliance did not actually mean much. Fleets came, transports with soldiers came, but nothing seemed to happen and the British still held New York. Far to the west a valiant troop of riflemen under Virginia's George Rogers Clark had made a storybook campaign across Illinois and Indiana, driving out the British and giving the nation a claim to the Northwest country; but that was a long way off and it offered little nourishment to people who were showing definite signs of war weariness. On the high seas a sailor of genius, John Paul Jones, boldly swept down the English Channel and up the Irish Sea with his warship *Ranger,* raiding the seaport of Whitehaven and taking H.M.S. *Drake,* and a little later he cruised in the North Sea with *Bonhomme Richard,* capturing the big frigate *Serapis* and sailing her off to France in triumph. Yet these exploits, while stimulating national pride and laying a foundation for the country's infant navy, were remote and unrewarding. Very real and close was the galloping inflation caused by the central government's inability to tax or control the separate states; despite the brave words that had been spoken, perhaps this really was just a brief alliance of little provinces rather than a united country, and perhaps independence itself, of one or of many, was a delusion that would vanish after definitive ceremonies in the Tower of London. Not in the dark fall of 1776 or the hungry Valley Forge winter did the cause come closer to final defeat than it did in 1780.

Clinton took an army and navy south for an attack on Charleston, one of the great cradles of the Revolution. Benjamin Lincoln had an American army of 5,500 men to hold the place, but Clinton refused to order the fleet to butt its way past Fort Moultrie and instead attacked by land from the southward; he boxed Lincoln's men in behind their defenses and on May 12 captured Charleston, Lincoln, and the entire American garrison. He then sailed back to New York, leaving Cornwallis in charge of a formidable occupation force.

Worse was to come. The French sent over an expeditionary army under the Comte de Rochambeau, who landed his men in Rhode Island and prepared to co-operate with Washington, but for the moment there was no way they could strike effectively. The British were secure in New York and beyond reach in Charleston, and the sands seemed to be running out. Cornwallis got South Carolina under control, began recruiting loyalist American regiments, and early in the summer moved north to take over North Carolina as well. There was nothing to stop him except some militia outposts, and although Washington sent the first-class Continental regiments from Delaware and Maryland down to help, under another of those invaluable German soldiers, the Baron de Kalb, Congress gave way to its weakness for wartime politics and sent Horatio Gates down to take top command.

Gates had perhaps 3,000 men, fewer than a third of them Continentals, and while this had been a winning combination at Saratoga it did not work at all in South Carolina. The two armies collided on August 16, 1780, near the town of Camden, and the American force was quickly routed. The Continentals hung on until they were almost annihilated, and the Baron de Kalb was killed, but the militia caved in when the formal redcoat line with its precise glittering bayonets moved up, and the panicked fugitives streamed away northward, formless and unmanageable, Gates well in the lead because he rode a very fast horse. The general came to a halt at last at Charlotte, North Carolina, sixty miles from the battlefield, his companions in misfortune halted in woods, swamps, and pastures all up and down the countryside, and now the British were the lords of both Carolinas—probably for keeps, as far as anyone could see.

And on September 25, 1780, Benedict Arnold attempted the greatest act of treachery in American history by trying to sell the important stronghold at West Point to the British.

Arnold was a magnetic leader of men and a great battlefield commander, and by any standard except the crucial one now up for measurement he was one of the country's best generals. His fellow Americans admired him, Washington trusted him implicitly, and he had all the gifts a soldier needs except integrity. He was vain, and he saw lesser men getting promotions he was denied; avaricious, with an expensive wife, he saw stay-at-homes growing rich while he went into debt; and in the end what he wanted for himself looked bigger than anything else within his range of vision. So he sold out.

By great good luck the Americans discovered his plot just in time. Arnold escaped, took service under General Clinton, wore the uniform of a British officer and collected his pound of flesh, and went at last to England to live out his days for whatever it may have been worth to him, his name surviving to this day as that of the one unrivaled scoundrel in the American story. Major André, the engaging young staff officer who had been Clinton's go-between in this affair, was captured by the Americans and was promptly hanged; Washington regretted the hanging very much and went ahead with it inexorably. Both sides then got on with the war and things were about as they had been . . . except that patriot morale had suffered a terrible shock. If Arnold was false who could be trusted? If he thought the American cause was doomed—and there was plenty to make a man think so this year —who could be hopeful?

The answer to both questions remained George Washington. The cause was still this man, surviving because he made it survive, hope reviving because he was there. Having reached bottom, the pendulum now began to swing upward—unexpectedly, almost unaccountably, but steadily.

When he went into North Carolina, Cornwallis detached a force of 1,400 loyalists under a capable British officer, Major Patrick Ferguson, to make a wide sweep in protection of the left flank, paying special attention to the need for restoring British authority in the mountain country. The possibilities were there, but the British lacked the touch; Ferguson tried to overawe the mountain folk by letting them know that he was going to knock their heads together, and as anyone who knew these people might have told him he got a bad response. Backwoods riflemen swarmed out to meet him, aided by other backwoods riflemen from western Virginia, and on October 7, 1780, they stormed his camp on King's Mountain, killing Ferguson himself and killing or capturing his entire command. It was a small fight at an unimportant outpost, but the same could be said of Trenton; it was a smashing victory won at a time when men despaired of victory, and it brought a revival of enthusiasm.

Then Nathanael Greene made his own contribution, which was not small.

When Gates fled so incontinently from the field at Camden he

of course galloped straight out of active service. Congress restored control to Washington, who at once put Greene in Gates's
place, and in December Greene reached Charlotte to take command. He did not take command of very much: present for duty
were perhaps 950 Continental infantry plus some artillery and
cavalry, and probably 550 militia, all of them hungry and ragged
in the best Revolutionary tradition, sullen but not ready to quit—
waiting to be shown. Greene began by seeing to it that they got
food and something to wear. Washington sent modest reinforcements, including militia regiments from Virginia; including also
that notable fighter, Daniel Morgan, who was just the man
Greene wanted.

Facing Cornwallis with an inadequate force, Greene did the
unimaginable by dividing his little army into two wings, putting
Morgan in command of one and taking direct charge of the other
himself. Cornwallis had another flanking detachment moving
about to the west, a mixed force of loyalist cavalry and regular infantry, led by a man the Southern folk had learned to hate—Colonel Banastre Tarleton, a graceful pretty-boy type by the
surviving paintings, gifted as such types often are with a cold and
brutal ferocity. He was notorious for his refusal to give quarter on
the battlefield—that is, he took no prisoners if he could help it,
bayoneting the submissive and the wounded—and all in all he
was a dangerous, hard-driving commander. His mission now
was to seek out the western wing of Greene's army, the part led
by Morgan, and on January 17, 1781, he found it at Cowpens and
swung up to the attack.

The result was a resounding American victory—another
King's Mountain, with bells on. Morgan's Continentals and militia took the worst Tarleton's men could give them and then coun-
terattacked and destroyed or blew away nine tenths of the British
force, sending the blood-and-thunder young colonel off in un-
dignified retreat with the fragment that remained. To make up
for this Cornwallis advanced vigorously, trying to knock out
Greene and invade North Carolina; Greene parried and retreated,

Morgan having rejoined him, and although Cornwallis pursued all the way across the state he could not bring the Americans to battle. Late in the winter, after many hard marches over miserable roads, Greene went north of the Dan River into Virginia and Cornwallis exulted that the Carolinas had been totally reclaimed.

Cornwallis was inexact and premature. The formal armies might be gone, but South Carolina held some effective bands of irregulars which became legendary—groups led by Francis Marion, the famous "Swamp Fox," whose hideout in the marshes the British never could find, and by Andrew Pickens and Thomas Sumter—and these raided British outposts and supply bases, constricted movement along the country roads, and kept South Carolina in ferment.

Even in his immediate front Cornwallis found the situation fluid. Greene pulled his army together and found that he had 4,000 men. Only 1,600 of these were Continentals, some of them fresh from Von Steuben's shaping hand without combat experience, and the rest were militia; but Greene had discovered something about the militia and made good use of what he had learned. A great deal depended on the man for whom the militiamen were fighting; if he understood them and had the right touch they could be very useful in combat. Not all generals had this touch, but a few did—Morgan, for example, that fallen Son of the Morning Benedict Arnold, and Greene himself; and now Greene put his regulars and militiamen on the road, recrossed the Dan, took position at Guilford Court House, North Carolina, and waited for Cornwallis to attack.

He did not have long to wait. Cornwallis had been trying for weary weeks to bring this army to battle, and he drove at it now, making a powerful attack on March 15, 1781, and bringing on one of the bloodiest and most hard-fought battles of the entire war.

Greene's mixed force stood firm, and the British attack was repulsed with heavy loss. An American counterattack made headway, but the militia, who had so far done all that was asked of them, got mixed up in the business of going from defense to of-fense; and although the priceless Delaware and Maryland Conti-nentals roughed up the bearskin-hatted British Guards, heavy artillery fire checked them, and as dusk came on Greene with-drew, leaving Cornwallis in possession of the field.

Greene had done about what he intended. He had inflicted far heavier losses than he had received, administered a decisive check, and saved his own army for further adventures. Corn-wallis showed what he thought of the affair by retiring to Wil-mington, on the sea-coast, to reorganize and re-equip under the guns of the royal navy, while Greene moved on south to get on with the job of recovering the Carolinas. Ahead of him he sent a crack 300-man troop of Virginia cavalry led by dashing Light Horse Harry Lee, with orders to work closely with Marion and the other irregulars—orders which Lee executed with skill and enthusiasm. (Long after the war Lee would father a son, named Robert, who would also become a soldier.)

Cornwallis wasted little time in Wilmington. He wanted to get out of Carolina, where he had met checks and frustration despite a victory or two on the field, and move into Virginia, where per-haps he and Clinton could work together and where the navy could guarantee his supplies and communications. On April 25 he marched north, sending up the curtain for the last great act of the Revolutionary drama.

—□—

On the banks of the James River he picked up reinforcements, raising his strength to 7,200 of all arms. Shortly after this he got perplexing orders from Clinton. He was told his reinforcements were needed elsewhere and he must send them to New York as soon as the navy provided transports. Then he got revised orders telling him to send the men to Philadelphia; then a further revi-sion told him to keep them and establish a secure base for the navy somewhere near the entrance to Chesapeake Bay. Cornwallis set about it, brushed off a small force led by Lafayette and Anthony Wayne, and settled at last on a pleasant town with a good defensive anchorage, a place named Yorktown, end of the line, the village where he and his army would wait, all inert, for the final blow to descend.

On the Hudson a short distance above New York an allied Franco-American army of some 12,000 men was waiting while the commanding generals, Washington and Rochambeau, looked for an opening. Rochambeau's force had been on American soil since the preceding summer, and although so far it had been able to accomplish nothing it was getting along remarkably well with its allies. The soldiers were on their good behavior and molested the civilian population not at all, and the civilians were cordial and did not profiteer at the soldiers' expense. Troops of the two armies had worked out some sort of understanding, Americans admiring the handsome uniforms, precise infantry drill, and strict discipline of the French, Frenchmen in turn finding the Americans informal in their dress and lacking in military equipment but seasoned, capable, and as tough as any fighting men needed to be. Washington and Rochambeau worked together harmoniously and understood one another well. But no victories were being won, and although a joint attack on Clinton's force in New York seemed to be indicated it was hard to see just how it could be arranged with good prospect of success.

Then, on August 24, 1781, came the news that changed everything. The French government had ordered the Comte de Grasse with twenty-eight ships of the line and transports bearing three regiments of infantry to sail from the West Indies and do whatever could be done to help the American cause. The one proviso was that action would have to be quick, because De Grasse and his force must be back in the islands by the middle of October.

This might give Washington, briefly, what he had always wanted but probably never hoped to get: command of the sea.

Although the time was brief the opportunity was great. Clin-

ton in New York might be almost invulnerable, but Cornwallis at
Yorktown was out on the end of an insecure limb, alive only as
long as British ships could keep him supplied and, in case of
emergency, reinforce him or take him away. If De Grasse could
bring his fleet to the Virginia capes and close them, Washington
and Rochambeau could do the rest. During the following week
the French and American armies crossed the Hudson and moved
south. Washington left some troops behind as a screen, and industriously spread rumors that an attack on New York was in prospect, while he hurried on through Philadelphia to the head of the
Elk River in Maryland, the place where Howe had brought his
troops ashore in 1777. There he learned that the French fleet had
indeed reached the Chesapeake and that French ships were immediately available to ferry his and Rochambeau's men down the
Virginia peninsula. The job was rushed, Washington overjoyed at
what had been done but tense with anxiety over what might have
happened between the French and British fleets after De Grasse's
arrival. The Franco-American force joined up with Lafayette and
Wayne on September 14, learning that the infantry that came up
from the Indies with De Grasse had already landed, and—the
final, incredible bit of good news—that De Grasse had fought
and beaten the British off the Virginia capes a week earlier, driving the whole British fleet back to New York and putting Cornwallis and his army entirely at Washington's disposal.

That sea battle between De Grasse and the British admiral,
Thomas Graves, was one of the great decisive battles in American
history, and it seems a pity that no American was present to take
part or even to watch and bear witness afterward. The fleets were
not badly matched, ship for ship, but the French had a first-rate
admiral and the British were led by a mediocrity. After a day
filled largely with maneuvering but climaxed by some hard toe-
to-toe slugging the British were driven out to sea, found that
many of their ships had been badly hurt, and limped off to New
York to repair and refit, while De Grasse sailed triumphantly into
the Chesapeake. From that moment American independence was
assured.

Washington and Rochambeau quickly got their men over to Yorktown and established siege lines. Between them they commanded probably 16,000 men, roughly half of them Americans and the other half French; combined, they had Cornwallis outnumbered two to one, and his case was hopeless, as he himself quickly realized. He was locked in, an overpowering force closing all the roads to him, the great French three-deckers and 74s closing the sea lanes. He could not get out and Clinton could not get in, and if he stayed where he was his army would starve. (It did not in fact occur to Clinton to try to help him until far too late; he had been thoroughly deceived, and up to the moment when Cornwallis was actually put under siege Clinton still imagined that Washington, Rochambeau, and De Grasse were going to attack New York.)

Cornwallis endured the bombardment, saw French and American assault columns take part of his works by storm, and came to the same conclusion Burgoyne had come to four years earlier. On the morning of October 17 a British drummer stood up on a parapet and beat the parley, a stuttering long roll that military men everywhere recognized as an invitation to talk things over. There was a truce, commissioned notables crossed the lines, conferred and agreed, and on October 19, 1781, there was a great ceremony of surrender, with British troops marching out between two long rows of victors, resplendent French on one side, Americans on the other. Not all Americans had uniforms even on this mighty day, and those who had none stood in the rear ranks. However, they carried loaded guns, and like the front-row men, they had in their hearts something that a long war had never extinguished.

Cornwallis was not quite able to face up to this ceremony, so General Charles O'Hara was delegated to be his agent. O'Hara came up with the waiting French and Americans and tried to save face: the British held that they had been beaten by French professionals, not by ragged American amateurs, and so it was the French to whom the surrender would be made. O'Hara rode over to Rochambeau to offer his sword; Rochambeau smiled, shook

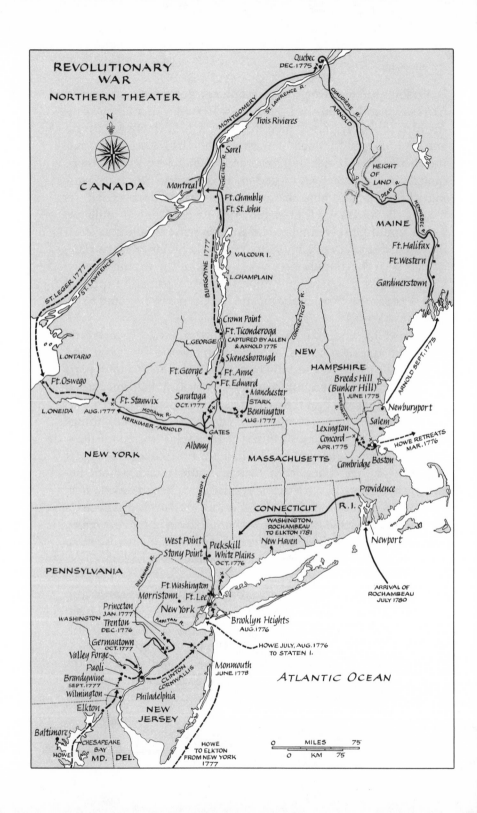

REVOLUTIONARY
WAR

NORTHERN THEATER

N

CANADA

Quebec
DEC. 1775

St. LAWRENCE R.

MONTGOMERY

Trois Rivieres

CHAUDIÈRE R.

ARNOLD

DEAD R.

HEIGHT
OF
LAND

Sorel

RICHELIEU R.

Montreal

Ft. Chambly
Ft. St. John

MAINE

KENNEBEC R.

Ft. Halifax
Ft. Western

Gardinerstown

St. LAWRENCE R.

ST. LEGER 1777

BURGOYNE 1777

VALCOUR I.

L. CHAMPLAIN

CONNECTICUT R.

L. ONTARIO

Crown Point
Ft. Ticonderoga
CAPTURED BY ALLEN
& ARNOLD 1775

Skenesborough

NEW

HAMPSHIRE

ARNOLD SEPT. 1775

Ft. Oswego

L. GEORGE

Ft. George

Ft. Anne
Ft. Edward

Manchester
STARK
Bennington
AUG. 1777

Breeds Hill
(Bunker Hill)
JUNE 1775

Newburyport

MERRIMACK R.

Salem

Ft. Stanwix

AUG. 1777

MOHAWK R.

Saratoga
OCT. 1777

HERKIMER-ARNOLD

GATES

Lexington
Concord
APR. 1775

HOWE RETREATS
MAR. 1776

L. ONEIDA

Albany

Cambridge Boston

NEW YORK

MASSACHUSETTS

Providence

HUDSON R.

CONNECTICUT

R. I.

WASHINGTON,
ROCHAMBEAU
TO ELKTON 1781

New Haven

Newport

West Point
Stony Point

Peekskill
White Plains
OCT. 1776

ARRIVAL OF
ROCHAMBEAU
JULY 1780

PENNSYLVANIA

DELAWARE R.

Ft. Washington
Morristown   Ft. Lee

New York

Brooklyn Heights
AUG. 1776

Princeton
JAN. 1777
Trenton
DEC. 1776

WASHINGTON

RARITAN R.

Germantown
OCT. 1777

Valley Forge

Paoli

Brandywine
SEPT. 1777

Wilmington

Elkton

CLINTON
CORNWALLIS

Monmouth
JUNE 1778

HOWE JULY, AUG. 1776
TO STATEN I.

ATLANTIC OCEAN

Philadelphia

NEW

JERSEY

Baltimore

CHESAPEAKE
BAY

HOWE

MD.   DEL.

HOWE
TO ELKTON
FROM NEW YORK
1777

0   MILES   75

0   KM   75

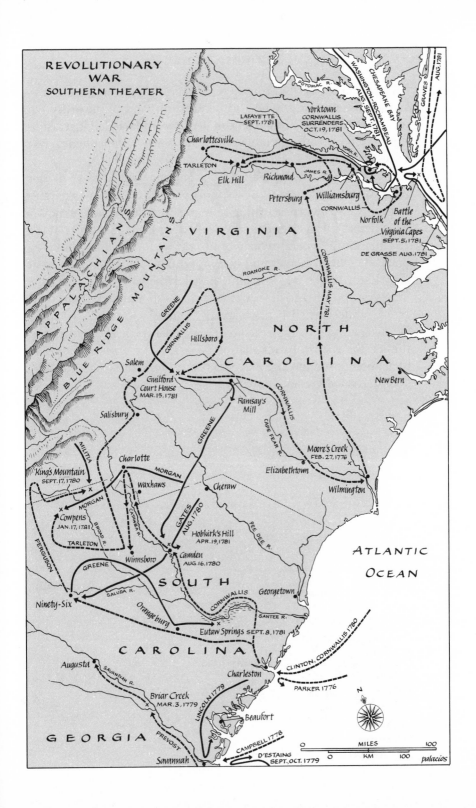

REVOLUTIONARY
WAR
SOUTHERN THEATER

APPALACHIANS

BLUE RIDGE MOUNTAINS

VIRGINIA

NORTH

CAROLINA

SOUTH

CAROLINA

GEORGIA

ATLANTIC
OCEAN

POTOMAC R.

CHESAPEAKE BAY

WASHINGTON-ROCHAMBEAU AUG.-SEPT. 1781

GRAVES AUG. 1781

LAFAYETTE SEPT. 1781

Yorktown
CORNWALLIS
SURRENDERS
OCT. 19, 1781

Charlottesville

TARLETON

Elk Hill   Richmond

Petersburg   Williamsburg

YORK R.

JAMES R.

CORNWALLIS

Norfolk

Battle
of the
Virginia Capes
SEPT. 5, 1781

DE GRASSE AUG. 1781

ROANOKE R.

CORNWALLIS MAY 1781

GREENE

CORNWALLIS

Hillsboro

Salem

Guilford
Court House
MAR. 15, 1781

Ramsay's
Mill

Salisbury

GREENE

CORNWALLIS

CAPE FEAR R.

New Bern

Moore's Creek
FEB. 27, 1776

Charlotte

MORGAN

Elizabethtown

Wilmington

King's Mountain
SEPT. 17, 1780

MILITIA

MORGAN

Waxhaws

Cheraw

Cowpens
JAN. 17, 1781

BROAD R.

CATAWBA R.

GATES 1780

Hobkirk's Hill
APR. 19, 1781

PEE DEE R.

TARLETON

FERGUSON

GREENE

Winnsboro

Camden
AUG. 16, 1780

Ninety-Six

SALUDA R.

Orangeburg

CORNWALLIS

Georgetown

SANTEE R.

Eutaw Springs SEPT. 8, 1781

CLINTON, CORNWALLIS 1780

Augusta

SAVANNAH R.

Briar Creek
MAR. 3, 1779

LINCOLN 1779

Charleston

Beaufort

PARKER 1776

N

Savannah

PREVOST

CAMPBELL 1778

D'ESTAING
SEPT., OCT. 1779

GEORGIA

0   MILES   100

0   KM   100   palacios

his head, and gestured to where Washington sat on his horse—
George Washington, who had taken command of the army before independence had even been declared and had led it at last to
this dazzling, unforgettable moment when independence was
visibly achieved.

Washington could be as starchy as anyone when it was a matter
of putting insolence in its place. Cornwallis had sent out a deputy
to give up his sword, scorning to come out himself and acknowledge defeat by an inferior; very well, it was a deputy and not the
commanding general who would receive it. Washington beckoned to General Benjamin Lincoln, who had had to surrender at
Charleston, and it was Lincoln who took the sword . . . and the
long column of British troops marched out and laid down their
arms, while French bands played "Yankee Doodle." By some
fantastic accident engineered by the eternal spirit of the fitness of
things, the British bands that came out, as by tradition, to play
their men down the line played a topical little ditty named "The
World Turned Upside Down."

CHAPTER 17

Free and Independent

YORKTOWN WAS not quite the end of the war, but it was the last important engagement. This was the second time in four years that an entire British army had surrendered to the rebels, and the Yorktown campaign had had a quality and a decisiveness—the Americans and their French allies had totally outmaneuvered and outfought their opponents on land and sea—that took all the remaining steam out of England's effort to subdue her former colonies. Soon there was hardly anyone left in the kingdom except George III who wanted to go on fighting; Lord North was driven from office in the spring of 1782, and the king had to accept a ministry that wanted peace. Only the terms remained in doubt; the fighting to all intents and purposes was over.

These terms required several months of rather intricate negotiation, even though the basic fact of American success was no longer in question. The delay stemmed chiefly from complications posed by the other belligerents. America's treaty of alliance contained a mutual pledge not to make a separate peace, and the commissioners Congress had sent to Europe in mid-1781 to seek a settlement were hampered by strict orders to keep France informed and to follow French advice and leadership in conducting their negotiations. The French themselves were ready enough for peace, their already overburdened financial system having been strained to the point of collapse by expenses in America. But France was also committed to her other ally Spain, and the Spaniards, who had entered the war in pursuit of their own ends in 1779, wanted to go on fighting until they had captured Gibraltar from Great Britain. Since their siege of the place was getting nowhere and was not likely to get anywhere, and since France had promised Spain to keep fighting until Gibraltar fell, the American attempts to find a basis for settlement within the confines of all these agreements and restrictions made little progress.

The American commissioners, fortunately, were an able group: John Adams, who had been in France since 1779 as minister plenipotentiary; tough-minded John Jay of New York, who had recently lost whatever remained of his naïveté after two years as American minister to Spain; and old Ben Franklin, who had never had any trouble beating Old World diplomats at their own game.

With Jay and Franklin carrying most of the load, the Americans eventually managed to find a way through the impasse. The two points that they had to get in any settlement with England were full recognition of United States sovereignty and independence—negotiations could not even begin until such recognition was forthcoming—and boundaries extending to the Great Lakes, the Mississippi River, and the 31st parallel (the southernmost version of the Florida border; Spain, it would develop, had another version). The Americans soon learned that British, French, and Spanish diplomats were conducting backstairs intrigue on both these points: France was encouraging British intransigence by hinting that it would not back the American demand for prior recognition of independence, and Britain and Spain were being urged to hold out for a boundary some distance east of the Mississippi, in trans-Appalachian territory both nations coveted.

From here on it was every country for itself, and the Americans maneuvered their way through the maze. Violating their instructions, they began direct talks with the British without seeking French advice or informing the French of details—taking care, however, to let the French know that talks had begun. The British commissioners proved eager enough to reach a settlement, and by no means reluctant to drive a wedge into the Franco-American alliance if they could. Before the end of 1782, playing shrewdly on the intricate network of European jealousies and rivalries, the Americans obtained everything they wanted except trading privileges within the Empire.

The preliminary treaty began with the acknowledgment that "the said United States . . . were free, sovereign, and independent. . . ." It went on to accord American fishing rights along the Grand Banks, promise withdrawal of all British troops from American soil, and accede to American demands for boundaries along the Great Lakes, the Mississippi, and the 31st parallel. (Upon reflection, the British preferred this to any arrangement that might permit Spanish or possibly French expansion into the trans-Appalachian country.) The United States Government in turn promised to do what it could to encourage restitution of confiscated Tory property, to prevent further confiscations, and to impose no obstacles to the collection of debts owed by Americans to British subjects. Having secured these terms, Jay and Franklin showed them to Count Vergennes, who until this point knew only that conversations between the American and British commissioners had been taking place.

All in all it was a stunning triumph for American diplomacy, and the French, more impressed than dismayed, proceeded to help everything else fall into place. Indeed, the American success enabled Vergennes to pressure Spain into calling it quits, and the Spaniards consented to give up on Gibraltar if Britain would relinquish Florida and Minorca. The British agreed. The final treaties ratifying all of this were signed at Paris in September 1783, and the American War for Independence was officially at an end.

— □ —

What had they really done, these onetime English colonies whose independent status as the United States of America was now confirmed after some eight years of armed conflict?

For many Americans it has been a source of comfort, especially after the world afforded comparative examples, to hold that the nation had not really undergone a revolution at all. It was more accurate to term it a war for independence, rendered necessary only because of the mother country's stubborn refusal to face reality. At the most it had been a conservative, polite revolution, waged properly within bounds by sober middle-class farmers and townsfolk and country gentlemen who never lost their respect for law and order. The American contents had simply been removed, unchanged, from the British box. There had been none of the frightening excesses of violence, social upheaval, and destruction or seizure of property made famous by the French in the 1790s and the Russians after 1917; no reign of terror, no guillotines or tumbrils or bloody purges, no mobs in the streets, no crowned heads rolling in the dust or going down before a hail of bullets in a back-country cellar.

According to this view, real revolutions were something perpetrated by foreigners—the foreign image in this context being a blurred compound of unkempt sans-culottes, volatile Latins, bearded Slavic bomb throwers, and ranting demagogues. By contrast, Americans had won their independence between two pinches of snuff, and had been so orderly and restrained that well-heeled descendants in the late nineteenth century and after, people whom Daniel Morgan's profane riflemen and Sam Adams' unruly fellow townsmen and Washington's ragged Continentals would neither have recognized nor liked very much, could organize patriotic societies and glory in the name of Sons or Daughters of the American Revolution.

A more scholarly rendition of the same idea stressed the point that colonial America was a land of small property owners and staid Protestants; these folk, long accustomed to freedom and self-government in a laxly run empire, were really doing no more than force Great Britain (their remonstrances having failed) to ratify a political situation that had long existed. With a minimum of violence and no alteration in their social and political institutions and leadership beyond what was rendered necessary by the departure of English officialdom and a few loyalists, the orderly transition from colonies to independent republic was marked by continuity and consensus. This view was challenged during the early twentieth century by progressive historians who detected signs of real social conflict and democratic gains during the Revolutionary generation, but the consensus-and-continuity school in one form or another has been the favorite. We have prided ourselves on being too practical and moderate a people to indulge in political excesses or utopian fancies.

Nonsense. Something far more epochal than a war for independence was under way after Lexington and Concord. There was little doubt at the time, in either America or Europe, that the English colonists were staging a full-fledged revolution. A glance at how they moved toward their goal and how they defined it may afford some clues.

From the beginning they had systematically proceeded to take the law into their own hands. This was admittedly where they were accustomed to having it, but from 1774 on they acted in open defiance of authority and without a shadow of legality. Revolution, reduced to its essentials, has been defined as an unlawful change in the conditions of lawfulness, and Americans were effecting precisely that. Their assemblies, prorogued by anxious royal governors as the final confrontation began, simply reconvened on their own initiative, reconstituted themselves as provincial legislatures, and proceeded to govern on their own authority. A whole network of committees of correspondence, town meetings, and conventions, many of which had been tuning up for years as the quarrel with England progressed, also sprang into operation. The colonists capped this homemade political edifice with a Continental Congress that had not the shadow of a legal basis for existence. This Congress in cooperation with the provincial legislatures then appointed a commander-in-chief and put an army in the field to pick up where the Minute Men and farm boys on the road back from Concord had left off—in armed opposition to law and order as represented by the king's troops.

As for the heralded moderation with which the patriots handled loyalists and their property (in contrast to the vengeful Jacquerie and Jacobin leaders in Revolutionary France, who seized the châteaux and expropriated the great estates and drove terrified nobles into exile or the guillotine), Professor Robert Palmer has made some interesting comparisons. On the theory that two good litmus tests of a revolution are the amount of confiscated property and the number of political exiles, he estimated that, in proportion to size and population, Revolutionary America sequestered about as much private property and drove about as many loyalists out of the country as Revolutionary France managed to do a decade and a half later.

It was true that the patriots did not resort to so grimly final a solution to political dissent as the guillotine, but the best explanation for this, in Palmer's judgment, is the relative weakness of Tory opposition in America. Had it been as strong and as determined as in Revolutionary France, it would almost inevitably have touched off sterner responses. The most ardent American loyalists, he adds—in contrast to the French émigrés—never returned after the struggle to perpetuate and fan the antagonisms between revolution and old regime.

Certainly there is scattered evidence, to say nothing of observable traits in the American character, to suggest that the patriots were prepared to come down upon disloyalty as heavily as the situation seemed to warrant. In New Jersey, for example, where political instability and turmoil were at a premium as contending armies maneuvered back and forth across the state, the inadequacy of provincial government led a determined group of patriots to form a committee of public safety and run the province through representatives on mission armed with arbitrary authority. The result was price fixing and other controls, loyalty oaths (often exacted at gunpoint), forced requisitions, property confiscation, and rule with an iron hand—all of which, as Professor Palmer notes, bore striking resemblance to the situation in Robespierre's France a short time later. When ardent Tories and ardent patriots collided they fought with the same intense savagery that characterizes any civil war, and in areas where patriots were worried about treasonous intrigue they had a way of resorting to the kind of window-smashing, tar-and-feather intimidation that the Sons of Liberty had employed against royal officials a decade earlier. In short, the people at the center of the American cause were playing for keeps and they played rough when they had to, which suggests that images of a mannered contest between English and American gentlemen are absurdly wide of the mark.

If this were not enough, the inhabitants of the new republic were staking their entire system upon two interrelated and downright epochal principles: a workable version of the hitherto abstract, illusory concept of popular sovereignty, and the cluster of ideas set forth in the preamble to the Declaration of Independence.

Americans did not invent the notion of the sovereignty of the people, but in the process of breaking from England they had done several things with it, and what they had done was revolutionary. Specifically, they had formulated and begun acting upon certain key assumptions: first, that the people literally "constituted" the state and the entire mechanism of government, neither of which had any other legal basis for existence; further, that this sovereignty belonged *only* to the people; and finally, that it belonged equally to *all* of them. Each of these items is worth brief attention.

The means whereby the people exercised their constituent power were developed during the war years, chiefly from the grass roots, as men searched for ways of protecting their rights from the encroachments of those in authority. (Even elected bodies, it was recognized, might exceed their powers.) The answer, emerging in several localities as the war progressed and formalized at the state level by Massachusetts in 1780, was a distinctively American contribution to political science. This was the constitutional convention: a one-shot, non-perpetuating assemblage specifically gathered for the single purpose of framing a document that would define and limit the powers of government and all government officials. Once ratified by the people, this constitution became a kind of higher law—the forthcoming federal document outspokenly called itself the supreme law of the land—to which all subsequent statutes and political procedures must conform. The Massachusetts example was followed by New Hampshire a few years later and by the nation itself in 1787. Thereafter the device of the constitutional convention became standard American procedure, a formal mechanism whereby the ultimate, unimpeachable sovereignty of the people could express itself and legalize the system of government under which they agreed to live.

The notion that this sovereignty did not have to be shared or ratified anywhere else—the people as court of last resort, so to speak—represented another American innovation. European philosophers had long conceded that a voice in the political process rightfully belonged to the "people" (variously defined, and often more in theory than in practice), but always as one voice among several: sovereignty was looked upon as shared or divided among estates or orders to countervailing elements like the traditional King, Lords, and Commons. America recognized only Commons.

The corollary to this—no estates, no privileged orders, no second-class citizens—was the most revolutionary concept of all. It was nothing less than the principle of human equality, which like the others had grown with a kind of haphazard logic out of the dispute with Great Britain. Freedom gradually came to be viewed as something more than a historic attribute of English citizenship. In order to mean what reflective colonists began to see in it, freedom could not be defined as anything less than humanity's birthright, belonging equally to everyone. Thomas Jefferson did not hedge this bet; he called it a self-evident truth.

It is impossible to study the Revolutionary generation without paying some sort of tribute to the collective wisdom and genius of the Founding Fathers. Although this genius is most often cited in terms of the Federal Constitution, a frame of government that has proved flexible enough to adapt to changing circumstances for nearly two centuries, the Fathers deserve even higher marks for that preamble to the Declaration of Independence. In a more radical way this explosive document has also shown its flexibility by proving infinitely expandable—or rather, by impelling repeated enlargements of the nation's working definition of citizenship.

In 1776 the document called for far more than America was prepared to deliver. But what it called for could never quite be forgotten or ignored, though each succeeding generation would contain men who tried. Those sweeping assertions remained, and our experiment had indisputably originated with them. As a result—slowly, painfully, haltingly, sometimes violently—their application has been extended and broadened.

Since the Declaration proclaimed human equality and inalienable rights for all even though the American political process excluded women, black slaves, and that not inconsiderable minority of the white male population which neither owned property nor paid taxes, it is easy to belittle the men of 1776 and their accomplishment. They can be dubbed inconsistent, if not insincere. Jefferson himself owned slaves; so did Madison and Washington and most of the other stars in that remarkable galaxy of Revolutionary Virginians. How (it was asked at the time, chiefly by disgruntled British observers and now and then by observant blacks) could a nation of slaveholders talk about universal rights to life and liberty? From then on, purist reformers have pounced on all of this as evidence that the Fathers were little more than pious hypocrites—while arch-conservatives have suggested that the Fathers never really meant to admit anyone but white male property owners to full citizenship, the implication being that later generations need not do so either.

Both views are off target. The Fathers were keenly, even painfully conscious of the discrepancy between the political ideals they put forth and the political reality in which they operated. ("I tremble for my country," slaveowner Jefferson wrote, "when I reflect that God is just.") They were men of affairs, most of them trained in the law and well versed in history and political thought. Their ranks included several who were uncommonly good with words, the pre-eminent example being the man they chose to put what they had been talking about into written form. The framers of the Declaration were neither abstract theorists debating some hypothetical ideal state nor propagandists trying to make their venture look good by employing noble phrases that said more than they meant.

They wanted it to look good, to be sure, and they did not scruple at resorting to propaganda. But above all they wanted it to *be* good, and they gave every evidence of weighing their words carefully. It should be remembered that the issue had not been settled in the early summer of 1776. It had barely been joined, and the formidable armada and army being deployed in and about New York by Admiral Lord Howe and his brother seemed well on the verge of settling it England's way. The signers of the Declaration were putting everything they had on the line, including their lives, and they knew it. They had thought through the implications of what they were doing and saying. And they meant what they said.

They deliberately meant, in other words, to speak for all humanity in that preamble. When they wrote it, there were large numbers of Americans who could claim little or no share in the rights being enunciated. But the door was being left ajar for them, and for voiceless, faceless legions of their kind the world over, and for millions yet unborn. It was being left open consciously, because all-inclusiveness—a better life and a stake in society for

everyone, regardless of race or sex or creed or previous condition
—was what the American dream at its highest had already come
to mean.

The Fathers (like their ancestors the Puritans, whom they resembled in more ways than one) were an indissoluble blend of realist and idealist: practical men of affairs who were also soaring
visionaries. They knew and partook of their own times well
enough to shy away from advancing immediate claims for those
whom gender or skin color or poverty had placed beyond the
pale. But their faith in humanity's ultimate destiny and capability
was such that they could use words like "all" in the confident belief that time would someday bring reality into line with theory.
And it would be more apt to do so, they knew, if the theory were
proclaimed at the outset without qualifiers. As practical men they
would not try to go beyond prevailing social attitudes. Yet as
children of the Enlightenment, which they were, they would
blithely proclaim that the sky was the limit.

For in America the idea that the sky was the limit—that a society of free people in a new, untrammeled land could in fact do
and be anything it chose—did not seem farfetched in the late
eighteenth century. In America, realist and visionary were one
and inseparable because the loftiest of visions had enough of reality in it to seem plausible.

Here lay the basis of a faith that could move mountains. The
course of human events had reached one of its decisive turning
points, and a great deal of human history for the next two centuries (and beyond) was going to be different because the men of
1776 had first enunciated the dream, in phrases that still contain
fire—liberty, equality, pursuit of happiness, inalienable human
rights—and had then proceeded to show that it just might work.
Whoever chose that tune for Lord Cornwallis' military bands at
Yorktown had known what he was about.

—□—

The actual advances in the direction of this millennial social vision during and after the Revolution were modest enough. (America's storied practicality and moderation lie not in the goals but in the mode and pace of trying to get there; long, slow tacks have usually been preferred over sailing directly into the wind. The deep vein of conservatism that runs through the national temperament has acted as a healthy restraining influence, forcing a society in quest of perfection to make haste slowly and recognize that the impossible takes a little while.)

Yet advances were made. Americans founded a spate of new colleges and academies, and their children encountered the first editions of Noah Webster's *Speller* and *Reader*. People took steps in the direction of separating church and state, with Virginia going the distance in 1786 when its legislature enacted Thomas Jefferson's draft bill into a law which provided that "no man shall be compelled to frequent or support any religious worship, place, or ministry whatsoever."

Aware of what their Declaration said and recognizing an incongruity when they saw one, they made the first stumbling efforts to contain and weaken the institution of slavery. The Northern states, which had few slaves and no important economic interests dependent upon them, moved at varying speeds to get rid of the institution altogether. Even in the South, where much of the economy and social structure were built upon it, more than one state responded to the flush of revolutionary enthusiasm by prohibiting the further importation of slaves. The number of Southern manumissions rose sharply, though not enough to make a dent in the system. Anti-slavery sentiment was visibly growing.

Such evidence strengthened a hope, compounded equally of revolutionary idealism and wishful thinking, that slavery was on its way to dying an easy natural death. Even as the hope flourished, a potent combination of economic, geographic, technological, and social facts was winding up to administer a knock-out blow: power-driven British textile mills with an insatiable appetite for cotton, rich black soil lying in wide belts across the Gulf coastal plain, and ideas already germinating in the fertile minds of a Yankee inventor named Eli Whitney and a Haitian slave named Toussaint L'Ouverture. Neither the hopes nor the prospects for slavery's easy natural death could withstand a blow with that much strength behind it.

However, if the institution was fated to survive and grow until it took a shattering head-on collision with the Declaration of Independence and assorted other forces to begin resolving the contradiction, the implications of the human equality clause had been glimpsed by sensitive Americans of both races and both sections. Quaker voices like that of gentle stubborn John Woolman had been raised and would not hush, and a humanitarian ground swell against slavery was also gathering force across the Atlantic. Slowly but perceptibly, the mills of God had begun to grind.

Though not exactly in bondage, the female half of the white population was also very much on the political sideline. The relative scarcity of women in colonial America had enabled them to improve their legal status, especially in the matter of inheritance; and several competent females had done well managing farms and other businesses. But only a few voices had begun protesting women's inferior status—the most notable being that of charming, irrepressible Abigail Adams, John's wife, whose perception and caustic wit were fully on a par with her husband's. Mrs. Adams had boldly informed him that women would not wait forever to claim their rightful share of the Declaration's promise. As yet, however, the movement for equality of the sexes was a cloud on the horizon no larger than a woman's hand.

The notion of equality was making faster headway against the status quo in other, less difficult areas. Most states lowered the property requirements for voting during the war years, although only Pennsylvania and Georgia went so far as to extend the franchise to all taxpayers. Larger property requirements for office-holding remained the rule everywhere, and Americans were still in general agreement that a degree of property ownership was necessary for the proper exercise of citizenship—on the old but still defensible theory that landless men were too vulnerable to pressure from landlords or employers. In any case, the wide diffusion of landownership did not make the property requirement a major violation of the equality clause, and land in America was still easy to come by.

Even so, concern for the debtor and the poor man was on the rise. A few states responded to the depressed, tight-money conditions of the 1780s by issuing paper currency and passing stay laws and other measures designed to give debtors a better chance to get out from under. But not everyone looked with favor upon this tendency, as we shall see.

The war undoubtedly widened and smoothed the path of social mobility (in both directions) by creating new opportunities. Enterprising debtors could take advantage of inflated prices and wartime demand to pay their obligations and acquire a stake; the disruption of old trading patterns and the hasty loyalist exodus wiped out many an established mercantile house and permitted ambitious men from the lower ranks of trade, especially those with an eye for army contracting or speculation in land and government securities, to rise to the top. A few small farmers improved their status by acquiring pieces of confiscated Tory property, although most of that real estate probably passed in large blocks into the hands of more affluent holders and speculators.

Democracy's biggest gains were undoubtedly the less tangible ones. Many farmers and mechanics and other plain folk who went to war displayed enough talent to become sergeants or line officers, and few among the thousands of men who served with the Continentals or the militia could fail to see the world and their place in it and the people around them with a new and sharper eye. The practice of deferring to one's betters had long been on shaky ground in America, and what remained of it was badly undermined by any war effort that talked of liberty and equality as readily as this one did.

Indeed, the concept of equality dealt most harshly with the time-honored notion of a social hierarchy with an elite patrician class at its apex. This notion still commanded many adherents and had a few days in court yet to come, but it was living on borrowed time. The upper classes had furnished vital leadership for the patriot cause both before and during the Revolution, and in a way they had co-opted themselves. Their own resentment of British authority had led them to rally the mass of ordinary citizens to their support back in the Stamp Act days, and the resulting coalition had inevitably taken on a more democratic cast as the debate with England over rights and liberties moved toward its climax. By 1776 the better sorts, without having quite planned it that way, found themselves leading an armed revolution committed to independence in the name of universal rights and rule by the people. The most conservative members of the American elite were so horrified by this that they became loyalists and fled. And for the majority of first families who stayed and continued to lead, it was a question of retaining large doubts about democracy but accepting it in order to win.

Now they had won, and the social and political climate would never be the same again. Ordinary voters still tended to choose their leaders from among the patrician element, but no longer with the old ready deference. The war and *Common Sense* and all those slogans had changed things. Affluence and blue blood no longer sufficed by themselves; leaders now had to have something special going for them, like proven ability or some combination of personal qualities that induced a positive response.

Even more important, Americans had tasted enough equality to form a deep-seated dislike of anything that smacked of special privilege—the very essence of an aristocratic system—and they were quick to detect signs of it. A storm of criticism greeted the formation of the Society of the Cincinnati by a group of Continental Army officers in 1783, and its members and meetings remained deeply suspect. A medical society in Connecticut that sought to improve standards by licensing doctors had trouble getting a charter because it proposed to grant life memberships. Except for a few semi-resident Englishmen, colonial America had never had a titled nobility, and the new nation was determined to keep it that way; state laws forbade American citizens to accept titles from foreign countries. From now on, believers in an ordered aristocratic society would be on the defensive, and a potent political rallying point lay in that fear of special privilege: the individual or group that was liable to the charge of having any—especially if it concerned a privileged position in or near the government—was sooner or later going to be in trouble.

The same pressure in the direction of more responsible and democratic government could be seen in the political system that emerged during the Revolution. The institutions were basically those of the colonial era, but in each state the reaction against uncontrolled and arbitrary authority led to a strengthening of the popularly elected lower house and a weakening of the executive and the upper house (the old royal governor and appointed council, a privileged element which had usually represented and upheld English authority). Governors were sometimes denied the veto, and in some states the powers of the lower house were extended to include that of choosing both the governor and the members of the state senate. States added bills of rights to their constitutions, so that there could be no doubt as to the existence and nature of those inherent attributes of a free people—jury trial, habeas corpus, free speech, the right to assemble, and so on—that government was forbidden to touch.

All of this reflected and reinforced a growing American conviction that they had indeed created a new and different society. What made it different from the prevailing Old World model, and infinitely superior, was the multitude of ways in which human rights had been established and safeguarded. Freedom not merely existed but had been defined and codified to render it safe from encroachment; an open society of enfranchised independent property owners offered the best guarantee against subversion or domination of representative government by a privileged minority; political power was sufficiently divided and circumscribed and close to the people to be safe from usurpation or dangerous misuse.

It is not surprising that a people with such an array of priorities would accord the most fragmentary and vestigial authority to their central government. This government was created by the Articles of Confederation, which the Continental Congress had drawn up in late 1777 and submitted to the states for approval. The Articles vested all national power—what there was of it—in a Congress, to which each state legislature appointed delegates and in which each state had a single vote. Congress could make war and peace, military and naval appointments, and treaties and alliances; it could send and receive ambassadors, coin and borrow money, create a post office, and regulate Indian affairs.

The Confederation government is best understood by looking at what it lacked. There was no national executive or system of courts, no power to levy taxes or regulate trade or act directly upon the citizen or even enact laws; Congress could only pass resolutions, ask the states for money, and govern by supplication. Important matters like war and peace and appropriations required the consent of nine states; amendments to the Articles required the consent of all thirteen. Delegates were elected for one-year terms and forbidden to serve more than three years in any six, which meant that Congress lacked continuity in membership. It also lacked a permanent capital, aimlessly occupying five different cities in as many years. Indifference or slowness in appointing delegates meant that it frequently lacked a quorum.

Congress did its best, setting up departments which, given real power, could have functioned quite adequately. Unfortunately it had no power to give them, and although highly capable secretaries were named they were not actually able to do very much. There was, for instance, a Department of Foreign Affairs, presided over first by Robert Livingston of New York and then by John Jay; there was a War Department under the redoubtable General Henry Knox, and a Department of Finance headed by

Robert Morris; and these men could do only what the states let them do and held the shadow of authority rather than the substance.

In short, the nation was little more than a league of sovereign states, each of which retained its "sovereignty, freedom, and independence, and every power, jurisdiction, and right" that the Articles did not expressly give to Congress. But this was the kind of national government most Americans wanted as they entered the postwar years. The loosest possible confederation of thirteen independent commonwealths was now on its own—and had embarked, willy-nilly, upon a sea of troubles. It remained to be seen whether a nation so constituted could handle them, or survive at all.

At this point the power of geography began to be felt. The thirteen independent states were banked up against the blue mountains that hid the sunset, no longer limited by them, powerfully drawn by what men could see through the gaps. Beyond the mountains there was what looked like limitless space linked to an entirely unlimited possibility, land that was empty except for Stone Age men who had begun to see what was going to happen but did not know how to stop it. This land was subject to certain claims. Many of the thirteen states had papers or charters or inflated ideas, and almost all of them had real estate dealers who were among the first Americans to see that although it was profitable to swindle the red man it could be much more profitable to swindle one another. This empty land, an empire unrealized, pulled the new nation on, molded it into shape, determined finally that it must be one nation and not a loose federation of independent principalities. It had to be attended to and it had to be attended to at once and not at some time in the hazy future.

The problem could be stated quite simply. Many of the states had territorial claims to the land west of the mountains; these lands, then, were territories—but territories of what? If the states claiming those territories became a nation, as they were trying to do, did these claims perpetuate the old divisions that set state apart from state or were they common property? Would they remain territories forever or would they grow up into statehood; and if they did, what sort of statehood would they reach? A powerful state with extensive claims to the Western lands—for example, Virginia, whose grandly worded charter included title to just about all the land from the Ohio Valley to the farthest Great Lakes—might presently become so great that all of the old antagonisms would be vastly intensified and the United States could turn out to be a federation of greatly unequal (and consequently jealous) states rather than a unified nation. There was a real danger here, and men saw it; and Maryland, finally, refused to ratify the Articles of Confederation unless each state gave up its Western rights and turned them over to the central government. (The fact that Maryland had no Western claims, but did have a fair number of well-placed speculators who did not want to be disadvantaged by rivals from states possessing such claims, was quite relevant to Maryland's posture here. Some of the states without claims—Pennsylvania was another; so was New Jersey—had some of the ablest speculators, a coincidence to which the ultimate triumph of a unified national policy with regard to the West owed a great deal.)

Arguments in favor of national unity, whether advanced by speculators or patriots—they were frequently one and the same —led Congress in September 1780 to urge the states to make "a liberal surrender of their territorial claims." For reasons in which calculations of national welfare and private gain were indissolubly mixed, the states were sooner or later persuaded to comply. Virginia, fittingly enough, led the way. In October Congress adopted a proposal submitted by two Virginians, Joseph Jones and James Madison, that lands ceded by the states should be held for the common benefit of the United States and should eventually be formed into new states that would enter the Union on a

basis of precise equality with the older ones. Not long after this —
on January 2, 1781 — Virginia's legislature, acting "for the sake of
the public good," turned over to the central government all of
Virginia's territory north of the Ohio River. Within the next few
years the other states with trans-Appalachian claims did likewise.

Virginia's act had been made conditional on the ratification of
the Articles of Confederation by all the states, which actually
meant by Maryland, the other twelve having ratified previously.
Maryland followed suit, the Articles were proclaimed on March
1, 1781, and the country now had a constitution.

Much more important, it had a solid and continuing reason for
existence; it owned an enormous territory in its own right which
it proposed to administer for the benefit of all the people. As a
matter of disillusioning fact, it took time to put this into effect.
Fired by Thomas Jefferson, the Congress in 1784 considered an
ordinance that would have provided for fourteen new states in
the West, would have prohibited chattel slavery everywhere west
and would have canceled all claims, concessions, and real estate
grants anywhere in the new land. In the end this was a little too
much to take, and although in 1785 Congress provided for government surveys of all of the great wilderness threaded by Indian
trails that led through forest twilight to the profound sunlight of
the prairie meadows, it developed that Congress, responsive to
people in all things, was not fitted to resist the pressures created
by important men who have money to make and would like a
permissive government. Chattel slavery would be ruled out only
north of the Ohio River, the provision for fourteen new states
was reduced to five, and by various compromises some of the
largest tracts of Western land were to be sold to the public by private speculators rather than by the central government.

More delay; then, finally, came the great Northwest Ordinance of 1787, which set forth the charter on which the country
north of the Ohio would be developed; set forth, in sober fact, the
enormous principle that although the new nation was developing
an empire it would not become an empire with subject colonies
but a republic of equal self-governing states, with one grade of

statehood just as there was one grade of citizenship. The Northwest country was blocked out into five territories, and a clear schedule was worked out. At first, when settlement had barely begun, a territory would be entirely under the control of the central government; later, when its population had increased, the developing territory would receive the right of self-government in all local matters—still a ward of the central authority, but a ward that could swiftly learn to walk alone. Finally, upon reaching a given level of population, the territory could attain statehood, not by petition but as a matter of right. Once it reached statehood it would stand on a basis of full equality with the older commonwealths. There were thirteen states at the time and now there are fifty, and the thirty-seven that have been formed since Yorktown all came up the same way.

Rarely has an American Congress passed a measure of greater importance or more far-reaching effect than this Ordinance of 1787. Once and for all, it determined what sort of country this was going to be; the concept of complete equality, so nobly voiced in the Declaration, was written into the basic document that would determine how the nation grew. It compelled men to look past their own dooryards to something unlimited beyond the horizon, and decreed that a man's place as a member of the American Republic would be forever greater than his place as a resident of a single state. The ordinance also set an important precedent by explicitly prohibiting slavery in the Northwest Territory, and in all states to be created therein.

Thus under the Articles of Confederation the Congress found the power to determine the future course the young Republic was going to take, and it acted with a daring and a breadth of vision that are still impressive. Unfortunately this Congress that could exert so much control over the future had almost no control over the present, and the road to what was going to be—exciting enough, by all odds—led straight across the formidable obstacles created by what already was.

———□———

It was one thing, for instance, to say how the Northwest country was going to be built, but it was quite another to get men out there so that they could start building. Under the Treaty of Paris the Americans had title to this country, but the British still held it—or held a good part of it, at any rate, and virtually controlled the rest—and the Congress had no power whatever to get them out. British military posts in places like Detroit and Michilimack-inac remained as they were, British flag overhead, redcoats on parade for the sunset gun at the end of day, British agents quietly counseling the Indian tribes to go on using the Western land as a vast hunting ground to which no white men would come except for a few friendly traders from Montreal.

In part this was (as the British loftily explained) because the Americans themselves had failed to carry out certain provisions of the Treaty of Paris, which provided for cash payments to émigré loyalists who had been dispossessed of their lands during the war and which also recognized the legal collectibility of pre-war debts owed to London merchants by American citizens. Yet Congress could do nothing whatever about these except "recommend" to the states that loyalists and creditors be assuaged. It had been clear all along that Congress lacked authority in this field, and the British had never actually expected anything to come of it. But it was convenient now to balance one failure to live up to the treaty against another, and so the British presence in the Northwest remained. The British continued to occupy the strategic forts and control the fur trade, quietly supported the Indians in their hostility to American settlers, and waited for the anticipated collapse of the brash young Republic. When that collapse came Britain proposed to be where she could pick up the pieces.

Collapse was predictable, London believed, because the American government was impotent. Of all the authorities belonging to a central government this one lacked the most fundamental—the power to tax. It could make requisitions on the states for needed funds, but if the states failed to meet the requisitions nothing could be done about it. In the same way Congress could call on the states to provide troops, but if the states refused, that ended the matter. Congress had the authority to make treaties and alliances, but each state could impose its own tariff laws, and when Congress tried to negotiate a treaty with Great Britain an official in London unkindly remarked that thirteen separate treaties would really be needed. In point of plain fact, Britain at this time controlled American trade as completely as it had done before Bunker Hill; and the thirteen states in their turn were erecting trade barriers against each other rather than trying to get united action for freedom of trade overseas. About all of this Congress could do absolutely nothing.

This was felt where it hurt. The multifarious works of men's hands and the varying bounty of the Lord on sea and land had always compelled Americans to live by trade, and one of the things leading to revolution had been the fact that the rules governing colonial trade had been devised to benefit the people back home rather than the outlanders who were doing the trading. Now, however, it began to be clear that restrictive British authority had offered certain benefits. Americans trading abroad before 1776 had had access to credit and financing, and to a share in lucrative markets which were closed to foreign traders; they had also enjoyed protection from the arrant lawlessness that made life at sea so eventful in those days. A case in point was provided by the merciless sea rovers sent out by Moorish states in the western Mediterranean; these corsairs considered infidel traders fair game, but ships from British colonies usually fared well because the royal navy always cruised not far beyond the horizon. Americans learned that trading in the Mediterranean without any protection could involve painful risks, and their government could offer no protection at all. The British West Indies market, long a mainstay for American producers and traders, was now closed to American shipping, and their government could not help them here either.

The difficulties were interrelated, and growing. American securities were worthless, America could gain no commercial treaties worth mentioning, American credit in Europe was non-existent, and the navy that might have checked the Barbary pirates could not be built because the American government could not levy taxes. Peace had brought an inevitable postwar depression. There was a woeful shortage of hard money, commerce was stagnating, and an unending pressure of debts bore down upon farmers, merchants, such bankers as there were, and on all units of government. If Britain was trying to pressure the Republic back into subservience she had everything in her favor. All the elements of collapse seemed to be present.

It was not just England. Out West the great opportunity that was compelling the new nation to take thought for a great future was simultaneously presenting it with a formidable problem. The vast rich acreage west of the Appalachians was a vacuum that pulled men irresistibly, so that a region subject to the haziest authority was becoming peopled by an eternally energetic breed that was going to establish a society here no matter what. And not only Britain but Spain, sullen because she had gone to war for a gain that never materialized, had taken an especial interest in these settlers and the land they occupied.

Spain was a mighty empire that had grown hollow at the core and feeble in its vital nerve centers, but it still wore the robes and ornaments of its days of greatness and was accepted by most men as if the present shadow still had its old weight. Spain held Florida and the land west of the Mississippi, reached out with palsied-majestic hands to control the entire river valley, and intrigued endlessly to extend its sway, steadfastly refusing to admit that the upstart Republic owned anything at all west of the mountains. The Treaty of Paris had given America title to everything east of the Mississippi River from the Great Lakes to Florida, whose northern boundary was fixed along the 31st parallel. But Spain had never signed that treaty and refused to accept its terms. As Madrid believed and tirelessly asserted, Florida extended some 175 miles north of the 31st parallel, and anyway because of various incursions by Spanish troops Spain virtually controlled everything south of the Tennessee River as far east as Georgia.

American settlers were already moving into the Ohio Valley and down into what are now Kentucky and Tennessee, and they began to see that they were in a bind. Their only hope of survival lay in their ability to send to the outside world, at a profit, the bulky cargoes of corn, pork, whiskey, hides, and lumber which were all they had to offer, and these products could not possibly afford to go to the eastern seaboard by wagon over the mountains. They could only go out by water, which meant by the Mississippi and its tributaries—and Spain controlled the Mississippi, controlled especially its mouth and seaport, New Orleans, through which everything produced in the interior had to pass. And in 1784 Spain closed the port and river to American shipping.

To make the lesson more pointed, Spain was ready to relax this restriction for American frontiersmen who might accept Spanish guidance, perhaps even Spanish sovereignty complete with Spanish flags over the Daniel Boone country, in return for the chance to market their produce and make a living. It might be that destiny was about to execute a bewildering side step so that the great American heartland would become a chain of Spanish colonies, with the immeasurable weight of a legendary Old World pride balanced on the muzzles of Kentucky rifles.

In the end of course it did not happen so, but many intrigues, treasonous plots, and fantastic schemes were born of this and they lay in the air like the distorting heat pulsations of an August noon in the corn belt, hard to decipher, impossible to ignore. To this day most of these convulsive veiled intents and purposes are hazy and indistinct, but their meaning is clear enough. The men who had gone on to occupy the great new land opened to them by the young Republic were going to hold and use and grow with that land, come what may. They would greatly prefer to live under the American flag but they were going to remain in any case, under any flag or under no flag, and they had the sinewy ruthless determination that had already emerged as a distinguishing American trait. If this powerless Republic could not help them now they might well decide to become part of a Spanish protectorate or a Spanish province or a Spanish something-or-other beyond the Appalachians. If it became Spanish, to be sure, it would be like no other Spanish dominion that ever was, and anyone who can imagine the toplofty dignity of Old Castile living unruffled amid the likes of Mike Fink is at liberty to do so. But the threat that America stood on the verge of being dispossessed in the great interior valley was real enough.

America's one friend among the imperial powers was France, but at the moment that asset had little cash value. The difficulty was that privately the French had America cast in the role of satellite, useful enough but not expected ever to have a real life of its own. The infection France had taken from the American Revolution had not yet developed its disturbing symptoms. For the time being the French monarchy was conscious of nothing more than an unpleasant shortness of breath and a dismaying weakness in the muscular areas; the men at Versailles went on making imperial plans just as if something might someday come of them, and America was a pawn to be played. The United States did have a commercial treaty with France, but its benefits were moderate. The great empires that conducted world affairs were economic as well as political entities, world trade was under their control, and one and all they were run by predators. America's government simply did not have the strength to defend the nation's interests in this area, and if economic independence could not be had, political independence was not likely to last long either.

— □ —

Be that as it may, government under the Articles of Confederation was functioning about the way most people wanted it to, which was hardly at all. To an extent that modern citizens find difficult to imagine, government two hundred years ago touched the ordinary American's life so rarely and so gently that he might well live his days without ever encountering it. Although the war had of course brought the state into many people's lives with a vengeance, even here the scope by modern standards was small: there was no conscription and no compulsory taxation, and aside from those whose loyalties were suspect or whose property stood in the path of the contending armies, involvement tended to be voluntary and readily terminable. For those who wanted no part of the struggle there was plenty of trackless wilderness or remote backwater to hide in.

And when the war ended nearly everyone assumed (in a fashion that would prove typical) that the need for active government had disappeared and things could go back to the way they were. Wars rarely permit this kind of luxury, but for a few years under their Articles of Confederation the American people came close to achieving a restoration of the good old days: a remote and ineffectual government that never bothered you and could generally be ignored, taxes and other important matters decided by one's friends and neighbors in town meeting or country court or at the statehouse, and freedom as most Americans defined it—freedom to be left alone—a very real and enjoyable possession indeed.

Since this was life the way nearly everyone wanted it, the burden of proof lay with that energetic minority who could see beyond the local horizon and wanted to make changes. To be sure, changes were needed. National government had no armed forces, no executive, no power to tax or regulate trade or enforce its will, and it faced an increasing number of problems which it was poorly equipped to handle. But the magnitude of these problems may loom larger in retrospect than it did at the time, if only because we know how things came out—Federal Constitution, stronger government, Hamilton and Marshall and Jackson and Lincoln successively reaffirming the power of the Union, one nation indivisible, and so on. It is all so logical that an alternative political system, such as the survival in slightly modified form of the government under the Articles of Confederation, seems virtually unthinkable.

Perhaps it was less unthinkable at the time. The proponents of change were swimming against the current in the 1780s. They succeeded anyway and have had a good press ever since, but a majority of their contemporaries would take some persuading. Outside of that diverse minority whose interests were being hurt —speculators and frontiersmen with Western ambitions, seaboard merchants cramped by foreign trading restrictions, investors bewailing the rock-bottom value of government securities, local manufacturers undersold by cheap British imports, and a few others—Americans were not suffering acutely. Postwar dislocation and depression had hurt, in some cases badly, but by 1786 the country was beginning to emerge from all of that. The prospects for most farmers, artisans, shopkeepers, and politicians were still contained within the bounds of the local community, and for such folk things tended to be satisfactory, or looking up, or at least manageable. The presence of British troops and hostile Indians and Spanish intrigue beyond the mountains and trading restrictions in the West Indies and Barbary pirates off the shores of Tripoli simply did not weigh heavily in most people's lives.

Something stood in rather delicate balance here. An American national spirit had come into being in the generation, more or less, that spanned Braddock's defeat at the Forks of the Ohio and Cornwallis' surrender at Yorktown, and a great many Americans had acquired a sense of country that went beyond attachment to one's province or home town. But this national spirit was a far cry from the screaming-eagle patriotism of later years, when responses to flag and Fourth of July and Lincoln's call for volunteers would show how deep and visceral the nation's hold upon people's loyalties had become. The eighteenth-century brand of nationalism was a tentative thing, a tender green shoot that had most of its growing still to do. As yet it consisted chiefly of a sense of shared values, a common heritage, and a cherished way of life, all of which in turn could be summed up in words like "liberty." Americans had fought Great Britain in the name of liberty and they had won, but their "Americanism" was as yet merely localism writ large: the hard-won liberty of each community to do as it chose with almost no outside restraints whatever. This in a way was what the war had been all about, and this kind of localism did not so much oppose American nationalism as embody it.

The matter went even deeper. Americans whose sense of unity went on further than a shared desire to be free from constraint were not being simple-minded. At bottom the whole dispute with England had revolved around the question of power: its location, its use and abuse, who exercised how much and by whose authority. If the American colonist had come out of that struggle with a single idea etched across his consciousness, it was a profound, abiding distrust of power and a determination to keep its exercise as fragmented and minimal and close to home as possible. Over a century before Lord Acton would reduce the idea to a brief and usually misquoted aphorism, Americans had learned—from British customs officials, royal governors, ministers, and Parliament itself, to say nothing of a few of their own countrymen—all they needed to know about the corrupting effects of power.

Hence the weak central government under the Articles of Confederation, unable to tax or make people feel the exercise of authority the way king and Parliament had made them feel it after the French war. Hence the clipped wings of state governors and upper chambers and the strengthening of popularly chosen representative assemblies. Power was "safe" (if at all) in direct ratio to its closeness to the people, which finally meant the local community. Any inconveniences or difficulties stemming from inadequate central government could be tolerated, because the alternative was to invite a return of the conditions that had caused the Revolution in the first place. There is more to this view than impatient centralists of the Hamiltonian stripe, then and later, have been willing to admit.

CHAPTER 18

From Many, One

B UT THE nationalists had a point to make, too, and if their sense of urgency was exaggerated their reasoning was sound. If the American experiment was to work, it would sooner or later have to develop bonds of unity that went beyond a shared aversion to government and a shared distrust of political power. Like it or no, the United States was a weak country occupying one end of a huge, sparsely settled continent that contained great wealth—involved, in other words, in a contest for big stakes, with big powers for rivals. Britain and Spain had seats around the western rim of the table, and France was less than casually waiting a chance to get back in the game.

The Indians were still to be reckoned with, as well, and they viewed the situation with a hard logic that held little promise for the American position. Europeans were not numerous in the American interior and they never figured to be, having their eyes chiefly on furs or precious metals or other wealth that could be commandeered from a distance; Americans were farmers who came to stay, and they kept coming. Without liking any white men very much, the red men knew which group of whites posed the greatest threat to their hunting grounds and their way of life. Most of the tribes were now tilting toward British or Spanish affiliation as they had once tilted toward the French.

The moral was inescapable. Unless the young Republic were willing to stay penned up east of the Appalachians and relinquish its Western claims and abandon the hopes and the settlers it had already planted there—back to square one, in other words, as though the French wars and the Revolution had never happened —it was going to have to find ways of meeting power with power. And if Americans opted for retreat instead, they had no guarantee whatsoever that the power already in existence out West would not move east across the mountains and come looking for them, since power was about on a par with nature when it came to abhorring a vacuum.

In case they had forgotten Franklin's comment about hanging together or hanging separately, Americans could ponder the example of Poland. Hamstrung by a notoriously ineffectual central government and surrounded by predators, Poland was well on the way to disappearing altogether; the unhappy kingdom had seen one third of its territory annexed in a concerted land grab by its three voracious neighbors in 1772 and was soon to be partitioned twice more, literally to the vanishing point.

The nationalists also had arguments closer to home. Along with pointing up the need for a government that could tax and regulate trade and create enough of an army and navy to make its writ run where it was supposed to run, they were beginning to enunciate genuine fears about the domestic situation. It seemed possible that freedom itself might be lost—by a decline through national impotence into sheer anarchy, or by a dictatorship born of the desire to have a stable society at any price. Probably the danger men feared was greater than the danger that actually existed, but men go by what they believe rather than by what is, and increasing numbers now believed that the worst was at hand. One of the decisive factors at this point was the fright thrown into moderate folk all up and down the Atlantic coast by the strange uprising in western Massachusetts generally known as Shays' Rebellion.

Shays' Rebellion found debtors and poor farmers rising in the Revolutionary manner to protest against grasping landlords, scheming lawyers, propertied men who could thrive in time of grim deflation, and the courts and legal authorities which such folk seemed to control. Postwar readjustment came hard, especially with trade at a standstill and farm produce almost unsalable, and when Massachusetts adopted a sound money policy in 1782, depressed prices went down further than ever and taxes rose beyond the poor man's endurance. In some states blanket measures of relief were adopted, ranging all the way from the issuance of scrip (Rhode Island had issued so much that creditors were reportedly fleeing the state rather than be paid in it) to laws suspending the collection of debts and mortgages for a term of years.

But the Massachusetts government was controlled by substantial folk along the seaboard, and these folk lived by the most orthodox economics. So in Massachusetts the legal officials foreclosed mortgages, jailed men for failure to pay taxes, and issued court orders under which a farmer's land, his livestock, his very household furniture were taken away from him—and suddenly the westerners had had enough. It began to look like 1775 all over again, with old Sam Adams' devices coming back into play—armed mobs to keep courts from opening, conventions meeting to declare grievances, committees of correspondence functioning to give local uprisings greater effect . . . all very embarrassing, one supposes, to Sam Adams himself, now a member of the Massachusetts senate, a leading citizen of Boston, and a believer in due processes. And by the fall of 1786 there was a force of insurgents at large in the Connecticut Valley and the Berkshires led by a western farmer named Daniel Shays, who had been a captain in the Revolution. Shays and his men compelled the state Supreme Court, meeting at Springfield, to adjourn, made an unsuccessful attack on the federal arsenal there, and frightened thoughtful people all the way from New Hampshire to Georgia.

In 1787 Massachusetts put more than 4,000 soldiers in the field under command of General Benjamin Lincoln. Shays' army was routed and driven off, Shays himself fled to Vermont, and the whole affair was over. There were pardons before long for the men who had taken up arms, pardon eventually for Shays himself, and nothing was left of the great uprising but the scare it had created—that, and the hardships that had provoked it in the first place.

The scare was what mattered. Here, it seemed, was anarchy itself, coming up unbidden because a government intentionally made weak had proved too weak to maintain order, and unruly men had set out to create mob government and redistribute property. Obviously a crisis was at hand and drastic action was demanded.

It is perfectly clear at this distance (and was clear enough then, to men who examined the matter thoughtfully) that Shays and his followers had no intention of destroying legitimate government or doing anything very drastic to anybody's property rights. Indeed, Shays' people were actually more or less on the side of the propertied people they were supposedly rebelling against. They were disturbed primarily by the collapse in trade and the grievous burden of taxes, and both groups really wanted the same thing: a scheme of government under which there could be a united, effective attack on the causes of collapsing trade, which would make it possible to bring the tax load down to manageable size.

A strange, momentous political blend was taking place. Popular rights were becoming identified with the far-reaching demands of a sturdy nationalism. Freedom demanded security, and the radical spirit that had destroyed one government to gain liberty for the individual was beginning to demand a new government strong enough to keep that individual's liberty alive and healthy. As it happened, when 1787 saw an end to Shays' Rebellion the worst of the economic storm was over. Prosperity was returning, and the dust-up in western Massachusetts made more and more Americans anxious to adjust their grievances peacefully without calling the Minute Man from his plow. Some settlement between the forces demanding and opposing centralization of power was obviously necessary, and it was going to be worked out by reasonable men who did not go armed to debate the issues that plagued them.

—□—

There had been some preliminary debating, even before the Shays affair created something like national concern. Advocates of concerted action in the areas of trade and public finance had begun to mutter when congressional attempts to establish a national revenue system failed twice, both times ignominiously. With such action requiring an amendment to the Articles, which in turn required unanimity, Rhode Island had blocked a national 5 per cent import duty in 1782, after twelve states had approved it; and New York thwarted an even more ambitious financial measure in 1786, after three years of sporadic debate had won the often grudging consent of most of the others.

Virginia and Maryland, wearying of congressional impotence and aware that certain problems simply could not be handled by individual state action, got together in 1785 to discuss common concerns on Chesapeake Bay and the Potomac River. Encouraged by their progress, the two states sought broader agreement and began by asking the co-operation of Pennsylvania and Delaware; from this emerged a convention at Annapolis in September 1786 attended by twelve commissioners representing five states. (Delegates from four other states had been appointed but did not appear.) The agenda centered on questions of American trade and commercial policy.

The Annapolis Convention did not represent enough states to get very far, but before adjourning it adopted and circulated a momentous report which reflected the handiwork of two brilliant young delegates—Alexander Hamilton of New York and James Madison of Virginia. Quite simply, the report called upon the states represented at Annapolis to appoint deputies and to encourage their sister commonwealths to do likewise, said deputies being invited to assemble in Philadelphia on the second Monday in May 1787.

This convention would have a broader mandate: far from merely resuming the trade talks, the delegates in Philadelphia were explicitly asked "to take into consideration the situation of the United States, to devise such further provisions as shall appear to them necessary to render the constitution of the federal government adequate to the exigencies of the Union; and to report such an act for that purpose to the United States in Congress assembled as . . . will effectually provide for the same"—in short, to propose alterations in the American frame of government as they saw fit.

Now neither the Annapolis gathering nor its call for a larger convention in Philadelphia, least of all the bold new agenda it had proclaimed, was exactly legal. The business of framing national policy and authorizing national conventions and proposing amendments to the Articles lay properly with Congress, which had not yet lent a shadow of countenance to any of this. But the Annapolis report went into circulation just as Daniel Shays began making news in western Massachusetts, and from here on the idea of reviewing the political system gathered force. Virginia and New Jersey were prompt to appoint delegates to represent them in Philadelphia, and within a few weeks four or five other states had done likewise. The whole thing acquired legal sanction in February 1787 when Congress, fortuitously blessed with a quorum and the presence of ailing but indefatigable little James Madison, passed a resolution authorizing a national convention and adopting the time and place that the Annapolis report had proposed. By mid-spring twelve states (all but Rhode Island, where a defiant majority was more than happy with the way things were) had named deputies; and by May 25, less than two weeks behind schedule, seven of the state delegations had arrived in Philadelphia. Having thus obtained a quorum, the convention could officially organize and get down to business. A national debate over the American governmental system was about to begin.

Americans were uncommonly fortunate, as they had been in 1776, to have some very able men on hand to join in the debate. Most of the leaders of 1776 were still present and available for duty, and neither their vision nor their grasp had been in any way impaired by a decade of revolution and experiments in independent government. The greatest single phase of the experiment was now at hand. The Declaration had staked the rebelling colonists to a lofty and improbable ideal, and it was still to be tested whether they could put together the kind of governmental machinery that would keep the ideal alive, protect it from present dangers beyond and within, and trundle it forward along the uncharted trail to fulfillment without grinding it up or shaking it to pieces.

This would have been a tall enough order, even if the eighteenth-century world had stayed more or less the way it was. But the social, economic, technological, and political currents that would change that world beyond recognition within the next hundred years were already in motion, and some of the men who went to Philadelphia had glimpsed enough of this—had contributed something to it, in fact, by actions taken a few years earlier—to realize that adjusting to the status quo would not be sufficient. The status quo itself was headed for trouble.

So men of no little skill and insight were needed, and the Republic had a fair share even though not all of them were available. Some of the best, like John Adams and Thomas Jefferson, were on diplomatic mission in Europe. A few of the firebrands of 1776, like Patrick Henry and Sam Adams, refused to participate in the Philadelphia gathering, having become local establishment figures and wary defenders of state rights and decentralized government. But there was some formidable talent on hand in Philadelphia. The caliber of the Virginia and Pennsylvania delegations alone was enough to ensure that the convention would amount to something and command a respectful hearing afterward, and nationalists found it both significant and heartening that these two key commonwealths would support the move for a stronger government in so impressive a fashion.

Virginia had led with her ace and appointed the nation's first citizen, George Washington. He was accompanied by such notables as George Mason, whose fame and eloquence as a spokesman for human rights were on a par with Jefferson's; George Wythe, influential jurist and professor of law; Edmund Randolph and John Blair, distinguished first-family leaders; and that peerless young host-in-himself, James Madison. Pennsylvania had matched Washington with doughty old Ben Franklin, still full of shrewd wisdom amid the gout and drowsiness and frailty of his eighty-one years. They had also sent General Thomas Mifflin, prominent businessman and political leader; two of Philadelphia's foremost merchants, Thomas FitzSimons and George Clymer; a canny lawyer-politician named James Wilson; and the two unrelated, talented Morrises: Robert Morris, noted banker, erstwhile superintendent of finance, ardent nationalist, financial wizard, and plunger; and Gouverneur Morris, a witty, worldly patrician from New York whose grasp of the ways of men and governments was unexcelled.

No other state could match Virginia and Pennsylvania, but there were good men from all over, and some few of the fifty-five names were widely known then and are worth remembering now: Roger Sherman and Oliver Ellsworth and scholarly William Samuel Johnson of Connecticut; distinguished John Dickinson of Delaware, the "Pennsylvania Farmer" whose letters to the press in the 1760s had sharpened many a colonist's sense of the issues; William Paterson and William Livingston of New Jersey; a Maryland Carroll; a Rutledge and two Pinckneys from South Carolina; John Langdon of New Hampshire; Hugh Williamson of North Carolina; Abraham Baldwin of Georgia. The Bay State had no Adams available for once and John Hancock had just been elected governor, but it was well represented by the likes of Rufus King and Nathaniel Gorham and Sam Adams' touchy sidekick Elbridge Gerry. New York's three-man contingent, appointed by Governor Clinton's anti-nationalist faction, was smaller and less favorably disposed than it might have been, but it did include Alexander Hamilton, who had enough talent and nationalist zeal for an entire delegation.

Taken together, the assemblage was rich in political experience, legal training, and worldly wisdom and accomplishment. The social and economic backgrounds varied, but the men were predominantly of established-family origins and comfortable or affluent circumstances, fairly representative of the educated planter-merchant-lawyer elites that had furnished America with most of its provincial leaders. All in all it was quite a group, and Thomas Jefferson's enthusiastic comment from Paris—"an assembly of demigods"—was the kind of exaggeration that the cumulative historical verdict of nearly two centuries has pronounced both pardonable and mild.

The men at Philadelphia had even more going for them than a high median level of talent and community standing. They had a political and constitutional heritage that went back through Great Britain's Glorious Revolution and Puritan Revolution to the earliest parliaments and the barons at Runnymede, and they were on speaking terms with nearly all of it. They were well versed in eighteenth-century theories of natural law and natural rights; by and large they subscribed to such theories and admired what Harrington and Montesquieu and Locke had written on the subject.

But their collective philosophy had more than one edge to it. To be sure, they believed in human liberty and government by consent, in checked and balanced power and the right of revolution; they extolled Hampden and Pym and Sidney and other Whig foes of arbitrary authority. Yet their view of the world was neither abstract nor doctrinaire. It went beyond natural rights to make room for such worldly and skeptical observers of the human condition as Hume, Hobbes, and Machiavelli, and it contained nothing whatever of naïveté. If the Framers were intellectual heirs of John Locke they were also spiritual heirs of John Calvin, who had never been very starry-eyed about man's natural tendencies. (In viewing human nature the delegates had their glasses on straight. Although they had more in them of secular rationalism than of any known brand of religious orthodoxy, they had seen too much of the world to credit the notion that the Enlightenment had in any way superseded the Old Testament.)

All of this reflected a habit of mind that promised to stand the Framers in good stead. Their book learning and their rational faculties, in both of which they placed considerable stock, were firmly grounded in their own practical experience—in politics, law, government, business, and life generally. The common fund of this experience that the delegates brought with them to Philadelphia was enormous, and most of it was strikingly relevant to the matter at hand. The belief that reason and experience were mutually supportive, and indeed of little value except in tandem, made perfect sense to observant Americans in the late eighteenth century: here alone, as we have seen, present conditions and past history seemed to offer proof that concepts like social contract, natural rights, and popular government were eminently workable. The closest thing to an illusion that the men of Philadelphia permitted themselves was the belief that America's unique circumstances afforded grounds for hope: that here, if the thing were carefully enough defined and hedged and watched, a government composed of fallible human beings might just possibly escape the snares and corrupting influences to which all institutions were liable.

Illusion or no, the most workable part of their rich political heritage was the part they knew most about, having grown up with it and taken it in with the air they breathed. This was the part that had been brought overseas in the seventeenth century and transplanted at Jamestown and Plymouth and Massachusetts Bay, later at St. Mary's and Providence and Charles Town and William Penn's new city along the Delaware, to flourish and mature in the New World environment: several generations of direct, firsthand, self-governing experience in town meeting, vestry, county court, and provincial assembly. This experience had been capped by the recent debate with Great Britain over the nature and location of sovereignty, which in turn had led to revolution and a greatly amplified set of experiences in making new constitutions and new governments and new efforts to balance the complex equation that contains both governmental power and human rights.

This culminating segment of their heritage was the biggest asset of all—partly, of course, because most of the Philadelphia delegates had themselves been active, sometimes instrumental, in making the history of the preceding twenty-five years come out the way it did; more basically because these men had simply lived in what may have been the most self-conscious, thoughtful, *participatory* generation that ever existed. Thinking about such normally abstract or esoteric concepts as federalism, representation, sovereignty, and the basis of government had become both necessity and habit for Americans in the period after 1760. And their political system had evolved in such a way as to make these thoughts habitual not merely among community leaders and educated folk; the habit reached down to raise the level of awareness among tradesmen, artisans, and farmers, including some of those who had recently fallen in behind Daniel Shays. (It was not the desperate ignorance of downtrodden and disfranchised men but the blunted aspirations of a politically alert citizenry that gave the Shays movement its impact. And there was comparable political awareness among the Massachusetts farmers who joined the militia and marched out to face his movement down.) This generation of Americans had acquired its political education on the job and the lesson had taken; leaders of a society with so finely tuned and sophisticated an electorate had to have their wits about them—especially if they hoped to find a marketable formula for change.

—□—

Several shades of political opinion were represented at Philadelphia, and the debates soon revealed numerous areas of disagreement. But on a few fundamentals the convention was substantially of one mind all along. The system they envisioned should be republican, with sovereignty residing in the people; it should be federal, with political authority divided in some fashion between state and national governments; and power should be so defined, separated, checked, and balanced as to prevent any one faction, interest, state, section, class, or branch of government from exercising too much of it or achieving dominance.

At the same time, most of the delegates had come to Philadelphia in the first place because they believed that their political system—no matter how republican, federal, and circumscribed its authority—had to be topped by a central government that could do what their present government could not do: tax, regulate trade, and enforce its decrees. They were sufficiently of one mind to agree upon secrecy during their deliberations and, until almost the very end, to maintain it; bitter ideological differences would have made such a course impossible. Yet despite this broad consensus, the attempt to apply so complex and tricky a set of political principles could easily have led to deadlock or failure if the group had not been seasoned in the ways of compromise and give and take.

The most artful and difficult of the compromises involved reconciling what most of the delegates really wanted with what their political antennae told them the American people could be persuaded to accept. Although the assemblage included a fair amount of state-rights sentiment and an even larger number whose desire for more centralization was in delicate balance with their fear of too much of it, the root-and-branch nationalists were ascendant. All that really restrained them was their own practical realism; they never let themselves forget that whatever they decided upon would have to pass muster in the country at large.

If left alone, these resolute nationalists would probably have come up with a proposal vesting the central government with nearly all power and reducing the states to little more than administrative departments. Certainly Madison's Virginia Resolutions, which were drafted and presented early enough to become a virtual agenda for the convention, were a blueprint for out-and-out centralization. Madison saw fit not to emphasize this during ratification, when he wrote essays that have been hailed as brilliant contributions to the federal principle, but there was precious little federalism in his Virginia Plan. It called for a popularly elected lower house, an upper house selected by the lower, and an executive and judiciary chosen by the two houses—the whole procedure by-passing the states altogether. Representation in both chambers would be by population. This Congress would be empowered to disallow state laws and use military force upon disobedient states, and the national government would have plenary power in areas where "the separate states are incompetent" or "the exercise of individual legislation" might disrupt "the harmony of the United States"—a clause elastic enough to permit almost any action the government wanted to pursue.

In adopting this bold plan as their agenda the delegates made no bones about the direction they were taking. They quibbled over several points and toned down some of the stronger phrases, but they did not really quarrel with Madison's basic propositions: that there should be a brand-new frame of government, not a mere tinkering with the Articles; that the new government would act directly upon the people rather than upon the states; that the national legislature, executive, and judiciary would be supreme; and that approval of the new document should be voiced not by state legislatures but through ratifying conventions "expressly chosen by the people."

All of this was a far cry from the cherished principle of state sovereignty—the idea that the nation was essentially an association of independent commonwealths which had agreed to delegate a few of their powers to a central government that would act in certain matters as their agent. This principle still had some important parts to play in America, but James Madison had dealt it a lethal blow at the very beginning of the Philadelphia convention. (He would soon regret having gone quite such a distance, but his nationalism never really wavered; even in his later opposition to the central authority he had done so much to create, Madison would invoke state rights as a useful political weapon rather than a sacred principle. His vision of the nation's destiny went immeasurably beyond a league of sovereign states; and toward the end of his life, more than forty years after Philadelphia, an elder statesman in retirement on his Virginia estate, he would deliver an uncompromisingly harsh and sweeping condemnation of John Calhoun's theory of nullification. On the general questions of union and national supremacy this remarkable little man stood squarely, first and last, with Andrew Jackson and Abraham Lincoln.)

The major alternative to the Virginia resolutions—the so-called New Jersey Plan offered by William Paterson in June—was only superficially a state-rights counterattack, although it did make more room for the states than Madison had. Essentially Paterson proposed to revise the Articles rather than create a new constitution. His big objection to the Virginia Plan lay in its provision for apportioning representation in Congress by population; Paterson advocated a retention of the one-state, one-vote principle contained in the present Congress.

Otherwise, however, Paterson was as firm a nationalist as Madison. He would strengthen the Confederation government by adding an executive, a judiciary, and the crucial tax-trade-enforcement powers. Furthermore, the New Jersey Plan permitted the national government to act directly on the individual citizen, sanctioned the use of military force if states did not comply with national legislation, and said explicitly what Madison's proposal had only implied: that acts and treaties passed by the national Congress would be the supreme law of the land.

What the New Jersey people were really voicing was not state-rights sentiment but political realism, together with a real fear that proportional representation in the new Congress would result in domination by the big populous states (the two biggest of which, far from coincidentally, were the most enthusiastic proponents of the Madison Plan—Virginia and Pennsylvania). Paterson and his supporters insisted that the Virginia Plan ignored provincial loyalties too blatantly to be politically marketable. "Our object," he reminded the convention, "is not such a Governmt. as may be best in itself, but such a one as our Constituents have authorized us to prepare, and as they will approve." From thoughtful John Dickinson came a similar warning. The Virginia Plan was "pushing things too far," he told Madison, adding that the small states "would sooner submit to a foreign power than . . . be deprived of an equality of suffrage in both branches of the legislature, and thereby be thrown under the domination of the large states."

The threat of a small-state alignment behind the New Jersey Plan undoubtedly sobered the Madison nationalists. Another possibility came out into the open on June 18 in an eloquent four-hour oration by Alexander Hamilton. While the delegates listened with a mixture of inattention and polite incredulity, Hamilton advocated a species of centralized government—Chief Executive and Senate to be indirectly chosen and to hold office for life, state governors to be appointed by the national government, and so on—that made the Virginia Plan sound almost anarchical. Thereafter, whether Hamilton had spoken with calculated intent or no, the specter of his powerful unitary state looming on one flank while the small-state bloc made noises on the other acted to make some scaled-down version of the Virginia Plan all the more attractive.

While its leading backers—Madison and the two resourceful Pennsylvanians, James Wilson and Gouverneur Morris—labored mightily to keep the substance intact, the Virginia Plan moved through a series of adjustments and changes that eventuated in a document nearly everyone could support. Many of the adjustments had a built-in logic to them, and most of the delegates knew how to compromise. But the product of all that debating and deliberating through the humid Philadelphia summer acquired its obvious and inevitable quality later, as generation after generation grew up under it and came to look upon the Federal Constitution as part of an almost divinely ordained plan. To its increasingly weary and irascible architects it could hardly have seemed so—at one point Gouverneur Morris dryly warned the assemblage "not to expect any particular interference of Heaven" in their behalf—and they arrived at the inevitable only after a good deal of very hard and painstaking work.

In any event, they got there. The biggest compromise had to do with bridging the representational chasm that separated the Virginia and New Jersey proposals. What they finally agreed upon seems eminently sensible in retrospect—representation by population in the lower house, each state equally represented in the upper—but the process of reaching this agreement strained the convention's collective wisdom and patience almost beyond their limits. In the absence of population statistics the delegates did some educated guessing and arbitrarily assigned each state its quota of representatives in the first Congress; thereafter they proposed to determine proportional representation by means of a national census every ten years. The idea was made more palatable to the small states by tying it to the requirement that direct taxes, too, would be apportioned among the states according to population.

This basic compromise was inextricably bound up with another, equally intricate, and even more indispensable if the nation were to stay united. (What might happen to this unity in the long run was quite beyond the reach of the men in Philadelphia. They were pragmatists who knew their society well enough to realize that short-run unity was the best they could get.) Even this was only obtainable at the cost of a few swallowed scruples and some dirt swept under the rug. So they swallowed, swept, and agreed that for purposes of apportionment and taxation five slaves would be counted as the equivalent of three citizens. The document also contained a clause facilitating the recovery of fugitive slaves, and another guaranteeing continuation of the foreign slave trade for at least twenty more years.

In thus extending the mantle of constitutional sanction and protection over slavery, the delegates revealed their discomfort by dodging the word itself and resorting to elaborate euphemisms—"by adding to the whole number of free persons . . . three fifths of all other persons"; "the migration or importation of such persons as any of the states . . . shall think proper to admit"; "person[s] held to service or labor." But they wrote slavery firmly and unequivocally into the document they were about to pronounce the supreme law of the land.

The debates on this issue merely dramatized what the delegates well knew: there was already a Northern and a Southern interest in the United States, and although part of the difference had to do with the sometimes divergent needs of commercial towns and staple-crop agriculture, what really crouched balefully at the heart of the matter was the institution of slavery. From Pennsylvania north and east, slavery was peripheral and on its way out; from Delaware Bay on south it had lodged itself so deeply into the marrow of the prevailing social and economic system that men who lived within that system displayed a hair-trigger sensitivity to whatever might threaten or jar it, however lightly. Slavery, under scrutiny, turned out to be a very special kind of interest, demanding special treatment. And its hold upon the people who ran the system seemed only a little less binding than it was upon the folk who labored under it. Northern delegates, and not a few of those from the South, were less than happy about yoking their new republican constitution to a system of property in man, but there could be no doubt that such a yoke was the price of union in 1787—even before Eli Whitney and Toussaint L'Ouverture.

The remainder, once these big compromises had been made, was largely a matter of hammering out details and patching up lesser disagreements, of which there were several. The final draft was still very much a nationalist document, but it contained enough federalism and enough checks and balances to reassure those who feared too much centralized power and enough hedges on majority rule to satisfy those who feared too much democracy. The Senate, with its members serving six-year terms and chosen by state legislatures rather than direct popular vote, was seen as a kind of advisory council for the executive and a bastion for conservatism and property rights. The independent judiciary, the executive veto, and the rather cumbersome device of the electoral college were regarded as further checks upon turbulent majorities. On the other hand, the people still mattered. The lower chamber was to be popularly elected every two years and had the sole right, like Britain's House of Commons, to initiate money bills. A two-thirds majority could override a veto, and the impeachment mechanism offered an ultimate safeguard against abuses of power. The new document guaranteed each state a republican form of government and offered other securities: there would be no titles of nobility, no bills of attainder or ex post facto laws, no religious tests for officeholding, and no suspension of habeas corpus except when rebellion or invasion threatened the public safety.

Behind all the hedges and safeguards, however, stood a frame of government with all the muscle its sponsors had intended to provide. The new Congress would have the power to tax, coin and borrow money, regulate trade, make treaties, create and maintain armed forces, summon and exercise control over the militia, admit new states, and administer the national territories.

States were expressly forbidden to levy import duties, make treaties with foreign nations or with one another, issue paper money
or allow anything but gold and silver to be accepted in payment
of debts (Rhode Island, though absent, was much on the convention's mind), keep troops or warships in peacetime, and so on.

To clinch the matter, the national government's enumerated
powers were buttressed by some catchall clauses, framed by men
who knew enough law to appreciate what good lawyers could do
with them. The Congress could employ its tax power to provide
for the general welfare, and it could pass any legislation it deemed
"necessary and proper" to enforce the government's writ. The
new document, and laws and treaties made by the new government, were explicitly designated as the supreme law of the land,
which all federal and state judges, officials, and legislators would
be oathbound to support.

Amendments required approval of three fourths rather than all
of the states, and the final article pronounced the document in
force as soon as nine instead of all thirteen states had ratified it
(Rhode Island once again: no longer would a single commonwealth be able to thwart the national purpose all by itself.)

By the time these and a variety of lesser matters had been settled it
was nearly autumn, and those delegates who had not already left
—for personal reasons, business reasons, or in disgust—were
more than ready to. The finished document won the assent and
the signatures of all but three of the forty-one who were still on
hand. (Aging John Dickinson had recently gone home in ill-
health but had authorized a colleague to sign for him.)

Two men from Maryland and Governor Clinton's two anti-
nationalist New Yorkers had also left—the New Yorkers long
since—out of open disagreement with the thrust of the new constitution. Several who remained had reservations, and three important delegates entertained them so strongly that they were

finally unable to sign the document. High-minded George Mason regarded the power of the new national government as excessive and deplored the absence of a bill of rights; his colleague Edmund Randolph and Gerry of Massachusetts opposed the document for the same reasons—not unmixed with awareness (in Randolph's case) that he would now have to go home and campaign for office in the presence of doubters like Richard Henry Lee and Patrick Henry, or (in Gerry's) that he would now have to go home and explain things to suspicious old Sam Adams.

The rest signed willingly enough. The delegates met for the last time on September 17, shook hands, adjourned, and set out for home or other duty—weary, glad to be finished, and fully aware that they still had a job to do. Congress would now have to be persuaded to transmit their handiwork to the states, where conventions "expressly chosen by the people" would then have to be persuaded to ratify it.

Congress proved to be no problem. The nine signers who were also members of Congress hastened from Philadelphia to New York to rejoin that body, anxious to be on hand when their document came up for consideration. (A tenth Framer, William Pierce of Georgia, had left the convention in June to return to his seat in Congress, and was there to greet and help his fellow delegates in September.) These men succeeded in getting their colleagues to vote unanimously, on September 28, 1787, to transmit the proposed constitution to the state legislatures "in order to be submitted to a convention of delegates chosen in each state by the people thereof." The price of unanimity was the absence of any accompanying recommendation in *favor* of the document, since some members were highly skeptical. But Congress interposed neither delay nor difficulty in voting to transmit, and the Constitution cleared its first hurdle with relative ease.

The real campaigns were waged in the states, where opposition began to generate steam as soon as copies of the new document passed into circulation. Its proponents had several advantages, not least of which was their ability to put each advantage to good use. At the top of their masthead were the names of Washington and Franklin, whose support was enough to settle the argument for many uncertain voters. Their adherents also included a clear majority of the established elites in each state, although a substantial number of eminent leaders could be found on the opposing side. Support for the Constitution was also disproportionately strong among those whom Clinton Rossiter termed the word-makers: editors, lawyers, ministers, teachers, writers; many of these put their talents to work on the document's behalf. On the whole, pro-Constitution men proved more gifted than their foes in the assorted arts of organization, manipulation, maneuver, and cajolery. They were generally more determined and purposeful, with a far clearer sense of what they wanted.

One of their telling strategies was to campaign as "Federalists," which was an altogether misleading name for their position. By rights they should have been called "nationalists" or "centralists" or perhaps "consolidationists"—all negatively loaded terms that would have cost them a great many votes. As it was, pro-Constitution men having pre-empted a more attractive but less accurate word, the opposition—far more "federalist" in outlook—was forced to fall back on the unimaginative and uninspiring "Antifederalist." It was a small matter, but symptomatic . . . and the Constitution makers had taken another trick.

To sum it up, the Federalists had the advantages of momentum, prominent and inspired leadership, political skill, determination, superior word power, and a good label; they exploited each to the full—and they needed every one of them. The Antifederalists had some assets too. They had enough influential leaders in their camp to make a real fight of it, especially in the three or four key states whose adherence was essential. There was enough apathy and ignorance in the backwater areas—even in this most politically conscious of generations there were many thousands of lives which the consciousness never penetrated—to have beaten the new Constitution soundly had sufficient numbers of such folk been mobilized; and in several places the Antifederalists almost managed it.

Nothing in the Federalist arsenal could quite match their opponents' chief talking point, which touched American sensibilities right at the quick: the new document represented a dangerous consolidation of power and threatened those precious individual liberties for which the people had recently fought a revolution. Many doubters shared George Mason's fears that the Constitution did not offer adequate guarantees for human rights and that the new national government could easily evolve into monarchy or tyranny. All the Federalists' persuasive powers were needed to counter these points, and despite their best efforts many of the doubters remained doubtful.

The first round of ratifications came easily and quickly, being from small states that saw a much better future for themselves in the new union than in the old one. By early January 1788, scarcely three months after Congress had passed the document along, four state conventions had met and ratified it without difficulty —Delaware, New Jersey, and Georgia unanimously, and Connecticut by a 3 to 1 majority.

Pennsylvania also provided a fast endorsement, although here it took ruthless maneuvering, organized mob pressure, and strong-arm tactics to carry the day. Outvoted 2 to 1, the Antifederalists—strongest in the remote rural and western districts, weakest in Philadelphia and the commercial farm belt between the lower Delaware and Susquehanna valleys—were the first to try to affix human-rights amendments to the new document. But the determined Federalists beat down their proposals and their attempts to gain time for more deliberation, and forced things through to a vote in December 1787. Pennsylvania Antifederalists felt cheated and misused, and would long remain bitter against the new government.

The first real contest took place in Massachusetts, where the tradition of resisting external authority stood in fine balance against a felt need for stronger government. This time the Federalists played their cards cautiously and delicately, aware that the opposition and the undecided vote would unfailingly combine to beat them if they tried any of the rugged tactics that had carried Pennsylvania. After much effort they won grudging support from Sam Adams and John Hancock, and on February 6, 1788, the Bay State voted to ratify by the narrow margin of 187 to 168.

Part of the purchase price was a Federalist pledge, later exacted by other conventions, to submit human-rights amendments to the first session of the new Congress. Pressure for a bill of rights was mounting, and the Federalists—not opposed in principle, but determined to resist the demand that a second constitutional convention be summoned to consider such amendments—readily made promises to put a bill of rights at the top of the first congressional agenda. In due time the pledges would be called, and honored.

Now the Federalists had six states, but the road was getting bumpier. The only way they could stave off defeat in New Hampshire, where a committed Antifederalist majority came to the convention in February 1788, was to persuade a few of the opposition to join them in voting to adjourn until June; during the interim they used all their influence to win over some of these delegates and get them released from their constituents' instructions, but the outcome was uncertain. Elsewhere, opposition was vocal in Maryland and strong in South Carolina, but large Federalist majorities carried the former state in April and the latter in May —again with proposed amendments that pointed toward a bill of rights.

This brought the total to eight, one short of the number necessary to declare the Constitution established. The ninth state was secured in mid-June when the adjourned New Hampshire convention reassembled with enough uninstructed or reinstructed delegates on hand to obtain a 57 to 47 Federalist majority. But everyone knew that this particular set of nine states could not form a viable union unless they were joined by Virginia and New York, where the hardest and closest battles over ratification were still very much in process and very much in doubt.

In Virginia the Antifederalist leadership, which included Mason and Patrick Henry and a host of others, was every bit as impressive as that of the Federalists, Washington and Madison notwithstanding. The exciting four-week debate in the Virginia convention saw eloquent past masters parading and exchanging arguments, and for a while it was touch and go. In the end the Federalists eked out a narrow triumph (89 to 79) based on a combination of luck, Madison's skill, the return of Randolph to a position of support, the news that a favorable decision was imminent in New Hampshire, and the palpable offstage influence of George Washington waiting at Mount Vernon to hear how his state would decide. (Not least among the Federalist talking points, in and out of Virginia, was the assurance that Washington would stand—in his case it would not be a question of *running*— for the presidency.) Both New Hampshire and Virginia accompanied their endorsement with demands for a bill of rights.

In New York the Antifederalists came to the convention in June 1788 with a big majority, and the task of prying enough votes loose required a superb Federalist effort—political adroitness, brilliant argument, good lines of communication, and a shrewd counterthrust. The man who provided all of these, singlehandedly or in concert, was Alexander Hamilton, who proceeded to make up for a rather indifferent performance in Philadelphia by a dazzling tour de force in his home state. Working tirelessly on and off the convention floor, Hamilton somehow found time to team up with Madison and John Jay to write *The Federalist*—a set of trenchant, well-reasoned essays analyzing, explaining, and defending the new Constitution. He also organized a system of couriers so that the favorable results of the New Hampshire and Virginia conventions—the ninth and tenth states, putting the Union over the top—could be hastened to New York and reported there at opportune moments.

And to bolster the high logic of the *Federalist* essays and the good news from elsewhere, Hamilton turned one of the opposition's biggest arguments completely around and fired it back at them. The Antifederalists, who drew most of their support from upstate to offset the Federalist stronghold in and around New York City, had been making much of the point that the new federal union could not hold together without the adherence of New York. Hamilton quietly reminded some of the delegates that if New York failed to join, the metropolis with its big Federalist majority might well withdraw from the rest of the state and ratify the Constitution all by itself. When it came to holding together, in other words, New York needed the Union as much as the Union needed New York. This was by no means a farfetched argument, and a few delegates were sobered by it. The Federalists had entered the convention with only 19 of the 65 delegates. In the end 11 Antifederalists switched sides and a few others abstained, enabling the Constitution to win a narrow 30 to 27 victory in late July. Requests for human-rights amendments were again attached.

New York had clinched it, of course. Later that summer North Carolina voted not to ratify, and stubborn Rhode Island refused even to call a convention, but what these laggard commonwealths did no longer mattered very much. The new federal union was now a fact. (North Carolina bowed to the inevitable and joined it in November 1789, while Rhode Island held out till May of 1790, over a year after the first Congress had convened.)

Once New York had ratified, the machinery of existing governments got in motion to set things up for the new one. The expiring Confederation Congress established timetables for federal elections and the convening of the new national legislature, and the eleven member states swung into action: in early 1789, while each legislature appointed its two United States senators, the citizens voted for representatives and chose presidential electors. This last was a formality; it had long been a foregone conclusion that George Washington would be the first President if the Constitution were adopted, and none of the electors even thought of casting their ballots for anyone else. On April 6, 1789, with the President-elect already making his preparations to leave Mount Vernon for New York, a quorum in both houses enabled the new Congress to convene. The new government of the United States of America came officially into existence.

— □ —

Posterity has treated the Framers of the Constitution with enormous respect, not unmixed with veneration, and the respect at least is fully deserved. Their document has worked well and proved remarkably adaptable. The mechanism it established has failed only once—understandably so, no contrivance of even the most gifted human intelligence being sufficient to keep the Declaration of Independence and the institution of slavery in harmony indefinitely.

If it is impossible not to admire their accomplishment, it is easy to get a distorted view of what they were trying to accomplish. Their own motives, and those of the men who supported or opposed them during ratification, are frequently obscured by what people of succeeding generations have wanted to see when they looked back there. This happens with all retrospection, of course. It has happened with particular force to the men of Philadelphia.

In the early years of the nineteenth century, outside of a few busy lawmakers and judges arguing about its true meaning, Americans were content simply to admire their Constitution as an eminently successful contrivance and its creators as patriot heroes: the thing worked, the country was thriving under it, and people were impressed. Then the sectional controversy began to heat up, and threw off smoke to cloud nearly everyone's perspective; from the 1820s until Appomattox, or thereabouts, men searched the wisdom and intent of the Framers primarily to find support for their own views about slavery, state sovereignty, the jurisdiction of Congress, the nature of the Union, and related matters. Both sides waged civil war in the conviction that they were upholding the true meaning of the Constitution.

For the next four or five decades a lofty, genteel conservatism dominated American constitutional thought. This view, advanced chiefly by earnest graybeards who admired the late nineteenth-century status quo and did not want it disrupted, regarded the Constitution as sacrosanct—an inviolable bulwark against irresponsible reform legislation. The Framers, correspondingly, were depicted as little less than godlike: disinterested Olympians bestowing governmental perfection from the mountaintop and rescuing America from economic stagnation, financial ruin, anarchy, and disintegration. Hardheaded progressives like Charles A. Beard challenged this view after 1900 by "exposing" the Founding Fathers as wealthy archconservatives who loathed the democratic excesses of the Confederation period and engineered a virtual coup d'état on behalf of property, law and order, and vested social and economic interests. The Beardian interpretation, in vogue among liberals for a generation or more, came under heavy fire in its turn. Although Beard's critics conceded the relevance of social and economic issues, they emerged after 1950 with a modified, tough-minded, secular version of the old Olympian approach: if not all-wise disinterested statesmen, the Framers were now praised, only a shade less reverently, for their shrewd foresight, practical wisdom, political sagacity, and superior understanding of what was best for the country.

In terms of sophistication and insight, each succeeding view represents something of an improvement over its predecessor. But all are flawed by a tendency to read latter-day political attitudes back into the 1780s, where they fit poorly. As a result, the contest over ratification somehow retains the overtones of a dispute between "conservatism"—whether favorably defined as community wisdom or critically unmasked as vested interest—and opposing forces rather vaguely depicted as less responsible or more democratic, or sometimes both.

The trouble with seeing the Federalist victory as a triumph of conservatism, however defined, is that it badly oversimplifies the political realities of 1787. There were many conservatives in the Philadelphia convention, to be sure, and the specter of armed mobs attacking property was partly what had drawn them there. But there were many conservatives outside of Philadelphia, too, and they by no means agreed on the need for a stronger central government. Americans were essentially a unit in their respect for property; if this was what defined conservatism in the 1780s, virtually everyone was a conservative, and the term becomes meaningless.

At best, it came in different shades. Although the nation contained a handful of radical levelers and out-and-out democrats on one fringe and a few reactionaries who longed for divine-right monarchy and hereditary aristocracy on the other, the vast majority of politically conscious folk occupied broad and not very distinct bands across the middle of the spectrum. The essential dialogue was between moderate republicans (to coin a term) who favored a somewhat greater popular voice in government and a more open, fluid society; and moderate conservatives (to coin another) who favored greater restrictions or checks upon popular sovereignty and a more stable, structured society. The politics of the next fifteen or twenty years would sharpen this distinction and greatly widen the gap, but in 1787 the two groups shared basic assumptions: both believed in some form of republican government guided and led by the better sorts, differing only in emphasis and degree. (Notions of egalitarian democracy and rule by the "common man" were still a generation or two in the future, although the way was being paved for them.)

The point, in any case, is that the distinction between moderate republican and moderate conservative—fuzzy enough, at best— cut squarely *across* the line that separated advocates and opponents of the new Constitution. Later generations tended to miss this, partly because of their own predilections and partly, too, because the ratification dialogue acted to conceal it. Enemies of the document voiced fears of centralized power and often made their point by invoking the image of colonists defending their liberties against the encroachments of king and Parliament. Yet distrust of the new Constitution might or might not stem from a genuine concern for individual liberty and popular government. Such concern existed, but the ordinary citizen's true friends could be found on both sides of the constitutional debate.

"Conservative" though some of them were, the Framers were mainly aiming at *balance*—not between national and state authority (where they tilted as heavily toward the former as their sense of the possible allowed them to) but among the assorted factions and interest groups that jostled one another for position in every part of the country. Angry debtors who might form mobs or vote a redistribution of wealth were not the only groups the Philadelphia convention wanted to contain, as a second glance at the "conservative" features of the new government might suggest.

Admittedly, the electoral college was supposed to encourage ordinary voters to choose electors from among each community's sagest pillars, who in turn would exercise their superior judgment in choosing a President—an indirection designed to prevent passion-crazed majorities from electing demagogues. On the other hand, two other agencies in the new government struck balances of a different sort. The Senate, for example, could be seen not only as a bastion for propertied aristocrats but as a means of isolating them; otherwise the influential eminences who were expected to occupy the Senate could dominate the lesser mortals in the lower house and hence control the whole legislature. (Even certified conservatives like Gouverneur Morris and John Adams spoke with frank approval of curbing the aristocracy's power by confining it to the upper chamber.) As for the strong national executive, recent political history in more than one country had revealed this as yet another sword that cut both ways, as able (and as apt) to push for liberal reforms and greater equity against entrenched hereditary privilege as to defend property from angry mobs. And the Framers knew it.

Support for the new document, in other words, was not necessarily a sign of elitist disdain for the rank and file; and opposition
to it, by the same token, did not always stem from a concern for
popular liberties. The real key to the Antifederalists can be found
in their fear of a new locus of authority that would obviously
overshadow those of state and local governments. And state
rights was not, in 1787 any more than in 1860 or 1954, an automatic synonym for human rights, although it is fond of parading
as such. More often, it was a device for keeping the local elites and
vested interests on top in their own bailiwicks, and if some of
these local groups consisted of horny-handed farmers and sober
townsfolk governing themselves in the treasured accents of the
New England town meeting, many—probably most—were
fairly tight little oligarchies and courthouse rings who dominated their communities and wielded considerable power. They
sometimes wielded it benignly, but they had no intention whatsoever of sharing it, losing it, or seeing it eclipsed by a greater
power center somewhere else.

This was a defensible position, often sincerely defended. But
there was seldom much democracy in it, and many recent supporters of Daniel Shays could vote for the new Constitution because they regarded it as a useful counterweight, an offset to the
domination under which they had long fretted at the hands of the
Bay State establishment (many of whom, for obverse reasons,
were supporting the new document too).

The debate over the Constitution, then, was both more and
less than a dispute between conservatives and democrats. As recent historians like Cecelia Kenyon, Stanley Elkins, and Eric
McKitrick have suggested, it is better understood as a contest between localism and nationalism, between men whose eyesight
tended to blur when they looked beyond their own region and
men who, in Hamilton's term, thought continentally. Inertia was
being challenged by motion, as an emplaced rock is attacked by a
river's current. As a group, the men of Philadelphia and their
hard-core support succeeded because they were more resolute,

adroit, and resourceful, perhaps also more unscrupulous, than their opponents. What they had in common was not a political philosophy, conservative or otherwise, but a sense of purpose and a sense of direction. They had come to identify their careers and their aspirations with the nation rather than with the states (such identification, with Crown or province, was often what had made loyalists or patriots out of people in the 1770s), and they moved toward their goal with the zest born of confidence. The Framers also had a distinct, decisive edge over the Antifederalists in youth, imagination, and above all faith and energy: faith in what a united republic with continental dimensions might do, and energy enough to create the necessary fabric of government, persuade their fellow countrymen to accept it, and stay around to put it to work. They did all of this, and they did it well—reason enough for their beneficiaries, regardless of political slant, to unite in honoring the charge they made.

CHAPTER 19

A Crack in Time Itself

THE TRIP was one extended triumphal procession. The towns and major river crossings on the route from Alexandria to New York formed a string of varicolored lights 250 miles long, each light glowing brightly in succession as he passed through. Accompanied by his old friend Colonel David Humphreys and by Charles Thomson, the secretary of Congress, who had ridden down from New York to notify him of his election, the first President left Alexandria on April 17, 1789, and reached New York on April 23, traveling an early version of the great Northeast corridor that so many millions of his countrymen would travel (by horseback, stagecoach, train, bus, auto) in the years ahead.

It began with a long ferry ride up the Potomac to Georgetown on the Maryland side, near the site where the city that would bear his name was soon to be laid out. Then they rode through the gentle Maryland hills and farmland to Baltimore, on along the indented marshy shores of the upper Chesapeake, another ferry for the broad Susquehanna, thence to Wilmington where Brandywine Creek flows into Delaware Bay. They crossed the Pennsylvania border and went on to the flimsy pontoon bridge over the

Schuylkill at Gray's Ferry in Philadelphia, then up the right bank of the Delaware to the crossing at Trenton, over the Jersey roads through Princeton and New Brunswick—not a town or a crossing that this man and his hard-pressed little army had not marched through or fought over a few years before—and finally to an arm of New York Harbor at Elizabeth Town Point, where a fifteen-mile boat ride to the foot of Manhattan would complete his journey.

America has always liked to celebrate things, and here was an unparalleled opportunity: one of its earliest chances and clearly one of its best. Naturally they overdid it a little, but the occasion and the central figure and the hopes that were riding with him fairly justified some extra exuberance. It was early spring, and the new green buds and first blossoms provided apt symbols for those who wanted to think of a young land bright with the promise of growth and rich harvests ahead. Times were markedly better than they had been a few years ago, and there was reason to believe that under a new government led by the nation's first citizen they would get better still.

So the towns along his route pulled out the stops and saw him through in style. The ceremonies were perforce rather brief—as he occasionally had to remind people, Congress was waiting for him, he was on his way to be sworn in, and the government could not really begin to function until he got there—but within the limits thus imposed each community used what imagination it had and did its best. The performances had much in common: the honor guards arrayed to greet him and escort him through town, trotting or marching self-consciously fore and aft of his carriage; the reception committees full of local dignitaries, including many former Continental officers and other old associates; delegations of war veterans or matrons or white-robed young ladies; banquets; long prepared addresses eulogizing the young nation and its heroic leader; toasts and salutes, odes and tableaux; occasional bridges all decked out with boughs of evergreen and laurel; and everywhere the curious eager crowds waving and cheering their first President on to his destination. Interspersed among all of this, fortunately, were long stretches of deserted road winding through empty countryside, quiet thoughtful miles between the last and the next escort contingent, and restful stopovers at rural inns or the homes of old friends.

George Washington bore it all with his usual grave dignity. Waving stiffly, bowing, nodding, acknowledging each tribute with whatever brief thanks the occasion demanded, he was pleased by some of the ceremonies and moved by others, now and then alarmed by the reverential, almost hysterical note of adulation in some of the receptions and on some of the faces. Expectations seemed impossibly high, and to this sober republican gentleman it must have smacked uncomfortably of Old World plaudits to divine-right monarchs on their way to be crowned.

The similarities were there, to the extent that this raw and not very monarchical nation was capable of staging things. Washington completed his journey in a custom-made 47-foot barge equipped with mast, sail, respendent red-curtained awning, and thirteen oars to a side, manned by veteran harbor pilots decked out in black caps and white smocks. While detachments of militia and regulars stood at attention and local notables waved and field artillery boomed a farewell salute from the Jersey shore, the barge and its august passenger, accompanied by delegations from the city of New York and both houses of Congress, moved majestically across the lower end of Newark Bay and along the Kill van Kull that separated Staten Island from the Bayonne peninsula, then turned northeast into upper New York Bay for the five-mile pull to Manhattan. Other craft fell in behind or came alongside to render passing honors which included, among others, earnest odes in four-part harmony and several appropriately reworded stanzas of "God Save the King."

A thirteen-gun salute from the battery on Staten Island was the signal for every vessel in the harbor to break out flags and bright bunting. The barge moved up the bay with a favoring wind at its back and porpoises wheeling across its bows and hordes of small boats bobbing in as close as they dared. The inner harbor echoed again and again to the bark of cannon. The Staten Island battery was answered by thirteen guns from a British packet and fifteen deeper notes from the larger guns of a Spanish corvette that swung to her anchor off Governor's Island, seamen manning her yards and the flags of some two dozen nations broken out on her rigging. The final salute came from the Battery at the foot of Manhattan, where people lined the shore and cheered as the oarsmen pulled their craft a short distance up the East River and made fast alongside Murray's Wharf at the foot of Wall Street.

Washington and his escort mounted carpeted steps to the landing where Governor Clinton and other dignitaries waited to greet him. The crowd gave cheer after cheer, local militia snapped to a full salute, and after courteously acknowledging all the greetings, Washington announced that he preferred to walk rather than ride to the house on Cherry Street a few blocks distant, which the government had reserved for him. Duly accompanied as he was by a parade of notables and an honor guard, it took the tall figure in cocked hat and blue and buff suit nearly half an hour to move through the dense throngs to his house. Here there was barely time for a glass of punch and more greetings before the governor's coach arrived to take him to a formal banquet at the governor's mansion. (It was a good omen, and a tribute to the restraint shown by both sides in New York's recent nip-and-tuck battle over ratification, that Antifederalist George Clinton was now so cordially in evidence to welcome the new President of a government he had been opposed to creating.)

A busy week of public affairs and visits to congressmen and formal dinners followed. In between times Washington received streams of callers, worked in collaboration with James Madison on his brief inaugural speech (fortunately deciding to scrap the 73-page address he had prepared before leaving Virginia), and got what rest he could. Congress, meanwhile, fell into a long and acrid wrangle over how to address the new Chief Executive, flirting with such inapt Europeanisms as "His Most Serene Highness"—this being the choice, oddly enough, of Vice-President John Adams, whose Yankee republican common sense was seasoned now and then with strong dashes of pomposity. They could not agree upon the final, unadorned choice—"the President of the United States"—until well after Washington's inauguration.

This took place on April 30, 1789, in a climactic round of ceremonies that nearly everyone in town had been working up to for days. Cannon and church bells began proclaiming the appointed day soon after it dawned, and crowds gathered at strategic places all through the morning. A joint congressional committee called at the Cherry Street house around noon to escort him to the swearing in, and the President-elect, clad today in sober brown homespun set off by bright silver buttons, white silk stockings, silver-buckled shoes, and a dress sword, rode in solitary splendor in a ponderous four-horse coach. Troops, aides, the congressional committee, and eminent officialdom formed a parade that marched ahead and beside and behind the stately vehicle. The procession moved slowly through several crowded blocks to the seat of government, then located in Federal Hall at the corner of Broad and Wall streets. Washington rode to the sound of band music and church bells and endless cheers that swelled and pulsed about his coach as it lumbered past.

The ceremony at Federal Hall (recently remodeled after the design of a talented French architect, Major Pierre L'Enfant, who would soon be laying out a magnificent street plan for the future federal capital on the Potomac) was brief and moving. Washington and his entourage walked the last two hundred yards to the building, entered and mounted the stairs to the Senate chamber on the second floor, where United States senators and foreign diplomats were seated on one side and representatives on the other. All rose as he entered. Bowing in acknowledgment, Washington walked down the center aisle to a dais containing three chairs at the north end of the room. Vice-President Adams greeted him there, escorted him to the central chair, and sat on the

President's right, while Frederick Muhlenberg of Pennsylvania, first Speaker of the House, seated himself on Washington's left. Then Adams stood, faced the President, and announced haltingly that all was in readiness. "I am ready to proceed," Washington replied. Bowing, Adams led the President back to the south end of the room and out onto a half-enclosed portico overlooking Wall Street. Crowds jamming the streets and nearby rooftops promptly broke into new rounds of cheering which reverberated across lower Manhattan as the President bowed again and again in response.

The portico contained a single chair and a table draped in red, topped by a Bible resting on a velvet cushion. Washington seated himself momentarily while the appointed dignitaries—Vice-President Adams, Governor Clinton, New York's Chancellor Robert Livingston, Generals Knox and St. Clair, and a few others —took their places on the portico. Washington rose to face Livingston, who stepped forward to administer the oath. The two men stood in profile to the street, and the secretary of the Senate (diminutive Samuel Otis, whose fiery, erratic brother James had fanned the early sparks of revolution in Boston twenty-five years earlier) stood between them, facing the crowd, to hold the Bible. While Washington placed his hand on it Livingston read the sonorous oath that every American Chief Executive would hear and repeat at the outset of his term; and Washington became the first to solemnly swear that he would "faithfully execute the office of President . . . and . . . preserve, protect, and defend the Constitution of the United States."

"So help me God," Washington concluded, bending forward to kiss the Bible. Livingston turned to face the crowd and made an expansive gesture. "It is done," he said. And then, as loudly as he could: "Long live George Washingston, President of the United States!"

Once again the waves of sound rose to beat against the building and the tall figure on the portico and the assembled worthies who flanked him. Cannon from the Spanish sloop of war and the harbor batteries thudded their accompaniment, and the city's church bells sounded faintly above the din. Washington bowed and bowed in response, then walked back inside the Senate chamber and took his seat while the great roar from without continued. Several minutes later, when everyone else had found chairs and the noise had subsided a bit, he rose and prepared to speak. The audience rustled into silence and rose with him.

Observers reported the President's demeanor as "grave, almost to sadness." He was visibly nervous, speaking in a deep, barely audible voice that trembled a little, and shifting his manuscript from one hand to the other several times as he read.

As state speeches go, this one was brief and unremarkable, yet —like nearly everything else this altogether remarkable man did —it was effective with the solid, steady effectiveness of things that ring true. Washington advised the Congress to steer shy of "local prejudices or attachments" and "party animosities." He urged extreme caution in amending the new Constitution but asked Congress to hasten those particular amendments that reflected "a reverence for the characteristic rights of freemen and a regard for the public harmony"—a reminder of the Federalist pledge to obtain a bill of rights. Deprecating his own talents and capacities, he revealed his sense of the largeness of the task before him by fervent appeals for divine guidance and the blessings of Providence. He spoke confidently of "an indissoluble union between virtue and happiness, between duty and advantage, between the genuine maxims of an honest and magnanimous policy and the solid rewards of public prosperity and felicity."

George Washington was no orator, but the very simplicity, modesty, and earnestness of the performance, together with the man's unimpeachable dignity and the solemnity of the occasion, moved nearly everyone, including crusty John Adams, to tears. When the address was over there was much applause and shaking of hands, after which the President left Federal Hall and walked between ranks of stiffly saluting militia and more cheering crowds to St. Paul's Chapel for formal religious services conducted by the Episcopal Bishop of New York. Although Washington was then permitted the luxury of a private meal in his quarters, the day's proceedings soon resumed with what must have seemed like an interminable round of receptions, illuminations, fireworks, toasts, and official formality. All in all the inaugural journey and ceremonies had been hugely successful. If the citizens of New York and the towns he had visited en route from Mount Vernon offered a fair measure of national sentiment, Americans were fairly ecstatic about their new chief of state.

Perhaps there was, as Washington feared, a danger in the kind of adulation he had received. Yet perhaps there was sound reason for it, too. The eager multitudes whose cheers were tinged with reverence were celebrating an end and a beginning that rarely dovetail with such symmetry: the wild experiment in rebellion which had begun with volunteer citizen-soldiers converging on Boston to besiege a British army after Lexington and Bunker Hill was now stabilized and domesticated, voluntarily constrained by a homemade central government committed to the formidable task of making freedom march in some kind of step with power. That this was a fulfillment rather than a subversion of the noble vision of 1776 was eloquently attested—hence the joyous note of exaltation in all those cheers—by the fact that the same man who had led the experiment in rebellion was on hand fourteen years later to lead the experiment in centralized power. Americans who hailed the return of their commander-in-chief were marking a singular achievement, and they sensed it. Their Revolution had come of age.

Exactly five days later, with far more lavish pomp and circumstance as befitted one of Europe's greatest powers and oldest monarchies, delegates of the three French estates—300 noblemen, 300 prelates and lesser clergy, and 600 bourgeois commoners—gathered with royal officials and courtiers amid the ornate splendor of Versailles to parade ceremoniously into session. The Estates-General, an ancient, moribund, almost forgotten institution, was assembling for the first time since 1614. It had been convoked by a desperate monarchy as a last resort in order to help bail the government out of an acute financial crisis, and although the court and the cream of French society and enthusiastic Parisian crowds welcomed the august convocation with stylish formality, its appearance after 175 years of disuse was proof that the royal government of Bourbon France stood, in more ways than one, irremediably and irreversibly on the threshold of bankruptcy.

Moreover, although relatively few of the chosen delegates and royal officials bowing and scraping at one another in the fabled palaces and gardens of the Sun King on that fateful fifth of May quite realized it, the occasion marked the formal beginning of the French Revolution.

New York and Versailles; America and France. It was fitting that two ceremonies should occur within the same week. The long era of action, reaction, and interaction had entered upon a climactic phase, and before the next quarter century of war and social turmoil was over the map of Europe would be remade several times and the political and intellectual configurations of the Western world would be changed beyond recall. One revolution had peaceably consolidated itself behind a new government; another revolution, peacefully enough in its hopeful opening pageant, had begun.

A great deal had happened in the hundred-odd years since Louis XIV's advances toward the Rhine and Iroquois-Algonquin clashes in the far-off Great Lakes country had summoned Count Frontenac to direct murderous Indian attacks upon colonial frontier settlements. The French were gone from the North American mainland, and the frontier settlements were now pushing relentlessly westward as the vanguard of a new independent nation.

The French Crown had contributed mightily, if unwittingly, to the changed relationship between Great Britain and her mainland colonies whereby that independence had become a possibility; later the French Crown had contributed knowingly, perhaps decisively, to the war effort whereby the independence had been achieved. Now America was paying off this debt, principal and interest, in ways that went well beyond anything the original creditors had had in mind.

The French Crown's days were numbered, although few of the notables parading through Versailles that spring had much inkling of this. Equally on borrowed time were the tenacious holdovers of Europe's feudal past—the whole complex structure of dues and obligations and rights and privileges whereby one small class had clung to power and place and dominated the social and political life of most of the Continent for the better part of a millennium. (Some of these privileges and powers would survive for well over a century after the Estates-General met to launch a new era in 1789; it would take the sustained holocaust of two twentieth-century world wars, which consumed millions of lives while the great European empires tore one another apart, to deal the old system its death blow. A few well-placed bluebloods would survive even this, but the system built on hereditary privilege and corporate exclusiveness and great landed estates, which had ridden the crest of Europe's surge toward world domination in the centuries after Columbus, was irretrievably gone by 1950 —as was the domination.)

It is an oversimplification to say that the French were starting a revolution because the Americans had just completed one. But the influence of the American example upon thoughtful Europeans, of whom France had a full share, was profound. It was not just that French expenditures on behalf of the American cause had hastened and deepened the financial crisis which was the proximate cause for summoning the Estates-General in 1789. What really mattered was the impact of America's success on the elements that would make France's financial crisis the occasion not merely for reform but for revolution.

By the final quarter of the eighteenth century the nations of

Western Europe contained something like an informed public opinion below the level of royal court and country estate— growing clusters of intelligent, educated, urban middle-class professionals and businessmen who were expanding their areas of knowledge and getting together to talk it over. They read newspapers and magazines, pamphlets and essays, knew more than a little about the writings of the *philosophes,* and were full of the confident belief in social progress and human betterment which the Age of Reason had fostered. They were, in short, ready for change, ready to applaud and join any movement that promised to free mankind from the dead weight of outworn institutions and advance the cause of human progress.

More specifically, these bourgeois reformers wanted liberation from the systems of government, taxation, law, and preferment that stifled their own initiative and gave undue advantage to the entrenched patricians at the top of every society. Individualism, equal opportunity, and free-enterprise capitalism lay at the root of their demands, whether they articulated it in precisely those terms or not. The Industrial Revolution had already begun in parts of Western Europe, and these were the folk who wanted to partake of it.

Expectant revolutionaries, they had been greatly excited by the American Revolution, seeing it as a harbinger of things to come, as proof that liberty could in fact triumph over tyranny— that the future worked. Most of them had rather farfetched and cloudy notions of what had really happened in America, and of what the American experience really had to say to their own societies, which were saddled with a good bit of heavy cultural baggage that America had cast aside. Nevertheless, events on the far side of the Atlantic had greatly quickened the European imagination. This was particularly true in France, where—as in England and two or three of the West German states—the view of America was built upon a shade more than coffeehouse fantasizing. Every social rank had had a little direct exposure, transmitted by thousands of veterans (from the Marquis de Lafayette on down) who had come back from America after Yorktown to talk about what they had seen, and to retain who knows how many restless impulses and impressions that surfaced in one way or another when the lid began to come off in 1789.

Inspired by the American example, these middle-class towns-folk responded the more quickly and the more boldly when the French monarchy proved unable to solve its financial crisis without summoning the Estates. From then on the Crown proposed but the Third Estate disposed; initiative soon passed into the hands of the French bourgeoisie, who were mainly responsible for the tangled course of political events whereby their country moved from royal absolutism through constitutional monarchy to full-fledged republic within three or four years.

It was heady stuff, beyond doubt. Conservatives were horrified, but most European intellectuals and literate townsfolk were exultant, at least for a while. A new era seemed to have begun, bright with promise and alive with hope. The Bastille fell; feudal dues and privileges blew away like autumn leaves before a storm. A new French Constitution proclaimed the Rights of Man and the Citizen; divine right gave way to liberty, equality, fraternity. Young William Wordsworth, a student at Cambridge when all of this began happening across the Channel, summed it up for an entire generation of hopeful European liberals: "Bliss was it in that dawn to be alive," he crowed, "but to be young was very heaven."

—□—

This, as older and more sedate Englishmen might have retorted, was all very well, but the forces set in motion by those eager Frenchmen were more powerful and deadly than they appeared, and in the end they were not going to be controllable. If the French Revolution was in good part a result of the contagion France had caught from America, it was soon spreading beyond France's borders with an epidemic virulence of its own—except that metaphors trip over themselves and cannot quite do justice to what began pulsing out of France in the 1790s. The impassioned slogans and explosive ideas of the Revolution that so exhilarated Wordsworth could travel airborne, so to speak, and some did, spread by letter and news column and word of mouth to be absorbed and begin doing their work in societies far removed from Paris streets. But mostly these ideas traveled on French bayonets, carried across the Rhine and the Alps by invading armies that marched beneath the Revolutionary tricolor flag, to be imposed in harsh and unsubtle fashion. The nearer neighbors of Revolutionary France were partly infected and partly steamrollered, and they split sharply over whether to welcome these spirited Gallic columns as liberators or conquerors.

They came in fact as both. Revolutions are respecters of neither logic nor consistency, and they almost always impose their own pattern upon the course of events. A revolution will overflow its banks and inundate the lowlands and carve strange shifting new paths across the landscape (the metaphors of flood and tide are as apt, and as imperfect, as those of virus and infection) unless its channel is deep and well lodged between high banks. Here, certainly, is one important difference between what happened in France and what happened in America. The Americans and their ancestors had in effect been at work upon a channel for their Revolution since the days of the Tudors and the Plantagenets, and the circumstances in both England and America had been uniquely favorable. Frenchmen, by contrast, did not really begin to think seriously about changing their political and social system until a few years before they tried it, and the French terrain was so overgrown with a tangle of deeply rooted institutions that there was no clear-cut channel for their sudden venture in revolution to follow. So it went where it would, and things got out of hand.

The best metaphor for this kind of sweeping alteration in the present scheme of things was coined by Stephen Vincent Benét: now and then, he said, there comes a crack in time itself. Benét was discussing the onset of the American Civil War, but the term

applies equally well to the revolutionary epoch that traced its seis-
mic scar across Western history between Lexington and Water-
loo. Since the advent of Christianity the Western calendar has
experienced two comparable fissures: the sixteenth-century Reformation and the turbulent period of more recent memory that
spans Sarajevo and Hiroshima. It is not always bliss to be alive at
such times, but it is rarely dull.

At home, the French Revolution kept accelerating and eventually engulfed not merely the Old Regime but its own leaders
and principles. The slogans and rhetoric remained, but the
abrupt, often violent political changes that took Frenchmen from
First Republic to Robespierre and the Terror, thence to Directory, Consulate, and Napoleonic Empire all within a twelve-
year span involved measures and actions several long removes
from liberty, equality, fraternity, and the Rights of Man.

The French were still in the early phases of their Revolution
when they became smitten with the idea of exporting it, and
things got out of hand even faster. This idea would probably have
occurred to them in any event; it took hold faster, and with
greater force, because of the way other countries reacted to what
went on inside France. What went on there—mobs in the street,
abolition of feudal privileges, nationalization of church property,
persecution of noble families—was sensational and alarming.
Other nations were not content merely to protest; they meddled.
Part of this was old-fashioned power politics: one of Europe's
strongest and most aggressive states was weakened by internal
disorder, and rivals could not resist trying to take advantage. But
it went well beyond power politics. A not inconsiderable body of
Europeans held with religious certitude to the conviction that the
future of civilization, morality, law and order, and all other good
things depended upon a stratified social hierarchy ruled by hereditary monarchs, held together by established churches, and
staffed at the top by privileged aristocracies. To such folk the
French Revolution was an abomination and a mortal threat. Since
this attitude numbered among its votaries nearly all of Europe's

crowned heads and ruling classes, some sort of meddling in French affairs was bound to happen.

The meddling began with noises of disapproval and went on to include giving aid and asylum to émigré aristocrats, encouraging sundry intrigues and plots against France's shaky constitutional monarchy of 1791, and canvassing the prospects of undoing the Revolution by means of forcible intervention. The French responded to these tactics with a bellicose universal-revolution rhetoric that confirmed the European establishment's worst fears, and the atmosphere fairly crackled with hostility. It surprised no one when France went to war with Austria and Prussia, the two loudest champions of the old order, in the spring of 1792. A combined Austro-Prussian army promptly launched an invasion and marched on Paris, which the allied commander threatened to destroy if any harm befell the French royal family.

This outside attempt to restore the Bourbon status quo backfired disastrously. Torn by internal conflict and seemingly on the verge of collapse, the French revolutionary impulse regrouped and acquired a terrible new momentum in the face of foreign attack. While factions scrambling for position at the crest of the French wave overthrew one another with increasing frequency, the wave gathered force and became tidal: within a year France became a republic, executed its king, launched the Terror, rolled back the invasion, and carried the war and the revolution outside its borders. Britain, Holland, and Spain joined the anti-French coalition in 1793, but the old powers were up against something new, and for a time they were badly overmatched. The French armed forces were in disarray when the war began, the Revolution having alienated or expelled the aristocratic officer corps. But Frenchmen soon found a potent substitute for the eighteenth century's small, well-drilled professional armies. Part of this was the almost invincible élan of the citizen soldier who believed to the point of exaltation in what he fought for, and part of it offered a grim portent for future conflicts: the *levè en masse,* or universal conscription, which gathered together enough of these citizen soldiers to create several large armies and put the rest of the populace to work equipping and supplying them.

Achieving something like total mobilization and firing her new armies with a combination of revolutionary and patriotic zeal, France took the offensive in 1793 and stayed on it for the better part of twenty years. The French armies mastered techniques and skill as they went, found able officers and commanders by sifting them through repeated trial by combat, and became the masters of Europe. (This proved impossible to accomplish at sea, where revolutionary zeal turned out to be insufficient. In the navy there was no substitute for professional leadership, iron discipline, or practical experience, all of which were in woefully short supply when untrained republicans replaced blueblood commanders on French quarterdecks. It was the navy deployed by the parliamentary government across the Channel that had all the professionalism and discipline, and in the end it was this navy that kept Revolutionary and Napoleonic France from carrying everything before them.)

They carried a good deal before them, nevertheless, and it took a rather heterogeneous combination of powers and circumstances to get the Continent out from under. For nearly a generation Europe's most hidebound autocracies—Russia, Austria, Prussia, Spain—were arrayed off and on with Europe's most advanced constitutional monarchy—Great Britain—in an all-out war against a revolution that somehow managed to fall under the sway of an imperial conqueror without losing any of its élan or dynamism. The conqueror marched with the Revolutionary tricolor and sought to impose his own order upon Europe beneath the slogans and a few of the principles of 1789. Change, upheaval, dislocation, and new regimes, often harshly oppressive yet often more justly and efficiently run than the ones they supplanted, followed in the wake of his armies; and his armies eventually extended French sway from the Tagus to the Dnieper.

All in all it was a confused and contradictory struggle. The real victors, finally, were modern nationalism and modern liberal capitalism, both of which came into their own during or soon after the conflict—reason enough, certainly, for calling this a revolutionary era, and for adding that very few of the participants knew what kind of revolution it was or where it would lead.

It was, in any event, the biggest war Europe had yet staged—a world war, really, with troops and squadrons maneuvering in both hemispheres—and because it was not only a war for empire and world hegemony but also a contest (confusingly aligned but earnestly waged) between starkly conflicting social and political theories, the implications were enormous, if not always clear. And no Western nation was so remote that it could avoid getting involved.

This included the new United States of America, where nearly everything that happened for twenty-five years after George Washington took the oath of office was shaped in one way or another by the political convulsions taking place in Europe. The ideas battling for supremacy in the Atlantic community after 1789 infused American politics with an antagonism, a shrillness, and a depth of theoretical disagreement that would only be surpassed in later years by the quarrel over slavery. Not until the middle of the twentieth century would international affairs play so pervasive a role in American life. Since the United States was a small nation seeking to steer an independent course amid what grew into an all-out war between the world's superpowers, France and Great Britain, foreign policy became a tense and intricate game in which not only trade and territory but peace and national survival were among the counters.

Yet the game was exciting as well as dangerous, because many of the counters were made of solid gold. Europe—the world's buyer, seller, distributor, and processor, where all the lines of trade converged—was continuously at war for the better part of twenty-five years. It massed great armies and kept mighty battle fleets on station, and its need for food, fiber, timber, iron, powder, and the ships to carry them was insatiable and beyond its own capacities. The United States was in a unique position to profit from all of this, and for most of the period it did so, enjoying a sustained commercial boom that laid the basis for the great nineteenth-century take-off into industrialization.

In short, everything the young Republic sought to do, at home and abroad, was carried on against a backdrop of world war, power politics, revolutionary ferment and intrigue, and economic opportunities of boundless scope and boundless peril. The United States resembled a brand-new sailing ship that took treasure on board and encountered a full gale on its shakedown cruise. No other quarter century in our history would offer so formidable and complex a set of challenges.

It was just as well, under the circumstances, that the nation and its new government were permitted two or three years in which to settle in on their new course before the high-pressure area building up in France began to be felt on this side of the Atlantic. There was more than enough to do, even in quiet times. Washington's first administration occupied itself mainly with domestic matters and the necessary business of creating some federal machinery and putting it to work.

This machinery was neither elaborate nor extensive by modern standards, but it represented considerably more than anything the American people had yet attempted in the way of government apparatus. Proceeding with all deliberate speed and occasional sharp disagreement, the men chiefly responsible for getting things started in those busy first months discovered right away that their new Constitution maintained a sphinxlike inscrutability on matters of detail and implementation. But expert opinions as to its meaning and intent were in good supply, a substantial number of the Framers having been elected to the First Congress.

Chief among these, by all odds, was James Madison, now a representative from Virginia (Patrick Henry's opposition had blocked his appointment to the Senate) and very much in evidence indeed. One can hardly say too much about this man's contributions to our early national years, yet beyond scholarly circles he has never had the attention he deserves. It is partly a matter of image. A self-effacing and not very imposing figure, Madison worked in the shadow of more conspicuous national leaders during every phase of his long career. Revolutionary America enjoyed the services of six men who can legitimately be called great: Franklin, Washington, Adams, Hamilton, Jefferson, and Madison. Various attributes of personality, presence, or character made each of the other five, in one way or another, larger than life; while Madison, who was if anything a shade smaller than life, tends to fade from view, like the shy child who is almost entirely hidden in the family snapshots by a cluster of photogenic big brothers.

He was not lost on his contemporaries, certainly not on those who worked with him; it is posterity that finds him forgettable. Even as President, when he had eight years at the center of the stage, he was overshadowed by larger world figures like Napoleon and Wellington or by flamboyant newcomers on the American scene like Andrew Jackson and Henry Clay. Moreover, Madison had the ill fortune to preside over a war that was highly unpopular in the region that would produce most of the nation's historians for the next seventy-five years. New Englanders wrote about the diplomacy and leadership of "Mr. Madison's War" with icy patrician disdain, and tended to couch their treatment of the fourth President in tones that resembled Washington Irving's patronizing portrait. "Poor Jemmy Madison," Irving wrote; "he's such a withered little applejohn." American historical writing has outgrown Irving and New England, but poor Jemmy Madison is still in the shadows.

Be that as it may, in the 1790s he was simply indispensable. A master of logic, persuasive argument, parliamentary tactics, and the written word, Madison moved about Congress with quiet efficiency and proved as instrumental in shaping and defining the contours of the new government as he had been in shaping and defining its charter. The United States would not have followed the course it took, or followed it as well, without him.

Representative Madison soon learned that getting his Constitution properly implemented was every bit as difficult as getting it drafted and ratified. In the Congress, as in the country at large, there were strong pockets of state-rights sentiment and many individuals who still entertained doubts and reservations about centralized power. Many who had been elected as Federalists shared some of these doubts, and there were others whose desire for harmony made them unduly eager to conciliate Antifederalist sentiment. If these folk had had their way, they would have managed to clip the wings of the new government in the process of getting it aloft. Madison was able to forestall such efforts in several key areas before the first session adjourned in the fall of 1789.

To begin with, there was the matter of fleshing out the executive branch. Congress established five executive departments— State, Treasury, War, and the offices of Attorney General and Postmaster General—and followed Article II of the Constitution in empowering the President to appoint the heads of such departments with the advice and consent of the Senate; this much was routine. But the Constitution was silent on the subject of removing these officers, and Congress considered requiring senatorial approval here as well. This pointed toward the emergence of a cabinet system along British lines, with department heads responsible to the legislature; and it reflected a long-standing American belief that the balance of political power should reside in the legislative branch. Determined to preserve executive independence, Madison persuaded his colleagues that the first clause in Article II, vesting executive power in the presidency, clearly implied an unrestricted right of removal. Congress finally agreed and authorized the President to remove his appointees without anyone's advice and consent.

Madison forestalled a similar inclination toward legislative supremacy when it came to locating the lines of authority for the Treasury Department. The Confederation Congress had exercised direct control over finance, delegating authority now and then to a treasury board that remained firmly under the congressional thumb. This was in keeping with the hallowed Anglo-American tradition of legislative power over the purse strings, and the new Congress was reluctant to part with any of it. In arguing that a single secretary responsible to the President could formulate and execute policy more efficiently than a board responsible to Congress, Madison cited the Revolutionary government's unimpressive financial record. The "inconsistent, unproductive and expensive schemes" resulting from the previous system, he said, were far worse than any "undue influence which the well-digested plans of a well-informed officer can have." Again Madison carried the day. (He was soon to learn some bitter lessons in the matter of just how much undue influence a well-informed Treasury Secretary's well-digested plans could have.) Congress did remain on guard against a too powerful executive by stipulating that the Secretary should make reports and provide financial information directly to Congress rather than through the President. Then, lest they be creating a kind of chancellor of the exchequer who could take the lead from them in money matters, they further stipulated that the Secretary should submit reports only when Congress asked him to rather than on his own initiative.

Madison had another battle on his hands over the federal judiciary, about whose structure and scope the Constitution offered few clues. He had to compromise a good deal here and fell some distance short of getting what the hard-core nationalists really wanted: a federal court system with all-inclusive jurisdiction presiding over a unified national system of law and justice—"One Whole," in Hamilton's term. This was far too much for the state-rights people. They would have met the call for a national judiciary in the narrowest possible fashion, by creating nothing beyond a Supreme Court and letting the state courts take over federal law enforcement at the lower levels. Both sides emerged with something in the Judiciary Act of 1789. The nationalists got a system of federal circuit and district courts beneath the six-man Supreme Court; the state-righters were able to limit the scope of federal jurisdiction and won implicit endorsement of the principle that state courts could hear cases involving federal law.

Although the jurisdiction of the national courts was narrower than Madison would have liked, the act of 1789 did contain a clause authorizing the appeal of certain cases from state courts to the Supreme Court. This explicit enactment of the principle that state legislation was subject to review by the federal judiciary, at least in the area of its jurisdiction, must have made Madison feel that the other concessions were worth while. The nationalists had not quite dared to write judicial review into the Constitution. Now they had it in a federal law, which was the next best thing.

Equally pressing, in its way, was the question of a bill of rights; a great many people who would otherwise have opposed the Federal Constitution had been promised that human-rights amendments would be the first order of business for the new Congress. Madison had hitherto opposed a bill of rights. He had held that they were important in a monarchy but scarcely relevant in a republic, where the lawmaking power resided in the people anyway. Listing specific rights, he had added, could have an adverse effect; a malevolently inclined government might construe the list as containing the only rights the people had. According to the Framers, the new government was one of enumerated and therefore limited powers, and civil liberties were outside its jurisdiction.

So, at any rate, the Federalists had argued. These arguments, coming as they did from such practical men, contained a dubious and strangely abstract sort of logic, and one is tempted to conclude that they were pursuing a strategy rather than speaking out of deep conviction. To cite a similar example, the *Federalist* essays that Hamilton, Madison, and Jay had written during ratification were superbly reasoned, but they had been designed to persuade;

the authors believed in some of what they were saying, but they were not saying everything. The point, in both instances, is that the Federalist logicians wanted a strong national government and were willing to manipulate words and ideas a little in order to get it.

There were indeed hidden agendas behind the bill-of-rights arguments, and not all of them hid behind James Madison's logic. He fully subscribed to the basic civil liberties, and now, from a position of great strength and influence—in effect the House Majority Leader, although there were no majorities and no parties as yet—he was prepared to do battle for them. His strategy of doing battle in Congress rather than during ratification derived from a keen sense of what many of the bill-of-rights proponents were really up to. Behind their pious rhetoric about safeguarding human freedoms lay a strategy no less calculated and even less straightforward than Madison's.

The Antifederalists had originally hoped to win by demanding that human-rights amendments be taken up at a second constitutional convention, where the document could be emasculated or talked to death; having failed to cripple the document, they now hoped to use the same proposals to cripple the new national government. Sifting through the 200-odd amendments that had been proposed by various state ratifying conventions, Madison concluded that human liberties were a far less genuine concern than the desire to curb the federal government's powers. (The most conspicuous and widely supported of the proposed amendments were designed to restrict the government's all-important right to tax.) Here, Madison believed, spoke the voice of provincial oligarchies, earnestly quoting libertarian scripture in order to keep their own interests safely vested and their own powers intact. If many of these amendments were adopted, the new government would be no more effective than the old one had been.

Convinced that it would be impolitic to ignore the sentiment and ruinous to consider the existing proposals, Madison calmly digested the material Congress had received and drafted some human-rights amendments of his own. These became the basis, after his colleagues had tinkered with them a bit, for the existing Bill of Rights. By August 1789 the House had approved a total of seventeen amendments, within a month the two chambers had agreed upon twelve, and the states eventually ratified ten, which went into effect in December 1791.

Madison had seen to it that these amendments were everything sincere friends of human liberty could have wanted. To intone them is to summon forth echoes of colonial grievances against the mother country and to be reminded once more of what it was about governments that made eighteenth-century Americans nervous. The first eight amendments guaranteed the people's right to assemble, petition, and bear arms; their right to freedom of speech, press, and religion; the right to due process and jury trial; freedom from self-incrimination, cruel or unusual punishment, unreasonable search or seizure, excessive bail, the quartering of troops in private homes, and so on. The Fathers had not been indifferent to these treasured rights; it had merely been a matter of waiting for the right moment to incorporate them.

Madison also saw to it that the wing-clipping features of the state proposals were eliminated from the final package; as Hamilton gleefully noted, Madison's amendments dealt with "scarcely any of the important objections which were urged, leaving the structure of the government, and the mass and distribution of its powers where they were." In a strategic retreat that further disarmed critics of consolidated government, Madison had added two summary amendments to the specific guarantees in the first eight. The Ninth (in keeping with his own fears) affirmed that the enumeration of certain rights "shall not be construed to deny or disparage others retained by the people"; and the Tenth soothed state-rights alarms by declaring that "powers not delegated to the United States by the Constitution, nor prohibited by it to the States, are reserved to the States respectively, or to the people." This last, which was copied almost verbatim from a restriction that had hobbled the Confederation government, looked like a much bigger concession than it actually was. The Articles had said that the states retained all powers not *expressly* delegated to the national government. In transposing this clause to the Tenth Amendment Madison had quietly dropped the word "expressly"—knowing, as a good lawyer, that this left wide open (which was how he wanted it) the crucial question as to exactly which *unstated* powers the national government might or might not have.

It had been a deft performance. In the space of six months Congress and its adroit floor leader had established the executive and judicial branches and got the federal apparatus in motion with its powers intact. The addition of the first ten amendments had quieted the fears that mattered and deprived the Antifederalists of their best argument. As a movement, and even as a sentiment, Antifederalism simply disappeared after 1789. The danger that the nation would be permanently split by the formation of an irreconcilable "anti-Constitution" party was gone before the new document had been in effect a year; public support for the Federal Constitution became almost total.

The prospects of a long divisive quarrel over the Constitution had barely subsided before the issues that would summon forth the American two-party system—with a deeper gulf between the parties than would ever exist again—had become government policy and a subject of fierce national debate.

Something of the sort was bound to happen, yet on this subject the Founding Fathers had been strangely myopic. They did not approve of political parties at all, and they had somehow concluded that in a properly run government there would be no need for them. Measured by eighteenth-century British and colonial examples, parties had come to be viewed, not inaccurately, as factions and cliques that formed and maneuvered for their own selfish advantage at public expense. Parties might be undesirable, but they were just over the horizon anyway. What the Fathers never seemed to appreciate was that the new government would inevitably raise questions of national import and provide a focus for national discussion; disagreements over such questions would thus acquire national scope. Furthermore, the Constitution had created no machinery whatever for nominating men to federal office. Efforts to gain public support for a position on some national issue and to create some sort of nominating machinery both pointed straight toward party organizations, and the embryos of such organizations began to take form early in George Washington's first term.

It was ironic, since the President so passionately deplored this development, that the issues around which America's first parties would form all came out of his own branch of government. Congress was where the disagreements appeared and hardened into controversy, but the presidency and its powers and policies were the focus. The Antifederalists had nothing to do with this; they melted away during 1789 like an April snowfall, only eight or ten certified Antifederalists had been elected to the First Congress anyway, and there would be no discernible correlation between a man's Antifederalist views during ratification and his political alignment when the two parties began to emerge in the 1790s. It was entirely from within the Federalist ranks that the new differences of opinion arose.

They arose before Washington had finished taking the oath of office, and they sputtered in and out of congressional discussion for months until a larger, related set of issues arrived to widen and sharpen the disagreement. It began, really, with the seemingly petty dispute over how to address the new Chief Executive. Federalist congressmen who agreed on nearly everything else found themselves at odds here, and beneath the flurry over whether to adorn republican simplicity with appellations like "His Elective Highness," and over whether Vice-President Adams was out of line in referring to the President's inaugural as "his most gracious speech" (which was the way they responded in England when the king spoke from the throne), lurked some honest fears and mis-givings.

Some men, including Adams, were afraid that the new presidential office would not command enough respect in the country unless it were buttressed with a variety of ceremonial trappings and, in Adams' words, "dignity and splendor." Others were afraid that these regal adornments would encourage the re-establishment of a monarchy—what Patrick Henry, who opposed the Federal Constitution in part for this reason, saw as a "bold push for the throne." It is much clearer in retrospect than it was at the time that the American people were through with royalty for good; although they retained a certain fascination for living examples, their interest in kings was akin to one's interest in tigers —splendid to look upon and contemplate, but only from a safe distance and not at large in one's neighborhood.

This did not, however, reduce the argument over kingly titles to absurdity. Whichever side they took, men were genuinely uncertain about the success of their political experiment, and both supporters and opponents of royal pomp were trying to act in the country's best interest. The lessons of history were not very reassuring. The American colonies had been planted by a monarchy and had been a part of one for all but a fraction of their existence. In 1789 they had been a republic for less than fifteen years, an officially recognized republic for less than eight. The monarchy from which they sprung had been in existence for centuries, as had most of its neighbors, and nearly every country that counted for anything was ruled by some sort of crowned head. Monarchies *worked*—the fate of the House of Bourbon was not yet apparent —whereas outside of the Netherlands, an example that was neither very comforting nor very applicable, and Switzerland, which was no example at all, the record of man's political activity since ancient times contained scant grounds for confidence in the viability of republics. One did not have to be a monarchist in order to feel that some of the trappings of monarchy might stand the country in good stead; anything that enhanced the ordinary citizen's respect for his leaders was a good thing. But not too much respect: Americans knew all about Caesarism and what had happened to the Roman Republic. And the fact that monarchies worked did not make them desirable; America's living memory of contacts with Great Britain was almost uniformly unpleasant. So they wrangled, and the victory for republican simplicity in the matter of titles was by no means the end of the argument.

Washington's own position here was equivocal. He was disgusted with the talk of royal forms of address, complaining that the subject had been raised "without any privity of knowledge of it on my part, and urged after I was apprized of it contrary to my opinion." He was not a monarchist, and it was duty rather than ambition that had impelled him to the presidency; its onerous and irritating features—the hordes of office-seekers, the endless official functions, the harsh and often unfair criticism—far outweighed whatever satisfaction he derived from it. (Jefferson describes the first President exploding over some issue at a cabinet meeting and thundering that "by god he had rather be on his farm than be made *emperor of the world*.")

He was no monarch, yet no American knew better how to act like one, and Washington agreed with Adams on the need to build public respect for the presidency. His public appearances were replete with pomp and show. He entertained by means of formal levees at which he circulated among the guests with august aloofness, observed rigid protocol, kept a retinue of powdered lackeys on hand in the presidential mansion, rode about town on a splendid white charger with gilt-edged leopard-skin saddle or in a carriage drawn by six marching cream-colored horses and accompanied by uniformed outriders—and generally conducted himself like the first citizen of his country, its former commanding general, and a Virginia gentleman to the manner born, none of which required playacting.

Traditionalists and lovers of ceremony adored this regal display, while men whose antennae quivered at every faint sign of incipient monarchy were alarmed by it. These same critics deplored a certain tendency on the part of the new United States Senate to act as though it were the House of Lords. (Many senators outdid John Adams in seeking to bestow Old World titles on republican offices and were resentful when the House of Representatives refused to concur.) Even Madison, who wanted a strong presidency and worked closely with Washington, groaned at the number of "sycophants and satellites" buzzing around the President—who, he felt, "had wound up the ceremonials of the government to such a pitch of stateliness which nothing but his personal character could have supported, & which no character save him could ever maintain."

So far the disagreement had been over matters of form, and perhaps everyone was overreacting a little. A few months later the executive branch produced an agenda full of substantive questions, and the waters got more troubled. The agenda came from the Treasury Department. Washington's cabinet appointments—he did not regard his department heads as a cabinet, but he sought their counsel often enough to set a precedent that became standard practice—included his fellow Virginian Edmund Randolph as Attorney General; his old comrade in arms Henry Knox, who carried over from Confederation as Secretary of War; and two of the Republic's best and brightest: Thomas Jefferson (not back from France to take up his new post until March 1790) as Secretary of State, and Alexander Hamilton as Secretary of the Treasury. In the fall of 1789, petitioned by government creditors and convinced that restoration of national credit was essential, Congress directed the new Treasury Secretary to prepare a report on the subject.

It was all the opening this Secretary needed. Initiative in the new government had hitherto belonged mainly to the President and the redoubtable Madison; for the next two or three years it belonged mainly to Alexander Hamilton, who was incapable of going anywhere or undertaking any assignment without making his presence felt. Of America's six great leaders Hamilton was the youngest (not yet thirty-five when he went to the Treasury Department), and his total public career was by far the shortest (the rendezvous with Aaron Burr on Weehawken Heights was only fifteen years distant). But none of his illustrious contemporaries would have a greater influence on the course of national development.

Born in the British West Indies, Hamilton had come to the mainland colonies in 1772, still in his teens, and attended King's College in New York, where he quickly got involved on the patriot side of America's dispute with Great Britain. The precocious young man wrote some attention-getting pamphlets and essays on the subject and got his career started with the war: captain of artillery, then secretary and aide-de-camp of General Washington, finally lieutenant colonel of infantry who performed with reckless daring and gallantry at Yorktown. He became a successful New York lawyer, married into New York's prominent Schuyler family, served in the Continental Congress, displayed a remarkable grasp of financial matters, and lobbied tirelessly during the 1780s for a stronger central government.

Now he was helping lead it, and his impact derived in fairly equal measure from what he did, from what he believed, and from what he was. He was (among other things) a complex and contradictory figure, easier to describe than to encompass, and about as easy to ignore as a live volcano. His outstanding traits included charm, boundless energy, talent bordering on genius, and a restless, driving ambition. Charm notwithstanding, Hamilton could be a tempestuous, sharp-tongued infighter and intriguer, which inspired resentment and made many enemies. Raised by his mother's family until he came to New York to seek fame and fortune, he was very much a self-made man and a climber; the illegitimate son of a West Indian planter's daughter and a ne'er-do-well Scot (which fact prompted unkind enemies to call him a bastard in both senses of the term), Hamilton had the polished manners, tastes, and inclinations of an aristocrat.

His outlook was a strange mixture indeed: hardheaded realist with an incurable romantic streak; conservative admirer of the British political and social system whose dreams of empire were downright Napoleonic; seventeenth-century mercantilist who foresaw the twentieth-century corporate state. No American of his day had a clearer sense of what he wanted the country to be or of how to get it there; few national visions were such an odd mix of tomorrow and yesterday. His economic outlook and grasp were decades ahead of his time, his social philosophy decades behind it. (Usually paired for contrast with his great adversary Jefferson, Hamilton remains a paradox. While Jefferson talked of school systems, Hamilton wanted to put children to work in factories because it made economic sense. Yet it was Hamilton and not Jefferson who transcended the racist assumptions of the era. The natural faculties of blacks, Hamilton said, "were probably as good as ours," adding that "the contempt we have been taught to entertain for the blacks makes us fancy many things that are founded neither in reason nor experience"—a truth that never quite dawned on Thomas Jefferson.)

Typically enough, Secretary Hamilton had already drafted the financial report that Congress asked for in October 1789. He came out with a comprehensive program designed to restore the nation's credit and lay secure foundations for national prosperity, and the program bore no small resemblance to the man: bold, brilliant, ambitious, successful, and controversial.

Hamilton's program had three components. Two were contained in his Report on the Public Credit, which he submitted to Congress in January 1790; the third came out a year later. First, he proposed to fund the entire national debt, principal and interest, foreign and domestic—amounting at the time to some $55 million, a large sum for a new country that was 95 per cent rural and perpetually short of cash. He would fund this debt at par, by issuing new interest-bearing government bonds and exchanging them, dollar for dollar, for all of the assorted securities, certificates of indebtedness, Treasury notes, unpaid interest coupons, and other pieces of paper issued by the previous government since 1776 and still outstanding. Secondly, he wanted the federal government to assume the war-incurred debts of the states, amounting in 1790 to some $25 million. Assumption, too, would involve a new bond issue, this time in a dollar-for-dollar replacement of all the state securities. The revenue wherewith to pay the annual interest on all these new government bonds would come primarily from two sources, which Congress under Madison's guidance had already provided for: a 5 per cent duty on imports and a set of tonnage duties that discriminated against foreign shipping. The third feature of his program, which he set forth in a report in January 1791, called for the establishment of a federally chartered national bank.

Funding, Assumption, National Bank: this was quintessential Hamilton, the great tripod on which his plan for financial recovery and economic development rested. Hamilton had figured it out with great care. Funding the national debt would accomplish three related tasks: it would restore the nation's credit at home and abroad; it would provide a needed supplement to the currency in the form of new negotiable bonds; and it would greatly strengthen the government by gaining the allegiance of wealthy capitalists and investors who dealt in government securities. The assumption of state debts would transfer the allegiance of state creditors to the federal government, which was where Hamilton wanted it; and, by eliminating the need for most state taxes, would give the federal government a virtual monopoly in the business of revenue collecting. A national bank would perform several useful functions. It would serve as the government's fiscal agent (acquiring, holding, transferring, and disbursing funds) and keep the credit policies of state-chartered banks under control; most important, it would issue bank notes which would circulate as legal tender and become the nation's principal medium of exchange. With credit and confidence restored and money available, investment in trade, transportation, industry, and agriculture would rise and the country would prosper.

Hamilton's program was duly enacted, and it began to happen so. Dutch, French, and Spanish creditors were delighted to exchange their old Continental securities for the new United States Government bonds and begin receiving regular interest payments at last. American holders also came forward with a rush, turning in old state and national certificates that had gone begging at twenty-five cents on the dollar or less for new government issues that bought and sold freely in the vicinity of par. Foreign capitalists, as the European political scene darkened with uncertainty, came to regard American bonds as a favored investment, and their market value rose even higher. National loans could henceforth be floated on good terms. And the American business community, as the major holders and buyers of the new bonds, lived up to Hamilton's expectations and waxed enthusiastic in their support of the government.

In 1791 the new Bank of the United States began its operations, and the business community became happier than ever. The bank was capitalized at $10 million, 80 per cent of which was to be held by private investors and 20 per cent by the government. (The same 4 to 1 ratio obtained on the board of directors.) Although it handled the government's finances and performed some of the functions of a central bank, the new corporation was very much a private profit-making institution, and Hamilton's arrangements were such that it began showing profits in a hurry. The bank was empowered to issue notes and lend them up to the value of its stock. (It could also lend against its deposits, once it had gone into operation and had customers with deposits to make; but initially its note issue was tied to its $10 million stock.) To be effective as a circulating medium, these bank notes had to be redeemable in hard cash—real money—on demand, and Hamilton's major achievement was the creation of some acceptable substitutes for real money. Had he not done so, the bank could not have been the success it turned out to be.

For the uninitiated this money question was hard to understand then and it is scarcely less so now. Nevertheless, it carried enough economic and political implications in Hamilton's time and later to be worth some attention.

Money and banking in the eighteenth century had become fairly sophisticated, but financial transactions had to rest ultimately, at times in practice and always in theory, upon hard cash, or what the capital market called specie—gold and silver bullion, coins of American or foreign mintage, bills of exchange on London or Amsterdam or Paris that could be converted into specie there and hence were literally "as good as gold." Hamilton's essential problem began at this point. The American colonies had always been short of specie and so was the Republic, for the simple reason that the country always paid more for its imports, which were mainly manufactures, than it received for its exports, which were mainly agricultural goods. Chronic cash shortage meant that much business had to be done on credit, which depended on the lender's confidence in the borrower and, more generally, on people's willingness to accept things other than hard cash in payment. Readily marketable commodities like furs or tobacco or barrels of whiskey could sometimes be used as cash substitutes, but this was a cumbersome device, and communities usually resorted instead to various forms of paper—certificates representing such produce, or land warrants, or other claims to ownership or obligation. Useful locally, such paper tended to be of less certain value the farther one went from its point of origin, often of no value at all when doing business with a banker or an importer, or when paying taxes or debts. It was no real substitute for a convenient, abundant, readily acceptable medium of national exchange.

This Hamilton provided. For the first time the economy actually had enough money on hand to expand and underwrite new projects and literally begin to cash in on its potential. The specie supply was as short as ever, but Hamilton had provided various paper substitutes in which the business community had entire confidence—and since the value of any and all money rests ultimately on public confidence in it, he had in effect created new money. Not everyone understood or liked it, as we shall see. But it worked.

Consider the Bank of the United States. In theory, a bank acquired the specie it would use as a reserve against its notes by selling stock for cash. Since the American investing community did not have enough specie to buy anything like $8 million worth of bank stock, Hamilton ruled that up to three fourths of this stock could be purchased instead with government bonds—now circulating close to par because of his Funding-Assumption program. The investing community had an abundance of these bonds and leaped at the chance to buy bank stock with them; as a result, the bank's entire subscription was gobbled up at once and hundreds of would-be investors were turned away. The bank, its stock selling at a premium because demand exceeded supply, thus acquired a small but satisfactory amount of specie and a large amount of good government securities. It began issuing notes against this reserve, and the notes immediately became an acceptable circulating medium because people had so much confidence in the bank's ability to redeem the notes that they hardly ever asked it to.

Public confidence was the key to the whole operation, and it was this that Hamilton had created first. Then he had created money, the form of pieces of paper which could be used as money because people would accept them as such. He had created paper in profusion, multiplying the nation's workable supply of capital many times over. First there were some $80 million worth of new government bonds, now marketable at par or better. Then there was the bank stock, also fetching premium prices because the bank was a dividend-paying investment right from the start. And finally there were the new bank notes, circulating nationwide as readily as newly minted coins. Bonds, stock, and notes together formed a big new pyramid of negotiable paper currency, all resting on a pittance of specie and an abundance of confidence. The confidence, based in turn upon the knowledge that the United States Government was now collecting taxes and meeting its obligations on schedule, enabled debt to be used as credit and money to flow. Business enterprise flourished accordingly, and the country prospered.

———□———

Successful though it was, Hamilton's Funding-Assumption-Bank tripod supported more than his plans for a healthy economy. His view of America, which we shall examine in a moment, rested there too. So did a big Pandora's box full of political, sectional, class, and personal antagonisms and—to mix the fables a little—a genie waiting to be summoned and to serve, a smiling expansive creature with gold dust on his fingertips and more powers for good and ill than anything ever contained in Aladdin's famous lamp.

Americans who thought they had devised a political system relatively free from partisan strife and corrupt self-seeking were about to learn something. Mainly they were going to learn things about themselves and one another, and the troubles that always ensue from the opening of that legendary box should not be blamed on Alexander Hamilton. He was not responsible for its contents or for having emplaced it ready to hand, and if he had not opened it somebody else would have.

Sooner or later, that is. Thanks to Hamilton it was going to be sooner, and a decision Americans did not yet realize they had already made was about to be dramatically affirmed. If it is errant fancy to invoke Pandora and Aladdin for anything so mundane as funding a debt and chartering a bank, perhaps more down-to-earth metaphors will provide some sense of the enormous difference between known past and unknown future that Americans were about to begin experiencing. They stood on a threshold before a mighty half-open door, and the red man's history offers an instructive contrast.

More than five thousand years earlier, in the Lake Superior country, the American Indian had become one of the world's first users of metal, making weapons, tools, and ornaments out of virgin copper, learning how to extract the copper from the quartz it was embedded in, learning how to anneal it as he worked it so that it would not become brittle. Living in one of the most metal-rich spots on earth, he stood on the verge of leaving the Stone Age altogether, scores of generations ahead of time . . .

. . . except that somehow he did not. Whether from sheer inertia or because in an uncanny way he knew something, he stopped working with copper and went back into the Stone Age, commiting himself to staying where he was. He was still there, essentially, when the white man came across him centuries later.

The American saw the red man as a savage and himself as vastly superior. But he too had a way of life that suited him, balanced midway between untamed Stone Age society and the decadent societies of Europe. The image he liked to use was that of a cultivated garden, neither trackless and shaggily overgrown like the raw wilderness nor hopelessly paved and crowded like a European city. With the wild forest slowly receding in the West and over 95 per cent of the people on farms or in villages, and the largest cities containing no more than forty or fifty thousand inhabitants, this garden image corresponded well with American reality in the 1790s. And this reality seemed the best of both worlds, a happy compromise midway between two undesirable extremes. In their quieter moments it was where Americans wanted to make *their* commitment.

The trouble was that they also wanted more than this. The Indian was a Stone Age man who had advanced to the threshold of technological breakthrough and then decided, well before white civilization arrived to plunder and debauch and finally break him, that he would stay on the Stone Age side of the door. White

Americans at the end of the eighteenth century had come a greater distance and stood at a higher threshold, but the similarity remained: on the hither side was the familiar, the known, the comfortable, everything that enabled a person to locate and define himself—the American garden. On the other side was . . . well, the works: combustion engines and Thomas Edison and Henry Ford, Pittsburgh and Detroit, change on a rising geometric curve, Chase Manhattan and IBM, megalopolis, man on the moon . . . the fire of Prometheus. (In describing the fabulous, one keeps returning to fable: it was after Prometheus stole fire as a gift for mankind that an angered Zeus visited Pandora's box upon them.) The works.

Britons and other Europeans were about to cross this threshold too, but the point was that Americans could not cross it and keep their garden intact at the same time, and unlike the Indian they did not really have a choice. This was where they were bound to go. For white Americans were not Stone Age men—or gardeners either, for that matter—but movers and shakers, a powerful advance guard of European expansion, Western civilization's sharp cutting edge, honed sharper still by their recent experiences and the land they occupied and the faith they swore by. At the moment they might be dressed in homespun and wield plowshares instead of swords, but they were still conquerors who sought gain and carried tomorrow in their backpacks—spiritual kin to Cortés and Pizarro, Da Gama and Cabral, Cartier and Champlain, Drake and Hawkins and Raleigh and all the other bearded Renaissance men who had worn breastplates and sailed bluff-bowed little ships across unknown seas in search of all there was to find. Had it been otherwise the colonists would not have left home in the first place, or crossed the mountains, or made a revolution.

But until now they could comfort themselves with the notion that they had only been making some needed improvements in What Already Was. Not any more. They had opted to cross that threshold long before Hamilton's program had been conceived or Hamilton himself had been born, and they could not be what they were and turn back. The trouble was that they could not take their garden with them, and this hurt.

Actually, only Alexander Hamilton and a few of his countrymen understood that a threshold was being crossed at all. For most Americans it was a matter of being baffled and disturbed by the things that started happening in the wake of his financial program. One of the results was prosperity, and this they liked, but the by-products worried them: the old order was changing, and so was the tempo of existence, and it was unsettling. What these Americans really wanted, of course, was to have it both ways: the cake and the eating, growth and opportunity without change, a garden fetching higher prices per acre. Several generations would pass before the nation fully grasped the idea that its comfortable middle ground between wilderness and metropolis was only a way station—that if you take the first step, as Rudyard Kipling pointed out, you will take the last.

PART THREE

HOPES AND FEARS

CHAPTER 20

First in Peace

THE FIRST major step was now at hand, and the taking of it set the tone and pace for the politics of the 1790s. Hamilton's ideas and methods made a lot of his countrymen uneasy, and the more they saw the uneasier they got. The Secretary of the Treasury, who at times was rather too articulate and outspoken for his own good, made no bones about the kind of system he wanted: an expanding, industrializing nation dominated by a commercial-financial elite working in close reciprocal harmony with a powerful central government. He sincerely wanted to benefit the entire country, and he was neither the first nor the last to operate on the notion that what directly and immediately benefited the merchant-capitalist-investor class would eventually benefit everyone.

But he also believed that benefiting this merchant-capitalist-investor group was a good thing in and of itself. These were the folk who mattered, whose support was essential for the continued success of the government, men whose ideas and talents were worth paying a premium for because they were of superior quality. As for the great mass of people who had not risen above the common herd—this was a British expression; Hamilton report-

□ 495

edly referred to them as a great beast—nothing positive could be expected, and nothing much was to be given beyond trying to keep them gainfully employed and ruled with a strong enough hand to prevent discontent from growing into rebellious outbreaks. Hamilton, in short, was an unabashed elitist. The only elite that could take the nation where he wanted it to go was the commercial-financial elite, and any policy that enhanced their power and influence was therefore a good thing.

Such an approach, in a society full of farmers and planters, was bound to encounter resistance. The resistance was compounded, moreover, because opponents of Hamilton's program could not fully understand part of it—the financial part, which worked beautifully and seemed to the uninformed like a species of black magic; while another part—the direct, immediate benefits to Hamilton's favored class—they understood all too well. The combination of what they could not understand and what they saw and disliked was potent; their opposition became deep-seated, strongly laced with fear and resentment.

It began quietly enough with a difference of opinion between Madison and Hamilton over an important detail in the Funding plan. Nearly everyone agreed that the existing national debt should be paid, and there was only perfunctory opposition to the idea of paying it in full; no one could really counter Hamilton's point that any scaling down would be a partial repudiation, hardly calculated to inspire confidence in the new government. The argument arose over exactly whom to pay.

Hamilton proposed to pay *all* present holders of the old debt, dollar for dollar, and Madison took exception to this. The original holders included many war veterans who had taken some form of Continental certificate in lieu of pay, and many merchants, storekeepers, artisans, and farmers who had accepted government promissory notes in payment for various goods and services. Everyone agreed that all of these folk should receive new securities up to the face value of their holdings. But Madison saw no need to extend this principle to later purchasers, mainly speculators, who had acquired large chunks of the old national debt at bargain prices before news of the funding plan enhanced their value. These people should only be compensated in part, Madison believed, and some consideration should also be given to those original holders—veterans, widows, farmers, and the like—who had parted with their securities at a fraction of their face value months or years ago out of pressing need for cash.

Madison's demand for equity had much to recommend it, but Congress, after making the proper clucking noises on behalf of veterans and widows, voted for Hamilton's version. It was the first time Madison had not been able to line up a congressional majority for something he wanted, and it marked the real opening of the dialogue that was about to make violent political partisans out of statesmen who deprecated parties.

Madison had lost because too many congressmen felt that his idea of compensating different classes of bondholders in different ways would be costly, formidably difficult to work out, and—Hamilton insisted—unjust: to discriminate against later purchasers, he said, would go against "established rules of morality and justice" and "render all rights precarious, and . . . introduce a general dissoluteness and corruption of morals."

Here Hamilton had gone to the nub. Exactly what constituted dissoluteness and corruption of morals depended on one's vantage point, and Americans were of two minds about this. To Hamilton, the only relevant morality was that of the market place and the counting house; the best government was one that gave priority to creating an atmosphere in which business could be transacted with confidence. This meant not repudiating debts, and not letting extraneous considerations like sympathy for losers interfere with old-fashioned sanctity of contract. A transaction wherein something changed hands for a price was a matter between buyer and seller: both should beware. The government's only duty was to the present holder of its debt, who should be paid in full regardless of when or how he acquired it, or at what price.

The morality of the market place did not yet have the field to itself in America, although it had already acquired an irresistible momentum. To the folk who began lining up behind Madison in the debate over Funding and Assumption (the two projects were part of the same bill and raised similar questions), the "general dissoluteness and corruption of morals" came from the shrewd financial types who were profiting greatly from their speculation in government securities. Indeed, from the outside it looked as though a fast shuffle was taking place—and some of those who were participating in the shuffle were also voting in Congress in favor of Funding and Assumption.

What had happened was predictable, inevitable, and quite within the bounds of Hamiltonian morality. It did not mean (although some suspicious souls found this hard to believe) that the fix was in; Hamilton did not use his office for his own enrichment and he did not deliberately tip anybody off. He did not need to. The commercial-financial-investor class whose allegiance he sought, because of their superior wisdom, had simply begun demonstrating that they possessed such wisdom by figuring out what was going to happen and moving to take advantage of it; what his enemies called speculative mania was to Hamilton no more than legitimate business enterprise. These men went out before the Funding-Assumption bill was introduced (agents armed with cash were going by fast ship or fast horse to the deep South and the back country during 1789 and 1790) to buy all the old national and state securities they could find. Some had begun doing this as soon as the Constitution was ratified, others when the revenue law of 1789 was passed, on the plausible theory that a government with the power to tax would eventually honor the old debts; more started doing it when Hamilton, whose views on the subject were no secret, became Secretary of the Treasury. Dutch bankers, too, were speculating in American securities in anticipation of a rise, buying some two or three million pounds' worth at an average price of five shillings to the pound.

These speculators were not betting on a sure thing, exactly, because they had no guarantee that Hamilton's Funding-Assumption bill was going to pass in the form he wanted. But being mainly from the commercial centers—New York, Philadelphia, Boston—and having good connections with Hamilton and his circle, they had a distinct edge in knowledge and awareness over the distant country folk whose old securities they now sought to buy at a few cents on the dollar. (Hamilton felt that crocodile tears were being shed over these rural bondholders, whose capacity to drive a shrewd bargain yielded little or nothing to the city slickers. The Funding-Assumption bill wavered between victory and defeat in Congress for six months in 1790, and many of its back-country enemies knew this well and were speculating on a fall in government paper every bit as calculatedly as its commercial friends were speculating on a rise.) Nevertheless, the image of crafty insiders conning innocent old soldiers and widows took on added dimensions when it developed that many of the congressmen who voted in favor of the Funding-Assumption bill were themselves speculating heavily in government securities. Evidence that the "speculative mania" was working both sides of the street in the contest merely added to the Madisonian conviction that a corrupting influence was indeed at work, and that Hamilton's attitude on the whole broad issue of profit and privilege left much to be desired.

Assumption was an even thornier matter. Like Funding, it touched off a nationwide scramble in and out of Congress to buy old war debts at bargain prices. It also jarred state-rights sensitivities and dramatized the sectional issue in stark and ominous fashion. Many people could see no need—beyond speculative opportunity, which they deplored—for the national government to assume the debts of the states, and they feared the centralizing tendency behind it. But the real sticking point lay in the fact that some states had done much better than others in paying off their war debts. And with the exception of South Carolina, nearly all of the least indebted states were below the Mason-Dixon line. If Assumption passed, taxpayers in those commonwealths stood in double jeopardy: having recently been assessed to help retire their own states' debts, they now faced federal levies designed to fund the indebtedness of other states. Southerners saw no reason why they should be taxed because a lot of New England securities were still outstanding.

Madison and Hamilton, close nationalist allies since the early 1780s, disagreed even more sharply over Assumption than they had over Funding. Madison's Virginia had retired a large portion of its war debt; Madison's Virginia colleagues and constituents were beginning to mutter that he was being less than true to the interests of the Old Dominion; and Madison's own long-standing desire for a strong central government was beginning to recoil as he observed what Hamilton was capable of doing with it.

Madison continued to believe in the supremacy of the nation over the states, but he did not accept the supremacy of commerce over agriculture. This was partly a matter of being a Virginia landed gentleman (and one who held elective office), but it was mainly a question of being a republican—far more so than Hamilton, whose confidence in republican government was never more than marginal. Madison's vision of a strong united nation was bound up with his notion of a society in which no interest or faction was powerful enough to dominate. His nationalism, in short, was built upon a balanced republic; Hamilton's, upon a commercial plutocracy. These were incompatible views, and the two great nationalists broke permanently.

Convinced that its undesirable features outweighed its benefits, Madison became the leader of congressional opposition to the Funding-Assumption bill, which prompted an angry Hamilton to charge him with "a perfidious desertion of the principles which he was solemnly pledged to defend." The Hamilton and Madison forces were evenly enough divided to throw Congress into a deadlock. Neither side could muster a reliable majority, and the deadlock went on for more than six months.

It also generated growing amounts of heat. Speculators on both sides continued their operations, the national debt went further into arrears, and tempers frayed. The Hamilton program, John Marshall observed, "seemed to unchain all those fierce passions which a high respect for the government and for those who administered it, had in a great measure restrained." Sectional antagonism flared quickly, and with vehemence. With some four fifths of the national debt and a comparable amount of the state debt in the hands of Northerners, Southerners began to feel that they were not merely being discriminated against but dominated by the commercial section. The receipt of a Quaker petition against slavery and the slave trade ignited an angry, portentous exchange between Northern and Southern congressmen on that explosive issue. A few New Englanders grew so exasperated over Virginia's intransigence on the Funding-Assumption bill that they muttered openly about secession, which Virginia's Senator Richard Henry Lee answered in kind by announcing that he considered disunion preferable to "the rule of a fixed insolent northern majority." Such exchanges afforded a brief, disturbing glimpse into the dark labyrinth where America's great dilemma prowled balefully at large and untamed, but they merely prolonged the deadlock over Hamilton's program.

In the end the principals worked out a compromise. Hamilton, realizing by midsummer of 1790 that neither his eloquence nor his influence was sufficient to get his bill through Congress and genuinely afraid that the Union might break up, intercepted Secretary of State Jefferson on the steps of the President's house one day and in effect asked for help. Jefferson, just back from France, was relatively unfamiliar with the details of the controversy and could not quite tell just what Hamilton had in mind, but he agreed to do what he could. A day later he brought Hamilton and Madison together and the three men made a deal: the Virginians would use their influence to swing some Southern votes in favor of the Funding-Assumption bill, and Hamilton would use his on behalf of a bill that would remove the federal capital from New York to Philadelphia for a ten-year interim, thence to a permanent location on the Potomac River, where it would presumably be more responsive to Southern needs. Hamilton duly helped secure the Potomac capital bill, and the two Virginians duly cooperated on behalf of Funding-Assumption, although a further compromise proved necessary before it passed: the final version included some compensation to those states that had already retired parts of their war debts.

Funding and Assumption became law in August 1790, and the benefits Hamilton had been predicting were soon in evidence. But not everyone felt them equally. Most of those who were enriched by the rise in value of government securities lived in the North. The annual interest payment on government bonds held by residents of Massachusetts totaled some $300,000 in 1795; Virginia bondholders received about one fifth of that amount. Long before such figures became known, the smoldering antagonism between the Secretary of the Treasury and the state of Virginia had burst into enduring flame. Patrick Henry, who had been uttering jeremiads about the dangers of centralization since before the Philadelphia convention, was now hailed as a prophet with honor; and George Mason remarked that Hamilton had done Virginia "more injury than Great Britain and all her fleets and armies." The Virginia legislature called his program "repugnant to the Constitution" and "dangerous to the rights and subversive of the interests of the people."

Hamilton was equally outraged. The Virginians were confirming his worst suspicions about the foolish particularity of individual states. Virginia's contention that the South had been sacrificed to Northern interests was, he said, "unsupported by documents, facts, or, it may be added, probabilities." *All* sections would benefit from his financial measures, he insisted, and Virginia's opposition was pernicious and misguided—"the first symptom," he fumed to John Jay, "of the spirit which must either be killed, or it will kill the Constitution of the United States." Hamilton made no effort to hide his conviction that the only effective solution was to carve Virginia up into a group of small unimportant districts (which, from the standpoint of political feasibility and lèse-majesté, was rather like suggesting that the Roman Catholic Church be reorganized on the congregational principle).

The lines had been drawn, and Hamilton's proposal to create a national bank ran into fierce opposition as soon as his report on the subject reached Congress in January 1791. By now the people who feared commercial-financial domination were in full cry, and the gulf between the Madison-Jefferson and Hamilton positions had widened irreparably. This time Hamilton had enough votes to get his bill passed, but Madison raised serious doubts as to the constitutionality of a federally chartered bank, and it seemed quite possible that President Washington, into whose ken the doubts had circulated, might veto the bill. Genuinely perplexed, Washington requested written opinions from Hamilton, Jefferson, and Attorney General Randolph. The opinions that counted were from Hamilton and Jefferson, the President's right and left bowers; they submitted thoughtful, persuasive legal briefs for different ways of interpreting the Constitution. (The views of Randolph, who was something of a lightweight, were in accordance with Jefferson's.)

In searching for the power to create a bank, both Hamilton and Jefferson took off from the "necessary and proper" clause in Article I, Section 8. Hamilton construed "necessary" to mean "useful" or "helpful" (so long as the action did not conflict with the legitimate ends of the federal government—in this case the collection of taxes and payment of debts); Jefferson construed the word to mean "indispensable," without which the thing could not be done. They were the classic statements on behalf of loose and strict construction, and what they boiled down to in this instance was that Hamilton found ample constitutional justification for a bank and Jefferson found none.

Both men were arguing in earnest—good lawyers always do —and both men argued well, and the fate of the national bank came to rest on the President's desk. Washington pondered it deeply. He might have been a shade slower on the uptake than either of his two brilliant, strong-minded department heads, but he was very much his own man, the final decision was entirely his, and he resolved at last in favor of his Secretary of the Treasury. His decision to approve the Bank of the United States was not a sign that the President was under anybody's thumb. Rather, it suggested that the bank proposal possessed enough merit to come under the careful scrutiny of a Virginia planter and still pass muster.

So by mid-1791 Hamilton had the third leg of his tripod, and his ideas had virtually become synonymous with national policy. In order to provide additional revenue to pay the costs of Funding and Assumption, he persuaded Congress to pass an excise tax on whiskey, which would eventually lead to trouble and a showdown in western Pennsylvania. Riding at full gallop, Hamilton also submitted a Report on Manufactures which called for an elaborate system of federal bounties, subsidies, protective tariffs, and other encouragements to new industrial enterprises. Had this measure passed, it would have involved the government so deeply with business as to launch the country in the direction of a planned economy. But Congress shelved most of this plan; only a few of the specific tariff proposals managed to find their way into law. Meanwhile the Secretary was also throwing his weight around in foreign affairs and generally acting like the man who ran the country, and by 1792 his enemies were alarmed enough to make opposition to Alexander Hamilton the basis for taking a stand.

The line was drawn for fair, and political parties with a sense of mission were starting to coalesce on either side of it. They did not think of themselves as parties, at first. Madison's following in Congress, increasingly a unit in their opposition to Hamilton, began referring to themselves as the republican interest, sometimes as the republican party. The capital letters came later and the formal organization came later still, but the congressional bloc was the nucleus of a cell that would grow. Regarding their opponents as a corrupt faction in the traditional British sense and themselves as representatives of the true national interest, the republicans were content for a time to keep their congressional ranks intact and support a newspaper—the *National Gazette,* which began appearing in late 1791 under the editorship of an ardent republican poet named Philip Freneau—to provide the public with a republican version of national issues and events (and, in short order, with violently partisan denunciations of the other side).

Before long these congressional republicans were in touch with friends of the same persuasion at the state and local level, seeking to bring about the nomination and election of right-minded candidates. As the decade wore to a close and lines hardened, the Republicans began using the capital letter and forming a committee network and other mechanisms and procedures by which a political organization gets its work done.

The other side began calling themselves Federalists, by way of affirming their link with the Constitution, although both nascent parties—Madison and Hamilton, after all, were the opposing leaders—came out of the group that had ratified and implemented the new document. The Federalists were even slower to organize outside of Congress. They saw themselves not as a party but as *the government,* with President Washington as their leader and the making of national policy as their official function; it was the Republican opposition that was behaving in partisan and self-seeking manner. The one newspaper that provided anything like national coverage before Freneau launched his venture in 1791 was John Fenno's *Gazette of the United States,* which was pro-Hamilton from the start and became as fiercely and scurrilously partisan as Freneau's paper once the battle had been joined. But aside from newspaper warfare the Federalists took a high-minded attitude about what they were doing and deplored political activity even as they engaged in it. Washington was still, in his own and nearly everyone else's judgment, a national rather than a party leader, and both sides urged him to stand for re-election in 1792. He did so, again without opposition, but by the start of his second term the issues and animosities and convictions around which the two parties would be built had already crystallized, and the process of party formation was irreversibly under way.

What helped give America's first parties their peculiarly intense quality, their tone, and their reason for existence was the conviction, born of a shared distaste for parties, that opposition must be badly motivated, wrongheaded, and downright disloyal, almost treasonous—because it was opposition not to a party but to the nation and the national interest. This conviction took root early on both sides.

The convictions were heavily reinforced by events on the other side of the Atlantic. Foreign affairs sliced into American sensitivities at many levels and from more than one direction, and they cut deep. These sensitivities were abnormally acute to begin with, because thoughtful people had the feeling that their national experiment was very much on trial, very precarious, and very vulnerable, unduly subject to pernicious influences from within and without. Foreign affairs in the 1790s posed an inordinate number of such threats, and their shadow somehow had a way of falling across everything Americans were trying to do.

After 1789 all trails led through Paris. Americans hailed the outbreak and early stages of the French Revolution, seeing it as another great step in mankind's march toward liberty and delighted that their ally was the first to follow the American example. But public opinion soon divided over the French question. The division grew sharper as the French Revolution picked up speed, and by 1792 American conservatives were vying with European conservatives in seeing it as a dire menace to stability, tradition, law and order, property, religion, and other eternal verities. Alexander Hamilton, who had become the chief spokesman of the emerging Federalist Party, was among those who felt this way, and the Federalists soon made opposition to France a cardinal item in their creed. Republicans, on the other hand, took their cue from Thomas Jefferson, who had been in France when the Revolution began and never really lost his enthusiasm for it. He regretted its excesses but felt that they were justified, since "the liberty of the whole earth" was dependent on its success; extreme measures in defense of liberty were sometimes necessary.

To the Federalists these extreme measures were precisely what made the French Revolution a mortal threat, and Jefferson's "softness" on this issue (at one point during the Terror, Jefferson remarked that he would rather see "half the earth devastated" than have the French Revolution fail) stamped him as dangerous and unreliable. At the grass roots, Americans who admired France had a way of celebrating Revolutionary achievements by donning liberty caps, erecting liberty poles, mouthing Revolutionary slogans, singing the *Ça Ira,* and generally parading about like so many Yankee sans-culottes. This sort of thing appalled the Federalists, who conjured up lurid visions of guillotines in American public squares and bloodthirsty mobs rampaging through American streets.

Beginning in 1793, when Great Britain joined the war against Revolutionary France, it became the Republicans' turn to find the opposition deeply suspect on a point of sound doctrine. The Federalists not only wanted the British to win, seeing British power as the best means of containing and crushing the Revolution; they were heard to express open admiration for the British social and political system—for its balance, stability, respect for tradition and the proper values, and so on.

To good Republicans this was heresy. America's War for Independence had been over for little more than a decade, and memories were green. Great Britain was the enemy. The British system, with its graft-ridden government, its decadent privileged aristocracy, and its brutal army and navy, had suppressed colonial liberties and driven the colonists to rebellion; escaping this iniquitous system was what the war had been all about. And Great Britain was *still* the enemy. Ten years after the Treaty of Paris she yet kept her empire closed to American shipping, kept her troops on American soil, agitated the Indians, and generally behaved toward the United States with an arrogant condescension which British officialdom had already raised to the level of a high art.

To the Republican way of thinking, Americans had to be on guard lest they slide back under British domination, and Federalist policies and attitudes were very apt to lead to this, either by making the nation a British satellite or by converting the American system into an unlovely New World copy of Britain's, complete with king and court and all the rest of it. (Hamilton's financial program, Republicans noted darkly, was very English in style and effect: a large public debt and a powerful national bank, each enabling unscrupulous stockjobbers and speculators occupying privileged positions to manipulate prices, corrupt public officials, and profit at the expense of honest producers. The United States under Hamilton's tutelage was becoming more like Britain all the time.)

Republican fears of "going the way of England," like Federalist fears of being engulfed by a French-style revolution, are worth a brief glance. They were real fears, deep-seated enough to verge on paranoia and entertained by some of America's most astute leaders and soberest citizens. It seems clear enough, in retrospect, that neither danger amounted to much. Americans were busy feeling their way into nationhood and the first stages of an economic boom, and these were absorbing tasks; they had no real inclination either to set up guillotines for Federalist patricians on Boston Common and lower Broadway or to re-enthrall American farmers and planters to a homemade monarch and House of Lords.

What then of the fears? Hindsight is what enables the historian to operate, but it can trip him up sometimes. If it tells him that such and such was an improbable occurrence, he is apt to get top-lofty about the motives of people at the time who thought such and such was about to occur. Every society has a few cranks who live in a world of their own and who believe on the basis of neither discernible evidence nor discernible logic that their worst fears are about to befall society—due to either insidious enemy plots or a decline in public morality, or both. In this case, however, the fears were woven not on the lunatic fringe but into the center strands of the American fabric, warp and weft. Seeing this, the historian is apt to look for political motives and conclude that leaders who voiced such fears were talking for effect, playing upon some popular prejudice in order to discredit the opposition.

Now politicians are never unmindful of this tactic, and few American leaders in the 1790s were so high-minded as to ignore such an opportunity. To the extent that Federalists could be identified as monarchists, or Republicans as Jacobins (the most radical of the French Revolutionists, who inspired in conservatives a degree of revulsion and hysteria akin to twentieth-century capitalist views about communists), the allegiance of many voters could be swung. The two American parties vied with each other increasingly to do just that, on precisely those terms.

We are still left with the fears themselves, and it will not do to dismiss the rhetoric they inspired as "mere" politics. The 1790s were like the years of Civil War and Reconstruction, when, as Eric McKitrick has observed, there was nothing "mere" about an American's political allegiance. The fears were expressed through the medium of politics, as all social fears are; this did not mean that men of the caliber of Jefferson and Madison and Hamilton were simply using them. Indeed, the reverse explanation makes more sense: far from exploiting the fears for political advantage, the Federalist and Republican leaders were driven to the distasteful extreme of resorting to partisan politics in the first place because they were so genuinely afraid of what they inveighed against.

One keeps returning, willy-nilly, to the special qualities of this final quarter of the eighteenth century—special qualities of which the people of the time were acutely aware, whether they gauged them correctly or not. The old order was changing; the world was turning upside down. Americans had embarked upon an experiment they knew to be perilous and fraught with uncertainty, and their fears for its success—had they trusted too much in popular wisdom? enough? could a republic survive in a world of imperialist powers?—were hugely compounded by the French Revolution, which seemed to be plumbing the fountains of the great deep and putting all the verities up for grabs. Upside down, for fair. The old stars by which men steered were being replaced by new stars not yet charted. Americans did not yet have the boundless confidence in their destiny that would propel them through most of the nineteenth century like an all-conquering host; in the 1790s they *wanted* to believe in what they were doing, but everything was too new, and visibility was poor. At times it seemed as though the seas had parted for their infant Republic as they had for the children of Israel; at other times as though the waves would surely close over them before the promised land could be reached.

So men were afraid, not altogether without reason. Some feared anarchy, which by all that history had to teach was what ensued when the common folk were subject to too little restraint, this in turn being the signal for demagogues (Jefferson, said the Federalists) to come forth and bend the multitude to their evil purpose. Others feared monarchy, which champions of privilege (Hamilton, said the Republicans) would try to reinstall as a means of keeping the populace subject to their evil purpose. In either case it was the end of the dream, twilight and finally darkness in the city on the hill, the Red Sea closing over the tribes of Israel—defeat.

The Virginians are of particular interest here. By any normal standards they were privileged aristocrats themselves—certainly they behaved as such, most of them—slaveowners, landed gentlemen, members of families who had run the province like a closed corporation for almost a century and would run the country, or at least the presidency, for thirty-two of its first thirty-six years. Yet these Virginians were more spooked than any other group in America by the prospect of a British-style monarchy (in which aristocrats of like pretensions throve)—and they had been spooked by it for thirty years and more, since the very beginning of the revolutionary agitation in the early 1760s. Their anti-British rhetoric, then and since, was far out of proportion to any real threat the British posed.

What were they really afraid of, these Virginia gentlemen, who by every canon of social standing, political influence, and world view were improbable revolutionaries and even less likely democrats? Back around the middle of the century Virginians had undergone a collective social trauma that had apparently been seared across their conscience with a red-hot iron: it was a brand they would continue to wear. A big financial scandal had been uncovered in the Virginia House of Burgesses, involving not merely the venerable and highly respected Speaker but a number of first families—whom the Speaker, out of concern for friends in need, had systematically aided over a period of years by advancing them large sums which he had in effect embezzled from the public tax receipts. What hurt was not so much the Speaker's misguided generosity as the revelation that so many prominent families had reduced themselves to straits where such assistance was necessary.

Taking a long look around, many young Virginians concluded that their prized social structure was visibly decaying from the top down: families going impossibly into debt with the purchase of luxuries and fripperies, young sons living like fops and wastrels, wining, dueling, wenching, and gambling away their inheritance—in short, an aristocracy afflicted with moral dry rot. The model after which this deplorable behavior was patterned, it seemed obvious, was the British one. Britain's aristocracy far outdid their transatlantic cousins in the whole matter of wasteful consumption and sustained debauchery, but the similarities were visible and the moral was clear: the British system was a contaminating influence, and Virginia society was degenerating to the British level.

A wave of something like regenerative fervor swept across Virginia's leaders in the 1760s, and much of their revolutionary rhetoric during the next decade was shot through with apocalyptic visions of the ruin and moral degradation that continued association with Britain would entail. In seeking to escape the evils of the British system these Virginians were hoping to purify their own. (One wonders what murky subconscious hopes and fears about slavery accompanied this quest for moral regeneration—might it be possible, if the British cancer were cut away, that slavery itself would somehow disappear or get purified too?) And the vague belief that the American environment was somehow more conducive to clean living and moral progress than that of corrupt old Europe suddenly acquired an explicit corollary: the British connection had to be severed.

In any case, the conviction that Great Britain represented a corrupt and decadent social order was as strong in the 1790s as it had been thirty years before, and it helps explain why so many Virginians remained supersensitive to any policy, foreign or domestic, that might encourage a return or recrudescence of British social and economic conditions. (Not all eminent Virginians thought alike, of course. Jefferson and Madison believed that a great national republic run according to their principles might keep the enemy at bay. Patrick Henry and George Mason and Richard Henry Lee had concluded that power anywhere outside the Old Dominion was not to be trusted. John Marshall, a Hamiltonian Federalist to the core, apparently felt that the American ship of state could carry British top hamper without behaving like a British vessel. And George Washington . . . was George Washington, wrapped in the cloak of his own integrity, big enough to face down threats from any quarter while he was in command, but caught between forces that were as far beyond him as they were beyond anyone. About all Virginia could still agree upon in the 1790s was that the country would be well advised to pursue a wary course toward Great Britain and, if supping with her were ever necessary, to use a long spoon.)

——□——

Whether Americans identified Britain with privileged decadence or social stability and France with the march of human liberty or the onset of chaos and terror, it was not just a matter of rooting for one's favorite from the sidelines. What brought it all into the realm of the immediate and the practical was that the two great powers were at war and America had connections with both and was going to be involved, perhaps at great cost and certainly at great risk, no matter what policy she followed.

Involved, and possibly at war, which Americans who were otherwise unalterably opposed could unite in seeking to avoid. Both parties wanted to keep America neutral, but they differed about how best to do this, and each party's "neutrality" had a way of inclining visibly toward the belligerent it favored. This was risky, and it inevitably kept partisanship in high gear.

France posed the first specific problem for American diplomacy. The treaties of alliance that France and the United States had concluded in 1778 were still in effect, and the French—now engaged, in their turn, in creating a republic and fighting Britain's monarchy—not unnaturally hoped that the Americans would leap to their assistance. France did not insist that the United States formally declare war upon Great Britain, but the aid being sought—help in defending the French West Indies against British attack, the use of American ports and American vessels for privateering operations against British commerce—would assuredly result in hostilities sooner or later. Yet the treaties of 1778 contained provision for such assistance.

Washington's two chief advisers, at odds by now on nearly everything, gave conflicting advice. Hamilton wanted to suspend the treaties, both out of distaste for Revolutionary France and in order to reduce the risk of war; Jefferson wanted to retain the treaties, both in order to keep French friendship and to be able to bargain from strength with the British. Steering a middle course, the President issued a formal proclamation of neutrality in the spring of 1793, assuring foreign nations that the United States would pursue a "friendly and impartial" conduct toward the belligerents and prohibiting American citizens from "aiding or abetting hostilities" or engaging in unneutral activity. The President also officially recognized the new French Republic and agreed to receive its diplomatic emissary.

This gentleman, Citizen Edmond Genêt, landed in Charleston that spring intending to travel overland to Philadelphia to present his credentials; and before long he managed to take the play completely away from the Washington administration and make a shambles out of Washington's neutrality proclamation. Genêt was a charming young man who rather resembled the republic he served: naïve, brash, zealous, overconfident, and prepared to make up the rules as he went along. Genêt saw no problem. His country was at war with England and Spain and allied to the United States, and from this premise his actions made a certain amount of sense. While pro-French crowds cheered and lionized him, the young Frenchman issued letters of marque to American citizens who wished to try their hand at privateering, set up prize courts in American ports for the condemnation of captured British prizes, and granted commissions in a volunteer army he proposed to form and use for the conquest of British and Spanish possessions in the New World. While news of these actions filtered northward, and American privateers began fitting out and the first captured British prizes were actually brought in, and brand-new American officers in the yet unmustered *Armée des Florides* and *Armée du Mississippe* swaggered a shade uncertainly about Charleston, Genêt made his trip to the capital a hero's journey, lingering in each town to acknowledge the cheers with appropriate Gallic gestures and fervid republican oratory.

The Administration was angry but nonplussed. They did not

approve of what Genêt was doing—reading from right to left, Hamilton began disapproving of Genêt before he arrived, Washington as soon as the first reports reached Philadelphia, Jefferson only after the man's incorrigibility had been amply demonstrated —but eighteenth-century communications were such that it was hard to catch up with him long enough to make their disapproval clear. Genêt did not let the disapproval impede his activities even after he learned about it, and he was able to start hares faster than anyone could stop them.

The French Revolution was still popular in much of America, though the popularity was neither as wide nor as deep as Genêt, who saw only the enthusiasts, came to believe. After a few weeks in Philadelphia this enthusiasm turned his head completely. When a tight-lipped Washington coldly informed him that his actions were in violation of American law and ordered him to stop, Genêt demanded a special session of Congress so that the lawmakers could uphold his actions, and loudly threatened to appeal to the people over Washington's head if the special session were not called.

At this point even the well-disposed Jefferson lost his patience, and the Administration demanded Genêt's recall and told him to start packing. (The final chapter in the Genêt story has an only-in-America twist. While the request for his recall was in transit it was learned that the Girondists, the French regime responsible for sending Genêt, had been ousted and replaced by the Jacobins, who were identifying many of their predecessors as enemies of the state. The new French government sent word that Genêt was under arrest and ordered him home, where a trial for treason and a probable appointment with the guillotine awaited him. A chastened Genêt asked for asylum, Washington granted it, and the erstwhile French minister proceeded to acquire a farm on Long Island, marry the daughter of the governor of New York, and live happily ever after.)

———□———

Genêt's conduct had damaged American neutrality, hurt the pro-French Republicans, and strained America's relations with France (to say nothing of America's relations with Great Britain, whose government was annoyed both by the Washington administration's apparent inability to curb Genêt and by the loss of more than eighty British merchantmen to Genêt's American privateers). But Jefferson's fears that the impulsive Genêt had jarred the United States into an anti-French posture were soon allayed by the British, who could generally be relied upon to outperform everyone else in the matter of giving grounds for offense. They gave so much offense to America during 1793 that the two nations seemed on the verge of going to war, the Republicans were even being joined by a few Federalists in clamoring for it, and President Washington finally dispatched a minister plenipotentiary to London in the spring of 1794 in a last-ditch attempt to see if the items in dispute could be negotiated.

The items in dispute were numerous, and most of them were tricky. The older ones included substantial sums owed since before the Revolution by American citizens to British citizens and still unpaid (many of these delinquent debtors were Virginians, which helps explain why Alexander Hamilton sneered when Virginia made pious noises about avoiding British corruption); and some equally venerable American claims against the British government for slave property confiscated during the war.

The British presence in the American West was a bigger and touchier sore spot, possibly the crucial one: while British troops continued to occupy strategic forts in United States territory, British traders controlled the American fur traffic and British officials kept Indian hostility well heated and well supplied. In a related matter, Spain still refused to let western Americans export their surplus by way of the Mississippi River—the only route to market which that surplus could afford to travel. The Washington administration's seeming inability to rectify any of these problems was producing the kind of intrigue and resentment among American frontiersmen in the Ohio Valley that could end by detaching the whole trans-Appalachian region from its loyalty to the United States. As far as Westerners could see, the new national government was as ineffectual as the old one: it could budge neither the British nor the Spaniards, and its two attempts to subdue the Indians—a military expedition under General Harmar in 1790 and a larger one under General St. Clair in 1791—had been utter disasters, the Indians having successively routed both forces in the Maumee Valley. Tribal depredations continued and tribal confidence mounted, and the American mood out west was bad.

The items in dispute that had the greatest impact back East were maritime and commercial. They provided an object lesson in the age-old problems faced by a weak neutral in dealing with a powerful belligerent, none the less insoluble for being familiar. Great Britain continued to keep her empire, and especially her West Indian islands, closed to American shipping. At war, the British operated as they had done for a century—refusing to let neutral vessels carry contraband items to enemy ports, defining contraband broadly and extending it to include just about anything they did not want the enemy to have, and indeed regarding all enemy consignments in the holds of neutral ships as fair game and confiscating such cargoes whenever they found them. When the French, desperate for shipping in the face of superior British sea power, suspended their navigation laws and opened the ports of their Caribbean islands to American vessels, the British invoked the so-called Rule of 1756, which stated that trade not permitted in time of peace (as France had kept her Caribbean ports closed to American ships) could not be permitted in time of war. Neutrals invariably protested these actions by invoking the principle of freedom of the seas, and Great Britain always responded by invoking the royal navy, which was all the authority she needed.

By way of rubbing America's nose in it, the British reinforced their West Indian squadron in the fall of 1793, alerted their frigate captains, issued an order in council authorizing the seizure of all neutral vessels trading with the French West Indies, and kept the order secret until large numbers of American merchantmen had accumulated in and about the French islands. Then the royal navy went into action, capturing some 250 American vessels in one big swoop and offsetting any conceivable damage that Citizen Genêt might have done to America's relations with France.

The British navy also had a practice which no other foreign country experienced the way the United States did—impressment, the dragooning of hapless civilians into a service that could never, especially in wartime, attract the men it needed by the volunteer system. Mostly the navy press gangs rounded up English merchant seamen or landsmen unlucky enough to be near some English waterfront, but at sea they supplemented this source of supply by stopping American ships and searching the crew for deserters from the royal navy—sometimes contenting themselves with able-bodied United States seamen whose citizenship was either suspect or unprovable. These seizures were an insult that did more over the years for America's dawning sense of nationality—and for its feelings toward the mother country—than anything that happened between Yorktown and the War of 1812.

The fine hand of British policy was further evident when Portugal, virtually a British satellite, concluded a treaty in 1793 with Algiers, one of the Moorish states along the Barbary coast whose pirate raiders had been snapping up merchantmen and enslaving or ransoming the people on board for generations. The Portuguese navy had hitherto kept the Strait of Gibraltar closed to the Barbary corsairs and had occasionally escorted American ships through the most dangerous part of the western Mediterranean. Once the treaty was signed these services ceased, Moorish pirates began operating in the Atlantic, American losses rose—thanks to the British, James Monroe wrote angrily, our ships were being "kicked, cuffed and plundered all over the ocean"—and in 1794 the United States submitted to the humiliation of purchasing security from further depredations by payment of a $750,000 tribute to the Dey of Algiers.

The list of grievances was long, and the United States was

woefully short on means of redress. With no navy at all and an army of insufficient size and quality to handle the Western Indians—Anthony Wayne was assembling a military force in the spring of 1794 to have another go at them in northern Ohio—the Americans could counter British highhandedness with little more than fist shaking and angry protests. They did an abundance of this, thanks to the Republicans, but Congress was too divided to agree upon a policy. The trouble was that the Republicans, whose resentment of Britain had burst at the seams, were opposed on grounds of both principle and cost to creating anything like enough armed forces to defend American rights; only their language was bellicose. The weapon the Republicans wanted to employ was economic. The most lucrative and important part of America's foreign trade was with England, and a mercantilist policy of discriminating against British ships and goods might coerce the island kingdom into better behavior. Madison had wanted to levy discriminatory duties on British shipping as early as 1789, but Northern merchants and congressmen had finally talked him out of it; when Madison and Jefferson pressed for even stronger anti-British commercial measures in 1793–94, Hamilton and the Federalists opposed them strongly.

Many Federalists were unhappy over recent British actions, and some of them favored creating a navy and enlarging the army so as to be able to deal from strength. But they were almost a unit in not wanting to jeopardize their trade with England. The result, said Hamilton, would be a drying up of British credit and a falling off in imports, and in the import duties on which his whole fiscal program rested. France, the logical and intended replacement as a trading partner, could never supply the United States as cheaply and capably as England did. Besides, Hamilton maintained, the British would fight before they submitted to the kind of discriminatory policies Jefferson and Madison were advocating.

It was a multiple irony: the Republican farmers and planters hated the British enough to risk war with them but insisted upon commercial retaliation rather than military preparedness; the commercial Federalists, whose ships and cargoes and crews were suffering most at the hands of Great Britain, preferred a military build-up so as to be ready for a war they did not want rather than risk losing their best customer and supplier by applying economic penalties. It would be a familiar theme, right down to 1812.

Anti-British sentiment culminated in the spring of 1794 in a proposal that the United States sequester the £4 million that American subjects owed to British subjects and use it to pry compensation out of the British government for the seizures of American cargoes in the Carribean. To a scandalized Hamilton this would result in a war for the worst of reasons—an attempt to welsh on a legitimate debt. The sequestration bill did not pass but it received a lot of support, and Republican demands for measures that could only lead to war grew in volume and intensity. The British, concluding from all the noises coming out of Philadelphia that a clash was imminent, enlarged their naval forces in North American waters and began constructing a new fort in western Ohio. The governor general of Canada exhorted Western chiefs to be ready to take strong action in the forthcoming conflict with America.

Washington, sensing that British arrogance and Republican saber rattling were about to produce a war, appointed Chief Justice John Jay as minister plenipotentiary and sent him to England in the spring of 1794 to seek the best terms he could obtain. Hamilton would not have minded going, but the President realized that the Republicans would never hold still for such an appointment or look with favor on anything he brought back, so he turned instead to Hamilton's long-time associate. Jay seemed a good choice: experienced negotiator, staunch Federalist, and New York patrician with no anti-British chip on his shoulder but with enough starchy self-assurance to be able to mingle easily in British social and diplomatic circles. It remained to be seen whether there was anything in America's long list of grievances that could be successfully negotiated.

—□—

Jay had barely embarked for England when the government faced a challenge to its authority from the West that raised the temperature of party animosities another degree or two. The cause of the difficulty was the excise on whiskey that Hamilton had persuaded Congress to pass in 1791. Westerners hated this tax, partly with the hatred that all men have for all taxes, partly out of the conviction that their livelihood was being destroyed. Whiskey was the standard medium of exchange west of the mountains, the only commodity (with the Mississippi closed) that could stand the cost of shipment to the seaboard market, and the excise amounted to some 25 per cent of the purchase price. Resentment simmered and grew, and in the summer of 1794 it boiled over in western Pennsylvania just as it had in western Massachusetts seven years earlier. Malcontents terrorized excise officers, stopped judicial proceedings, overpowered a small contingent of federal troops guarding an excise inspector's house, and —fired, one suspects, by a good many ounces of the stuff they distilled—talked of marching on Pittsburgh.

Neither a government proclamation demanding dispersal nor an offer of amnesty in exchange for obedience had any effect, and the Federalists, feeling their oats, decided to face this threat down with a show of strength that the Pennsylvanians and any other potential dissidents would note and remember. The government pulled together more than 12,000 militia, mustered them into federal service, and with George Washington himself in command (more troops, it would be observed, than he had ever been able to deploy during the Revolution), marched them across the wooded Alleghenies to where the trouble had started. Washington stayed with the army long enough to get it going, and Secretary Hamilton, determined to meet this challenge to government authority in person, went the whole way. Republicans never lost sight of the vision of Alexander Hamilton marching at the head of an army to put down a domestic squabble, and people with memories of Major Pitcairn leading his men through Lexington exchanged grim nods.

By the time Hamilton's army got to the scene of the crime, the trouble and the rebel leaders and nearly everyone else had vanished. The government rounded up a few frightened and very unmilitant locals, brought them back East, tried and imprisoned and later pardoned them, and pronounced itself satisfied. Hamilton felt that the government had gained "reputation and strength" by this show of force; Jefferson dryly noted that "an insurrection was announced and proclaimed and armed against, but could never be found."

Still feeling their oats, the Federalists went on to attack the so-called Democratic Societies that had been formed here and there during 1793 out of grass-roots enthusiasm for the French Revolution. There were over forty of them in all. Patterned after similar groups in France (Genêt had helped get the first one started), the societies kept one another informed in the manner of America's own Revolutionary committees of correspondence. Committed to the destruction of monarchy, aristocracy, and Hamiltonian finance (terms they used interchangeably), they acted as pressure groups on behalf of right-minded political candidates, supported the emerging Republican Party, and frightened sober Federalists into thinking of them as so many Jacobin cells fomenting revolution.

President Washington himself, believing that the societies were responsible for the Whiskey Rebellion and if not counteracted "would shake the government to its foundations," denounced them pointedly in his message to Congress in November 1794. It was an ill-advised move. The societies, whose only connection with the whiskey rebels appears to have been a shared resentment of Federalism, melted away in due course during the next few months, intimidated by Washington's blast and increasingly alienated by events in France. But the chief effect of the President's attack was to weaken his own position as a leader who stood above the battle. His condemnation, which verged on questioning the right of peaceful assembly, was an act of angry partisanship that placed him squarely in the Hamiltonian camp, and the Republicans began to include the President in their attacks on the Federalists.

They included him even more sharply when John Jay came back from England in 1795 with a controversial treaty in his pocket. It was by no means a totally bad treaty and it was the best that could be had, since Great Britain held most of the high cards. But it contained enough unsatisfactory provisions to infuriate the Republicans, damage Washington's prestige, and bring partisanship to an angry fever pitch that would continue for the balance of the decade.

Jay had been instructed to obtain a commercial treaty, and Britain had consented to open India to American shipping, under certain conditions, and to permit American trade with the West Indies—provided that the vessels were under 70 tons burthen and that the goods obtained there would be taken only to the United States. Jay had also been instructed to demand evacuation of American territory in the Northwest, and the British had agreed to do this. Two of the items in dispute—the debts American citizens owed British citizens, and American claims growing out of the recent British seizures in the Caribbean—were referred to joint commissions of arbitration, with both governments pledging that the claims would be paid.

In return for these British concessions, such as they were, Jay had fully accepted the British version of wartime commercial regulation: the Rule of 1756, the extended contraband list, no freedom of the seas. Jay had also agreed to give England "most favored nation" treatment in the matter of tariff and tonnage duties —promising, in other words, that no other country's ships or goods would be allowed to enter American ports on better terms than those accorded to Great Britain. The treaty spoke to British concerns in two other areas of recent activity: the United States pledged that there would be no sequestration of private debts, and that Britain's enemies would not be permitted to use American ports as bases for privateering operations. The treaty said nothing at all about compensating American owners for slaves emancipated by British forces during the Revolution, and it said nothing about the impressment of American seamen.

In short, the British had obtained a lot and had given very little, and Americans could hardly be blamed for regarding the Jay Treaty as a set of capitulations. The first public outcry, Washington observed, was "like that of a mad dog." Republican outrage was boundless, sustained, highly vocal, and shared by many Federalists. Jay was burned in effigy, denounced as pro-British and little better than a traitor, and damned from one end of the country to the other; there was talk of impeaching him. Washington hesitated long before signing the treaty, and an equally reluctant Senate could muster a two-thirds majority (without a single vote to spare) only after striking the section that impossibly restricted America's rights in the British West Indies. Ratification took place in June 1795, but the House of Representatives was so angry that it debated the measure halfway through 1796 and came within an ace of voting not to implement it.

The indignation was understandable and much of it was justified, but John Jay and his controversial treaty, the President, and the other men who relucantly engineered its passage were soon vindicated by the course of events. There was only one kind of alternative to John Jay. Anything more than the treaty he got was unobtainable, and anything less would have been no treaty at all. This in turn would have led to a war which America was even less prepared to fight than she would be in 1812, and which in the political atmosphere of the 1790s would probably have split the nation into weak unstable fragments, with independence and the bold dream going up in the smoke of British broadsides and civil war.

Great Britain was riding high when Jay arrived. The war with France was going her way at the moment, and she was not prepared to make any concessions whatever to her upstart former colonies if they were moving as close to joining the French as the utterances of men like James Monroe and other Republicans suggested. (Young Monroe had been appointed minister to France at about the time Jay went to England, and he was lauding the Revolution and the present French regime in accents that London found disgusting and alarming.) The British regarded the Federalists about the way the Federalists regarded themselves—as a bulwark against the triumph of Jacobinism in the United States —and the urbane, conservative Jay struck just the right note and undoubtedly got the most out of a situation in which there was not much to be had.

And what little there was proved far more important than the infuriated critics could see at first glance. Some of the treaty's worst features turned out to be bearable, others were less unfortunate than they appeared, and its best feature enabled things to fall into place for the United States in the area that mattered most. The wartime grievances—impressment, seizures of neutral cargoes, and the like—were going to last as long as the European war did, and for the shipping interests most directly involved they were a supportable burden: if neutral commerce was a high-risk operation it was also highly profitable, and the most enterprising American merchants were quite willing to take their chances at sea. As for the mercantile restrictions that America found so galling, the inexorable logic of war took care of these to her advantage too. Soon after the United States indignantly rejected the crippling terms by which Britain had condescended to permit trade with her Caribbean islands, the royal governors of those islands urgently in need of American timber and foodstuffs and American shipping, threw their ports wide open to American trade. The home government, which was run by realists, upheld these actions, and the Republic's valuable West Indian traffic began to flourish once again.

Meanwhile, Jay's treaty broke a log jam that enabled the mighty Western current to begin flowing smoothly and strongly for the first time since 1783 and provided the first real security for America's title to the trans-Appalachian country. A share of the credit for this must go to Anthony Wayne, who marched his little army out to Ohio and became the first American commander to perform with distinction in the West since the days of George Rogers Clark. Wayne met a large Indian force near the falls of the Maumee at a place called Fallen Timbers in August 1794 and beat them decisively, while Britishers in a nearby fort coldly and prudently kept their distance. Disillusioned and beaten, the tribes agreed to come to terms, signing a treaty at Greenville in 1795 in which they buried the hatchet and recognized American title to nearly all of present-day Ohio together with the sites of Vincennes, Detroit, and Chicago. News of Wayne's victory undoubtedly contributed to the British willingness to evacuate the seven forts they had been occupying on American territory, abandon the one they had been building in western Ohio, and move their troops back to the Canadian side of the Great Lakes-St. Lawrence border. The lands north of the Ohio were safe at last, and settlers began pouring in.

The Jay Treaty paid another big Western dividend by jarring satisfactory terms out of Spain, which no previous American negotiator—including Jay, who had tried it ten years earlier—had ever been able to obtain. Spain's policy in the American interior resembled Great Britain's. The Spaniards still claimed title to nearly everything south of the Tennessee and west of Georgia, occupied forts and kept troops there, aided and abetted Indian attacks on United States settlements, conducted shadowy intrigues among Indians and frontiersmen in an effort to maintain and enlarge Spanish control, and kept a tight grip on the key to the whole interior heartland—the port of New Orleans and the mouth of the great river. As long as this artery was closed to American commerce there was no future for the Western settlements except possibly as an adjunct of Spain, which was as real a possibility in 1795 as it had been during the Confederation period.

But Jay's treaty and related international developments forced the Spaniards to re-examine their policy. In 1794, badly hurt by the European war and preparing to withdraw from the coalition against France, fearful that American frontiersmen might be planning to attack Florida and Louisiana, Spain indicated a willingness to review its treaty relationships with the United States. When Thomas Pinckney of South Carolina arrived in Madrid in mid-1795 to undertake this task—Pinckney came from England where he had been American minister, present during the Jay negotiations—he found the Spaniards in an unusually co-operative mood.

No longer England's ally in the war against France, Spain now feared that the Jay Treaty marked the beginning of an Anglo-American alliance, one of whose objectives might well be an attack in concert upon Spain's North American possessions. Eager to forestall this, Madrid readily acceded to American demands, and the Pinckney Treaty gave the United States nearly everything it wanted: recognition of American claims to the disputed territory north of the 31st parallel, evacuation of the Spanish forts in that area, a promise (by both sides) to restrain rather than incite Indian hostility, and, most important of all, the opening of the Mississippi to American navigation and the port of New Orleans as a place of deposit for American goods awaiting transshipment. Spain refused to open its empire to American ships but agreed with America's concept of neutral rights: freedom of the seas, a narrow definition of contraband, and the right of neutral ships to trade at belligerent ports unless they were actually under blockade or siege.

Back home, Thomas Pinckney was as widely acclaimed for his diplomacy as John Jay was condemned for his, yet the latter's effort had made Pinckney's success possible. In any event the American West had been the real victor in all these negotiations, which suggests that American statesmen either knew or sensed that the nation's true path to fulfillment lay not on the oceans but through the great interior. The new Western states were already trooping in, beginning to alter the old territorial balance along the eastern seaboard. Kentucky joined the Union in 1792, Tennessee in 1796, and settlement was booming in the newly pacified region north of the Ohio. (Vermont, a disputed offspring of New

Hampshire and New York which had defied the claims of both states and functioned as an independent republic since 1777, edged out the Westerners by joining the Union as the fourteenth state in 1791.)

——□——

As the end of his second term approached, George Washington issued a farewell address in which he made an eloquent plea for impartiality and no unwise entanglements in foreign affairs and for an end to violent partisanship at home. This partisanship had cast a cloud over his final years in office; he had been embittered and badly hurt by it (when Washington called for an end to partisanship he was thinking entirely of Republican partisanship), and his relief at the prospect of returning to Mount Vernon was equaled only by his regret that what he had always felt to be disinterested acts of statesmanship should have encountered such intemperate and hostile criticism.

He left office a sadder and less universally respected man than when he had entered it, and yet the record of those eight years had been remarkably good. The government worked; it was collecting taxes, enforcing its writ, learning its way. Its courts were open and its credit fully restored. Thanks to its diplomacy and its muscle, the West was secure at last—two new Western states already added and the Ohio territory filling up with people, most of the Western tribes subdued or pacified, the British back in Canada where they belonged, the great Mississippi waterway open. The country was prosperous and at peace. Americans were laying out turnpikes, investing money, moving west, speculating in land, building ships, and clearing new acres because a brisk international trade kept enlarging the market for whatever they produced.

The famous contrivance of Eli Whitney, barely three years old, had already begun to move the cotton frontier inland from the sea-island region along the Georgia and Carolina coast, where the long-staple variety could be separated by hand. In the interior the short-staple variety could be grown profitably now that Whitney's simple machine was available to draw the fiber from the husk; short-staple cotton could flourish in the Georgia uplands and the Alabama black belt and the Mississippi bottomlands and all the way to what was still Spanish Louisiana. Men with cotton gins and slave labor were moving west to plant it, and British mills were prepared to buy all the cotton America could grow. Cotton exports had been negligible when George Washington became President. They totaled 6 million pounds during his last year in office; five years later they would exceed 20 million pounds—and this was the barest beginning. The outlines of a vast, powerful, tragic Southern empire were already taking shape as the century wore to a close.

To be sure, the issues that would bedevil Washington's successors were also present: American ships and commerce continually subject to the seizures, depredations, and arbitrary changes in policy of which great powers at war were capable; political parties maneuvering for advantage and drawing a sharp battle line across which to exchange invective and animosity of such virulence that not even George Washington's enormous prestige could insulate him from it. A price had had to be paid for all the achievements of those first eight years, and Washington had paid his share. But neither war clouds abroad nor angry political dialogue at home could long obscure the value of what he had accomplished—or the value people would place upon it. After the presidency he was permitted only three short years of relative peace at Mount Vernon, but before they were over he would be back where he belonged—above party, above the battle, first in the hearts of his countrymen.

CHAPTER 21

Perils of Neutrality

T HE REPUBLICANS had begun to vilify him, but the election
of 1796 did not become America's first presidential contest
until after Washington made it clear that he would not seek a third
term. Then the race figured to be close. The two parties were
more or less equally represented in Congress; resentment of England and John Jay and the Hamilton program were in approxi-
mate equilibrium with national prosperity and fear of France and
satisfaction over the new Spanish treaty. Antagonisms ran deep,
but they were not well mobilized; partisanship had not yet discovered the levée en masse. Neither party had assumed more
than a hazy dot-to-dot outline of organization or structure, and
there was a refreshing informality and tentativeness—perhaps
because none of the major figures had fully accepted either the
fact or the desirability of parties—about the way they went about
choosing and electing candidates.

Washington's great opposing counselors, Hamilton and Jefferson, were the two most prominent political leaders, but neither
had the field to himself or ran a one-man show. They had retired
from public office before Washington did—Jefferson to Monti-
cello at the end of 1793, Hamilton to a New York law practice a

year later—but they had not retired from politics. With Washington out of the running, their posture and influence in the election of 1796 figured to be decisive.

The Republican high command was on its way to becoming a triumvirate consisting of Jefferson, Madison, and a talented young Swiss patrician named Albert Gallatin, who had emigrated to Pennsylvania during the War for Independence and quickly rose to prominence—respected local leader, influential moderate during the Whiskey Rebellion, senator and then representative from Pennsylvania, Republican floor leader in Congress after Madison retired in 1797, and as skilled and knowledgeable in financial matters as Hamilton himself. Madison and Gallatin were greatly respected, but there was little question in the Republican camp that the distinguished Jefferson should be their candidate. For Vice-President, though he was by no means a unanimous choice, the party chose the shrewd, ambitious leader of the New York Republicans, Aaron Burr.

Hamilton, the most influential Federalist and the party's major spokesman, was much too controversial a figure to run for President; the most respected and most likely Federalist candidate was Vice-President Adams. The Federalist congressmen caucused and nominated Adams, then chose the popular Thomas Pinckney, widely hailed for his recent success in Spain, as Adams' running mate. At this point Hamilton, who wanted to direct things from behind the throne and had grave and justifiable doubts about his chances of directing John Adams, proceeded to launch a behind-the-scenes maneuver that very nearly cost the Federalists the election and did cost them the lower half of it.

The procedure for choosing a President was not yet geared to the party system, and it had a lot of play in it. There were no national conventions to nominate candidates or draw up platforms, no instructed delegates or firmly pledged slates of electors, no formal machinery whatever above the state level. The electors (some chosen by state legislature, some by popular vote) each cast two ballots, with the Presidency going to the highest vote-getter and the vice-presidency to the second highest. Hamilton wanted Pinckney to be President rather than Adams, and his idea was that if a few Federalist electors voted for Pinckney and threw away their second vote (rather than casting if for Adams), the South Carolinian would win. It was arranged so, but the Adams people heard about it—Hamilton was never very good at keeping his intrigues secret—and they persuaded some New England electors to vote for Adams but not Pinckney. Both groups did as instructed, the Adams electors on a somewhat larger scale, with the result that Jefferson almost won the presidency. Adams barely edged him, 71 electoral votes to 68, and Jefferson did finish ahead of the unfortunate Pinckney, who came in third with 59.

This meant that Republican Jefferson was going to be Federalist Adams' Vice-President, a situation which displeased both sides. Nearly everyone, in fact, began the new four-year term in a state of disgruntlement. Hamilton was chagrined at the miscarriage of his plan and worked at cross-purposes with the new President from the very start. Jefferson and Adams, though they admired each other, did not see eye to eye about England, France, or much of anything else on the current political scene except Hamilton, whom both distrusted. Adams was especially bitter at Hamilton for having tried to steal the election and deprive him of the presidency. Pinckney, for whatever it was worth, felt done out of the vice-presidency. And something was clearly going to have to be done about the electoral process. The fourth-place finisher in the balloting, Aaron Burr, had received only 30 votes to his running mate's 68, and he was indignant to discover that 15 Virginia Republicans had cast their second ballot for (of all people) Sam Adams. Burr would remember all of this four years later, and proceed to make the need for electoral reform imperative.

It was not an auspicious beginning for poor John Adams, but it set the tone for his presidency, which saw the United States hover on the brink of war and total political disruption for nearly all of his four years in office and ended in disaster for his party. Foreign affairs and domestic politics were intertwined in the ugliest kind of tangle. Adams was caught between the French and the English, who were earnestly competing to see who could give America the rougher treatment; and between the Federalists and the Republicans, who were competing in both paranoid behavior and vituperative language—with the President almost as much a target of his own party as he was of the opposition. His Cabinet, which it did not occur to him to replace until much too late, consisted mainly of holdovers from the Washington administration: second-rate men who took their orders from Hamilton and undercut the new President at almost every turn.

Almost none of this was Adams' fault. He deserved better of his contemporaries in the late 1790s than he received, and he kept his head better than anyone else did. His flinty independent mind and prickly personality made him easy to dislike, and he was vain, egotistical, jealous, crotchety—and as wise, sane, and dedicated a leader as America has ever had. He had the courage and insight to resist political pressure and public clamor and keep the country out of war, thereby also keeping the Federalists and Republicans from drifting into such total antagonism that the country would probably have fallen apart. Canny and perceptive about many things, he was strangely blind to the machinations of his Cabinet; the Adamses were statesmen who refused to master the art of politics, apparently never realizing that politics is part of statecraft too, and that if statesmen do not resort to it they risk being sandbagged by nonstatesmen who do. But if his career suffered at the hands of such men, his stature grew.

The bane and focal point of the Adams administration were America's relations with France. The French had been spoiling for trouble since before the election, and they persisted until they found it. From the American standpoint each new French regime turned out to be more heavy-handed and arrogant than its predecessor, and the Directory, which came to power in 1795, was the worst yet; their minister to the United States was one Citizen Adet, who managed to make Citizen Genêt appear a model of diplomatic rectitude by comparison.

The French hated the Federalists and made no bones about it, regarding them as enemies of the Revolution, of the people, of the rights of man, and of France. Specifically they resented the Jay Treaty, which they interpreted to mean that the United States favored Britain over France. Taking their cue from some of Jefferson's utterances and nearly all of James Monroe's, who was in Paris making the most extravagant pro-French noises, the French government concluded that Americans were basically a right-minded people groaning beneath the yoke of Federalist tyranny and needing only a little encouragement to rise up and throw it off. The idea was that such an uprising would replace the Federalists with a well-disposed Republican regime which would repudiate the Jay Treaty, honor the French alliance, and join France in the holy war against perfidious Albion.

The French way of bringing down the Federalists was to apply crude pressure. During the campaign of 1796, Citizen Adet allowed confidential diplomatic material to be published as campaign propaganda against the Administration, and delivered official pronouncements to the effect that France was suspending diplomatic relations and commencing to seize American vessels that traded with England. When the Federalists won the election anyway, despite or perhaps because of these French tactics, the angered Directory stepped up its seizures of American merchantmen, ordered the American minister home, and made threatening noises about confiscating all American cargoes that included any British goods.

Relations had deteriorated to the breaking point, and President Adams, with Hamilton's concurrence—it was almost the only time during Adams' tenure that the two men agreed on anything —decided to send a special mission to France to try to negotiate the difficulties. He sent three men: the recently expelled minister to France, Charles C. Pinckney (Thomas' brother); future Chief

Justice John Marshall of Virginia; and Elbridge Gerry of Massachusetts. The mission got nowhere. The Directory's foreign minister was Charles Maurice de Talleyrand, one of the most successfully corrupt members of an increasingly corrupt regime. Talleyrand kept the Americans waiting for weeks and then informed them (through a trio of agents whom the bewildered Americans knew only as Messrs. X, Y, and Z) that the price of improved diplomatic relations would be a $250,000 payment to Talleyrand himself a "loan" of several million dollars to the French government. Pinckney and Marshall threw up their hands and went home in disgust while Gerry lingered in a vain attempt to see if anything could be negotiated without the bribe.

President Adams saw to it that all of the papers and correspondence pertaining to the XYZ affair were made public in the spring of 1798, and the nation reacted with an angry howl. The pro-French Republicans were badly discredited and saw their voting strength dwindle, while the Administration enjoyed a wave of popular support and the United States strode purposefully to the brink of war with France. (Adet, Talleyrand, and the Directory had behaved abominably, but the extent and vehemence of America's reaction were enough out of proportion to the magnitude of the offense as to suggest that national frustration over foreign affairs and the arrogant behavior of foreign powers had reached flash point.)

Adams, at the peak of his own popularity, had no trouble persuading Congress to pass various retaliatory measures. The government repudiated the treaties of 1778, suspended all trade with France, created a Navy Department and began building a navy. Three big frigates had been authorized and launched in 1797, as the French crisis heated up; these vessels—*Constitution, Constellation,* and *United States*—were hastened to completion in the summer of 1798, the first American warships larger than a revenue cutter to come into existence since the end of the Revolutionary War. The government also authorized the purchase or construction of some two dozen other naval craft. Congress appropriated money for arms and ammunition and the fortification of harbors and ordered an increase in the size of the regular army.

For the next two years the United States and France waged an undeclared but very real maritime war. French privateers seized American vessels on the open ocean, in the West Indies, and right off the Atlantic coast; American warships and armed private vessels, confining their operations to French naval craft and privateers, drove the latter away from our shores and captured some eighty enemy vessels altogether. As far as Americans were concerned the two peak moments in this quasi war were provided by U.S.S. *Constellation* under Captain Thomas Truxtun, who pounded one French frigate into submission in a single-ship action in early 1799 and reduced another to a total wreck a year later.

The undeclared naval war had barely begun in the summer of 1798 when the more extreme wing of Adams' party, the so-called High Federalists, moved boldly to take the initiative from the President. In so doing they managed also to take leave of their senses.

Apparently believing that their hour had come, and that public opinion was ready to support them in launching a victorious war against the Jacobin menace both abroad and at home, the Federalists went on a legislative spree. They authorized an "Additional Army" of 10,000 men (over and above existing armed forces), to be mustered immediately and kept while the present dispute with France lasted; and a "Provisional Army" of 50,000 men, to be raised in case the dispute widened into a full-scale war. They passed a series of new direct taxes on houses, land, and slaves in order to pay for all these new soldiers. They persuaded the ailing Washington to come out of retirement and accept command of this big new army, with the understanding that the former President would be no more than a nominal commander-in-chief. For the post of second in command, and hence the actual ranking officer on active duty, the High Federalists persuaded Washington to pressure John Adams into passing over his own choice, General Henry Knox, and also to pass over the other two highest-ranking general officers—Daniel Morgan and Benjamin Lincoln—so as to confer the appointment on none other than Alexander Hamilton, who very much wanted the job! The High Federalists accompanied all this activity by pressing as hard as they could for a declaration of war against France.

Nor did they forget the home front. In that same busy summer of 1798 they secured the passage of a set of laws known as the Alien and Sedition Acts. In sum, these laws lengthened the period of naturalization for foreign immigrants from five to fourteen years, made resident aliens subject to deportation if they were deemed a threat to the public safety, and in effect made it unlawful to say or print anything of a critical nature about the government, its laws, or its elected officials. The Sedition Act was the one with all the hooks in it, and lest anyone mistake the intended target, the law was slated to expire in March 1801—when the incumbent party would be either safely back in office and in no need of further protection, or freshly voted out of office and in need of the freedom to criticize the recently elected officials of the opposition party. Wasting no time, the government moved briskly against the Republican press. They prosecuted some twenty-five Republican editors under the Sedition Act and obtained ten convictions, which carried jail sentences as well as stiff fines.

Paranoia had clearly reached an acute stage, where it could begin feeding upon itself. The High Federalists, who seem to have convinced themselves that French influence and Republican attacks demanded such draconian legislation, had contributed to a self-fulfilling prophecy—resorting to the kind of autocratic repressive measures that confirmed the Republicans' worst fears.

John Adams was caught in the middle by this spate of Federalist activity, and badly torn. He was enough of a Federalist, and sufficiently disturbed by the intemperate hostility of Republican attacks, to sign the Alien and Sedition Acts. He signed the army measures against his better judgment, pointing out that the country had no need of a big army in any conceivable struggle with France. And he was furious over being forced to accept Hamilton as ranking major general. ("You crammed him down my throat!" he cried out at one point.) The President was as alarmed as the Republicans were by the use Hamilton wanted to make of that Provisional Army: he spoke grandly of leading it on expeditions of conquest into Florida and Louisiana and possibly even into Central and South America, revealing an imperial dream with dimensions that would have impressed Bonaparte himself. And Republicans had a fairly clear notion of what else this ambitious man on horseback might do with his new army.

The Hamilton appointment made Adams so angry that he refused to be pushed any further. Digging in his heels, he resisted the High Federalist demands for a declaration of war on France. His party split wide open on the issue, but while the High Federalists fumed and denounced him and maneuvered behind his back, Adams appointed William Vans Murray as minister to France in early 1799 and instructed him to seek a settlement. The opposing wing was able to add two other men to the diplomatic mission, but they could neither prevent it from going nor prevent it from succeeding. Bonaparte was now essentially in charge of French policy, and he wanted to end the trouble with the United States.

France agreed to void the old 1778 treaties, thus ending the alliance that the United States had found so troublesome. The French also agreed to accept the American version of neutral rights—freedom of the seas, and so forth—and to stop seizing American ships. The quarrel was over. Thanks to Adams, the country had achieved its ends by a judicious combination of firmness and diplomacy. The High Federalists were furious, but Adams undoubtedly gained more support than he lost in the country at large. His handling of the French crisis had apparently been in accordance with what most Americans wanted: they were tired of being pushed around, but they did not really want an all-out war if satisfactory terms could be had.

The Republicans meanwhile, were mobilizing to recoup their losses and turn recent developments to their advantage. The Federalists had provided them with some potent ammunition: oppressive new taxes, a bigger standing army (with none other than Hamilton in command), and a stringent Sedition Act. There was a parallel in the American experience, and the Republicans did not ignore it. In the hands of a capable editor, the recent Federalist legislation could be used to conjure up memories of the Stamp and Townshend duties, the arrival of British regiments in New York and Boston before the war, the acts of Parliament in 1774 that banned the Boston town meeting and prorogued the Massachusetts assembly—in short, monarchical repression of the rights of a free people. This had been answered with armed resistance in 1775, the editor might continue; but in 1800 it could be answered at the polls, in a root-and-branch rejection of the monocrat Federalists!

The Republicans had some potent issues and made the most of them. They also took steps to improve the party organization, setting up a pyramid of county and state committees topped by a caucus of congressional Republicans, which assumed primary responsibility for party policy. By way of making official remonstrance and attracting public attention to the matter, Madison and Jefferson persuaded the legislatures of Virginia and Kentucky to pass resolutions in 1798 and 1799 condemning the Alien and Sedition Acts as unconstitutional—the Kentucky set, drafted by Jefferson, went so far as to pronounce them "void and of no force" and went on to suggest that nullification by the states was the proper remedy for an unconstitutional law. (Madison and Jefferson were sowing dragon's teeth here. They were employing the legislatures as a conveniently able forum in a political contest and did not regard state rights as much more than a useful political weapon. But a precedent for challenging the authority of the federal government had been set.)

Momentum was with the Republicans in the campaign of 1800, but the election was close. As in 1796, the opposing candidates were Thomas Jefferson and John Adams. The two parties were roughly equal in voting strength. The Federalists were stronger in New England, in the towns, among merchants and commercial farmers, in older and more established communities; they also had some appeal among Southern planters, especially in South Carolina with its thriving port. The Republicans were stronger in the South and West, in the back country, among immigrants and planters, and in more recently settled communities. They were also gaining more support among businessmen and merchants in the Northern cities, especially New York and Philadelphia; the commercial classes were far from unanimous in their allegiance to Federalism.

Republican strength was growing, helped by the Federalist split and the new taxes and the fears raised by the Alien and Sedition Acts. The Federalists had lost their nerve somewhere along the way and then had overreached themselves, and they were on the beginnings of a permanent downhill slope. Yet Adams himself retained enough popularity to make a race out of it, and Jefferson's winning margin was not large. With Pennsylvania and Maryland dividing their votes evenly between the two candidates, Adams carried all of New England, plus New Jersey, Delaware, and one third of North Carolina, for a total of 65 electoral votes. Jefferson had 73, carrying New York, Kentucky, and Tennessee, and everything south of the Potomac except for 4 votes in North Carolina. The two crucial states had been New York, where Burr's influence finally proved decisive, and South Carolina, which had enough Federalist strength to give the Adams forces hope until the very end; had he carried this state, he would have been re-elected.

Instead the Republicans had won, but the nation's electoral machinery had created another problem. Anxious to avoid the trouble the Federalists had brought on themselves four years ago, the Republicans used their new party organization and discipline effectively and enjoined all of their electors not to throw away any votes. The electors obediently complied, with the result that Jefferson and his running mate, Aaron Burr, finished in a tie. Under the Constitution this threw the election into the House of Representatives, where the Federalists controlled enough states to keep things tied up if they chose. Burr, instead of withdrawing, simply held himself aloof and waited for things to happen. The Federalist congressmen first voted en bloc for Burr and created a deadlock, but after thirty-five ballots Hamilton decided to intervene. Disapproving of Jefferson far less than he distrusted Burr, Hamilton finally persuaded Federalists in two or three key states to submit blank ballots, and Jefferson thereupon won the necessary nine states and was declared elected. Congress later took steps to see that this kind of tie-up never happened again and approved the Twelfth Amendment in 1803, which required separate balloting in the electoral college for the offices of President and Vice-President.

Jefferson liked to refer to his triumph as the Revolution of 1800, so large a difference did he see between Republican and Federalist leadership. Revolution was probably too strong a word, but something important had happened. For one thing, the nation had proved that it could transfer power from one party to another in peaceful and orderly fashion, despite the inflamed passions and dire predictions that had accompanied the campaign. The governmental system had absorbed the party system and continued to work.

The new President was convinced that in getting the nation back on the republican tack, as he put it, he and his party had effected a vitally important change. Certainly the tone and emphasis were going to be different. Jefferson wanted as small and as frugal a government as possible, on the historically demonstrable theory that nearly all of the injustice, suffering, cruelty, war, and repression man had undergone down the ages had been visited upon him by governments wielding too much power and spending too much money. Yet Jefferson was a pragmatist who would not hesitate to wield power or spend money for something he found necessary; the difference, as he saw it, was that right-minded *believers* in small government (in contrast to the centralizing Federalists) could more safely be trusted to stretch its powers on occasion.

There were other differences. Jefferson's answer to the old conservative fears of rule by the people was to point out that if men were incapable of governing themselves it made little sense to let them govern others. When the Federalists responded that some men were better fitted to govern, Jefferson would assent— with the stipulation that the talented leaders should be recruited from neither a hereditary nobility nor an entrenched plutocracy; he believed instead in a natural aristocracy which in an open society would rise to the top like cream in a pan of milk. He preferred an agricultural society, both out of personal taste and in the belief that agriculture was a more ennobling and somehow a more *moral* vocation than industry or trade. He disliked big cities for the reasons that people in all ages have disliked big cities, fearing that masses of propertyless urban dwellers could more readily be bought or intimidated by the rich and powerful or swayed by demagogues.

But, like Madison, he wanted a balanced society—ideally, one that was predominantly agricultural but possessed of enough commerce and industry to be free from dependence on foreign powers—and he was willing to change with the times; he was a witness to the great growth in American commerce and the beginnings of American industry, and he conceded that this was all right if the people wanted it that way. Trust of the people's judgment underlay much of this attitude, and it may constitute the largest single difference between Jefferson and the Federalists.

Furthermore, in electing the party of Jefferson and Madison

and Gallatin the American people had made a truly momentous decision. So much was at issue, and so much was at stake, and these men who had become so fiercely partisan were seeing it in bits and pieces. Part was the voice of agriculture against the voice of commerce and money and banking—America's garden brought to bay by America's destiny. Part was localism against centralism, state against nation, the hills of home against a continental empire. (Here the party lines were already blurring and shifting.) Another important part was South against North, because geography had long ago decreed that certain regions in America would thrive on staple-crop agriculture and certain others would live by trade and ships and double-entry bookkeeping.

But these were only bits and pieces—each partly true, and each incomplete. Behind it all were two opposing visions of society, and the rural-urban, farm-commerce, South-North, state-federal antagonisms were symptoms rather than essence. In opting for a strong central government as opposed to a league of sovereign states, Americans had voted to provide a canvas and a framework big enough for their energies, which had all the explosive potential of the hydrogen atom. What they were still in process of deciding was how to direct that energy—whether in a closed and planned society led by a privileged class, or in a wide-open, free-wheeling society built on equal opportunity and no special favors. In electing Jefferson they were indicating a preference for the latter.

To pose it in those terms is to make the issue sound more clear-cut than it actually was, and the distinction would always have a murky quality because so many of the people who lined up on the wide-open and free-wheeling side were agrarians and state-rights men and slaveholders and Northern capitalists on the make; and the desire of these folk for equal opportunity often extended no further than the opportunities of their own group.

And yet equal opportunity was a genuine principle, shimmering hazily through the smoke clouds thrown up by the heat of partisan conflict, and the two Virginians who became the partisan rallying point for opposition to Alexander Hamilton were enunciating the principle in terms that struck a responsive chord. These Virginia gentlemen were also slaveholders, and some of the elements that rallied behind their leadership were as predatory and as crassly motivated as the worst of the speculators who buzzed about the Treasury Department. The fact remained that Hamilton's program, supported by taxpayers' money, had been systematiclly used to enrich a favored class of people, and a majority of Americans had become so alienated by this that they would be hostile to anything smacking of special privilege (including, eventually, the special privileges enjoyed by slaveholders) from this time forward.

Equal opportunity harked back to the Declaration of Independence, and was being invoked now by the man who had written it. The idea of a privileged class enjoying special government favors harked back to the system from which Americans had rebelled. For all their contributions, which were enormous, Hamilton and his ideas stood on one side of this question and Jefferson and Madison stood on the other, and in the end it was the decisive question. American energies would soon start rocketing across the landscape and developing the country in ways that embodied more of Hamilton's instincts than of Madison's or Jefferson's. But these energies would not be containable within an elitist system or march into the future behind a privileged economic class. And the principle of equal opportunity would ensure that free-enterprise capitalism, even at its worst, would be more susceptible to reform influences and arguments on behalf of society's unfortunates and society's outcasts than Hamilton's plutocracy would ever have been. Perhaps "the Revolution of 1800" is not too strong a term, at that.

Taken all in all, Thomas Jefferson's first six years in office were about as happy and successful a period as the nation would ever know. Difficulties of course existed, but they were generally small and generally manageable. There was a running, acrimonious dispute between the new Republican President and the new Federalist Chief Justice (one of John Adams' biggest contributions to his country's future was the appointment of John Marshall to the Supreme Court in 1801), in which, among other things, the latter established the principle that the Supreme Court could declare an act of Congress unconstitutional. Toward the end of Jefferson's first term his restless and erratically brilliant Vice-President immersed himself in notoriety and deep trouble —first by running for governor of New York in 1804 and getting so angry at the crucial role played by Hamilton in his defeat that he challenged Hamilton to a duel and killed him; then by getting involved with the perpetually intriguing and perpetually untrustworthy James Wilkinson in a hazy empire-building foray out West: when Wilkinson ratted on him halfway through the enterprise, Burr found himself under arrest and on trial for treason. He was eventually acquitted, but his reputation and career were in tatters.

Yet on the whole everything went well. The Federalists were in visible and continuing decline, sulking on the sidelines and watching their support dwindle. The Republicans had solid majorities in Congress and in all of the states outside New England, and even here they were making inroads. The party triumvirate was in command and doing well: Jefferson appointed Madison Secretary of State and Gallatin Secretary of the Treasury. The government quietly cut down the size of the Hamiltonian apparatus without dismantling it: Gallatin reduced the size of the debt, cut expenses, ran an efficient and frugal operation. Frugality enabled the Administration to eliminate the hated taxes levied during the French crisis, and Jefferson also repealed the whiskey excise, thereby immortalizing himself west of the mountains. The Sedition Act was simply allowed to lapse.

They were highly prosperous years. American farm produce had good and growing markets. The thriving re-export trade in the varied products from Spanish, French, Dutch, and British possessions continued apace. Ocean freight rates were so high that new vessels could pay for themselves in a voyage or two, which touched off a boom in American shipyards from Maine to Savannah. The shipping boom had a multiplier effect, stimulating activity in sawmills, ropewalks, forges, and necessary commercial apparatus like docking and warehousing facilities and marine insurance companies. Profits made in shipping and international trade were piling up, soon to be available for manufacturing enterprises, and for transportation projects which more and more Americans in the hinterland, as they were drawn into an expanding overseas market, were coming to demand.

The biggest event in Jefferson's first term was the purchase of the whole Louisiana territory, which extended America's frontier from the Mississippi to the Rockies. When the United States learned that Spain had ceded this vast region to Napoleon in a secret treaty in 1800, Jefferson took alarm. His concern was the port of New Orleans, vital river outlet for interior produce. He saw no problem in decrepit Spain but a large problem indeed in France under Bonaparte, who was planning to expand the French overseas empire and use Louisiana as a source of supply for the French sugar islands. In 1802, Spain, still holding the territory but about to cede it, made noises about closing the port and the river to American goods, and Jefferson interpreted this as forthcoming French policy. His response was blunt. "The day that France takes possession of New Orleans," he said, we will be forced to "marry ourselves to the British fleet and nation."

These were strong words indeed from such a quarter, but the President tried another solution before resorting to the marriage. He sent James Monroe to Paris to aid Robert R. Livingston, the American minister, in an attempt to buy New Orleans from France. All he wanted was the port and the mouth of the river, but by the time Monroe and Livingston began making their pitch Napoleon had changed his mind about a New World empire and abruptly offered to sell the whole Louisiana territory. (What made him change his mind is worth noting. A series of slave revolts in Haiti led by Toussaint L'Ouverture had brought nearly all of the rich island of Hispaniola under Toussaint's control by 1800. Bonaparte had sent a French army to recapture it and put down the revolt, and a combination of yellow fever and brilliant black generalship had decimated and thoroughly checked the French forces. This setback persuaded Napoleon to cut his losses and get out of North America altogether: one result was the Louisiana Purchase; another, already noticeable in the 1790s when Toussaint's revolt began to succeed, was the implanting of a fear of black insurrection in the hearts of Southern slaveowners. The fear would never leave them, and it would vastly complicate the attempt to end slavery in the United States.)

Flabbergasted by Napoleon's offer, Monroe and Livingston talked it over and decided that it was too good an opportunity to miss. They agreed to buy, settled on a purchase price of $15 million, and came home with a draft treaty that would add New Orleans and some 850,000 square miles of trans-Mississippi wilderness to the United States.

Jefferson was equally astounded, and equally persuaded that it had indeed been a worthwhile bargain. (He was disappointed that West Florida had not been included in the package but calmly reasoned that "all in good time" the United States was bound to obtain the Floridas.) The President had to do some wrestling with his conscience and apply some Hamilton-style loose construction in order to make the purchase conform to the Constitution, which nowhere explicitly authorizes the acquisition of territory. But he was a practical man, more than equal to this exercise, and he suggested that the treaty-making power *implied* (how Hamilton must have smiled) the right to acquire new territory. The Senate, despite some caustic comments from the Federalists, ratified the treaty by a vote of 24 to 7. The United States took formal possession of New Orleans in late 1803 and the upper region, centered on St. Louis, in early 1804.

The nation then wrote its signature with a flourish all the way across the new territory by sending a big expedition under Meriwether Lewis and William Clark on a two-year journey up the wide Missouri to its headwaters, across the continental divide, and down the Columbia to the Pacific. The expedition collected a great deal of valuable information about the geography, plant and animal life, and trading possibilities of the region and helped set America's sights on the far Pacific slope.

They had been years of achievement, and Thomas Jefferson was easily re-elected along with big Republican majorities in 1804. Times were very good indeed. But the young Republic and its high-minded President had been having it both ways—prosperously at peace, and prosperously enjoying fat profits as carriers and suppliers for someone else's war. This was not the kind of war that would permit such a happy state of affairs to continue indefinitely. The Louisiana Purchase had forestalled one European effort to spill over into America's back yard; but America's back yard, thanks to the lucrative re-export and carrying trades, had extended itself all over the transatlantic and Caribbean sea lanes and beyond. The two great belligerents were striking at each other wherever they found a target, and the neutral ships belonging to a country that had no navy to speak of offered such a target, as they had in the past. The European war was growing in scale and intensity. And there was no conceivable way for the United States to remain indefinitely both prosperous and at peace in a world where the two final arbiters were Napoleon Bonaparte and His Britannic Majesty's navy.

—□—

Their war had become, by the end of 1805, the fabled struggle between the elephant and the whale. Napoleon was supreme on the Continent and Britain was supreme on the high seas; fighting to the death, these two gigantic powers were unable to get at each other. Because of this fact the struggle inevitably involved America.

The British concluded that the only way to bring Napoleon down was to throttle him. To do this the mighty fleet would cut off all French seaborne trade; except for goods that could move wholly by land, Napoleon's empire would have no imports and no exports. In the long run this might very well be fatal—to Napoleon, to the Grand Army, to France . . . and, as a by-product, to the United States of America. For by far the greater part of the trade Britain proposed to destroy was carried in American ships.

America was vulnerable because of her growth and success as an independent nation. Doing what they could do best, opportunity and their own talents pointing in that direction, Americans had made Europe's affairs part of their own lives. They built a great fleet of merchant vessels—sloops, brigs, schooners, ships with tall masts and rounded sails white in the morning sun—and sent them out to trade where they could; and before the nineteenth century was five years old they were the largest neutral carrier of goods in the world. In 1790 the American merchant fleet had a carrying capacity of some 100,000 tons. Fifteen years later this had increased tenfold. The nation's total of imports and exports had been multiplied by four. In addition, these ships were carriers for others, sailing from Latin America and the Caribbean islands to Europe, going for months without ever touching at a home port, carrying an increasing part of the trade between France and her colonies. By 1805, in fact, with the French and Spanish merchant marines practically swept from the seas, just about all of the trade to and from the French and Spanish colonies was carried under the American flag.

This made a prodigious hole in the British blockade and London moved to plug it. The British announced the revival of the Rule of 1756, which Americans had first encountered in the 1790s: trade forbidden in time of peace (as France and Spain had forbidden foreigners to trade with their New World possessions) could not be made legal in time of war.

American shippers worked out a way to evade this rule. A ship with a Caribbean cargo for a French port would first put in at some American port, unload the cargo, and pay a duty on it. Then the cargo would be reloaded, the duty would be quietly refunded, and the ship would sail serenely for France, innocent as a lamb in spring, carrying a cargo loaded in an American port on a perfectly legal voyage.

This worked for a time—a short time. In July 1805 a British admiralty court held that this arrangement was a sham, and British cruisers were deployed along the American coast to stop and search American merchantmen and send doubtful cases into Halifax for adjudication. Not unnaturally, the frigate captains found most cases doubtful, and it was equally natural for the admiralty court to agree with them. The best an American shipper could hope for was permission to resume his voyage after a long and costly delay.

Implicit in all of this, of course, was the British feeling that what America thought was of no importance. James Monroe, now American minister at London, reported that many Britishers believed the United States, "by the nature of their government, incapable of any great, vigorous or persevering exertion." Out of this conviction, as Admiral Mahan pointed out long afterward, grew "that unconciliatory and disdainful attitude towards the United States which made inevitable a war that a higher bearing might have avoided."

Things speedily got complicated. A sweeping British order in council dated May 16, 1806, proclaimed a blockade of the European coast and required neutral ships to pay fees and get British permits to carry non-contraband items through the blockade. Hitherto, the general international understanding was that a blockade was legal only when warships were actually present off the entrance to the blockaded port. This order implied a vast extension of the powers of the nation applying the blockade; now a British frigate cruising within sight of the Carolina sandbanks could make prize of an American ship that had just cleared for some port on the Elbe, even though no British warship was on patrol anywhere near the mouth of that river. The fee-and-permit business could be classed as a gratuitous insult.

Napoleon retaliated as soon as he heard about this order, and the American shipping community suffered even more. In November 1806 he issued the Decree of Berlin, which proclaimed a blockade of the British Isles—off whose shores no French cruiser dared show itself—outlawed all trade in British goods, and (supplemented a year later by the Decree of Milan) held that no vessel which had touched at a British port could be received in any port under French control. These decrees were about as expensive to American shippers as the British order in council; a host of French privateers infested the waters near the French coast to snap up all American ships that came within range, and some were confiscated while anchored in French ports. The matter grew even worse when the British retaliated in January 1807 with another order in council forbidding neutral ships to sail from one port to another if those ports were so far under French control that British merchantmen could not visit them. This hit the Americans with especial force as they often sailed from port to port in Europe seeking markets or looking for a pay load to take back home.

Both the British and the French were proclaiming paper blockades, illegal in ordinary times, adopted now by a win-the-war desperation that made all weapons legal. America would have found little to choose between the two ruthless tyrannies that were closing the oceans to her, except that the royal navy was continuing that abomination that outweighed all the others: the practice of impressment.

When British merchantmen entered home ports press gangs would come aboard and take some of the sailors for the navy. Merchant ships were stopped at sea for the same purpose. Under British law a Briton remained a Briton all his life, and the cruisers that overhauled American merchantmen looking for contraband often seized any sailors who, in the opinion of the officer in charge of the boarding party, were of British origin. (The officer's opinion was final and there was no appeal.) All of this was utterly at odds with the American belief that an American citizen was free from British control when he was not actually on British territory.

For the victim of impressment, life in the royal navy was several degrees worse than life in a penitentiary—with, as Dr. Johnson remarked, the added chance of being drowned. The food was appallingly bad, living conditions were on a level with the food, discipline was ferocious, and many sailors spent years without shore leave because their captains feared, quite justifiably, that if they once got off the ship they would never come back. A British deserter, knowing no other trade than that of sailor, would naturally want to go to sea again, and over the years increasing numbers shipped on American merchantmen. A good many of these, used to the man-o'-war's life, finally enlisted in the American navy, where the food and general level of treatment were better than anything in the royal navy. Probably there was not an American warship that did not have British deserters on its rolls. Under American law these men became United States citizens when they enlisted and took the oath; by British law they remained British to the day of death.

The royal navy knew of course that British deserters helped man American warships, and decided not to put up with it. When the royal navy makes up its mind not to put up with something it takes direct, unmistakable action. Accordingly—

Morning of June 22, 1807; U.S.S. *Chesapeake,* 36 guns, Captain James Barron, left her anchorage at Hampton Roads and sailed out through the Virginia capes on a routine peacetime cruise, her decks still cluttered with stores not yet struck below, no guns loaded, everyone intent on making sail and getting to sea. She passed Lynnhaven Bay, just inside Cape Henry, and perceived a British squadron at anchor there; two French cruisers were lying off Annapolis, one hundred miles up the bay, and the British were waiting for them. As *Chesapeake* went out, H.M.S. *Leopard,* 50 guns, detached herself from the British squadron, quietly cleared for action, and sailed in pursuit; hailed *Chesapeake* and demanded that she stop while a small boat came over with a message. Barron complied, and the boat and message arrived—an order from Vice-Admiral Berkeley, British commander in North American waters, requiring *Chesapeake* to heave to so that an armed guard might search her to see whether she harbored British deserters, who, if found, would immediately be arrested and taken back to England. Barron indignantly refused, whereupon *Leopard* opened fire, slamming in several broadsides, inflicting twenty-one casualties and causing extensive damage to hull and rigging. *Chesapeake* was in no shape to make a fight of it, what with coiled hawsers and bales of dry goods stacked at random on her gun deck. Barron made a frantic effort, managed to get one gun cleared and loaded, fired it, and then struck his flag. The British sent a party aboard and extracted four men whom it designated deserters from the royal navy. *Leopard* then sailed away, leaving *Chesapeake* to limp back to Hampton Roads.

This was the turning point. Freedom of the seas was an abstraction about which most Americans neither knew nor cared a great deal, but all Americans were pugnaciously touchy about national independence. Paper blockades and orders in council were resented not so much because they caused financial loss as because they implied that America was not really an independent nation. Now, suddenly, the old unendurable arrogance was in view once more. Continental congresses, continental armies and finally continental unity once came into being because of it; here it was again, the essence of everything America had rebelled against. If this action stood there was going to be war.

Yet war was delayed for five years. Thomas Jefferson was no apostle of non-resistance but he could add—warships, soldiers, military assets in general—and he thought there might be a better way to assert American rights than to fight against overpowering odds. He decided to apply economic sanctions, transferring the struggle to a field where his country had genuine power. In December 1807 Congress at his instigation passed the Embargo Act, which in substance suspended foreign trade. If England and

France were trying to destroy American trade, America would reply by abolishing that trade altogether. She would export and import nothing. England and France desperately needed American goods—and in England's case the American market as well —and perhaps this would force them to adopt milder tactics.

Perhaps. The trouble was that economic sanctions were most expensive and difficult to apply. There was a good deal of leakage —some ships slipped out despite the law, the ancient art of smuggling was revived (by experts), and there was a good deal of funny business by shippers who got papers for coastal voyages and then slipped over to British or French markets—which weakened the effect of the law overseas. At home it produced a sharp economic depression, and in New England there was a revival of embittered Federalism, and bankers and merchants began denouncing Jefferson with all the blind venom of economic royalists denouncing Franklin Roosevelt a century and a quarter later. The thing simply did not work. It became clear that to enforce the act rigidly would call for a most un-Jeffersonian interference with the doings of individual citizens. Some of this interference was in fact applied, much to the resentment of shippers whose vessels or warehouses were targets of federal search and seizure. England and France seemed unshaken, New England Federalists were talking openly about secession—and obviously the Embargo had to go.

This did not mean a political victory for the Federalists. The South and West continued to support the Republicans, and the popularity of the Louisiana Purchase helped make up for the unpopularity of the Embargo. James Madison was elected to succeed Jefferson when the latter's second term expired in 1808, and the Republicans were to enjoy sixteen more years in power; the Federalists, complaining bitterly, remained a vocal minority fated to wither and die on the vine, impotent outside of New England and not as strong there as they sounded. All that had happened was that an attempt to win respect for American independence by steps short of war had dissolved in failure. On

March 1, 1809, the Embargo Act was formally repealed. Three days later James Madison became President.

It was fairly apparent that America was going to go to war, even more apparent that when war came—as it did before the end of Madison's first term—it would be a war against Britain. In his interference with American sea-borne trade Napoleon was as high-handed as London, his interference as costly to American shippers, but Britain aroused the anger that made men want to fight. Impressment was not costly; it was just intolerable, and *Leopard-Chesapeake* made it unforgettable, resented in the trans-Allegheny West as much as in the seagoing East. The West as a matter of fact had its own grievance against Great Britain, and in the end the strongest pressure for war came from there.

In the West things had looked so bright. Clear through the rich Northwest Territory, across the Mississippi, and on to the magically unknown country that ran to the crest of the Rockies, a continent lay at America's disposal—except that it did not seem possible to go ahead and possess it. William Henry Harrison, governor of the Northwest Territory, burst out in angry complaint: "Is one of the fairest portions of the globe to remain in a state of nature, the haunt of a few wretched savages, when it seems destined by the Creator to give support to a large population and to be the seat of civilization, of science and of true religion?" The border line set by the Greenville Treaty of 1795, in which the Indians had ceded certain lands north of the Ohio, was breaking down, and Harrison had recently acquired for the United States an insecure title to 2,500,000 acres in the Wabash Valley—but the wretched savages were refusing to get out of the way.

Their refusal was inspired and voiced by Tecumseh, a Shawnee chief who was one of the sturdiest and canniest leaders of men the North American tribes ever produced. Dimly visible behind Tecumseh, giving him encouragement and support, were the British, who wanted to retain their monopoly on the fur trade and also hoped to see the establishment of an Indian nation that would block America's way to the Louisiana country. As far as the West-erners were concerned the outrage perpetrated by *Leopard* simply added fuel to a fire that was already burning briskly. All of this was in James Madison's mind when he delivered his inaugural ad-dress.

His speech was guarded; he spoke of "the peculiar solemnity of the existing period" and remarked that American efforts to keep the peace and meet the obligations of neutrality had been thwarted by the belligerents, who were behaving in a manner "equally contrary to universal reason and acknowledged law." He did not say, however, what ought to be done next, although he was clear in his own mind that America was going to have to fight someone—perhaps Britain, perhaps France, depending on how those nations acted now that the embargo had ended. He lost little time letting them know that he felt that way.

Repealing the Embargo Act, Congress had passed a Non-In-tercourse Act, which prohibited the importation of French or British goods but authorized the President to suspend this ban on imports against whichever nation would stop violating Ameri-can commercial rights. Madison notified the American ministers to Great Britain and France that Congress would meet in May to consider the situation, voicing his belief that if either nation re-pealed or materially relaxed its restrictions Congress would "au-thorize acts of hostility on the part of the United States against the other." The ministers were authorized to tell their hosts what was afoot, and the same information was given to David Erskine, British minister in Washington.

For a short time it looked as if Madison had won a great success. Erskine sent word that he had new instructions from London; Britain would revoke the orders in council if America would repeal that part of the Non-Intercourse Act that applied to Britain. Madison accepted this as authentic, and on April 19, 1809, he announced that Erskine, "by the order and in the name of his sovereign," had declared that the orders in council would have been revoked by June 10; so he, James Madison, had set June 10 as the day on which United States trade with Great Britain should be resumed.

Much rejoicing. Madison became briefly popular even in New England, and a whole fleet of merchantmen spread their wings and followed the westerlies to the British Isles.

Then came the letdown. There had been a mix-up somewhere; Foreign Secretary George Canning announced that Erskine had exceeded his powers and was being recalled, and said that the orders would be revised in no essential particular. Madison had to recall his announcement—scores of American ships, bearing goods that Britain needed very badly, had already docked in British ports—and a most iridescent bubble was cruelly punctured. Britain sent over a new minister, one Francis James Jackson, widely known as a hatchet man for the Foreign Office—that is, he was usually assigned to a country earmarked for some unpleasant experience. He had a genuine flair for being offensive; 150 years later a British historian commented that "it is impossible to imagine a more disastrous British representative in the United States."

In his message to Congress in the fall of 1809 Madison pointed to one good side effect: dependence on foreign supplies, principally manufactured goods, was declining. America was learning to make things for herself. Ironworks, tin and copper mills, plants for making textiles and glass and paper, even shops to make such machine tools as were needed in those days, were beginning to appear. They were not numerous, but they were significant, and they appeared not only in New England and New York but also in western Pennsylvania, even in parts of Ohio and Kentucky.

This was encouraging. American self-confidence rose, and a

perky belligerence along with it—coupled, strangely, with a refusal to prepare for the war that clearly was coming. In 1810 Madison found it impossible to get a proper defense budget. For one thing, Secretary Gallatin pointed out that the country could not afford an increase in military spending. Beyond that, the Republicans did not really believe in a standing army or navy. On land the militia could do the job, on sea the privateers plus the spirit of John Paul Jones and the guidance of a thoughtful Providence. The logical move to accompany a drift toward war by a preparation for war was not made.

One thing Congress did do: it passed a bill brought forward by Representative Nathaniel Macon of North Carolina, which subtly modified the Non-Intercourse Act. The new act removed trade restrictions and invited the two belligerents to do likewise, declaring that if one side did this while the other did not, America would stop trading with the offender. Not wholly invisible behind it was the tacit offer of an alliance—with Britain, if she would go America's way; otherwise, with France.

Britain had no intention of repealing the orders in council, and made the fact clear. Napoleon, however, saw the opening and reached out for it, characteristically turning his act into a sleight-of-hand performance. In August 1810 his government formally notified the American minister that, inasmuch as America had canceled her Non-Intercourse Act, "the decrees of Berlin and Milan are revoked, and that after the first of November they will cease to have effect; it being understood that in consequence of this declaration the English revoke their Orders in Council and renounce the new principles of blockade . . . or that the Americans shall cause their rights to be respected by the English."

Napoleon thus was accepting much and promising little. The thing amounted to a trap, and John Quincy Adams, America's minister to Russia, warned Madison about it; but Madison accepted it at face value, hoping that he might thus win some concessions from the British. What he wanted was fairly simple:

reparation for the *Leopard-Chesapeake* outrage and repeal or sharp modification of the orders in council. So he went ahead, making public announcement that France had lifted trade restrictions and that Britain had not, and that accordingly the Non-Intercourse Act would go into effect against the latter nation on March 2, 1811.

With spring came a fresh complication.

American merchantmen sailed for Europe in response to Napoleon's lifting of trade restrictions, and British cruisers fanned out along the American coast to stop them. Madison sent warships out to protect American rights, at least in American waters, and on a spring evening Commodore John Rodgers in the frigate *President* spotted a British man-o'-war and sailed after her to see what she was up to. The two craft came together just as darkness fell, confused ship-to-ship hails brought no identification, someone fired a gun—to this day no one is sure which ship fired it—and at last there was an exchange of broadsides and a vicious sea fight that ended forty-five minutes later with the British vessel staggering out of action. It turned out that she was the 20-gun corvette *Little Belt,* no match for the powerful *President,* and she was all but wrecked, with thirty-two men dead or wounded. Each side insisted that the other was the aggressor, and Rodgers carefully explained that in the darkness he had not known his opponent was a mere corvette. He was not sorry he had fought; he just did not want to be accused of attacking someone too small to make a good fight.

So the last hope that there might be reparation for the attack on *Chesapeake* vanished, and with it, piece by piece, went the hope that America's argument with Great Britain might be settled by quiet men shuffling papers around a table in a room where nobody raised his voice. Violence: in the crashing broadsides Americans perceived a rough and wholly satisfying justice. Public patience was at an end.

As if a dark conclusion had been reached offstage, William

Henry Harrison in November 1811 moved in on Tecumseh's Indians along the Tippecanoe River in Indiana (in Tecumseh's absence), won a victory, destroyed the Indians' chief village, and gained a nickname that he would ride to the White House nearly three decades later. . . . Years of frustration and impotent anger found an outlet at last in the smashing of *Little Belt* and the destruction of a Shawnee village.

When congressmen chosen in the fall elections of 1810 met in Washington at the end of 1811 it was obvious that the men who actively wanted war—the War Hawks, they were called—were much stronger than they had been earlier, not so much by a great increase in numbers as by the election of some vigorous, able young leaders, notably Henry Clay of Kentucky and John C. Calhoun of South Carolina. Clay became Speaker of the House of Representatives, giving to that office the prestige and the potential for leadership it has had ever since, and he began to put the demand for war into focus. More and more, this demand centered on the need to end British domination in the West. It began to be coupled with demands for the conquest of Canada.

There was precedent for this idea of gaining new territory. The long West Florida panhandle, running along the Gulf Coast clear to New Orleans, was owned by Spain, which was falling into sad disarray. America had long claimed West Florida as properly going with the Louisiana Purchase, and in 1810 Madison had quietly taken over enough of it to round out the present state of Louisiana. Now America wanted the rest of it. And if Florida, why not Canada? The Westerners grew enthusiastic about the idea.

There may have been more froth than substance to this. Men like Madison and Clay probably wanted Canada only as a counter in a game, a means of forcing Britain once and for all to stop blocking American westward expansion. Once suitable peace terms had been reached, Canada could be given up. America would be busy enough without it.

But there was a powerful resurgence of heady nationalism, rising to a point where anything seemed possible. Americans were beginning to believe not merely in themselves but also in their future, which had come to look real, indefinable but boundless, and the belief pulled them on through greed and folly, cruelty and war, to an unstained magnificence lying just beyond the western horizon.

And at last the countdown began.

CHAPTER 22

Dawn's Early Light

IN APRIL 1812 Congress voted to impose a ninety-day embargo. If there was going to be war there seemed no point in letting Britain stock up on American supplies. Shortly after this the British minister notified Madison that there was no prospect that the orders in council would be rescinded, and on June 1 Madison asked Congress to declare war.

The House, firmly under Clay's control, acted promptly, voting for war on June 4. The Senate took longer, and spent some time debating a quaint proposal that the country declare war on both Britain and France together; rejected the idea at last, and on June 17 voted for war with England, 19 to 13. Madison signed the resolution next day and the war was on.

It entered to a devastating note of irony.

All along Madison had hoped that economic sanctions would compel Britain to respect American rights. He finally concluded that this was impossible, demanded and got a declaration of war —at precisely which moment the British government caved in. On June 16, one day before the Senate voted, Britain's new foreign secretary, Lord Castlereagh, announced that the orders in council would be lifted immediately as far as America was concerned.

If there had been a transatlantic cable in 1812 things might have gone differently, but of course there was not; it took from one to two months for news to cross the Atlantic, and the only result of this just-too-late concession was to leave some good men on both sides wondering what the new war was all about.

It is easy to show that the War of 1812 was totally meaningless. The principal cause was removed before the war started and the bloodiest battle was fought after the war ended; the peace treaty never mentioned any of the issues that had led to war in the first place, and in the end the two nations agreed to turn the clock back and restore the situation that had existed before the war began. If there could be magic in words solemnly put down on paper this war would be as if it had never been fought.

But it *was* fought, and its overall effect was anything but meaningless. Wars rarely go as planned and they never leave a situation the way they find it; they invariably defy all attempts to turn the clock back, and at the very least they bring an unpredictable illogic into the sober processes of history. So this war that need not have occurred became one of America's most significant experiences. It ended one era and began another. It changed the way Americans thought about themselves and their future; after it was over they talked increasingly about their "destiny" and turned what had been a soaring dream into solid belief. Until now they had merely hoped that someday their country would do great things. Hereafter they simply expected it.

Ineffective moves toward peace were made the day after the war began when the British minister, Augustus Foster, called on Madison to suggest that hostilities be suspended until the American declaration of war was received in London; he himself would take it there, along with any proposition the President cared to submit. Madison pointed out that this war had been declared by Congress, and he as President could not exactly suspend it—but he added that the American chargé d'affaires in London, Jonathan

Russell, would stay there to act as U.S. agent for prisoners, and America would be glad to have the secretary of the British Legation remain in Washington on the same basis. That, said Foster, could hardly be; still, two American seamen who had been snatched from U.S.S. *Chesapeake* were going to be returned—at last, five years late!—and the secretary could stay in Washington to handle that business. So a thin but potentially useful channel of communication would remain open.

All of which was slightly fantastic. Before the war was a week old the two governments were trying to stop it; were at least thinking about stopping it and setting up machinery that could be used if they actually meant to stop it. Nobody in America knew that Britain had repealed the orders in council and the American declaration of war had effectively canceled the repeal anyway, so that both sides would have to begin all over, but the climate seemed to be good. If both the orders and impressment could be abandoned Madison felt that an armistice and a lasting peace were quite possible.

Unfortunately, Britain had no intention of giving up impressment; unfortunately, also, Western America had no intention of calling off the projected assault on Canada, which might or might not end in annexation but which if successful would enable the Republic to sweep the Indians out of the way of westward expansion. Furthermore, neither side had any notion that it could possibly lose this war.

The British case rested squarely on the royal navy, largest and strongest the world had ever seen, with more than 600 warships in service, including 120 ships of the line and 116 frigates. Most of these were busy enough in European waters, but the American navy hardly seemed worth considering; it contained a total of 16 vessels (of which several needed a major overhaul before they would be of service), no ships of the line at all, and a "first line," if that expression could be used, consisting of three 44-gun frigates and three more of 38 guns. At best, such a navy could be no more than a minor nuisance to the world's greatest sea power. The

American Secretary of the Navy, who was both an alcoholic and a pessimist, suggested in early 1812 that if war came the best thing to do with these ships was to put them in a safe navy yard and take them out of commission before somebody sank them. He seemed to be talking sense. The only people who disagreed with him were a few ardent naval officers and President James Madison.

On land the case looked different. The United States contained six million white people (black folk and the red folk who originally owned this land not being counted) and Canada had only 500,000, of whom scarcely a fifth lived in Upper Canada, or Ontario. From Montreal to Fort Malden at the western end of Lake Erie the Canadian frontier was some 650 miles long; from Fort Malden north to the mouth of the St. Mary's River at the top of Lake Huron it was 300 more. To hold this long line Britain had some 4,000 British regulars and 3,000 Canadian regulars, together with as many militia as they could get: 3,000 by close figuring, although the estimate was not at all solid. Seven thousand troops, then, to start with; of these only 1,700 were in Upper Canada.

On the American side the figures looked better, as long as they were not examined too closely. Congress had recently voted to raise the regular army to a strength of 35,000, although because it specified five-year enlistments the new men came in slowly; when the war began the army contained rather fewer than 18,000, of whom 5,000 were raw recruits. The regulars were scattered all over the country. If Canada was to be molested the chief reliance would have to be on the militia, far outnumbering any force Canada could raise.

To a country brought up on the gorgeous memory of untrained farmers slaughtering the king's finest troops at Bunker Hill this was quite satisfactory. But there were certain angles.

What was needed was an outright invasion; specifically, an attack on Montreal, whose capture would automatically mean the fall of all Upper Canada. To take Montreal would require an army made up largely of militia. The best militia in the country, supposedly, and the nearest to the Montreal theater, was that of New England, and New England was Federalist in complexion and had little enthusiasm for what was already being called "Mr. Madison's War." Furthermore, there was a constitutional question—of which, as one who had had much to do with the writing of the Constitution, James Madison was acutely aware. The Constitution said that the state militia could be called into federal service to execute the laws, to suppress insurrection, and to repel invasion. To invade Canada?

Looking foggily ahead to war, Congress had shown one gleam of foresight; it had authorized a volunteer corps, to be enlisted in the states with the President empowered to name the officers. This, it was argued, in addition to making it possible to by-pass local magnificoes who wanted military fame, converted the volunteers into regulars, at least to the extent that they could be sent across the international boundary without running afoul of the Constitution. But the only levies immediately available were the state militia. Massachusetts was urged to send a force to defend the frontier in case Britain launched an invasion, and difficulties arose. Governor Caleb Strong referred the question to the state Supreme Court, which evolved a delightful ruling: the President indeed had power to call out militia to repel invasion, but he did not have power to determine when invasion was threatened. This could be done only by the militia's proper commander, the governor. If he held (as in this case he did) that no invasion was threatened, the militia could not be called into federal service.

So a shadow lay across the bright dream of a patriot army sweeping the British away from the Lakes, the St. Lawrence, and the great wilderness to the west. It grew deeper when one looked at the human elements involved. Secretary of War was Dr. William

Eustis of Massachusetts, an estimable gentleman who was totally lacking in energy and administrative ability; a fatal defect, inasmuch as the entire War Department consisted of the Secretary and eight clerks, who had to build, organize, supply, and direct the force that must be raised and so needed energy and administrative ability in vast quantities. Congress had recently refused to create two assistant secretaries, probably because it distrusted Secretary Eustis so much that it saw no sense in strengthening any department he controlled.

Senior officer in the army was Major General Henry Dearborn, who had been Secretary of War under Jefferson and who was now turning sixty; a good man, regrettably past his prime. Before the war Madison had told him that the grand strategy called for an offensive against Montreal, with subsidiary offensives on the Detroit and Niagara rivers and at the foot of Lake Ontario, where the British had a naval base at Kingston. Dearborn agreed, opened an office at Albany, and then went to Boston where he spent two months perfecting coast defenses and consulting with New England governors about the help which they did not propose to provide. A month after war was declared he wrote plaintively to Secretary Eustis confessing that he did not know the extent of his authority or the field of his command. (He commanded everything along the Canadian border, from Maine to Michigan, and controlled everybody in it; he had never thought to ask about it before, nor had Eustis thought to tell him.)

The British were quite willing to see him dawdle. The high command just then was Lieutenant General Sir George Prevost, Governor of Lower Canada and also governor general and commander-in-chief of all the provinces. He did not think the projected American offensive was going to amount to much, and he saw no point in hasty action. He therefore sent Dearborn a flag of truce proposing an armistice: he had just learned about London's last-minute repeal of the orders in council and it seemed to him that the chief reason for fighting had vanished. Dearborn, who may have felt the same way, agreed to act on the defensive until he heard from Washington.

When he learned about this Madison promptly annulled the armistice and told Dearborn to get on with the war; specifically, to take the British posts at Niagara and Kingston in order to protect his flank when he advanced on Montreal. Dearborn notified Prevost that the deal was off and took thought for the offensive . . . but the campaign in the East was hardly being pushed with vigor.

What would be done in the West would be up to another aging officer, Major General William Hull, Governor of Michigan Territory and commander of the Army of the Northwest. A Revolutionary War veteran, Hull suspected that the British would move against the forts at Detroit and Mackinac in order to strengthen their influence over the Indians, who were following Tecumseh in the dark belief that American settlement in the West had to be stopped. It seemed to Hull that if the British tried to do these things they would probably succeed; what happened in the Northwest would depend entirely on naval control of the Lakes, and the British had a fleet on Lake Erie whereas the Americans had nothing at all. Against logic, Hull hoped that if he held Detroit with a strong army the lack of a fleet would not matter much.

A strong army the government tried to give him. The governor of Ohio, one Return Jonathan Meigs, raised 1,200 volunteers, and these were joined by the 4th U.S. Infantry; Hull took command in Ohio, some weeks before the war began, and set off for Detroit.

Taking an army to Detroit in those days, if one could not go by boat on Lake Erie, was almost impossible. There was no road, so Hull's men had to build one as they went, Western woodsmen going in advance to blaze a trail. From the mouth of the Maumee to the upper part of the River Raisin in Michigan lay an almost impassable swamp: mile after soggy mile of it, the bottom of some lake in prehistoric times, looking as if it would need little encouragement to become a lake bottom once again. To march an army with wagon train and artillery across forty miles of this muck was all but impossible. At the falls of the Maumee (fifteen miles above present-day Toledo) Hull chartered a schooner, which he loaded with supplies and headquarters papers and sent off to Detroit. Thus lightened, corduroying roads as it went, his army floundered through to Frenchtown at the mouth of the Raisin, where the town of Monroe now stands. It got there on July 2 and learned that war had been declared; also that Hull's schooner had been captured, which meant that the British now knew all about his strength, his plans, and his orders.

Hull reached Detroit three days later, and after getting established he took two regiments across the river, captured the town of Sandwich, and announced that he would soon attack Fort Malden, the strong point vitally needed by the British fleet on Lake Erie. Then he began to worry. His supply line was long and vulnerable, and the idea of seizing Fort Malden grew dim. Hull's mind centered on the business of holding Detroit and getting more supplies from Ohio.

It was a bad time to fumble, because the permissive system under which General Prevost was allowing General Dearborn to operate in the East did not prevail in the West. The British war effort here was directed by a soldier of intelligence and vigor— Major General Isaac Brock, Governor of Upper Canada. He was under Prevost's orders, but communications were so slow that Brock had two or three months to operate according to his own ideas. He used them.

Meanwhile Hull had developed the vapors. He took refuge in the Detroit fortifications, forgot about Fort Malden, sent an inadequate force to the River Raisin to rescue a supply party sent up by Governor Meigs, saw this party driven back by a mixed force of British and Indians—and learned that the British had captured Mackinac Island.

Before the commander at Mackinac even knew that the war

had begun Brock sent a force against him—500 Indians and Canadian militia stiffened by a few companies of regulars with two field pieces, organized at a British outpost on St. Joseph Island in the St. Mary's River. They sailed past Mackinac in the darkness, landed on the western side of the island, marched across it during the night, and occupied a hilltop overlooking the fort. Fort Mackinac resembled the more elaborate fort the British built years later at Singapore—invulnerable to attack by sea, defenseless against a land attack.

So Lieutenant Porter Hanks, commanding at Mackinac, awoke on the morning of July 17, 1812, to see a hostile force in his rear placed where it could shoot him out of the fort without difficulty. The British sent in a note demanding surrender, thoughtfully adding that if the place had to be stormed the Indian allies, always hard to control, would probably kill and scalp every prisoner. Hanks surrendered, there being nothing else he could do, the Indians restrained themselves, and the northern key to American control of the upper Lakes dropped out of sight.

This was exactly what Hull had been afraid of. He suspected (correctly) that it would activate a host of red men on his flank and rear, and he sent word to Captain Nathan Held, commanding Fort Dearborn, where Chicago is now, ordering him to evacuate the fort and march east with all speed. Held obeyed, setting out on August 15. He had gone but a few miles when 500 Potawatomi warriors attacked, killing half of his party and taking the rest prisoner.

Meanwhile Brock reached the Detroit River in person. He met Tecumseh, with whom he hit it off at once—as fighting men these two were cut from the same pattern—and then crossed the river to attack Detroit. He had a force of 700 regulars and militia, less than a third the size of Hull's command. But Tecumseh and his Indians were visibly present, Hull by now was at a low ebb and on August 15 Brock demanded surrender. He added that if he had to fight for the place the Indians would be totally out of control.

Hull gave up, and on August 16 the flag came down and the British marched in, taking 2,500 prisoners. They sent the regulars off to prison camps in Lower Canada but released the volunteers on parole, and Brock announced that he considered the whole Michigan Territory to be British soil once more.

—□—

So here was a humiliating end to all the fine talk. Instead of taking Canada, America in two months had lost the West—lost it in ignominy, too, with a senile general giving up an army he had not even put into battle. Now the Administration might lose the presidential election this fall. Madison had been nominated by confident congressional Republicans in caucus; running against him was another Republican, De Witt Clinton of New York, nominated by his state legislature but also supported by the die-hard New England Federalists, who knew they had no chance of winning without New York and that they could not possibly carry New York with any of their own men. They were beginning to beat the drums. When they heard about Detroit the drums would beat much louder.

It took time for news from the interior to reach the seacoast. Detroit fell on August 16, but nobody in the East knew about it until well on in September . . . and on August 30 U.S. *Constitution*, Old Ironsides in wood and canvas, battle flags at her mastheads and honorable scars on her decks and bulwarks, came sailing into Boston bearing as prisoners Captain James Dacres and the other survivors of H.M.S. *Guerrière*, which had struck her colors after a sharp fight and had gone to the bottom of the Atlantic next day, *Constitution*'s Captain Isaac Hull having found her too badly damaged to bring home.

Here was a triumph to set the country ablaze, brought into the heartland of disgruntled Federalism—which also happened to be the place of all American places most certain to appreciate and exult in a victory at sea. The royal navy simply did not lose single-ship actions . . . but it had lost this one in the most dramatic way imaginable, with the king's ship a mastless hulk rolling her bulwarks under at the close of action while Yankee sailors (including, just possibly, a few British deserters whom the press gangs had missed) transferred the survivors to the victor's decks before setting fire to the wrecked craft, which at last blew up and sank when the flames reached her magazine. Here was a splendid offset to the news from the West. Fittingly, Captain Hull was nephew to the general who surrendered at Detroit.

Constitution's victory vindicated the American navy, which had managed to acquire a distinctive character despite the prevailing democratic dogma that standing armies and navies were menaces to the people's liberties and rallying points for tyranny. The peacetime army had been kept small, a thin force of regulars to be fleshed out with militia in wartime. The same idea applied to the navy: maintain a few regular warships, and in war fill the gaps with privateers. But somehow the men who wanted to make a real navy had established two guiding principles from the start: American warships should be bigger, faster, and stronger than their counterparts in foreign navies. Also: when war came they must *fight*.

Thus the big frigates, of which the Republic had just three— *Constitution, Constellation, United States*—were unquestionably the strongest frigates afloat. Rated at 44 guns, they actually mounted more than 50; they were twenty feet longer than British vessels of the same class, they were "sharp built" and hence fast, they had what amounted to a complete spar deck over the gun deck, and in addition to the 30 long 24-pounders in the main battery they carried some 20 42-pounder carronades topside, plus two long 24s on forecastle for chase guns. This armament was too heavy, put a great strain on the hull, and harmed sailing qualities —but at close range that spar deck full of carronades had a fearful smashing power, and if *Guerrière* was dismasted and destroyed in a brief fight there was reason for it.

Along with this went the conviction that the officer corps

should have a high sense of duty and responsibility. This belief was rigidly followed, and it supported the first principle: where American craft were basically no stronger than their British rivals, at the level of brigs and sloops of war, they were better served. American officers quickly trained their crews—having generally better material to work with than the shoreside flotsam the press gangs brought to the British fleet—and when the war came the American ships had abler gunners and as fighting machines were superior simply because they were better manned.

This was good as far as it went, but the royal navy still had an overwhelming superiority in numbers, including all those line-of-battle ships; *Constitution* might be the best frigate afloat, but she could not hope to stand up to a British 74, and no American officer deceived himself about it. Two of the best of them, Captains John Rodgers and Stephen Decatur, had worked out a plan in advance: when war came, take what ships were at hand, form two squadrons, and send them far out across the ocean, even into British home waters. The effect might be to lighten the blockade along the American coast; privateers and the navy's brigs and sloops could get out, and the mistress of the seas might find the war unexpectedly troublesome. Secretary of the Navy Paul Hamilton, who had suggested hiding the navy before the British fleet hurt it, demurred and found himself overruled by President Madison, who expressed confidence in the navy; it did not have many ships, but "it would do its duty."

Madison talked to some of the fire-eating officers, who said they believed they could win any single-ship action, but the winning ship might be so knocked about that it would be unable to escape if it met a superior British force. Was the President prepared to face that? The President was. "It is victories we want," he said. "Give us them and lose your ships afterward. They can be replaced by others."

So when war came Hamilton made out orders along the lines proposed by Rodgers and Decatur, and on June 22 these orders were issued. There would be two squadrons—*President* and *Hor-*

net, under Rodgers, and *United States, Congress,* and *Argus* under Decatur. Rodgers sailed from New York, Decatur from the Virginia capes, both squadrons bound east; now the British would have to protect their own shipping and could not concentrate so heavily along the American coast, and more American merchantmen could come and go. (Quaintly enough, many of these American ships were supplying Wellington's army in Spain with its food, and others did the same for the British army in Canada. The British had no desire to stop this trade, War of 1812 or no, and their blockade of New England, where most of the supplies came from, was kept noticeably porous even before the voyages of Rodgers and Decatur.)

While those little American squadrons were on their way, Hull in *Constitution,* which had been fitting out in the Chesapeake, sailed for New York to join Rodgers and instead ran into a powerful British squadron—one ship of the line, four frigates, and two lighter craft. There followed a two-day flight for life, in which the wind died entirely, leaving the ships immobilized. Get out the small boats, then, and try towing; also try kedging: carry an anchor far ahead of the vessel, drop it, work the windlass aboard ship until she came up with the anchor, and then repeat the process. . . . All very wearisome, and ultimately a losing game because the British could put several times as many men to work in the boats. *Constitution*'s crew was at the point of exhaustion, fresh water and other stores were thrown overboard to lighten ship—and finally, in a way Hollywood could not improve on, a wind sprang up, filled the American sails first, and enabled *Constitution* to get away and reach Boston. Taking on new stores, she put to sea again and met *Guerrière* in August.

All very well, and this greatly eased the pain created by the news from Detroit. The trouble was that all of the news from the army was bad. By the time the shameful business at the far end of Lake

Erie had been digested the Americans learned that there had been a low-comedy fiasco at the eastern end of the lake.

The British held the Canadian side of the Niagara River at either end: at Fort Erie, where the river flows out of Lake Erie, and at Fort George, where it enters Lake Ontario. A few miles upstream from Fort George was the town of Queenston. On the American side there was Buffalo on Lake Erie, with Black Rock a little downstream, and at the river's mouth on Lake Ontario there was Fort Niagara, with the town of Lewiston not far upstream. Halfway between the lakes were Niagara Falls and its gorge, which of course were impassable, but the river could be crossed easily in small boats both above and below those spectacular obstacles. If the Americans could take the British forts and hold the river crossings they could control the eastern end of Lake Erie and the western end of Lake Ontario, which might lead to the recovery of what Hull had given up.

Nothing worked. General Dearborn, busy farther east, had entrusted the command here to Major General Stephen Van Rensselaer, a distinguished citizen of New York who had had no military experience. Second in command was Brigadier General Alexander Smyth, a regular, a former member of the Virginia legislature, an orator of repute but a soldier of no consequence, whose one enduring distinction is that eventually he was retired from the army by special act of Congress.

By October there were 6,000 American troops on the Niagara line. They had little discipline, skimpy supplies, and abominable leadership, and across the river there was General Brock. He had only 1,600 soldiers and 300 Indians, but unlike the Americans he knew what he was doing. He waited attentively now, watching his enemy.

Van Rensselaer planned a two-handed attack. One force would cross from Lewiston and go north to take the high ground at Queenston Heights; at the same time Smyth would cross at the river's mouth, capture Fort George, and strike the rear of the British defending Queenston Heights. The upstream force, somewhat skeletonized, went over on schedule and made good progress, partly because of the presence of two young regular officers who assumed leadership after the commander was shot— Captain John Wool and a towering lieutenant colonel named Winfield Scott. Downstream, however, nothing happened; Smyth thought the attack ought to be made above the falls, did not think a mere militia general like Van Rensselaer had any business giving him orders, and as a result did not move at all.

The British inevitably won this battle. Smyth's inactivity enabled them to bring up a strong relief force from Fort George; the American militia on the New York side, watching what was going on, were ordered to cross and help and remarked that under the Constitution they were not obliged to fight on foreign soil, and did not stir; and the men who had taken Queenston Heights were surrounded and compelled to surrender. But it cost the British more than they could afford to pay; General Brock was killed in action, and the one man big enough to block America's drive in the West was removed from the scene. General Van Rensselaer, whose men were deserting in droves, asked to be relieved. General Smyth replaced him.

Smyth got enough Pennsylvania militiamen to bring the army's strength back to about what it was before this fight. Early in November he acted. He got 400 men across above the falls, moved them here and there, and then brought them back again. Then he scheduled a new crossing by the entire command, canceled it, ordered it afresh, canceled it again, ordered still another, postponed it and finally called a council of war and announced that the invasion was put off until next spring.

Obviously nothing could be done with him. He resigned his command and went back to Virginia, and Congress passed an act suspending his old post of inspector general, thereby legislating him out of the army. He later ran for Congress, got elected, and found in that cave of the winds full scope for his oratorical talents. In Samuel Eliot Morison's words, "he continued to bray for many years."

The farce on the Niagara was played too late to affect the presidential election. Madison lost New York and other middle states, and all of New England except Vermont, but he carried Pennsylvania and the entire South and West and was handily re-elected. And when word of Smyth's ineptitude at last filtered back east, good news came once more from the navy to overshadow it.

First, sloop of war *Wasp* met the British brig *Frolic,* a vessel of her own rating, fought her in a rising gale, pounded her into wreckage, and forced her to strike her flag; that a British 74 came up while *Wasp* was repairing damage to her rigging and compelled her to surrender did not dampen the rejoicing—Madison had been warned about this, and had said that victories were vitally needed even if the victors did not survive to tell the story. Right after this came bigger news: Decatur in *United States* had beaten the new British frigate *Macedonian* and had brought her into port as a prize. Now the young navy could do what very few European navies could do—count a British-built warship, still wearing her British name, as a part of its own fleet. And in early January *Constitution,* now commanded by William Bainbridge, met the frigate *Java,* dismasted her, forced her to surrender, and then—as had happened with *Guerrière*—found her too badly shot up to bring into port and burned her. Finally, James Lawrence in the sloop of war *Hornet* beat the British brig *Peacock.* Striking her flag after a short, savage action, *Peacock* was so badly hurt that she sank soon afterward.

Something to crow about, indeed: five single-ship actions and five victories, in six months of war with the world's greatest sea power! The royal navy had lost some of its tail feathers and no little prestige, and a few of its troubles were self-induced. British officers knew perfectly well that ships like *Constitution* were superfrigates that should be avoided; but an incurable arrogance derided them as "fir-built" monstrosities too clumsy to be handled by colonials who lacked the tradition and the breeding to make proper naval officers, and anyway a captain in the royal navy who shied away from a single-ship action was endangering his whole career. So commanders like Dacres sailed blithely into certain destruction.

The Admiralty grew testy. At year's end Sir John Warren, commander-in-chief on the North American station, was curtly reminded that he had ninety-seven ships in his command, including eleven of the line, thirty-four frigates, and thirty-eight sloops; yet he had let those American frigates get out, not to mention a pestiferous cloud of privateers. British commerce had suffered painfully, and in home waters the Admiralty had had to divert six ships of the line and various frigates and sloops to protect the sea lanes. In the end, this produced a tight blockade of the American coast and a convoy system in transatlantic waters, all to the detriment of the American effort. Still, there was a heady flavor to the whole business that made Americans think they were winning the war even when most of the evidence pointed the other way.

Evidence pointing the other way was heavy and oppressive. The great campaign to take Canada had fizzled out completely. While the tale of misfortune was being compiled at both ends of Lake Erie, General Dearborn finally massed some 6,000 men at Plattsburg, New York—militia, mostly, with a detachment of regulars for stiffening—and in mid-November he moved out to the Canadian border, where Prevost sent 1,900 British and Canadian troops to meet him. Dearborn's regulars crossed the border, skirmished lightly with the enemy, and sent back for the militia when the redcoats drew away. As at Queenston, the militia clung to the constitutional safeguard and refused to cross the border. In the shifting back and forth that grew out of this the Americans fell into confusion and fired on some of their own detached parties; and at last, on November 23, the whole force retired. The regulars went into winter quarters at Plattsburg and Burlington, the militia went home, the campaign of 1812 was over, and nothing at all had been accomplished.

Clearly it was time for a shake-up. Secretary of War Eustis resigned, to be replaced after a brief interim by Brigadier General John Armstrong—self-willed, opinionated, hard to handle, but a man of driving energy unlikely to tolerate deadwood in the army command. Shortly afterward the navy also got a new Secretary, Paul Hamilton having resigned when Congress rejected his request for the building of some 74-gun line-of-battleships. (Congress did not like the idea of building battleships, for reasons deep-rooted and obscure; had refused to build battleships before the war, when the idea was most timely, and refused to build them now.) Hamilton was replaced by William Jones of Philadelphia, merchant and Revolutionary War veteran, a capable executive who believed in giving full support to the naval effort on the Lakes.

—□—

This was intelligent of him. Unless it was to accept outright defeat, America had to regain what had been lost in the West, and it could never do this without winning naval control of Lake Erie. The overland route was too tough, as Hull had discovered and as a far abler soldier, William Henry Harrison, was now in process of learning.

Kentucky, heart and center of the drive for westward expansion, had reacted vigorously to the news of Hull's surrender, making Harrison a major general of Kentucky militia and raising a substantial militia force for him to command. Endorsing this, Madison gave Harrison a general's commission in the regulars and made him commander of the Western Army. Harrison was strongly reinforced—the idea was that eventually he would have 10,000 men—and he set out for Detroit. But the autumn rains had begun, and that infernal swamp north of the Maumee became totally impassable for so large an army. He put up fortifications on the Maumee and settled down to wait for cold weather, when the ground might become solid enough for marching men and wheeled vehicles.

He was able to move in December, but an advance party that went on to establish a forward post at Frenchtown, on the Raisin, was snuffed out when the British commander, Colonel Henry Procter, brought 1,200 soldiers down to make a surprise attack across the snow in the dark hours before dawn. The entire party surrendered. Procter took his prisoners back to Fort Malden, leaving those who were too sick or wounded to march, some thirty or forty in all, at Frenchtown with Indians for guards; the Indians looted the American camp, found whiskey and drank it, and then slew all of the prisoners. Angry patriots had a new slogan: "Remember the River Raisin!"—but winter campaigning was out of the question. Harrison snuggled down as well as he could along the Maumee and waited for spring. His army dwindled as the terms of his militiamen began to expire.

If the overland route had once again proven a bottomless pit, the navy was already at work upon the alternative. In November 1812 Captain Isaac Chauncey was given top naval command on fresh water, and he started with Lake Ontario; his goal was to control the inland water routes between the United States and Canada—the only place on earth where America had a chance to establish naval superiority over Great Britain and the one place where the nation's existence might depend on its ability to gain and use that superiority.

Chauncey went to Sacket's Harbor, a lonely little port at the eastern end of Lake Ontario, to establish a naval base. With him went one of those indispensable men who come to the surface in wartime: Henry Eckford, a New York shipbuilder. Eckford brought a force of carpenters and riggers, had woodsmen cut timbers from the surrounding forest, set up building ways, and began to show a talent for building good ships in a hurry.

The struggle for dominance on Lake Ontario became largely a battle of shipwrights. For actual warships, Chauncey had *Oneida,* a 14-gun brig, to begin with; he captured a 12-gun Canadian schooner, renamed it *Scourge* and took it into his own force, got a number of light craft and gave them such arms as they were able to carry, and saw to it that Eckford got what he needed for his building program. North of the lake the royal navy took over from the Canadian Provincial Marine and put energetic Captain James Yeo in command. Yeo brought in shipwrights and matériel and set up two yards, one at Kingston near the eastern end of Lake Ontario and the other at York, then a modest provincial capital that would eventually become the city of Toronto.

Two yards, of course, could build ships faster than one yard, and this would upset the balance. Chauncey planned a blow at Kingston, abandoned the idea when he was informed (erroneously, as it happened) that the British had 6,000 men there, and settled instead for a raid on York. Dearborn provided 1,600 troops under a good regular, Brigadier General Zebulon Pike, Chauncey took such ships as he had, and on April 27, 1813, this force sailed up to York. The warships opened a bombardment while Pike took his men ashore and headed for the shipyard and its fortifications, which were weakly manned

. . . The trails west crossed at improbable places. Here was Zebulon Pike, most of whose professional career had been spent on the work that had to be done before America could possess the empire Thomas Jefferson had bought. He had led an expedition into northern Minnesota, looking for the headwaters of the Mississippi, and then he had scouted the great and perilous emptiness that stretched down toward Spanish Santa Fe, giving his name to a spectacular mountain peak in present-day Colorado and reporting that this southwestern country was a great American desert —an expression that clung, to be applied later to much of the trans-Missouri country. Now he was fighting in Upper Canada, still trying to clear the western trail and enable the Republic to use it. For Pike the trail ended right here. He stormed the fortifications and seized the shipyard, and then a magazine blew up and Pike and a number of his men were killed.

The Americans went on to destroy the shipyard, burn a half-completed frigate, and carry off a good deal of military booty, including thirty naval guns which British forces on the Lakes missed greatly a little later. The burned frigate might well have given Yeo control over Lake Ontario, and altogether the Americans had done a good day's work; but with Pike's death the troops got out of hand and went rampaging through the town of York, carrying torches and destroying, among other things, the modest buildings that housed the provincial government. This was a costly mistake; any Canadians inclined to side with the American cause were cured of that notion, and the idea of burning the enemy's Capitol came home to roost when the British occupied Washington a year later.

The immediate follow-up was more important. Chauncey took the American force over to the mouth of the Niagara and Colonel Winfield Scott (duly exchanged after his capture at Queenston Heights) led a column that captured Fort George. This caused the British to give up the whole Niagara line, abandoning Fort Erie and retreating to the neighborhood of present-day Hamilton. As a result, a modest American fleet at Black Rock —a corvette taken from the British in a daring cutting-out raid some months earlier, and a few lighter craft—was able to get out of the river and coast along the south shore of Lake Erie to the spacious harbor of Presque Isle, where the Pennsylvanians a few years earlier had built the town of Erie.

Here things were happening. A young naval officer named Oliver Hazard Perry, the sort for whom the word "dashing" was invented, sensing that there was going to be action on the Lakes, had asked Chauncey for a job. Chauncey sent him to Lake Erie to build a fleet, and Perry was now hard at work creating a naval base and rounding up timber for the shipwrights, who were under a New York builder named Noah Brown. Brown had certain assets: the harbor was spacious and well protected, and there was easy communication with Pittsburgh, which was beginning to be a supply center of some importance. A turnpike road, good by the standards of that time and place, led south from Erie over the height of land to a point on the upper Allegheny that could be reached by Ohio River keelboats, and the Pittsburgh foundries were already a useful source of ironwork, from anchors to cannonballs and guns. Pittsburgh also had shipyards and could supply workers for Noah Brown, and cordage, and western Pennsylvania could send up provisions, including excellent Monongahela grog.

There were drawbacks: chiefly the fact that the good harbor into which Perry and Brown would launch their new ships carried only six feet of water at its entrance. The only way to get the ships out was by means of "camels"—cumbersome barges, flooded until just barely awash, then lashed firmly to the ship's sides and pumped out; as they rose they would bring the ship up with them, and if she had been properly lightened beforehand, stripped of guns and stores and everything movable, ship and camels could be hauled over the bar into deep water. This, in turn, would be possible only if the British fleet stayed away, and the officer Yeo had sent to Lake Erie, Commander Robert H. Barclay, showed an annoying tendency to cruise not far off shore, keeping an eye on things.

Barclay had his own problems. He was short of men and supplies, and his strongest ship had no guns and could not well get any because of the losses at the York shipyard. In the end he armed her after a fashion by taking army guns from Fort Malden. He had to devote most of his attention to keeping the lake clear between the mouth of the Detroit River and Long Point, on the north shore, the beginning of an overland route to the British position at the western tip of Lake Ontario. This was most unsatisfactory but it was Britain's only supply line for her Western forces once Scott had occupied the Canadian side of the Niagara. Barclay did his best but he could not spend all of his time cruising off Presque Isle, and late in the spring of 1813 Perry got his ships over the bar, rearmed them, and sailed west to get in touch with General Harrison at Sandusky.

Like Barclay, Perry was short of men, and he made a deal with Harrison, getting a hundred Kentuckians who had never seen anything bigger than a Green River skiff but who went aboard Perry's fleet and became acceptable sailors. (In addition, some 25 per cent of Perry's crewmen were blacks. Their performance prompted him to remark that neither the cut of a man's coat nor the color of his skin was any indication of his worth—a truth that most white Americans would be an unconscionable time learning.)

Perry's two biggest ships were massive brigs built by Noah Brown at Erie, each bearing two long 12-pounders and eighteen 32-pounder carronades—*Niagara* and *Lawrence,* the latter name bearing a story. James Lawrence, after his notable victory in *Hornet,* had been given command of U.S.S. *Chesapeake.* It was this frigate which H.M.S. *Leopard* had overpowered off the Virginia capes in 1807, dragging away alleged deserters from the royal navy, and when Lawrence took her to sea early in 1813 her luck had not improved; off the New England coast she ran into H.M.S. *Shannon,* a crack ship under a crack commander, Philip Broke. *Chesapeake* was overwhelmed and captured, and Lawrence was mortally wounded; carried below to die, just before *Chesapeake* struck her flag, he cried despairingly, "Don't give up the ship!" and his words became a battle cry. Perry had them stitched on a banner which his flagship, *Lawrence,* wore at her masthead; and early in September 1813 he took his fleet out of its anchorage at Put-in Bay and sailed to intercept Barclay, who was cruising to Long Point.

Along with *Lawrence* and *Niagara,* Perry had the brig *Caledonia,* armed with three pivot guns, and six lightly armed schooners. Barclay had six warships in all, and although Perry's fleet, relying largely on carronades, would have the advantage at close quarters Barclay had more long guns and could fight more effectively at long range. On the almost windless morning of September 10 the fleets sighted each other and drifted slowly into action.

The Americans got off to a bad start. Somehow *Niagara* held back when Perry took *Lawrence* in to fight at close range, and the American flagship was surrounded, engaged in a thunderous duel close up with most of the British fleet. She was all but wrecked, with heavy casualties, and by the standards of that day Perry would have been justified in surrendering. Instead he took a long-shot gamble: hauled down his "Don't give up the ship!" banner and tucked it under his arm, got into a small boat, and had four sailors row him across the battle zone to *Niagara*. By some miracle of good luck or good management he got through unharmed; boarding *Niagara,* he sent its captain off to bring up the lighter craft, ran his battle flag to the masthead, and sailed into the melee around his crippled flagship.

About this time *Lawrence* struck her flag, but the British never had a chance to take possession. Dying hard, the flagship had all but wrecked her assailants, and when Perry came in with *Niagara* firing both broadsides at once, and *Caledonia* and the schooners got up close, the British ships fell out of action. Then, suddenly, it was all over, the whole enemy fleet had surrendered, *Lawrence*'s colors were raised again, and Perry wrote a historic message to General Harrison: "We have met the enemy and they are ours; two ships, two brigs, one schooner and one sloop." The British no longer had a man-o'-war above Niagara Falls. Harrison and his army made it to the Detroit River, and when the British evacuated Fort Malden and set off overland for Lake Ontario, Tippecanoe marched in pursuit; won a hot rearguard action on the Thames River, killed Tecumseh and broke up his band of warriors, and destroyed Britain's last chance of controlling the upper Lakes.

Not that the British would give up trying. Before Perry even got his fleet out of Presque Isle, Yeo had convoyed a force of some 800 regulars under General Prevost across Lake Ontario for an attack on Sacket's Harbor. This failed when an American militia general named Jacob Brown led an unexpectedly valiant defense, inflicting heavy losses and forcing Prevost to get his men on their transports and go back to Canada, but the fight for Lake Ontario had hardly begun.

And then the Americans returned to their old habit of fumbling. An invading force, sent from the Niagara River to drive the British away from their base near the site of Hamilton, advanced incautiously and was overwhelmed when British troops made a surprise attack at night. The survivors retreated to Fort George; a fresh American expedition prowled west from Queenston, ran into a force of Indians with a thin seasoning of redcoats, found itself partially surrounded, and listened attentively while a British officer repeated the old, old refrain—if the American camp had to be taken by storm, the uncontrollable Indians would probably massacre all the prisoners. Surrender promptly followed, and old General Dearborn, who still held top command in this area, was relieved at his own request.

Unfortunately, Secretary Armstrong picked Major General James Wilkinson, who had been in command at New Orleans, as his successor; Wilkinson had been involved in some shadowy, near-treasonous dealings with the Spanish before the war, and in addition was most incompetent as a field commander. Between Armstrong and Wilkinson, an American army was moved out from upstate New York to attack Montreal. It was checked by a smart British counterattack near the St. Lawrence rapids, and withdrew after a defeat that failed to become an actual rout only because of a stout fight put up by Jacob Brown's brigade. Dismayed, Wilkinson pulled the troops back to American soil and ordered them into winter quarters at French Mills, New York, just south of the Canadian border.

Then the war returned to vigorous life along the Niagara. Lieutenant General Gordon Drummond, a Canadian-born British regular, sent out troops that recaptured Fort George, drove the Americans from Canadian soil all the way along the river, crossed to storm Fort Niagara, and then went rampaging upstream to take and pillage Lewiston, Black Rock, and Buffalo. Indian war parties also crossed and began ravaging the countryside. American naval control of the upper Lakes was not affected by all of this, but so far the war around Lake Ontario had been little less than disaster and the British began meditating an outright invasion of the United States. From what they had seen of American generalship so far, the idea had unmistakable appeal.

—□—

Meanwhile, as an offstage sound played unobtrusively by wood-winds, beaten down by the trumpets and kettledrums of battle, peace negotiations were going on. Peace negotiations of a sort.

Late in 1812, with Napoleon in Moscow, Tsar Alexander I tried to bring this American war to a close—moved in part by his humanity, and even more by his belief that Britain might bother Napoleon more if it no longer had to think about America. Alexander offered to mediate the dispute. Madison promptly accepted, and sent Albert Gallatin and James A. Bayard of Delaware to Russia to join John Quincy Adams, the American minister, as a negotiating team. Lord Castlereagh rejected the Russian offer—Napoleon was leaving Moscow now, so Alexander did not mind—and suggested that Britain and the United States begin discussions of their own. Madison agreed and ordered his negotiators to Ghent, in Belgium, to be reinforced there by Henry Clay and the American minister to Sweden, Jonathan Russell. By the middle of 1814 Americans and Englishmen were sitting around a table, talking peace.

For a while their talks got nowhere, due in part to the immense time gap. Reliable accounts from the American war zone took from two to four months to reach the men who were trying to bring the war to an end. They were always talking from the vantage point of a situation that had changed materially by the time they began to talk and would change even more by the time their words got back to the scene of action. When Castlereagh sent his men to Ghent he knew that America had lost Mackinac and Detroit and that her fumbling efforts to attack Canada had been disgraceful failures. Furthermore, Napoleon was clearly losing the war in Europe. As far as Castlereagh could see, Britain had the winning hand, and although his primary objective was to withdraw with suitable dignity from a war that was little more than a pesky nuisance, there was no sense in failing to exploit a victory that was taking shape before his eyes. Besides, England was annoyed. The royal navy had lost face, and what happened on Lake Erie did not improve matters. But on dry land the Americans obviously offered nothing to fear, and if the navy buckled down and set up a blockade that a few overblown frigates could not evade, the army could move in and make a killing. There were plenty of seasoned troops to spare, now that the war in Europe was closing. Send them overseas, put some real muscle into this war, and make the Americans sorry they ever started it.

Extensive plans were made. Prevost in Canada would be given and army of 10,000 men, made up largely of tough regulars who had been fighting Napoleon, and he would move south along Burgoyne's old path, up Lake Champlain and over to the Hudson on an invasion aimed at the heart of the United States. A secondary expedition sailed for the Chesapeake, which the royal navy had firmly under control, to strike northward and do whatever damage it could to Washington and Baltimore. Most ominous of all, 8,000 of Wellington's veterans were started for New Orleans to seize that port and then stand by for further orders. And as the transports started out across the Atlantic the Americans at Ghent were shown the new British peace terms.

American territory in Maine, upper New York, and west of the Lakes would be annexed to Canada. No peace could be made that did not provide for an independent Indian nation south of the Lakes, which would prevent Canada and the land-hungry Americans from rubbing against each other and would also prevent American expansion westward.

These terms, of course, were unacceptable, and the great British offensive began. If it succeeded—and it was not easy to see how it was going to be stopped—the final peace terms obviously would be much more severe. America faced outright catastrophe: loss of a great part of her territory, loss of access to the Louisiana country, loss of the all-important port at the mouth of the Mississippi . . . ultimately, indeed, probable loss of national identity. It escaped no one's notice that an airtight naval blockade and an armed invasion moving down the Champlain-Hudson route from Canada might well detach the anti-war New England states from the Union altogether; and to lose New Orleans and the lower Mississippi would probably be to lose the entire West.

The world that had been turned upside down at Yorktown might be turned other side up again, in which case the dream that Americans lived by would flicker out and leave a cinder to go tumbling down through the empty spaces beyond the stars.

. . . Not yet. If the dream ever dies it will die because people cease to believe and desire and so cause a warp in the continuum where what man wants meets what man can get, and not because man himself has dreamed something too big for him to carry. So it is time (getting back to earth) to consider the militia, the temporary soldier, the volunteer, the eternal amateur, on whom American defeats thus far had been blamed and on whom success finally would depend. And as the British bared their fangs at Ghent it was beginning to be seen at home that the trouble with the war effort had been not the militiaman but his generals. The American amateur soldier could do anything that was asked of him *provided* he was asked by people who knew what they were about. So far the asking had been done by men who were incapable of evoking the right response. One by one these men were being unloaded, and real leaders were being found.

John Armstrong was an inadequate Secretary of War, but now and then he did the right thing: most notably at the beginning of 1814 when he made Jacob Brown a major general in the regular army and put him in charge of operations along the Niagara River, and then made Winfield Scott a brigadier and placed him in Brown's command. These two went to work in earnest, drilled their men hard, got proper uniforms and equipment for them, and early in the summer took them north from Fort Erie to drive the British away from Burlington Heights. Chauncey and his fleet were to join them when they reached the Lake Ontario shore, they could all go on together and take York once more, and then they might swing eastward, capture Kingston, and win permanent control of the lake. (This would put a severe crimp in Prevost's projected invasion of the United States, although the two generals did not yet know about this plan.) They had 3,500 men in all—two brigades of regulars and one of militia—and they ran into the British by the Chippawa River near Niagara Falls, beat them in a spirited little battle, and moved on to Queenston to await Chauncey and his warships.

It developed that Chauncey was not coming. He was busy administering the affairs of his new fresh-water navy, he had convoys to guard and Yeo's enemy ships to look out for, and he did not like having the army call signals for him; so he did not show up. Unable to go farther without the navy, Brown withdrew to the Chippawa, and when a British force approached, the Americans moved out on July 25, 1814, and brought on the desperate, bitterly fought battle of Lundy's Lane. The fight was pretty much a standoff, with heavy losses on both sides. Both Brown and Scott were wounded, and the Americans retreated to Fort Erie.

A fortnight later the British made a driving attack, seized what looked like a key part of the defensive line, losing 900 men in the process, found they could go no farther, and tried to make a siege of it. Late in September Brown, recovered from his wound, returned to action and led 1,600 men, mostly militia, in a counterattack that broke the British line at a cost of 500 casualties on each side.

So the American offensive had failed, but somehow the whole operation had been impressive. The militiamen had made no difficulty about fighting on foreign soil; when put into action they had teamed up with the regulars to give a solid professional performance, and it was clear that under capable leaders American soldiers could meet the king's troops on an equal footing.

Among those who noticed this was General Sir George Prevost.

Leading a solid army of 15,000 men, Prevost crossed the border on September 3 and marched for Plattsburg on the western shore of Lake Champlain. Plattsburg was well fortified, held by a substantial garrison, but late in August Armstrong had ordered most of the defenders to Sacket's Harbor, 150 miles away, leaving

General Alexander Macomb to defend the place with 1,500 militia and raw recruits. By the time the British drew near, Macomb had managed to get reinforcements—more militia, and odd lots of details called in from scattered outposts—but he was hopelessly outclassed and outnumbered and Prevost could have swallowed him whole if he had made one determined lunge. But Macomb put up a bold front; and Prevost, already impressed by the fighting qualities Americans were unexpectedly displaying this year, was not the sort to make an aggressive lunge anyway. He considered the enemy lines too strong to be stormed but felt that an attack upon the American right might succeed if the American fleet, cruising off Plattsburg in support of the defending troops, could be demolished or driven off. Accordingly Prevost called on the royal navy for help.

When the war began neither nation had anything that could be called a fleet on Lake Champlain. The British woke up first, and early in 1813 they armed a few small craft, started to build more, and for about a year controlled that narrow waterway. Then the Americans sent Captain Thomas Macdonough in to take charge, and gave him shipwright Noah Brown, who had built Perry's fleet. Macdonough and Brown set up a navy yard on Otter Creek, near Vergennes, Vermont, and Brown got to work. The British were at work on Isle aux Noix, where Champlain's overflow starts down to the St. Lawrence, but Brown was a driver and there was no beating him. (Perry and Macdonough get the fame for saving the waterways whose loss would have meant the loss of the war, but Noah Brown was the man who made their victories possible. Somewhere he ought to have a small monument.) And when Prevost asked Captain George Downie, British commander afloat, to brush the American ships out of his way Macdonough had a formidable little fleet ready and able to fight.

Macdonough had anchored his ships inside Plattsburg Bay. To get at him Downie would have to move against the prevailing wind into a narrow pocket—"sail uphill," as he put it—and if the Americans retreated they could anchor under protection of the army's batteries. Downie could see no profit in it—nor much point, because the American fleet was just far enough offshore to be unable to protect the army's flank if Prevost made a serious attack. And by fighting in the bay Downie would lose the advantage which his preponderance of long guns would give him in a battle on the open lake. But Prevost, overbearing and insulting, was after all the governor general of Canada, so Downie buckled down to it.

On the morning of September 11 he brought his ships into the bay—flagship *Confiance,* ship-rigged, of 27 guns; brig *Linnet,* 16; two lighter craft, *Chub* and *Finch;* and ten or twelve row galleys, each mounting one gun, waiting outside to come in when needed. Macdonough was waiting on the ship *Saratoga,* 26, with the brig *Eagle,* 20, schooner *Ticonderoga* with 7 light guns, and sloop *Preble,* 7. Like Downie, he had a handful of row galleys on call in the background.

As the British ships came in, smoke clouds taking form here and there as gunners tried ranging shots, it seems to have occurred to no one that the decisive battle of the war was beginning.

There ought to be something grand and spectacular about a decisive battle. Here there was nothing of the sort, except for such grandeur as may arise when young men willingly die for a cause bigger than they. All anyone could see was two homemade squadrons fighting in a remote corner of a landlocked lake for possession of an unimportant harbor that few people on either side had ever heard of. But if the British won, Prevost's army could go where it chose and Britain could do as it wished with the American Republic; and if the British were stopped here they were stopped everywhere, Prevost would have to go back to Canada, and the most Britain could get from the war would be a stalemate.

The fleets met in a tremendous crash of exploding gunpowder and splintered wood. There was no subtlety and no finesse; just flail away at the enemy and hope that he gives out before you do. Both sides were badly hurt. Downie was killed, his *Confiance* shattered; *Saratoga*'s whole starboard side was wrecked, and so was *Eagle*'s, and four of Britain's row galleys got into action and drove *Preble* close inshore under the protection of the army's guns. *Chub* stumbled through the American line, ran hard aground, and struck her flag; *Finch* ran aground on an islet to the south, kept her flag flying, but did no more fighting; and the noise and the killing went on, and the smoke of their torment went up to the September sky.

Perry had saved the day on Lake Erie by getting into a rowboat and making a heroic dash through the firestorm to bring a fresh ship into action; Macdonough won on Lake Champlain by taking thought beforehand, anchoring his principal ships with springs on their cables so that they could be turned around in place regardless of wind or battle damage. He used this maneuver now, and suddenly the undamaged port sides of *Saratoga* and *Eagle* came into play. The British tried it with *Confiance* and *Linnet,* but they had to rely on wind and sail power and they could not make it—rigging all broken up, crews dreadfully thinned, a fickle breeze refusing to blow when it was most needed. So now the Americans had all the advantage; they hammered broken *Confiance* unmercifully and at last she had to surrender. *Linnet,* shot up as badly as her flagship, followed suit. The battle was over, a victory as decisive as Perry's, but the American ships were all crippled; when the row galleys that had driven *Preble* out of action got out of the bay and headed north the Americans could not pursue because none of their ships could spread any canvas.

It did not matter. Prevost was beaten. He had 15,000 soldiers and he had lost fewer than 250, but when Downie and his fleet were destroyed Prevost's hope died with them; he pulled away and marched back to Canada. While General Macomb sent out patrols to make sure that the British were really leaving, Macdonough put his repair gangs to work, and news of what had happened went slowly back to Europe—sailing ships riding down the wind to let the men at Ghent know that everything must be recalculated. In London the news led the government to try to play its ace: top command and full powers for peace or war in America were offered to the Duke of Wellington, who had driven Napoleon's armies out of Spain. Wellington read the dispatches, studied the maps, and declined: the ace refused to be played. If Britain did not control the inland waterways—as by virtue of Perry and Macdonough she did not—then Britain (said Wellington) could not invade the United States and might as well make peace and be done with it.

But this shapeless, formless war had to run its own course, because of that four- or five-month time lag between an American event and the return of orders from England based on that event. British forces in America continued to go by orders issued earlier, when the whole American defense seemed to be cracking. And so Major General Robert Ross, with 2,500 veterans from Europe via Bermuda, came on to join Vice-Admiral Sir Alexander Cochrane's fleet in Chesapeake Bay, committed to making a punishing raid where America would feel it most. Cochrane took him up the Patuxent River and set his force ashore at Benedict, Maryland, and Ross took four regiments of infantry, a battalion of royal marines, and a naval contingent hauling three cannon, and set out for Washington.

Washington was given over to a confusion and frantic mindless fumbling uncommon even for this war, where confusion was normal. Armstrong refused to believe that the British would attack Washington because it was a place of no military value, so he did little to defend it until the foe was at the gates. President Madison, who had had enough, was in the act of removing Armstrong and putting James Monroe in his place but the act had not yet been consummated and all three men were more or less on duty, riding about desperately and accomplishing very little. Immediate military command was given to Brigadier General William Winder, who rode harder, farther, more at random and more desperately than anybody else and accomplished least of all. He had little to work with: 2,000 half-trained men in a District of Columbia brigade, a levy of 3,000 militia of whom only 300 actually showed up, and a contingent of sailors and marines under Commodore Joshua Barney, with some artillery. Winder skirmished fruitlessly as Ross advanced, and on August 24, 1814, the Americans formed a battle line at Bladensburg, just east of the District of Columbia line. Ross's veterans blew the militia out of the way without working very hard, found Barney's naval force a tougher nut to crack, finally cracked it after losing 500 men — and then the American force dissolved and the British marched into the American capital.

They found little to do when they got there, Washington being a small country town with few rewards for a conqueror. Remembering what had happened at York, Ross burned the Navy Yard, the White House, and the Capitol (President and Mrs. Madison having decamped just in time), restrained his troops from loot and pillage, and twenty-four hours later, finding nothing there to detain him, marched back to the Patuxent. He had profoundly humiliated his foes but he had inflicted no real injury, and so he re-embarked on August 30 to sail up the bay and take Baltimore, which as a major seaport and one of America's principal cities was a prize worth grabbing. It was also a shipbuilding center of note, and many of the swift privateers that were making the British community thoroughly tired of this war had been built here; if taken, Baltimore could expect rough treatment.

Baltimore got the kind of protection Washington needed but did not get. In charge of defense was a lively sixty-two-year-old militia officer, Major General Samuel Smith, and out of militia regiments, regulars, and some sailors kept ashore by the British blockade he put together a force of 13,000 men and placed them in a well-built line of fortifications. Ross came up, led a spirited attack on this line, and was killed; 300 of other ranks fell with him, and no breakthrough was made. The British canceled the land attack and brought up the fleet for a twenty-four-hour bombardment of the strong point of Baltimore's harbor defense, Fort McHenry.

It is an old story now, worn smooth by constant handling— cannonade going on all day and all night, bombs and rockets and a firelit clang of broken metal against masonry, with a young American named Francis Scott Key huddling on a British warship to see how it would end. Then daylight, and beyond the heavy smoke our flag was *still there,* sign and symbol for future generations saying that this country would endure . . . and for all its musical deficiencies the national anthem was pretty well chosen. The British sailed away, and the thrust at America's heart had been averted.

Actually the crisis was over—a remark that calls for two qualifications: it took most people a long time to see it, and in this illogical war anything could happen, no matter where logic pointed.

In midsummer, before the news from Plattsburg got overseas, the British were wearing all their war paint. Admiral Cochrane wanted to do as much damage as possible before peace came and predicted America would lose command of the Mississippi and the northwest frontier. Gallatin warned that the enemy meant to inflict "a severe chastisement" by way of showing that "war is not to be declared against Great Britain with impunity." The string of American victories at sea was broken. Brig *Argus* was taken by the Brigish brig *Pelican,* sloop *Frolic* fell to the frigate *Orpheus,* and the famous frigate *Essex,* which had rounded the Horn and enjoyed fantastic success capturing British whalers and merchantmen in the Pacific, was blockaded in Chilean waters by H.M. frigate *Phoebe* and sloop *Cherub.* Trying to slip out, she was caught, gunned down, and forced to surrender. There were a few American victories: a new *Wasp* cruised to the Channel, destroyed two British man-o'-war brigs, and then went missing with all hands in an Atlantic gale; sloop *Peacock* took the British brig *Epervier.* But the great days were over, the blockade along the American coast got tighter and tighter, and although America

at last began to build some 74-gun ships of the line it seemed unlikely that they would be finished in time to fight in this war.

By the summer of 1814 Federalist New England got its dislike
of the war into high gear. The Massachusetts legislature called a
New England convention to air these views, and although Vermont and New Hampshire did not accept the call, Rhode Island
and Connecticut did. The convention met at Hartford on December 15, 1814, holding its sessions in secret. The secrecy
seemed ominous; Federalist partisans had been talking wildly of
disunion for some time, and now the word went around that outright secession was being planned—which, coming in the middle
of a war, would of course have been nothing less than treason.
Luckily, this was not the case; when they got right down to it the
fire-eaters went on a blander diet, and in the end they simply invoked the principle of state rights and called for a series of constitutional amendments, expressing the real basis for their grievance
in the last two: no President should serve more than one term,
and there could not be two Presidents in a row from the same
state. (Madison and the Virginia dynasty were the real targets.)
The Hartford Convention finally adjourned, and nothing came
of its laboriously composed amendments and resolutions—but
the Federalists had given their own party a mortal wound, and
before long it would disintegrate, its departure widely un-
mourned. It had narrowly avoided actual treason and had used
the crisis of a war to try to force through its own political program, and the whole operation had left a bad taste in everybody's
mouth. It was time for the Federalists to go out of business.

Meanwhile the men at Ghent were working for peace. In midsummer 1814, while the British braves were counting coups and
slashing the air with menacing words, the terms London was offering were clear and grim. People who fought wars thought in
terms of land that might be grabbed, and the British offered peace
on a basis of *uti possidetis*—the diplomat's way of saying that each
side would get title to all of the other side's land it was actually occupying when the treaty was signed. America then held no Brit-

ish land at all, but Britain held half of Maine, Prevost was moving down into New York with 15,000 men, Ross and Cochrane were about to gouge out a substantial homestead along the upper Chesapeake, and an army of Wellington's veterans was under orders to go to New Orleans and take possession there. If all of this went as planned the American Republic had had its day. When the American delegates digested this they prepared to break off the talks and go home. In Ghent they could do nothing but agree to their own destruction.

—□—

News from America came just in time. Macdonough had slammed the door in the face of Prevost, if Washington had been burned the Stars and Stripes remained flying over Fort McHenry, a sturdy reception committee was being prepared for the prospective callers in New Orleans, and the British were not winning the war after all. *Uti possidetis* indeed; the Americans resumed their chairs at the council table and offered peace on the basis of *status quo ante bellum,* or as you were. Territorially it would be as if the war had never been fought.

It was at this point that the British appealed to Wellington and got his discouraging verdict, with the blunt advice to make peace while they could. The look of things in Europe reinforced his views. Napoleon was in exile, but Elba was not far from France and there were disturbing rumors; the victorious allies were falling into discord and there was no telling what might happen next. The people at Ghent suddenly found that they were reaching agreement.

In many ways it was an odd agreement. The Americans quietly dropped their demand for an end to impressment. With the end of the war in Europe, Britain no longer needed to impress seamen and had discontinued the practice; she was not prepared to bind herself not to do it again, but the Americans were happy enough to accept the situation as it was and did not press the point. Similarly with the orders in council and the whole business of freedom of the seas and neutral rights; from a practical viewpoint this was solving itself and the treaty could ignore it. There were other matters—fishing privileges in American and Canadian waters, rights of navigation on the Mississippi, and details regarding minor boundary adjustments in Maine and the Northwest—but these were simply put aside, with a general agreement to settle them later in the ordinary course of peacetime diplomacy. Obviously, both sides wanted the war to end quickly, and a treaty was drawn up and signed on December 24, 1814. Once it had been ratified in London, sent across the Atlantic and ratified in Washington, and the ratifications exchanged, the war would be officially over.

. . . Except that Lord Liverpool, British Prime Minister, was hedging his bet. The peace terms had been arranged, the treaty signed and on its way to Washington, but Liverpool suspected that President Madison would either refuse to ratify it or "play us some trick"—so that army of veterans was going to New Orleans to nail everything down. It was to have been commanded by General Ross, and when he died in the attack on Baltimore Sir Edward Pakenham, Wellington's brother-in-law and his chief of staff in Spain, was sent over in his place. Pakenham had 10,000 men and he had Admiral Cochrane to take him wherever he wanted to go, and his orders revealed that tricks did indeed lie back of this treaty. After he captured New Orleans (his ability to do this was not for a moment doubted) he was to take the bulk of his troops to the Chesapeake and stand by. Then if Madison refused to ratify or did anything else unfortunate, the British would immediately try to make a separate peace with New England. With secessionist noises already coming out of Hartford, and Pakenham and Cochrane and their irresistible forces as persuaders, "we have good reason to believe that they would not be indisposed to listen to such a proposal." From the moment Britain knew it was going to end the war there was plenty of time to cancel Pakenham's orders. They were not canceled, and there is nothing in the record to indicate that Britain would meekly surrender an important conquest just because it had been made after the war ended. No matter what the men at Ghent finally signed on December 24, this was a battle America had better win.

Washington at least put the job in good hands, thereby bringing to the national stage a man who would be a long time getting off of it—Andrew Jackson. Jackson was a lawyer, land speculator, cotton planter, slaveowner, and politician, master of an imposing 640-acre homestead near Nashville, and commander-in-chief of Tennessee's militia by virtue of his political influence and inborn driving force. Jackson liked to fight. He especially liked to fight the British, who had given him rough treatment during the Revolution when they occupied South Carolina and he was an orphaned fourteen-year-old. He also liked to fight the Indians, for he believed the entire Southwest ought to be opened to white settlement and did much to bring it about. (He was happy, as a matter of fact, just to fight, and if necessary he would trust the luck of the draw to provide an opponent.) He was called out in 1813 to suppress the Creeks, a formidable people who thought Indian lands ought to be occupied by Indians. Tecumseh had assured them that when they fought the Americans the British would help; and if the Creeks had timed their effort better Tecumseh would doubtless have been proven right; to have that tribe on the warpath in the immediate American rear during the campaign to take New Orleans would have tempted the British to give them all possible aid.

Jackson's troops were backwoods militia, and he found them disobedient and panicky; he shot a few of them, threatened to shoot more, marched them hard and drilled them mercilessly, made soldiers of them and drew from them the resentful comment that he was as tough as old hickory. When Jackson finally broke the Creeks, once and for all, in a desperate fight at Horseshoe Bend, Alabama, on March 27, 1814, the whole country heard about this frontier general whose troops called him "Old Hickory." It seemed a good nickname, and it stuck. After this victory Madison made Jackson a major general in the regular army and gave him command of the forces being assembled to defend New Orleans.

There is a haunting echo from this war against the Creeks. In the summer of 1814 Jackson had to make a treaty by which the Creeks (signing with a horse pistol against the ear) gave up a vast swath of their homeland—more than half of Alabama and a good slice of Georgia. An important group of Creeks had fought on Jackson's side during the campaign, and these now learned that they would lose their land along with those who had fought against him. They complained, but Jackson was deaf. He wrote to his wife that it was a "disagreeable business," but he went ahead and did it anyway, and the friendly Creeks lost all they had along with the hostile Creeks. The tragic story of the Trail of Tears got its first chapter then and there.

Singular. This leader who became the symbol of freedom and fair treatment for the man at the bottom of the heap took it for granted that that man had a white skin. Robbing the red man of his home was a disagreeable business but the white man needed it. There were after all grades and conditions of men . . . the American dream needed a good deal of developing.

Too late, the British saw possibilities in an Indian counterattack that would cripple the defenders of New Orleans, and late in 1814 a small British force landed at Pensacola, in Spanish Florida, and tried to create a diversion. It was not much of an effort (the British apparently never thought of putting large numbers ashore farther west, say at Mobile, and marching them overland to the Mississippi above New Orleans to attack the city from the rear), and Jackson reacted promptly. Without waiting for orders from Washington—technically, Spanish Florida was neutral territory—he moved on Pensacola, stamped out the rising and its supporting force, and then turned to New Orleans itself.

Geography played against the British here. They could not bring their fleet up the river because of Fort St. Philip, forty miles below the city, a barrier wind-driven warships could not pass; so they coasted west along Mississippi Sound to Lake Borgne, transferred troops and guns to open boats, the lake being too shallow for regular warships, and after much labor got their force ashore on an open plain between the Mississippi and the western end of Lake Borgne some ten miles below New Orleans. The country was flat and soggy, water on two sides, nothing much in the rear, and Andrew Jackson dead ahead, his troops well dug in behind a sluggish canal. There was a week or more of skirmishing, long-range bombarding, and general flexing of muscles, and Jackson perfected his defenses while British sappers prepared fascines and scaling ladders with which the infantrymen could cross the canal and scale the eight-foot embankment behind which the Americans were waiting for them.

Andrew Jackson was matter-of-fact, not given to flights of fancy, but for this fight he had an army straight out of fable. He had his own troops, to begin with: Kentuckians and Tennesseans, some of them the legendary riflemen you hear about, others just homespun militia. There were a couple of regiments of regulars, two volunteer battalions of Free Negroes of New Orleans, a battalion of wellborn New Orleans white folk and a band known as the New Orleans sharpshooters. There was also a contingent of Choctaw Indians, apparently undismayed by what had happened to the Creeks; and finally, unforgettably, there were Jean Lafitte's pirates, who had a lawless little principality of their own in the bayou country south of New Orleans and preyed on all shipping in prescribed pirate fashion. When Lafitte offered their services Jackson snorted at the idea of using a set of conscienceless banditti, but he cooled off when he learned that Lafitte could provide needed guns, powder, and other supplies; and so now he had 1,000 pirates in his ranks. They seem to have turned out partly for fun and partly because they figured these Americans were about to become bosses of the delta and it might be well to get purged of sin.

Jackson got this unlikely army lined up behind a thick, solid breastwork too high for assailants to climb. His men looked down on the canal and the muddy plain beyond, and on January 8, 1815, they saw the red-coated line take form just out of range to

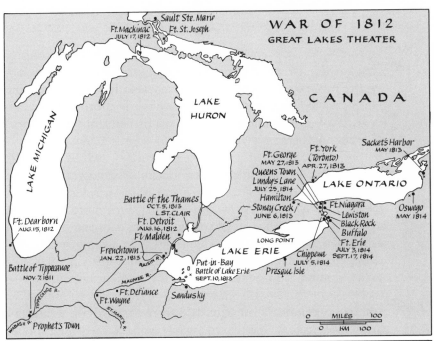

WAR OF 1812
GREAT LAKES THEATER

Sault Ste. Marie
Ft. St. Joseph
Ft. Mackinac
JULY 17, 1812

LAKE HURON

CANADA

LAKE MICHIGAN

Sacket's Harbor
MAY 1813

Ft. George
MAY 27, 1813
Ft. York
(Toronto)
APR. 27, 1813
Queens Town
Lundy's Lane
JULY 25, 1814
Hamilton
Stoney Creek
JUNE 6, 1813

LAKE ONTARIO

Oswego
MAY 1814

Ft. Niagara
Lewiston
Black Rock
Buffalo
Ft. Erie
JULY 3, 1814
SEPT. 17, 1814

Battle of the Thames
OCT. 5, 1813
L. ST. CLAIR
Ft. Detroit
AUG. 16, 1812
Ft. Malden

LONG POINT

Ft. Dearborn
AUG. 15, 1812

Frenchtown
JAN. 22, 1813
RAISIN R.
LAKE ERIE
Chippewa
JULY 5, 1814

Put-in-Bay
Battle of Lake Erie
SEPT. 10, 1813
Presque Isle

Battle of Tippecanoe
NOV. 7, 1811

MAUMEE R.

Ft. Defiance
Ft. Wayne
Sandusky

TIPPECANOE R.
ST. MARY'S R.

WABASH R.
Prophet's Town

MILES 100
KM 100

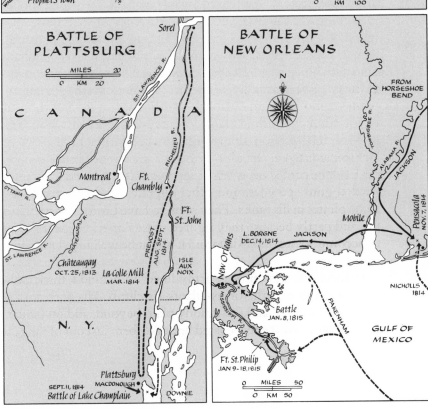

BATTLE OF PLATTSBURG

MILES 20
KM 20

C A N A D A

Sorel

ST. LAWRENCE R.

Montreal
Ft. Chambly

OTTAWA R.

ST. LAWRENCE R.
CHATEAUGAY R.

RICHELIEU R.

Ft. St. John

Châteaugay
OCT. 25, 1813

La Colle Mill
MAR. 1814

PREVOST AUG. SEPT. 1814

ISLE AUX NOIX

N. Y.

Plattsburg
MACDONOUGH
SEPT. 11, 1814
Battle of Lake Champlain

DOWNIE

BATTLE OF NEW ORLEANS

N

FROM HORSESHOE BEND

TOMBIGBEE R.

ALABAMA R.

JACKSON

Mobile

Pensacola
NOV. 7, 1814

L. BORGNE
DEC. 14, 1814
JACKSON
JACKSON

New Orleans

MISSISSIPPI R.

PAKENHAM

NICHOLLS
1814

Battle
JAN. 8, 1815

GULF OF MEXICO

Ft. St. Philip
JAN. 9-18, 1815

MILES 50
KM 50

the south. At last General Pakenham—moved by memories of Spain, where British troops now and then had stormed French lines too strong to be carried, moved also by the feeling that Americans did not need to be taken seriously—ordered his men forward to break the ignorant backwoodsmen from the swamps of upper nowhere.

It was no contest. The redcoats came on—white crossbelts bright, muskets tilted at the port, gaiters splashing through the mud—they came on, precisely arrayed, valor directed by stupidity, doomed forever. (A few years earlier, writing to a friend in England, Wellington had observed: "I begin to be of opinion with you that there is nothing as stupid as a gallant officer." Apparently this was the sort of thing he had in mind.) The first ranks carried scaling ladders to get over the high breastworks, and never used them because they did not live long enough. The Americans stood at their ease, laid their weapons on the heavy earth embankment, and blazed away. Cannon fired, muskets and rifles crackled at a target no one could miss. British ranks dissolved and the fragments were picked up by the ranks behind them, these ranks were blown to fragments, and when Pakenham rode up to pull everyone together he was killed and what was left of the assault column broke up into fugitives fleeing for safety; and suddenly the battle of New Orleans was over and the war was over and a new light came down from the sky on the road to the West, where the great gate was swinging open.

Andrew Jackson wrote to President Madison. The British, he said, had lost 700 men killed, 1,400 wounded, and 500 captured; the American loss was 7 killed and 6 wounded, and he confessed that these figures "must I know excite astonishment and may not everywhere be fully credited." As he wrote, General Jacob Brown was in Washington proposing a spring offensive against Montreal by 20,000 regulars and 30,000 New York and Vermont volunteers, led by himself. That one would have worked . . . but fortunately the packet from England arrived, the treaty was sent to Congress, Congress ratified it, and on February 17, 1815, Madison proclaimed the war at an end.

CONCLUSION

Rendezvous

I N A W A Y, measured against what had happened in Europe since 1789, the War of 1812 was an absurd side show, a drawn battle that started just as they agreed to avoid it, went on after they had agreed to stop it, and settled none of the issues over which it had been fought—a comedy of misconceptions and poorly executed plans in which clumsy amateurs and distracted professionals outfumbled each other across the wild North American landscape.

. . . Except, of course, that there was nothing fumbling or comic about Isaac Brock or Tecumseh, Harrison or Jacob Brown or Winfield Scott, Perry or Macdonough, Andrew Jackson, the sea captains and the men those fighters led; nothing that Napoleon or Nelson or Wellington could have taught them about bravery or leadership or the victor's touch.

Besides, the war had settled something fairly substantial. Americans had fought the world's greatest power to a standstill and had won when it counted—on Lake Erie and Lake Champlain, at New Orleans and on the high seas—and the sense of achievement deriving from those victories had more than supplied whatever Americans might have been lacking in self-confidence or security. Now their independence was unquestioned and complete, once and for all, and there would be no more acquisitive foreign powers edging at their boundaries or infringing on their rights. Suddenly, for the first time, they were alone with America, free to have their way with it.

Something as vast and unconfinable as the human spirit was entering upon a great testing ground. In the preceding century, as Henry Steele Commager has observed, Europe had invented the Enlightenment and America had begun acting it out—proclaiming to all the world that liberty and a better life could in fact be achieved, that the pursuit of happiness was a legitimate pursuit, to be protected by government, that these things were part of humanity's birthright belonging equally to everyone, and that man's reach need not exceed his grasp. It was as bold and magnificent a dream as human beings had permitted themselves since the birth of Christ, and this time its sponsors were contending that the good things of which they spoke were attainable here on earth, today or tomorrow or the day after, by one's own efforts.

Bold and magnificent, surely—and also dangerous, strewn with pitfalls, tragically flawed and woefully incomplete (as red men and black men and others would continue to bear witness), perhaps no more than presumptuous folly born of the pride that goes before destruction, deceptively easy to twist or pervert into a cruel travesty of its noble aim, always in need of men who could point out the flaws and reaffirm the true meaning and see the need for a humble and a contrite heart.

To put Franklin Roosevelt's injunction into broader perspective, Americans were a people of whom much had been asked and to whom much had been given, and their rendezvous with destiny had fairly started—an ongoing destiny, to be partaken of and defined and applied in different ways by each generation in turn. The time, the place, and the means were at hand: one hundred years of absolute national security in which to devote themselves to the pursuit of their own ends, free from foreign threat or foreign entanglement; natural abundance that was incredibly varied and seemingly infinite, a vast continental treasure house stretching out beyond the sunset to rainbow's end; and human energies fired to awesome proportions by the nation's commitment to its dream. Here, if anywhere, perhaps the thing could be done; here, by all odds, it was going to be tried.

Selective Bibliography

WHAT FOLLOWS is hardly a conventional bibliography, chiefly because this is not a very conventional book. It is neither a college text based upon an extensive survey of the latest scholarly writings nor a historical monograph based upon original sources. It is rather (if a label can be concocted) a combination of narrative and interpretive essay, and we have sought not to break new ground but to impose our own thoughts and order upon conventional historical material.

Like all historians we owe an enormous and incalculable debt to the work other people have done, and a list of such works that made any attempt at completeness—including monographs, articles, biographies, essays, studies of particular periods or events or themes, and the like—would require more space than is either available or pertinent in a book of this kind.

The real basis for the substance of this volume lies in something like a career and a half devoted in a variety of ways to American history—to writing it, teaching it, reading it, experiencing and watching isolated parts of it, and simply talking and thinking about it year after year with friends, relatives, students, colleagues, and most of all with each other. With a few exceptions, it would be impossible to identify our specific indebtedness to this or that scholarly work; too much of the debt is cumulative, acquired piecemeal over the years as we variously read, reviewed, wrote, lectured, edited, criticized, discussed, examined, and pondered.

The following, then, represents a partial and rather haphazard listing of the works, recent and not so recent, which in one way or another have been helpful to our command of the facts or to the shaping and sharpening of our view of what America is all about.

We would not be historians if we did not include a few qualifiers. First, our familiarity with European history is, by and large, confined to literature of the textbook and survey variety, and we are painfully aware of how thinly we have stretched our knowledge in this vast area. Second, our decision to include a few venerable works in this bibliography—and we are venerable enough to have included several—does not mean that we are unmindful of intervening modifications and revisions of those authors' views. And finally, the inclusion of *any* volume, old or new, does not mean that we share all, or necessarily any, of its author's conclusions.

In any case our gratitude to these and other writers is heartfelt, and we are sorry that the scope of this acknowledgment is so greatly overshadowed by the size of the debt.

GENERAL WORKS, TEXTBOOKS, SURVEYS, ETC.

Allen, Harry C. *Great Britain and the United States: A History of Anglo-American Relations, 1783–1952.* New York: St. Martin's, 1955.

Billington, Ray A. *Westward Expansion: A History of the American Frontier.* 3rd ed. New York: Macmillan, 1967.

Blum, John, et al. *The National Experience: A History of the United States.* 3rd ed. New York: Harcourt, Brace, 1973.

Chapelle, Howard I. *The History of the American Sailing Navy.* New York: Norton, 1949.

Dillard, Dudley. *Economic Development of the North Atlantic Community.* Englewood Cliffs, N.J.: Prentice-Hall, 1967.

Franklin, John Hope. *From Slavery to Freedom: A History of Negro Americans.* 4th ed. New York: Knopf, 1974.

Garraty, John A. *The American Nation: A History of the United States.* 2 vols. 3rd ed. New York: Harper, 1975.

McNeill, William H. *The Rise of the West: A History of the Human Community*. Chicago and London: University of Chicago Press, 1963.

Malone, Dumas, and Rauch, Basil. *Empire for Liberty: The Genesis and Growth of the United States of America*. 2 vols. New York: Appleton-Century-Crofts, 1960.

Morison, Samuel E.; *The Oxford History of the American People*. New York: Oxford University Press, 1965.

Morison, Samuel E.; Commager, Henry S.; and Leuchtenburg, William E. *The Growth of the American Republic*. 2 vols. 6th ed. New York: Oxford University Press, 1969.

Palmer, Robert R., and Colton, Joel. *A History of the Modern World*. 3rd ed. New York: Knopf, 1967.

Strayer, Joseph R.; Gatzke, Hans W.; and Harbison, E. Harris. *The Course of Civilization*. 2 vols. New York: Harcourt, Brace, 1961.

Trevelyan, George M. *History of England*. 3 vols. 3rd ed. London: Longmans, Green & Co., 1945. (Doubleday Anchor edition 1953)

Thematic and Interpretive Studies

Berthoff, Rowland. *An Unsettled People: Social Order and Disorder in American History*. New York: Harper, 1971.

Billington, Ray A. *America's Frontier Heritage*. New York: Holt, Rinehart & Winston, 1966.

Boorstin, Daniel J. *The Genius of American Politics*. Chicago: University of Chicago Press, 1953.

Brinton, Crane. *The Anatomy of Revolution*. Rev. ed. New York: Prentice-Hall, 1952.

Brown, Richard D. *Modernization: The Transformation of American Life, 1600–1865*. New York: Hill & Wang, 1976.

Bruchey, Stuart W. *The Roots of American Economic Growth, 1607–1861: An Essay in Social Causation*. New York: Harper, 1965.

Caruso, John A. *The Great Lakes Frontier: An Epic of the Old Northwest*. Indianapolis: Bobbs-Merrill, 1961.

Commager, Henry S. *The Empire of Reason: How Europe Imagined and*

America Realized the Enlightenment. Garden City, N.Y.: Double-day, 1977.

Cutler, Carl. *Greyhounds of the Sea*. New York: Putnam's, 1930.

Davis, David B. *The Problem of Slavery in the Age of Revolution, 1770–1823*. Ithaca, N.Y.: Cornell University Press, 1975.

———. *The Problem of Slavery in Western Culture*. Ithaca, N.Y.: Cornell University Press, 1966.

Degler, Carl. *Out of Our Past: The Forces That Shaped Modern America*. Rev. ed. New York: Harper, 1970.

DeVoto, Bernard. *The Course of Empire*. Boston: Houghton Mifflin, 1952. (Sentry ed. 1962)

Eccles, William J. *France in America*. New York: Harper, 1972.

Genovese, Eugene. *The Political Economy of Slavery: Studies in the Economy and Society of the Slave South*. New York: Random House, 1967.

Gibson, Charles. *Spain in America*. New York: Harper, 1966.

Hartz, Louis. *The Liberal Tradition in America*. New York: Harcourt, Brace, 1955.

Hofstadter, Richard. *The American Political Tradition and the Men Who Made It*. New York: Knopf, 1948.

Jordan, Winthrop D. *White over Black: American Attitudes Toward the Negro, 1550–1812*. Chapel Hill, N.C.: University of North Carolina Press, 1968.

Josephy, Alvin M. *The Indian Heritage of America*. New York: Knopf, 1968.

Kammen, Michael. *People of Paradox: An Inquiry Concerning the Origins of American Civilization*. New York: Random House, 1972.

Koch, Adrienne. *Power, Morals, and the Founding Fathers: Essays in the Interpretation of the American Enlightenment*. Ithaca, N.Y.: Cornell University Press, 1961.

North, Douglass C. *The Economic Growth of the United States, 1790–1860*. Englewood Cliffs, N.J.: Prentice-Hall, 1961.

Palmer, Robert R. *Tha Age of the Democratic Revolution: A Political History of Europe and America, 1760–1800*. 2 vols. Princeton, N.J.: Princeton University Press, 1959, 1964.

Quinn, David B. *North America from Earliest Discovery to First Settlements: The Norse Voyages to 1612.* New York: Harper, 1977.

Rossiter, Clinton. *Conservatism in America.* 2nd ed. New York: Random House, 1962.

Savelle, Max. *Seeds of Liberty: The Genesis of the American Mind.* New York: Knopf, 1948.

Tawney, R. H. *Religion and the Rise of Capitalism.* New York: Harcourt, Brace, 1926. (Mentor ed. 1947)

Washburn, Wilcomb. *The Indian in America.* New York: Harper, 1975.

Wiebe, Robert H. *The Segmented Society: An Historical Preface to the Meaning of America.* New York: Oxford University Press, 1975.

Woodward, C. Vann. *American Counterpoint: Slavery and Racism in the North-South Dialogue.* Boston: Little, Brown, 1971.

THE OLD WORLD

Alexander, Henry G. *Religion in England, 1558–1662.* London: University of London Press, 1968.

Ashton, T. S. *The Industrial Revolution, 1760–1830.* London: Oxford University Press, 1948.

Atkinson, William C. *A History of Spain and Portugal.* London: Penguin, 1960.

Bindoff, S. T. *Tudor England.* Baltimore: Penguin, 1950.

Braudel, Ferdinand. *The Mediterranean and the Mediterranean World in the Age of Philip II.* 2 vols. New York: Harper, 1972, 1973.

Bridenbaugh, Carl. *Vexed and Troubled Englishmen, 1590–1642.* New York: Oxford University Press, 1968.

Brinton, Crane. *A Decade of Revolution, 1789–1799.* New York: Harper, 1934.

Bruun, Geoffrey. *Europe and the French Imperium, 1799–1814.* New York: Harper, 1938.

Clark, Sir George. *Early Modern Europe, from About 1450 to About 1720.* New York: Oxford University Press, 1960. (First published 1954.)

Clark, G. N. *The Seventeenth Century,* 2nd ed. London: Oxford University Press, 1947.

Collinson, Patrick. *The Elizabethan Puritan Movement*. London: Jonathan Cape, 1967.

Davis, Ralph. *The Rise of the Atlantic Economies*. Ithaca, N.Y.: Cornell University Press, 1973.

Deane, Phyllis. *The First Industrial Revolution*. Cambridge: Cambridge University Press, 1965.

Dietz, Frederick C. *An Economic History of England*. New York: Holt, 1942.

Dorn, Walter L. *Competition for Empire, 1740–1763*. New York: Harper, 1940.

Elliott, J. H. *Europe Divided, 1559–1598*. New York: Harper, 1968.

———. *Imperial Spain, 1469–1716*. London: Edward Arnold, 1963. (Penguin ed. 1970)

Elton, G. R. *Reformation Europe, 1517–1559*. Cleveland: Meridian, 1964.

Friedrich, Carl J. *The Age of the Baroque, 1610–1660*. New York: Harper, 1952.

Gershoy, Leo. *From Despotism to Revolution, 1763–1789*. New York: Harper, 1944.

Hale, J. R. *Renaissance Europe, 1480–1520*. London: Fontana, 1971.

Hill, Christopher. *Change and Continuity in 17th-Century England*. London: Weidenfeld & Nicolson, 1974.

———. *God's Englishman: Oliver Cromwell and the English Revolution*. New York: Dial, 1970.

———. *Intellectual Origins of the English Revolution*. Oxford: Clarendon Press, 1965.

———. *Reformation to Industrial Revolution: A Social and Economic History of Britain 1530–1780*. London: Weidenfeld & Nicolson, 1967.

———. *Society and Puritanism in Pre-Revolution England*. New York: Schocken Books, 1964.

Hobsbawm, E. J. *The Age of Revolution, 1789–1848*. New York: New American Library, 1962.

Huizinga, Johan. *Waning of the Middle Ages*. Garden City, N.Y.: Doubleday, 1954. (Orig. pub. London: E. Arnold & Co., 1924.)

Hurstfield, Joel. *Elizabeth I and the Unity of England*. New York: Harper, 1960.

Longford, Elizabeth. *Wellington: The Years of the Sword*. New York: Harper, 1969.

Mantoux, Paul. *The Industrial Revolution in the Eighteenth Century: An Outline of the Beginnings of the Modern Factory System in England*. New York: Harper, 1961. (First pub. 1928.)

Mattingly, Garrett. *The Armada*. Boston: Houghton Mifflin, 1959.

Morison, Samuel E. *Admiral of the Ocean Sea: A Life of Christopher Columbus*. Boston: Little, Brown, 1942.

———. *The European Discovery of America*. Vol. 1, *The Northern Voyages*. New York: Oxford University Press, 1971. Vol. 2, *The Southern Voyages*. New York: Oxford University Press, 1974.

Nef, John U. *Cultural Foundations of Industrial Civilization*. Cambridge: Cambridge University Press, 1958. (Harper Torchbook ed. 1960)

Notestein, Wallace. *The English People on the Eve of Colonization, 1603–1630*. New York: Harper, 1954.

Parry, J. H. *The Establishment of the European Hegemony, 1415–1715*. New York: Harper, 1961. (First pub. as *Europe and a Wider World*. London: Hutchinson & Co., 1949.)

———. *The Spanish Seaborne Empire*. New York: Knopf, 1966.

Pirenne, Henri. *Economic and Social History of Medieval Europe*. New York: Harcourt, Brace, 1937.

Roberts, Penfield. *The Quest for Security, 1715–1740*. New York: Harper, 1947.

Rowse, A. L. *The Elizabethan Renaissance: The Cultural Achievement*. New York: Scribner's, 1972.

———. *The Elizabethans and America*. New York: Harper, 1959.

———. *The England of Elizabeth: The Structure of Society*. London. Macmillan, 1951.

———. *The Expansion of Elizabethan England*. New York: St. Martin's, 1955.

Smith, Lacey B. *Elizabeth Tudor: Portrait of a Queen*. Boston: Little, Brown, 1975.

Stone, Lawrence. *The Causes of the English Revolution, 1529–1642*. London: Routledge & Kegan Paul, 1972.

Stoye, John. *Europe Unfolding, 1648–1688*. New York: Harper, 1969.

Wedgwood, C. V. *The King's Peace, 1637–1641*. New York: Macmillan, 1955.

———. *The King's War, 1641–1647*. New York: Macmillan, 1959.

———. *The Thirty Years War*. Garden City, N.Y.: Doubleday, 1961.

Williams, Neville. *Elizabeth I, Queen of England*. New York: Dutton, 1968.

Wilson, Charles. *The Dutch Republic and the Civilization of the Seventeenth Century*. New York: McGraw-Hill, 1968.

Wolf, John B. *The Emergence of the Great Powers, 1685–1715*. New York: Harper, 1951.

THE AMERICAN COLONIES

Bailyn, Bernard. *The New England Merchants in the Seventeenth Century*. New York: Harper, 1955.

Barnes, Viola F. *The Dominion of New England: A Study in British Colonial Policy*. New Haven, Conn.: Yale University Press, 1923.

Battis, Emery. *Saints and Sectaries: Anne Hutchinson and the Antinomian Controversy in the Massachusetts Bay Colony*. Chapel Hill, N.C.: University of North Carolina Press, 1962.

Boorstin, Daniel J. *The Americans: The Colonial Experience*. New York: Random House, 1958.

Bremer, Francis J. *The Puritan Experiment: New England Society from Bradford to Edwards*. New York: St. Martin's, 1976.

Bridenbaugh, Carl. *Cities in Revolt: Urban Life in America 1743–1766*. New York: Capricorn Books, 1955.

———. *Cities in the Wilderness: Urban Life in America 1625–1742*. New York: Ronald Press, 1938.

———. *Myths and Realities: Societies of the Colonial South*. Baton Rouge: Louisiana State University Press, 1952. (New York: Atheneum, 1963)

————. *The Spirit of '76: The Growth of American Patriotism Before Independence, 1607–1776*. London: Oxford University Press, 1975.

Buck, Solon J., and Buck, Elizabeth H. *The Planting of Civilization in Western Pennsylvania*. Pittsburgh: Pittsburgh University Press, 1939.

Craven, Wesley Frank. *The Colonies in Transition, 1660–1713*. New York: Harper, 1968.

————. *The Southern Colonies in the Seventeenth Century*. Baton Rouge: Louisiana State University Press, 1949.

Dickerson, Oliver M. *American Colonial Government, 1696–1765: A Study of the British Board of Trade* . . . New York: Russell & Russell, 1939.

————. *The Navigation Acts and the American Revolution*. Philadelphia: University of Pennsylvania Press, 1951.

Gaustad, Edwin S. *The Great Awakening in New England*. New York: Harper, 1957.

Hall, Michael G. *Edward Randolph and the American Colonies, 1676–1703*. Chapel Hill, N.C.: University of North Carolina Press, 1960.

Hansen, Chadwick. *Witchcraft at Salem*. New York: Braziller, 1969.

Harper, Lawrence. *The English Navigation Laws: A 17th-century Experiment in Social Engineering*. New York: Columbia University Press, 1939.

Hawke, David. *The Colonial Experience*. Indianapolis: Bobbs-Merrill, 1966.

Hofstadter, Richard. *America at 1750: A Social Portrait*. New York: Knopf, 1971.

Kammen, Michael, *Empire and Interest: The American Colonies and the Politics of Mercantilism*. Philadelphia: Lippincott, 1970.

Lovejoy, David. *The Glorious Revolution in America*. New York: Harper, 1972.

Miller, Perry. *Errand into the Wilderness*. New York: Harper, 1956.

————. *The New England Mind: From Colony to Province*. Cambridge, Mass.: Harvard University Press, 1953.

————. *The New England Mind: The Seventeenth Century*. New York: Macmillan, 1939.

————. *Orthodoxy in Massachusetts 1630–1650*. Cambridge, Mass.: Harvard University Press, 1933.

————. *Roger Williams: His Contributions to the American Tradition*. Indianapolis: Bobbs-Merrill, 1953.

Morgan, Edmund S. *American Slavery, American Freedom: The Ordeal of Colonial Virginia,* New York: Norton, 1975.

————. *The Puritan Dilemma: The Story of John Winthrop*. Boston: Little, Brown, 1958.

————. *Roger Williams: The Church and the State*. New York: Harcourt, Brace, 1967.

————. *Visible Saints: The History of a Puritan Idea*. New York: New York University Press, 1963.

Morison, Samuel E. *Builders of the Bay Colony*. Boston and New York: Houghton Mifflin, 1930.

————. *Samuel de Champlain, Father of New France*. Boston: Little, Brown, 1972.

Morton, Richard L. *Colonial Virginia*. 2 vols. Chapel Hill, N.C.: University of North Carolina Press, 1960.

Parkman, Francis. *A Half Century of Conflict*. Boston: Little, Brown, 1893.

————. *The Conspiracy of Pontiac and the Indian War After the Conquest of Canada*. Boston: Little, Brown, 1880.

————. *Count Frontenac and New France Under Louis XIV*. Boston: Little, Brown, 1877.

————. *LaSalle and the Discovery of the Great West*. Boston: Little, Brown, 1879.

————. *Montcalm and Wolfe*. New York: Macmillan, 1962. (Orig. pub. Boston: Little, Brown, 1884.)

————. *The Old Regime in Canada*. Boston: Little, Brown, 1880.

Peckham, Howard H. *The Colonial Wars, 1689–1762*. Chicago: University of Chicago Press, 1964.

————. *Pontiac and the Indian Uprising*. Chicago: University of Chicago Press, 1961.

Reich, Jerome R. *Leisler's Rebellion: A Study of Democracy in New York, 1664–1720*. Chicago: University of Chicago Press, 1953.

Rutman, Darrett B. *American Puritanism: Faith and Practice*. Philadelphia: Lippincott, 1970.

Simpson, Alan. *Puritanism in Old and New England*. Chicago: University of Chicago Press, 1955.

Sydnor, Charles S. *Gentleman Freeholders: Political Practices in Washington's Virginia*. Chapel Hill, N.C.: University of North Carolina Press, 1952. (Reprinted by Macmillan in 1965 with title *American Revolutionaries in the Making*.)

Tolles, Frederick B. *Meeting House and Counting House: The Quaker Merchants of Colonial Philadelphia, 1682–1783*. Chapel Hill, N.C.: University of North Carolina Press, 1948.

Vaughan, Alden T. *American Genesis: Captain John Smith and the Founding of Virginia*. Boston: Little, Brown, 1975.

———. *New England Frontier: Puritans and Indians, 1620–1675*. Boston: Little, Brown, 1965.

Ver Steeg, Clarence W. The Formative Years, *1607–1763*. New York: Hill & Wang, 1964.

Winslow, Ola. *Master Roger Williams*. New York: Macmillan, 1957.

THE REVOLUTIONARY ERA, 1763–89

Alden, John R. *The American Revolution, 1775–1783*. New York: Harper, 1954.

Andrews, Charles M. *The Colonial Background of the American Revolution*. New Haven, Conn.: Yale University Press, 1924.

Bailyn, Bernard. *Intellectual Origins of the American Revolution*. Cambridge, Mass.: Harvard University Press, 1967.

Beard, Charles A. *An Economic Interpretation of the Constitution of the United States*. New York: Macmillan, 1957. (First pub. 1913.)

Becker, Carl L. *The Declaration of Independence: A Study in the History of Political Ideas*. New York: Knopf, 1956 (First pub. 1922.)

Berkhover, Robert F., Jr., ed. *The American Revolution: The Critical Issues*. Boston: Little, Brown, 1971.

Dabney, Virginius, ed. *The Patriots: The American Revolution Generation of Genius*. New York: Atheneum, 1975.

Dumbauld, Edward. *The Constitution of the United States*. Norman, Okla.: University of Oklahoma Press, 1964.

Elkins, Stanley, and McKitrick, Eric. "The Founding Fathers: Young Men of the Revolution." *Political Science Quarterly*, June 1961.

Farrand, Max. *The Framing of the Constitution of the United States*. New Haven, Conn.: Yale University Press, 1913.

Ferguson, E. James. *The Power of the Purse: A History of American Public Finance, 1776–1790*. Chapel Hill, N.C.: University of North Carolina Press, 1961.

French, Allen. *The First Year of the American Revolution*. Boston and New York: Houghton Mifflin, 1934.

Gipson, Lawrence H. *The British Empire Before the American Revolution*. 15 vols. Caldwell, Idaho: Caxton Printers, 1936–70.

———. *The Coming of the Revolution, 1763–1775*. New York: Harper, 1954.

Hawke, David. *A Transaction of Free Men: The Birth and Course of the Declaration of Independence*. New York: Scribner's, 1964.

Heimert, Alan. *Religion and the American Mind, from the Great Awakening to the Revolution*. Cambridge, Mass.: Harvard University Press, 1966.

Jacobson, David L., ed. *Essays on the American Revolution*. New York: Holt, Rinehart & Winston, 1970.

Jellison, Richard M., ed. *Society, Freedom, and Conscience: The Coming of the Revolution in Virginia, Massachusetts, and New York*. New York: Norton, 1976.

Jensen, Merrill. *The Articles of Confederation: An Interpretation of the Social-Constitutional History of the American Revolution, 1774–1781*. Madison: University of Wisconsin Press, 1940.

———. *The Founding of a Nation: A History of the American Revolution, 1763–1776*. New York: Oxford University Press, 1968.

———. *The New Nation: A History of the United States During the Confederation, 1781–1789*. New York: Knopf, 1950.

Kenyon, Cecelia. "Men of Little Faith: The Anti-Federalists on the Nature of Representative Government." *William & Mary Quarterly,* 3rd Ser., XII (1955).

Ketchum, Richard M. *Decisive Day: The Battle for Bunker Hill,* Garden City, N.Y.: Doubleday, 1974.

———. *The Winter Soldiers.* Garden City, N.Y.: Doubleday, 1973.

Knollenberg, Bernhard. *Origins of the American Revolution, 1759–1766.* Rev. ed. New York: Collier, 1961.

Lewis, Paul. *The Man Who Lost America: A Biography of Gentleman Johnny Burgoyne.* New York: Dial, 1973.

McCardell, Lee. *Ill-starred General: Braddock of the Coldstream Guards.* Pittsburgh: University of Pittsburgh Press, 1958.

McDonald, Forrest. *The Formation of the American Republic, 1776–1790.* Baltimore: Penguin, n.d. (First pub. under title *E Pluribus Unum.* Boston: Houghton Mifflin, 1965.)

———. *We the People: The Economic Origins of the Constitution.* Chicago: University of Chicago Press, 1958.

Main, Jackson T. *The Antifederalists: Critics of the Constitution, 1781–1788.* Chapel Hill, N.C.: University of North Carolina Press, 1961.

———. *The Social Structure of Revolutionary America.* Princeton, N.J.: Princeton University Press, 1965.

Mitchell, Broadus. *A Biography of the Constitution of the United States,* 2nd ed. New York: Oxford University Press, 1975.

———. *The Price of Independence: A Realistic View of the American Revolution.* New York: Oxford University Press, 1974.

Morgan, Edmund S. *The Birth of the Republic, 1763–1789.* Chicago: University of Chicago Press, 1956.

———. *The Challenge of the American Revolution.* New York: Norton, 1976.

Morgan, Edmund S., and Morgan, Helen. *The Stamp Act Crisis: Prologue to Revolution.* Chapel Hill, N.C.: University of North Carolina Press, 1953.

Morris, Richard B. *The American Revolution Reconsidered.* New York: Harper, 1967.

———. *The Peacemakers: The Great Powers and American Independence.* New York: Harper, 1965.

Nelson, William H. *The American Tory.* New York: Oxford, 1961.

Nettels, Curtis P. *George Washington and American Independence.* Boston: Little, Brown, 1951.

Palmer, John M. *General Von Steuben.* New Haven, Conn.: Yale University Press, 1937.

Peckham, Howard H., ed. *The Toll of Independence: Engagements and Battle Casualties of the American Revolution.* Chicago: University of Chicago Press, 1974.

Rossiter, Clinton. *Alexander Hamilton and the Constitution.* New York: Harcourt, Brace, 1964.

———. *The First American Revolution: The American Colonies on the Eve of Independence.* New York: Harcourt, Brace, 1956.

———. *1787: The Grand Convention; The Year That Made a Nation.* New York: Macmillan, 1966.

Scheer, George F., and Rankin, Hugh F. *Rebels and Redcoats.* Cleveland: World Publishing Co., 1957.

Schuyler, Robert. L. *The Constitution of the United States: An Historical Survey of Its Foundations.* New York: Macmillan, 1923. (Reprinted by Peter Smith, 1952.)

Shy, John W. *A People Numerous and Armed: Reflections on the Military Struggle for American Independence.* London: Oxford University Press, 1976.

———. *Toward Lexington: The Role of the British Army in the Coming of the American Revolution.* Princeton, N.J.: Princeton University Press, 1965.

Smith, Page. *A New Age Now Begins: A People's History of the American Revolution.* 2 vols. New York: McGraw-Hill, 1976.

Van Doren, Carl. *Secret History of the American Revolution.* New York: Viking Press, 1941.

Ver Steeg, Clarence. *Robert Morris, Revolutionary Financier.* New York: Octagon, 1972. (First pub. 1954.)

Wickwire, Franklin, and Wickwire, Mary. *Cornwallis: The American Adventure.* Boston: Houghton Mifflin, 1970.

Willcox, William B. *Portrait of a General: Sir Henry Clinton in the War of Independence*. New York: Knopf, 1964.

Wood, Gordon S. "Rhetoric and Reality in the American Revolution," *William & Mary Quarterly*, January 1966.

Wright, Esmond. *Washington and the American Revolution*. New York: Collier, 1962.

————, ed. *Causes and Consequences of the American Revolution*. Chicago: Quadrangle Books, 1966.

THE NEW NATION AND THE FOUNDING FATHERS

Adams, Henry. *The United States in 1800*. Ithaca, N.Y.: Cornell University Press, 1955. (The first six chapters of Volume I of Adams' *History of the United States During the First Administration of Thomas Jefferson*. New York: Scribner's, 1889.)

Borden, Morton. *Parties and Politics in the Early Republic, 1789–1815*. New York: Thomas Y. Crowell, 1967.

Brant, Irving. *James Madison*. 6 vols. Indianapolis: Bobbs-Merrill, 1941–61.

Brown, Roger H. *The Republic in Peril: 1812*. New York: Norton, 1971.

Buel, Richard, Jr. *Securing the Revolution: Ideology in American Politics, 1789–1815*. Ithaca, N.Y.: Cornell University Press, 1972.

Chambers, William N. *Political Parties in a New Nation: The American Experience, 1776–1809*. New York: Oxford University Press, 1963.

Charles, Joseph. *The Origins of the American Party System*. New York: Harper, 1956.

Chinard, Gilbert. *Honest John Adams*. Boston: Little, Brown, 1933.

————. *Thomas Jefferson: Apostle of Americanism*. Boston: Little, Brown, 1929.

Coles, Harry L. *The War of 1812*. Chicago: University of Chicago Press, 1965.

Cunliffe, Marcus. *George Washington: Man and Monument*. New York: New American Library, 1958.

————. *The Nation Takes Shape, 1789–1837.* Chicago: University of Chicago Press, 1959.

Cunningham, Noble E., Jr. *The Jeffersonian Republicans: The Formation of Party Organization, 1789–1801.* Chapel Hill, N.C.: University of North Carolina Press, 1957.

————. *The Jeffersonian Republicans in Power: Party Operations, 1801–1809.* Chapel Hill, N.C.: University of North Carolina Press, 1963.

Dauer, Manning J. *The Adams Federalists.* Baltimore: Johns Hopkins Press, 1953.

Fischer, David H. *The Revolution of American Conservatism: The Federalist Party in the Era of Jeffersonian Democracy.* New York: Harper, 1965.

Flexner, James T. *George Washington.* 4 vols. Boston: Little, Brown, 1965–72.

————. *Washington, the Indispensable Man.* Boston: Little, Brown, 1973.

Freeman, Douglas S. *George Washington: A Biography.* 7 vols. New York: Scribner's, 1948–57. (Vol. 7 was written in collaboration with J. A. Carroll and M. W. Ashworth.)

Hofstadter, Richard. *The Idea of a Party System: The Rise of Legitimate Opposition in the United States, 1780–1840.* Berkeley: University of California Press, 1969.

Horsman, Reginald. *The War of 1812.* New York: Knopf, 1969.

Howe, John R., Jr. *The Changing Political Thought of John Adams.* Princeton, N.J.: Princeton University Press, 1966.

Ketcham, Ralph. *James Madison: A Biography.* New York: Macmillan, 1971.

Koch, Adrienne. *Jefferson and Madison: The Great Collaboration.* New York: Knopf, 1950.

Kurtz, Stephen G. *The Presidency of John Adams: The Collapse of Federalism, 1795–1800.* Philadelphia: University of Pennsylvania Press, 1957.

Mahan, Alfred T. *Sea Power in Its Relation to the War of 1812.* 2 vols. Boston: Little, Brown, 1905.

Malone, Dumas. *Thomas Jefferson and His Time.* 5 vols. Boston: Little, Brown, 1948–74.

Miller, John C. *Alexander Hamilton: Portrait in Paradox*. New York: Harper, 1959.

———. *The Federalist Era, 1789–1801*. New York: Harper, 1960.

Mitchell, Broadus. *Alexander Hamilton*. 2 vols. New York: Macmillan, 1957–62.

Morris, Richard B. *Seven Who Shaped Our Destiny: The Founding Fathers as Revolutionaries*. New York: Harper, 1973.

Perkins, Bradford. *Castlereagh and Adams: England and the United States, 1812–1823*. Berkeley: University of California Press, 1964.

———. *The First Rapprochement: England and the United States, 1795–1805*. Berkeley: University of California Press, 1955.

———. *Prologue to War, 1805–1812*. Berkeley: University of California Press, 1961.

Peterson, Merrill D. *Thomas Jefferson and the New Nation*. New York: Oxford University Press, 1970.

Sisson, Daniel. *The American Revolution of 1800*. New York: Knopf, 1974.

Smelser, Marshall. *The Democratic Republic, 1801–1815*. New York: Harper, 1968.

Van Doren, Carl. *Benjamin Franklin*. New York: Viking, 1941.

Index